CONSTANTINE

AND

EUSEBIUS

CONSTANTINE

AND

EUSEBIUS

TIMOTHY D. BARNES

HARVARD UNIVERSITY PRESS
Cambridge, Massachusetts
London, England

Publication of this book has been aided by a grant from the Andrew W. Mellon
Foundation

Library of Congress Cataloging in Publication Data

Barnes, Timothy David.
    Constantine and Eusebius.
    Bibliography: p.
    Includes index.
    1. Constantine I, Emperor of Rome, d. 337.   2. Eusebius, of Caesarea,
Bishop of Caesarea, ca. 260–ca. 340.   3. Church history—Primitive and early
church, ca. 30–600.   4. Rome—History—Constantine I, the Great, 306–337.
I. Title.
DG315.B35   937'.08'0922   81-4248
ISBN 0-674-16530-6 (cloth)   AACR2
ISBN 0-674-16531-4 (paper)

PREFACE

The present work is neither a biography of Constantine nor a comprehensive study of Eusebius as a writer and thinker. Nor, strictly speaking, is it a history of the age of Constantine. It may best be described as an interpretative essay. I have deliberately concentrated on Constantine and Eusebius as individuals, attempting first to delineate an accurate portrait of each man separately, then to depict their relationship to each other. I have not tried to present a comprehensive picture of the age of Constantine with all the available or recoverable details, but rather to establish the main features of the period by emphasizing the career, character, and policies of the first Christian ruler of the Roman Empire and the viewpoint and assumptions of the most important writer of Constantine's time. More can be done, but further work will require methods different from those employed here and will necessarily be more speculative. It is advisable to establish the basic framework first, lest hostile critics seize upon the speculations as casting doubt upon the underlying facts themselves.

In a sense, the present work forms a sequel to my study of Tertullian (completed ten years ago), for it amplifies and develops the view of Eusebius I adopted there as a historian whose interpretation of early Christian history is circumscribed by both his prejudices and his sources. But my main impetus to study Eusebius in depth derived from the strange and obvious failure of modern scholarship to put the study of the age of Constantine on a proper footing.

Eusebius is the most voluminous extant writer of the late third and early fourth centuries—Greek or Latin, Christian or pagan. Yet, while biographies of Constantine abound, much of Eusebius' vast output lies neglected. No complete modern edition of his work exists, many of his writings lack competent commentaries of any sort, some have never been edited critically, and the two most important modern attempts at a rounded presentation of his career and writings (by J. B. Lightfoot and E. Schwartz) have both been articles in encyclopedias. Worse still, most historians of the Roman Empire and its institutions decline to read Eusebius' theological, exegetical, and apologetical works, and even historians of the Christian church overlook precious nuggets of information which lie buried there. I decided, therefore, to redress the balance, and I have tried not only to set Eusebius in his historical milieu, but also to use the full range of his writings to illuminate the age in which both he and Constantine lived.

My work has been rendered possible by the generosity of three institutions. The University of Toronto has supported me since 1970, and my colleagues in the Department of Classics have provided me with an intellectual ambience in which I have felt able to think and to write without inhibition. In 1976–77, the University granted me a year's sabbatical leave, and the American Council of Learned Societies awarded me a Leave Fellowship, thus allowing me to take advantage of the incomparable hospitality of the Institute for Advanced Study in Princeton.

Among scholars who have written about the Constantinian period, I have learned most from Otto Seeck, whose technical brilliance and alert accuracy far outweigh his prejudices and occasional errors of historical judgment. And among the many friends with whom I have discussed topics covered in this book I owe most to Fergus Millar and John Rist, both of whom gave me much helpful advice during its composition and penetrating comments on the penultimate version. My most profound debt, however, is to my wife—for fifteen years of constant encouragement.

Something should perhaps be said about my apparent disregard of much modern scholarship. Since there already exist several excellent guides to the learned literature on Constantine, yet another attempt at bibliographical comprehensiveness would be ostentatious rather than useful. In the notes, I have tried to acknowledge fully and honestly what I owe to other scholars and to indicate areas of serious doubt and uncertainty. But at the same time I have decided to eschew polemic and, for the most part, simply not to record modern opinions which new evidence has disproved outright or which I consider to be the products of nothing more profound than ignorance, inaccuracy, misunderstanding, or a blind refusal to abandon positions which have become untenable. Consequently, if the work of a modern scholar is cited rarely or never, it does not necessarily follow that I have not studied or read it. A companion volume, entitled *The New Empire of Diocletian and Constantine,* deals with many vexatious problems, both large and small, and I have often assumed here conclusions which are there argued in detail. I must apologize in advance for the inevitable cases where I have overlooked ancient evidence or modern discussions of genuine value, and I hope that such omissions will not damage my central theses. Throughout, I have endeavored to confront the evidence directly and to expound solutions for problems without hedging and without sheltering behind the authority of others. If my interpretation of Constantine and Eusebius provokes salutary criticism, so much the better.

T.D.B.

CONTENTS

 O N E
CONSTANTINE

I. Diocletian and Maximiam   3
II. Galerius and the Christians   15
III. The Rise of Constantine   28
IV. The Christian Emperor of the West   44
V. Constantine and Licinius   62

T W O
EUSEBIUS

VI. Origen and Caesarea   81
VII. Biblical Scholarship and the *Chronicle*   106
VIII. The History of the Church   126
IX. Persecution   148
X. Eusebius as Apologist   164

T H R E E
THE CHRISTIAN EMPIRE

XI. Before Constantine   191
XII. The Council of Nicaea   208
XIII. Ecclesiastical Politics   224
XIV. The New Monarchy   245
XV. Eusebius and Constantine   261

Epilogue   272

Chronological Table   277
Editions and Translations of Eusebius   280
Abbreviations   284
Notes   286
Bibliography   406
Index of Passages of Eusebius Discussed   443
General Index   445

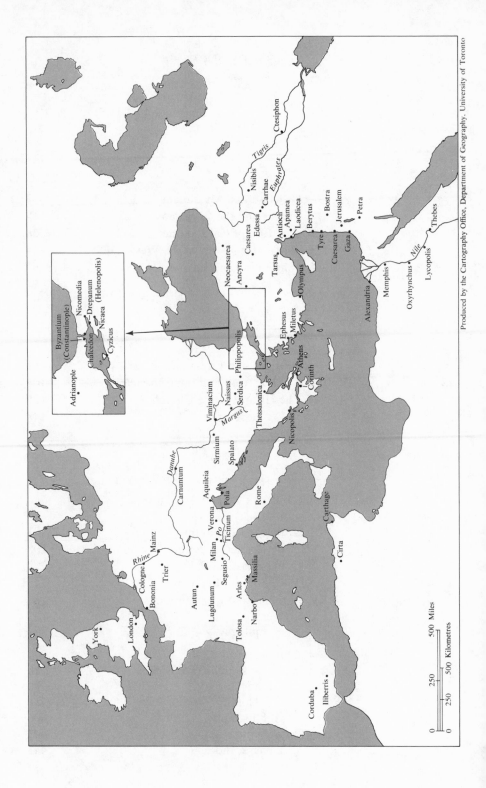

Produced by the Cartography Office, Department of Geography, University of Toronto.

Ctesiphon

Nisibis
Carrhae
Caesarea
Edessa

Neocaesarea
Ancyra

Tarsus
Antioch
Apamea
Laodicea
Berytus

Tyre
Caesarea
Gaza

Bostra
Jerusalem
Petra

Thebes

Memphis
Oxyrhynchus
Lycopolis

Alexandria

Olympus
Ephesus
Miletus

Byzantium
(Constantinople)
Nicomedia
Drepanum
Nicaea (Helenopolis)
Chalcedon
Cyzicus

Adrianople

Philippopolis

Athens
Corinth

Viminacium
Naissus
Serdica
Thessalonica

Nicopolis

Sirmium
Spalato

Carnuntum
Aquileia
Pola

Rome

Verona
Milan
Ticinum
Segusio

Mainz

Cologne
Bononia
Trier

Autun
Lugdunum

Arles
Massilia

Narbo
Tolosa

Cirta

Carthage

York
London

Corduba
Iliberris

Tigris
Euphrates
Nile
Rhine
Po
Danube
Margus

ONE

CONSTANTINE

I

DIOCLETIAN AND MAXIMIAN

Constantine was born on 27 February soon after the year 270 (probably 272 or 273).[1] He saw the light of day near Naissus, a military city on the Danube.[2] His father, Flavius Constantius, appears to have been a native of the region later known as the province of Dacia Ripensis,[3] while his mother, Helena, was a woman of humble origin from Drepanum in Bithynia.[4] Constantius' original social standing is unclear, but by the time of his son's birth he was an officer in the Roman army: he fought in Syria under Aurelian and had risen to become governor of Dalmatia in 284/5 when the proclamation of a new emperor offered the opportunity for further promotion.[5] By 289 Constantius was the emperor Maximian's praetorian prefect in Gaul,[6] and on 1 March 293 he himself entered the imperial college as a Caesar.[7] At the age of twenty or twenty-one, therefore, Constantine, as a Caesar's son, automatically became a candidate for future appointment as emperor, and he soon proceeded to the court of Diocletian, where he resided as an heir presumptive to the throne.[8]

By that time, Constantius had divorced Helena. His second wife matched his newly acquired social and political prestige. She was Theodora, the daughter of Maximian, and Constantius married her before 289 while praetorian prefect of her father.[9] No fewer than six children are known from this marriage, of whom

3

one, scarcely born later than 300, bore the significant name Anastasia.[10] The Jewish and Christian overtones of the name point unmistakably to the religious sympathies of Constantius.[11]

Diocletian, Maximian, and Constantius, together with the Caesar Galerius, formed a college of four emperors which Diocletian created in 293 to buttress and enhance his own position as Roman emperor. Like the régime which it supplanted, the régime of Diocletian arose from usurpation. Diocletian had been born about 244, probably at Salonae in Dalmatia.[12] His original name was Diocles, which he changed when emperor to the more impressive Diocletian, and so low was his original status in Roman society that hostile writers claimed that his father was a scribe, or the freedman of a senator.[13] The first four decades of Diocletian's life are totally obscure: he burst upon the stage of history in 284 as commander of the bodyguard of the emperor Numerianus, whose father had himself seized power only two years earlier.[14]

In 282 M. Aurelius Carus, praetorian prefect of the apparently secure emperor Probus, gathered an army in Raetia and Noricum and rose in rebellion. The army of Probus, who was at Sirmium, declined to fight against Carus, mutinied, and killed their commander. The new Augustus Carus immediately elevated his sons Carinus and Numerianus to the rank of Caesar and began to plan a campaign against Persia. In 283 Carinus, the elder son, received charge of Illyricum, Gaul, and Italy; he went to Gaul, restored the Rhine frontier and announced a German victory, and perhaps suppressed a revolt in Britain. Meanwhile, Carus took Numerianus with him and exploited an opportunity offered by civil war in Persia. The Roman army advanced to Ctesiphon without encountering serious opposition, and Carus, Carinus, and Numerianus all assumed the title *Persici maximi* in celebration. But then disaster struck: Carus was killed near Ctesiphon, allegedly by lightning, and his army retired to Roman territory.[15]

On their father's death, the Caesars Carinus and Numerianus became Augusti, and by January 284 Carinus was in Rome, awaiting the return of his brother and their joint triumph.[16] Numerianus, however, did not hasten westward, perhaps being loath to surrender his father's court and entourage to his elder brother. In March 284 Numerianus was still in Syria; in November, still in Asia Minor.[17] He suffered from a disease of the eyes and traveled in a closed litter. When the army reached Bithynia, Numerianus did not appear in public for several days, and it was discovered that he was dead. His generals and tribunes then held a council at which they chose Diocles, the commander of Numerianus' bodyguard, as emperor. The choice of the leaders was ratified by the army. On 20 November 284, on a hill three miles outside Nicomedia in Bithynia, the soldiers saluted the new Augustus, who as Valerius Diocletianus assumed all the normal titles pertaining to the imperial office.[18]

Diocletian acted at once to consolidate his position. He swore upon oath that Numerianus had died through no oversight or plot of his: the true culprit was the praetorian prefect Aper, who (Diocletian asserted) had both perpetrated and concealed the emperor's death. In full view of the army, Diocletian drew his sword and plunged it into Aper. The public execution was followed by a happier ceremony. Carus and Numerianus had been accompanied on their eastern expedition by a number of distinguished senators, as was the custom when emperors spent long periods away from Rome. Among the *comites* of Numerianus was L. Caesonius Ovinius Manlius Rufinianus Bassus, a member of a senatorial family from Campania who had earlier been consul, proconsul of Africa for three years, and chosen by Probus for a signal distinction.[19] Diocletian chose Bassus as his consular colleague, and the two men assumed the *fasces* as consuls in place of Carinus and Numerianus.[20] The gesture had a double significance. Diocletian did not desire to become emperor with Carinus as a senior colleague: he took a consular colleague of his own choosing in order to advertise his total rejection of the existing régime. But he selected a prominent senator, not a general: he needed the support of the Senate, or at least its neutrality, since he proposed to liberate Rome from what he depicted as a tyrannical oppression.[21]

Diocletian was not the only rival who threatened Carinus. Northern Italy and Pannonia were under the control of one M. Aurelius Julianus, described before his rebellion both as a *corrector* and as Carinus' praetorian prefect. But Julianus presented no great military danger, and Carinus suppressed him easily with a swift march through northern Italy.[22] Diocletian, to whom the eastern provinces rapidly swore allegiance, represented a peril of a different order.

In the spring of 285, the armies of East and West advanced cautiously until they faced each other across the River Margus in Moesia, between the Mons Aureus and Viminacium. Carinus led the stronger army, but its loyalty was vulnerable. Subsequently it was alleged that Carinus had not only maltreated the Senate and its womenfolk but also seduced the wives of his officers. Even if that charge was false, Carinus had certainly alienated men on whose support his success depended. When battle was joined, assassination decided the outcome: Carinus was killed by a soldier under his command, and Diocletian became undisputed ruler of the Roman Empire.[23]

After his victory Diocletian marched to Italy, perhaps even visited Rome,[24] and established his rule on a solid basis. The prefect of the city of Rome was dismissed and replaced by the Bassus who had been Diocletian's consular colleague.[25] Bassus himself soon left office, perhaps because of illness or death, and his successor (also consul in 286) is a mere name.[26] But the next prefect, Pomponius Januarianus, who entered office on 27 February 288 and was also ordinary consul in that year, had been prefect of Egypt under Numerianus: he had presumably transferred his allegiance to the new régime with alacrity and performed useful services.[27] Diocletian was generous to servants of the former government, some of whom may secretly have aided his cause before the battle at the Margus. Ti. Claudius Aurelius Aristobulus was the praetorian prefect of Carinus and consul with Carinus in 285; Diocletian maintained him in both functions, declared a general amnesty, and continued most of Carinus' officials and governors in their posts.[28]

Recent history, however, showed the vulnerability of a single emperor, and Gaul was troubled by both a peasant uprising and seaborne raids from the north, while the Danubian frontier was restive. Diocletian needed a lieutenant whom he could trust. His choice fell on Aurelius Maximianus, a man aged about thirty-four from the vicinity of Sirmium who had served for many years in the Roman army, gradually rising through promotion. Maximian was an old friend of Diocletian, to whom he had doubtless displayed conspicuous loyalty during the campaign against Carinus.[29] Probably on 21 July 285 at Milan, Diocletian appointed Maximian Caesar and dispatched him to Gaul.[30]

Having arranged the government of the West, Diocletian returned to the East. He marched slowly down the Danube, encountering and defeating Sarmatian raiders in the autumn. The winter he spent in Nicomedia, which he had chosen as one of his permanent residences. During the summer of 286 he visited Palestine, then turned westward and presumably spent the winter at Nicomedia.[31] A rebellion in the East may have occurred, because early in his reign Diocletian brought settlers from Asia to people deserted farmlands in Thrace.[32] In 287, perhaps by threatening to fight, Diocletian scored a diplomatic triumph: the king of Persia sent to him envoys laden with precious gifts, professed friendship, even invited Diocletian to visit him, and acknowledged Roman suzerainty over territory to the west and south of the Tigris.[33] At the same time the Persian monarch ceased to claim Armenia as a province of his empire, and a Roman nominee was installed as ruler of its western districts. In 252/3, when the Persians overran Armenia and made it into a Persian province, the royal infant Tiridates had been removed to a refuge in the Roman Empire; he was now restored as ruler of part of his ancestral domains.[34]

Maximian was less successful than Diocletian in accomplishing his imperial duties. A brisk campaign sufficed to quiet the interior of Gaul: the Bagaudae, though they might put up a pretender to the imperial throne, were no more than a disorganized rabble, ill-equipped and ill-trained rustics against practiced legionaries. But Maximian did not suppress the peasant uprising before it had provoked a barbarian raid. Two marauding armies, one of Burgundians and Alamanni, the other of Chaibones and Heruli, crossed the Rhine and broke into Gaul. Maximian let the first army perish of hunger and disease; the second, he intercepted and defeated. Already, however, so it seems, Maximian had made a decision which ultimately had profound consequences. He put another in charge of operations against the Frankish and Saxon pirates who were harassing northwestern Gaul; then he retired to Milan for the winter.[35]

The commander chosen was Carausius, a Menapian who had distinguished himself against the Bagaudae. At Bononia, probably in the autumn of 285, Maximian commissioned him to build a fleet and clear the sea of pirates. Carausius performed the task entrusted to him with efficiency, but not without dishonesty. He took some of the recaptured booty for himself instead of returning it all to the provincials or surrendering it to the imperial treasury. These actions soon provoked a crisis. Maximian, raised from Caesar to Augustus on 1 April 286, was at Mainz on 21 June and probably proceeded from there toward the theater of war. Carausius feared the advent of the emperor, who was reported to have ordered his death. He preferred rebellion to trial, execution, or murder, and he proclaimed himself Augustus. In the autumn of 286, not only Britain but also much of northwestern Gaul renounced allegiance to the central imperial government.[36]

Maximian could not suppress Carausius. And danger still threatened from beyond the Rhine. While the emperor was celebrating his assumption of the consular *fasces* on 1 January 287, the ceremonies were disrupted by news of a barbarian raid. Maximian laid aside his toga, donned his breastplate, and sallied forth. The raiders were suitably chastised, and Maximian returned in triumph and celebrated a victory. Yet to repel a raiding party was not enough to secure the frontier. Maximian devoted the whole of the campaigning season of 287 to a German expedition, crossing the Rhine and parading Roman strength far beyond the imperial frontier.[37]

In the following spring, serious preparations began for the suppression of Carausius, with the building of fleets on every river which could serve to transport troops against the rebel.[38] Diocletian lent his aid: he marched up the Danube to Raetia and invaded Germany from the south. The strike added territory to the empire, and the two Augusti conferred before Diocletian again withdrew to the eastern provinces.[39] Maximian once more entrusted a vital task to another: Flavius Constantius, his praetorian prefect and already the husband of his daughter Theodora, undertook an expedition against the Franks, with whom Carausius appears to have allied himself. Since they controlled the estuaries of the Rhine, they could in effect protect the rebel from attack by sea. Constantius advanced, spreading slaughter, and soon reached the shores of the North Sea. The Franks sued for peace and came before Maximian in a body; he confirmed Gennoboudes as their king and settled them on deserted land near Trier.[40]

On 21 April 289, the orator Mamertinus, who perhaps held the post of *magister memoriae*, delivered a panegyric to Maximian in which he confidently predicted the defeat of Carausius.[41] However, a storm at sea destroyed the imperial fleet.[42] Carausius, now secure, sought to legitimize his position and presented himself no longer as a rival to Diocletian and Maximian, but as their colleague.[43] There is no reason to believe that the two established Augusti ever admitted the claim, however long they failed to assert their supremacy.

His failure to suppress Carausius made Maximian feel insecure. In 290 he toured the cities of Gaul receiving homage;[44] but beneath the adulation rendered to Maximian his subjects perhaps harbored grave doubts about his capacity as emperor. Maximian had probably ceased to lead troops on active campaign; his army fought now under the command of Constantius, who prosecuted warfare on the Rhine with vigor and perhaps with ostentation. At some date between 289 and 293, the praetorian prefect captured a barbarian king and laid Germany waste from Mainz south to the headwaters of the Danube.[45]

The Augustus crossed the Alps into Italy in late December 290 in order to meet Diocletian in Milan. The meeting was a solemn and impressive occasion, with much pomp and pageantry. Political decisions were doubtless made, but they were made in secret. And the Roman Senate took the opportunity to renew its contacts with emperors whom it never normally saw: a deputation from Rome attended on the emperors and may have heard news of future imperial policy.[46] After the conference, Maximian returned to Gaul and perhaps made a last feeble attempt to expel Carausius from Gaul.[47] Otherwise, his activities cannot be documented until 1 March 293, when he invested Constantius with the imperial purple, probably in Milan, which probably now became his principal residence.[48]

Diocletian could see the dangers inherent in the existing situation. His colleague had permitted a usurper to seize control of a large part of his domain and to retain it for several years. Moreover, Diocletian found increasing difficulty in attending to every emergency himself. In 288 he had invaded Germany and conferred with Maximian, in 289 he needed to repel an invasion of Dacia and reestablish the Danube frontier, and in 290 the eastern frontier required his attention. The Saraceni being restive, Diocletian went to Syria and quickly restored order; then he traveled westward to confer with Maximian, and after their meeting in Milan in late December 290 or January 291, he took up residence on the Danube, probably at Sirmium. Here, in the course of the next two years, Diocletian formulated a plan for restructuring the Roman state.[49]

On 1 March 293, two Caesars were appointed, junior in rank to the Augusti but members of the imperial college and possessing most of the privileges of their senior colleagues. The senior of the pair was Constantius, who was to take charge of the military operations which Maximian had bungled: he was assigned Gaul and Britain, and he immediately set about his task.[50] The junior Caesar was Galerius Maximianus, a man perhaps not much older than thirty, and perhaps the praetorian prefect of Diocletian. He received Syria, Palestine, and Egypt, with responsibility for the defense of the eastern frontier.[51]

The Roman Empire was in theory an elective monarchy: the Senate or the preceding emperor would appoint a new emperor solely on the basis of his fitness to rule.[52] In practice, however, succession was always hereditary: no emperor whose rule was secure had ever excluded his sons from the succession, and emperors who appointed heirs not of their blood customarily adopted them in a formal ceremony.[53] In 293, therefore, Diocletian and Maximian, who, as Augusti, styled themselves brothers, adopted Galerius and Constantius as their sons.[54] The Augusti and the Caesars were also linked by marriage: Constantius had married Theodora, the daughter of Maximian, at least as early as 289, and it must be suspected that Galerius' marriage to Valeria, the daughter of Diocletian, also antedates his elevation to the purple.[55]

These alliances by marriage did more than bind the four reigning emperors to one another. They advertised to the world the identity of their prospective heirs. In 289 the panegyric of Mamertinus had looked forward to the education of Maximian's young son Maxentius as his father's successor.[56] The proclamation of two Caesars in 293 did not diminish the status of Maxentius or impede his prospects. On the contrary, his standing was enhanced, at an unknown date, by his marriage to Galerius' daughter, the only legitimate child of the Caesar.[57] Moreover, Diocletian may have summoned Maxentius to his court to groom him for the throne.[58] The adult son of Constantius was the other obvious candidate for the imperial succession. Constantine was soon summoned to Diocletian's court, and a mosaic in the banquet room of the imperial palace at Aquileia depicted his departure from the West in a scene with Fausta, the young daughter of Maximian, offering him a plumed helmet which gleamed with gold and precious jewels.[59]

In 293, therefore, the prospects for the succession seemed clear enough: only two of the emperors had sons, and each of these sons was expected to marry another emperor's daughter. But the oldest of the reigning emperors had not yet turned fifty. There might be no new emperors for many years, and who could foresee what might occur before any of the present imperial college died? Constantius' second marriage proved unusually fertile. The prospects of Constantine and Maxentius, bright enough in 293, might dim with the passage of time.

Each of the four emperors had his own court. After 293 Maximian resided in northern Italy, while Constantius occupied Maximian's former capital of Trier. Between 293 and 296 Diocletian spent much of his time traveling or on campaign, but Sirmium can be identified as his preferred place of residence, and Galerius probably chose Antioch as his capital.[60] Each emperor also had a praetorian prefect, a court, administrative officers for the transaction of routine business, and a standing army. Each of these four armies (some alleged) exceeded in size the army of any earlier emperor who had ruled alone.[61]

Diocletian saw that the larger army required a more efficient collection of taxes and supplies, and he reorganized the administrative structure of the Roman Empire with this end in view. Northern Italy was put on the same administrative level as the provinces,[62] and Diocletian divided the existing provinces into smaller units, doubling their number from fifty to almost one hundred.[63] The new provinces were grouped in twelve dioceses, and a new type of official, described as a deputy of the praetorian prefects (*vicarius* or *vices agens praefectorum praetorio*), was created to govern the new dioceses.[64] Moreover, the *vicarii* and the *praesides* of the new provinces had functions different from most provincial governors of the early empire. Whereas earlier governors commanded troops and administered justice while procurators supervised taxation, under the new system, at least in theory, *vicarii* and governors were responsible for both justice and taxation, while *duces* independent of the civil administration were in charge of troops other than the four central armies.[65] Reducing the size of provinces and creating the *vicarii* implied a devaluation of the status of governors, and few senators were interested in serving as the *praeses* of one of the new provinces. Some provinces, however, continued to be governed by senators, who were still willing both to hold an annual proconsulate of Africa, Asia, or even Achaea and to serve as a *corrector* in an Italian province.[66]

Diocletian greatly increased the number of financial officials in the provinces. Far more *rationales* and *magistri privatae* are attested under Diocletian than before; their function was not only to manage imperial properties but to supervise closely the collection of badly needed revenue.[67] Diocletian's new administrative structure enabled a closer surveillance of the empire and a more systematic exaction of the goods and services the government needed.[68] Diocletian also reformed the monetary system through which the taxes collected were turned into coin to pay the armies and the bureaucracy. For the first years of his reign he minted on the debased standard inherited from his predecessors. In 294 new mints were opened, and a large and uniform coinage was issued in three metals.[69]

Furthermore, it was probably Diocletian himself who inspired the jurists Gregorius and Hermogenianus to provide imperial officials with up-to-date legal guidance in the exercise of their duties.[70] Before 293, the handbooks of jurisprudence available belonged to the Severan age or earlier and did not reflect the conditions of the later third century.[71] Gregorius published a collection of imperial rescripts from the time of Hadrian down to 292, and Hermogenianus supplemented this *Codex Gregorianus* with a collection, probably complete, of rescripts issued by Diocletian in 293 and 294 which later received some haphazard additions.[72] Shortly after 293 Hermogenianus compiled comprehensive *Iuris Epitomae,* while in the West there appeared a compendium known as the *Sententiae Pauli,* which survives in an abridged form; both served as handbooks to instruct governors in the administration of criminal law.[73]

Diocletian's reforms were bold and imaginative, but reality sometimes resisted his neat formulas. It was a small matter that some of his provincial divisions needed revision, either very soon after 293 or early in the fourth century.[74] More serious was his inability to control the monetary system established in 294, which was undermined by a sharp rise in the market price of gold. Since gold coins circulated at their value as bullion, the ratios on which Diocletian's reform rested were destroyed.[75] On 1 September 301, therefore, Diocletian abruptly doubled the value of the silver and bronze coinages in order to restore the original ratios.[76] Perhaps partly as a result, the inflation of prices became worse, and in late November or early December 301 Diocletian issued an edict fixing maximum prices for an enormous range of goods and services. The long preamble explains and justifies his actions.

With the help of the immortal gods (Diocletian declares), the emperors have rescued the Roman Empire from foreign invasion and have restored peace and tranquillity. But the avarice of a few imperils the well-being of all, and the emperors must intervene to establish the justice which mankind cannot provide for itself. If the emperors have done nothing yet about prices despite many years on the throne, it is because they charitably expected a natural amelioration of an intolerable situation. Now, however, prices are rising so quickly that avarice and rapacity must be checked by imperial action. Worst of all, the safety of the empire is imperiled because soldiers cannot afford to buy the necessities of life: a single trivial purchase (Diocletian complains) consumes all their normal pay and bonuses. The emperors decree, therefore, that a maximum price shall be set, valid throughout every province of the Roman Empire, for all normal articles used in everyday life and for a wide range of services. Since audacity and greed have caused the trouble, it shall be a capital offense to sell (or buy) above the prices stated in the lists which follow the emperors' pronouncement.[77]

The edict with its attached schedule of maximum prices was published throughout the eastern empire, prominently displayed on public buildings or walls in the centers of cities. Fragments survive from more than forty different cities,[78] as well as the letter in which the governor of Phrygia and Caria ordered the publication of the price edict in his province: he praised the foresight of the emperors in laying down a fair price for all goods and services by means of a law which would last forever.[79] No fragments have ever been found, however, of any copy published in the West: although Diocletian issued the edict in the name of all the emperors and speaks as if legislating for the whole empire, it is clear that Maximian and Constantius never even promulgated it in their domains.[80]

The price edict probably had a far more restricted purpose than its rhetoric and widespread publication imply. Diocletian set a limit to what the administration would pay for goods and services: the circumstances in which he acted indicate that the rise in prices was sudden and recent and that his central concern was to procure adequate supplies for the army and the court.[81] According to one witness, despite the price edict much blood was shed, prices rose still higher, goods disappeared from the marketplace—and the law was soon abrogated.[82]

The ideology of the "Tetrarchy," as well as a vivid sense that the accession of Diocletian marked a new age, are reflected in official pronouncements, on coins and monuments, and in the surviving oratory of the period.[83] Panegyrists might occasionally salute an emperor as a god on earth, hailing Diocletian as Jupiter and Maximian as Hercules,[84] but officially the emperors themselves no longer laid claim to divine status. They were not gods, but the chosen instruments of the gods, their deputies on earth, and in some sense their sons. Diocletian was considered to be under the special protection of Jupiter, and Maximian under that of Hercules; relations between the two emperors were held to reflect the divine order: Diocletian commanded; his faithful helper put his wishes into effect.[85] A more complicated scheme was needed to accommodate the Caesars and other prospective successors. From 293, therefore, there was both a Jovian and a Herculean dynasty. Constantius, though the senior Caesar, was Herculius, for it was Maximian who invested him with the purple, while Galerius took the sobriquet Iovius from his adoptive father.[86]

Yet Constantius and Galerius also had their own patron deities. As the imperial coinage shows, the Caesars were under the protection of Mars and Sol Invictus, also identified as Apollo. But the correlation of the Caesars and their tutelary deities was not rigid; indeed, a contemporary poet likened Diocletian and Galerius when they went forth to war to Jupiter and Apollo setting out from Crete and Delos.[87] On the most precise definition, however, just as Jupiter and Hercules were the *conservatores* of the Augusti, so Mars was the *conservator* of Galerius, who declared that he was fathered by Mars, and Sol or Apollo was the *conservator* of Constantius.[88]

Many of Diocletian's subjects were grateful for the blessings of his reign. Effusive orators spoke of the golden age being reborn and gave detailed reasons for their optimism. Peace ruled everywhere. The Rhine, the Danube, and the Euphrates again formed secure frontiers guarded by Roman troops. Defeated barbarians had been assigned to recover deserted farmland for cultivation. Plowed fields replaced forest, the granaries were filled, there was almost too much produce to harvest. Cities long overgrown with vegetation or abandoned to wild animals were being rebuilt, restored, and repopulated. Men lived longer and reared more children. How different from the preceding epoch! Then famine and plague stalked the empire, and people died in enormous numbers. Nor had the imperial government then been able to protect its subjects from robbery and murder. Under Gallienus the empire had been mutilated. The Persians claimed superiority, the Palmyrenes equality. Egypt and Syria rebelled. Raetia was lost, Noricum and Pannonia ravaged. Italy itself grieved at the sack of many of its cities. And in the reign of Probus a band of Franks roamed the Mediterranean with total impunity. They seized ships on the Black Sea, raided Greece and Asia, landed in Africa, captured Syracuse, and then sailed unmolested out into the Atlantic Ocean.[89]

Diocletian and Maximian (their panegyrists averred) had changed the situation completely. Italy, Africa, Gaul, Spain, and the Danubian provinces all felt secure. The emperors had often raided the territory of the Alamanni and Sarmatians, had often defeated Juthungi, Quadi, and Carpi in battle, had constrained the Goths to seek peace, and had induced the Persian kings to show a proper respect for Rome. The credit for all this could be assigned to the rulers: forgetful of their own comfort, they surveyed the world to see what needed their attention; they passed their days and nights in incessant concern for the safety of all.[90]

Admiration, however, was not universal. A contemporary Christian writer has left a very different assessment of the emperors. He presents Diocletian as avaricious and timid. He complains that Diocletian so multiplied the army and administration that farmers deserted their fields because they could not pay their taxes, that he plundered the provinces to transform Nicomedia into a new capital which was to equal Rome, and that he frequently had his subjects unjustly condemned so that he could confiscate their villas or farms. Yet even this hostile critic admits that Diocletian possessed great political sagacity, for he had the enviable ability to garner for himself the credit for actions which proved popular while saddling others with the responsibility for failures or mistakes. Maximian, according to the same observer, shared Diocletian's basic attitudes but differed from him in being more open and more interested in enjoying the sensual prerogatives of his position. The Caesars differed totally, both from the Augusti and from each other. Galerius had an animal quality. He was huge of stature and stout like a giant, brutal, arrogant, and ambitious. Hence, though an adherent of the traditional religion, he struck the cultured classes as alien and semibarbarian.[91] Constantius, in contrast, practiced the traditional moral virtues and sought always to remain on good terms with the established aristocracy while at the same time showing himself sympathetic to Christianity.[92]

The writer who provides these vivid vignettes of Diocletian and his colleagues, L. Caecilius Firmianus Lactantius, was an African who came to Nicomedia in the reign of Diocletian to teach Latin rhetoric.[93] In Nicomedia, Lactantius was converted to Christianity while it was not only fashionable but also safe.[94] In 303 he lost or resigned his chair and began to compose works of Christian apologetic.[95] He appears, however, to have completed his *Divine Institutes,* in seven lengthy books, not in Bithynia or elsewhere in the East, but somewhere in the West, perhaps in his native Africa while the usurper Domitius Alexander ruled (308/9).[96] Lactantius then became the tutor of Constantine's eldest son.[97] When persecution of the Christians ended in 313, he probably became entitled to resume the chair which he had forfeited ten years earlier,[98] and it seems that he returned to Nicomedia.[99]

Between 313 and 315 Lactantius composed a pamphlet entitled *On the Deaths of the Persecutors,* which he dedicated to Donatus, a confessor who had spent six years in prison in Nicomedia.[100] The work has a violent and aggressive tone, with no attempt to disguise its author's bias, his profound admiration for Constantine, his deep loathing of Constantine's political adversaries. Lactantius' prejudices and strong opinions foster the suspicion that he must have tailored the facts to suit his thesis.[101] It has further been held that he wrote as a mere propagandist for Constantine, subserviently disseminating a version of his rise to power which the emperor had deliberately falsified.[102] But coins, inscriptions, and papyri confirm innumerable details of the narrative.[103] Moreover, the theories of falsification assume that Lactantius wrote *On the Deaths of the Persecutors* in Gaul between 318 and 321, and hence that he must intend to mislead when he depicts Constantine and Licinius as allies acting in harmony, because Licinius, ruler of the whole of the eastern empire from 313, went to war with Constantine not long after the latest event which Lactantius describes.

But those theories demonstrably err in assuming that Constantine and Licinius fought for the first time in October 314: when the war is correctly dated to 316/7, then the case against Lactantius collapses.[104]

Lactantius wrote *On the Deaths of the Persecutors* while Constantine and Licinius were still at peace with each other, and he wrote it in Nicomedia as a subject of Licinius, not of Constantine.[105] He may be regarded, therefore, as an independent observer whose earlier reception at the court of Constantine need not impair the value of his testimony. On the contrary, if Lactantius was in Nicomedia in 305 and in Gaul before the Battle of the Milvian Bridge, then he was in a position to know what standing Constantine enjoyed at the court of Diocletian and what legal privileges Constantine granted to his Christian subjects in Gaul before his conversion. Lactantius affirms in explicit terms that in 305 Constantine was regarded as heir presumptive to the throne and that in 306, when proclaimed emperor, Constantine immediately released the Christians of Britain, Gaul, and Spain from any form of persecution and granted them full freedom of worship.[106] He deserves to be believed.

II

GALERIUS AND THE CHRISTIANS

Diocletian and his colleagues ruled an empire which could no longer impose its will on neighboring states by diplomacy but which often needed to resort to warfare.[1] Although an orator in 291 boasted that Rome's enemies were slaughtering one another on every imperial frontier,[2] the Roman Empire did not enjoy security. The Caesars appointed on 1 March 293 at once set forth for war.

Constantius had been appointed to suppress a rebellion. He left Italy and marched across Gaul to the English Channel. The rebel régime of Carausius, who ruled Britain, still controlled the port of Bononia and much of northwestern Gaul. Constantius surrounded the town by land, blocked the entrance to its harbor, and offered the rebels favorable terms. Bononia rapidly capitulated.[3] Gaul was restored to Roman rule, Constantius enrolled the rebel troops in his own army, and Carausius fell from power: his henchman, Allectus, replaced him as Augustus in Britain.[4] Since Constantius lacked a fleet, he postponed the recovery of Britain and turned his immediate attention northward.

Before his defeat, Carausius had entered into alliance with the Franks, who with his encouragement occupied the Batavian districts. Constantius marched to the estuaries of the Rhine and the Scheldt, spreading devastation and terror. It was the first victory over foreign foes by a member of the new imperial college, and all four emperors took the title "Germanicus maximus."[5] Constantius knew how to consolidate a victory. He transported Franks, Chamavi, and Frisii from their native districts to the depopulated farmlands of Gaul, where they were put to work as slaves or serfs.[6]

It was not until 296 that a Roman expedition at last sailed for Britain to suppress Allectus. Constantius divided his forces into two. He himself sailed from Bononia, while his praetorian prefect, Asclepiodotus, and a second army embarked near the mouth of the Seine. Allectus, with the bulk of his army, awaited the emperor somewhere on the Kentish coast, having stationed his fleet near the Isle of Wight to prevent Asclepiodotus and his forces from effecting a landing.

The expedition sailed in bad weather. Asclepiodotus avoided the British fleet in a sea mist, landed, burned his boats, and began to march on London. Allectus, compelled to intercept him or lose the capital, marched swiftly westward. When the two armies met, probably in Berkshire or northern Hampshire, Allectus' Frankish mercenaries could not withstand the Roman legions, who cut them to pieces. Allectus perished in the battle. Constantius (it seems) was prevented by the bad weather from disembarking his own army as he had planned, and he returned to Gaul. But a large portion of his troops, separated from him in the fog, landed on the English coast and marched unopposed on London, where they encountered and butchered the fleeing remnants of Allectus' already defeated army.[7] Constantius now sailed in good weather to the reconquered island, whose inhabitants greeted him as a liberator, a savior, and "the restorer of eternal light."[8]

During the British expedition, Maximian stood guard on the Rhine.[9] He was soon summoned by news of trouble in Africa, where a confederation of tribes was vexing the Mauretanian provinces.[10] Maximian went there by way of Spain, which he perhaps defended against Moorish raiders.[11] By the spring of 297 he had begun an offensive campaign against the African tribes.[12] The war dragged on: Maximian retired to Carthage for the winter of 297/8 and spent another season campaigning before he at last returned to Italy in 299 and entered Rome in triumph.[13] Thereafter, Maximian relapsed into his customary life of idleness in north Italy, except for a visit to Rome in 303/4 which enabled him to bask in Diocletian's reflected glory.[14]

Maximian was even less successful in politics than in war. It is alleged that he terrorized the Senate and condemned leading senators to death on false charges—and it seems that the man who had been prefect of the city of Rome in 301/2 was disgraced and executed.[15] Constantius, in contrast, maintained good relations with the senatorial class and actively defended the empire. Residing at Trier, he took the offensive against the Franks in 300 or 301, and in the following years (302–304) he needed to repel three different groups of Germans who invaded Gaul across the Upper Rhine.[16]

Warfare against external foes had become a constant preoccupation of the Roman emperors and was to remain so throughout the fourth century. The persecution of the Christians occurred not at a time of peace, when the emperors could concentrate exclusively on internal policies, but against a background of war. A military crisis in the East enabled the Caesar Galerius to undermine the theoretical ascendancy of Diocletian in the imperial college. Galerius won glory in war, which he attempted to turn to his own political and dynastic advantage—and against that of Constantine.

In the spring of 293, Diocletian escorted his new Caesar, Galerius, from Sirmium to Byzantium before returning to Sirmium, where he spent the following winter and spring.[17] In the campaigning season of 294, Diocletian won a victory over the Sarmatians and built forts north of the Danube,[18] while the two following years saw more operations in the field and a further consolidation of the frontier, with a victory over the Carpi.[19] In the East, Galerius was occupied with military problems in remote Upper Egypt for nearly two years, until he went to Syria (probably in 295) and prepared for war against a newly aggressive Persia.[20]

The martial Shapur, who had captured the emperor Valerian in 260, died in 272 and was succeeded by a series of weak kings who surrendered royal prerogatives to the Zoroastrian clergy.[21] In 293, however, Narseh, a son of Shapur who had been passed over on his father's death, made himself king and adopted an aggressive policy against the Romans.[22] Although Galerius easily repelled his first offensive,[23] Narseh attacked again in 296 with a larger and stronger army. He overran Tiridates' kingdom in western Armenia, seized those parts of Mesopotamia which Vahram had ceded to Rome in 287, and invaded Syria, brushing aside the Roman defenses.[24] Galerius, feeling unable to meet the threat unaided, appealed to Diocletian, who came to the East late in 296; in the following spring Augustus and Caesar took the field together.[25] Narseh was forced to retire, but only after defeating a Roman army. Much will always remain obscure about this battle, which was fought between Carrhae and Callinicum, but when the emperors returned to Antioch, the official version of events became obvious to all. Galerius shouldered the blame for the defeat and was publicly humiliated: while Diocletian entered the city in a chariot, his Caesar, still wearing the imperial purple, walked before him on foot.[26]

News of the Roman defeat inspired a revolt in Egypt, where Diocletian's attempt to assimilate its tax structure more closely to that of the rest of the empire had aroused deep discontent.[27] In July or August 297 Alexandria and much of Egypt recognized one L. Domitius Domitianus as emperor,[28] and Diocletian went to Egypt to suppress him. The revolt collapsed, except at Alexandria, where Aurelius Achilleus organized the defense of the city. By the end of December the imperial government controlled the countryside, though Alexandria held out for several months more, probably until March.[29] Nor could Diocletian depart even then, for he needed to reorganize the administration and the southern frontier of Egypt.[30]

During the summer of 298 Diocletian sailed up the Nile and made a peace treaty with the Nobatae and Blemmyes which was to endure for more than two centuries. The boundary of Roman territory was withdrawn northward to the island of Philae, where Diocletian established a garrison and religious shrines; the Nobatae settled in the vacated territory and, with the Blemmyes, received an annual subsidy in gold.[31] Diocletian then returned north with all speed: in September 298 he was still in Upper Egypt, but by February 299 he was again in Syria.[32] During his absence, Galerius had retrieved Roman honor and won a victory unparalleled since Trajan's Parthian War.

After the initial defeat by the Persians, the Romans collected a new army from the Danube. When it arrived in the East, probably in the spring of 298, Galerius took a deliberate risk: he marched into the mountains of Armenia. The gamble succeeded. Narseh allowed himself to be drawn into Armenia too. Local help enabled Galerius to surprise the Persian army. He routed the enemy, capturing Narseh's wife, harem, and treasury.[33] Galerius marched on, from Armenia into Media and then into Adiabene. In each region he won a victory in the field.[34] Nisibis was captured before 1 October 298.[35] Galerius pressed forward, driving home his advantage. He sped down the Tigris to Ctesiphon, which he captured, and officers in his army were able to gaze on the ruins of Babylon, or at least what passed for such.[36] Galerius then returned to Roman territory, ascending the course of the Euphrates.[37]

A peace advantageous to Rome could now be negotiated. Narseh had already, perhaps even before Galerius invaded Mesopotamia, sent a trusted court official to seek the return of his wives and children. Galerius reminded Narseh's ambassador how Shapur had treated Valerian, how he had ordered the skin of the dead emperor to be removed and preserved for public exhibition. Galerius then summarily dismissed the envoy.[38] Serious negotiation for a treaty began in the spring of 299, when Diocletian and Galerius conferred at Nisibis. They sent Sicorius Probus, the *magister memoriae,* to present their terms to the Persian king. There were five main points: Persia was to cede territory to Rome, with the Tigris forming the boundary between the two empires; Nisibis was to be the only place of commercial exchange between Roman and Persian traders; the whole of Armenia was to be under Roman protection, with the fort Ziatha as its boundary; the king of Iberia was to owe allegiance to Rome and to be a Roman appointee; and Rome was to exercise suzerainty over the five satrapies which lay between the Tigris and Armenia. When Narseh raised a quibble over Nisibis, Probus stated bluntly that he had no mandate to revise the terms offered, and Narseh saw the necessity of submission.[39] Tiridates recovered not only his throne, but also his entire ancestral domain, Roman provinces were restored and enlarged, and the empire acquired a wide zone of influence beyond the Tigris.

Diocletian and Galerius returned to Syria. In 299 while the emperors were engaged in sacrifice and divination, some Christians in their household made the sign of the cross to ward off demons. The haruspices failed to discover normal marks on the entrails of the sacrificed animals, and repeated attempts could not produce the desired divination. The master of the haruspices detected the cause: profane men were interrupting the sacrifices. The enraged emperors ordered all the members of the imperial court to sacrifice to the gods. Further, they sent letters to all military commanders: all soldiers under their command were to sacrifice or else to quit the army.[40]

This sudden purge reflected the increased political influence of Galerius. Diocletian was prepared to tolerate Christianity: in Nicomedia the Christian church was visible from the imperial palace, there were avowed Christians at his court, and even his wife and daughter were believed sympathetic to the religion.[41] Galerius, on the other hand, was a fanatical pagan, and success in war had increased his prestige. Diocletian now feared him; and Galerius did not forget how Diocletian had humiliated him. Always arrogant and ambitious, the Caesar now resented his subordinate position and began to express his dissatisfaction openly.[42] Contemporaries considered Galerius the main instigator of the persecution of the Christians.[43] They correctly saw that persecution was not part of Diocletian's grand design for the Roman Empire, that conflict was not inevitable. Persecution came after a generation of peace, and it came through the efforts of a group of men whose motives may not have been exclusively religious.

The initial purge had no immediate sequel. The Persian War successfully completed, Diocletian and Galerius changed stations. The Augustus resided at Antioch for three years, visiting Egypt in the winter of 301/2, when he instituted a distribution of free bread in Alexandria.[44] The Caesar took charge of the defense of the Danube and resided in Thessalonica, where he constructed an enormous palace, a mausoleum, and a triumphal arch depicting the Persian War; the engraved reliefs of the arch presented Diocletian and Galerius almost as equals and left no doubt in the mind of any beholder which of the two had won the victory.[45] From Thessalonica, Galerius probably urged Diocletian to issue a general law against the Christians.

Galerius was able to persuade Diocletian to persecute the Christians partly because he could argue that the official ideology of the Tetrarchy presupposed religious conformity. The emperors, with all the enthusiasm of provincials risen to power, desired to be even more Roman than Romans of impeccable ancestry.[46] They never denied their Pannonian origins, but their coinage proclaimed their devotion to the *genius* of the Roman people,[47] and Diocletian endeavored to make the empire truly Roman: Latin became the language of government even in the Greek-speaking East,[48] and Diocletian continually reaffirmed the predominance of Roman law over local law and custom with the plausible justification that all who possessed Roman citizenship (as virtually all the inhabitants of the Roman Empire had since 212/3) should obey the Roman law which united them, rather than local laws which varied from region to region.[49]

An intense moral fervor can sometimes be detected in the laws of the period. An imperial edict issued at Damascus in 295 affirms that Roman laws of marriage shall be valid everywhere.[50] The forbidden degrees of kinship are specified: they naturally repeat what had long been Roman law. The edict not only declares that all marriages contracted after a certain date contrary to the "honor of the Roman name and sanctity of the laws" shall be null and void but also denounces such marriages as wicked, manifestly criminal, and deserving of severe punishment. (In their clemency, the emperors allow previous offenders to escape the execution they deserve but declare all offspring of the forbidden unions bastards.) The harshness follows from the premises of the edict: the pious and religious emperors have a strict duty to venerate and uphold the chaste and sacred precepts of Roman law. For the immortal gods will favor the Roman name, as they have in the past, if the emperors ensure that all their subjects lead a pious, religious, peaceable, and chaste life. Marriages contrary to Roman law (it is proclaimed) are like the lustful promiscuity of cattle or wild animals who cannot understand morality. Such arguments, if pressed to their logical conclusions, would obviously encourage a legislator to prescribe conformity in religion as well as in conduct.[51]

Diocletian had no objection to religious persecution as such. On the contrary, he shared traditional Roman prejudices against novel religions.[52] Some followers of the Mesopotamian visionary Mani were denounced before the proconsul of Africa. The proconsul consulted Diocletian and received a rescript from Alexandria issued on 31 March in a year which can only be 302.[53] The emperor ordered the leading Manichees burned alive together with their abominable scriptures, their followers executed with the sword, or, if they were persons of status, sent to work in the mines of Phaeno or quarries of Proconnesus. (The property of all the guilty was naturally forfeited to the imperial treasury.) When seeking advice from Diocletian, the proconsul had described the Manichean religion in some detail. This revelation of superstition and vice stung the emperor and moved him to use language of extreme vehemence. The immortal gods (he declared) had ordained that what was good and true should be tested and established by the verdict of many good, eminent, and wise men; it was wrong to dispute their verdict, and an old religion ought not to be impugned by a new one. To call into question what the ancients had fixed and defined once and for all time was the greatest of crimes. Hence the emperor must hasten to punish the depraved obstinacy of miscreants, who wantonly reject the gifts of the gods, and who set up a novel and unheard-of creed in opposition to the established religions. The Manichees were of foreign origin, they destroyed the domestic peace of the empire, they corrupted the pure morals of the Roman race. In brief, they deserved extermination.[54]

Despite his strong disapproval of religious nonconformity, Diocletian still declined to make any further move against the Christians. But in the autumn of 302, when Diocletian was in Antioch, the deacon Romanus came to the city from Caesarea in Palestine. Romanus saw men, women, and children thronging pagan temples, and he decided to protest. He came into court just as the sacrifice which was the normal preliminary to official business was being performed. Romanus interrupted and denounced the practice in a loud voice. He was arrested and at first sentenced to be burned. But Diocletian devised a more appropriate punishment for the offense committed: Romanus' tongue was cut out and he was consigned to prison, where he was executed a year later (on 17 November 303).[55]

Diocletian, enraged by the presumption and perversity of this Christian, proceeded to Nicomedia for the winter. Galerius joined him, insistent for persecution, and set out to wear down the reluctance of the senior emperor. His first step was to persuade Diocletian to seek the views of the emperors' leading counselors. Civilian governors and military commanders were asked their opinion in order of rank. Those who hated the Christians urged that the enemies of the gods and of the public cults should be destroyed; those who felt otherwise could see what Galerius wished and acquiesced, either through fear or to curry his favor. When Diocletian still hesitated, Galerius played on his religious emotions. The oracle of Apollo at Didyma was consulted. The god, or at least his priestess, whose ravings were interpreted by a prophet, replied that "the just on earth" hindered him from giving true oracles. Eager exegetes in the palace expounded the god's real meaning for Diocletian, who was at last induced to act. The festival of the Terminalia, on 23 February 303, was chosen as the day which would terminate the Christian religion.[56]

It is not easy to estimate how much support the persecution of Christians had at first. Disagreement existed in the imperial administration at all levels: at least one emperor disapproved; the palace and the army, despite the purge of 299, still contained men who were prepared to become martyrs; and some provincial governors declined to enforce at all strictly the legislation which the emperors transmitted to them.[57] The mass of the population was probably indifferent to the persecution. Long before, in the second and early third centuries, popular clamor had often encouraged or even compelled provincial governors to execute Christians.[58] More recently, when Christians were executed by imperial order under Decius and Valerian, crowds still openly jeered at martyrs and their sympathizers.[59] In the "Great Persecution," however, evidence of similar hostility is almost entirely lacking; by the last decades of the third century, the Christian church had become an established and respectable institution.[60]

Articulate enemies of Christianity could be found among the traditional urban aristocracies and in the imperial service. After the purge of 299, and still more when persecution began in earnest in 303, they began to applaud the change in imperial policy and to argue, as the Platonist Celsus had, more than a century before, that Christianity was intellectually disreputable. Most prominent among the pagans who now raised their voices was Porphyry, the pupil of Plotinus, who had recently put out a complete edition of his master's writings.[61] Porphyry published a work *Against the Christians* in fifteen books, contending that Christianity was incompatible with civilization. Christians were denounced as barbarians, as apostates from ancestral religion, as atheists who deserved punishment. Specifically, Porphyry argued that the profession of

Christianity ought rightfully to be considered a capital crime.[62] Such an argument was not an idle, theoretical, or academic exercise: Porphyry desired to encourage the imperial authorities in a policy of bloody repression.

Porphyry probably wrote in Italy.[63] In the east, an anti-Christian tract was put out by Sossianus Hierocles, who was successively *vicarius,* probably of the diocese of Oriens, and governor of Bithynia.[64] It seems that he originally published his *Lover of Truth,* which he claimed to have composed "to the Christians," not "against the Christians," in Syria before persecution began.[65] Hierocles was, therefore, a known foe of the Christians when, as a member of the imperial *consilium* early in 303, he urged Diocletian toward a policy of persecution. Moreover, when laws were promulgated against the Christians, Hierocles enforced them in Nicomedia with enthusiasm, and it was as a Roman official that he recited the *Lover of Truth* in the imperial capital.[66] At the same time, a philosopher produced a pamphlet, in three books, against the Christians. His identity is unknown, though he might have been a pupil of the Neoplatonist Iamblichus who taught at Apamea.[67] More significant than his identity was his social standing: this philosopher dined frequently in the imperial palace.[68] It was again socially and intellectually acceptable for pagans to affirm that Christians deserved to die simply for being Christians.

At dawn on 23 February 303, the praetorian prefect came with generals, tribunes, and financial officials to the Christian church in Nicomedia. The doors were torn down, copies of the Bible found and burned, and the rest of the church's contents plundered. The church was then razed. On the following day, a copy of the imperial edict, by virtue of which the praetorians had destroyed the church, was posted in the city. A Christian by the name of Euetius, a man of some social standing, took the document down and tore it into pieces, mocking its references to victories over the Goths and Sarmatians. He was arrested for treason, tortured, and burned alive that very day.[69]

The edict issued on 23 February 303 and published on the following day contained a variety of provisions designed both to prevent Christians from worshiping their God openly and to compel them to make a token act of conformity to the established religion. Assembly for Christian worship was declared illegal. In order to enforce the prohibition, Diocletian prescribed the destruction of all churches—and of any private house where copies of the Scriptures or items of church property might be discovered. All copies of the Bible and any liturgical books were to be surrendered and burned, all the paraphernalia of the Christian cult to be confiscated for the imperial treasury. Individual Christians who refused to recant were deprived of any official status and legal privileges they might possess, so that they became liable to torture, and Christian freedmen in imperial service were reduced to slavery. The edict specified very precisely that anyone who came to plead in any court, criminal or civil, should sacrifice to the gods before he was heard. This requirement was a devastating blow for any Christian who owned property. Lactantius complained that the enemies of a Christian could now seize his goods, steal his wife, and assault his person with impunity: Diocletian had totally deprived him of legal redress.[70]

The first persecuting edict was promulgated throughout the Roman Empire. Even Constantius, who mitigated its effects and allowed no executions in his domains, demolished churches.[71] How the law worked in practice can perhaps be seen most clearly in Africa, where Maximian encouraged stricter enforcement. In the edict, Diocletian had provided that the local magistrates and leading men of each city should supervise the suppression of the Christian cult. In one African town, the *curator* arrested a priest, two lectors, and the elders of the congregation and demanded their holy books. When they replied that the absent bishop had the books, the magistrate kept them in custody until the bishop returned. He admitted having Scriptures but refused repeated requests to surrender them for burning. The *curator* then sent the bishop under escort to Carthage, where the proconsul sentenced him to death.[72] The *curator* of Cirta in Numidia, who was also *flamen perpetuus* of the city, performed his commission with greater success. When he arrived at the church, the bishop had no copies of the Scriptures, but he voluntarily surrendered a large amount of church plate, together with a quantity of shoes and clothing presumably kept in the church for distribution to the needy. The building was then searched, and various other objects came to light. Finally, the *curator* tracked down the lectors who were said to have the Scriptures: codices were seized from several persons, their houses being searched if the *curator* deemed it necessary.[73]

The edict itself probably specified no penalties for failure to comply with its terms, simply assuming that the normal practices would apply: recalcitrants would be executed, either by the sword or in a more brutal fashion.[74] As a result, an individual governor could enforce the edict either with comparative mildness or with extreme severity. The proconsul of Africa and the *praeses* of Numidia chose the latter course. More than sixty years later, their ferocity was still remembered. The Christians in their provinces could nowhere feel safe, even though they steadfastly avoided pagan temples and altars. By physical force, they were compelled to burn incense, to deny Christ, to join in the destruction of churches, and to consign the holy Scriptures to the flames.[75] Anullinus, the proconsul of Africa, added his own interpretation to the imperial edict: besides the surrender of the Scriptures and the destruction of churches, he ordered that Christians should sacrifice to the gods.[76] Similarly, during the summer or autumn of 303 at Milevis in Numidia, where Valerius Florus was the governor, there were "days of incense burning" which cost Christians their lives.[77]

The edict of 23 February 303 provided the only legal basis for the "Great Persecution" in the West.[78] In August 304 a Christian in Sicily could still be executed under its provisions.[79] In the East, however, Diocletian and Galerius adopted a more stringent policy of repression.[80] In the spring or summer of 303, protests against the emperors in Melitene and Syria produced ephemeral rebellions,[81] and thereupon a new edict ordered the Christian clergy arrested and imprisoned.[82] The prisons could not accommodate the crowds of bishops, priests, deacons, lectors, and exorcists. Accordingly, Diocletian declared an amnesty to mark his approaching *vicennalia* on 20 November. But sacrifice to the gods was a condition for release, and many clergy endured torture and death rather than secure their release on such terms. Nevertheless, the prisons were emptied, sometimes by obtaining merely nominal compliance with the imperial order: some Christians were physically forced to perform a sacrifice over which they had no control, while others were deemed to have sacrificed even when they did nothing.[83] In the early months of 304, a fourth and more severe edict went out: the inhabitants of each city, men, women, and children, were to gather in a body and collectively offer sacrifice and libations to the gods.[84] This edict was already being enforced in Thessalonica in April 304, and it reached Palestine not long after.[85] Maximian and Constantius neither enforced nor even promulgated it in their domains.

In Nicomedia itself, the first persecuting edict was followed by a mysterious fire. Before the end of February, part of the imperial palace burned down. Years later Constantine, who had been there, spoke of lightning and fire from heaven.[86] At the time, Christians and pagans blamed each other. But it was Galerius who had Diocletian's ear. He accused the Christians of plotting with the eunuchs of the palace to destroy both emperors. Diocletian was frightened and enraged. An investigation began, and although nothing was discovered, executions commenced. The victims included many members of the imperial household, among them the eunuchs Dorotheus and Gorgonius. The emperors presided over many of the trials and tortures in person. When Peter, another member of the imperial household, appeared before them, they had him stripped, raised high, and scourged all over. They then poured salt and vinegar in his wounds and slowly roasted him alive.[87]

The pogrom continued violently in Nicomedia until at least 24 April, when the bishop Anthimus was beheaded, together with five others.[88] Not all those arrested met their deaths. The scholarly priest Lucian, in prison when the bishop died, was destined to live several years longer.[89] The priest Donatus, probably first arrested in the spring of 303, was not brought before the emperors but before the praetorian prefect Flaccinus, who tortured him. Donatus neither yielded nor received a sentence of death. Despite further tortures from Sossianus Hierocles and Priscillianus, who succeeded Hierocles as governor of Bithynia, Donatus survived, spending years in prison. In 311 he emerged from jail, with many other confessors, and later received Lactantius' *On the Deaths of the Persecutors* with its invaluable account of the circumstances in which he had suffered.[90]

Sixteen days after the first fire, there occurred a second. Galerius at once departed from Nicomedia declaring the city unsafe;[91] nor did Diocletian remain many weeks longer. He set out for Rome to celebrate his *vicennalia* and the

Persian victory. The journey occupied most of the year. Diocletian entered Rome shortly before 20 November 303 and celebrated, with Maximian, the *vicennalia* of both Augusti, the *decennalia* of the Caesars, and a triumph for Galerius' victory over the Persians.[92] But Diocletian had lived too long in the atmosphere of a servile court whose ceremonial reflected his supreme power. At Rome people expected him to play the citizen and magistrate, not the autocrat. Irritated and annoyed, Diocletian left Rome before the ceremonies marking the start of his ninth consulate, which he assumed on 1 January 304 at Ravenna. On the journey, he contracted a slight illness but spent the spring and early summer of 304 inspecting the Danube frontier.[93]

The illness Diocletian had contracted continued to affect him. He traveled now, for the most part, in a litter. When he reached Nicomedia (by 28 August), the malady became still more serious. On 20 November, Diocletian appeared in public to dedicate the circus adjoining the palace. Soon afterward, he collapsed. Prayers were offered for his life, until on 13 December he seemed to have expired, and the palace and the city plunged into sudden mourning. The following day, however, a rumor that the emperor was still alive swept through the city, and mourning was put aside—though some alleged that Diocletian's death was being deliberately concealed until Galerius could arrive. Such suspicions were not allayed for many weeks. Only on 1 March 305 did Diocletian appear again in public, emaciated and scarcely recognizable from his long illness.[94] His judgment and his will power were now impaired.

During the month of March, Galerius arrived on the gravest of political business. He wished to reconstitute the imperial college: Diocletian and Maximian were to abdicate after he appointed two of his own nominees as Caesars. Galerius had already met Maximian and terrified him into acquiescence. When he reached Nicomedia, he urged Diocletian to resign his power, and the two emperors deliberated in secret, perhaps at some length and with acrimony. Whatever was in fact said or threatened, the result was entirely as Galerius desired.[95]

In the spring of 305, it still seemed obvious who would replace Diocletian and Maximian in the imperial college. Only two of the four emperors had adult sons, and Constantine and Maxentius had long been groomed for the succession.[96] Perhaps as early as 293 (and certainly no later than 296), Constantine came to the East, where he served as an officer in the Roman army, first in the campaigns of the Persian War and later under Galerius on the Danube.[97] By 301/2 he was with Diocletian's court: when the emperor traversed Palestine, Constantine rode at his right hand, in the place of honor.[98] Constantine was in Nicomedia in both March 303 and March 305[99] and had presumably accompanied Diocletian to Rome in the interval. By March 305 Constantine was a man of thirty-two or thirty-three whose rank in the Roman army and accomplishments in war rendered him a candidate for the purple on the grounds of merit as well as descent.[100] Maxentius too (were the truth on record) had probably served under Galerius, and he was either in Nicomedia or at his father's court in Italy, waiting to become the Caesar of the West.[101] Neither Constantine nor Maxentius concealed his personal dislike of Galerius,[102] and neither was likely as Caesar to accord Galerius the respect he considered his due. Moreover, when they came to power, both Constantine and Maxentius immediately abrogated the legislation against the Christians.[103] It is possible that they were already known to be sympathetic towards Christianity before 303[104] and that Galerius urged Diocletian to adopt the policy of persecution partly in order to embarrass or discredit the two princes.

On 1 May 305 Diocletian summoned an assembly of generals, troops who habitually accompanied him, and representatives from distant legions. They gathered about three miles outside Nicomedia at the very spot where Diocletian had been proclaimed emperor. Before a column surmounted by a statue of Jupiter, his patron deity, a weeping Diocletian addressed his men: he told them that he was weak, needed rest, and must entrust the empire to stronger hands. Few doubted what would follow. All eyes looked to Constantine. But Diocletian named Severus and Maximinus as Caesars. Constantine stood there, shocked like the rest. Then Galerius produced Maximinus. Diocletian removed his purple robe and put it on the new Caesar.[105] On the same day, Severus, whom Galerius had sent secretly to Milan, received the imperial purple from the hands of Maximian.[106]

The new emperors were a disparate pair. Severus was a practiced soldier, middle-aged, violent, and hard-drinking—a creature of Galerius.[107] Maximinus had even a closer tie, for he was Galerius' nephew. He was young, despite having been a foot soldier, a bodyguard of the emperor, and a tribune.[108] He may also have appealed to Diocletian for superstitious reasons. Maximinus was born on the same day—and possibly in the selfsame year—as Diocletian became emperor.[109]

After 1 May 305, the imperial college still comprised two Augusti and two Caesars, among whom Constantius took precedence over Galerius, and Severus over Maximinus. The new emperors took the divine epithets which they received from their adoptive fathers: Severus was the son of Constantius, and hence Herculius, while Maximinus became Iovius as the son of Galerius.[110] And the retired emperors retained an honorary position in the imperial college as "senior Augusti and fathers of the Augusti."[111]

A new territorial division of the empire was made.[112] Constantius received Spain to add to Gaul and Britain;[113] Galerius added Asia Minor to the Balkans and Greece; Severus was assigned Italy and Africa, and perhaps also part of Pannonia; Maximinus got the large diocese of Oriens.[114] Galerius was the great gainer from the redistribution. Residing now at Serdica, he ruled directly over the vast area from the boundaries of Italy to the mountains of the Taurus, with Severus in Milan and Maximinus in Antioch as virtual dependents. Beyond the Alps, Constantius was supreme for the present. But illness and age (he was fifty-five) rendered an imminent decease probable. Galerius then hoped to extend his authority over the whole empire.[115]

Galerius, however, though brutal by nature and hardly a man to flinch from shedding blood, either had scruples which prevented him from removing potential threats to his supremacy or else lacked the opportunity. It seemed of no significance that Diocletian should retire to his homeland to the palace which he had built at Spalato, or Maximian to a life of ease and luxury in fashionable Campania and Lucania.[116] The disappointed heirs stationed themselves in strategic positions. Maxentius took up residence outside Rome, in a villa on the Via Labicana, and ostentatiously comported himself as a Roman senator.[117] Constantine joined his father in Britain.

Within a few years of his arrival, Constantine and his propagandists had put out a colorful tale about his journey to Constantius. In this official story, Constantine fled Nicomedia the moment he had gained leave to depart, hamstringing horses to prevent pursuit or interception by Severus, and arrived in Britain to find his father on his deathbed.[118] The reality, if more prosaic, reveals more about Constantine's position in 305/6. Whatever the circumstances of his departure, Constantine left the court of Galerius not long after 1 May 305. He found his father about to cross from Bononia to Britain. Father and son crossed the English Channel together and sped north. Constantius marched beyond Hadrian's Wall, defeated the Picts, and before the end of the campaigning season of 305, claimed a victory.[119] Constantine was always at his father's side, again a destined heir to the imperial purple.

On 25 July 306 at York, Constantius died, with the children of both his marriages in attendance.[120] His army and his entourage, led (it was later said) by a king of the Alamanni, saluted Constantine as emperor in his father's stead. Constantine may have made a conventional show of reluctance, but no one was deceived. Both then and later Constantine asseverated most categorically that the dying Constantius had made him his heir in the fullest sense—as the ruler of Britain, Gaul, and Spain with the rank of Augustus.[121]

III

THE RISE OF CONSTANTINE

Constantine was in his thirty-fourth or thirty-fifth year when proclaimed emperor. Long groomed for the throne, he knew the realities of power and a monarch's need for genuine popularity. His first actions as emperor reveal his unerring astuteness in exploiting a political opportunity. The new Augustus at once decreed a formal end to the persecution of Christians in his domains and restored Christianity to its former status and privileges.[1] Constantius had enforced only one of the persecuting edicts, and that without bloodshed. But Constantine did more than merely continue his father's policy of passive toleration. He gave the Christians in his domains full restitution of what they had lost under the first of the persecuting edicts. This political gesture had a wide significance: Constantine asserted his right to legislate for his own subjects, dissociated himself from the policies of his imperial colleagues, and proclaimed himself a potential liberator for persecuted Christians elsewhere. He had perhaps already perceived how vulnerable was the hold of the other three emperors on the loyalty of those under their rule.

Although Constantine could only be called a usurper on the most tendentious of definitions, he at once set out to put his legitimacy beyond any possible doubt. He dispatched the traditional laureled image of himself to Galerius,

28

now the senior member of the imperial college. In the accompanying announcement of his accession, Constantine described himself as Augustus and Galerius' colleague. Strict protocol had been observed, and Galerius was faced with a difficult problem. He had no desire to have Constantine as a colleague. But Constantine had seized control of Constantius' territories, was acting as an emperor, and could advance an indisputable claim to have received appointment from his father in due form. Moreover, Galerius felt insecure even within his own territory.[2] In 306 the Augustus of the East ordained that the urban population of cities throughout the empire should be included on the census lists and taxed. New taxes are always resented, but loss of this traditional exemption stirred passions everywhere, and attempts at evasion necessitated a dangerous number of executions.[3] The unpopular census might produce insurrection, and to attempt to remove Constantine was impossible. Galerius accordingly presented him in turn with a dilemma. He accepted the laureled image and Constantine's right to the throne, but he dispatched a purple robe from the East to indicate that it was he, not Constantius, who had made the appointment—and he proclaimed Constantine Caesar only, promoting Severus to replace the dead Augustus.[4]

Constantine reacted with mature sagacity. He accepted the appointment as Caesar and thereby removed any possible doubt about the legitimacy of his rule. He could always revive the claim that his father had raised him to the rank of Augustus on the day he had died, whenever he deemed it advantageous or appropriate. For the present, he was content to rule with the title of Caesar in Britain, Gaul, and Spain. He established his credentials as a warrior when he crossed to the continent, repelled a Frankish raid, and exhibited two captured kings in triumphal games at Trier.[5] Implacably ambitious, Constantine was determined to become sole ruler of a united Roman Empire. But, secure within his own realm, he could confidently await the course of events. Whatever might happen elsewhere in the empire would probably bring him some political advantage.

Galerius' fiscal policy produced more than vague feelings of outrage among his subjects. He extended the imperial census to peninsular Italy and to Rome itself.[6] To tax Rome was an innovation which shocked many, even though the continuing exemption of the former capital had become an anomaly after Diocletian began to exact tribute from Italy north of the Appennines as if the area were a province like any other. In the autumn of 306 imperial commissioners arrived in Rome to register the populace. Moreover, Galerius had recently removed the bulk of the praetorian guard from Rome; since its principal function was to guard emperors, he had presumably decided to incorporate these much needed soldiers in his own army. A few praetorians, however, remained in the camp at Rome.

Maxentius, chafing at his idleness and jealous of Constantine, seized his opportunity and plotted insurrection. He gained the support (it appears) of the three tribunes of the urban cohorts, and with their help killed Abellius, the *vi-carius* of the *praefectus urbi* who commanded these cohorts but who had refused to join the conspiracy. The remnants of the praetorian guard still in Rome then mutinied, joined the discontented people, and on 28 October 306 invested Maxentius with the imperial purple.[7]

Maxentius, like Constantine, sought recognition and legitimacy from Galerius. Indeed, he went further than Constantine in modesty and styled himself merely *princeps,* deliberately avoiding the official titles of Augustus or Caesar until he should receive appointment from the senior emperor.[8] Galerius refused. He hated his son-in-law, and a fifth emperor would destroy the symmetry of an imperial college of two Augusti each aided by a Caesar.[9] Since Maxentius could not retreat, he assumed the title of Augustus and prepared to defend his position by force.[10] In January 307, the consuls for the new year were announced in Rome. The choice neatly defined Maxentius' attitude: he rejected Galerius' nomination of Severus as consul, substituting Galerius himself, but he acknowledged the Caesar Maximinus as the other consul.[11] That can only mean that Maxentius still hoped for recognition as a member of the imperial college.

When he heard of Maxentius' coup in Rome, Galerius summoned Severus and urged him to suppress the rebel. Before the winter ended, Severus marched south from Milan. But he overestimated his hold on his troops, many of whom had served in the army of Maximian. Many also retained happy memories of Rome, where they would rather live than on the northern frontier. Maxentius too made a miscalculation. Not feeling wholly confident of success (he had few troops for a pitched battle), he decided to seek his father's aid. He sent a purple robe to Maximian and saluted him as "Augustus for the second time." Maximian, ever resentful of his enforced retirement, eagerly joined the fray.

When Severus approached Rome, Maxentius used bribery to seduce his army. Severus' men began to desert; even Severus' praetorian prefect came over to Maxentius' side. The Augustus of the West fled to Ravenna, where Maximian besieged him. Since the city seemed impregnable, Maximian offered terms. Severus accepted them, surrendered on a promise of his life, and divested himself of the purple. Maximian took him to Rome as a hostage.[12]

Severus' failure had immediate political consequences. Maxentius may again have sought recognition from Galerius only to suffer a second rebuff; at all events, in April 307 he rejected the consulate of Galerius and Maximinus which he had proclaimed in January.[13] Galerius pretended officially that Severus was still emperor, and he prepared to suppress Maxentius himself.[14] He was, however, probably delayed by trouble on the Danubian frontier, where between the proclamation of Constantine as emperor and his own invasion of Italy he won a victory over the Sarmatians.[15] Not until the summer had almost passed was Galerius ready to advance into Italy. Severus, kept in custody at Tres Tabernae outside Rome, could now serve no useful purpose for Maxentius and Maximian. He was removed, either by execution or enforced suicide.[16]

Maxentius and Maximian stood in sore need of allies to face Galerius, whose skill as a general was known to all. They sought the friendship or neutrality of Constantine and offered him Fausta, the sister of Maxentius, in marriage.[17] A decade or more earlier, Constantine had probably been expected to marry Fausta,[18] though subsequently he had married Minervina, who bore him a son before she died.[19] As a widower, he welcomed the opportunity of a royal bride. But he insisted that Maximian, who had proclaimed Constantius Caesar, should formally promote him too to the rank of Augustus. The double ceremony was celebrated in the late summer of 307, and the panegyric then recited in joint praise of the two emperors survives.[20] The orator stressed the dynastic connections of the Herculean dynasty, the modesty of Constantine in waiting for Maximian to promote him, and Maximian's devotion to duty in refusing to abandon Rome in her hour of need. His audience no doubt understood the allusion. Although the speech names neither Galerius nor Maxentius, even by a periphrasis, all knew that the two were about to confront each other beyond the Alps.

Galerius entered Italy about September 307 and marched on Rome. The walls of Aurelian provided sufficient protection, and the city shut its gates. Galerius had no hope of storming the city, and his army, though large, could not surround the whole circuit of the walls and mount an effective siege. He camped by the Tiber, and then attempted negotiation. He sent his lieutenants Licinius and Probus to seek an interview with Maxentius. They promised that if Maxentius would make a formal submission to Galerius, he could peaceably receive all he wished. Maxentius spurned the offer, either because he suspected a trick or because he knew the weakness of Galerius' position. Several legions of the besieging army soon deserted, Maxentius was wooing the rest, and Galerius feared the fate of Severus. But Galerius was a far better general than Severus, and he had the able Licinius as his chief lieutenant. He fell on his knees before his men, made them extravagant promises—and retained the loyalty of the great majority. The army, not yet in disarray, retreated north, laying Italy waste to revenge themselves and to hinder pursuit.[21] Galerius thus avoided a decisive defeat and extricated himself from peril. Maxentius, though he ruled Italy and Africa more firmly than before, was still a usurper.

The consuls of 308 reflect the altered political situation. Galerius assumed the *fasces* himself for the seventh time with Diocletian as his colleague, and he begged the retired Augustus to emerge from his Dalmatian retreat.[22] He needed the advice and authority of Diocletian to sanction the appointment of new emperors. For Galerius put a strict interpretation on the actions of Constantine. He reasoned that Constantine, by allying himself with the usurper in Italy against the senior legitimate emperor and by proclaiming his own consuls in Gaul in 307, had forfeited his membership in the imperial college.[23] About September 307, Galerius' mints dropped Constantine from the imperial coinage, and official documents in the East began to employ dating formulas which treated Galerius and Maximinus as the only legitimate emperors—and Galerius maintained the same official attitude to Constantine after his invasion of Italy.[24] Constantine of necessity pretended that his status as emperor remained unimpaired, and in 308 he accepted Diocletian and Galerius as consuls of the year.[25] Maxentius too adopted a conciliatory posture: in Rome in January 308 the consuls were announced as "those whom our lords the Augusti shall ordain."[26]

In April 308 a sudden crisis supervened. Maximian ruled conjointly with his son, but as an inferior both in real power and in official rank. The old man, who had enjoyed twenty years as the only or the senior emperor in the West, resented his subordination and attempted to depose his son. Assuming that his former army would support him, Maximian convened an assembly of soldiers and civilians. He discoursed on the ills of the state, denounced Maxentius as the main author of its calamities, and ripped the purple from his son's shoulders. Maxentius leaped down from the platform where they both stood, and the soldiers took his side. Maximian fled from Rome with all haste.[27] On 20 April 308 Maxentius proclaimed himself and his son Valerius Romulus consuls of the year in Italy and Africa.[28]

Maximian fled to Gaul, where Constantine received him, probably with embarrassment, despite a show of amity.[29] For Maximian was an obstacle to Galerius' official recognition of Constantine as a legitimate emperor. On the other hand, since Galerius had totally lost control of the West, he needed to come to terms with one of its two rulers, and his breach with Maxentius was the more irreconcilable. Constantine could only gain by waiting patiently. Galerius (it seems) was occupied on the lower Danube during the summer of 308; he campaigned against the Carpi and proclaimed an imperial victory.[30] In the autumn he conferred at Carnuntum with Diocletian, who emerged briefly from retirement. Maximian came too. On 11 November 308, with both former emperors present, Galerius appointed Licinius, a trusted friend and comrade in arms, to be Augustus in place of the dead Severus.[31] The ceremony occurred, appropriately, in the military camp of Carnuntum, where the four emperors dedicated a newly restored shrine of Mithras, both in their own name and on behalf of the two absent Caesars.[32]

The settlement at Carnuntum reconstituted the imperial college as a tetrarchy, and Constantine was again, on any criterion, a legitimate emperor. Maximian was once more compelled to divest himself of the purple.[33] Galerius returned to Serdica and probably soon took up residence in Thessalonica.[34] Licinius chose Sirmium for his capital, awaiting an opportunity to reunite Maxentius' territories with the rest of the empire.[35]

The Caesars were discontented. Augustus in his own domains, Constantine hoped that the emperors at Carnuntum would concede his right to the title—and there is no evidence that he ever accepted demotion.[36] In the East, Maximinus attempted to argue with Galerius. Still Caesar and officially the third member of the imperial college, he contended that he ought to be superior in rank to the new emperor. Galerius sent envoys to urge him to respect his arrangements and to yield to Licinius' age and grey hair. When he failed to assuage the Caesar's anger, Galerius divised a new title and styled both Maximinus and Constantine "sons of the Augusti."[37] Too timid or too insecure for open defiance, Maximinus appeared to accept the compromise.[38] A little more than a year later, however, perhaps precisely on 1 May 310, Maximinus' army saluted him Augustus, and he began to use the title openly.[39] Galerius of necessity acquiesced, though he may have promoted Maximinus to second place in the imperial college of four Augusti tardily and with reluctance.[40] The promotion of Maximinus and Constantine spelled the end of the successive imperial colleges of two Augusti and two Caesars. But if all the emperors were Augusti, then the imperial college was no longer a tetrarchy on the Diocletianic model—and it could then contain either more or less than four members.

Licinius, appointed Augustus at Carnuntum in order to suppress Maxentius,[41] began his task in the next campaigning season (309). The prospects for victory were favorable, for a rebellion in Africa (probably begun in the summer or autumn of 308) was endangering the stability of Maxentius' régime.[42] Valerius Alexander, who had served as *vicarius* of Africa for at least five years,[43] proclaimed himself Augustus, sought an alliance with Constantine, made himself master of the sea, seized control of Sardinia, and cut off the corn supply to the city of Rome.[44] Maxentius reacted decisively. Few regular troops were stationed anywhere in Africa. Alexander was enrolling Gaetulians and Moors in his army, but was vulnerable to a swift attack.

Maxentius sent his praetorian prefect, Rufius Volusianus, to suppress the rebel. His army, though small, was well led and well trained. Volusianus crossed to Africa with a few cohorts and routed the ill-armed rebels. The victorious troops rampaged through Carthage and other African cities. Alexander fled to Cirta, which was stormed and sacked,[45] and the rebel was captured and brutally strangled.[46] Maxentius' subordinates then conducted a purge of known and suspected supporters of Alexander in which many were killed and those who escaped with their lives were stripped of their property.[47] As for the rebel army, it swore allegiance to Maxentius and went to reinforce the defense of Italy.[48] Maxentius himself celebrated a triumph in Rome.[49]

In the same year as the African expedition (309), Maxentius closed the northern Italian mints of Ticinum and Aquileia,[50] presumably because he feared that they might fall into the hands of Licinius, who had probably already seized the outlying provinces of the Italian diocese. For in 309, so it seems, Licinius attacked Istria;[51] in 310 the Istrian town of Parentium honored Licinius as its sovereign, but the fact that Licinius' name was later erased may indicate that Maxentius subsequently recovered Istria for a period.[52] Licinius was now busy elsewhere: on 27 June 310 he won a victory over the Sarmatians,[53] and thereafter the political and military situation in the Balkans claimed his attention. In the spring of 310 Galerius was unexpectedly afflicted by a disease (perhaps cancer of the bowels), which rendered him incapable of strenuous action.[54] His Christian subjects were doubtless already saying what they were to reiterate with jubilation after he died: that the illness came from God.[55] Whatever its nature or origin, the illness of Galerius had profound political consequences: it distracted Licinius and enabled Maxentius to strengthen the defenses of Italy against invasion from Pannonia.

Nor had Maxentius anything to fear from Constantine, at least for the present. If Alexander had styled himself the ally and colleague of Constantine, there is no sign that Constantine accepted his overtures, still less helped his cause in any way.[56] Constantine had one overriding political aim in his early years: to secure his political base in Gaul and Britain. To this end, he visited Britain twice (apparently in 307 and late in 310),[57] traveled through Gaul advertising his benevolence towards his subjects, and campaigned assiduously on the German frontier. In the first months of his reign he had defeated a Frankish incursion, in 308 he crossed the Rhine to devastate the territory of the Bructeri, and in 310 he was again on campaign against the Franks when an internal crisis challenged his authority.[58]

Constantine's absence offered Maximian an irresistible temptation. Maximian had left Carnuntum in November 308 disgruntled at a second forced abdication. Constantine received him again into his household, as a private citizen but also as his father-in-law and as an apparently trusted adviser. Little more than a year had passed since Maximian conferred on him the rank of Augustus, which Diocletian and Galerius now denied him. Even if Constantine had not needed Maximian's assistance, he could not entirely deny him access to the palace (and hence to influence) nor wholly suppress his inclination to meddle in public affairs. In fact, however, Constantine probably needed Maximian as a lieutenant, should he become embroiled in war on two flanks. In 310, while he marched north to fight on the lower Rhine, he sent his father-in-law south with part of his army. Although it was subsequently alleged that Maximian tricked him into dividing his forces, the political situation suggests that Constantine feared an attack from Maxentius in southern Gaul.

Maximian hurried to Arles, announced that Constantine was dead, and donned the imperial purple for a third time. He then seized all the public or imperial funds he could find, gave a donative to the soldiers who saluted him emperor, and promised equal generosity to all who would forsake Constantine. The attempt to seduce Constantine's army failed: most of his troops remained loyal. Constantine abandoned his campaign against the Franks and swiftly marched up the Rhine. At Cabillunum, he embarked his army on waiting boats: they rowed down the sluggish Saône until the rapid current of the Rhone carried them south from Lugdunum.

Maximian did not await their arrival. He left Arles and shut himself up in Massilia, which could withstand a long siege. When Constantine arrived, however, the citizens of Massilia opened its gates. The rebel was dragged before Constantine, who reproved him for his crimes. The discredited Maximian soon hanged himself. A panegyrist who addressed Constantine only a few weeks later avowed that the guilty man refused to accept clemency, deeming himself unworthy to live any longer. He doubtless received strong encouragement to commit suicide.[59]

The death of Maximian ultimately strengthened Constantine's real authority over his court and administration. But part of his army had proved disloyal, and there were other sons of Constantius available for the purple, should anyone emulate Maximian and challenge Constantine's position. In the summer of 310, therefore, Constantine felt insecure and resorted to a dynastic fiction which shows a real flair for propaganda. A speech delivered before Constantine shortly after 25 July not only narrates the story of the rebellion of Maximian, but mirrors very accurately what the Constantine of 310 wished his subjects to believe about their monarch and his right to rule.[60]

The orator begins by revealing a closely guarded secret: there flows in the veins of Constantine the blood of Claudius, who defeated the Goths when they poured over the Danube and through the Hellespont, and thus first restored order to the Roman Empire.[61] (Significantly, Constantine's precise relationship to Claudius is not vouchsafed: the inventors of the pedigree vacillated between grandfather and great-uncle.)[62] Constantine was the third emperor in his family. He was the sole rightful heir of Constantius, being his eldest son, begotten when his father was in the prime of youth, and in every way resembling him.[63] Not that birth constituted Constantine's sole claim to the purple: on the contrary, so far as his age allowed, he pursued a military career with distinction, performing deeds of valor in hand-to-hand combat with the enemy. But it is one thing to strive laboriously uphill from the plain to the ridges of a mountain, another to start at the summit, and to have fortune in hand rather than merely in expectation. The felicity of those who rise through the ranks of the army to become emperor deserves admiration (the allusion is to Licinius), but Constantine entered the imperial palace of Trier not as a candidate for power, but as a designated heir.[64]

Constantine, the orator continues, accompanied his father on his last expedition, when Constantius sought not merely a triumph in Britain but a closer approach to the gods who were summoning him to their midst. When the heavenly temples opened to receive the dying emperor, Jupiter welcomed him and asked whom he desired to name as his successor. The gods ratified Constantius' choice of Constantine by unanimous verdict. The terrestrial proclamation followed. As soon as Constantius departed this earth, all his army and all his subjects fixed on Constantine as their new emperor, despite an obvious and emphatic reluctance which led him (so the disingenuous orator avers) to mount a horse and attempt to flee. Unwilling to disappoint the wishes of his loyal subjects, Constantine consulted the senior emperors, who confirmed his appointment to the imperial college.[65] Constantine at once began to display the virtues of a good, wise, and brave ruler: he defeated the Franks who dared to invade Roman territory, he secured peace along the frontier, he conducted raids deep into hostile territory, and he built a bridge over the Rhine at Cologne in order to increase Roman authority over the German tribes.[66] Admittedly, there was trouble on the Rhine when Constantine went south to suppress Maximian. But the news of Constantine's success quieted the restive barbarians at once.[67]

The Constantine whom the orator of 310 describes is a dutiful member of the imperial college, which reigns in harmonious majesty: if the orator praises Constantine alone, he intends no disrespect to the other emperors, whom he would praise too if they were present.[68] Hence he lauds Diocletian (which is remarkable in itself and in contradiction to Constantine's true opinions). That "divine man" (he is not named), the first both to share and to abdicate the empire, has no regrets: he does not consider lost what he voluntarily resigned, he is truly happy and blessed because so many emperors revere him as a private citizen. He rejoices in the protection of Constantine, whom he regards as his own offspring and whose successes he treats as his own.[69]

The speech also contains another disconcerting element—a vision attributed to Constantine. On his way to Massilia, the emperor made a brief diversion to "the fairest temple in the whole world"—presumably, since it was a temple of Apollo, the shrine of Apollo Grannus at Grand.[70] There (so the orator asserts, in words which betray the fiction) Constantine saw Apollo, accompanied by Victory, offering him four laurel crowns which each signified thirty years of success, and which together promised him as long a life as a man could enjoy.[71] Better still, Constantine recognized himself in Apollo: young, handsome, joyful, a bringer of salvation, the world ruler whose advent Virgil foretold.[72] After his victory, Constantine fulfilled the vows to the immortal gods which he had made on his journey south, and showered the shrine of Apollo with lavish gifts.[73]

It is not necessary to believe that Constantine ever saw such a vision.[74] The orator speaks as he does not because the emperor had revealed to him his private thoughts, but because he wants to persuade Constantine to extend imperial generosity to the cult of Apollo in Autun, where (he brazenly informs Constantine) the god's hot spring punishes perjury.[75] The orator, who came from Autun, was alert to the possibility that his native city, with its grove, temple, and spring of Apollo, might benefit from Constantine's recent adoption of Sol or Apollo as his patron deity.[76]

In the ideology of the Tetrarchy, Constantius was both Herculius and, at least while Caesar, under the special protection of Sol Invictus, conventionally identified with Apollo.[77] In the early years of his reign, the coinage of Constantine advertised his especial patron as Mars, the god of war.[78] In 310, however, the coinage of Constantine replaces Mars with Sol—a change clearly connected with the usurpation of Maximian.[79] In the new political situation, that change had clear advantages. Since Sol was the god who protected Constantius, emphasis on Sol stressed Constantine's status as his father's heir;[80] devotion to Apollo, the patron of culture and of the emperor Augustus, would appeal to the civilized parts of Gaul—and solar monotheism was far less objectionable than the normal pagan pantheon to the Christians, who formed an influential section of Constantine's subjects.[81]

Despite the events of 310, Constantine was firmly in power. The régime of Maxentius in Italy lacked similar stability. Worse, it was flawed by a fundamental contradiction. Although Maxentius came to power with the support of the Roman people, and probably of the Senate, he was never able to satisfy all their expectations of him. They had rebelled against Galerius when he assessed them for direct taxation. But when Maxentius gained an army from Severus and Galerius, he needed to maintain and supply his troops, which protected Italy from invasion, by raising money within the territory he controlled, that is, Italy, Africa, and the Mediterranean islands. Under Maxentius, therefore, Rome and peninsular Italy could not seriously hope either to enjoy the rewards of empire or to escape its burdens. Moreover, if Maxentius could count on the acquiescence of the Senate, a warm alliance never developed. Although he gave senators a greater influence in public affairs than they had enjoyed for a century, and employed a senator as praetorian prefect and commander of troops in the field,[82] only two senators held the ordinary consulate,[83] which Maxentius himself held four times in six years, twice without a colleague.[84] By 312 the civilian population of Italy tolerated Maxentius rather than supported him with active enthusiasm.

When Maxentius went down to defeat in 312, both silence and obloquy rapidly traduced his memory and damned his administration as a savage tyranny.[85] Hence the Maxentius who dominates the historical tradition is the usurper whom Constantine wished people to believe that he defeated. Some scattered items of fact contradict that superficial story of tyranny and permit a juster appreciation of how Maxentius governed.[86] Even if the fundamental weakness of his position produced continual crises, he ruled Italy for six years, and his policies bore a greater resemblance to those of Constantine than the latter dared to admit.

In late 306, Africa declared for Maxentius at once.[87] But he may not have exercised effective control. The *vicarius* of Africa, Alexander, was a man well advanced in years who had been appointed before 303 and was thus a nominee of Maximian.[88] Not long after Maximian fell out with his son, Alexander proclaimed himself emperor.[89] In 308 Alexander interrupted the supply of African grain needed to feed the population of Rome.[90] Riots ensued in the city, and Maxentius (it appears) used the praetorian guard to quell the disturbance.[91] Rioters were slaughtered in the streets, and the number of dead may have amounted to six thousand.[92] Although Alexander was subsequently suppressed and the grain supply restored, the Roman people did not forget the episode.

Maxentius' program of public building was also unsuccessful in winning genuine popularity. Outside the walls of Rome on the Via Appia, he constructed a circus. Inside the city, he rebuilt the temple of Rome which had burned down, commenced a vast, new basilica near the Forum, and constructed baths in the imperial palace.[93] But neither the temple nor the basilica was completely finished by October 312, and Constantine received the credit for their completion.[94] Moreover, Maxentius needed to raise money to pay for these buildings. Later sources report that he required senators and other landowners to contribute gifts of money to his treasury,[95] that he levied a tax in gold on the whole population of Rome;[96] and two lists of names from fragmentary inscriptions appear to document donations of money for some purpose by Roman senators at precisely this period.[97]

Nor did Maxentius' religious policy bring him the popularity he expected. Very soon after being acclaimed emperor, he proclaimed toleration for the Christians in his realms.[98] A formal announcement of the emperor's indulgence went to Africa, where years later a Christian of Cirta could still remember the exact day when "peace" came to his city.[99] However, at this stage, Maxentius ordained only toleration: the Christians of Italy and Africa could not yet recover property confiscated in 303/4—and Maxentius also took actions that later Christians construed as tantamount to persecution.

The promulgation of the first persecuting edict in the spring of 303 had left the Roman church in disarray. The bishop Marcellinus disgraced himself as a *traditor*: he complied with the imperial edict and surrendered copies of the Scriptures.[100] What happened next is extremely obscure.[101] At all events, there was a lapse in the Roman see.[102] Marcellinus appears to have died on 25 October 304,[103] but his apostasy had presumably left the church without a generally acknowledged bishop since the preceding year.[104] The accession of Maxentius and his grant of toleration permitted an election. The new bishop, Marcellus, whose consecration is probably to be dated to November or December 306, was a rigorist who damned the memory of Marcellinus and expunged his name from the official list of bishops.[105] The lapsed Christians who were still alive and performing acts of penance were outraged. The dispute produced discord, quarrels, rioting—even murder. Maxentius banished the bishop Marcellus from Rome, and Marcellus died in exile on 16 January 308.[106]

The next episcopal election probably occurred immediately after Maximian left Rome. The coincidence is hardly accidental: Maxentius was again attempting to win the support of the Christians. Eusebius was elected bishop on 18 April 308,[107] but the Roman church was still split into two factions. Eusebius was the candidate of the moderate party, which allowed apostates repentance, while Heraclius opposed the readmission of the lapsed. Again rioting ensued. Maxentius exiled both Eusebius and Heraclius, and the bishop died in Sicily on 21 October.[108]

The see then remained vacant for nearly three years, until an episcopal election again occurred in response to the political situation. Miltiades became bishop on 2 July 311, when war with either Constantine or Licinius had become inevitable.[109] Maxentius now gave his Christian subjects what Constantine gave the Christians of Gaul, Spain, and Britain five years earlier. He ordered that property confiscated in the persecution be returned, and the new bishop, Miltiades, sent two deacons with letters from Maxentius and his praetorian prefect to the prefect of the city allowing the Christians to recover property taken during the persecution.[110] This measure, tardy and probably reluctant, availed Maxentius little. By 312, the Christians of Africa had still not recovered all that they had lost[111]—and the Christians of Italy could see that Constantine was far more sympathetic to their well-being than Maxentius.

In April 311 Galerius lay close to death. The persecution had failed. He decided, as his last political act, to rescind the persecuting edicts and thus to relieve his successor of potential embarrassment. In the name of the imperial college, he issued a recantation in the form of a letter to provincials (though many called it an edict), and it was posted in Nicomedia on 30 April. The aim of the persecution (Galerius explained) was noble: the emperors, devoted to the ancient laws and public discipline of the Romans, desired that the Christians, who had deserted the religion of their forefathers, should recover their common sense. Unfortunately, he continued, the imperial command to return to ancient customs subjected many to danger and harassment, and the majority of Christians were now worshiping openly neither the established gods nor their own. Clemency demanded, therefore, that the Christians be allowed once more to exist and to assemble in an orderly fashion. Galerius concluded humbly with a request for Christians to pray for his safety and for that of the state, on which their own security depended.[112] The novelty or importance of this measure should not be overestimated. The Christians of Italy and Africa already possessed all that Galerius now granted to his eastern subjects, and those of Gaul, Spain, and Britain possessed far more. Although the prisons were opened and confessors in the mines regained their liberty,[113] Galerius made no provision for Christians to recover confiscated buildings or property.

Galerius wished to die where he was born, at Romulianum on the Danube, and he set out on his last journey. As his condition worsened, he entrusted his wife and bastard son Candidianus to Licinius, who had joined him. Finally, Galerius expired in great pain, in the province of Dardania, and his body was escorted to Romulianum, where it was buried.[114]

The news of Galerius' death had immediate political consequences. Maximinus seized his opportunity. Since 305 he had ruled the vast diocese of Oriens, residing in Antioch and for a period, it seems, at Caesarea in Palestine.[115] In 310 he had taken the field against the Persians and won a victory; all the emperors took the title *Persici maximi*, and Maximinus proclaimed an extension of the imperial frontiers.[116] In 311 an empire-wide census was in progress when Galerius died.[117] On hearing of Galerius' death, or perhaps even before, Maximinus canceled the registration of city dwellers in the diocese of Oriens. He then invaded Asia Minor, occupying every province from the Taurus to the Bosporus. In each Asian province in turn, he introduced the relief from taxation already granted in Syria and Egypt and thereby gained a great and immediate popularity.[118]

Maximinus had in effect bid for the support of the civilian population against Licinius, who inherited Galerius' fiscal policies. On 9 June 311, Licinius was still at Serdica. He countered Maximinus' action with an appeal to the pockets of his soldiers. He addressed to a man named Dalmatius (who was either a *vicarius* or a military commander) a letter which proceeds from the principle that soldiers who exert themselves on behalf of the state deserve some profit from their labors while they serve, and peace and security when they retire. Accordingly, Licinius prescribed that all soldiers under his command, whatever their rank or status, should be allowed to exempt five *capita* from the census and the tax payments computed thereon and to retain this exemption when they retired. He further allowed a soldier who had already gained an honorable discharge, either after completing twenty years of service or as a result of wounds, to deduct two *capita* (defined as the veteran's own and that of his wife) from his tax assessment.[119] Licinius then departed to confront his rival. The armies of Europe and Asia faced each other, but war did not ensue. The two emperors met on board a ship and came to terms, professing peace and friendship.[120]

Already in control of Asia Minor, Maximinus took up residence in Diocletian's capital of Nicomedia[121] and introduced his religious policies to his newly acquired territories.[122] Although Galerius had issued his edict of toleration in the name of all the legitimate emperors, Maximinus frustrated its application and declined to publish copies of the original enactment. Instead, his praetorian prefect wrote to provincial governors instructing them to disregard the persecuting edicts but not explicitly granting toleration.[123] And within six months of that letter, Maximinus began to persecute again openly: on 26 November 311 his agents surprised, arrested, and executed the bishop of Alexandria, and in Nicomedia on 7 January 312 Maximinus himself tried the scholar Lucian and sentenced him to death.[124] Constantine protested, but the deaths and torture of Christians continued in the East.[125]

Galerius' last illness and Maximinus' seizure of Asia Minor diverted Licinius and rendered him incapable of military action on his western flank. When Maxentius was suppressed, it was not Licinius, as Galerius had intended, but Constantine who conquered Italy. Surprisingly, however, Constantine was not the one who initiated hostilities. In the summer of 311, Maxentius gambled all on a sudden offensive while Licinius was occupied in the East. He declared war on Constantine, vowing to avenge the murder of his father.[126] Unfortunately, the actions which supported these threats are lost to history, since the victorious Constantine desired them to be forgotten. Nor is it known how Constantine parried the thrust. His propaganda, however, reflected the aggression of Maxentius.

In 310, the conspiracy of Maximian was presented by Constantine as a family tragedy, his death as contrary to Constantine's wishes. The retired emperor sinned by fate or fortune, surrendered at Massilia, then decided that he did not deserve to enjoy Constantine's pardon and met an entirely voluntary death.[127]

In 311, however, Constantine damned the memory of his father-in-law, ordering the erasure of his name from public inscriptions and the destruction of his statues.[128] A second plot was now revealed, of which there was no hint before. After failure at Massilia and subsequent pardon (so it was alleged), Maximian planned to murder Constantine with his own hand while the emperor slept. Fausta forewarned Constantine, who placed a eunuch in his bed. Maximian was apprehended when he killed the substitute. Suicide being permitted, he hanged himself forthwith.[129]

Constantine was a master of diplomacy as well as propaganda. To prevent Licinius and Maxentius from allying themselves against him, he offered Licinius the hand of his sister in marriage. Maximinus realized where his own interests lay and encouraged Maxentius by offering him recognition as a legitimate emperor. Envoys came to Rome with letters. Maxentius welcomed the overtures and displayed the Augustus of the East as his colleague.[130] It was at this juncture (it seems) that Diocletian died, after hearing how closely the *damnatio memoriae* visited on Maximian had touched him. His own statues and pictures were torn down together with those of his former colleague. Despair added to illness, and Diocletian died on 3 December 311, perhaps partly of his own volition.[131] If time can be reckoned by events rather than by mere span of years, an age had passed since his abdication.

In 312 Maximinus left Nicomedia, visited Antioch in July or August and was on campaign in Mesopotamia by the autumn.[132] In Italy, Maxentius expected an attack from Licinius and stationed an army at Verona, presumably to guard against an expected invasion from Pannonia.[133] But Constantine anticipated his colleague and struck first. A panegyrist later asserted that Constantine acted from divine inspiration, against the expectations of men, against the advice of his advisers and generals.[134] The claim may be true, despite its credentials. Constantine could discern the political weakness of Maxentius and the need for immediate action: if Licinius suppressed Maxentius, then his own hope of ruling the whole empire would be at an end. Constantine needed to conquer Italy for political reasons, even if the purely military calculation of his prospects were adverse.

In 312, probably as early as the weather permitted, Constantine crossed the Alps and descended on Italy with a quarter of his total army—an expeditionary force of somewhat under forty thousand men.[135] The town of Segusio stood in his path, heavily fortified and containing a military garrison. It shut its gates. Constantine ordered the gates set on fire; scaling ladders were brought to the walls, and the assault was swiftly successful. Constantine forbade plunder and advanced into the northern Italian plain.[136]

Before he reached Turin, he encountered an opposing army with heavily armed cavalry. Victory was easy (or so it appears), and Turin refused to admit the fugitives from the defeated army.[137] It opened its gates to Constantine, however, and the other cities of northern Italy began to send embassies of congratulation. He proceeded to Milan, where his welcome surpassed expectation. The rejoicing was probably unfeigned, for the victory of Constantine would remove the fear of further war, reunite Italy with the empire, and restore to northern Italy an importance of which the régime of Maxentius, centered on Rome, had temporarily deprived her. Constantine stayed in Milan for some time before continuing the campaign.[138]

Verona was held for Maxentius by an army under the command of his praetorian prefect. Constantine advanced from Milan and met and routed a detachment of cavalry near Brixia. Verona itself was protected by the fast-flowing and rocky River Adige, which rendered a direct assault impossible and seemed to ensure the city access to reinforcements and supplies from the rear. Constantine crossed the river upstream, where it could be forded and where an attack was not expected, and invested the city. Several attempts at a breakout failed before the prefect Pompeianus evaded the besiegers to fetch reinforcements. He returned to Verona with a large army. Constantine, faced with the threat of encirclement or simultaneous attack from front and rear, refused to lift the siege. He divided his army. The fight was desperate, but decisive. Pompeianus was killed, and the relieving army surrendered. Aquileia came over, Verona soon capitulated, and Constantine was finally the undisputed master of northern Italy.[139]

Constantine could now march on Rome with every confidence of success. He proceeded slowly and deliberately, waiting for the opposition to crumble. The régime of Maxentius now rested on naked military force. If the people of Rome could remember the bloody suppression of riots, and Christians the exile of bishops, the Senate had a more recent reminder of what the presence of an autocrat entailed.[140] Maxentius had a reputation for seducing the wives of respectable men. One woman who attracted his attention was a Christian and the wife of the prefect of the city. When the emperor's agents came to summon her to his presence, her husband was afraid to resist them. His wife asked for a brief delay to don appropriate dress, withdrew to her room, and in solitude stabbed herself in the breast.[141] The suicide and her husband can plausibly be identified as Junius Flavianus and his wife. Although the prefecture of the city normally changed hands on the anniversary of Maxentius' accession, Flavianus left office on 9 February 312.[142] It may be inferred that he resigned in consequence of his wife's death.[143]

Maxentius proposed to repeat the tactics which defeated Severus and Galerius.[144] He stayed in Rome and prepared for a siege. The Milvian Bridge and presumably all the other bridges over the Tiber were cut. Religion added its sanction: the gods (it was alleged) counseled this course of action. Pretending to be secure behind the walls of Rome, Maxentius continued to behave as if nothing were amiss. Finally, however, the tensions within the city came into the open. With the army of Constantine encamped outside Rome, the population rioted and proclaimed Constantine invincible.

Maxentius now knew the inevitable outcome of a long siege and decided to fight. He constructed a temporary bridge of boats across the Tiber over which his army could advance to battle and removed his wife and son from the palace to a private house. He then approached the *quindecimviri sacris faciundis,* who had custody of the Sibylline books, in which he discovered an oracle which, if ambiguous, at least enabled him to save face: it declared that the enemy of the Romans would die that very day. The date was 28 October 312, the sixth anniversary of Maxentius' assumption of the purple. He left Rome, crossed the Tiber, and confronted Constantine.[145]

The army encamped beyond the Milvian Bridge had an unusual appearance. Constantine was preparing to fight under the banner of Christ. Some believed that during the night before the battle the emperor had been commanded in a dream to place the sign of Christ on the shields of his soldiers.[146] That belief is probably no more than an attempt to give Constantine's unexpected action a conventional religious explanation.[147] Constantine himself, years later, gave a fuller account, whose truth he asseverated emphatically and upon oath.[148] One afternoon on their march, both he and the whole army had seen a cross of light in the sky and the words "in this conquer": during the next night, in a dream, Christ appeared to him with the heavenly sign and instructed him to make standards for his army in this form. On waking, Constantine questioned the Christians in his entourage, who probably included Ossius, the bishop of Corduba. They explained that Constantine had indeed seen Christ and that the sign signified immortality and victory over death.[149] Constantine then took a public and significant step. He replaced the pagan standards of his troops with a new Christian sign which either bore or soon acquired a name which reflects its origin: the *labarum*—a Gallic word, as befitted the largely Gallic and German army of 312.[150]

The battle was brief. The Maxentian forces soon fled in disarray towards Rome, and the bridge of boats broke. Maxentius himself descended into the Tiber, clad in heavy armor and riding his horse: he may have preferred drowning to an ignominious capture.[151] Constantine already had Christian bishops in his entourage as he marched on Rome, and he publicly declared himself a Christian before battle. It seems natural to conclude that he was converted to Christianity before the Battle of the Milvian Bridge. But the moment of psychological conviction may have followed, rather than preceded, his open avowal: it perhaps occurred during the battle, at the moment victory became certain.[152] In the ultimate reckoning, however, the precise details of Constantine's conversion matter little. After 28 October 312 the emperor consistently thought of himself as God's servant, entrusted with a divine mission to convert the Roman Empire to Christianity.

IV

THE CHRISTIAN EMPEROR
OF THE WEST

Constantine entered Rome on 29 October 312.[1] Crowds thronged the streets in greeting and congratulated their liberator with a joy which almost all genuinely felt. Constantine came in triumph and as a Christian. Unlike his pagan predecessors, he declined to ascend the Capitol to perform the customary sacrifices and to give thanks to Jupiter for his victory.[2] Constantine now owed allegiance to another God, outside the pantheon of the Roman state. Pagan writers were later to affirm that this gesture caused great offense and alienated the Senate and the people of Rome.[3] It is not certain that the inhabitants of Rome resented Constantine's action or even perceived its historic significance. In October 312 more attention went to the political consequences of Constantine's victory: the conqueror decreed that those who had lost their property under Maxentius should receive it back again, he recalled exiles, and he released those who languished in prison for their opposition, real or suspected, to the previous ruler of Italy.[4]

Maxentius' body was recovered from the Tiber and mutilated. His head was stuck on a spear, paraded through the streets of Rome, and abused by his former subjects. Constantine then sent it to Carthage to prove that his foe was truly dead, and the supporters of Maxentius in Africa offered no further resistance.[5] In Italy, Constantine disbanded the praetorian guard completely and removed the legion II Parthica from Alba.[6] Even without troops, however, Rome might cause trouble, and Constantine could foresee the possibility of conflict with an eastern emperor. Necessity, therefore, recommended cooperation with the Roman Senate. Master of Italy and Africa by right of conquest, Constantine now needed to devise a political settlement which would ensure the loyalty of his new territories in the coming years.

During the night between Constantine's victory and his entry into Rome, the leading senators presumably met to consider the new political situation. Although many had held office under Maxentius and collaborated with his régime, they could argue that they acted under compulsion. Moreover, some senators may have communicated secretly with Constantine before the Battle of the Milvian Bridge, while many had probably made his acquaintance when Diocletian visited Rome in 303.[7] So much for the past. What of the future?

The Senate as a body could, if it chose, confer prestige on Constantine and strengthen his control of Italy and Africa through its very real political influence in these areas, and it needed little percipience to discern that Constantine neither wished nor would dare to rule by force and terror. Not many months had passed since Licinius seemed destined to recover Italy and reunite it with the rest of the Roman Empire. Constantine was the new master of Italy only because he anticipated Licinius in an inevitable conquest. But there would soon be war in the East between Licinius and Maximinus, whose alliance with the now dead Maxentius had clearly been directed against Licinius. If Maximinus won, Constantine would certainly not wish to allow him to enjoy the spoils of victory or to threaten his own position. On the other hand, were Licinius victorious, he might not refrain from exploiting any obvious opportunity to embarrass Constantine.

Such were the circumstances in which Constantine acted, astutely combining common sense and propaganda. He spoke in the Senate and announced a new dispensation. The evils of the preceding régime were blamed on Maxentius himself and a few henchmen. The usurper had bound followers to his cause by presenting them with the wives of other men and the property of his innocent victims; devoted to their vile master and prepared to commit any crime, his cronies suppressed, terrorized, silenced any opposition. In contrast, Constantine, who came as a conqueror, came in mercy and peace and forbade bloodletting. Revenge had no place. Constantine discouraged political accusations, issued edicts to the people which prescribed sentence of death for informers, and even protected (it was claimed) men who had committed murder while the tyrant ruled.[8] He annulled Maxentius' rescripts, with the limiting proviso that rightful decisions should stand.[9] And though he invalidated honors which Maxentius had bestowed on leaders of the Senate, he took care not to diminish the standing of individuals who had held office under the previous government. He retained in office for a month the prefect of the city whom Maxentius had appointed on 27 October 312.[10] The next two prefects had also held office under Maxentius, and Constantine presumably appointed them mainly in order to preserve their rank and status. One of them, C. Ceionius Rufius Volusianus, who had also been praetorian prefect of Maxentius and ordinary consul in 311, soon became a *comes* of Constantine and held the *fasces* as ordinary consul in 314, with Constantine's praetorian prefect as his colleague.[11]

When Constantine enounced his policies in the Curia, he promised to restore to the Senate its ancient authority and prerogatives and to keep its memory ever fresh in his breast. His later actions did not belie his initial declaration of policy: under Constantine, senators again attained high office at the imperial court. If the emperors of the third century showed an increasing preference for men who were not senators to administer the empire, Constantine disregarded the rigid distinction between Senate and knights and thus again made it possible for the landed aristocracy of the West to aspire to office and power at court.[12] That was a very practical consequence of Constantine's claim to be the liberator of Rome and the restorer of the Senate.[13]

The Senate reciprocated. They decreed that Constantine was the senior member of the imperial college, that he was not merely Augustus but "the greatest Augustus."[14] It is not clear what concrete advantages Constantine gained, beyond the right to name the consuls of the year,[15] but the "title of the first name" meant that Constantine's name stood first in all official documents. More tangible were buildings and objects dedicated to Constantine. He received a gold shield and a gold wreath as the liberator of Italy, and the Senate consecrated a statuette of Victory in his honor in the Curia.[16] Most spectacular of all, Maxentius' vast new basilica was dedicated to Constantine.[17] In it soon stood a huge statue alluding to recent events. At the focal point of the hall, Constantine was depicted in stone, ten times larger than life, gazing heavenward in devotion and holding the Christian *labarum* in his hand. The inscription made explicit the message which even the illiterate could hardly fail to imbibe: by this sign Constantine had freed Rome from the yoke of the tyrant and restored the Senate and people to their ancient splendor.[18]

A speech survives, delivered at Trier in the late summer or autumn of 313, which depicts Constantine from a pagan perspective.[19] Unlike previous panegyrics, this speech carefully avoids naming any pagan god.[20] Although the orator of 313 emphasizes Constantine's close familiarity with the divine, he was a pagan, as were many in his audience, and he therefore practices a studied ambiguity designed to offend neither the Christian emperor nor any adherent of traditional beliefs. Constantine (he declares) shares the secrets of that divine mind which delegates the care of ordinary men to lesser gods but which reveals itself to the emperor alone.[21] And the peroration, where a prayer to the gods was almost obligatory, invokes the great creator whose names are as diverse as the languages of mankind, who may be either a force which permeates the world or a remote power beyond the visible heavens.[22] The formulations of the speech are culled from philosophy and poetry,[23] but the orator has a practical end in view: whatever their personal creed, all men can recognize the supreme deity in the god who protects Constantine. Two years after this speech, when the Senate dedicated to Constantine the commemorative arch which they decreed in the autumn of 312, they chose similar language: the emperor liberated Rome and destroyed the tyrant and his faction through his own greatness of mind, at the prompting of the divinity.[24]

The speech of 313 reveals how Constantine wished the war of 312 to be remembered. Much of the orator's account is predictable and presents the stereotype of a virtuous, brave, and pure emperor defeating a wicked, cowardly, and depraved tyrant.[25] But some passages reflect a deliberate distortion of the truth for political reasons. When Constantine distributed largess to the Roman people, he did so in front of the columns which the Senate had dedicated in 303 to mark the *vicennalia* of Diocletian and Maximian and the *decennalia* of Constantius and Galerius.[26] The choice of venue signified Constantine's claim to be the true successor of the Tetrarchs. But Maxentius was the son of Maximian and the brother of Constantine's wife, and in 311 Constantine had damned Maximian's memory as a traitor and murderer. After October 312, Constantine coolly substituted propaganda for history. The wife of Maximian swore publicly that she conceived Maxentius in adultery.[27] The orator repeats the theme: the fallen tyrant was a supposititious son of Maximian, a dwarf with twisted and deformed limbs.[28] Maximian and Maxentius being dissociated, the former could be rehabilitated: by 318 he has become Divus Maximianus and joins Divus Constantius and Divus Claudius on coinage celebrating the imperial forebears of Constantine as "the best of emperors."[29]

Constantine, like any other emperor, was not only head of the state and of the state religion; he was also expected to be a patron of the arts.[30] Constantine took to the role with genuine interest. To be sure, a normally well-informed writer accuses him of lack of education,[31] but his allegation is disproved by abundant and varied evidence.[32] Constantine spent some years at Diocletian's court, where philosophers, poets and other literary men were welcome. There he learned to speak Greek and acquired some knowledge of Greek philosophy.[33] While he governed Gaul, he appointed men who studied rhetoric in Autun to govern his provinces and chose Lactantius to teach his son.[34] Constantine encouraged the liberal arts, especially literature, and liked to read, write, and listen to speeches recited by his subjects.[35] Before Constantine left Rome in January 313, a senator who had probably served Maxentius gave him the opportunity to affirm his patronage of Latin literature.[36]

Publilius Optatianus Porfyrius sent a poem to Constantine.[37] It was a technopaegnion, a poem in which the author hid a message which the inscriber revealed by picking out the letters forming the significant pattern in inks of different colors. The emperor acknowledged this presentation in an extant letter.[38] He addressed the poet as "dearest brother," complimented him on his technical virtuosity, and expressed pleasure at receiving an example of his talent. The emperor also attempted to set his own attitude to literature into a cultural tradition reaching back to Homer and Virgil: although poets have sometimes failed to enjoy the success which they deserve because of the temper of the times, the age of Constantine represents an artistic renaissance. A kindly reception, like a gentle breeze, will greet writers and orators, and the emperor will give literature tangible evidence of his appreciation. Porfyrius should rejoice in the successes of the present time and pursue the glory which he merits by continuing to exercise his talent—presumably in praise of Constantine.

Porfyrius was to send the emperor much more poetry, some of it beautifully inscribed in gold and silver on luxurious purple parchment.[39] The letter which accompanied the second presentation survives.[40] In it Porfyrius strikes just those chords which Constantine would most have wished to hear. The piety, virtue, clemency, and eternal felicity of Constantine furnish the poet's inspiration. The greatest of emperors, ever unconquerable and first in rank, the emperor of the whole world, victorious in war and a legislator in peace—the poet carefully intones a subtle blend of reality and propaganda.[41]

The army which defeated Maxentius on 28 October 312 fought under the *labarum,* an avowedly Christian banner. After this momentous step, the army of Constantine became officially Christian, whatever private religious sentiments his troops might cherish.[42] Constantine gave his Christian soldiers leave to attend church on Sundays and ordered that his pagan soldiers assemble every Sunday to recite in Latin a monotheistic prayer.[43] The date of these innovations is not expressly attested, but the reported content of the prayer recited by Constantine's pagan soldiers corresponds closely to a prayer which Licinius administered to his army on 30 April 313 when about to do battle with Maximinus—and Licinius may have modeled his prayer on one which Constantine originally devised for his own army to recite before the Battle of the Milvian Bridge.[44]

The court and its ceremonial reflected the emperor's new religion. Bishops dined at Constantine's table and accompanied him wherever he went,[45] and within three years of his conversion, a silver medallion minted at Ticinum depicted Constantine with the Christian monogram on his helmet.[46] The new ideology naturally took time to make its effects felt everywhere, and the Constantinian mints continued to portray the originally pagan Sol Invictus as the emperor's divine *comes,* protector, and patron for several years more.[47] That fact attests not imperial devotion to a vague solar monotheism,[48] but the dead weight of iconographic tradition.[49] It is Constantine's innovations and deliberate actions which reveal his true beliefs and the strength of his Christian convictions. The apparent ambiguity of his religious attitudes is a sign of caution, not of doubt or hesitation in his own mind; it represents the shrewd assessment of a skillful statesman that he must make haste slowly.[50]

Where tradition did not hamper him, Constantine could act swiftly and decisively. As courtesy demanded, he immediately wrote to Maximinus, who ruled in the East, announcing the defeat of Maxentius and his own victory. The letter also contained two substantive points. Constantine informed Maximinus that, by virtue of a decision of the Roman Senate, he was now the senior member of the imperial college, and that in this capacity he was making a peremptory demand that Maximinus desist from persecuting his Christian subjects.[51] Constantine wrote this letter, as protocol demanded, in the joint names of himself and Licinius, and at least one subject of Maximinus, who described it as a "most perfect law on behalf of Christians," gave Licinius equal credit for the démarche.[52] Nevertheless, the letter of late 312 which ordered Maximinus to issue instructions to stop the molestation of eastern Christians was in fact the work of Constantine alone.[53]

In his newly acquired territories Constantine hastened the still incomplete restoration of Christian property confiscated during the persecution.[54] Moreover, before he sent officials to Africa to replace Maxentius' appointees, he interviewed them and gave them *mandata* which reflected a new attitude to the Christian church. A letter which he wrote early in 313 reveals that Patricius, the *vicarius* of Africa, Anullinus, the proconsul, and Heraclides, the procurator of the imperial estates, had standing instructions to provide money to the bishop of Carthage on request—which they had received from Constantine in person.[55]

Everywhere in the West, Constantine now gave freely from the imperial treasury, both to build or enlarge churches and to decorate them richly.[56] The most spectacular examples of such generosity were in Rome, for which an early list of Constantinian foundations and their endowments fortunately survives.[57] On the site of the former camp of the *equites singulares* (once part of the property of Plautius Lateranus, from whom the church derives its name), Constantine built a splendid basilica, with a baptistery close by, to serve as the principal church of the city.[58] The distribution of the imperial estates which comprised the endowment of St. John Lateran (all within provinces Constantine ruled before 316/7) suggests an early date for the foundation.[59] Equally significant, Helena, the emperor's mother, began to reside in Rome and constructed a new church in the Sessorian palace for her own devotions (Santa Croce in Gierusalemme): its endowment was similar.[60] Nor did Constantine neglect the Roman church after 312: before the end of his reign (sometimes demonstrably after 324), he provided funds for the construction of shrines commemorating Roman martyrs, above all for the Church of the Apostle Peter on the Vatican.[61] Constantine also aided Christian charitable endeavors. He gave money, clothing, and shelter to the poverty-stricken, he supported orphans and widows—though in their case his generosity took a form which will have embarrassed many Christians: he provided dowries to enable indigent women to find second husbands.[62]

Constantine was not content merely to patronize Christianity as a benefactor within the established institutional framework. He changed the legal status of the Church and its place in Roman society. However, Constantine did not need to confer on the Christian church a corporate legal existence or the right to own property.[63] Churches had long owned cemeteries, places of assembly, and all the paraphernalia of worship, and emperors before Constantine had expressly confirmed a right which no one in the late third century challenged, whatever its precise origin in public law.[64] The confiscations of 303 were soon rescinded, in Constantine's domains at or perhaps even before his accession, in Italy and Africa five years later, and in 313 throughout the rest of the Roman Empire.[65] The churches thereby resumed possession of their property. Nor again did Constantine probably need to bestow on the Church the ability to receive legacies from testators (as is commonly supposed);[66] his surviving law on the subject has in fact a more subtle and more fundamental purport. Constantine allowed a dying man, by a simple verbal expression of his wishes, to bequeath to the Church as much of his property as he desired.[67] Constantine thereby set the tie of religion above the bonds of family. When Constantine became a Christian, the Church (or at least the Christian community of any Roman city) already existed as a corporate entity. His contribution was to elevate Christianity to a privileged position among the religions of the Roman Empire.

The process, begun immediately after his conversion, was one whose stages are not entirely easy to discern.[68] Often the innovative laws have perished, and the official codes compiled under Theodosius in the fifth century and Justinian in the sixth preserve only later modifications of the original law. The Christian clergy received immunity from public liturgies and probably from all taxes which might be levied on their persons or property. The exemption from liturgies is attested in 313 in documents which state the emperor's motivation. Constantine did not wish the clergy to be distracted from their function of divine worship: since God bestowed prosperity on mankind, the due performance of God's worship would aid in maintaining the happiness and prosperity of the Roman state.[69] The Syro-Roman lawbook of the late fifth century credits Constantine with more: it states that he freed the clergy from all taxes in money and from the *potestas* of their fathers.[70] This testimony has often been denied credence, since the complete exemption of clergy from payment of taxes in money as well as from the performance of public service appears not to be expressly asserted in surviving laws before the reign of Constantine's sons.[71] But that it was indeed Constantine who granted at least partial exemption from taxation emerges indirectly from a letter of 333, in which the emperor threatens to add ten *capita* and the taxes thereon to the census assessment of any who try to found a heretical church.[72]

The new status of priests was reflected in laws which established manumission in church as a valid legal act whereby a slave could be freed and become a Roman citizen. Lawyers of the fifth century knew three laws on the subject,[73] but the official codes have omitted the earliest and most important law. Its main provisions are stated in two extant reaffirmations and extensions. On 8 December 316 Constantine wrote to the bishop Protogenes (clearly the bishop of Serdica) extending the law to territories recently conquered in war. It was already the case that masters could give their servants freedom in a Catholic church, provided that they did so before the congregation in the presence of bishops who could ensure that a written record of the transaction be produced, duly authenticated by themselves. In 316 Constantine assured Protogenes of his right to preside over such transactions.[74] Some years later, Constantine addressed a letter to Ossius, the surviving extract of which states two substantive points. First, those who give their slaves liberty in church are deemed to have given it in the form which ensures the possession of Roman citizenship, provided that bishops witnessed the act. Second, clergy are allowed to grant full liberty to their own slaves on their deathbed by a mere expression of their wishes.[75]

Most of these privileges accorded to the Christian clergy had precedents in laws regulating the status of imperial soldiers and pagan priests.[76] But even soldiers, who were not liable to *patria potestas* or public liturgies, and could make legally binding wills in any form, lacked the complete exemption from taxation which Constantine may have conferred on Christian priests.[77] A still more striking innovation, the legal definition of *episcopalis audientia,* seems to have purely Christian precedents and a purely Christian justification.[78] The apostle Paul had scolded Christians of the first generation for taking their legal disputes with one another to pagan law courts.[79] Constantine (it seems) legislated that any Christian engaged in a civil lawsuit with another Christian could transfer the case, at any stage and even without the consent of the other party, from the court of the secular magistrate to the arbitration of a bishop. Again, the innovatory law is lost. Its existence is inferred from two subsequent laws dealing with the practical problems episcopal arbitration produced. The earlier is of uncertain date, and the surviving text is obviously corrupt and lacunose: its main purpose appears to be to prevent a secular magistrate from accepting and acting on one party's biased or inaccurate report of the bishop's decision.[80] The later is a rescript issued on 5 May 333 to the praetorian prefect Ablabius; a collection of canon law preserves it in full. The ruling arose out of a case before the prefect where one party argued that cases involving minors could not be referred to espiscopal arbitration. Constantine expressed surprise that the Christian Ablabius needed to consult him about past legislation or his present wishes. He then restated the law on the subject as he intended it to operate. In any type of civil case in whatever court, if a litigant at any stage (even when the magistrate has begun to read his verdict) expresses a wish that the case be judged by a bishop, then the presiding magistrate shall send the litigants to the bishop, even if the other party objects. The bishop's decision shall be final and not subject to any sort of appeal or revision.[81] Constantine does not place any explicit limits on episcopal jurisdiction, but it might be that these rules applied only to cases where both litigants were Christian.[82]

Constantine also began to remold Roman law and the attitudes of Roman society in a Christian direction. He abolished crucifixion as a legal punishment and forbade the disfiguring of the face, the image of divine beauty, ordering instead that the crimes of those condemned to gladiatorial school or the mines should be tattooed on their hands or ankles.[83] The observance of Sunday as a holy day was prescribed for all. A law of 321 (not necessarily the first on the subject) prohibited all official business and the manufacturing of artifacts on the Lord's Day, though it allowed agricultural work, if God granted fine weather, and the emancipation or manumission of slaves in church.[84]

More fundamental were changes which Constantine introduced in the law of marriage. Augustus had long before encouraged his subjects to beget a large progeny, establishing legal privileges for the fathers of many children and imposing legal disabilities on the unmarried.[85] Although the legislation was largely ineffective, it stood unrepealed, and later emperors of Rome sometimes amended it in order to attempt strict enforcement.[86] But, whereas Augustus assumed that marriage and the procreation of children were natural and desirable in themselves, Christianity preached a different set of values, setting virginity and celibacy above the married state.[87]

Constantine acted on the assumption that those who lacked children because they were sterile deserved pity, not punishment, while those who chose celibacy from love of God should be admired, not penalized.[88] He removed all the ancient restrictions on the ability of the unmarried and childless of either sex to receive gifts and inheritances. He made one exception, however, a significant one: there was to be no change in the laws concerning the transfer of property between married couples—whose often deceptive caresses (he complained) were scarcely held in check by the rigor of the law.[89] Furthermore, Constantine made divorce and remarriage more difficult: he laid down that a wife could divorce her husband only if he were a murderer, poisoner, or tomb violator, while a husband could divorce his wife only for adultery, poisoning, or running a brothel.[90]

A direct attack on paganism was not yet possible. It was deferred until no pagan emperor existed who could turn such a policy to Constantine's political disadvantage. But Constantine began to regulate the art of divination. The official standing of haruspices, though ancient and venerable, was less secure than that of other priests.[91] Already in 313 a pagan panegyrist praised the Christian emperor for disregarding the advice of the haruspices when about to invade Italy.[92] Constantine drew a distinction between public and private divination. The latter was prohibited. A haruspex who entered a private house for purposes of divination was to be burned alive, while the man who invited him was to lose his property and to be exiled to an island. Constantine offered rewards for an accuser, in place of the penalties normally imposed on informers.[93]

Public divination, however, Constantine allowed as a relic of the past.[94] In 320, when lightning struck the Colosseum, the haruspices publicly consulted the auspices, and the pagan prefect of the city informed the *magister officiorum* of the event and its interpretation. The *magister officiorum* informed Constantine, who wrote to the prefect. In his letter the emperor reaffirmed that private sacrifices were prohibited, but he allowed public divination in the old form if ever the palace or any public building should be struck by lightning—provided that he be informed forthwith.[95] Political preoccupations are clearly relevant to Constantine's attitude.[96] Yet the distinction between two types of divination underscores his basic hostility to an ancient and hallowed practice: he assumes that divination is a superstition and therefore, by definition, evil.[97]

Constantine did not at once think through the full implications of his new religion. Condemnation to gladiatorial school was a penalty which clearly presupposed the existence of gladiators, gladiatorial schools, and gladiatorial displays. In 315 Constantine, in a rescript, declared that slaves or freedmen convicted of kidnaping be thrown to the beasts, and that men of free status guilty of the same crime be sent to a gladiatorial school to be cut to pieces before they learned how to defend themselves.[98] Many Christians disapproved strongly of gladiatorial shows, partly on moral grounds, partly because of their pagan origin and associations.[99] By 325 Constantine believed that such cruel spectacles were unacceptable and totally forbade gladiators.[100] The entertainment long survived despite the prohibition, especially in Rome, but it very soon ceased to be a normal form of public entertainment subsidized by the emperors.[101] Constantine (it may be suggested) reorganized public entertainment, replacing the gladiator in the arena with the charioteer in the hippodrome—and thus unwittingly giving the Blues and Greens a greater importance in public life.[102] Before 337 there was scarcely any facet of Roman public life unaffected by the official Christianization of Roman society which Constantine began at the Battle of the Milvian Bridge.

The early history of the Christian church in the West is so badly documented that no narrative of its expansion can be written. The surviving evidence, however, clearly indicates that Christianity had thoroughly permeated provincial society long before Constantine became emperor.[103] The voluminous works of Tertullian sometimes assert, and frequently presuppose, that the Christians of Carthage in the very early third century formed a numerous community drawn from every social category, including the provincial aristocracy.[104] A generation later, Minucius Felix depicted members of the ruling class of Cirta as Christians, while the career, treatises, and correspondence of Cyprian, bishop of Carthage from about 247 to 258, reveal a network of influential Christian communities throughout the African provinces.[105]

In the imperial capital in 251, the Christian community employed the services of forty-six priests, seven deacons, seven subdeacons, forty-two acolytes, and fifty-two exorcists, lectors, and doorkeepers, and it supported more than fifteen hundred widows and beggars—which implies that the total number of Roman Christians exceeded thirty thousand.[106] For Gaul, there is nothing from the third century to show how the persecuted community of humble folk which existed at Lugdunum about 177 subsequently grew and prospered.[107] In Spain, however, sudden illumination comes from the eighty-one canons enacted by a council of nineteen bishops who met at Iliberris in Baetica not long before Diocletian decreed persecution.[108]

Many of the canons relate to delinquencies which inevitably arise in any community whose rules forbid men and women to indulge their natural desires for excitement or sexual pleasure.[109] Others prescribe penalties for acts which any civilized society will regard as abhorrent and illegal,[110] while others again relate to specifically Christian problems of organization.[111] But a few reveal the size of the Christian church in Spain and the high social standing of some of its members. Parents are forbidden to marry their daughters to pagans, heretics, or Jews: there seems to have been an abundance of nubile virgins of the Christian faith.[112] One canon prohibits the chief magistrates of cities from entering a church during their year of office, while another prohibits holders of local pagan priesthoods from entering a church for two whole years, even if they avoid sacrificing or subsidizing the worship of idols.[113] Three canons lay down similar rules for *flamines,* that is, for Christians who hold the provincial high-priesthood of the imperial cult after baptism. Christian *flamines* who have sacrificed are excommunicated until they die, while *flamines* who have not sacrificed but only given gladiatorial games must perform penance and can only be readmitted to communion when near death. But *flamines* who are catechumens and refrain from sacrifice are admitted to baptism after three years have lapsed.[114] Before 303, therefore, Christians in Baetica were holding magistracies and priesthoods like any other municipal or provincial aristocrats—and one canon even implies that some Christians had already attempted to destroy pagan shrines by violence.[115]

When persecution came, it touched Spain only lightly. Bishop Ossius of Corduba, who had attended the Council of Iliberris, was imprisoned briefly, earning the title of confessor,[116] and there were clearly some martyrs elsewhere in the Iberian peninsula.[117] But in Spain, as in Gaul, the persecution seems to have had no permanent effect on the Church. In Africa, by contrast, persecution was more severe, and it had results which soured the atmosphere of African Christianity for generations.

In 303, C. Annius Anullinus, the proconsul of Africa, and Valerius Florus, the governor of Numidia, zealously enforced the first edict and even exceeded its provisions by requiring sacrifice of everyone.[118] Christians reacted variously. There were martyrs, confessors, and apostates alike among laity, clergy, and bishops. When persecution abated, angry recriminations began. Worse, the quarrels soon produced a schism in the African church in which both parties accused the other of *traditio,* of surrendering the Scriptures to be burned at the emperors' command.[119]

The differences of attitude which converted a disputed episcopal election at Carthage into a schism became evident immediately after the persecution. Mensurius, who was bishop of Carthage in 303, surrendered some books but later wrote to Secundus of Tigisis, the senior bishop of Numidia, to assure him that they were not copies of Scripture. By his own account, Mensurius hid the sacred manuscripts in his own house, replacing them in his basilica with some heretical writings. The authorities found, removed, and burned these writings without making further inquiry. Some members of the Carthaginian city council then informed the proconsul and suggested that Mensurius be forced to surrender the Scriptures, but the proconsul did nothing. Secundus, however, refused to make even a gesture of compromise: when the centurion and *beneficiarius* who came to seize the Scriptures proposed to satisfy their orders by taking discarded and worthless objects, he refused their offer and was imprisoned.

The difference in their conduct reflected deep moral and theological disagreement between the two bishops. Mensurius, in his letter to Secundus, derided some recent martyrs as criminals and debtors seeking release from a wearisome existence, absolution for their crimes, or material benefits from Christians who treated them as heroes. Moreover, he forbade his congregation in Carthage to honor as confessors those who had offered themselves for arrest or volunteered the information that they possessed copies of the Scriptures which they would refuse to surrender.[120] These were extreme views, and not typical. At Catania, while the governor of Sicily was conducting official business, one Euplus interrupted with the shout "I am a Christian, I want to die," and entered the governor's *secretarium* flaunting a copy of the Gospels. After his imprisonment and execution, no one denied Euplus the title of martyr.[121] Had he died in Carthage, however, he would have fallen under Mensurius' interdict. Secundus replied firmly but amicably to the letter from Carthage. He described the persecution in Numidia and praised the constancy of Numidian martyrs who preferred death to an act which they considered apostasy.

Immediately after the persecution an episcopal election occurred at Cirta. There were two candidates: the subdeacon Silvanus and one Donatus. It was later alleged that the majority of the congregation wanted Donatus and rejected Silvanus as a *traditor* for surrendering some church plate, and that Silvanus obtained election as bishop by bribery and by the support of people like gladiators and prostitutes.[122] That story can hardly be both true and complete. Whatever transpired in the election, Silvanus was consecrated by a dozen Numidian bishops, who met in a private house because the churches had not yet been restored (probably on 13 May 307).[123] Shortly thereafter, these same Numidian bishops intervened in an episcopal election at Carthage.

Sometime earlier the Carthaginian deacon Felix had composed a scurrilous letter about a persecuting emperor (presumably Maximian); when Felix was denounced, some said he was hiding in the house of Mensurius. The bishop of Carthage refused to give him up, and the emperor was consulted. He summoned Mensurius to court. Before he departed, Mensurius entrusted the church plate, which he had hidden in his house, to the *seniores* Botrus and Caelestius, and he left an inventory with an old woman, who was to give it to his successor when persecution ended, should he fail to return. The bishop set out for Italy, defended himself successfully, but died during the return journey.[124]

Persecution ended during the winter of 306/7, and at the behest of Maxentius the Christians recovered their freedom. The Carthaginian congregation unanimously elected Caecilianus as their new bishop. Felix of Abthungi at once consecrated Caecilianus, who recovered the church plate. The next step was later attributed to the avarice of Botrus and Caelestius: disappointed of their hope of embezzling the church plate, they withdrew from communion, secured the support of a rich widow, and concocted false charges against Caecilianus.[125] Again, that cannot be the whole truth: as early as 313 Donatus was alleged to have created a schism at Carthage while Caecilianus was still a deacon.[126]

Be that as it may, the Numidian bishops intervened in the dispute. Secundus of Tigisis first sought to avoid a schism by appointing an *interventor* to perform Caecilianus' duties until his right to be bishop was decided. The *interventor* was murdered in his church.[127] Secundus then presided over a council of about seventy bishops (clearly not all Numidian), which Caecilianus refused to attend. Against Caecilianus himself, no action which merited disqualification from clerical office could be proved. But the council pronounced Felix of Abthungi guilty of *traditio* and declared his consecration of Caecilianus invalid. The bishop of Carthage, therefore, offered to be consecrated a second time, by the council. The compromise was refused. The council elected the lector Maiorinus bishop in Caecilianus' stead and communicated their decision to churches outside Africa. In Carthage itself, Caecilianus enjoyed the support of the Christian congregation and retained possession of the see.[128]

Unfortunately, nothing is known of the progress of the schism between the council at Carthage, which probably met in 307/8,[129] and the defeat of Maxentius. Bitter controversy presumably spread throughout the African provinces. When Constantine became master of Africa late in 312, he confronted a deeply divided church. Yet his first contacts with the African church deliberately declared that he supported one party.

In the winter of 312/3, Constantine wrote at least three letters to Carthage. The first, to the proconsul Anullinus, ordered that Christian property seized in the persecution be restored with all haste to "the catholic church of the Christians in every city," no matter who now possessed it.[130] The second letter informed Caecilianus, as bishop of Carthage, that the *rationalis* Ursus would give him three thousand *folles:* these the bishop must then distribute to specified "ministers of the lawful and most holy catholic religion," listed on a schedule which Ossius had sent him. Constantine, moreover, assured Caecilianus that he had given instructions to the proconsul and the *vicarius* of Africa to support the bishop, should any persons of unsound mind try to disturb the most holy and catholic church.[131] The third letter, again to Anullinus, instructed him to release the clergy of "the catholic church over which Caecilianus presides" from all public liturgies.[132] Since Constantine defined the recipients of his bounty so explicitly and carefully, it must be presumed that he already knew of the schism before he acted. When the adherents of Maiorinus appealed to Constantine, they were not invoking the aid of an emperor ignorant of their existence but of one who had already committed himself.[133]

On receipt of the letter, the proconsul announced in Carthage that clergy of the catholic Church were exempt from liturgies. A few days later some petitioners approached Anullinus denouncing Caecilianus. They gave him two documents, one sealed and containing charges against Caecilianus, the other unsealed, and they asked him to forward both to the emperor. On 15 April 313 Anullinus wrote to Constantine.[134] The petition he forwarded deliberately avoided any reference to Constantine's own Christianity. Instead, it praised his justice and asked Constantine to send arbitrators from Gaul, where his father had not persecuted the Church.[135] Now a Christian, the emperor believed it improper for him to decide disputes between bishops, and he granted the request in a manner which the petitioners cannot have foreseen: although he named the bishops Maternus of Cologne, Reticius of Autun, and Marinus of Arles as arbitrators, they were not to decide the issue by themselves. They were to go to Rome to hear representations from Caecilianus and ten African bishops from each side, with the bishop of Rome presiding.[136] In the event, however, the hearing was not an arbitration in the form prescribed by Constantine, but a Church council according to ecclesiastical precedent.[137]

The bishop of Rome presided over the council in a house which the empress Fausta had either given to the church of Rome or lent for the occasion.[138] The council comprised fifteen Italian bishops in addition to himself and the three from Gaul. On 2 October 313 they rendered a decision. Caecilianus was acquitted, since his opponents could not substantiate any charge against him. On the other hand, the council condemned Donatus, who had replaced Maiorinus on his death, for an offense against ecclesiastical propriety. Donatus had observed the normal African practice that Christian laymen who had lapsed in persecution should be rebaptized and that lapsed bishops needed reconsecration. Rebaptism was now declared illegal, and Donatus was condemned for requiring it. The bishop of Rome also tried to isolate Donatus from his African supporters by offering to write letters of communion to bishops consecrated by Maiorinus to explain that where there were two rival bishops, the one elected first should remain, while the other would be assigned to a different see.[139]

This decision did not end the conflict, and the schism became more bitter than before. Constantine was again approached, this time in person. He was already concerned about the scandal caused by the schism: Christians were disgracing themselves and giving pagans material for denigration. And he felt that God, who had entrusted everything on earth to his care, might be angry with him for allowing dissension to prevent his subjects from rendering due worship to their creator. But he was moved to reopen the case by a specific allegation of prejudice: the council (the petitioners asseverated) did not hear the whole case but shut themselves up in secret and delivered a biased verdict. Accordingly, despite his own conviction that the bishops at Rome had reached a just and honest decision, Constantine summoned a council of bishops from all the western provinces to meet at Arles on 1 August 314. He provided free transport and lodging for the bishops (each accompanied by two priests and three servants), and instructed the *vicarius* of Africa to send delegations of supporters and opponents of Caecilianus to arrive in Arles before the council began.[140]

The council met. Constantine was present, sitting as a layman, without any armed bodyguard, accompanied only by Christian courtiers.[141] The assembled bishops made several decisions about general matters of Christian faith and practice.[142] Therein lay the ultimate historical importance of the council. For on the specific issue for which it was convened, the council merely reiterated the findings and the decision of the earlier council. The Donatists lodged an immediate appeal. Constantine ordered the Donatists in Gaul to be kept at his court and wrote to the *vicarius* of Africa to send any Donatists there to court. He then addressed an angry and impassioned letter to the bishops before they departed. He affirmed most categorically that the decision of bishops should be respected just as if God himself sat in judgment, and he denounced the Donatists with all the ferocity of a man who believed that the renewed appeal called his own sincerity into question. They were insane, deluded agents of the Devil, who arrogantly refused to see the truth.[143]

The Donatists had already made their next move. In Carthage, on 19 August 314, one Maximus appeared before one of the chief magistrates of the city and announced that the case against Caecilianus and Felix needed to be argued before the emperor. To support his contention, he produced prima facie evidence that Felix of Abthungi had complied with the imperial edict of 23 February 303 ordering churches to be destroyed, the Scriptures burned and church property confiscated. The evidence was a letter written by Alfius Caecilianus, who had been *duovir* of Abthungi in 303 and thus charged with local enforcement of the edict. Caecilianus swore to the authenticity of the letter, which he had, however, written only recently. It was addressed to Felix and described how Caecilianus discharged his duties in 303 by burning the Scriptures. A postscript added that Felix, afraid of having his house destroyed if the Scriptures were found there, promised to produce them in the place of worship— where Caecilianus found them and seized them in accordance with the imperial edict. Alfius Caecilianus was an old man, too old (Maximus observed) to travel to Constantine in Gaul. His testimony and his letter, therefore, were read into the records of the *duovir* at Carthage, and the *duovir* transmitted a report to the emperor.[144]

The new evidence gave Constantine pause. The bishops of two councils (he must have suspected) seemed to have been mistaken about the facts of the case. He accordingly instructed the *vicarius* of Africa to investigate the matter more closely. The inquiry dragged on until 15 February 315: the *vicarius* Aelius Paulinus was replaced, and his successor fell ill.[145] Then the proconsul Aelianus, who conducted the investigation in place of the indisposed *vicarius,* pronounced Felix innocent of the charges against him. In the part of the proceedings which survives, Caecilianus swears that his letter of the previous year is misleading and partly forged. He never wrote the damaging postscript; it was added by Ingentius, who persuaded him to write the letter. Under threat of torture, Ingentius confessed. Caecilianus wrote only the genuine part of the letter as what he thought was a favor to Felix. Ingentius came to Caecilianus with a request, allegedly from Felix, that Caecilianus declare that, as a magistrate eleven years before, he had burned the Scriptures, for Ingentius did not now wish to return to the church eleven valuable codices which were in his private possession.[146]

Constantine's actions before he received Aelianus' verdict seem vacillating and mysterious. Perhaps he received an interim report whose tenor differed from the final verdict. Whatever the reason, at some date in the winter of 314/5, he summoned the bishop Caecilianus to court. On the other hand, before Caecilianus arrived, he acceded to a petition from the Donatists that he should allow them to return to Africa and should send special envoys to settle the dispute there.[147] On 28 April 315 four Donatist bishops and a priest received a document, issued at Trier by the praetorian prefect, permitting them to use the *cursus publicus* in order to return to Africa.[148] A few days later, however, Constantine canceled their permission to leave and reversed his earlier decision: the Donatists should confront Caecilianus before the emperor—who promises that they will win their case if they sustain a single charge against the bishop.[149]

The cause of Constantine's sudden change of mind is clear: the report of Aelianus arrived, exculpating Felix. The emperor wrote at once to the new proconsul of Africa. He requested him to send Ingentius to court, under suitable escort, so that the Donatists could hear from his own lips how futile it was to stir up resentment against Caecilianus.[150] When that happened, Constantine hoped that dissension would cease.

The known events of the next months cannot (it appears) be combined to form a coherent narrative. Either in early May or during the summer of 315, Constantine sent the bishops Eunomius and Olympius to Carthage. Perhaps they were instructed to attempt a compromise by appointing someone other than Caecilianus or Donatus as bishop. In the event, the Donatists rioted, and Eunomius and Olympius confirmed the verdict of 313 acquitting Caecilianus. During the mission of the two bishops (it is stated) Caecilianus was detained at Brixia on the suggestion of the courtier Philumenus, after Donatus himself requested and was refused permission to return to Carthage.[151] Moreover, for reasons which are unknown, Constantine ordered both parties to appear before him in Rome, which he entered on 18 July 315 and left in late September. Caecilianus failed to present himself there, and the case was adjourned to Milan. After some Donatists attempted to flee on the journey, Constantine heard the case at Milan in October 315 and made his final decision.[152] Caecilianus, exonerated again, returned to Carthage, where Donatus had already arrived. Rioting continued unabated.[153] Constantine was consulted twice. On the second occasion, he vowed to come to Africa to settle the matter finally in person.[154]

The war against Licinius intervened, and Constantine never visited Africa. But the issue was decided, at least in the emperor's mind. It only remained to draw the logical and legal consequences. On 10 November 316 Constantine wrote to Eumelius, the *vicarius Africae,* reviewing the dispute between Caecilianus and his enemies.[155] It was perhaps in this letter that he ordered all churches belonging to the Donatists to be confiscated.[156] Repression followed. On 12 March 317, the schismatic sect gained its first martyrs when Roman soldiers and a Carthaginian mob attacked Donatist churches, allegedly at the instigation of Caecilianus, and killed several Donatists, among them two bishops of small African towns.[157] Thereafter, the *comes* Ursacius, and perhaps the *dux* Leontius, continued to harass the Donatists, but with what degree of effectiveness it is difficult to estimate.[158] Moreover, an official inquiry conducted at Cirta in December 320 by the *consularis* Domitius Zenophilus may originally have been intended as a prelude to stern measures in Numidia.[159]

The year 321, however, saw a complete reversal of imperial policy, despite the intransigence of the Donatists.[160] Constantine was not yet at war with Licinius, but there were different consuls in the East and West, and armed conflict was obviously approaching. Constantine intended to fight the coming war as a champion of Christianity, rescuing his fellow believers in the East from pagan persecution. But he himself was persecuting Christians, even if they belonged to a schismatic church. The contrast between reality and propaganda might become too blatant. On 5 May 321, therefore, Constantine instructed Verinus, the *vicarius* of Africa, to recall all Donatist exiles.[161] Another letter justified the change of policy to the bishops and laity of the Catholic church throughout Africa: revenge was consigned to God, who would surely regard any sufferings which the Donatists might inflict on their opponents as martyrdom.[162]

Such a concession, once made, was hard to revoke, and the Donatist cause prospered. In 324 Constantine sent some bishops from the newly conquered East to urge concord.[163] The result of their visit to Africa is not recorded, but may be surmised. Although the Donatists never shared in the legal privileges which Constantine gave to the Catholic church, their local influence in the cities of Africa could defeat the emperor's intention to confer benefits on the Catholic church alone. In Cirta, the Donatists forced lectors, subdeacons, and other clerics into the local senate, and they took possession of the Christian basilica which Constantine built. The emperor ultimately bowed to reality and allowed them to retain the basilica. On 5 February 330 he wrote to the Catholic bishops of Numidia a letter which breathes a pathetic air of resigned impotence. Unable to restore the basilica to its intended users, Constantine provided land and money to build a second basilica for the exclusive use of the Catholics.[164] Some years later, the Donatists held a council in Carthage. Two hundred and seventy bishops attended.[165] Despite Constantine's intervention, a schismatic group now dominated the African church.

V

CONSTANTINE AND LICINIUS

When Constantine left Rome in January 313, he went to northern Italy to cement his alliance with Licinius by giving him, as agreed in 311, his sister in marriage.[1] At the very beginning of February, Licinius left Carnuntum and traveled swiftly to Milan, where he married Constantia.[2] The two Augusti also had weighty matters of state to discuss. War between Licinius and Maximinus seemed not only inevitable but desirable. Even if Maximinus had formally ended persecution in late 312, his Christian subjects sensed his insincerity and still feared to exercise their rights openly.[3] Moreover, even in the Danubian provinces which Licinius ruled, the Christians, though tolerated, had probably not yet recovered buildings and property lost in the persecution. Constantine, therefore, pressed Licinius to extend the policy of restoration to his territories. Licinius agreed, and the defeat of Maximinus was to extend it to the whole of the Roman Empire.[4]

The ruler of the East, to his embarrassment, was compelled to fight a campaign in Mesopotamia which began in the late summer of 312 and dragged on through the autumn.[5] When it was concluded, Maximinus turned his attention westward. Before the end of winter, perhaps while Licinius was still in Milan, he marched across Asia Minor in great haste. Despite enormous losses of transport animals in the rain, snow, mud, and cold, he soon reached Bithynia and crossed into Europe. The garrison which held Byzantium for Licinius resisted bribes and promises, then repelled an armed assault. After eleven days, however, despairing because of their small number, they surrendered. Maximinus moved on to Heraclea, where he again took several days to induce the garrison to surrender. Licinius was now at Adrianople with a hastily assembled army. Maximinus, after further brief delay, advanced eighteen miles from Heraclea. There he discovered that Licinius was at the next guard post but one, some eighteen miles away, preparing to fight despite his inferiority in numbers— thirty thousand (it was estimated) against his own seventy thousand.[6]

Battle was joined under the opposing banners of paganism and monotheism. Maximinus vowed to Jupiter that if he gained the victory, he would utterly extinguish Christianity. Licinius, in contrast, distributed a prayer to "Great, Holy God" for his men to recite. It was said that an angel appeared to the emperor in a dream and dictated the prayer; it is at least equally probable that Constantine furnished the text for use in precisely these circumstances. Be that as it may, Licinius' army waited confidently, intending to give battle on 1 May so that Maximinus, like Maxentius, should fall on the anniversary of his accession. Maximinus opined that his *dies imperii* was more suited for a triumph than for battle. On 30 April, he drew up his army and advanced. A bare and desolate plain lay between the armies. Licinius' forces, also drawn up for battle, suddenly halted, laid aside their shields and helmets for a moment, and in unison recited their new prayer three times.[7]

A brief colloquy between the emperors preceded the hostilities. Maximinus refused to withdraw in peace, hoping that Licinius' army would desert. Licinius ordered his men to begin the attack. The opposing army adopted a rigidly defensive pose, while Maximinus urged the attackers to change sides. Unsuccessful, he abandoned the attempt. His own men, although they stood firm, could not repel the assault. The army of Licinius gradually began to prevail. When Maximinus realized that the day was lost, he exchanged the imperial purple for a slave's dress and fled. Their leader gone, his army broke: part surrendered, part scattered in flight. Licinius stopped to consolidate his victory. He enrolled the surrendered troops under his own standards and carefully distributed them in dispersed postings. Then, after a few days, he crossed to Bithynia and entered Nicomedia.

Maximinus passed through Nicomedia on 2 May. Pausing only to collect his wife, children, and a few trusted advisers, he fled eastward. In Cappadocia, however, he halted, donned the imperial purple again, and put himself at the head of an army formed of fugitives and the soldiers from Oriens.[8] Further resistance could be offered only at the Cilician Gates. Maximinus, therefore, went south from Cappadocia and attempted to hold the passes through the Taurus Mountains. When Licinius' army broke through, his situation became hopeless. He retreated to Tarsus, where, under siege, probably in July 313, he committed suicide, slowly and painfully. Christians soon claimed that he repented at the end, imploring the aid of Christ to save him from everlasting damnation.[9]

Licinius remained in Nicomedia for more than a month (until at least 13 June) before he proceeded eastward.[10] By the autumn he was in Antioch, enjoying the rewards of victory and arranging the administration of his new territories. The memory of Maximinus was condemned. His statues were destroyed or defaced, his name and titles erased from public inscriptions.[11] Supporters of his régime were hunted down and killed—and Licinius used the opportunity to remove all possible dynastic rivals. Candidianus, the bastard son of Galerius, greeted Licinius at Nicomedia and was received with apparent honor. But Licinius ordered his death, and the unsuspecting Candidianus was assassinated. Severianus, the son of Severus, had accompanied Maximinus to the end. Accused of wishing to become emperor in place of Maximinus, he was formally tried for treason and executed. At Antioch, the wife and children of Maximinus (a son of eight and a daughter of seven) were killed. Nor were the widows of still respected emperors safe. While at Nicomedia, Licinius ordered that Valeria too, the widow of Galerius, be put to death. She escaped. Fifteen months later, however, she was apprehended at Thessalonica, where she and her mother, Prisca, the widow of Diocletian, were publicly beheaded, and their bodies then cast into the sea.[12]

The purge ordered by Licinius was directed particularly against those who had persecuted Christians. The wife of Maximinus was thrown into the Orontes, where she had often herself ordered Christian women to be drowned.[13] Peucetius, a close confidant of the fallen emperor, Culcianus, a former prefect of Egypt, and Firmilianus, who governed Palestine from 308 to 310, all notorious persecutors, were put to death.[14] At Miletus, the priest of Apollo was sought out and killed. In the winter of 302/3 he had helped to produce an anti-Christian oracle which swayed Diocletian: the victors now had their revenge.[15] When Maximinus ruled in Antioch, the *curator* of the city, Theotecnus, raised a statue of Zeus Philios and organized a cult around it, with initiations, mysteries, and oracles. He used these rites to harry the Christians, and the emperor rewarded him with an appointment as a provincial governor. When Licinius came to Antioch, he executed Theotecnus and all his associates after torturing them until they confessed that their theosophy was nothing but fraud and trickery.[16]

During the summer and autumn of 313, each provincial governor in Asia Minor and the East received a letter from Licinius which defined the new legal position of the Christians. Those issued for Bithynia and Palestine, as posted in Nicomedia and Caesarea, survive.[17] Both make the same essential points. At their meeting in Milan, Constantine and Licinius decided that all their subjects should have complete religious freedom. The letter instructs each governor, therefore, to remove all the conditions which have previously restricted imperial acts of toleration for the Christians—a clear allusion to Maximinus' attempts to circumvent Galerius' edict of 311. All are now to enjoy full freedom of worship. In addition, the Christian churches shall receive, without payment, delay, or dispute, all the buildings and movable property seized from them in the persecution, whether still owned by the imperial *fiscus* or now held by private citizens. In the latter case, the *vicarius* of the diocese, upon being petitioned, will indemnify the owner for his losses. This provision was significant. Whereas the edict of 311 justified persecution as right in principle, even if attended by disastrous consequences, these letters of 313 disown the previous imperial policy of persecution as mistaken, perhaps even as morally wrong. The persecution which had lasted in the East for more than ten years was now at an end. The Christians began to rebuild their churches, to hold councils, to resume the rhythm of an existence interrupted for a decade.[18]

The Christians may also have lent Licinius aid in a political matter. It seems that in late 313 or 314 the emperor campaigned on the Persian frontier, fighting in Cappadocia and Adiabene, in Media and Armenia.[19] In the summer or autumn of 314, a council of bishops met at Caesarea in Cappadocia and consecrated Gregory as primate of Armenia: he then journeyed solemnly from Caesarea into Armenia, where he baptized King Tiridates, who declared his kingdom officially Christian.[20] Soon, however, Licinius was needed on the Danube; he crossed the Hellespont and, before the end of 315, celebrated a victory over the Goths.[21] The frontier re-established, Licinius made a symbolic gesture: he rebuilt the city of Tropaeum Traiani and perhaps restored the reliefs on the great monument celebrating Trajan's conquest of Dacia.[22] The eastern emperor now took up residence in or near one of the great cities near the Danube.[23] There he must have begun to contemplate the political situation, for a new factor impinged on his relationship with Constantine. In 315, the quinquagenarian emperor acquired an heir when Constantia gave birth to a son.[24] The event had obvious dynastic implications for Licinius' western colleague.

In the spring of 313 Constantine returned to Gaul, presumably after waiting in northern Italy to discover the outcome of the war in the East.[25] Had Maximinus prevailed, Constantine would doubtless have annexed Illyricum: in the event, he needed to transform his ally into a legitimate enemy. When news of the battle near Adrianople came, Constantine too damned the memory of Maximinus and annulled Maximinus' current consulate, eventually substituting Licinius as his colleague.[26] By 28 May Constantine was in Trier.[27] In the late summer or autumn he fought on the lower Rhine: although a contemporary speech speaks grandiloquently of a campaign which will advance the Roman frontier to the Elbe, no victory worthy of official commemoration was won.[28] Shortly after the speech, probably in the autumn of 313, Constantine appears to have conducted a brief expedition to Britain,[29] but at several dates between 3 November 313 and 1 June 314 his presence is attested at Trier, and he traveled south to attend the Council of Arles, which opened on 1 August 314.[30]

After the council, military matters again demanded Constantine's attention.

The emperor proceeded to the Rhine, and the imperial coinage soon began to advertise widespread victories, the adversaries being named on one issue as Franks and Alamanni.[31] Constantine spent the following winter (314/5) in Trier, before traveling south to celebrate his *decennalia* in Rome.[32] He entered the imperial city in July and departed on 27 September.[33] The visit allowed time for celebration and propaganda—and perhaps for political initiatives designed to prepare the way for war.[34]

From Rome, Constantine returned to Gaul by way of Milan and again spent the winter at Trier.[35] In the spring of 316 he moved south and passed the summer in southern Gaul, preparing for war.[36] On 7 August 316, Fausta give birth to a son at Arles,[37] and within two months Constantine invaded the territories of Licinius in a campaign designed to win the rest of the Roman Empire for himself. The preliminaries to this war, though obscure, ineluctably imply that Constantine was the aggressor.

The official story presented Licinius as deceiving Constantine and trying to murder him.[38] One source, however, furnishes details which set the latter charge in a precise context.[39] Constantine sent Constantius (presumably his young half-brother) to Licinius with a proposal to create a new emperor: Bassianus, the husband of Constantine's sister Anastasia, should be Caesar and rule Italy. That was surely not the whole plan. The proposal appealed to the precedent set by Diocletian and Maximian; therefore, Constantine must be suspected of proposing the creation of two Caesars, the other being his son Crispus. As transmitted, the proposal lacks a precise date and convincing motivation. Both can be divined. The marriage of Constantine and Fausta, celebrated in 307, was barren until 316. But Licinius and Constantia, married in 313, produced a son within two years or a little more. Constantine's plan was surely designed to preclude Licinius' newly born son from the imperial succession by nominating his own son and his brother-in-law as Caesars: in the new tetrarchy, as in the old, there would be no room for a fifth emperor, and Constantine might claim that his position as senior emperor entitled him, not Licinius, to name the next Augustus or Caesar in the East.

Licinius declined the proposal. He then (it was alleged) induced Senecio, the brother of Bassianus, to persuade Bassianus to murder Constantine. Caught in the attempt, Bassianus was confronted with his guilt and killed. Senecio fled to Licinius, who refused to surrender him to justice. War was the consequence, and Constantine justified going to war with the additional charge that Licinius had ordered pictures and statues of Constantine on display at Emona, close to the frontier between the two emperors, to be pulled down and destroyed.[40]

Chronology suggests a cynical view of Constantine's conduct. Licinius' son was born in the spring or summer of 315. During the winter of 315/6, it became obvious that Fausta, after more than eight years of marriage, was pregnant. If she should bear a son, he would deserve the imperial purple more than Bassianus. Constantine's brother-in-law was expendable, and vulnerable: through Constantine's proposal, he had become a potential rival to the emperor's sons.

He may have taken precipitate action or uttered unwise words, but he may equally well have been innocent of any malfeasance. His alleged crime bears a suspicious similarity to that imputed to Maximian—not the open rebellion of 310, but the secret attempt at assassination subsequently invented.[41]

The affair of Bassianus may have had wide ramifications. Rufius Volusianus, once an active supporter of Maxentius, had rallied to Constantine at a timely moment: he became *comes* of the emperor, prefect of the city of Rome, and in 314, ordinary consul. On 20 August 315, while Constantine was in Rome, Vettius Rufinus replaced Volusianus as prefect.[42] Volusianus subsequently fell into disgrace, and the Senate exiled him.[43] The date of Volusianus' fall is unknown, but it clearly cannot precede his departure from the urban prefecture, and the mysterious episode of Bassianus may be relevant to his exile. Further, the poet Publilius Optatianus Porfyrius, apparently a relative of Volusianus, was languishing in exile in 324: he (and others) may have been exiled at the same time as Volusianus.[44]

Be that as it may, the essential facts about the war are well attested. On 7 August 316 Constantine's second son was born and immediately received his father's name.[45] On 29 September the emperor was in Verona, and on 8 October he attacked Licinius near Cibalae, more than two hundred miles inside his territory, on the road leading to the great city of Sirmium.[46]

Constantine led twenty thousand men against thirty-five thousand—which implies that Licinius had not properly concentrated his forces.[47] In the battle (it was estimated) Licinius lost more than twenty thousand infantry; under cover of darkness, he then retreated to Sirmium with the greater part of his cavalry. Collecting his wife, son, and treasury, he fled thence to Serdica, where he proclaimed as emperor Valens, the *dux* in charge of defending the frontier. Valens assembled a vast army at Adrianople. Licinius then sent ambassadors to Constantine, who was now at Philippopolis. Constantine dismissed them, preferring the hazards of battle. The armies met near Adrianople.[48] The fighting was intense, and the outcome long doubtful, but Licinius again yielded and again escaped as night fell.

Twice victorious in the field, Constantine believed the war won. He advanced rapidly toward Byzantium, doubtless expecting resistance to collapse. But Licinius was an experienced and skillful general who had fought in Galerius' Persian and Italian campaigns.[49] He divined Constantine's intentions. Licinius and Valens withdrew not toward Byzantium, but obliquely toward Beroea. When Constantine rashly pressed on, they were able to break his lines of communication. Genuine negotiation now being possible, Licinius sued for peace. Terms were quickly agreed upon. Constantine demanded the deposition of Valens, whom he denounced as a "vile slave." Valens was removed, and Licinius soon put him to death. Licinius ceded all of Europe except Thrace, Moesia, and Scythia Minor to Constantine. On 1 March 317 at Serdica, the compact was ratified in a solemn ceremony.[50] Constantine invested his sons Crispus and Constantinus as Caesars, with Licinius' son as a third Caesar intermediate in rank. The dynastic implications of that arrangement seem clear: should Licinius die, the imperial college would again become a tetrarchy, with Crispus promoted to be Augustus in the East.

After the war, Licinius, who had lost the great cities of the Balkans, transferred his capital to Nicomedia, where he resided for the next seven years.[51] A group of contemporary letters vividly illustrates the disturbed circumstances in which Licinius' court left Sirmium and reveals something about Licinius' contacts with prominent pagans in the East. The letters were written to the philosopher Iamblichus by an unknown pupil, who had perhaps attached himself to the court in 313/4 when Licinius was in Syria.[52] One of the letters lists a series of discomforts recently experienced: the din of battle, the anguish of siege, wandering in flight, all kinds of terrors, severe storms, dangerous diseases, and countless varied disasters in a journey from Upper Pannonia to the Straits of Chalcedon.[53] But the writer was now safe: he wrote to Iamblichus from Nicomedia, and he entrusted the letter to a soldier in the imperial bodyguard who came from Apamea and claimed to know the philosopher very well.[54]

Iamblichus maintained contact with the imperial court from Apamea, where he resided, probably after teaching in Antioch for a period.[55] Before the war of 316/7, the philosopher had received a copy of a speech which his correspondent composed at Licinius' command, and his favorite pupil, Sopater, spent a winter near the Danube, clearly in attendance at court.[56] Sometime after the war, Sopater came on an embassy from Apamea to Nicomedia; he brought a letter from Iamblichus to his other pupil, who wrote back both to Iamblichus and to Sopater's son at Apamea.[57] These men were all pagans. Hence, when they hailed Iamblichus as "the universal blessing of the Hellenes" and "the Savior of virtually the whole Hellenic world," they implicitly underscored the conflict between pagans and Christians which was to undermine Licinius' régime.[58]

A realistic picture of how Licinius governed the East is not easily formed. After September 324 Constantine derided his defeated rival as "the common enemy of the civilized world."[59] His subjects took up the theme and elaborated it. Licinius was a monster of depravity and lust, a tyrant who oppressed his subjects with every refinement of injustice and cruelty.[60] But even the blandest of panegyrists could not avoid an embarrassing contradiction. In 313, Licinius had conquered Asia Minor and the East as a liberator, rescuing the Christians from persecution.[61] How was that possible for the tyrant of 324? Some attributed his transformation to madness, while others suggested that he revealed the utter wickedness of his true character only at the end.[62] No prudent subject of the victor would attempt to question the caricature of his fallen rival which Constantine wished to be disseminated. Nevertheless, later accusations and some contemporary evidence suffice to indicate, in outline, the nature of Licinius' government of the East between 313 and 324.

Licinius' administration cannot have differed markedly from that of his predecessors or of his rival.[63] Like any other emperor, Licinius professed concern for the safety of his subjects, respect for the legislation of his imperial predecessors, and a belief that ancient customs merited preservation.[64] Moreover, more than a hundred years after Licinius died, the compilers of the Theodosian Code included at least two of his edicts—whose provisions, therefore, must still have been valid in the fifth century. These two pronouncements concern the administration of justice and the imperial civil service.

Before the end of 313 Licinius checked the purge which followed the death of Maximinus by reasserting the traditional rules governing criminal accusations. Accusers (he laid down) should by all means be allowed to prefer charges. But they become liable to punishment themselves if they fail to prove their allegations. Further, in cases of *maiestas,* an accuser who cannot produce overwhelming proof shall be liable to torture, and without a formal accusation, charges should not be entertained at all. Specifically, informers should not be heard but punished; slaves or freedmen who accuse their masters or patrons are to be crucified to deter others from such presumptuous conduct, while anonymous accusations must be torn up or burned and their authors, if discoverable, suitably punished.[65]

Some years later, on 21 July 317, a law addressed to the province of Bithynia regulated access to four honorary ranks or titles: *perfectissimus, ducenarius, centenarius* and *egregius.* Men who had served in the imperial palace, governed provinces, held high administrative office, decurions or *principales* who had fulfilled all their obligations in their city, and leading centurions who had completed their military service were all allowed to receive such titles.[66] Forbidden to acquire the titles were *monetarii* and decurions who wished to escape their duties: any who obtained honorary rank were to lose it until they had discharged their local obligations.[67] Treasury officials (*Caesariani*) were allowed to hold the titles only after they retired from office with a clear record.[68] These regulations may echo a law of Constantine;[69] if so, the fact will merely emphasize the similarity of the two administrations.

In some areas, however, Licinius adopted policies at variance with his colleague and with ancestral custom. The charge that he seized the wives of noblemen for his henchmen, and debauched virgins and married women, need be no more than mindless repetition of the stereotyped crimes of the textbook tyrant.[70] Allegations that Licinius altered the laws concerning marriage and the legal rights of dying persons are another matter; even though no confirmation exists, Licinius may be supposed to have made changes, which many of his subjects resented, to benefit the imperial treasury.[71] The emperor of the East was tightfisted, in fact as well as by reputation. In 321 a census of the whole empire was due, and both emperors needed money for their approaching war.[72] Their actions reveal the difference between political genius and mediocrity.

Constantine devised a new type of official to advertise fairness in the census: his title was *peraequator census* and his function to hear appeals against assessments for tax liability.[73] Constantine also took care not to change the basic principles of assessment, though he may have increased his total revenue. Licinius, in contrast, provoked hostility through innovation. One of his former subjects later charged that the size of lots was exaggerated and that men long dead were included in the tax registers; the truth underlying these allegations is presumably that Licinius ordered a fresh and accurate survey of landed property and raised the age of exemption from the poll tax.[74] What appears to be a petition of early 325 shows a man of seventy-two applying for exemption from liturgies: it may be deduced that Licinius raised the age of exemption from both liturgies and taxation to seventy, and that in 324 Constantine lost little time in reducing the age of exemption again.[75] Similarly, he restored to retired soldiers the exemption from liturgies and curial duties which Licinius had canceled.[76]

Licinius' ultimate failure was intimately connected with his religious policies, which show an inherent contradiction. In 313 he rescued the Christians from persecution and restored all that they had lost, but his actions in 313 were inspired by Constantine, in whom the Christians of the East gradually came to recognize an authentic fellow believer such as Licinius would never be. Unable or unwilling to commit himself irrevocably either to militant Christianity or to militant paganism, Licinius drifted from toleration of Christianity to implicit disapproval, and finally toward active intolerance.

Licinius' attitude remained ambivalent to the end. Even after the army and civil service had been purged of Christians, Eusebius, the bishop of Nicomedia, retained a prominent position at court.[77] Eusebius had originally been bishop of Berytus, but from Berytus he soon moved to Licinius' capital, perhaps enticed by a desire to be close to the center of political power.[78] Eusebius (it appears) was related to Julius Julianus, who served Licinius as praetorian prefect from at least the spring of 315 until September 324.[79] The bishop of Nicomedia established himself as a firm favorite of Licinius' consort—the sister of Constantine—and thereby gained an influential voice to support his opinions in theological controversy when Constantine conquered the East.[80]

The attempt to please both parties brought Licinius no political advantage. No pagan subjects of Constantine are known to have turned against him through a desire to have a pagan emperor. But many Christian subjects of Licinius (as he well knew) were potentially or actively disloyal. When war came in 324, the Christians of the East prayed for the success of the Christian emperor, and not merely passively or in secret. The aged Lactantius added to his *Divine Institutes* an invocation of Constantine which invited him, as a pious emperor, to rescue "the just in other parts of the world" which he did not yet rule, and hence, by implication, to depose the persecuting emperor.[81] Constantine was justified in presenting the final campaign against Licinius as a Christian crusade. Despite his hesitations, Licinius had, by slow and inexorable stages, adopted a policy which again produced Christian martyrs and confessors—and a Christian liberator.

Licinius' first step was to expel Christians from the imperial palace.[82] Perhaps he purged his entourage of Christians very soon after the war of Cibalae. But those who left his service suffered no further molestation. Arsacius, a keeper of the imperial lions, immured himself in a tower at Nicomedia, where he remained for many years.[83] Auxentius, a *notarius,* accompanied Licinius into a courtyard of the imperial palace where there was a fountain, a statue of Dionysus, and a large, leafy vine. Licinius ordered Auxentius to cut a particularly fine cluster of grapes. When Auxentius did so, the emperor ordered him to lay it at Dionysus' feet. Auxentius refused. Licinius ordered him to obey or to leave his service. Auxentius left the palace at once. Many years later Auxentius became bishop of Mopsuestia. It may be significant that his younger brother, Theodorus, subsequently bishop of Tarsus, was educated in Athens—since 317 in the territory of Constantine.[84]

At a later date, Licinius ordered that all members of the imperial administration either sacrifice or forfeit their rank and be discharged.[85] An inscription from the camp at Salsovia shows how conformity was secured in the army: in accordance with the imperial order, all the troops stationed there consecrated a statue of Sol every year with incense, candles, and libations.[86] Such an order to sacrifice was sometimes extended to private citizens and civilians, to whom zealous subordinates of Licinius thought it ought to apply. On 25 December 323 Constantine issued a threatening law. Learning that clergy and other Christians had been compelled by men of other religions to sacrifice at the *quindecennalia* of Licinius, he promised condign punishment for any who forced Christians to participate in pagan rites.[87] It is not clear how much earlier Licinius had issued the law prescribing sacrifice for soldiers.

A series of measures attempted to regulate, or to hinder, Christian worship and corporate life under Licinius' rule. The emperor forbade assemblies and councils of bishops, apparently ordering each bishop to remain permanently in his own city.[88] Christians resented the ban, even though its stated object was to quiet doctrinal strife, because it prevented the consecration of new bishops according to normal ecclesiastical practice. Another law forbade men and women to worship together, or women to receive instruction from priests or bishops: only women could teach women.[89] A third law, which perhaps applied only to meetings held to elect a new bishop, ordered that Christian assemblies must be held outside the city gates in the open air.[90] More insidious still, Licinius canceled the tax privileges of the clergy: he enrolled priests in local councils and forced them to perform the public liturgies incumbent upon decurions.[91]

If these measures hardly constitute official persecution of the Christian name, it is nevertheless clear that provincial governors recovered the power to punish Christians in all the ways which Roman law allowed. Although virtually all of the documents purporting to describe the execution of martyrs under Licinius are fictitious, there is at least one strictly contemporary and unimpeachable witness of the persecution.[92] Eusebius of Caesarea began to write his *Preparation for the Gospel* and *Proof of the Gospel* shortly after Licinius defeated Maximinus in 313, and he completed the double work before Licinius fell eleven years later.[93] The *Preparation,* which was completed before 320, never alludes to persecution as a reality or even as a threat; the *Proof* does, in several striking passages. Magistrates (Eusebius observes) still treat Christians as self-confessed criminals, punishing those who proclaim belief in Christ, though they have committed no other crime, and releasing apostates immediately. The churches are flourishing and full of worshipers, but they are surrounded by visible and invisible foes of Christ's teaching who wish to extinguish it utterly.[94]

Some of Licinius' Christian subjects probably made the easy transition from sympathy with Constantine to acts of treason gainst their lawful emperor. Shortly before 1 March 321 Persian envoys visited Constantine to seek his friendship.[95] With Armenia officially Christian since 314, it seems that Licinius feared encirclement and suspected disloyalty on the sensitive eastern frontier.[96] He instructed governors to punish dissidents. The bishop of Amaseia and other bishops in Pontus were put to death, and churches were destroyed or closed.[97] The repression suited Constantine excellently. In 324 he made war on Licinius, on the plausible excuse that he wished to prevent a general persecution of eastern Christians.[98]

In 317 Constantine began to reside in the lands he had recently conquered.[99] He proclaimed that Serdica was his Rome and he spent much time there.[100] But he also resided in Sirmium, the former residence of Diocletian and Licinius, and his presence is also attested elsewhere: in 318 he visited northern Italy, and it was from Thessalonica that he launched campaigns in 323 and 324. In the war of 316/7, Constantine had acquired Greece and its islands in addition to most of the Danubian lands.[101] Hence Athens, one of the intellectual centers of the Greek world, passed under his sway, and Constantine added the patronage of Greek culture to his existing obligations. At an unknown date, perhaps not long after 317, he was elected hoplite general at Athens, and repaid the honor by granting the city a free annual supply of wheat.[102] After 324, Nicagoras, torchbearer of the Eleusinian mysteries, obtained Constantine's permission to use the imperial post to visit Thebes in Egypt,[103] and the pagan Praxagoras, at the age of twenty-one, sought imperial favor with a history chronicling the rise of Constantine.[104] It is not surprising, therefore, that, again at an unknown date, one Dionysius dedicated a work on music to the emperor, saluting him as a lover of the art, a finder and giver of all kinds of culture.[105]

Residing on or near the Danube, Constantine entrusted the administration of Gaul to his son Crispus, now a young man of twenty or more. Crispus had a court of his own at Trier, with the appropriate bureaucracy and army. The choice of praetorian prefect in 318 was significant: he was Junius Bassus, probably a Christian, whom Constantine maintained in office for fourteen years.[106] An emperor was clearly needed on the Rhine: Crispus waged war against the Franks in 319,[107] and probably on the middle or upper Rhine four years later.[108] Moreover, Crispus received a wife, who produced a daughter in October 322 and was probably pregnant again two years later.[109] Crispus' wife had the same name as Constantine's mother, to whom she might have been distantly related.[110]

Concord and amity between the Augusti did not endure. On 1 January 321 an open breach was apparent in the consular nominations. In the West, the consuls were the Caesars Crispus and Constantinus, who entered office at Serdica in the presence of their father.[111] In the East, Licinius proclaimed himself and his son consuls, and he refused to accept Constantine's consuls in any of the next three years.[112] In 322 the consuls nominated by Constantine were Petronius Probianus and Anicius Julianus, in 323 Severus and Vettius Rufinus, all leading senators.[113] In 324 another consulate of the Caesars Crispus and Constantinus portended war.

The initiative was Constantine's. Two almost contemporaneous speeches survive which reveal much about Constantine at this juncture—or at least about how Constantine wished others to regard him. One speech was recited in Rome on 1 March 321; it is a panegyric of Constantine which celebrates the *quinquennalia* of the Caesars.[114] Constantine himself delivered the other speech, either at Serdica or at Thessalonica, on a Good Friday in a year which should fall between 321 and 324; spoken in Latin, it regrettably survives only in an often obscure official Greek translation which Constantine may have dispatched for circulation in the East before 324.[115]

In Rome on 1 March 321, the rhetor Nazarius delivered an accomplished panegyric of a traditional type, which blandly avoids dangerous topics. An innocent reader would never suspect that other emperors existed besides Constantine and his two sons. Nazarius never lets slip the merest hint of the most recent civil war. Crispus' victories in Gaul were a safe topic and receive full, if brief, praise.[116] But Nazarius devotes the bulk of the speech to the events of 312, when Constantine liberated Rome—material doubtless familiar from frequent repetition, designed to comfort all and distress none. Nor does the peroration bring any surprises. Nazarius assures his audience that peace reigns abroad, and plenty at home. Cities have been refounded or marvelously adorned. New laws define morality and check vice, and the dangerous ambiguity of the old laws has been removed. Chastity, marriage, property are all safe. Rome lacks only one felicity: the presence of its rulers.[117] In this conventional speech only a few remarks betray a Christian viewpoint—and perhaps indicate that Nazarius himself was a Christian.[118]

The *Speech to the Assembly of the Saints* offers a total contrast. It is a sermon, not a panegyric. Its tone is firm, honest, and sincere, with few concessions to convention. Whether Constantine himself delivered the whole of the *Speech* in its extant form has often been doubted.[119] Such doubts, however, arise from an assumption that Constantine was an ill-educated soldier, with little or no knowledge of literature or Greek philosophy.[120] That assumption is vulnerable. Constantine might (for all that is known to the contrary) have studied philosophy in his youth—and he spent several years at the court of Diocletian, where philosophers were welcome.[121] Constantine resided in Nicomedia while Lactantius taught rhetoric there, and he later chose Lactantius as tutor to his son in Trier.[122] The emperor, therefore, had ample opportunity to converse with Lactantius, and several passages in the *Speech* not only resemble Lactantius' *Divine Institutes* in thought and diction but also appear to betray direct intellectual indebtedness.[123] Moreover, it can be argued that Lactantius persuaded Constantine to peruse the Sibylline Oracles for himself.[124] Still more significant, the philosophical content of the *Speech* exhibits a marked similarity to Calcidius' commentary on Plato's *Timaeus*: Calcidius dedicated his work to an Ossius who ought to be the Ossius, bishop of Corduba, who stood close to Constantine.[125]

By the standards of his time, Constantine was an educated man, and there is nothing in the *Speech* which he cannot have written or dictated himself. Even if the emperor lacked a philosophical training in Greek (which is not certain), he could have read Calcidius' Latin translation of the first part of the *Timaeus* and his commentary thereon. Ossius knew Greek well and could have introduced Constantine, who certainly spoke Greek, to the writings of the Platonic philosophers of the second century from whom both the *Speech* and Calcidius derive ideas.[126] Ossius may even have provided notes for Constantine or aided him in composing his oration.[127] But nothing in the text indicates that the *Speech,* once delivered, was retouched for its subsequent publication.[128] On the contrary, so much of the *Speech* reflects the same personality revealed elsewhere that Constantine should be supposed to have spoken the original text entire.[129] Although he may have incorporated ideas and expressions from others, in uttering them publicly the emperor made them his own.

Constantine delivered the *Speech to the Assembly of the Saints* to a Christian audience.[130] He appears to salute the bishop, and he prefaces the body of the speech with a remarkable statement of diffidence: if he makes any doctrinal mistake, those who know God's mysteries must correct him, not lamenting the lapse but welcoming the sincerity of the attempt.[131] Although the argument is often difficult to follow (and the Greek translators seem often to have muddled the Latin original), the main exposition falls into three sections: the philosophical basis of Christianity, the Incarnation, and God's role in recent history.[132]

The first section seems to show knowledge of Numenius of Apamea, whose ideas are modified in a Christian direction.[133] Numenius posited the existence of a "first god" and a "second god," and held that the latter was the demiurge of the *Timaeus* who created the universe.[134] The *Speech* commends Plato for distinguishing between the first god, who is above the real world, and the second god, who is inferior to the first: they have distinct essences, though a single perfection, and the second god derives his existence from the first. But the demiurge is the first god, God the Father, the Creator of all things.[135] It may be suspected that the argument of the whole section is heavily indebted, not necessarily at first hand, to Numenius' treatise *On the Good,* of whose five books only small fragments survive.[136] But the conclusions which Constantine derives from philosophy are markedly Christian. Behind much that seems irrelevant (and often disguises the drift of the argument), the equivalence of Platonic and Christian theology is consistently asserted: God the Father is the Good, the First God, and the Demiurge, while the Second God of the *Timaeus* (as traditionally interpreted) is God the Son, Christ, the Logos.[137]

The second main section of the *Speech* equates virtue with Christianity and vice with failure to believe in the Christian God.[138] It thus stresses both the moral and historical importance of the Incarnation. Constantine argues, here as throughout, that idolatry leads to disaster, adducing the destruction of Memphis and Babylon, both ruins which he has seen with his own eyes.[139] He also appeals to two authors whom Lactantius had invoked in the *Divine Institutes* as confirming the predictions of biblical Prophets.[140] But Constantine does so more systematically and more confidently, going beyond the probable source of his inspiration. He quotes thirty-four lines from the eighth book of the Sibylline Oracles, whose initial letters form an acrostic in Greek of the words "Jesus Christ, Son of God, Savior, Cross";[141] the original *Speech,* like the extant translation, probably quoted the lines in Greek.[142] Constantine then produces an exegesis of Virgil's Fourth Eclogue, claiming that the eclogue confirms the Sibyl because Virgil foretold the approaching birth of Christ. Constantine quotes most of the poem a few lines at a time and gives a running commentary based on the Latin.[143]

The final section of the *Speech* explains the relevance of Christianity to recent history, for the most part, admittedly, in somewhat allusive terms.[144] God rewards the just and punishes the bad, on earth as in heaven. The city where he is speaking itself bears witness to the fate of Galerius, who instigated persecution of the Christians and perished miserably after turning his victims into heroes. Persecutors, like Decius, Valerian, and Aurelian, never prosper for long and always die shamefully.[145] Diocletian was on the verge of madness when he issued laws against the Christians; God's vengeance involved harm to the state, and the persecution led inexorably to Constantine's victories in civil war and to the liberation of the city where he spoke.[146]

The *Speech to the Assembly of the Saints* fits into no recognizable literary category, for it combines homily, philosophy, apologetic, and literary exegesis into an expression of its author's personality. Throughout, Constantine assumes and asserts that God has given him success.[147] He confesses a mighty obligation: he must persuade his subjects to worship God, he must reform the wicked and unbelieving—and he alludes to his own conversion in the prime of life.[148] But the *Speech* is also a political manifesto. Constantine the Christian denounces persecutors, he thanks God for liberating the persecuted, and at the same time he alludes to his own defeat of an ignoble person who had wrongfully seized the imperial throne.[149] On the Good Friday of any year between 317 and 324, the reference to Licinius was transparent. As so often, Constantine's religious prejudices neatly coincided with his political interest. By dishonoring Christians, Licinius forfeited his moral right to rule: God chose Constantine as the instrument of liberation.

Despite the open avowal of hostility in 321, Constantine maintained a formal peace during which he built a harbor at Thessalonica and prepared a fleet in the Aegean.[150] He could afford to wait and goad his rival into unwise reaction. A barbarian invasion provided the opportunity for provocation. In the spring of 323, while Constantine was at Thessalonica, the Sarmatians crossed the Danube and ravaged Thrace and Moesia.[151] On hearing the news, Constantine canceled all military leave and decreed that any who aided the barbarians or handled the spoils should be burned alive.[152] He then took the field in person, expelled the invaders, and pursued them across the Danube.[153] Fighting is recorded at Campona, on the River Margus, and at Bononia, all within Constantine's territories.[154] But Constantine did not respect the frontier with Licinius, beyond which part of his army appears to have strayed, and he proclaimed a victory and issued coins advertising the defeat of the Sarmatians.[155] Licinius complained of the violation of his territory and prohibited the circulation of the coins.[156]

Constantine spent at least some of the winter of 323/4 at Sirmium.[157] In the following spring he returned to Thessalonica, where an enormous expeditionary force was ready—an army with a fleet of more than two thousand transports to aid its eastward advance.[158] Another fleet was concentrated at the Piraeus. Licinius collected an army reportedly still larger, advanced beyond Adrianople, and took up a defensive position, his army spread along the east bank of the Hebrus. Constantine camped west of the river, and the armies faced each other for many days. Finally, Constantine forced a crossing of the river and defeated the opposing army; during the battle he was slightly wounded in the thigh. Licinius fled when night came. On the following day (4 July 324), the remains of his army surrendered.[159] Constantine pursued Licinius to Byzantium and commenced a siege when Licinius took refuge there.

The progress of naval operations is not altogether clear, but Constantine's fleet, under the command of Crispus, won a decisive victory.[160] Licinius' admiral, Abantus, held the Hellespont with a fleet of three hundred and fifty triremes. After the battle at Adrianople, Crispus, aided by the winds, destroyed or captured almost the whole of Abantus' fleet and forced the straits. Having lost control of the sea, Licinius could no longer hold Byzantium: he withdrew to Chalcedon with much of his army and his treasury.

Licinius had not yet abandoned all hope. He appointed Martinianus, his *magister officiorum,* to be Augustus and sent him to Lampsacus to prevent an army from crossing the Hellespont into Asia.[161] If a crossing into Asia could be prevented, then fresh armies from the East might yet turn the fortune of war. These hopes were vain. Constantine concentrated his fleet near Byzantium and sought a safe crossing. He found one nearby and transported his army to Holy

Point, some twenty miles north of Chalcedon. Licinius summoned Martinianus, though his main strength now lay in a Gothic contingent under its own chieftain. On 18 September 324 at Chrysopolis outside Chalcedon, the two armies met: Constantine was again victorious.[162]

Byzantium and Chalcedon opened their gates. Licinius fled to Nicomedia. On the day after the battle, he offered submission. His wife, Constantia, sister of Constantine, and Eusebius, bishop of Nicomedia, came to the victor's camp requesting that Licinius be allowed to live out his remaining days in peace.[163] Constantine swore to spare his life. Licinius then came in person, laid his imperial purple at Constantine's feet, performed homage to his new emperor and master, and sought pardon for his past actions. Constantine ordered Martinianus to be executed but sent Licinius to Thessalonica with a promise that his life should be safe.

Constantine entered Nicomedia in triumph.[164] He came as a conqueror, nearly twenty years after he had departed as a disappointed heir. To mark the occasion he took the title "victor,"[165] and he began to stamp his personality on the administration of the eastern provinces. Among his new subjects was an elderly scholar and bishop who would later become his biographer.

T W O

E U S E B I U S

VI

ORIGEN AND CAESAREA

Caesarea in Palestine derived its name from the first Roman emperor. A small town had existed on the site from the days of the Persian Empire, clustered around a fortified harbor known as Strato's Tower after the dynast of Sidon who built it. Strato's Tower became a Greek city while the Ptolemaic and Seleucid kings fought over Palestine. About 100 B.C. the city was incorporated in the Hasmonean kingdom and probably received large numbers of Jewish settlers, but forty years later Pompey restored the city to the control of its gentile citizens. Strato's Tower subsequently became subject to Herod, who ruled from 37 to 4 B.C. as king of Judaea. Herod renamed the city after Augustus Caesar and transformed it totally: henceforward he was regarded by all, Jews and gentiles alike, as the founder of Caesarea.[1]

Herod rebuilt Caesarea with all the conveniences and trappings of a Hellenistic capital and a Roman metropolis. He laid out the new city on a grandiose scale and embellished it with marble imported from abroad at great expense. The center of the city was dominated by a luxurious palace, by lavish public buildings, and by marketplaces, and the harbor rivaled the Piraeus of Athens: protected by a mole, it had abundant sheltered anchorage and was overlooked by a temple of Rome and Augustus. Newly constructed sewers and aqueducts ministered to the material needs of the citizens, while Herod provided a stone theater, an amphitheater, and a hippodrome for their entertainment and for his own advertisement.[2] The places of amusement were a striking success; in the fourth century, Caesarea was famous for its circus, and it trained pantomime performers for the whole Syrian area.[3]

When Judaea became a Roman province, Caesarea became its administrative capital and the normal residence of its governor.[4] Its importance was only enhanced when the Jews rose against Rome twice (in 66–73 and in 132–135). While Jerusalem lost its role as the center of Jewish political and religious life, and Jews were forbidden upon pain of death to set foot in Jerusalem or its surrounding territory,[5] Caesarea was raised to the status of a Roman colony by Vespasian, who settled veterans there, and the city received exemption from provincial taxation.[6] The resurgence of Sassanian Persia in the third century made Caesarea even more important to the Roman government: the city became a collection point for men and supplies destined for imperial campaigns against Persia,[7] and later, in the early fourth century, so it seems, Maximinus deemed Caesarea worthy to be, at least briefly, the residence of a Roman emperor.[8]

By the third century, Caesarea was a cosmopolitan city perhaps containing as many as one hundred thousand inhabitants. Its population, moreover, was mixed, and no race or creed either formed a majority or could dominate the others. Officially, the city was pagan and, as long as its own mint existed, the coinage of Caesarea emphasized the Tyche who was the presiding deity of the city.[9] But there was also a thriving and important Jewish community, in which rabbinical studies flourished, and a Samaritan community, perhaps of almost equal size, which continued to be important in Byzantine times.[10] Clearly smaller, if more dynamic, was the Christian community, which had presumably existed in Caesarea since apostolic times.[11] However, no bishop is attested before about 190,[12] and it was only in the third century that Caesarea became a center of Christian scholarship, principally through the activities of Origen, Pamphilus, and Eusebius. In the cosmopolitan milieu which was the Caesarea of Origen and Eusebius, a Christian was less likely to suffer death or injury from overt acts of pagan hostility than to be compelled to stand a continual comparison with Jews in the moral and intellectual spheres.[13]

Origen was born in 185/6, apparently of Christian parents who lived in Alexandria; he was the oldest of seven children. His father, who possessed considerable wealth, recognized early the precocious talent of his son and not only gave him a good education in the traditional Greek curriculum but also supervised his learning to recite the Bible by heart. During an outbreak of persecution when Laetus was prefect of Egypt, Origen's father was arrested for being a Christian. Not yet seventeen, Origen wrote an exhortatory letter bidding his imprisoned father not to change his mind because of his family. Origen's father was executed, and Origen would (it was said) have rushed out to join him in martyrdom had not his mother hidden his clothes.[14] Origen never forgot that he was the son of a martyr.[15]

The property of condemned Christians was normally confiscated by the imperial treasury. Origen's family was now destitute, and only the generosity of a rich Christian widow enabled the young man to continue his studies. She took him into her household, where there already resided as her special protégé an Antiochene named Paul, described as a leading heretic in Alexandria at that time. Origen, it thus appears, lived briefly among a heterodox, probably Gnostic, sect. But he did not neglect the education on which his future livelihood appeared to depend: soon he set himself up as a *grammaticus*, teaching Greek literature and earning an adequate income.[16]

While teaching, Origen continued to study, and he attended the lectures of the philosopher Ammonius, making the acquaintance of Heraclas, who had already been Ammonius' pupil for five years.[17] In 206 persecution broke out again, with the arrival of Subatianus Aquila as prefect, and the bishop and most of the clergy hid, leaving many catechumens without the instruction in the faith which they needed for baptism. Origen took the place of the absent clergy, giving instruction to converts and other Christians, in addition to his normal teaching, until his neighbors denounced him and soldiers tried to arrest him at home. Origen escaped and continued to teach the faithful in other private houses. At least seven of Origen's pupils died as martyrs. When they were arrested, Origen visited them in prison; when they were tried, he was in court as a spectator; when they were about to be executed, he saluted and embraced them; after their deaths he escorted their bodies to the cemetery, and then returned to resume his instruction of catechumens who were equally willing to die for their new faith.[18]

When persecution abated, Origen resumed giving instruction as a *grammaticus* and also expounded the Bible to all who came to hear him. The bishop Demetrius encouraged him and perhaps bestowed some form of official recognition on Origen's teaching of catechumens.[19] Then, suddenly, Origen experienced a conversion to asceticism. He closed his school, condemning the time he spent on grammar as unprofitable and as a hindrance to sacred learning, and he disposed of his whole library of classical writers, accepting in return from their purchaser the small but secure income of four obols a day. On this he lived simply: he lay down to rest on the floor, he slept little, he fasted, he walked barefoot, he abstained from wine, he devoted himself entirely to studying the Bible and interpreting it for others.[20] Origen also marked his conversion by a brave, irrevocable, and controversial act. He took Jesus' benediction of those "who make themselves eunuchs for the sake of the kingdom of Heaven" (Matthew 19:12) quite literally and castrated himself.[21]

Origen's fame spread. A governor of Arabia wrote to the prefect of Egypt and to the bishop of Alexandria requesting them to send Origen for an interview: Origen went, presumably to Bostra, the capital of the province of Arabia, conversed with the governor, and returned.[22] Shortly thereafter, almost certainly in 215 when Caracalla visited the city, Origen left Alexandria secretly and went to Palestine, where he taught at Caesarea until Demetrius persuaded him to return.[23] It was presumably during this absence from Egypt that Origen visited Rome, since he was there when Zephyrinus, who died about 217, was still bishop.[24] The purpose, circumstances, and duration of this journey are obscure, but Origen appears to have traveled through Greece: at Nicopolis near Actium, where the philosopher Epictetus once lived and taught, he found a fifth Greek translation of the Psalms which differed from the four which he already knew.[25] Thereafter Origen returned to Alexandria, where he continued to study and to teach for several more years, still as a layman, and commenced writing. One Ambrosius, a Valentinian, was converted to orthodoxy by hearing Origen and became his patron, protector, and support. Ambrosius urged Origen to compose commentaries on the Bible and provided shorthand writers and copyists to take down Origen's dictation and reproduce it in multiple copies.[26]

Shortly after 230, Origen left Alexandria, never to return.[27] He set out for Greece, allegedly on an urgent matter of ecclesiastical business, but perhaps with the intention of settling in Athens—a Christian teacher in the home of Greek philosophy.[28] When he reached Caesarea, however, Origen was ordained a priest by Theoctistus and Alexander, the bishops of Caesarea and Jerusalem, who had formed a friendship with him when he first visited Palestine.[29] After his ordination, Origen proceeded to Athens, where he may have spent a year or more.[30] He returned to the East by way of Asia Minor, visiting Ephesus and Antioch.[31] It was probably at this juncture that Julia Mamaea, the mother of the emperor Severus Alexander, who was conducting war against Persia, summoned Origen to her presence with a military escort and listened to him explain Christian teaching.[32] The amicable interview symbolizes the respectability which a Christian teacher now enjoyed in the eyes of the Roman ruling classes.

During his absence from Egypt and Palestine, Origen had been the center of a bitter controversy. Demetrius, the bishop of Alexandria, objected to Origen's ordination as a priest, summoned a synod which pronounced it invalid, and transmitted this decision to the bishop of Rome, who also presided over a synod which nullified Origen's ordination.[33] Theoctistus and Alexander held an opposing synod of bishops from Palestine, Arabia, Phoenicia, and Greece, which declared that, on ceasing to reside in Alexandria, Origen had freed himself from Demetrius' jurisdiction: hence he was validly ordained a priest by other bishops.[34] The controversy (like most in the history of the Christian church) gave rise to much vituperation and dishonesty: Origen's castration was publicly discussed, his works were interpolated in order to convict him of heresy, and he was compelled to write long letters in defense of his personal life and opinions.[35] In 233 Demetrius died, and Heraclas, who had taken over Origen's instruction of catechumens, succeeded to the see of Alexandria.[36] He was no more amicably disposed to Origen than his predecessor.[37] Origen settled permanently in Caesarea, where Ambrosius soon joined him with his household, and together they established some form of Christian academy with a communal organization.[38]

Valuable testimony for Origen's activity as a teacher in Caesarea survives in the speech of thanksgiving delivered by a pupil about to return to his native province.[39] Gregory, who appears to have been called Theodorus until his baptism, was born into a pagan family in Cappadocia.[40] He had, however, some Christian relatives, for when his father died, he was compelled to become a Christian at the age of thirteen. His mother arranged for Gregory to study rhetoric, and then Latin, in order to become a lawyer and rise in the world. Finally, it was decided that Gregory should complete his legal studies in Berytus, a more Roman city famous for its legal instruction. But the governor of Palestine invited the husband of Gregory's sister, already a practiced lawyer, to serve as an adviser, and he went at once, in haste and alone. Gregory's brother-in-law then sent a soldier to bring Gregory and his sister to Palestine; they came to Caesarea, where Gregory was detained. Though at first he wished to escape to Berytus or his homeland, Gregory was soon introduced to Origen, who had recently taken up residence in Caesarea, and Gregory later construed the events which preceded this meeting as the operation of divine providence and his own guardian angel.[41] On the human plane, it may be that Gregory's brother-in-law decided that his talented relative should receive instruction from the most famous Christian teacher of the day.

Origen greeted the young man warmly and employed every effort to convert him from his chosen career and wordly ambitions to philosophy and true religion.[42] Gregory was won over. He stayed in Caesarea willingly and studied with Origen for several years.[43] Origen gave him a course of instruction which represented a gradual ascent to biblical truth. He first (to use Gregory's own metaphor) prepared the ground by clearing his pupil's soul of weeds: in long Socratic conversations he taught him how to think philosophically and dialectically. He then progressed from logic to the physical sciences, and thence to ethics, which he taught as both an intellectual system and a way of life; he sought to make Gregory impervious to the grief and pain resulting from evil: disciplined, balanced, truly godlike, and happy. Origen taught Gregory to identify irrational emotions and thus to master them, and to cultivate the four traditional virtues of justice, wisdom, temperance, and bravery, of which he stressed that the mother, the beginning, and the end is piety. Origen treated philosophy as a preparation for theology: with his pupil he read widely in the Greek philosophers, pointing out what was useful and true, and finally he read with him the Bible, which he interpreted as the repository of all truth and wisdom.[44]

Gregory regarded his years with Origen as a time in paradise. When he was leaving Caesarea, he spoke as if he were about to abandon light for darkness, day for night, the holy city for Babylon, about to travel into a strange country, even though it was his native land where his father had lived. He was going (he said) to experience tumult and strife instead of tranquillity, a disordered existence instead of a quiet and orderly life, slavery instead of freedom; and he spoke as if he were contemplating the life of a lawyer immersed in the concerns of men, with no further leisure for the divine word or philosophy.[45] Within a few years, however, Gregory became bishop of Neocaesarea in Pontus, where he contributed greatly to the diffusion and organization of Christianity.[46] He lived through the barbarian invasions of the 250s and 260s, reorganizing ecclesiastical discipline after the breakdown of ordinary social life and civilized standards.[47] On some occasion Eusebius met him and his brother, also a bishop in Pontus and his companion as a pupil of Origen.[48]

After he settled in Caesarea, Origen still traveled far abroad on occasion; one of the few surviving letters reveals that he spent some weeks in Nicomedia, accompanied by Ambrose together with his household.[49] Caesarea, however, remained the focus of Origen's life, despite his occasional absences, for almost twenty years. In Caesarea he taught and wrote, from Caesarea he explored the sacred sites of the Holy Land, and from Caesarea he ventured forth as a theological expert when synods of bishops investigated heretical opinions in neighboring provinces.[50] About 248, when he saw persecution approaching again, he composed a long refutation of Celsus' *True Reason,* a polemical work against Christianity written some seventy years earlier.[51] The imperial order to sacrifice to the gods came, and Origen stood firm. He was arrested and imprisoned, tortured on the rack, and urged repeatedly by the governor to sacrifice.[52] Despite his persistent contumacy, Origen was not in fact executed but set free when imperial policy changed. Prison and torture, however, had broken his health: in the reign of Gallus, sometime before his seventieth birthday, Origen died and was buried at Tyre.[53]

Origen combined two quite disparate talents: he was both a speculative theologian of unparalleled boldness and imagination and an interpreter of the Scriptures who combined technical expertise with dazzling exegesis. His theology was alluring and dangerous. Origen drew a rigid distinction between the teaching of the Church as transmitted by tradition from the apostles to the Church of his own day (the "ecclesiastical and apostolic tradition") and matters on which it was legitimate to speculate. The holy apostles had clearly laid down what they deemed necessary for all Christians to believe; they intended that their more studious followers who made themselves capable of receiving philosophical truth should exercise their intelligence in asking why, how, and whence.[54] Within the groundwork of prevailing definitions of the faith Origen speculated freely. But later generations regarded the definitions of the early third century as inadequate; and as the field of legitimate theological speculation was narrowed, much of Origen's teaching came to seem heretical.[55]

The strength and attractiveness of Origen's theology lay in his knowledge and use of contemporary philosophy: he read the recent philosophers on whom Plotinus lectured at Rome, he entered into the philosophical debates of his own day, and he achieved a far more detailed synthesis of Platonism and Christianity than any earlier Christian thinker.[56] Origen, like the pagan philosophers of the second and third centuries, is concerned above all with the relationship of God and man, with the role of divine providence, with God's revelation of himself, with the status of demons, with free will and determinism. Like the Platonists of his own times, he thinks in terms of a God distinct from creation, of immortal and pre-existing souls, and of the possibility of becoming like God by contemplation. Like these Platonists too, Origen has jettisoned much of Plato (his dialectic and the theory of forms) and concentrates on a few works, principally the *Timaeus,* the *Phaedrus,* the *Laws,* and the *Letters,* including the crucial *Second Letter,* which reflects later Pythagorean ideas alien to Plato. And again, like his contemporaries, Origen blends his Platonism with what he considered best in other systems; in particular he takes much of his logic, ethics, and psychological vocabulary from Stoicism.[57] Thus Origen could argue with pagan philosophers on equal terms and speak with authority, and thus, too, the fundamentals of his thought remained attractive for philosophical theologians of the fourth century, who, like Origen, set their Christianity in a Middle Platonic mental framework.[58]

Origen gives a systematic exposition of his theology in a work entitled *On First Principles,* which he composed not long before he left Alexandria, probably to dissuade intellectual Christians from flirting with Gnosticism.[59] He begins by stating the doctrines "plainly transmitted by apostolic teaching" and by indicating what is not so transmitted. First, there is one God, who created the world out of nothing, the God of both Old and New Testaments who sent Jesus, as his prophets foretold, to summon first Israel, then the gentiles. This God is just and good; he himself gave the Law, the Prophets, and the Gospels. Jesus Christ is God's son, "begotten of the Father before all creation," who became man without ceasing to be God. He assumed a body like ours, except that it was born of a virgin and the Holy Spirit: he truly died, truly rose from the dead, and ascended into heaven. The Holy Spirit is equal in rank and dignity to the Father and the Son and inspired the writers of Old and New Testaments alike. However, it is not stated clearly and authoritatively whether the Holy Spirit is born or unborn, or even whether the Holy Spirit should be considered a Son of God.

The soul, which has its own substance and life, will be rewarded when it departs from this world, either with eternal life and happiness or with eternal fire and punishment; there will be a resurrection of the dead when this corruptible body will rise in glory (1 Corinthians 15:42–53). For every soul has free will, because we can choose and be rewarded for virtue or sin. But Scripture does not explain how the soul is united with the body, whether it is transmitted from the parents at conception or comes into the body from outside, whether it is created or uncreated and immortal.

The Church teaches authoritatively that the Devil and his angels exist but not what they are or how they exist. Most Christians, however, think that the Devil is an apostate angel who persuaded other angels to join him in rebellion.

The Church also teaches that the world was made at a definite time and will some day come to an end. But it is unclear what existed before the world or what will exist after it. The whole Church agrees that the Scriptures are divinely inspired and have not only an obvious sense but a deeper meaning which escapes most readers (for what is written are the "forms of certain sacraments and images of divine things"); the true meaning is known only to those aided by the Holy Spirit in wisdom and knowledge.

Finally, the word "incorporeal" is not found in canonical Scripture. Hence it must be investigated whether God, Christ, the Holy Spirit, indeed every soul and rational nature, are corporeal and have a shape or are of a nature different from physical bodies. Nor is it clear at what point in time the guardian angels of whom the Church's teaching speaks were created and what attributes they have, or whether the sun, moon, and stars have souls.[60]

Having thus defined the area within which human reasoning can be allowed to operate, Origen proceeds systematically. God is incorporeal, immaterial, uncreated, and unbegotten, beyond normal human comprehension; and, as the Monad or One, God is the "mind and source from which is the beginning of every intellectual nature or mind," the father of the universe who created and ordered all things.[61] Christ is God's only-begotten Son, begotten not in any human sense, but eternally, just as a ray of light is generated by its source. He is the image of God, the Word of God, an emanation of the glory of God, of a different substance from God, and in a sense almost material, because he "shows himself and puts himself into the minds of those who can receive his virtues and knowledge." He is the wisdom of God of which Solomon spoke (Proverbs 8:22–36).[62]

So far Christianity corresponds to pagan philosophy. But Christianity is unique in asserting the existence of the Holy Spirit, which must be created, since every thing which exists received its capacity to exist from God. The Holy Spirit is revealed only to the holy and, together with the Son, assists the Father: all things or beings receive existence from God, while those which can reason are rational because they participate in Christ, the Word and Reason, and those rational beings which are also holy acquire holiness through the operation of the Holy Spirit. Nevertheless, Origen maintains, none of the three members of the Trinity is greater or less than the others; Father, Son, and Holy Spirit merely operate differently, so that fallen creatures may cast off the taint of ignorance and attain sanctity and happiness.[63] Yet, despite Origen's protestations, there is an inequality between the Father and the Son in his Trinity: the immanent Word is a mediator between the transcendent God and the created world.

God's attributes of creation, beneficence, and providence can never have been inactive; therefore, there must eternally have existed rational beings in a purely spiritual universe.[64] These first "rational natures" were the angels, of whom some, namely the Devil and his angels, rebelled against God and were expelled from heaven: since they could rebel, they possessed free will, for they were capable of choosing to do good or to do evil. Origen explains what man is in reference to good and bad angels. The souls of men are the spiritual beings which neither sinned so much that God made them demons when the Devil rebelled nor erred so little that they could remain angels. After this primal revolt, God created the world and bound the souls (which, as rational beings, are immortal) in bodies as a punishment. Nevertheless, these souls, though fallen from their former bliss, can ascend again to the rank of angels, becoming "sons of God" and transcending their corporeal nature to be made pure spirit again. As men, they have free will, are responsible for their actions and will be rewarded or punished when the world ends with the last judgment. Origen also implies that the sun, moon, and stars also contain incarcerated spiritual beings.[65]

God created the sensible world out of nothing, by which Origen means that he created matter itself, and he will some day destroy it; in the meantime, his providence watches over the course of history but without infringing on man's free will, which Origen defends and justifies at length.[66] Matter, as opposed to the qualities which inhere in it, cannot be destroyed, only transmuted, but about its exact status Origen reaches no firm conclusions. If matter is eternal, then the resurrection body will be like our earthly body but glorified and radiant; if spiritual beings can exist without bodies of any kind, then the material order may come into existence and dissolve again from time to time; or it may be that the visible world will be totally destroyed, while corporeal nature becomes purified and thoroughly spiritual.[67]

Although he leaves the question theoretically open, Origen inclines to the third view, for he believes that only the Trinity is absolutely incorporeal.[68] He insists continually, however, that the world had a beginning and will have an end, with the corollary that mankind is involved in the cosmic battle between God's providence and the opposing power of the Devil. But God is the doctor of our souls and desires our education and perfection. The highest good is to become like God, toward which end every rational nature strives. Hence, at the end of the world, evil will cease to exist, and creation will return to its pristine condition; the same souls which have sinned will be reconciled to God and summoned to bliss, together with their purified bodies, which will be their eternal habitation.[69]

Among the rational beings who loved their creator in varying degrees, one soul remained inseparably devoted to its creator. This soul was united with God's Word to become a single spirit which, with the substance of the soul mediating between God and flesh, was born as God-man: Jesus Christ the incarnate word of God. Hence Christ has a soul like all other souls, capable of both good and evil, even though in fact he never had the slightest desire or impulse to sin, and he not only urges and aids all towards salvation but also serves as its pattern and model in his resurrection and ascension.[70] When the holy die, they go to paradise, a place on the earth where, as if in a school for souls, they are taught the reason for what they have seen on earth. As they progress in their course of instruction, they ascend into the air between earth and heaven, which is occupied by rational beings with souls, and they gradually rise by a series of stages to the heavenly kingdom, where they receive a perfect revelation from God about the heavenly bodies and about God himself. Then they are truly God's sons.[71]

If men desire to know God's truth and the causes of things, how can they gain true wisdom? God reveals himself, albeit imperfectly, through the Holy Scriptures. But why should the Bible be regarded as inspired? In order to answer this question, Origen deserts metaphysics for history. The laws of Moses and the precepts of Jesus are of divine origin because of their astonishing success in winning adherents throughout the world, and the Old Testament is inspired because its prophecies have been fulfilled by the Incarnation and the fate of the Jewish people. Jesus' sojourn on earth provided clear proof that the Old Testament was inspired, that the law and the prophets were written "with grace from heaven."[72]

But how are the Scriptures to be read and understood? In order to avoid the errors of Judaism and heresy, one must interpret the Bible not literally but spiritually. Some passages (such as Lot lying with his daughters) must have a mystical meaning, and others (such as the building of the Tabernacle) a figurative or typological significance, while others again are obscure. Origen accordingly propounds the theory that Scripture has three levels of meaning corresponding to the three parts of man:

> Everyone must register in his soul the meanings of the Holy Writings in three ways; so that the simpler may be built by the flesh (as it were) of Scripture (for thus I call the obvious significance), while he who has made some progress may be built from its soul, and the perfect, who is similar to those of whom it is said by the apostle *I speak wisdom among the perfect, a wisdom not of this age nor of the declining rulers of this age, but I speak the wisdom of God hidden in a mystery, which God determined before all ages for our glory* (1 Corinthians 2:6–7), from the *spiritual law* (Romans 7:14) which *contains the shadow of things to come* (Hebrews 10:1). For, in exactly the same way as a man is composed of body, soul, and spirit, so is Scripture, which was designed by God to be given for man's salvation.

Not all passages, however, have a bodily meaning, useful though it is to true and simple believers. The Holy Spirit which, by God's providence, inspired the prophets and apostles, was intended to reveal the truths of theology and philosophy to holy souls while concealing them from others in a text full of the normal stuff of history. The Bible contains some offensive, ridiculous, and impossible things precisely in order to show that its value and importance never lie in the literal meaning, but in the deeper, more divine, spiritual sense.[73]

The treatise *On First Principles* justifies Origen's concentration on biblical exegesis, and his practice of it reflects his view that different audiences required different levels of instruction. For much of his life, Origin preached frequently, perhaps almost daily, to simple believers: he took successive passages of each book of the Bible as his text for successive homilies, which he delivered as extemporaneous discourses and which he long refused to allow to be copied and circulated.[74] On a completely different level, Origen dictated learned and weighty commentaries (called tomes) for a more scholarly audience, and he appears also to have made brief notes on individual passages, either for his own future use or for his pupils.[75] Origen dedicated his commentaries to his patron, Ambrosius, who provided shorthand writers and copyists to take down and record every word carefully in multiple copies.[76] Here he discussed problems, including textual ones, in a scholarly fashion for a Christian reading public.[77]

The treatise *On First Principles* does not attempt to describe the scholarly work on the Bible which provided the basis for Origen's biblical exegesis. Origen applied the techniques of Alexandrian scholarship to the textual criticism to the Bible—or at least to the Old Testament, for there is no evidence that he collected or collated manuscripts of the New. He compiled a synopsis of different versions of the Old Testament, written out, or at least revised and corrected, in his own hand and intended primarily for his own personal use. It bore the name Hexapla ("sixfold") and contained six columns.[78] In the first stood the Hebrew text, each line containing a single word or brief phrase which was transliterated into Greek in the second column.[79] Then came the Greek translations of Aquila and Symmachus, the former excessively literal and made by an orthodox Jew about 100, probably in Palestine, the latter apparently the work of an Ebionite in the late second century.[80] The fifth column contained the Septuagint, and the sixth, the translation ascribed to Theodotion, which Christians preferred to the Septuagint in some books (most notably in Daniel).[81]

Origen did more than reproduce the text of the Septuagint. Where it contained something for which the Hebrew had no equivalent, he obelized the additional word, phrase, or passage, and where the Septuagint lacked part of the Hebrew text, he added the missing passage, marking it with an asterisk before and a sideways obelus after.[82] Moreover, for some books there were more than the four Greek versions: of the Psalms, Origen himself found a fifth version at Nicopolis near Actium. He included this version with variants, presumably added from another manuscript with a closely similar text; he also possessed a sixth version "found with other Hebrew and Greek books in a jar near Jericho during the reign of Antoninus, the son of Severus."[83]

Besides the Hexapla, Origen also compiled a Tetrapla, which contained only the four Greek versions (Aquila, Symmachus, Septuagint, Theodotion).[84] What is the relation between the two? It is attractive to conjecture that the Tetrapla was the earlier and represents Origen's first attempt to compare versions of the Old Testament, and that toward the end of his life he produced for some books a synopsis which expanded the Hexapla as the Hexapla had expanded the Tetrapla.[85] But the Tetrapla did not contain a transliteration of the Hebrew text, and it is not plausible to suppose that Origen heard of the version of the Psalms found near Jericho only some thirty years after its discovery. It seems more probable that Origen composed the Hexapla first (perhaps before 215) and designed the Tetrapla to be an instrument more convenient for travel.[86]

Be that as it may, the order of the columns, with the Septuagint following the translations of Aquila and Symmachus, and the sometimes inaccurate vocalization in the transliterated Hebrew strongly imply that Origen used a pre-existing Jewish synopsis.[87] What precisely did this contain? A good case can be made for attributing such a synopsis to Symmachus, who perhaps added his own more elegant version to a still earlier synopsis containing the Hebrew text, a Greek transliteration, and Aquila's literal translation.[88] However, it may have been Origen himself who added Symmachus' version, for he received tracts and translations by Symmachus from the widow Juliana, who had obtained them from Symmachus himself.[89] It was certainly Origen who added, in the last two of the six columns, the two much earlier versions which the Christian church had taken over from Judaism in the first century.

Why did Origen perform this immense labor? When writing to Julius Africanus, who asked why, in a public disputation, Origen had appealed to the story of Susanna, when the Hebrew (in fact, Aramaic) does not contain the passage.[90] Origen replied that he knows the differences between the Greek and the Hebrew Bible: divine providence has given the one to guide the Church, but the other is necessary for argument with Jews.[91] Perhaps, therefore, Origen drew up the Hexapla because of apological or polemical motives.[92] But to discover any sign of its employment for such purposes is difficult. Origen's *Commentary on Matthew* discloses a more pertinent motivation: where manuscripts of the Septuagint differed, he used the other five versions to decide which reading was correct.[93]

How well did Origen know Hebrew? Eusebius vaunts his mastery of the language, and he certainly both received instruction from a Jewish rabbi in Alexandria and discussed linguistic problems with Jewish scholars in Palestine.[94] Yet he rarely speaks with the confidence of an expert, and he makes some obvious blunders.[95] The Hexapla, therefore, must surely have aided Origen in comprehending the Hebrew Bible.[96] Its main purpose, however, may be nobler and profounder. If Jews accused the Septuagint of perverting and falsifying the text, Origen realized that any version, even the Hebrew text available to him, might contain mistakes or corruptions.[97] Hence he designed the Hexapla as a means of discovering the original Hebrew text of the Old Testament: it is, in a sense, a critical edition with variant readings.[98]

On the biblical text thus established, Origen allowed his intelligence to roam freely. His celebrated distinction of the three senses of Scripture neither explains nor describes his normal technique of exegesis. Admittedly, he does sometimes distinguish between the literal, moral, and spiritual senses of a passage.[99] Predominantly, however, he writes as if there are two senses, the literal and the spiritual.[100] There was a rich tradition of typological and allegorical interpretation available for the biblical exegete. Christian writers had always used typology, which was current in Palestine in the first century.[101] Origen also knew the writings of Philo, who had used Hellenistic allegory to empty the Old Testament of historical content and replace it with a philosophical and moral message.[102] Moreover, he had read pagan philosophers who allegorized Greek religion, Greek mythology, and Greek literature.[103] Hence Origen could interpret any passage he wished as enshrining a spiritual truth which he had in fact derived from a source other than the biblical text.[104]

Origen characterizes the literal intepretation as Jewish, suitable only for the less intelligent Christians.[105] In some passages indeed, he maintains, the literal interpretation is impossible.[106] Origen looks consistently for the deeper meaning, in which the moral and intellectual senses fuse with the spiritual by means of allegory. His application of allegory, however, follows no discernible rules. Origen reads his own philosophy into Scripture, and his method, though brilliant, is wholly subjective. He bound himself with a principle which encouraged extravagance; for, if all Scripture has a spiritual sense, then some passages will compel the exegete to allegorical fantasy. Origen was a philosopher and speculative thinker. In his exegesis, as in that of Philo, the historicity of much of the biblical narrative tends to melt away, and the ancient laws of Moses, suitably interpreted, become a pattern of Christian doctrine, morality, and ecclesiastical practice.[107] In brief, Origen was not a biblical scholar, either by instinct or by training; he was a philosopher who used biblical exegesis as a vehicle for expressing views not derived from the sacred text but read into it.

Origen presumably had followers in Caesarea to preserve his intellectual heritage in the generation after his death, and Theotecnus, bishop of the city for many years in the late third century, was a product of Origen's school.[108] Yet Caesarea owed its subsequent reputation as a center of Christian scholarship largely to the efforts of Pamphilus and his disciples, among whom Eusebius was the most prominent. By birth, Pamphilus belonged to the local nobility of Berytus, where he studied as a young man and apparently held political office. From Berytus he went to Alexandria, where he became a pupil of Pierius, nicknamed "Origen the younger"; from Alexandria he came to Caesarea and settled there, probably early in the reign of Diocletian.[109] Pamphilus was ordained a priest at Caesarea. He lived a simple and austere life, and devoted his wealth (which was considerable) to founding a library, which continued to exist for several centuries.[110] The writings of Origen show that Ambrosius must have provided him with a working library in Caesarea; this collection presumably survived and formed the basis of Pamphilus' library, for Eusebius' *Preparation for the Gospel* shows a knowledge of Greek literature which clearly reflects Origen's interests: no comedy, tragedy, or lyric poetry, but a complete Plato and a wide range of later philosophers, mainly Middle Platonists from Philo to the late second century.[111]

The main function of the library, however, was not to preserve pagan literature, but to promote sacred learning. The biblical manuscripts included the Hexapla and Tetrapla which Origen had devised to deepen his study of the Old Testament. Nor was the New Testament neglected, although Origen had never labored on its text: the library possessed (or so it was claimed) a copy of the original Aramaic text of Matthew's Gospel.[112] Pamphilus carefully sought out and often copied in his own hand Origen's voluminous writings.[113] He attempted a complete collection, and the surviving list of Origen's works documents the extraordinary extent of his success.[114]

The subscriptions in several extant manuscripts refer to the revision and correction of biblical texts by Pamphilus and his pupils or friends, including Eusebius.[115] One has an especial interest: "Copied and corrected against the Hexapla of Origen, corrected by himself. The confessor Antoninus collated. I, Pamphilus, corrected the roll in prison."[116] Even persecution did not prevent Pamphilus from disseminating the results of Origen's scholarship and his own.

Eusebius bore the name "Eusebius, son of Pamphilus," and the patronymic inexorably implies that Pamphilus adopted him as his son.[117] He was born shortly after 260, about a decade after Origen died.[118] His association with Pamphilus began soon after the latter settled in Caesarea; Eusebius was then a young man, probably between twenty and twenty-five. Eusebius was soon helping Pamphilus to enlarge the library and to make the texts it contained available to others. He compiled a "Collection of Ancient Martyrdoms," which presumably took its place alongside other Christian texts Pamphilus had assembled to complement Origen's own library and writings.[119]

Pamphilus and Eusebius regarded themselves as the intellectual heirs of Origen and devoted their lives to scholarship in the tradition which he had founded. While Pamphilus was in prison (in 308 or 309), the two men began a *Defense of Origen*, completing five books, to which Eusebius added a sixth after Pamphilus' death as a martyr.[120] Eusebius remained loyal to his master's ideals, composing a *Life of Pamphilus* in three books, which included a catalogue of the library.[121] He continued to live, teach, and write in Caesarea, becoming bishop of the city in about 313 and occupying the see until his death on 30 May 339.[122]

Eusebius was a biblical scholar both by instinct and by training, but he was not by nature a philosopher or theologian. Hence his relation to Origen is not a simple one. On the one hand, Eusebius admired Origen and continually appealed to him as an authoritative or divinely inspired interpreter of Scripture. And he owed to Origen the technical instruments with which he could study the Bible in a scholarly manner—the Hexapla and Tetrapla, voluminous commentaries, and a Hebrew glossary. Moreover, he regarded himself as an intellectual heir of Origen, concerned to defend him against charges of heresy and accepting on trust many of his philosophical and theological views. On the other hand, Eusebius had no direct contact with Origen, and it should not be assumed that a "school of Caesarea" founded by Origen enjoyed a continuous existence to preserve its founder's traditions. Origen appears to have directed his teaching towards sympathetic pagans, whereas Eusebius gave biblical instruction to committed Christians.

Pamphilus and Eusebius disseminated the results of Origen's biblical scholarship. It was through their efforts in copying and revising manuscripts that a hexaplaric text of the Septuagint gained popularity in Palestine and Syria.[123] Yet this diffusion of Origen's text by no means reflects his original intentions; he designed for his own use a scholarly tool from which Pamphilus and Eusebius extracted and reproduced one element in isolation. That fact illustrates Eusebius' attitude towards the heritage of Origen, which exercised a formative influence on him. He accepted it consciously and in full, but he unintentionally and inevitably introduced modifications reflecting his own personality and the historical changes of a later generation.

A direct comparison of Eusebius with Origen as biblical exegetes can be made in their treatment of Psalm 37 (38). Eusebius' commentary is published in full among the doubtful works of Basil of Caesarea,[124] while Origen's interpretation is represented by two homilies in a group of nine homilies on Psalms 36–38 (37–39) which Rufinus translated into Latin and published together.[125] Hence some obvious differences in technique which reflect differences in genre: Origen adopted a homiletic style suitable to the popular audience whom he was addressing in church after the psalm had been read aloud, while Eusebius was writing for learned pupils and adduces variant readings which Symmachus and Aquila attest in their translations.[126] Yet the most basic differences in the two approaches have little or nothing to do with the level of discussion or the nature of the audience.

Psalm 37 (38) is a psalm of lamentation, probably composed not long after the reconstitution of the Jewish community under Persian protection (that is, in the late sixth or early fifth century B.C.).[127] Modern exegetes tend to view it either as a personal, private psalm of lamentation provoked by the poet's sickness, or as a psalm intended for use in the temple by suppliants afflicted by diseases.[128] It begins and concludes with an appeal to God (verses 1–2, 21–22), but the main part of the poem describes the sufferings of the subject (3–10), the indifference of his friends and the malice of his enemies (11–16), and the hopelessness of his plight (17–20). The text, however, contains no explicit indication whether it is a man speaking or the nation Israel, nor whether the sufferings are moral as well as physical. The heading of the psalm describes the poem as "a psalm of David" and states its function or occasion by means of a vague infinitive ("to revive memories").[129] Although the heading is clearly secondary (and obscure), both Origen and Eusebius took it into account in their exegesis of the psalm.

Origen assumed that Psalm 37 (38), like those which immediately precede and follow it, had a wholly moral significance; his exposition, Rufinus observed, exhibited precepts for a better life and showed the way to conversion and repentance, absolution from sin, and progress in virtue.[130] Hence Origen's first homily on Psalm 37 (38) begins from the general propositions that God has included in the Scriptures medicine to aid the human soul, and that God has entrusted the art of spiritual medicine to Christ and, through Christ, to the Church. Origen then applies these propositions to the text:

> This psalm, which has now been read, shows us, if we are ever by chance involved in sins, how and with what emotion we ought to pray and ask our spiritual doctor for help with our pains or infirmities. Hence, if the enemy ever surprises us and wounds our soul with his flaming arrows, this psalm teaches us first, that after sinning we should admit the sin and record the offense in our memory, so that our heart, roused through recollection of its fault and disturbed because of its offense, may rein itself in and restrain itself betimes, so that it commits nothing further of the sort. For this reason I think that the psalm is headed "Psalm of David, in memory." What "in memory" is, he explains through the whole body of the psalm itself. Let all of us sinners, therefore, if we are found in any offense or ought to say or do anything, see how, when we have learned this in Holy Scripture, we may succeed in obtaining a cure for our wound.

The whole exegesis is couched in moral terms, with the ostensible author, David, and the heading receiving no further discussion.

With his usual pyrotechnics, Origen hints at the "deeper meaning" of the text and is able to deduce the most far-reaching conclusions from the psalmist's laments: the words "there is no soundness in my flesh because of thy indignation" (verse 3) are converted into an exhortation to mortify the flesh in order to save the spirit. Origen treats the psalm as truly penitential in nature: it tells the repentant sinner in detail what he is to do and how he should behave, and Origen often seems to assume that the author (whom he consistently calls "the prophet") writes with a knowledge of Christian doctrine about the afterlife and Christian penitential practices. Hence he adduces both the New Testament and contemporary practice to illuminate the psalmist's moral message.[131]

Eusebius' approach diverges sharply. Admittedly, there are some points of contact, as when he follows Origen in taking "arrows" (verse 2) to mean "the words of God."[132] But the overall conception is totally dissimilar. Eusebius starts from the heading and expounds the whole psalm historically. He notes that Psalm 6 begins with exactly the same verse ("O Lord, do not rebuke me in thy anger") but has a different heading, and he construes "to bring to remembrance" in the heading of Psalm 37 (38) as a reference back to this earlier psalm. Both heading and psalm are ascribed to David himself, and the whole text is expounded as David speaking *in propria persona* of his own sins:

> He addresses a supplication to God, by which he seeks to turn aside the anger which hangs over all sinners, and he tries to propitiate the good Lord with expressions of excessive confession. When he says "O Lord, do not rebuke me in thy anger," he is not asking to be excused rebuke, but rebuke with anger, and when he says "Nor punish me in thy wrath," he does not shun punishment, but asks to obtain punishment without anger . . . David then begs not to be rebuked by evil powers, nor punished by the dispatch of evil angels but with words of salvation and useful lessons. Or he asks not to be kept till the day of wrath and revelation and the judgment of God, but to pay for his sins on earth and in the present life, before he dies. And he obtained his goal. For he seems to have paid the penalty by what he suffered before his death. Or else he punished himself, inflicting all sorts of chastisement on himself in his methods of confession.[133]

The explanation of each verse, therefore, is to be sought in the Old Testament. David alludes (according to Eusebius) to the rebellion of Absalom (verse 2), to the threats of his political foes (verse 19) and, more generally, to his own misdeeds; hence, though the psalm yields the implicit moral lesson that God forgives and rewards the repentant sinner,[134] it must still be interpreted historically to discover its full meaning. Eusebius was immersed in the Bible and in biblical ways of historical and quasi-historical thinking to a degree which Origen would have found alien and unspiritual.

Eusebius appears to have composed only two biblical commentaries, on Isaiah and on the Psalms.[135] This highly significant choice reveals what is central to Eusebius' thought. Isaiah and the Psalms contain more passages than any other books of the Old Testament which Christians had traditionally construed as messianic prophecies, and Eusebius considered the Incarnation to be the pivot of human history. The date of the extant commentaries must not be allowed to mask the true direction of Eusebius' intellectual development. Eusebius wrote the *Commentary on Isaiah* and completed the *Commentary on the Psalms* toward the end of his life, when Constantine was the sole ruler of an officially Christian empire.[136] But it does not follow that he was an apologist or historian before he became a biblical interpreter. For the extant commentaries are the final reflections of a man who had meditated on the sacred text for fifty years or more, perhaps not always profoundly, but with a deep sense that the Bible provided the key to understanding God, man, and history. Despite their date, therefore, the commentaries on Isaiah and the Psalms may legitimately be used to illustrate Eusebius' debt to Origen, the techniques of exegesis which he used throughout his literary career, and his basic intellectual assumptions.

Eusebius' debt to Origen stands revealed on every page of his two biblical commentaries. Most obvious and pervasive is Eusebius' use of the Hexapla: though he takes his lemma from the Septuagint, time and time again he quotes, compares, and comments on the variant versions of Aquila, Symmachus, Theodotion, and, in the Psalms, the anonymous fifth and sixth versions.[137] Sometimes too, he quotes the Hebrew or compares the Hebrew reading in the passage under discussion with that in another.[138] He occasionally notes that a phrase of the Septuagint is obelized, because it occurs neither in the Hebrew nor in the other translators.[139] Moreover, Eusebius presumably consulted Origen's onomasticon frequently when he wished to discover what Hebrew names meant, even though he had some genuine knowledge of the language and its grammar.[140]

Many features of Eusebius' treatment of the text recall Origen and presumably derive from him. In at least one passage Eusebius diagnoses textual corruption in the Septuagint, arguing that its "they ran in thirst" (Psalm 61:5 [62:4]) is a mistake which has crept in for the "in falsehood" attested by all the other versions.[141] He frequently draws a distinction between the literal sense of a passage and its deeper significance, between the bare words and their true meaning. Eusebius, like Origen, derides the Jews for interpreting the Old Testament too literally and stigmatizes literal interpretation as a characteristically Jewish or Judaizing error which degrades the Bible. A Jew is mere flesh and blood; he interprets in a fleshly and bodily sense, unlike the man "educated in divine teachings," who can see that Israel (in Psalm 75:2 [76:1]) is the man with spiritual insight and knowledge who sees God in contemplation.[142] God's promises, given to David, are divine and heavenly, not, as the Jews think, earthly and corporeal.[143] The Jews, because they do not properly understand the Scriptures, have an anthropomorphic God, subject to human emotions, about whom they spin many strange and degrading myths.[144] Jewish interpretation is essentially false, and proved false by the verdict of history.[145]

Eusebius sometimes argues that the literal sense of a passage is so trivial or impossible that there must be a deeper meaning, which can be discovered by employing the laws of allegory. When David says "Hear my cry, O God, listen to my prayer" (Psalm 60:2-6 [61:1-5]), the sentiments voiced are so commonplace that one must ask why the Bible includes this particular prayer. Eusebius argues that men of discernment selected it for inclusion because it is really a disguised prophecy of the Incarnation.[146] When Moses says "he satisfied him with honey from the crag and oil from the flinty rock" (Deuteronomy 32:13), the physical impossibility shows that he intended his words allegorically: the rock is Christ.[147]

Again, a passage where David prays for the death of his enemies (Psalm 54:16 [55:15]) is incompatible with David's virtuous and mild nature, with his steadfast loyalty towards Saul; therefore, the prayer must really be prophetic, and the whole psalm in fact foretells how Jesus will be betrayed and arrested.[148] Similarly, another psalm can only be interpreted without violence to the text when it is referred to the Crucifixion.[149] On occasion too, traces of Origen's celebrated distinction between the three senses of Scripture can be found. Although the "mountain of God" (Isaiah 2:3) might be taken in a physical sense to be a mountain in Palestine, its real meaning is the high and heavenly word of God in the gospel; but the apostle Paul advances a third interpretation when he teaches us that it is the heavenly Sion, the Jerusalem above "which is the mother of us all" (Hebrews 12:12; Galatians 4:26).[150]

When Eusebius launches into allegorical exegesis, he does so in ways reminiscent of Origen, and he often employs interpretations which can be documented from Origen's commentaries. For Eusebius, as for Origen, different material objects signify allegorically a single spiritual reality, while a single material object named in different passages may signify several different spiritual realities.[151] The mountains Carmel and Libanos (Isaiah 29:17) signify Jews and gentiles, though elsewhere, both in the Psalms (71:16 [72:16]) and in the Prophets (as in Ezekiel 17:3), Mount Libanos often denotes Jerusalem.[152] But mountains which afford God's people peace (Psalm 71:3 [72:3]) are the angels and the still higher divine powers.[153] Water (Isaiah 55:1) signifies the gospel message or Holy Scripture trampled by Jews and gentiles (Isaiah 32:20); waters (in the plural), the living waters of salvation which the Holy Spirit pours forth for the Church of God from the Old Testament and the New (Isaiah 41:17–18).[154] Scripture can also be a table (Psalm 68:23 [69:22]), while wine and milk (Isaiah 55:1) and the milk of nations (Isaiah 60:16) are the mystery of the Incarnation and the teaching of the gospel.[155]

Scriptural waters, however, are not always beneficial; by *waters* (in the plural) the Divine Word commonly signifies assaults, persecution, and repression by the ungodly (Psalm 68:2 [69:1]).[156] Alternatively, the waters may be the multitudes of Christian churchmen of every race, while the depths of the ocean in the same passage are the armies of unbelievers who persecute them (Psalm 76:17–18 [77:16]).[157] If mountains can signify angels, so too can both clouds (Psalm 77:23 [78:23]) and cedars (Psalm 79:11 [80:10]).[158] The vines which grow on the cedars are prophetic souls (Psalm 79:11 [80:10]), but prophetic souls which shower God's teachings on less perfect souls can also, like angels, be called clouds (Psalm 56:11 [57:10]).[159] Sandals too sometimes designate souls which serve the will of God, especially the souls of the apostles (Psalm 59:10 [60:8]).[160]

Eusebius' theology is deeply indebted to Origen.[161] Admittedly, many of the philosophical ideas Eusebius expresses are commonplace and need not derive from Origen.[162] Yet Eusebius formulates even the commonest ideas in ways which recall Origen, and he sometimes repeats opinions of Origen which few, if any, other early Christian writers held—for example, asserting quite boldly that "only the only-begotten Word of God is capable of nourishing every rational being."[163] Moreover, a passage such as the following seems to attempt to philosophize as Origen had done:

> Light, truth, and reason sent from the highest God do not lack being or substance; for it is not possible for a thing without substance to be sent. Just as the Word (Logos) is intended to be capable of producing healing and salvation, so in the present passage the same is called pity, as being an agent of the Father's love of mankind; and similarly he is called truth, as truly existing and vested with being through activity. Our reason (Logos), having its substance in syllables, words, and names, and being uttered by tongue and voice, would not properly and truly be called reason. It had another which begets it, which one may properly call true reason: this they say is immanent reason. The reason immanent in us, which may properly be called true reason, has substance, existing as a being, and is different from the one which sends it forth.[164]

But such ratiocination did not come easily or naturally to Eusebius, and it is rare in his biblical commentaries. Although Eusebius had learned from Origen to express the Christian view of God and man in terms of Middle Platonism,[165] he never completely mastered the philosophical issues. He tends to lack clarity, and even lapses into occasional confusion. Philosophers who agreed that there were two Gods disagreed over whether Plato's creator-god, the Demiurge, was the first and highest God or the second God who mediated between the first God and the world. Numenius argued the latter view, while the pagan Origen wrote a treatise entitled "The King Alone [that is, the first God] is Creator."[166] Eusebius uses language which appears to confuse the generally agreed distinction between the functions of the first and second persons of the Christian Trinity: God the Father is "the only Creator and Demiurge and King of the universe," "the Creator of the universe and Savior," whereas the Word of God not only endows those creatures who possess them with sensory perception, ability to reason, and intelligence, but is also "the maker of the world and creator of all."[167] The commentaries on Isaiah and the Psalms are not the product of a keen philosophical intelligence.

Despite a profound indebtedness to Origen, Eusebius moves in a different world. He has abandoned Origen's boldest and most vulnerable theological speculations, and he interprets the Bible from a perspective which is basically historical, even if much of the history is legendary or mythical. Nevertheless, Eusebius' point of departure can be found in Origen, who deduced that the Bible must be inspired by the Holy Spirit, because Christianity both fulfilled the prophecies of the Old Testament and enjoyed a worldly success which confirmed its divine origin.[168] Eusebius consistently founds his interpretation of the Bible (and hence of human history) on the same two inferences.[169]

Eusebius followed Origen in holding that the Holy Spirit is the ultimate author of all Scripture, speaking through the medium of the ostensible authors.[170] He also followed him in holding that the principal message of the prophets concerned the coming of God's Word at the Incarnation. Like Origen too he held that the Old Testament prefigures the New, that in a sense it contains the whole of the gospel message.[171] Thus Isaiah was called from a lowly station, filled with divine inspiration and wisdom, and became both an evangelist and an apostle.[172] Eusebius, however, marks a far sharper and more insistent distinction between the two Testaments, forever stressing the inferiority of the Old. Moses prescribed observation of the Sabbath as "shadows and symbols" of the great Sabbath of God's kingdom. The Jewish Law was temporary, and those who announced the gospel to the gentiles were dispensed from observing it, except for the precept to trumpet forth the word of salvation (Psalm 80:4 [81:3], on which Eusebius adduces Leviticus 23:24). The rules announced by Moses were mere types, symbols, and images: the true circumcision, the spiritual Sabbath, the spiritual sacrifices, the spiritual law—all these belong to Christianity.[173]

Eusebius regarded the Bible as the key to a correct understanding of human history. He also believed, like Origen, that it revealed the truths of philosophy and theology. But it is the historical sweep of the Bible which engrosses him, and as a result, he differs from Origen on the origin and ultimate fate of human souls. About their origin, he gives no clear statement, but he appears to assume the common-sense view that souls do not come into existence before their possessors, and he follows Paul and popular opinion against Origen in peopling the air with malignant and demonic powers.[174] On the ultimate destiny of mankind, Eusebius rejects any notion of universal salvation. There will be a last judgment, when Christ will come again in glory to judge the living and the dead, and everyone will be rewarded for his actions: Christ will receive all those who received him on earth into the kingdom of God, but those who hardened their hearts against him will be excluded from the joys of the heavenly Sabbath.[175]

Eusebius accepts the basic eschatology of the New Testament: a person's final destiny in the hereafter depends wholly on his actions in this world, and the course of history, in which good and evil are inextricably entwined, runs toward an end when the pious will be rewarded and the impious punished. And Eusebius believes that the Bible charts mankind's course on this journey. He will not be deceived by statements apparently made in the past tense:[176] Isaiah and the Psalms foretold the significant events in history from the time of writing to the end of the world, concentrating especially on the life, death, and resurrection of Jesus, the consequent ruin of the Jews who rejected him, and the triumph of the Christian church.

Eusebius dwells constantly on the contrast between contemporary Judaism and Christianity and argues that the contrast shows clearly which of the two has inherited God's promises to David of worldly success. The Jews lack a king, a high priest, prophets, even scribes, Pharisees, and Sadducees; their patriarchs are feeble and stupid boys; they are permitted neither to worship in nor to set foot in Jerusalem, which is now inhabited by gentiles; and their temple no longer exists.[177] The Church, despite frequent and sometimes violent persecution, is populous and successful everywhere; as was prophesied by Isaiah (42:11–12) and in the Psalms (59:10 [60:8]), the people of Arabia throng Christian churches, which exist now in the city of Petra, a stronghold of superstition, in the country districts around Petra, and even in the desert among the Saraceni.[178] Although the commentaries on Isaiah and the Psalms often reflect conditions which did not exist before Constantine conquered the East in 324, they express throughout an optimistic view of history which Eusebius had formed in his youth, long before Constantine became a Roman emperor.

Eusebius' interests led him to differ from Origen in matters of both the text and the interpretation of Scripture. Origen designed the Hexapla as a means of discovering the original text of the Old Testament. Eusebius consistently assumes that if there are variants, then the reading most susceptible of messianic interpretation must be correct.[179] Thus, in a passage about the suffering servant (Isaiah 53:2), he prefers Aquila's "from untrodden ground" for the "in thirsty ground" of all the other versions, and the Hebrew, because he can take *untrodden* to signify *virgin* and thus allude to the Incarnation.[180] Similarly, Eusebius prefers Symmachus' "My mouth shall announce thy justice, thy salvation every day" (Psalm 70:15 [71:15]) to the rendering "the whole day" in the other versions, so that he can claim fulfillment of prophecy in the daily reading of Scripture, in which the Savior speaks to all men.[181] Occasionally, Eusebius' assumption that a messianic allusion guarantees correctness produces bizarre theorizing. The penultimate verse of Psalm 86 (87) presented the following variants:

> The Lord will record in a roll of nations and of these rulers who lived in her. (Septuagint)
> The Lord will record when writing down nations: This one was born there. (Aquila)
> The Lord will count as he registers nations: This one was born there. (Symmachus)
> The Lord will record in a roll of nations: This one was born there. (Theodotion)

Eusebius naturally cannot resist so transparent an allusion to the Incarnation in the uncanonical translations. But what of the Septuagint? He suggests that the translators deliberately concealed the correct meaning because in the time of Ptolemy, when it was made, the Savior had not yet appeared on earth.[182]

Eusebius' constant search for messianic prophecy also led him to employ the distinction between the literal and the deeper sense of Scripture in very different ways from Origen. The opening paragraph of the *Commentary on Isaiah* makes a statement of principles:

The Spirit showed its meaning to the prophet sometimes clearly, so that there is no need of allegorical figures in the interpretation of his utterances and one uses only the bare words themselves, but sometimes through symbols of other things, which offer a different meaning by expressive words and names, as in his dreams *eleven stars* seemed to *bow down* before Joseph, thus meaning *his brothers,* and on another occasion he saw *his brothers* gathering *sheaves,* thus alluding to the famine (Genesis 37:5–10). So, too, to the present prophet most of the divine messages were seen through symbols, and very many things are said in a complicated fashion with different parts of the same passage intended literally and in a deeper sense.[183]

Hence Eusebius can find either a literal or a figurative sense in any passage, and often both together. But he has dropped Origen's notion that the deeper sense always has a primacy of regard. He tends rather to put both on the same level, or even to prefer the literal. Thus, on one passage of Isaiah he observes that "I think that the figurative exegesis is forced" but argues that another passage "forces even the unwilling to adopt a figurative exegesis."[184] He will attempt to save the literal interpretation or to excuse a figurative one which he feels compelled to adopt.[185]

Eusebius can even ridicule the allegorical interpretation of a passage as completely absurd. He sees in the sea monster whom God destroyed (Psalm 73:13 [74:13]) an allusion to Pharaoh and the Egyptians drowned as the Israelites crossed the Red Sea, but he will not allow its spiritual interpretation:

Perhaps someone will tackle the passage figuratively and refer this to invisible and unseen powers, saying that they are the serpents named here, that the sea is figuratively their habitation, and that the ruler of the evil spirits himself is indicated by the many-headed serpent, to which one might apply the text *thou didst break the serpent's heads, thou gavest him as food to the Ethiopians.* Such a person will also seek some Ethiopians by the laws of allegory, saying that they are those with blackened souls. He will also say that they eat the aforesaid serpent, corresponding to those who eat the flesh of the Word of salvation; and to be consistent with this, he will try to render figuratively the fountains which break into torrents and the rivers which dry up. But we, having given the meaning according to the letter, will pass on to what follows.[186]

Commenting on Matthew (7:9–11), Origen assumed an exegesis of the passage very close to the one which Eusebius pillories.[187]

Eusebius grounds his exegesis of Isaiah and the Psalms in the history of ancient Israel. Isaiah uttered all his prophecies (for Eusebius there is, of course, only one Isaiah who wrote the whole book) in the reigns of kings Uzziah, Jotham, Ahaz, and Hezekiah (1:1). Each psalm was composed at a definite and, in principle, discoverable date. If David composed a particular prayer in a cave, then it must be either the cave at Engeddi or the cave of Adullam.[188] Eusebius consistently combines the evidence of the text of the psalm under discussion, its heading, and the historical books of the Old Testament to date a psalm as accurately as possible.[189] He assumes not only that the Holy Spirit spoke through David and the other psalmists but also that those who collected, arranged, and provided titles or headings for the originally scattered corpus worked under divine guidance.[190]

Eusebius, therefore, attaches great significance to the order of the Psalms, commencing his discourse on each psalm with discussion of its relation to other psalms, of its date, and of its heading. In addition, he provides an introduction to each group of psalms with the same heading (for example, the twelve psalms headed "of Asaph").[191] He finds coherence, significance, and a messianic relevance in the arrangement within a group. Thus the fifteen psalms of pilgrimage which are inscribed "of the ascents" (119–133 [120–134]) foreshadow the history of the Jews and of the Christian church. Eusebius identifies their subjects, in succession, as the main themes of his interpretation of history: the first seven of these psalms record the exile in Babylon, the return to Judaea, the rebuilding of Jerusalem; the eighth prophesies "the second capture (of the temple), the final fall and desolation of the building on which they labored at the hands of the Romans, after their disbelief and impiety towards Jesus Christ our Savior"; and the last seven foretell the calling of the gentiles, the victory of the Christian church and its martyrs over persecution, the worldwide extension of Christianity, its beneficial effect, and its universal availability to the benighted who genuinely desire enlightenment.[192]

Eusebius lived and wrote in an area where the Christian religion had already set down deep and firm roots. Moreover, during his formative years, Roman emperors and their officials not only tolerated the open profession of Christianity but treated the Christian church as an organization whose rights and privileges might receive legal sanction and protection under their administration. Eusebius reached middle age before serious persecution again threatened the Church, and he was a man of more than sixty before he became the subject of a Christian emperor. These facts are fundamental for understanding his intellectual development. He did not compose his major works under the influence of Constantine, nor was he primarily an apologist who wrote to defend the Christian faith at a time of danger.[193] As Eusebius grew to manhood, the peaceful triumph of Christianity seemed already assured: Eusebius began as a scholar, made himself into a historian, and turned to apologetics only under the pressure of circumstances. All of his works, even those which he wrote toward the end of his long life, reflect attitudes formed in Caesarea when he was a young man and the pupil of Pamphilus. The three dominant characteristics of his thought are a continual emphasis on the Bible, an intellectual framework which derives from Origen, and celebration of the success of Christianity in the Roman world.

VII

BIBLICAL SCHOLARSHIP
AND THE *CHRONICLE*

No work of Eusebius illustrates better than *On the Place-Names in Holy Scripture* how he was able to create something original and lasting by applying what he had learned from his mentors and predecessors.[1] In the sense in which ancient scholars understood the terms, Eusebius' work is neither pure geography nor pure lexicography. It is rather a combination whose genre a modern scholar instinctively recognizes: *On the Place-Names in Holy Scripture* is a biblical gazetteer, which is still the main literary source for the historical geography and territorial history of Palestine both in biblical times and under the Roman Empire.[2]

The gazetteer is in fact the fourth and last part of a composite work; in the preface to this part, Eusebius explains that the first three parts (now lost) comprised a translation into Greek of the Hebrew names in the Bible for the peoples of the world outside the Holy Land,[3] a description or map of ancient Judaea which concentrated on the territorial divisions between the Twelve Tribes of Israel,[4] and a plan or description of ancient Jerusalem and the temple which quoted the evidence relevant to identifying each site. The preface to the gazetteer also states very explicitly Eusebius' purpose and his method of working: "I have set out the meaning, the location, and the contemporary name, whether similar to the ancient or different, of the cities and villages which occur in the Holy Scripture in the original language. I shall collect the entries from the whole of the divinely inspired Scriptures, and I shall set them out grouped by their initial letters so that one may easily perceive what lies scattered throughout the text."[5] Eusebius, therefore, has not used any earlier compilation of a similar type; he worked through the Bible collecting his material and arranging the entries himself.

The entries in *On the Place-Names in Holy Scripture* are arranged in a manner which reflects their genesis. Those for each letter are arranged book by book; and within each book, in the order of their occurrence, so that, for example, the entries under T read as follows:[6]

Letter T

From Genesis

Tigris (2:14): a river which goes out of paradise, flowing, as Scripture says, *opposite the Assyrians,* and falling "into the Red Sea," as Josephus says[7]—and that it is called Tigris because of its swiftness, as similarly the animal of the same name.

Terebinth—tree at Shechem (35:4): under which Jacob buried *the foreign gods,* near Neapolis.

From Joshua

Tina (15:22): of the tribe of Judah.
Telem (15:24): of the tribe of Judah.
Tessam (15:29): of the tribe of Judah.
Tyre (19:35): of the tribe of Naphthali.

Judges

Tabath (7:23): where they fought against Midiam.
Tob (11:3): land where Jephthah settled.
Topheth (2 Kings 23:10): *in the valley of the son of Hinnom,* where the people committed idolatry, in the suburbs of Jerusalem.[8]
Tanis (Isaiah 19:11): city of Egypt. In Isaiah and in Ezekiel (30:14).
Taphnas (Hosea 9:6): city of Egypt. In Hoseah and in Ezekiel (30:18) and in Jeremiah (43:7). Where the Jews who went into Egypt with Jeremiah settled.
Trachonitis (Luke 3:1): territory also called Ituraea, of which Philip was tetrarch according to the evangelist Luke. Also entered above.[9] It is beyond Bostra in the desert to the south as if facing Damascus.

The entries quoted are not an untypical selection. Some are brief in the extreme and based on nothing but the passage of the Bible where they occur, or rather where they occurred in the manuscript or manuscripts which Eusebius employed. Others of those quoted add a geographical location, while one entry adduces Josephus not only for the location of the Tigris but also for the meaning of the name of that river. In a similar fashion, the whole work juxtaposes long and short entries and is based above all on the Bible and Josephus.[10] The copy of the Bible from which Eusebius actually worked may or may not have been the Hexapla itself, but the Hexapla was available to him, and he clearly consulted it when he thought the occasion demanded.[11] Josephus' *Jewish Antiquities* is quoted in a dozen places,[12] and other material not explicitly ascribed to any source may also come from Josephus.[13] Eusebius presumably perused the Jewish historian in search of evidence relevant to his undertaking.

A number of entries contain information of a different nature from those already quoted. For example, the entries for Arnon (Numbers 21:13) and Ashtaroth (Deuteronomy 1:4) read as follows:[14]

> Arnon: *the wilderness which extends from Amorite territory.* It lies between *Moab and the Amorites,* and is *the Moabite frontier,* which is Areopolis in Arabia. To this day is shown a very difficult place with ravines, called the Arnonas, stretching to the north of Areopolis, in which garrisons of soldiers keep guard everywhere because of the frightening nature of the place. Of old it belonged to Sihon, the king of the Amorites, who had taken it from the Moabites. Then the territories beyond the Jordan came under the control of the sons of Israel, stretching from Arnon to Mount Hermon and Lebanon.

> Ashtaroth: ancient city of Og, in which the giants dwelled, which became part of the tribe of Manasseh. It lies in Batanaea about six miles from Adraa, a city in Arabia. (Adraa is twenty-five miles distant from Bostra.) It is also entered above as Ashtaroth-Karnain (Genesis 14:5).

Neither the text of the Bible nor Josephus supplied such information. Where then did Eusebius obtain such knowledge? Two sources of an official nature have been inferred: an official map of the Roman roads of Palestine and a document listing the disposition of Roman troops in the province—both of which may plausibly be supposed to have existed in Caesarea, where the governor of Palestine normally resided and presumably kept his archives.[15] But it is not necessary (and perhaps not plausible) to imagine Eusebius consulting administrative documents in the governor's official residence.[16] Whether or not Eusebius, like Origen, had tramped over the Holy Land following the footsteps of Jesus and the Old Testament prophets,[17] he could draw on his own general knowledge of his native land, and he could ask others about areas which he knew imperfectly. The presence of Roman troops in a place was no secret,[18] and the location of the places for which he gives precise distances from an important city suggests oral informants from certain areas rather than an official map of the whole province.[19] Moreover, the not infrequent entries which state that something "is shown to this day" clearly derive either from a visit by Eusebius or from the report of a contemporary.[20] Nevertheless, it might not be prudent to exclude completely the use of geographical sources.[21]

Eusebius states that he compiled *On the Place-Names in Holy Scripture* by working through the Bible piecemeal: he presumably first noted explanations and identifications in the margin of one manuscript, then transcribed the relevant lemmata and glosses together to a series of separate pieces of papyrus or roll, and finally produced a continuous text from these separate fragments. Eusebius' originality, therefore, can only be denied by disbelieving what he says about the composition of the work. Such distrust has in fact been evinced[22]— and, on the other side, the work as extant has been claimed to be a mere draft which Eusebius left incomplete and which was published posthumously.[23] Yet the finished product amply confirms Eusebius' account of his procedure, and the formal preface implies that the work has received what its author at least considered its finishing touches.[24] It should thus be judged and assessed as it stands.

In Eusebius' day, lexicography already had a long history,[25] and *On the Place-Names in Holy Scripture* conformed to the practice of contemporary scholarship in various ways: each lemma (it may be assumed) began a new line; different forms of the same name sometimes appeared as separate entries; most entries were brief; and the entries were arranged in a loosely alphabetical order.[26] Admittedly, most earlier onomastica and lexicons were compiled by scholars more interested in the form and stylistic propriety of names and words than in their meaning. But there are at least two analogs of Eusebius' work. In the second century, one Diogenianus had published a geographical lexicon entitled "Collection and Map of the Cities Throughout the World," which was perhaps a unique phenomenon.[27] And lexicons of a single author or text certainly existed. Full Homeric lexicons had developed out of short lists of glosses, and the arrangement of entries within them became more strictly alphabetical over the course of centuries; the sophist Apollonius had produced a particularly famous Homeric lexicon in the second century.[28]

Eusebius' procedure in *On the Place-Names in Holy Scripture* was to apply the methods of traditional lexicography to a new subject. The way had been prepared by Origen, whose influence can be detected in several entries, most obviously in the entry for Bethabara (John 1:28):[29] the name occurs in none of the earliest and most authoritative manuscripts of the New Testament but is known to be Origen's emendation for Bethany.[30] Origen can be shown to have used philosophical dictionaries, lexicons, and scholarly works of reference for etymology.[31] It may accordingly be presumed that the library at Caesarea contained various types of lexica which Eusebius could easily consult. Moreover,

Origen produced a biblical onomasticon of which Jerome's Latin translation (*Liber Interpretationis Hebraicorum Nominum*) survives in full,[32] and of which a papyrus of the third or fourth century preserves a probable fragment.[33] Origen seems to have done little more than revise and expand an earlier Jewish onomasticon which Jerome, and presumably, therefore, Origen himself, ascribed to Philo. It set out to explain the meaning of Hebrew names in the Old Testament, and its arrangement, which Origen took over from the earlier onomasticon, reflects its purpose as an aid for the biblical commentator: the entries are ordered first by the books of the Bible, then within each book by initial letter and the order in which the names occur in the text. Since Eusebius also compiled *On the Place-Names in Holy Scripture* as an aid to exegesis,[34] the contrast between the two works reflects all the more faithfully the fundamental difference between the two men: if Origen always sought a spiritual meaning behind the words of the Bible, Eusebius was more interested in history, in geography, in concrete reality—or at least he found these aspects of the Bible more congenial to his talents. Philosophically and theologically, Eusebius was always a faithful disciple of Origen, but the desire for useful scholarship led him to be original in a very different way.

The date of *On the Place-Names in Holy Scripture* is crucial to understanding Eusebius' intellectual development and literary career. Although its composition has often been assumed to belong to the fourth century,[35] and although the work has sometimes been dated as late as the third decade of the fourth century,[36] it was probably compiled before the end of the third. The criteria available for dating it are of two types: Eusebius' references both to Christianity and paganism and to the Roman administrative divisions of Palestine and Arabia suggest that he was writing long before 325. Eusebius says virtually nothing about Christianity, and he describes only three villages as having a wholly Christian population (namely, Anaia, Jetheira near Eleutheropolis, and Kariatha). He makes no mention whatever of Constantine's building of churches in the Holy Land, and states that the pagan ceremonies at the sacred oak of Mamre, which were suppressed in 326, still continue.[37] Moreover, it is not plausible (though perhaps not altogether impossible) to imagine Eusebius at work on a biblical gazetteer during the persecution of 303–313 or during the following decade.

More precisely, those few entries which refer to, or reflect, Roman administrative boundaries imply that Eusebius was engaged on the compilation in the 290s. Whereas two entries describe Petra, the former capital of the Nabataean kingdom, as "a city of Arabia," a third has the description "a famous city of Palestine," even though Eusebius is here adducing a passage where Josephus states that Rekem "ranks highest in the land of the Arabs."[38] This alteration from Arabia to Palestine must have been deliberate and appears to reflect the fact that Petra belonged to the Roman province of Palestine when Eusebius penned the entry. Now Arabia Petraea had certainly been incorporated in the

Roman province of Palestine by 307—and was probably united to it in 293 or very shortly thereafter.[39] Hence, if the statement in the other two entries that Petra belongs to Arabia also reflects the provincial boundaries at the time the entries were written, and is not the result of mere habit, carelessness, or inattention, it follows that Eusebius was compiling *On the Place-Names in Holy Scripture* when Petra became part of Palestine.[40]

Eusebius probably completed *On the Place-Names in Holy Scripture* before the end of the third century. So early a date has extremely serious implications for the chronology of his major historical works. In the preface to his Latin translation, Jerome alleges that the gazetteer was composed after the ten books of Eusebius' *Ecclesiastical History* and after the *Chronological Canons* which Jerome had already translated.[41] That cannot be strictly true, since Eusebius' *Chronicle,* from which Jerome rendered the *Canons* into Latin, concluded with the *vicennalia* of Constantine in 325/6.[42] However, Jerome is presumably reporting, or making an inference from, something Eusebius said in the preface to the whole work of which *On the Place-Names* formed the last part; Jerome's statement, therefore, implies that the first editions of the *Chronicle* and the *Ecclesiastical History* preceded the biblical gazetteer. But if that is so, then Eusebius also composed both of these works before the end of the third century.

This conclusion is consonant with the internal evidence of the *Chronicle* and the *History*[43] and helps to explain a puzzling feature of the second edition of the *Chronicle.* Under Olympiad 264.3, which corresponds to the second year of the Roman emperor Probus, occurs an entry recording Anatolius, the bishop of Laodicea and an accomplished philosopher. There immediately follows, occupying the whole width of the page, a note which reads: "The second year of Probus is year 325 in the calendar of Antioch, year 402 in the calendar of Tyre, year 324 in the calendar of Laodicea, year 588 in the calendar of Edessa, and year 380 in the calendar of Ascalon."[44] All these equivalences (except the Olympic year, which should be 264.4) are correct for 276/7.[45] Why did Eusebius give them? He may have wished to contradict Jews of the third century who believed that the Messiah would come during the fifty-year period of the eighty-fifth jubilee.[46] Eusebius marked the beginning of each tenth jubilee (that is, intervals of five hundred years) from the forty-first jubilee to the eighty-first—and the elaborate synchronism quoted occurs for the year Eusebius entered as the beginning of the eighty-sixth jubilee.[47] However, Anatolius' Easter cycle probably commenced with the same year, and Anatolius is discussed at the end of Book Seven of the *Ecclesiastical History.*[48] Eusebius surely ended the first edition of the *Chronicle* at precisely this point to make an implicit compliment to the scholarship of Anatolius.[49]

Eusebius' *Chronicle* is not only a historical text of great importance for a wide variety of fields but also a literary text which poses problems of peculiar intricacy on several levels.[50] At the most basic level, the transmission of the text has seriously hindered a just appreciation of Eusebius' achievement: the textual tradition is complicated and defective and has been the subject of great scholarly controversy.[51] Fortunately, however, the salient facts now seem to be agreed by most competent judges. Versions in no less than four languages are in question, and the *Chronicle* comprised two parts whose attestation differs greatly: the first part was a *Chronography* which quoted, discussed, and summarized the available sources for the chronology of different races, and the second combined the separate chronologies obtained in the first part and set them out in chronological tables or *Canons,* which also noted historical events and their dates.[52]

An Armenian translation preserves the whole of the *Chronicle,* though with lacunae, some of them quite substantial. The translation is extant in three manuscripts, of which one (written in 1696) is an obvious copy of one of the other two. Neither of the latter was written before the thirteenth century, and one may be a descendant of the other rather than its sibling. Only one modern "edition" takes account of all three manuscripts: a German translation with textual notes and commentary.[53] The Armenian translation itself perhaps dates from the sixth century; it was made directly from the Greek and was probably revised in part from a Syriac version.[54]

Jerome's Latin version of the *Canons* is much earlier and is preserved in much earlier manuscripts. Jerome composed it in Constantinople in 380/1 and seems to have revised it in 382 when he traveled to Rome.[55] One manuscript of the fifth century survives almost complete; of another, enough fragments survive to identify two later apographs which enable it to be reconstructed in its entirety, and there are several manuscripts of the seventh and eighth centuries: these early witnesses attest securely not only the text of Jerome's version but, equally important, its arrangement of the columns of numbers and of the entries on each page of the original.[56]

Although the original Greek has perished, substantial fragments of it can be identified in two ways.[57] There are explicit, direct quotations by later Greek writers, and lengthy passages in Greek, not expressly attributed to Eusebius, which correspond in content and phrasing to the extant Armenian and Latin versions.[58] The former category is not large, but the latter is important, especially for the long fragments which the *Chronography* quotes from earlier Greek historians. Some of these late Greek quotations or extracts (whether derived directly from Eusebius or not) enable corrupt readings in the Armenian version to be corrected or supply a word, phrase, or paragraph which the extant Armenian omits.[59] The *Chronicle* was also translated into Syriac, perhaps more than once; two Syriac epitomes of the *Chronicle* have been published, and traces of yet another Syriac version have been discovered.[60] Their value for constituting the text, however, appears to be negligible.

The facts of the transmission of the text are highly relevant to discovering precisely what Eusebius' original *Chronicle* contained. For the constitution of the text, the Syriac tradition can be ignored, and the Greek fragments and quotations are in practice useful only for supplying the original wording of passages whose substance the Armenian and Latin versions provide. For reconstructing the *Chronography,* therefore, the problem is in principle simple and essentially philological: the Armenian translation provides the structure of the text and the substance of what Eusebius wrote,[61] and Greek fragments and quotations enable the original Greek to be deduced for some passages. The *Canons* offers a challenge of a different order: the Armenian translation survives in a few, late manuscripts, but Jerome's version, of which very early and reliable manuscripts exist, was not intended by its author to be a mere translation. Jerome explains what he had done quite precisely. His Latin version (he states) falls into three distinct parts: as far as the fall of Troy it is a straight translation; from there until the *vicennalia* of Constantine the translator has felt free to expand existing entries and to add new ones to compensate for Eusebius' neglect of Roman political and literary history; and from 325/6 to 378 it is all Jerome's own composition.[62] Jerome's statement seems clear enough, and he deserves to be believed when he describes the nature of his work, for the extant product reflects the initial promise.[63] Admittedly, the execution was hasty: there are errors of comprehension and translation, and Jerome has added a few glosses in the section which he describes as straight translation.[64] But almost all of Jerome's additions and alterations in Eusebius' entries can be identified from their content and from comparison with other Latin writers; hence the task of reconstructing Jerome's exemplar, though laborious and intricate, can be performed by careful and patient work.[65]

One final hurdle remains before the *Chronicle* can be approached directly. Both the Armenian translator and Jerome used the second edition of the *Chronicle,* which ended with the *vicennalia* of Constantine in 325/6, when it was presumably composed.[66] The first edition is much earlier: although composition about 303 is normally assumed,[67] the available evidence points rather to a date at least a decade earlier, with the chronological tables terminating with the second year of the Roman emperor Probus, that is, with A.D. 276/7.[68] By singular good fortune, Eusebius himself has preserved, in a work completed no later than 320, a long quotation from the preface to the first edition of the *Chronological Canons;* the provenance of the quotation is certain, but its importance has rarely been recognized.[69] Comparisons of the quotation with Jerome's translation of the preface to the second edition reveals that the first edition lacked the polemic against Porphyry which occurs near the beginning of the second.[70] There is, therefore, no reason to infer from the preface (or from any other part of the work) that Eusebius composed the *Chronicle* mainly as a historical apologia for Christianity.[71] The *Chronicle* may be interpreted rather as primarily a work of pure scholarship.

The first part, or first book, of the *Chronicle,* which is expressly entitled *Chronography,*[72] opens with a claim to impartial, or at least to reliable, scholarship. Eusebius has perused (he states) the historians of the ancient Near East and ancient Greece with the aim of dating Moses and the prophets in relation to the Incarnation and of correlating sacred history with events in the history of Greeks and barbarians. Such research is necessary, because a universal chronology cannot be discovered from part of the evidence alone, not even if that part be Holy Scripture. Moreover, the evidence needs careful sifting: each chronological system must be established by careful documentation and then scrutinized for accuracy and credibility before the results of the individual inquiries can be integrated into a single chronology. And Eusebius claims to be suitably qualified for such detailed and intricate research: "I prize truth above all else."[73]

Eusebius' method corresponds to his intentions and professions. He quotes and discusses the evidence for each race separately, ending each time with chronological lists, so that he can subsequently write out the chronological tables for which the *Chronography* was designed to provide the foundation. The series of discussions begins with the Chaldaeans; the main authorities are Alexander Polyhistor and Abydenos, but Eusebius also quotes Josephus, Castor, Diodorus, and Cephalion, and the section ends with lists of the kings of Assyria, Media, Lydia, and Persia.[74] Eusebius then turns his attention to Jewish history, for which he names Josephus and Africanus as his authorities, together with the Bible. In the event, he also adduces Clement of Alexandria. This section is of great interest and reflects Eusebius' Caesarean milieu in a very specific way: Eusebius is not content merely to quote the Septuagint as the standard authoritative text of the Old Testament, but he compares its chronology to that of both the Hebrew and the Samaritan text. Admittedly, Eusebius pronounces in favor of the Septuagint, but it is significant that he decided to discuss the other versions and that he could see one of the axioms of modern textual criticism: the translation could derive from uncorrupted exemplars of the current Hebrew text.[75] Egypt comes next; Manetho is the authority adduced for the thirty-one dynasties preceding Alexander's conquest, Porphyry for the Ptolemaic monarchs.[76]

Eusebius then passes to Greek history, which he tackles in three sections. First, he discusses the ancient, often mythical kings of five cities (Athens, Argos, Sicyon, Sparta, and Corinth); then he reproduces a list of rulers of the sea (the so-called thalassocracies) and a list of Olympic victors in the stadion; and finally, he discusses the early kings of Macedonia and the successors of Alexander who ruled in Macedonia, Thessaly, Syria, and Asia. The text names Castor, Porphyry, and Diodorus as Eusebius' authorities. But the section seems in part confused: Eusebius departs from his stated order and fails to indicate the provenance of the list of Olympic victors, which ends with the two hundred and forty-ninth Olympiad (in A.D. 217).[77] Nevertheless, here as elsewhere, Eusebius has chosen his authorities wisely: his quotations of Porphyry still provide one of the main foundations of Hellenistic chronology.[78]

The final section of the *Chronography,* now incomplete, is devoted to Roman history, from Romulus to Eusebius' own day: before the text breaks off, Eusebius has quoted Dionysius of Halicarnassus, Diodorus and Castor on the foundation of Rome and on the kings, and has promised a list of emperors from Julius Caesar to his own time with consular and Olympic dates.[79] Here, it is clear, the Republic was omitted: Eusebius appears to have relied on Castor's statement of the number of years which separated the consulate of L. Junius Brutus and L. Tarquinius Collatinus (traditionally 509 B.C.) from that of M. Valerius Messala and M. Piso (61 B.C.) to link the kings of Rome with Julius Caesar and thus with the Roman emperors from Augustus onward.[80]

The primary technique employed in the *Chronography* is quotation, followed by the extrapolation of dates. Sometimes, however, kings appear in the concluding lists who have not been mentioned in the quotations; thus, for example, six of the eight Median kings listed are nowhere named in the preceding excerpts, so that the list has presumably been extrapolated without acknowledgment from Castor, who is quoted for the Assyrian kings, or from a source which had itself excerpted Castor.[81] Interspersed among the quotations are discussions designed to aid the subsequent synthesis, but not entirely lacking critical acumen. Comparison of Babylonian accounts of a great flood with that in the Bible leads Eusebius to argue that the Xisuthros of Alexander Polyhistor and Abydenos should be identical with Noah, and the one hundred and twenty *saroi* of Chaldaean saga (he contends) must represent not 3600 years each (as Alexander claimed) but some very brief period which allows the synchronism. The reality of the flood Eusebius defends from his own experience: in his own day the remains of fishes are found on the high ridges of Mount Lebanon.[82] And he is aware of the deficiencies of some of his evidence, expressly commenting on the uncertain chronology of Greek history before the fall of Troy and the lack of materials between that event and the first Olympiad. Furthermore, Eusebius begins the *Canons* not with the creation of the world or with Adam's expulsion from paradise but with the birth of Abraham—in the reigns of the Assyrian Ninus and of Europus, the second king of Sicyon, at the beginning of the sixteenth Egyptian dynasty.[83]

The *Chronography* was primarily a collection of raw material, with a little preliminary excerpting and reworking, intended to document and substantiate the second part of the work—the *Canons*. Eusebius equipped these chronological tables with a separate preface, which advanced a claim to originality and indicated how he regarded his own achievement:

> That Moses of the Hebrew race, who first of all the prophets before the advent of our Lord revealed the divine laws in sacred literature, lived at the time of Inachus, very learned men have recorded, the Christians Clement, Africanus, and Tatian, and the Jews Josephus and Justus, repeating monuments of ancient history. (Inachus preceded the Trojan War by five hundred years.) But I, traveling a newer way than those named, will use the following method. Since the coincidence is admitted between the period of the Roman emperor Augustus and the birth of our Savior, who began

the teaching of the gospel of Christ in the fifteenth year of Tiberius Caesar, if anyone wishes to compute the number of years from this point, ascending to the period of Darius, the king of Persia, and the restoration of the temple at Jerusalem under him, which happened after the Jewish race returned from Babylon, he would find from Tiberius to the second year of Darius 548 years. For the second year of Darius corresponds to the first year of the sixty-fifth Olympiad, while the fifteenth year of Tiberius coincides with the fourth year of the two hundred and first Olympiad.[84]

The second year of Darius and the fifteenth year of Tiberius are the twin foci of the *Canons:* from the first equation Eusebius can correlate sacred and profane history in the period of the Old Testament, while the second ties the history of Christianity to that of the Roman Empire. Eusebius also explained that he had tried to set out his results as clearly as possible:

> Lest the long list of numbers cause confusion, I have divided the whole series of years into decades, which I have gathered from the histories of each separate race and placed opposite one another, so that it may be easy to discover in the lifetime of which Greek or barbarian the prophets, kings, and priests of the Hebrews lived, and those of different races who are falsely believed to be gods or demigods, when each city was founded, what famous philosophers, poets, leaders, and writers of various works existed, and whatever else antiquity deemed worthy of memory. All these facts I shall put in their appropriate places with the utmost brevity.[85]

The arrangement of the *Canons* on the page fulfilled the initial promise.[86] Eusebius attempted to exhibit synchronisms as graphically as possible. As far as the second year of Darius, the *Canons* spread over a double page. The basic layout was simple and is clearest at the beginning (down to year 160 of Abraham). At the left was the column of figures representing Assyrian regnal years. Every tenth year of Abraham was marked at the extreme left by an underlined numeral, and the corresponding numerals in all the *fila regnorum* were similarly underlined. To the right of the column for kings of Assyria came a space, in which items from Jewish history were entered, and a column of figures representing Jewish chronology (at first the years of the patriarchs, later of the judges and kings). These two columns and the space between them occupied the whole of the left-hand page, while the right-hand page was similarly arranged, with the regnal years of the kings of Sicyon and Egypt framing a space in which items of gentile history were noted when appropriate.

Eusebius carefully observed the basic principle that columns of figures (*fila regnorum*) should frame separate spaces for sacred and secular history (*spatia historica*) on the left- and right-hand pages when he introduced additional columns of figures. On the left, the Assyrian kings give way to the Median, and they in their turn to the Persian. The Hebrew column is first moved to the left of the space, so that Eusebius can accommodate more columns of figures in the center; then it requires one column for each part of the divided monarchy (from year 1021 to year 1270 of Abraham). The central group of columns grows from two including Hebrew dates, to three and then to four excluding them: besides the Sicyonian column, there appear and disappear, at the appropriate dates, columns for the kings of Argos, Athens, Mycenae, Latium (later Rome), Macedonia, and Lydia. And at the extreme right the Egyptian kings are joined successively by those of Corinth and Lydia. Moreover, after the year 1240 of Abraham, the figures are divided horizontally into groups of four by the notation of each Olympiad. It should also be noted that, to preserve the proper alignment of the columns, each change of king, and later the notation of each Olympiad, requires the space of a line or more to be left completely blank across the whole width of the text.

After the second year of Darius, when the sacred history of the Old Testament was soon to cease, a single page sufficed for the synchronisms. Each Olympiad was noted on a separate line, and every tenth year of Abraham was marked at the extreme left throughout the rest of the work. Otherwise the arrangement of the material was much simpler than before. At the left of each page came a single column of figures, first for Persian kings, then of Ptolemaic regnal years, and finally for Roman emperors, from Julius Caesar onward. The center of the page contained the historical entries (which Eusebius probably still divided into separate columns for Jewish and gentile history), and to the right were additional columns of figures for the kings of Macedonia down to Perseus, of Egypt down to Nectanebo, for the Seleucid dynasty and (briefly) Antigonus the One-Eyed and his son, and for the Jewish kings from the time of the Maccabees to the capture of Jerusalem. From this point (Olympiad 212.2) the absence of columns of figures except at the left afforded Eusebius the opportunity of placing notices of Christian bishops to either side of the column or columns of historical entries, and he began to enter systematically the bishops of Rome, Antioch, and Alexandria.[87]

Eusebius intended the *Canons* to do more than merely tabulate the chronological results which the *Chronography* had established. Strictly, the first part of the *Chronicle* is devoted to justifying and demonstrating only the *fila regnorum,* the chronological framework. Into this Eusebius has inserted historical notices, in order to provide "a summary of history of every type."[88] It must be asked, therefore, what sources Eusebius used for these notices. The answer to this question has extremely serious implications for estimating Eusebius' purpose and achievement in composing the *Chronicle,* and even for assessing his intellectual probity. To generations of scholars it has seemed obvious that the *Chronicle* owes an enormous and unacknowledged debt to Julius Africanus and hence that Eusebius' originality must be less than he claims.[89] In particular, the *Chronological Canons* has often been regarded as little more than a transcription from Africanus' *Chronographiae,* which Eusebius modified in detail and sometimes distorted through carelessness.[90] But is that verdict just? It has recently been challenged by an analysis of Eusebius' sources which places him firmly within the Greek chronographic tradition and allows him to be credited with genuine and substantive originality.[91]

The *Canons* contains at least four types of material, whose sources may be different. Both the chronological framework and the *spatium historicum* which it surrounds can be divided into the sacred and the secular. The sources of the chronology and historical notices for the Jews and Christians can be identified easily. The *Chronography* names the Bible, Josephus' *Jewish Antiquities,* and Africanus' *Chronographiae,* and the *Canons* appends to the notice of Nehemiah's rebuilding of the walls of Jerusalem the statement: "To this point the divine Scriptures of the Hebrews contain the annals of the times. Their history after this point, however, we shall exhibit from the book of the Maccabees and the writings of Josephus and Africanus, who in succession pursued universal history down to the Roman period."[92] It is a reasonable inference that the Bible and Africanus are Eusebius' main sources for sacred chronology and history.[93] But his occasional direct consultation of Josephus and Christian writers other than Africanus cannot safely be denied.[94]

The identification of Eusebius' sources for secular chronology and history is far more problematical, not least because none of the works of Eusebius' predecessors is extant, except in fragments.[95] Discussion must begin, therefore, from a passage in the *Chronography* where Eusebius names his sources for Greek and Oriental chronology:

> After the whole of what has been discussed is collected from the records, which are here listed in order:
> Alexander Polyhistor;
> Abydenus, who wrote histories of the Assyrians and Medes;
> Manetho's three books of Egyptian antiquities;
> Cephalion's nine books named after the Muses;
> Diodorus' Library—40 books, in which he gives a brief summary of history down to Julius Caesar;
> Cassius Longinus—18 books, in which he has summarized 228 Olympiads;
> of Phlegon, the freedman of the emperor, 14 books, in which he has selectively summarized 229 Olympiads;
> Castor's 6 books, in which he has summarized from Ninus as far as 181 Olympiads;
> Thallus' three books, in which he has summarized briefly from the Fall of Troy to the 167th Olympiad;
> Porphyry, the philosopher and our contemporary, from the Fall of Troy to the reign of Claudius [A.D. 268–270]—
> it is time to turn to the chronology of the Roman Empire.[96]

Seven of these authorities have indeed been cited by name and quoted at length while Eusebius was investigating Greek and Oriental chronology. Yet there are three whom the text of the *Chronography* as extant does not in fact name: Cassius Longinus, Phlegon, and Thallus. That is puzzling, since Eusebius clearly claims to give a complete list of his authorities so far, except those for Jewish chronology named at the appropriate point.[97] An obvious explanation is that Eusebius has actually used Africanus as his source, and that he names not his immediate source but the authorities his source had used.[98] Use of Africanus would also explain discrepancies between the *Chronography* and the *Canons:* if, for example, the second part of the *Chronicle* presents a different list of the kings of Media from that apparently established in the first, then Eusebius may have copied Africanus instead of attempting to apply his own chronology in every instance.[99] Moreover, the case for Eusebius' unacknowledged use of Africanus seems to be confirmed by the fact that the list of Olympic victors quoted by Eusebius ends with the 249th Olympic Games in A.D. 217;[100] Africanus was writing in the consular year A.D. 221, presumably before the next celebration of the games in the late summer of that year.[101]

Such a view of Eusebius' use of sources implies a certain lack of honesty, even when allowance is made for the ancients' toleration of plagiarism, for it discounts Eusebius' claim that he will adopt a novel method, different from that of earlier Christian writers, Africanus included.[102] But Eusebius' honesty and originality can be vindicated.[103] Other evidence renders it improbable that Africanus' *Chronographiae* contained all the material Eusebius has been supposed to derive from him. In particular, Africanus had no good reason to include a list of Olympic victors in this work. He did indeed use Olympic dates, and he used them to synchronize biblical events and Jewish history with gentile history,[104] but his main interest lay in biblical and Christian chronology, to which the names of Olympic victors were quite extraneous.[105] Moreover, the name of Cassius Longinus almost certainly does not derive from Africanus. A scholar of that name is known: the teacher of Porphyry and a prominent intellectual figure when Eusebius was a boy, he served Zenobia against Aurelian and was executed when Aurelian defeated her (A.D. 272).[106] Longinus or his pupil Porphyry may be the immediate source of Eusebius' list of Olympic victors, and Phlegon and Thallus the authorities whom Longinus used in compiling it.[107]

Eusebius' method of working and the nature of his achievement can now be described. The materials which the *Chronological Canons* employs derive from three types of source. First, there was sacred history from the Bible and Julius Africanus, supplemented by Eusebius' own reading of Josephus and other Christian writers. Second, there was the Greek chronographic tradition. In Eusebius' day it was already seven centuries old, for it derived ultimately, in its oldest parts, from scholars such as Hippias of Elis and Hellanicus of Lesbos.[108] The dominant figures in this tradition were the Alexandrian scholars Eratosthenes, who established a consistent chronology based on Olympiads, and Apollodorus, whose dates for events in Greek history were almost universally adopted from the second century B.C. onward.[109] If Eusebius is not dependent on Africanus, then he has (as he claims) drawn directly on this tradition. It matters less to discover precisely which authors and works Eusebius used directly; they certainly included Castor of Rhodes, Porphyry's *Chronicle* and his *Philosophical History,* and one or more sources which transmitted Apollodorus' dates for a multiplicity of individual persons and events.[110] In addition, there are entries for which no specific written source need be invoked: although perhaps not numerous in the first edition, entries of this type must predominate in the section Eusebius added for the second (that is, between Olympiads 264.4 and 276.2).[111]

The *Chronography* began the task of drawing these disparate strands together, and the *Canons* presented the results of his researches in tabular form. Eusebius appears to have introduced a genuine innovation. Earlier chronographers compiled lists of kings or officials, but so far as can be ascertained, none had ever arranged these lists in parallel vertical columns to exhibit synchronisms.[112] The idea of tabulation may have been suggested by the parallel columns of the Hexapla. It appealed to Eusebius because of the universality of his approach: he wished to investigate and demonstrate in detail the relationship between different chronological systems, and his *Chronological Canons* included a summary history of mankind from a Christian viewpoint.[113] Paradoxically, Eusebius' *Chronological Canons* is also the earliest representative of the Greek chronographical tradition still extant in full.[114]

These facts must be taken into account by any modern scholar who wishes to use the *Canons* as a historical source. Although in the *Canons* Eusebius names a source only on rare occasions, the chronographical and historical traditions which he reproduces can often be identified. Hence very few dates in the *Canons* can be taken by themselves and made the basis for chronological deductions: even when a date is unambiguously and consistently attested in the surviving derivatives (a rare event), it must be correlated with other relevant evidence to determine what tradition Eusebius reports or whether he had any precise evidence at all.[115] For everything before the middle of the third century, Eusebius perforce depended on written sources, which often lacked precise dates, and he can sometimes be convicted of error on points where exact evidence was available.[116] It is imprudent, therefore, to base any historical arguments on the exact dates which the *Chronicle* offers; the modern scholar should show his respect for Eusebius' achievement not by repeating his sometimes erroneous dates but by applying his intelligence (as Eusebius did) to the substantive problems.

Although the *Chronicle* and its sequel, the *Ecclesiastical History,* expanded Eusebius' intellectual horizons, he never forsook biblical scholarship. Most of his apologetical and theological writing either consists of the quotation and exegesis of biblical passages or applies similar techniques to other material,[117] and his surviving commentary on Isaiah indicates by incidental allusions to the contemporary scene that it belongs to the last years of his life.[118] Study of the Bible (it is clear) formed an important part of the curriculum of the school at Caesarea where Eusebius taught until the end of his life.[119]

The most influential product of Eusebius' labors on the Bible is probably his concordance to the Gospels.[120] An introductory letter to Carpianus, his "beloved brother in the Lord" (otherwise unknown), describes and explains the nature and the purpose of this scholarly aid:

> Ammonius the Alexandrian, having employed much industry and effort (as was proper), has left us the fourfold Gospel, placing the corresponding passages of the other evangelists beside the Gospel of Matthew so that the continuous thread of the other three is necessarily broken, preventing a consecutive reading. So that you may know the individual passages of each evangelist, in which they were led to speak truthfully on the same subject, with the whole context and order of the other three still preserved, I have taken my point of departure from the work of the man already mentioned, but proceeded by a different method, and have produced canons for you, ten in number, which follow—
> The first contains numbers in which the four, Matthew, Mark, Luke, and John have said similar things.
> The second in which the three, Matthew, Mark, and Luke.
> The third in which the three, Matthew, Luke, and John.
> The fourth in which the three, Matthew, Mark, and John.
> The fifth in which the two, Matthew and Luke.
> The sixth in which the two, Matthew and Mark.
> The seventh in which the two, Matthew and John.
> The eighth in which the two, Mark and Luke.
> The ninth in which the two, Luke and John.
> The tenth in which each of them wrote about something in an individual manner.
> This then is the underlying purpose of the following canons; their clear application is as follows: Before each section of the four Gospels stands a number in the margin, beginning with the first, then the second and third, and proceeding in order throughout until the end of the books. And underneath each number is marked a note in red, indicating in which of the ten canons the number occurs. (For example, if it is 1, it is clear that it is in the first canon; if 2, in the second; and so on as far as 10.) Hence, if you were to open any one of the four Gospels, and wish to light upon any chapter whatever, to know who else has said similar things and to find the relevant passages in each, in which they treated of the same things, then find the number marked against the passage which you have before

you, look for it in the canon which the note in red has suggested, and you will immediately learn from the headings at the start of the canon how many and which have said similar things. If you then find the numbers of the other Gospels which lie parallel with the number which you have before you in the canon, and look for them in the appropriate places of each Gospel, you will find those passages which say similar things.

No paraphrase or explanation could improve on the deviser's own words. His remarks about Ammonius, whose work is otherwise unattested, are carefully chosen and deserve to be believed; the term *Ammonian Sections,* which has conventionally been employed, does Eusebius a grave injustice, for the division of the Gospels into numbered sections is his idea.[121] As with *On the Place-Names in Holy Scripture,* Eusebius may have derived the idea from pagan scholarship,[122] but the result achieves true originality. The letter to Carpianus, the ten canons, and the system of numbered sections form a Gospel concordance whose usefulness is well illustrated by the success it enjoyed in later centuries, both in its original form and with slight modifications, not only in Greek but also in Latin, Syriac, and other translations.[123]

The concordance to the Gospels cannot be dated with any confidence. But it may belong to Eusebius' youth, for the canons boldly omitted the spurious last twelve verses of Mark;[124] later in life Eusebius was more disposed to accept the idea that nothing transmitted in the Gospels should be totally rejected.[125] More conventional, and more precisely datable, are two works which Eusebius composed toward 320: *Questions and Answers on the Genealogy of our Savior Addressed to Stephanus* and *Questions and Answers on the Resurrection of our Savior Addressed to Marinus,* of which there survive later epitomes in Greek and Syriac (the latter being in some places fuller than the former) and Greek fragments culled from catenae on the Gospels.[126] The form of the work was not new: Philo of Alexandria had composed *Questions and Answers* on both Genesis and Exodus (which in effect amount to commentaries on these books), and the Christians Tatian and Rhodon had written works with the title "Problems in Holy Scripture."[127] But Eusebius used the conventional form very selectively. The problems he discusses all concern the Incarnation and the Resurrection, and they are all of a nature to permit Eusebius to give a purely historical (and sometimes philological) solution.[128] Both series of *Questions and Answers* may well have been designed for instructional purposes in Caesarea.[129]

The four questions discussed in the extant epitome of the work addressed to Marinus give the flavor of the whole:[130]

1. How does the Savior appear after his Resurrection "late on the Sabbath" in Matthew, but "early on the first day of the week" in Mark?
2. How, when according to Matthew Mary of Magdala has seen

the Resurrection "late on the Sabbath," does the same woman according to John stand and weep by the tomb "on Sunday morning"?

3. How, when according to Matthew Mary of Magdala has touched the Savior's feet with the other Mary "late on the Sabbath," is the same woman told "on Sunday morning" according to John "Do not touch me"?

4. How in Matthew has Mary of Magdala with the other Mary seen from outside the tomb one angel sitting on the slab of the tomb, and how according to John does Mary of Magdala see two angels sitting inside the tomb, whereas according to Luke two men appeared to the women, and according to Mark a young man was there sitting on the right side of the tomb visible to Mary of Magdala, Mary the wife of James, and Salome?

In answering the questions, Eusebius draws freely on ideas and facts which he had developed or documented elsewhere. For example, the idea that life according to the gospel is identical with the life of the patriarchs in Genesis, an ideal existence from which the Mosaic Law was a deviation, is brought in to help explain why Matthew mentions Tamar,[131] and Eusebius solves the second of the questions proposed by Marinus by arguing that Matthew composed his Gospel in Hebrew, but that the Greek translation misrepresented the original.[132] He also employs philological criteria, removing contradictions by close attention to punctuation and considering carefully the exact meaning of the Greek phrase translated here as "late on the Sabbath." Moreover, at least on one level, he avoids dogmatism and propounds alternative solutions depending on whether the last twelve verses of Mark are spurious or genuine or on whether two evangelists speak of the same Mary or different ones.[133]

The basic assumptions, however, are essentially dogmatic and uncritical, and Eusebius tries most often to remove an apparent contradiction by accepting both sides but referring them to different persons or episodes. Thus he explicitly infers that there were two women called Mary of Magdala, in order to avoid any suspicion that the evangelists may have erred, and he accepts both Matthew and Luke on the infancy of Jesus: after Jesus was born, he was circumcised in the temple and taken to Nazareth (Luke), but two years later Joseph and Mary went to Bethlehem again, whence they fled to Egypt (Matthew).[134] The device of multiplying events or persons is not unintelligent (indeed it still has its devotees among modern historians of the ancient world),[135] and Eusebius will long continue to find imitators of his methods of removing the contradictions between Matthew and Luke.[136] Unfortunately for modern Christians, it now seems certain that King Herod, in whose reign Jesus was born according to Matthew (2:1–19), died some nine years before the census of A.D. 6 with which Luke synchronizes the Incarnation (2:1–7).[137] Eusebius, however, has an excuse which modern students of the New Testament lack: despite his honesty and his historical techniques, he was writing in an age when all accepted divine intervention in history and the divine inspiration of their own sacred documents.

Eusebius' standing as a biblical scholar received official recognition when he became the subject of a Christian emperor. The new city of Constantinople contained many churches which needed Bibles for use in divine service. Constantine, therefore, wrote to Eusebius requesting him to furnish fifty copies of the Bible, well written and easy to read. Funds for their production were provided by the *rationalis* of the diocese of Oriens, and arrangements were made for their transport by official channels.[138] Eusebius readily obeyed, sending expensively produced volumes to the emperor three or four at a time.[139]

This episode prompts two conjectures about Eusebius' influence on the form and content of the text of the Bible. It may be argued (albeit very speculatively) that Eusebius added chapter headings to the Gospels,[140] and that he played some role in establishing the "Byzantine" text of the Gospels, that is, the recension of the Gospels which in later centuries established itself as authoritative in the imperial capital.[141]

Most of the Greek manuscripts of the Gospels exhibit a division of the text into numbered chapters (68 in Matthew, 48 in Mark, 83 in Luke, and 18 in John), each of which has a title of the form "About the Marriage at Cana" (preceding John 2:1). The opening of each gospel is left unnumbered, presumably as being of an introductory nature, and a list of the titles often precedes the Gospel by way of summary.[142] The argument for ascribing these chapter divisions and chapter headings to Eusebius is circumstantial and twofold. First, Eusebius normally equipped his works both with headings to each chapter, either interspersed through the text or in the margin, and with an index preceding each book and comprising a list of these chapter headings.[143] What was more natural, therefore, than that Eusebius should provide each Gospel with index and chapter headings? Second, the distribution of the standard chapter divisions and titles in manuscripts of the Gospels suggests a link with Eusebius: they occur in many manuscripts of the Byzantine recension and in the Codex Alexandrinus (which was probably written in Constantinople) but are lacking in old and independent manuscripts like the Codex Bezae and Codex Sinaiticus.[144] Admittedly, a pre-Eusebian origin for the chapter divisions and titles has been argued,[145] but the known facts suggest that Eusebius himself may be the originator.

The influence of Eusebius on the actual text of the Old or New Testament is normally regarded as negligible. On the standard theory, the prevailing biblical text in Constantinople by about 380 was a recension produced by Lucian of Antioch and his school.[146] But the very existence of a "Lucianic recension" of either the Septuagint or the New Testament can be called into question.[147] On *a priori* grounds it seems improbable that, in Constantinople at least, within fifty years another type of text should totally have supplanted that supplied by

Eusebius. However, a distinction must be drawn. The hexaplaric text of the Septuagint never attained pre-eminence outside Palestine and Syria,[148] and Eusebius does not necessarily claim that he supplied copies of both Old and New Testaments. It could be that Eusebius' fifty Bibles contained the New Testament alone. The quotations in his extant works do not necessarily contradict this hypothesis,[149] and, in at least one passage (Matthew 13:35), he firmly rejects a reading which is normally classified as Caesarean.[150] If early and explicit evidence deserves preference over later generalization and modern inference, then Eusebius should not be denied an important role in the transmission of the text of the New Testament.

VIII

THE HISTORY OF THE CHURCH

Eusebius expounded his historical views most fully and most explicitly in the *Preparation for the Gospel* and the *Proof of the Gospel.* But these apologetical works, composed long after the first editions of the *Chronicle* and the *Ecclesiastical History,* merely defend, amplify, render more precise, and modify but slightly views which Eusebius had long espoused.[1] In the *Chronicle,* Eusebius saw no need to justify or explain his underlying interpretation of history. The *Ecclesiastical History* necessarily contains a brief exposition of it, since Eusebius wished to define his subject, and he could explain what the Christian church was only by stating, however briefly, its role in the divine scheme and in the history of mankind.[2]

Christianity, for Eusebius, was not a new religion but the primeval religion from which the traditional religions of mankind were mere offshoots or declensions. The Christ who was crucified in the reign of Tiberius was the Divine Word, the Son of God, the Wisdom of God, the Light of the world, the first and only-begotten Son of God. He was, in philosophical terms, the second cause and hence partner with God the Father in the creation of the universe and its inhabitants. Since the dawn of history, the human race has been divided into two classes. The righteous and reverent (who included Abraham and the Jewish patriarchs, Moses and the prophets) have always worshiped the Son of God, who has acted as a mediator between God and man, instructing the pious in the knowledge of his Father by the theophanies which the Old Testament records.

The majority of the ancients, however, neither worshiped the Son of God nor originally possessed the capacity to receive his teachings. Adam disobeyed God, forfeited a life of blessedness and delight, and was condemned to a mortal and accursed existence. Adam's immediate descendants filled the earth and, with few exceptions, lived no better than beasts: they had no care for political organization, for law and morality, or for intellectual activity, but lived as nomads. Their self-inflicted wickedness destroyed their natural reason, and they indulged in all types of unholiness, even preparing to go to war with their creator. God, therefore, chastised them with floods, fires, famines, plagues, and wars. Yet, when mankind was sunk in a drunken torpor of wickedness, the Word of God appeared to some of the ancient worshipers of God, who planted the seeds of godliness on earth and soon made a whole nation devoted to godliness. They were the ancient Hebrews, on whom God enjoined, through the prophet Moses, religious practices which were the images and symbols of a spiritual reality not yet clearly revealed. The laws of Moses became widely known and had a gradually civilizing effect throughout the world. Hence, when the Roman Empire came into existence, the whole world, including the gentiles, was ready to receive knowledge of the Father. The Word of God, therefore, appeared on earth as the savior of all mankind. His birth, life, miracles, teaching, death, and resurrection had all been predicted exactly by Moses and the prophets of the Old Testament, who even revealed, to those who could read the Bible aright, that the incarnate Word would be called Jesus Christ.

Christians are the worshipers of Jesus Christ, the Son and Word of God, who has given them heavenly life, not through images and symbols but in very truth. The Christian religion, therefore, Eusebius holds, is not novel or strange, even though the Christian church and teachings explicitly designated as Christian have existed for less than three centuries. Christianity acquired its name when Jesus appeared on earth and created an organization which rapidly became the most populous of all nations, sustained and succored by God's help to overcome all perils and tribulations. But the way of life and the religious beliefs manifested in Christianity are much older. Christianity is identical with the religion of the patriarchs, and the worshipers of God from Adam to Abraham were Christians in all but name. Eusebius draws a rigid distinction between the Hebrews (the original Christians) and the Jews, whose way of life derives from the laws of Moses. The ancient Hebrews, like the later Christians, exhibited the moral virtues and held the theological beliefs inherent in true religion, without needing Jewish customs such as circumcision, the Sabbath, and abstention from certain foods as external symbols of inner piety. Thus Christianity is the most ancient and most venerable of all religions: accepted of old by Abraham and the patriarchs, now proclaimed to all mankind through the teaching of Christ, Christianity is the original, the only, the true way to worship God.[3]

The *Ecclesiastical History* is the history of the Christian church from its foundation by the Son of God. Admittedly, the literary character of the work, with its normally flat style, its copious quotations and its heterogeneous subject matter, might seem to imply that Eusebius has collected the materials for a history, rather than composed a proper history in the ancient sense of the word.[4] But Eusebius himself regarded his work as a genuine history which would treat the Christian church as a nation whose history could be written on the same basis as the history of any city, country, or race.[5] Moreover, the Christian "race," because it has a principle of cohesion different from racial, linguistic, or cultural homogeneity, is not merely one race among many; it is the most numerous of all, and it stands in a special relationship to God.[6] Hence the *Ecclesiastical History* is a national history of a morally superior type, and Eusebius can contrast its edifying content with ordinary histories. Other historians record wars, victories, conquests, the prowess of generals, and the brave deeds of soldiers, all defiled by the blood of countless murders committed to defend children, fatherland, and material possessions. But the historian of the divine polity will engrave on everlasting monuments peaceful wars waged for the repose of the soul, the actions of men who showed bravery for the sake of religion and truth rather than for fatherland and family; he will preserve forever a record of the steadfastness, bravery, and endurance of the champions of piety, their victories over demons and unseen adversaries, and their glorious crowns of martyrdom.[7]

The *Ecclesiastical History*, however, is more than a novel kind of national history. It is inevitably also a literary or philosophical history which chronicles the writings and teachings of Christian thinkers and attempts, like some earlier works about philosophical schools, to establish the lines through which correct doctrines have been transmitted from the incarnate Word to Christians of the late third century. In addition, the *History* is a sequel to the *Chronicle,* supplying a full account where the chronological tables gave a bare summary or epitome.[8]

Eusebius originally wrote the *Ecclesiastical History* (it seems) before the end of the third century, and it originally comprised seven books.[9] The first two books chronicle the origins of the Christian church—its significance, its foundation, and its emergence as a historical entity before the outbreak of the Jewish war under Nero, which marked the permanent breach between Judaism and Christianity. Book Three treats of the Jewish war (66–73) and of the Christian church in the following generation, and it sums up the age of the apostles. Book Four tackles the largest span of years, from the reign of Trajan (98–117) to that of Marcus Aurelius (161–180), while Book Five advances only to the end of the second century; neither book has a single focal point and their narrative frequently becomes disconnected and discursive. Book Six, in contrast, is arranged around the figures of Origen and Dionysius, and proceeds from persecution in the reign of Septimius Severus (193–211) to the Decian persecution (250/1). The seventh book (the last of the original edition) symbolically ushers in the peaceful Sabbath of the Church: after a decade of harassment (250–260), persecution ceased and Eusebius could describe the state of Christianity during his own lifetime. In conformity with tradition, Eusebius remained silent about the deeds and achievements of living contemporaries, and he probably brought the *History* to a close with a brief statement of the names of the bishops who occupied the principal sees at the time of writing.[10]

The fabric of the *Ecclesiastical History* is woven from a number of quite disparate strands or themes. Eusebius recognized its composite nature and proclaimed it in the sentence which opens the work:

> The successions from the holy apostles, together with the periods of time which have elapsed from our Savior to ourselves; the important transactions reported in the history of the Church, and those who led and governed it with distinction in the most famous communities; those who in each generation were ambassadors of the divine word either by speech or by writings; the names, number, and dates of those who fell into utmost error through desire for innovation and proclaimed themselves introducers of *knowledge falsely so-called* (1 Timothy 6:20), ravaging *the flock* of Christ unsparingly like *grievous wolves* (Acts 20:29); in addition, the disasters which beset the whole nation of the Jews as a result of their plot against our Savior; the extent, nature, and dates of the wars waged by the heathen against the divine word, and the character of those who from time to time underwent the contest of blood and torture for its sake—these it is my intention to commit to writing.[11]

Six distinct subjects are here identified: the chronological framework of bishops and emperors; the internal history of the Church; Christian writers and teachers; the development of heresy; the fate of the Jews; and the persecution of Christians. There is a seventh main strand, duly acknowledged in a later passage, which reflects the author's training and interests: Eusebius provides what is in effect a history of the text and canon of the Bible in the early Church.[12]

Book One, as Eusebius himself conceded, falls outside the stated categories, even apart from its introductory theological material.[13] Its narrative chapters are devoted to the life of Jesus from birth to ascension into heaven, and they seem almost more concerned to argue than to narrate. While Eusebius describes the foundation of the Church by Jesus Christ during his lifetime on earth, he presents the evidence of the New Testament as confirmed by external testimony. He quotes Josephus several times, and Africanus at length, on the genealogies of Jesus according to Matthew and Luke.[14] Moreover, in its present form Book One concludes by quoting the correspondence between Jesus and King Abgar, translated from a Syriac document preserved in the public archives in Edessa—though the quotation of this recently produced document may not have occurred in the original edition.[15] Books Two to Seven, however, weave together the disparate strands of the *History* into a narrative which proceeds chronologically.

The chronological framework of the *Ecclesiastical History* is taken from the *Chronicle* and comprises two basic elements: the reigns of Roman emperors and the episcopates of the bishops of the main apostolic sees.[16] Both the *Chronicle* and the *History* provide apparently complete lists of the bishops of Rome, Alexandria, Antioch, and Jerusalem. But for the bishops of Jerusalem, even Eusebius lacked dates which he regarded as reliable, except in a few cases, and he twice states long lists of bishops without any indication of individual dates.[17] On the bishops of Antioch, the practices of the *Chronicle* and the *History* diverge: the *Chronicle* normally gives a precise date for the accession of each bishop, which Eusebius must often have computed from imprecise evidence; the *History* indicates only approximate dates and never the length of an episcopate.[18] It is the bishops of Rome and Alexandria alone, therefore, who provided the framework within which the *History* dates ecclesiastical events from the reign of Nero down to the late third century. But Eusebius consistently and explicitly correlates their episcopates with the reigns of Roman emperors. With each new bishop of Alexandria or Rome, he normally states the number of years the previous incumbent had served and the regnal year in which his successor took office.[19] Hence it was an easy matter for Eusebius to decide where to include items (historical or literary) which he could assign to the reign of a Roman emperor or to a bishop of Rome or Alexandria.

The internal life of the early Church was known to Eusebius almost exclusively from the letters, sermons, and other writings of bishops and teachers. In practice, therefore, he could not neatly separate the history of the Church as an organization from the history of Christian literature: throughout the *History* Christian writers appear both as literary figures and as witnesses to historical events. Eusebius adopts a broad definition of Christianity which allows him to claim Philo and Josephus, both Jews by race and religion, as virtual Christians and to use them as valuable evidence for the first century.

Philo, according to Eusebius, conversed with the apostle Peter in Rome and described, in his work *On the Contemplative Life,* the occupations, meetings, communal meals, and whole way of life of the early Christians. Eusebius can thus use what Philo reports about the Jewish Therapeutae to prove that the Christians of Philo's day lived a life similar to the more ascetic and philosophical Christians of the late third century. Eusebius deduces from Philo that the earliest Christians formed a large community concentrated in Alexandria but with members elsewhere. They renounced their property and led frugal and abstemious lives devoted to study of the Bible in special colonies: men and women living as celibates and celebrating the divine festivals.[20] On the strength of this description, Philo is enrolled as a quasi-Christian, and Eusebius lists nearly thirty of his works, which he presumably found in the library at Caesarea.[21]

Similarly Josephus, used frequently as an authority for the life of Jesus, for the earliest days of the Church, and for Jewish history, finally receives discussion as a literary figure in his own right, and his works are duly noted and described.[22] Christian writers receive exactly the same treatment. Much of Books Two to Four is based on Hegesippus, Justin, and Irenaeus; in each case, the writer is first adduced as evidence and quoted at length, then located in time, with an account of his career and writings.[23] If this is Eusebius' normal procedure, it follows that he probably had not read for himself the Christian writers he adduces as evidence but fails to note as authors in their own right.[24]

One writer whom Eusebius did not know at all well was particularly important for his presentation of Christianity as a phenomenon which achieved both immediate and permanent importance in the Roman Empire. He is Tertullian, who wrote in Carthage under Septimius Severus and Caracalla; of his numerous writings, Eusebius had read only one, the *Apologeticum,* and that in a Greek translation of dubious accuracy.[25] Nowhere in the *History* does Tertullian receive proper discussion as a Christian writer. Eusebius was clearly unable to list Tertullian's works or to give an account of his career, and he mistakenly thought that Tertullian delivered his *Apologeticum* before the Senate in Rome.[26]

Tertullian is cited in five significant passages, three times as Eusebius' sole authority, once each in the company of Hegesippus and Apollinarius. Eusebius repeats Tertullian's story that the emperor Tiberius, on receiving a report from Pontius Pilate, proposed to enroll Jesus among the gods of the Roman pantheon, and that when the Senate demurred, the emperor gave Christians legal protection. Eusebius infers that the gospel rapidly became known in every corner of the Roman world: as early as the middle of the first century, churches existed in almost every city and village, filled with converts from the superstitions of their ancestors.[27] Tertullian is next adduced three times to show that only the emperors who suffered *damnatio memoriae,* like Nero and Domitian, instituted general persecutions of the Christians; Trajan stopped general persecution, though not entirely protecting Christians from their enemies.[28] Eusebius appeals to Tertullian for the fifth and last time in order to establish that Marcus Aurelius Caesar recognized that the prayers of Christians had secured rain when his army was dying of thirst, and that he threatened to punish with death all who harassed or accused the Christians.[29]

Philo and Tertullian have an importance out of proportion to the space Eusebius allots them; the historical assertions which he bases on their testimony document the static picture of Christianity to which his overall interpretation of history predisposed him. Christianity, though an ancient and venerable religion, was revealed in its full glory only when the Son of God became man. The Incarnation thus became the nodal point of all human history.[30] But was it credible that the final revelation of God's majesty within history should have little or no immediate effect? Eusebius welcomed evidence that the contemporaries of Jesus recognized his significance, that the Christian church had always been as numerous, respectable, and prosperous as it was in his own life-time. Hence he eagerly interpreted ambiguous or insufficient evidence as proof that Christianity permeated the higher echelons of Roman society at an early date. Domitian exiled his cousin Flavius Clemens and his niece Flavia Domi-tilla, the wife of Clemens, on a charge which the earliest available evidence re-ports as "atheism and Jewish customs": Eusebius, appealing in the *Chronicle* to a senator's account of the victims of Domitian, construes Domitilla's alleged crime as Christianity.[31] Similarly, the *History* generalizes from the case of Apollonius, and asserts that in the reign of Commodus, the divine Word was leading every soul from every race to the worship of God, so that many of the richest and most prominent inhabitants of Rome sought salvation with their whole family and household.[32] The modern concept of "the mission and ex-pansion of Christianity" was alien to Eusebius: for him the apostles and their immediate followers had spread the gospel everywhere;[33] the history of the Church was not primarily a story of gradual expansion in either a geographical or a social sense.

Eusebius was equally hampered, in discussing Christian writers and teach-ers, by his inability to contemplate theological development. For Eusebius there could be no improvement on the truths revealed imperfectly in the Old Testament and fully in the New. Hence his account of the internal history of the Church and of Christian literature is less a coherent narrative than a series of disconnected notes. Eusebius summarizes the Acts of the Apostles (with an-notation from other sources); and duly chronicles the subsequent fates of the protagonists in Acts: the stoning of James, the brother of the Lord, in Jerusa-lem; the martyrdoms of Peter and Paul in Rome under Nero; the exile of John to Patmos, his restoration by Nerva, and his death in Ephesus; and the death of Philip, who left four virgin daughters to prophesy at Hierapolis.[34] The tradi-tions of the apostles (Eusebius notes) were perpetuated by Polycarp of Smyrna and Clement of Rome, of whom the martyred Ignatius of Antioch and Papias of Hierapolis were contemporaries.[35] But after Book Three of the *Ecclesiastical History* the idea of an apostolic succession fades away, and Books Four and Five lack a unifying principle or any intrinsic pattern other than mere chronol-ogy. Hence the second half of Book Four, which professes to cover the first six-teen years of the reign of Marcus Aurelius, has the following succession of main items juxtaposed:

15. The martyrdom of Polycarp, paraphrased and quoted at length, with a summary of other *acta martyrum* preserved in the same document.
16. The martyrdom of Justin.
17. A description of the trial of Christians by the *praefectus urbi,* quoted from Justin.
18. Justin's writings.
19–20. The bishops of Rome, Alexandria, and Antioch.

21. Names of writers of this period.
22. Hegesippus.
23. Dionysius of Corinth.
24. Theophilus of Antioch.
25. Other writers against Marcion.
26. Melito of Sardis.
27. Apollinarius of Hierapolis.
28. Musanus.
29. Tatian and the Encratites.
30. Bardesanes of Edessa.

Parts of Books Five, Six, and Seven are equally disjointed: only an episode like the controversy over the date of Easter when Victor was bishop of Rome (about 189–199) or the long career of Origen enabled Eusebius to approach a connected narrative when presenting the history of the Church and Christian writers and teachers.[36]

The treatment of heresy has a greater unity: here Eusebius wished to argue a thesis, or at least to present an interpretation, and to do so he needed to arrange the material in a logical manner. In the late second century, Irenaeus had argued that the various Gnostic sects were all secondary accretions to an original and authentic Christianity which the apostolic succession of bishops preserved in its purest form.[37] Eusebius endorsed this view by echoing the title of Irenaeus' *Refutation of Knowledge Falsely So-Called* (itself an allusion to 1 Timothy 6:20) in the first sentence of his work.[38] Irenaeus' argument was not entirely original. Two earlier writers, both quoted by Eusebius, had attempted to identify the precise origin of heresy. Toward 150, Hegesippus published five *Memoirs,* which seem to have combined defense of Christianity, philosophical argument against heresy, and disquisitions on the early fortunes of the churches of Jerusalem, Rome, and Corinth.[39] In Hegesippus' view, no "vain teachings" defiled the Church until Symeon was chosen to succeed James, the brother of Jesus, as bishop of Jerusalem. Then Thebuthis, disappointed at not becoming bishop himself, began to corrupt the truth by introducing the teachings of Jewish sects, from which came Simon, Dositheus, and other heretics, from whom in turn the prominent heresies of the second century derived.[40] For Justin, however, the arch-heretic was Simon, a magician from Samaria who, unmasked as a fraud in Judaea, came to Rome, performed miracles, and was worshiped as a god.[41] It is Justin's view of the origin of heresy which Irenaeus and Eusebius accept.

Eusebius describes the career of Simon under the reign of Claudius (41–54) in the middle of Book Two, carefully segregating Simon from the later heretics who followed the Apostolic Age. Menander, the first of these, was a Samaritan like Simon, and no less a magician than his master.[42] To Menander are subjoined the Ebionites, a sect which observed the Jewish law and denied that Jesus was God or that he existed before Mary conceived, the Chiliastic

Cerinthus, and the Nicolaitans, to whom the Apocalypse refers (Revelation 2:6).[43] According to Eusebius, the great efflorescence of heresy occurred after the Jews rebelled against Hadrian, when the Devil, no longer able to attack the successful Church through persecution, sent cheats and deceivers to lead men away from salvation. Menander taught the heretics Saturninus of Antioch and Basilides of Alexandria, who regarded apostasy as a matter of indifference. Their contemporary was Carpocrates, who first explicitly laid claim to a secret knowledge, or *gnosis,* which enabled him to secure salvation by magic. Hence pagans believed ill of all Christians, and new forms of heresy were incessantly devised until the ever-increasing "splendor of the one, true, worldwide Church" silenced slander by its obvious modesty and purity. From the middle of the second century onward, Eusebius asserts, Christianity was universally recognized as a sober and respectable philosophy against which no one dared to revive the ancient calumnies.[44]

The heretics Valentinus and Cerdon were well known in Rome early in the reign of Antoninus (139–161). Cerdon, whom Eusebius presents as the predecessor of Marcion and as the true founder of Marcion's system, took his material from the followers of Simon, while Valentinus and his associate Marcus were "past masters in the art of magic trickery".[45] During the reign of Marcus Aurelius (161–180) are noted the Encratites, a rigorist sect founded by Justin's pupil Tatian and later revived by one Severus, who rejected Acts and the Pauline epistles.[46] But the fullest accounts of heresy occur in Book Five, where Eusebius spends seven consecutive chapters on Montanism and a heresy in Rome; these chapters are among the most successful in the whole work.[47]

The origins of Montanism are documented principally from two contemporary sources, each of whom Eusebius quotes at length. The first is an anonymous treatise addressed to Abercius Marcellus, which describes how Montanus began to prophesy in Phrygia, apparently about 170, and gathered a following which included ecstatic female prophets.[48] Eusebius also quotes and summarizes an attack on the Phrygian heresy by Apollonius, and he notes that Apollinarius of Hierapolis and Serapion of Antioch wrote letters denouncing the New Prophecy of Montanus, to which many other bishops subscribed.[49] At the same period, two men against whom Irenaeus wrote were active in Rome: the schismatic Blastus, and the heretic Florinus, who denied that God created evil.[50]

Book Five closes with yet another heresy: that of Artemon (or Artemas), the teacher of Paul of Samosata.[51] Eusebius quotes from a work whose author and title he does not name (and presumably, therefore, did not know): Theodoretus reports that it was entitled *The Little Labyrinth,* and the quotations reveal that it was written in Rome, apparently while Zephyrinus (about 199–217) was bishop.[52] The extracts which the *History* quotes do not mention Artemon but assail Theodotus, a shoemaker whom Victor, the previous bishop of Rome, had excommunicated: Theodotus' pupils studied Euclid, admired Aristotle and Theophrastus, and venerated Galen.[53] Eusebius (it appears) is guilty of a strange confusion: Artemon was still alive when Paul of Samosata was deposed, and the area of his activity must have been the East.[54]

Book Six of the *History* chronicles four heresies, more for their relevance to Origen and Dionysius of Alexandria than for their intrinsic interest. Beryllus of Bostra denied that the Son was a divine person separate from the Father or that he existed before the Incarnation. A council of bishops was convened, and Origen persuaded Beryllus to abandon his unorthodox views.[55] Similarly, when some in Arabia asserted that the soul dies with the body but will come to life again with the body at the resurrection, Origen changed their opinions at another synod.[56] Origen also (Eusebius erroneously asserts) quenched the heresy of the Elchasaites when it suddenly arose in the reign of Philip (244–249).[57]

The Novatianist schism is also classified as a heresy. In 251, after the Decian persecution, Novatus in Carthage and Novatian in Rome advocated harsher treatment for apostates than their bishops judged prudent. The two dissident priests joined forces, a synod met in Rome, and letters were exchanged with bishops in the East, among them Fabius of Antioch and Dionysius of Alexandria.[58] It was from the letters of Dionysius (especially those on baptism) and from letters preserved at Antioch that Eusebius derived his knowledge of this western schism; his account unfortunately conflates Novatus with Novatian and thus unduly simplifies the complex story.[59] It is Dionysius too who provides the only two references to Sabellianism; the *History* passes over Sabellius himself in silence, though it quotes a passage of Dionysius which shows that Sabellians were active shortly after 250 at Ptolemais in Libya, and it records that Dionysius composed letters and treatises against Sabellius.[60] Eusebius' silence about Sabellius probably indicates mere ignorance: although he refers to a work of Hippolytus entitled *Against All the Heresies,* he betrays no awareness of the fact that Callistus, bishop from about 217 to 222, expelled Sabellius from the church of Rome as a heretic.[61] Now Sabellius deviated from orthodoxy because he stressed the identity of God the Father with God the Son and argued that the two descriptions applied merely to different aspects of a single divine being.[62] Had Eusebius written the *Ecclesiastical History* twenty years later, Sabellianism would have had a sharp, contemporary relevance.[63]

One of Eusebius' stated themes was a demonstration of how political disasters afflicted the Jews as a direct result of their treatment of Jesus.[64] The theme is foreshadowed in Book One, where Eusebius presents the death of Herod (in 4 B.C.) as a divine punishment for his slaughter of innocent infants at Bethlehem (Matthew 2:6).[65] It receives full illustration in Books Two and Three, with two postscripts in Book Four.

The misfortunes of the Jews began immediately after the Crucifixion: Eusebius quotes Philo and Josephus on the policy of Caligula (37–41), which he interprets as God's vengeance for their protestation before Pilate that they had no king but Caesar (John 19:15).[66] From the reign of Claudius (41–54) riots, wars, and internecine strife never ceased in Judaea until a Roman army captured Jerusalem.[67] Eusebius adduces Josephus to show that the death of Herod

Agrippa in 44 was a consequence of his execution of James, the brother of John (Acts 12:2), and more important, that even some Jews admitted that the stoning of James, the brother of Jesus, was a cause of the siege of Jerusalem.[68] Divine punishment visited Jerusalem and the rest of Judaea when the Christian church of Jerusalem deserted it and moved to Pella beyond the Jordan.[69] Then came the utter disaster foretold both by prophets and by Jesus himself (Luke 19:42–44; 21:20–24).[70] Thousands of Jews were slaughtered, and Judaea was laid waste. Eusebius quotes Josephus' description of the famine inside the besieged Jerusalem, and adds that it was "the reward of the Jews for their wickedness and impiety towards the Christ of God."[71]

Nor was that all: another disaster followed in the reign of Trajan. The Jews of Egypt and Cyrene rebelled and were suppressed with much loss of life, whereupon Trajan ordered Lusius Quietus to clear his new province of Mesopotamia of Jews and then appointed him governor of Judaea.[72] The final humiliation of the Jews occurred under Hadrian: after a revolt led by Bar Kochba, so Eusebius asserts, the emperor refounded Jerusalem as a gentile city and prohibited any Jew from setting foot in the city or even in its surrounding territory.[73] The prohibition still stood in Eusebius' day, and his apologetical works repeatedly use it as proof that Judaism is a historical failure.[74]

For Eusebius success was a mark of truth, and his treatment of persecution reflects this belief—which was to receive emphatic validation from the persecution in his own day.[75] Eusebius does not present the early Church as a hated and persecuted minority gradually attaining security and respectability. For him the Christian church normally enjoyed respect and toleration, even in its earliest days.[76] For him it was persecution, not (as for moderns) the triumph of Christianity, which represented an aberration from the predictable course of history and thus required an explanation. Hence he presented persecution as a rare and unusual phenomenon which reflected not any underlying hostility by an established order toward a potentially subversive religion but the machinations of the devil, the moral depravity of a Roman emperor, or the envy of despicable individuals.

Persecution, Eusebius argues, began with the Jews: although God allowed them forty years to repent of killing Jesus, they persevered in hatred of the divine Word and persecuted the apostles.[77] The first Roman emperor who persecuted the Christians was Nero, whose total depravity needed no demonstration.[78] Next, Domitian, after killing many others, began to exile and to execute Christians. Further, so Eusebius reports from Hegesippus, he ordered that all Jews of the family of David were to be executed; but when the grandsons of Jude, the brother of Jesus, were brought before him, he saw that they were poor peasants and set them free, also putting an end to further persecution. After Domitian was killed and the Senate annulled his acts, the apostle John returned from exile to Ephesus.[79] Persecution, however, was not confined to the reigns of bad emperors. Under Trajan, popular pressure led to deaths in some cities. Symeon, the son of Clopas, bishop of Jerusalem for forty years, was executed by the governor of Palestine; Symeon's enemies alleged that, besides being a Christian, he was of the house and lineage of David.[80] Elsewhere, Pliny executed martyrs and consulted the emperor. Trajan's rescript prevented what Eusebius calls "open persecutions," but "partial persecutions in particular provinces" continued, since Trajan still allowed governors and private citizens "pretexts" to do Christians evil.[81]

From Trajan onward, Eusebius attempts to trace each emperor's attitude toward Christianity. The apologists Quadratus and Aristides addressed defenses of the faith to Hadrian, who issued a rescript to a proconsul of Asia preventing Christians from being tried "without a charge and reasonable accusation."[82] Antoninus too protected the Christians in a letter to the provincial council of Asia.[83] In the joint reign of Marcus Aurelius and Lucius Verus there were martyrs: at Smyrna, Polycarp and, at about the same date (so Eusebius categorically asserts), Pionius; in Pergamum, Carpus, Papylus, and Agathonice; in Rome, Justin, whom the Cynic philosopher Crescens denounced, and other martyrs, whom Justin himself records.[84] Melito of Sardis is subsequently quoted to document contemporary persecution in Asia—and the essential harmony of Christianity and the Roman Empire.[85] The peak of persecution occurred after Eleutherus became bishop of Rome in the seventeenth year of Marcus Aurelius; lengthy extracts are quoted from a letter of the churches of Vienne and Lugdunum describing a pogrom in the latter city. Eusebius gives the episode both emphasis and prominence: it begins Book Five of the *History* and leads him to reflect on the nature of Christian historiography.[86]

At this point in the *Ecclesiastical History* a strange confusion intrudes. The emperor who sanctioned the execution of Christians at Lugdunum is named as "Antoninus Verus," while the contemporaneous emperor who had Christians in his army and protected the faith is identified as "Marcus Aurelius Caesar," the brother of "Antoninus," that is, as the emperor conventionally known as Lucius Verus.[87] What can be the explanation of this bizarre confusion? To suspect deliberate falsification of history for political ends is uncharitable.[88] Eusebius is probably attempting to remove a contradiction in his evidence by adopting the hypotheses that Marcus and Lucius, though they ruled conjointly, pursued different policies toward the Christians.[89] If the letter of the Gallic churches showed that Marcus considered Christianity a capital crime, then (Eusebius must have reasoned), the attested protector of Christians must be his brother Lucius. Eusebius' reasoning is fallacious and anachronistic: Lucius was not the Caesar of Marcus in the Diocletianic sense, nor did he pursue policies divergent from those of Marcus.[90] Eusebius was the prisoner of assumptions which predisposed him to credit the tendentious claim of two Christian writers (Apollinarius and Tertullian) that a Roman emperor called Marcus Aurelius protected Christianity. To disallow such evidence completely was psychologically impossible for Eusebius.

With the reign of Commodus (180–192) came peace, even though Apollonius was martyred at Rome after trial by the praetorian prefect.[91] But Septimius Severus, according to Eusebius, stirred up a persecution which raged with particular intensity in Egypt.[92] Eusebius makes no comment on the religious policies of Caracalla, Macrinus, and Elagabalus. But with Severus Alexander (222–235) and succeeding emperors he correlates alternations in religious policy with the presence or absence of Christians at the imperial court. When Julia Mamaea was at Antioch, she summoned Origen to her presence.[93] When Maximinus replaced Alexander, he reacted against the Christian sympathies of Alexander's régime and ordered the execution of bishops.[94] Philip, who came to the throne in 244, is presented as a Christian, and his successor, Decius, was moved to persecute the Church by his enmity toward the emperor he supplanted.[95]

For the decade of intermittent persecution between 250 and 260 Eusebius had the detailed and explicit testimony of Dionysius of Alexandria, around whose writings he structures his account. In Alexandria, anti-Christian riots preceded the official persecution—and Eusebius unfortunately allows Dionysius' vivid description of this local happening to displace any account of Decius' edict of winter 249/250 or its enforcement.[96] Decius died in 251; his successor, Trebonianus Gallus, prospered until he drove away the holy men who prayed for his welfare.[97] Eusebius' account of persecution by Valerian is also based on Dionysius, and the *History* again devotes more space to the adventures of Dionysius than to imperial policy. At the start of his reign, the emperor showed greater sympathy to the Christians than even Philip had done. Later, however, he fell under the influence of the evil Macrianus, "the teacher and ruler of the synagogue of the Egyptian magicians," and commenced persecution.[98] When Valerian was captured by the Persians (in 260), Gallienus reversed imperial policy: he granted the Christians toleration and restored the churches and cemeteries which the imperial treasury had recently confiscated. After the accession of Gallienus, sporadic executions of Christians occurred (Christianity remained technically a capital crime), but the Christian church began to enjoy toleration everywhere.[99]

Within the Christian church the Bible has a special status. The *Ecclesiastical History* repeatedly draws attention to the opinions early Christian writers held about what should be considered authoritative holy Scripture and about the circumstances under which the books of the New Testament were written. On the Old Testament Eusebius is brief and dogmatic. The Jews of Palestine adopted a canon of inspired books identical with the modern Old Testament: they numbered twenty-two or twenty-four in different computations, and comprised the Law, the Prophets (including the historical books), and the other "Writings."[100] But the Jews of the Diaspora had a Bible which also included the Apocrypha. Many Christian communities clearly put the apocryphal books, most of which are of Hellenistic origin, on almost the same level as the Law and the Prophets; indeed, it is Christian manuscripts which have preserved the apocryphal books in full from antiquity to modern times.[101] Eusebius discusses the canon of the Old Testament three times and quotes Josephus, Melito, and Origen in support of the canon of twenty-two or twenty-four books.[102]

The canon of the New Testament was more problematical, but Eusebius states his own views with admirable candor. There was no doubt about the Gospels, Acts, the Epistles of Paul, 1 John, and 1 Peter; with them Eusebius also felt obliged to class Revelation, despite his own doubts. All of these books everyone acknowledged without dispute. The disputed books comprise five epistles, namely, James, Jude, 2 Peter, 2 John, and 3 John. But Eusebius classes as spurious, rather than disputed, the Acts of Paul, the Shepherd of Hermas, the Revelation of Peter, the Epistle of Barnabas, the Teachings of the Apostles, and probably the Gospel of the Hebrews. Yet these works contain genuine edification and must be distinguished from base forgeries concocted by heretics, such as the gospels of Peter, Thomas, and Matthias or the acts of Andrew, John, and other apostles.[103] Eusebius does not rigorously distinguish between the characteristics of the second and third categories:[104] though denying that the apostle Peter wrote 2 Peter, [105] he still classifies this letter as disputed, not spurious, as strict logic appears to demand. Eusebius implied that the seven "Catholic Epistles" formed a collection which circulated together, and it may be inferred that the much stronger evidence for apostolic authorship of 1 John and 1 Peter ultimately persuaded the Church to admit the other five to the canon.[106] Eusebius discusses most of the spurious writings and the forgeries in a brusque fashion, merely repudiating their claims to higher status.[107] Sometimes, however, he records favorable opinions from earlier writers: both Papias and Hegesippus quoted the Gospel of the Hebrews, while Clement of Alexandria, in his *Hypotyposeis,* commented on the Epistle of Barnabas and the Revelation of Peter with the rest of the New Testament.[108]

The apostolic origins of the undisputed books receive much fuller documentation and discussion. Eusebius' earliest authority is Papias, bishop of Hierapolis, who wrote five books expounding "the sayings of the Lord," early in the second century.[109] Eusebius also appeals to Irenaeus to establish the authority of Papias, and he notes the views of Clement and Origen.[110] Eusebius presents Matthew as the earliest of the four Gospels, John as the latest.[111] Matthew originally wrote his Gospel in Hebrew for Jewish Christians before he began to preach to gentiles, and the missionary Pantaenus found it still circulating in its original language in India in about 200.[112] Mark was a follower of Peter and wrote his Gospel to preserve Peter's preaching; Eusebius dates its composition to the reign of Claudius, before Mark founded the church of Alexandria—though he later quotes Irenaeus' clear statement that Mark wrote after Peter died.[113] Luke, a doctor from Antioch and the companion of Paul, wrote his Gospel from Paul's preaching and closed the narrative of Acts at the point where he parted from Paul.[114] John's Gospel, composed in Ephesus, is less historical and more philosophical than the other three; the context of Eusebius' discussion implies that he dates the composition of John's Gospel to the reign of Trajan.[115]

Eusebius accepted fourteen Pauline epistles as written wholly by Paul, including the Epistle to the Hebrews.[116] He knew that some rejected Hebrews as written by another, but he found their arguments invalid. The skeptics, including Origen, correctly held that its composition and style was not Pauline.[117] Eusebius believed that Paul wrote the letter in Hebrew and that it was translated into Greek by someone else—either Luke or, more probably, Clement of Rome, with whose letter to the church of Corinth it has obvious affinities.[118] Eusebius states summarily that the letters 1 Peter and 1 John are universally acknowledged as the work of their ostensible authors,[119] but he questions the credentials of Revelation, even though he knew of no early writer who denied Johannine authorship.[120] Irenaeus dated Revelation to the end of the reign of Domitian; Eusebius twice quotes the relevant passage, and he concedes that Justin and Origen both ascribe it to John.[121] Yet he appeals to Papias for proof that there were two Johns, the apostle who wrote the Gospel, and a younger, far less authoritative John who wrote Revelation. The idea that a different John wrote Revelation derived from Dionysius of Alexandria, whose arguments against the traditional attribution to the apostle Eusebius quotes at some length.[122] The cause of Eusebius' unease can readily be diagnosed. Revelation breathes an atmosphere of persecution, with an oppressed minority in a hostile world hoping for a glorious vindication in heaven; Eusebius believed that God intended his Church to prosper on earth.[123]

No survey or summary can adequately convey what a wealth of detail the *Ecclesiastical History* contains. Eusebius did not apply strict criteria of relevance, and his quotations illustrating one topic often preserve extremely valuable information about others, not always within even his purview. The letter of the Gallic Christians in Book Five, for example, provides important evidence for all aspects of life in Roman Lugdunum.[124] Similarly, the correspondence of Dionysius of Corinth and of Alexander of Jerusalem casts a vivid light on ecclesiastical politics in the early third century,[125] while the letters of Dionysius illuminate conditions in Alexandria some decades later.[126] Hence the *Ecclesiastical History* will always be an indispensable quarry for historians of early Christianity and of the Roman Empire. But it is also itself a work of history which reflects the interests and the limitations of its author. Eusebius had no predecessors in attempting to write the history of the Church. In describing his undertaking, he uses images which emphasize his loneliness and perplexity: he set out on a lonely and untrodden path with only a few distant beacons to light the way. He also employs a metaphor which implicitly avows the imposition of an interpretative structure: to compose a narrative of events before his own lifetime, he culled suitable flowers from the meadows of Christian literature.[127]

A close inspection of the text and a comparison of the *History* with the documents and writers employed as sources immediately discloses several grave deficiencies. When Eusebius paraphrases, he feels free to rewrite, to omit or to expand passages, to alter the emphases of the original, and he often misreports, just as if he had composed his paraphrase from memory. When he quotes extant writers directly, Eusebius often truncates his source, beginning or ending a quotation in the middle of a sentence. As a result, he sometimes misrepresents his authority or renders the mutilated sentence unintelligible. Sometimes too, Eusebius leaves out a section in the middle of an extract, with consequent alteration of its overall meaning. It must be inferred that the quotations of lost documents and lost writers have undergone similar alterations. The quotations, moreover, are often preceded by introductions or paraphrases which partially contradict or are contradicted by their contents. It seems probable, therefore, that Eusebius trusted a scribe or assistant to insert the quotations and neglected to remove the inconsistencies which he introduced.[128] In any event, it is unwise to rely on Eusebius' reports as reproducing exactly the precise tenor, or even main purport, of lost evidence.

That Eusebius sometimes used forged documents, that he could not detect Christian interpolations in Josephus, that he evinced bias towards heretics and persecutors, that he sometimes contradicted himself, that he tamely believed miracles which a less credulous age rejects will occasion no surprise.[129] A danger exists, however, that the evident care and honesty of his scholarship may be assumed to guarantee the accuracy of his results.[130] It is requisite, therefore, to ask how far Eusebius' interpretation of early Christian history corresponds with reality.

The first historian of the early Church was confronted with a mass of letters, sermons, and documents of many types, which he needed to arrange in chronological order. How did Eusebius proceed? Clearly, he first looked for passages referring to emperors or bishops whose dates the *Chronicle* tabulated. Failing that, he sought vaguer synchronisms, or even similarities of content. In every case, error could arise through faulty reasoning or simple oversight. Eusebius knew a dialogue by one Maximus entitled *On Matter,* whose subject he describes as "on the origin of evil and that matter had a beginning." He dated the dialogue to the reign of Septimius Severus.[131] But it seems probable that Maximus' work is in fact the extant dialogue conventionally entitled *On Right Belief in God* and ascribed to an unknown "Adamantius," and that Maximus wrote it not long after the death of Origen.[132] Similarly, Eusebius assigned Bardesanes to the reign of Marcus Aurelius, even though Bardesanes was born in 154 and died in 222/3.[133] The cause of his error is evident. Bardesanes composed a dialogue *On Fate* addressed to an Antoninus.[134] Eusebius simply made a mistaken identification of the addressee.[135]

Sometimes Eusebius' reasoning can be seen to reflect his general interpretation. He regarded the reign of Antoninus (137–161) as a time of peace for the Church but the succeeding reign of Marcus Aurelius (161–180) as a period of persecution. Hence he assigns the martyrdoms of Ptolemaeus and Lucius to the latter reign.[136] Since Justin is his only source, the guess was plausible. But the date is wrong: the *praefectus urbi* who executed the martyrs probably entered office in 146 and died in 160.[137] Eusebius also assigns to the reign of Marcus three groups of martyrs whose deaths were described in a single document which Eusebius had included in his *Collection of Ancient Martyrdoms*.[138] Presumably the date derives from Eusebius' belief that the persecutions which "threw Asia into turmoil" belonged exclusively to Marcus' reign.[139] Although that date might be correct for the third group of martyrs (Carpus, Papylus, and Agathonice), it is demonstrably wrong for the first two. An appendix to the *Martyrdom of Polycarp* names the proconsul who executed Polycarp as Statius Quadratus.[140] It is hard to deny that this proconsul is identical with the Athenian L. Statius Quadratus, ordinary consul in 142, whose proconsulate of Asia should fall around 156/7.[141] On Pionius the error is grosser, for the extant *Passion of Pionius* refers to the emperor Gordian (238–244), carries the consular date of 250, and manifestly reflects the circumstances of the Decian persecution.[142]

Eusebius was limited by more than his inability to date and evaluate all his evidence correctly. He projected the Church of the late third century back into the first two centuries and assumed that Christian churches had always been numerous, prosperous, and respectable. He thus could not perceive or document one of the crucial transitions in early Christianity. In 180 the Christians were an obscure sect, widely believed to enjoy "Oedipodean incests and Thyestean banquets."[143] Within a generation, however, there were Christians or Christian sympathizers at the imperial court and in the Roman Senate: an apologist could soberly inform a proconsul of Africa that if the proconsul wished to rid his province of Christians, he would need to decimate his own staff and social circle, and a governor of Arabia could ask the prefect of Egypt to send him a Christian teacher for an interview.[144] It is by no means easy to discover when a majority of the population of the Roman Empire (or any area within it) became Christian. The more significant stage in the transformation of Roman society occurred when figures like Tertullian in Africa, Clement and Origen in Alexandria, and, a little later, Cyprian in Carthage demonstrated the moral, social and intellectual respectability of their religion.[145] Eusebius' picture of the Church before 200 is fundamentally anachronistic.

The *Ecclesiastical History* can be compared not only with the writings which it quotes but with writers whom Eusebius had not read. Eusebius knew the writers of Egypt, Syria, and Asia Minor well, but Christians who wrote in Greek in Greece or Italy were less familiar to him. He shows no awareness, for example, of Athenagoras, who composed an apology for delivery to Marcus Aurelius and Commodus, apparently when they visited Athens in 176.[146] Of Latin writers Eusebius knew virtually nothing: of Tertullian's voluminous output he had read only the *Apologeticum* in a Greek translation; of Cyprian, only letters to be found in Antioch; of Minucius Felix and Novatian, nothing at all.[147] As for the history of the Church in the West, Eusebius reports events in Rome itself with relative frequency. For Italy and the western provinces, however, his information was meager: he could glean something from the New Testament; he had read Irenaeus; he possessed a dossier of letters and other documents sent from Gaul to Phrygia in the late second century[148]—and practically nothing else.

The earliest Christian writings in Latin, therefore, should not be interpreted (as has traditionally been the practice) within a Eusebian historical framework. They should be allowed to speak for themselves in their own authentic tones. Tertullian directed his *Apologeticum* and *Ad Scapulam* to magistrates in Carthage, not to Roman emperors; he chose these addressees because in the late second and early third centuries the attitude of provincial governors affected most Christians far more immediately and far more directly than the attitude of the emperor. Eusebius was unaware of this basic fact about the persecution of the Christians in the Roman Empire.

The polemics of Tertullian bring Severan Carthage to life. In a city where the annual arrival of a new proconsul could portend persecution, and where popular riots and attacks against Christians were not uncommon, the Church seethed with incessant controversy. Tertullian behaved like a contemporary sophist and derided heresy with as much vigor as he attacked paganism. Into this charged atmosphere there suddenly arrived the New Prophecy of Montanus, which found an initial welcome in the Carthaginian church. Tertullian accepted Montanus and his closest associates as genuinely inspired mouthpieces of the Holy Spirit and became the advocate of the New Prophecy, voluble and ever more hysterical as the church of Carthage repudiated Montanus' ideas.[149]

Minucius Felix documents the spread of Christianity in Africa outside Carthage: the protagonists of his *Octavius* are members of the local aristocracy of Cirta, and the dialogue (probably written about 240) presupposes that they died as Christians.[150] And the treatises and correspondence of Cyprian, bishop of Carthage from about 248 to 258, when he was martyred, document every aspect of the life of the Church in Africa in the middle of the third century.[151] Eusebius might have been surprised to discover that there were probably martyrs in Africa in the reigns of Roman emperors whom he regarded as protectors and champions of Christianity.[152] He sometimes gives his general statements about Christianity a universal application which the Latin evidence contradicts.

From 260 the *Ecclesiastical History* ceases to be merely a record of the past compiled from written sources—though it continues to use and to quote the letters and other writings of Dionysius of Alexandria, as it had earlier. Eusebius now writes about his own lifetime and begins to draw on his own experience and conversation with older contemporaries. Eusebius knew of three men of Caesarea who became martyrs in the persecution by Valerian, and of a woman martyr who was a Marcionite.[153] After Gallienus rescinded his father's legislation, Christianity remained technically a capital crime, as it had been before Decius. At Caesarea, not long after 260, the soldier Marinus was about to receive the staff signifying his promotion to the rank of centurion. A rival suddenly claimed the vacant post, alleging that Marinus was legally debarred from promotion because he was a Christian who did not sacrifice to the emperors. The governor, Achaeus, questioned Marinus and, when he discovered that Marinus was a Christian, gave him three hours to reconsider. As Marinus left the court, the bishop Theotecnus led him into his church and stressed the nature of the choice which confronted him: a soldier's sword or the divine Gospels. Marinus chose God, affirmed his choice in court, and was beheaded. Astyrius, a Roman senator acquainted with emperors, witnessed the execution, recovered Marinus' body, and gave him a sumptuous burial.[154]

Eusebius reports that Astyrius also put an end to a pagan practice at Caesarea Philippi. Each year the inhabitants used to throw a sacrificial animal into the spring from which the Jordan takes its source. When Astyrius was present one year, he prayed to God to confound the demon of error: the victim, instead of disappearing miraculously, as was normal, floated to the surface of the water, and the rite was never again celebrated.[155] In Caesarea Philippi (Eusebius continues) stood a bronze relief depicting a woman kneeling before a man, and a strange herb with marvelous healing power grew beside a stone supporting the relief; the scene depicted Jesus healing the woman with an issue of blood (Matthew 9:20). Eusebius saw the monument, which Maximinus later removed and destroyed. He also saw statues of Peter and Paul, paintings of Jesus, and the episcopal throne of James, which successive bishops of Jerusalem continued to use.[156]

Eusebius gives a detailed account of an important episode which illustrates how fully the Christian church had integrated itself into the ordinary institutional life of the Roman Empire. Paul, a native of Samosata, became bishop of Antioch, succeeding Demetrianus about 260.[157] Within a few years, the conduct and the theology of the new bishop caused enough offense to ensure his deposition. The opposition to Paul was led by Malchion, a priest at Antioch who taught as a sophist in a Greek academy. A synod convened at Antioch in the winter of 268/9, and Malchion interrogated Paul, much as Origen had interrogated Heracleides or Beryllus of Bostra, with stenographers taking down the question and answers.[158] When their decisions were made, the assembled bishops addressed a letter to Dionysius of Rome, Maximus of Alexandria, and all other bishops everywhere, which Eusebius quotes in part.[159] The council deposed Paul and installed Domnus, the son of Demetrianus, as bishop in his stead. The deposition was not a hasty action, but one forced on the council by Paul's persistence in heresy. Firmilianus had twice come from Cappadocia and presided over two earlier assemblies which stopped short of deposing Paul when he undertook to amend his beliefs. Paul adopted a view of the Trinity which entailed that Jesus was by nature an ordinary man. This assertion was, predictably, taken out of context and pilloried: it derived from premises which cannot fully be reconstructed from the existing hostile reports of Paul's teachings, but which may have included the proposition that God and the Word are "of one substance."[160] The Council of Antioch (it is stated by three writers of the fourth century) condemned the term *homoousios* as heretical.[161]

Eusebius is brief on the theology of Paul of Samosata, showing more interest in his conduct as bishop. Paul became rich through his episcopal office, taking bribes (so his enemies state) for deciding lawsuits between Christians. He acted like an imperial procurator, strutting in the marketplace with a large body-guard in attendance, reading and dictating letters as he perambulated. In his church, Paul habitually sat on a raised throne, again like a secular magistrate, separate from the congregation, whom he organized, as if in a theater, to applaud and wave their handkerchiefs when he signaled. He allowed bishops and priests from other cities to deliver panegyrics to him, and he trained a female choir to sing psalms which included praise of himself as a divine emissary. Worse still, Paul and his clergy openly lived with women. In theory, a celibate existence of this form represented a noble asceticism, since it required the ability to resist incessant temptation, but the youth and beauty of Paul's two constant companions aroused suspicions of misconduct.

Paul, though deposed and denounced by a council of bishops, retained the loyalty of his supporters in Antioch. He refused to surrender the church to Domnus, whom the council named as his successor, and his enemies were unable to dispossess him. The issue was resolved by appeal to the Roman emperor. Aurelian, who assumed the purple in September 270, ordered that the church building be restored to "those with whom the bishops of the doctrine in Italy and Rome should communicate in writing"; the form of the emperor's rescript perhaps reflects a petition presented to him in Italy by a deputation of Italian bishops. Paul was then expelled with indignity.[162]

The Christian church of Antioch under Gallienus was clearly numerous, rich, and powerful, and it could function almost as if it were a separate community within the city: Paul heard lawsuits and received petitions like any Roman magistrate. But when Christians had a dispute which they could not resolve within their own institutional framework, the ultimate court of appeal was the emperor. That should occasion no surprise: as a worldwide organization, the Church resembled the "ecumenical synod" of Dionysiac artists or the like, which treated the emperor as the obvious patron of its activities.[163] Once the Church enjoyed toleration, it was natural that it should copy all other organizations in the Roman Empire in regarding the emperor, simply because he was emperor, as patron, protector, and arbiter.[164] For the Christians of the third century there was no incongruity in inviting a pagan emperor to intervene in ecclesiastical affairs. Aurelian (many believed) was on the point of issuing decrees which adversely affected the status of Christians when he was killed (about September 275).[165] Christians construed his murder as God's intervention to protect the Church, and the legal position of Christianity was unchanged when the first edition of the *Ecclesiastical History* was completed.[166]

The final chapter of the original edition of the *Ecclesiastical History* discussed the career and writings of two bishops of Laodicea.[167] Eusebius and Anatolius were both Alexandrians, and both had been active when a Roman army was besieging Alexandria, probably during the rebellion of Aemilianus in 261/2.[168] Anatolius was with the besieged, Eusebius with the Roman commander. Eusebius obtained a promise of pardon for deserters, whereupon Anatolius persuaded the rebels to allow all the aged, women, and children to leave the beleaguered city. Some time later, Eusebius went to Syria on business connected with Paul of Samosata and was persuaded (or compelled) to stay as bishop of Laodicea. Anatolius was a philosopher skilled in mathematics, rhetoric, and all the sciences; he held the chair of Aristotelian philosophy in Alexandria, and may have taught Iamblichus.[169] Theotecnus intended Anatolius to succeed him in Caesarea and ordained him as his co-adjutant. But the Council of Antioch summoned Anatolius, and Eusebius of Laodicea died while Anatolius was in Syria. The church of Laodicea thereupon retained him as Eusebius' successor. Anatolius composed an *Introduction to Arithmetic* in ten books, and an Easter cycle. Anatolius' nineteen-year cycle represented an improvement on Dionysius' eight-year cycle, though it assumed that the vernal equinox occurred on 19 March. Both Dionysius and Anatolius were concerned to ensure that Easter always fell after the vernal equinox, even though it was possible for the Jewish Passover to precede the equinox. Eusebius quotes Anatolius' attempt to prove that the authentic Jewish computation likewise ensures that Passover on the fourteenth day of Nisan always occurs after the equinox.[170] Anatolius' Easter cycle was probably designed to come into effect in the second year of the emperor Probus (276/7), and it was precisely at this point that the first editions of both the *Chronicle* and the *Ecclesiastical History* probably concluded.[171] Eusebius may have noted at the very end that, at the time of writing, Stephanus was bishop of Laodicea, Agapius of Caesarea.[172]

Even when writing about his own lifetime, Eusebius is not immune from serious chronological errors. It appears that he twice misread the list of Roman bishops, so that he gives Xystus (257/8) a tenure of eleven years (instead of months) and Eutychianus (275–283) a tenure of less than ten months (instead of eight or nine years).[173] Perhaps partly as a result, the *History* states a false date for the Council of Antioch, a date which evidence at his disposal contradicts: Eusebius assigns the council to the reign of Aurelian, who was proclaimed emperor in September 270, even though its synodical letter is addressed to Dionysius of Rome, who died in December 268.[174]

Despite his valiant efforts, chronology was not Eusebius' forte. The value of the *Ecclesiastical History* lies less in its narrative, which depends on Eusebius' often faulty chronology and interpretation, than in its plethora of detail—and in the mere fact of its composition. The first seven books of the *Ecclesiastical History* reflect the optimistic assumptions of a Christian writing in the reign of Diocletian before persecution threatened. Eusebius wrote the history of the Church, not as the story of a long and difficult struggle for recognition, but as the story of a community founded by the Son of God which had always, apart from brief interruptions, enjoyed prosperity and success. For the Christians of the late third century persecution belonged to the past.

Since 260, although technically still illegal, Christianity had enjoyed effective toleration from emperors and provincial governors.[175] As a result, the Church prospered mightily. Worshipers thronged church services. Many communities built new churches to hold larger congregations. In the reign of Diocletian, Christians could be found among the officers of the Roman army, governors, financial officials, and their staffs, and Christian governors were discreetly permitted to omit the normal preliminary of sacrifice when they conducted public business.[176] The situation in Nicomedia symbolized the aggressive confidence of Christians everywhere immediately before the "Great Persecution." A large new church on a hill could be seen from Diocletian's palace, and from the palace came part of its congregation. Not only had many imperial slaves and freedmen embraced Christianity, but Prisca and Valeria, the wives of Diocletian and Galerius, were believed to adhere secretly to the faith.[177]

IX

PERSECUTION

Eusebius completed the original version of his *Ecclesiastical History* at a time when a renewal of persecution, which had effectively ceased in 260, scarcely seemed possible. But he had compiled a collection of ancient martyrdoms, and persecution was one of the main themes from which the web of the *History* was woven.[1] It was natural, therefore, when persecution came again, that Eusebius should desire to bequeath to posterity a permanent record of the martyrs of his own day. He penned no fewer than three accounts of the persecution which began in 303, in the *Martyrs of Palestine* (which survives in two recensions) and in the books added to the *Ecclesiastical History* after 313.

Eusebius continued to reside in Caesarea during the troubled decade of persecution. He refers to his presence there in 305/6, and he aided Pamphilus with his *Defense of Origen* while Pamphilus was imprisoned in Caesarea between late 307 and early 310.[2] During the persecution, however, Eusebius traveled outside Palestine, visiting Phoenicia and Egypt, and possibly also Arabia.[3] In both Tyre and the Thebaid Eusebius witnessed the deaths of Christian martyrs.[4] These visits (despite the contexts in which Eusebius alludes to them) probably belong to the second bout of persecution between 311 and 313, since the whole tenor of the *Martyrs of Palestine* implies that before 311 Eusebius encountered no martyrs outside his native province. Moreover, when Eusebius quotes a rescript which Maximinus dispatched to many cities in June 312, it is the copy posted at Tyre which he explicitly adduces.[5] In Egypt, Eusebius was apparently arrested and imprisoned. Many years later, in 335, the bishop of Heracleopolis taunted Eusebius with being a coward and an apostate: when the two were imprisoned together during the persecution, Potammon lost an eye, while Eusebius was released unharmed. Eusebius (his enemy insinuated) must have done something compromising to secure his release.[6] It is unfortunate that the reticence of Eusebius prevented any allusion to the episode in his own writings: the full story of his imprisonment would be valuable on many counts.

Eusebius observed the onset of persecution from a perspective which differs greatly from that of the only other contemporary who has left a detailed narrative. In 303, Lactantius was in Nicomedia, where Diocletian resided, close to the center of events and acquainted with intrigues within the imperial palace.[7] Eusebius lived in a provincial city remote from the emperors, able to experience the effects of imperial policy, but not to observe its causes. Yet this provincial viewpoint endows Eusebius' account of the persecution with its individuality and with great intrinsic value; he saw at first hand how the persecution affected Christians in Palestine and in other provinces of the eastern empire. Moreover, from 305 until 313, Eusebius was a subject of the emperor Maximinus, who visited Caesarea and perhaps even resided there for a period.[8] Eusebius' description of the persecution contains the fullest surviving account of how Maximinus governed his portion of the Roman Empire.

When news arrived in May 311 that Galerius had decreed toleration, Eusebius began to write. Within a few weeks, or at most a few months, he completed the first version of the *Martyrs of Palestine,* of which the complete text survives only in an ancient Syriac translation.[9] This version, commonly known as the long recension, claims to cover "the entire time of the persecution": it envisaged persecution as ending in 311, and the last full year of persecution which Eusebius chronicled was the eighth, which ended shortly before Easter 311.[10] Eusebius could not quote Galerius' edict of toleration, which Maximinus did not promulgate in the East,[11] but he clearly believed that it had ended the persecution. Such optimism was possible only between May and December 311: Maximinus soon decided to resume the policy of persecution, and the bishop of Alexandria was suddenly arrested and killed on 26 November 311.[12]

In Asia Minor and the East, the persecution begun in 303 finally came to an end in the summer of 313, when the dying Maximinus conceded Christians the rights which they already enjoyed elsewhere.[13] But the *Martyrs of Palestine* no longer covered "the entire time of the persecution"; only in 313 could Eusebius undertake a definitive account of the whole decade of persecution. His first attempt utilized his earlier work. He rewrote the *Martyrs of Palestine,* abbreviating it to produce the short recension, which he incorporated in a second edition of the *Ecclesiastical History.* To the original seven books, slightly retouched (especially at the end), Eusebius now added two more. Book Eight comprised the rewritten *Martyrs* with a new preface for its context in the *History,* the text of Galerius' edict, and a concluding paragraph; Book Nine, an account of the last phase of persecution under Maximinus.[14] Soon, however, Eusebius came to feel that this edition of the *History* was unsatisfactory. He must have sensed that the *Martyrs of Palestine,* even in its rewritten form, offered too local a perspective for a persecution which involved the entire Roman Empire. Before the autumn of 316, therefore, Eusebius produced an edition of the *History* in ten books. He replaced the *Martyrs* with the present Book Eight and added a tenth book with two main components: a sermon which he delivered at Tyre and six documents of 313 and 314, in which Constantine and Licinius manifested their benevolence and generosity toward the Christian church.[15] As for the *Martyrs of Palestine,* Eusebius appears at some stage to have intended the short recension to stand as a separate work; perhaps he envisioned a third edition of the *Martyrs* as a sort of appendix to the third edition of the *History.*[16]

Thereafter, the *Ecclesiastical History* received only minor modifications. A fourth edition reflected Constantine's victory in 324: Eusebius deleted or rewrote every passage where he had earlier named the defeated and discredited Licinius as a champion of religion and virtue.[17] He also removed the documents which concluded the third edition and in their place added a brief account of Licinius' policy of persecution and his overthrow.[18] Finally, in or after 326, Eusebius removed from this concluding passage the name of Constantine's son, Crispus, executed in that year, whom the fourth edition associated with his father.[19]

Among Eusebius' accounts of the persecution, therefore, the long recension of the *Martyrs of Palestine,* the Ninth Book of the *Ecclesiastical History,* and the sermon at Tyre deserve a primacy of regard. Closer to the events than the later revisions, they possess an immediacy of their own, for they present Eusebius' successive reactions to the apparent end of persecution in 311, to the real end in 313, and to the consequent restoration of the Church. Nevertheless, an account of the persecution in the East cannot neglect valuable and authentic details from Eusebius' later rewritings—or from any other source.

Easter was approaching when the governor of Palestine published the edict of 23 February 303 ordering the churches to be razed, the Scriptures to be burned, and Christians who refused to sacrifice to be deprived of their rank and of the right to plead cases in law courts.[20] Eusebius gives no description of how the local officials of eastern cities enforced the edict. But no one below the governor, who normally resided in Caesarea, possessed the legal power to execute recalcitrants. Hence Christians elsewhere in Palestine who failed to obey the imperial order were usually sent to the city where Eusebius lived. The first martyr falls into this category. He was sent to Caesarea from Scythopolis, where he was a lector, an interpreter of Syriac, and an exorcist. Brought before the governor, he was asked first to sacrifice to the gods, next to pour a libation to the emperors. In answer, he quoted Homer: "the lordship of many is not good; let there be one lord, one king." Hearing this treasonable utterance, the governor beheaded him at once. The martyr's name was Procopius, the date 7 June 303. Eusebius (it is important) does not disclose the fate of the companions of Procopius, to whom his narrative incidentally alludes.[21]

Soon there arrived in Palestine an order for the arrest of the Christian clergy, and many were imprisoned in Caesarea.[22] The order seems not to have prevented Eusebius from continuing his *General Elementary Introduction,* whose sixth book refers to the suppression of Christian worship and the incarceration of bishops.[23] The large number of prisoners exceeded the capacity of the prisons, and Diocletian marked his *vicennalia* on 20 November 303 by proclaiming an amnesty for all who sacrificed. The amnesty produced varied results. At Caesarea (if Eusebius' general statements may be given a particular application), the local authorities aimed at the release of clergy: they made some of the prisoners sacrifice by sheer physical force and then released them, together with others whom they had not compelled to undergo even this charade of compliance.[24] That is understandable in a city whose population contained Jews, Samaritans, pagans, and Christians in almost equal numbers.[25] But Caesarea was also the provincial capital. When Flavianus, the governor, returned from business elsewhere, he tortured and executed Zacchaeus, a deacon from Gadara, and Alpheus of Eleutheropolis, a reader and exorcist at Caesarea.[26]

Zacchaeus and Alpheus were martyred on 17 November 303. The next martyrdom in Palestine recorded by the *Martyrs* took place in the following spring. When the new governor, Urbanus, published the fourth edict, which ordained universal sacrifice, the pagans of Gaza made an example of one Timothy, denouncing him to the governor, who executed him.[27] On the same occasion, Urbanus sentenced Agapius and Thecla, also of Gaza, to fight with wild beasts, but he retained them in custody until suitable games were held. All three were clearly accused of disobeying the fourth edict—and they are the only Christians of Palestine whom Eusebius' account of 304/5 names as suffering under that edict. The next group of martyrs known comprises six young men who provoked arrest and two who ministered to them in prison. When it was rumored that Agapius and Thecla would be exposed to the beasts in Caesarea (perhaps on 20 November 304), six young men accosted Urbanus as he entered the amphitheater. They were arrested and imprisoned for a long time, finally being executed on 24 March 305.[28] There were probably many other victims of the fourth edict whom Eusebius does not name, for he alludes in passing to Montanist companions of the imprisoned Thecla, who was herself a Montanist.[29]

On 1 May 305, Diocletian invested Maximinus with the imperial purple. The new Caesar left Nicomedia at once, intending, his enemies alleged, to oppress and trample the diocese of Oriens.[30] In Palestine the Christians felt the effects of his hostility before many months had passed. The edict of 304 was difficult to enforce, because the authorities lacked lists of the inhabitants of cities who owned no agricultural land.[31] In 306 Galerius removed this obstacle. New census lists were compiled that year; they contained not only the names of all who paid taxes on land (whether landowners or tenants), but also the names of all heads of households living in cities, together with the number of their dependents.[32] Galerius proposed to tax city dwellers, whether or not they owned property.

Maximinus may have disapproved of the innovation, because in 311, at the next census, he again exempted the urban population in the East and in Asia Minor from registration in the census.[33] In 306, however, he seized the opportunity to enforce religious conformity. Local magistrates were instructed to make the whole population of their cities gather together to sacrifice and pour libations. In Caesarea heralds proclaimed a summons for men, women, and children to attend the temples, while military tribunes and centurions used the census lists to fetch individuals from their homes. Apphianus, a well-born Lycian who was studying with Eusebius in the household of Pamphilus, protested in an ostentatious and provocative fashion. On 31 March 306, as Urbanus prepared to pour a libation, Apphianus dashed past the governor's bodyguard, seized Urbanus' hand, and urged him to desist from the adoration of lifeless idols and evil spirits. The soldiers, perhaps fancying that Apphianus was an assassin, struck him, threw him to the ground, and stamped on him. The next day Urbanus questioned the Christian under torture. Apphianus steadfastly refused to say who he was, whence he came, or where he was staying, and on the third day Urbanus ordered him to be thrown into the sea.[34]

The next martyr of Palestine whom Eusebius records was the Agapius condemned by Urbanus two years before. Since then, Agapius had on several occasions been brought from prison into the arena and taken back again. Finally, on 20 November 306, he gained the crown of martyrdom when Maximinus was in Caesarea celebrating his birthday. Agapius was led out into the arena with a placard proclaiming him a Christian. The governor ordered him to be offered to the beasts, together with a slave who had murdered his master. Maximinus arrived and in his clemency pardoned the murderer. He then urged Agapius to deny God and obtain release too. When he persistently refused, the emperor had him exposed to be savaged by a bear. Agapius survived this ordeal. The next day he was thrown into the sea with stones tied to his ankles.[35]

At the start of the fifth year of persecution (which began shortly before Easter 307), Theodosia, a virgin from Tyre, was arrested when she conversed with Christians in court who were about to be tried by the governor. Urbanus bade her sacrifice. She refused. Theodosia was tortured, but the girl's cheerful serenity was not shattered. Feeling himself mocked, Urbanus condemned her to be thrown into the sea; while the confessors whom Theodosia had addressed were consigned to the copper mines at Phaeno.[36] Similar condemnations were perhaps common, though Eusebius characteristically concentrates on one episode: the varied punishments Urbanus handed out in a single day.

On 5 November 307, Urbanus sentenced Domninus to be burned alive, three nameless youths to fight as gladiators, a priest to be exposed to the beasts, Silvanus, bishop of Gaza, and his companions to work in the copper mines, and many others (among them Pamphilus) to be kept in prison. Much more cruel, he ordered some young men to be castrated and delivered three maidens to notorious brothel keepers. Urbanus himself, however, was soon dead. One day he was governor of Palestine, condemning Christians, surrounded by an escort of soldiers, and a guest at Maximinus' table, the next he was suddenly denounced, stripped of rank and honor, and sentenced to death by Maximinus, who tried him in person.[37]

Urbanus' successor, Firmilianus, was a trusted confidant of Maximinus and an experienced soldier who was later to pay for his loyalty with his life.[38] At Diocaesarea (Sepphoris) in the spring of 308, Firmilianus tried ninety-seven confessors sent to him from the porphyry mines in the Thebaid; after the tendons of their left ankles were destroyed with hot irons, their right eyes put out and the sockets seared, he dispatched them to the mines in Palestine.[39] Not long after, the three youths condemned to train as gladiators fought at Caesarea, together with others, while many Christians, including a group from Gaza who assembled for reading Scripture, suffered the loss of feet and eyes. Two virgins, Ennatha of Gaza and Valentina of Caesarea, were publicly lacerated and burned alive, and on the same day (25 July 308), the confessor Paul was beheaded. Soon Caesarea saw a second consignment of Egyptian confessors, one hundred and thirty in number; Firmilianus mutilated them all and sent some to Phaeno, others to Cilicia.[40]

Eusebius marks a respite from persecution at this point, but without indicating precisely how long it lasted.[41] Moreover, the text of the *Martyrs* fails to note where the sixth year of persecution ended and the seventh began, while the dates in the chapter headings betray some inconsistencies. It appears, however, that Eusebius records no Palestinian martyrs between 25 July 308 and 13 November 309.[42] For when the series of martyrs resumes after the respite, the first four diurnal dates recorded are 13 November, 14 December, 10 January and 16 February. The months are clearly consecutive, since the martyrs of 16 February include Pamphilus, who was put in prison in November 307 and kept there for more than two full years before his death.[43] The "short relief and calm," therefore, lasted from the summer of 308 until the autumn of 309. The political context should be relevant: the conference of Carnuntum met in November 308, and Maximinus spent the succeeding months haggling with Galerius about his status in the imperial college.[44]

In the autumn of 309, however, Maximinus issued letters which intensified the pressure on Christians to conform to prevailing customs. He instructed the praetorian prefect and provincial governors to urge local officials to repair temples and to compel all the inhabitants of each city to offer sacrifice and libations and to taste sacrificial meat. Further, all articles brought into a marketplace for sale were to be sprinkled with a libation or sacrificial blood, while guards posted at the entrance were to sprinkle all persons who entered public baths.[45] Immediately, three Christians interrupted Firmilianus at sacrifice: he beheaded all three. On the same day (13 November 309), he also executed Ennathas, a virgin from Scythopolis, after a tribune had stripped her half-naked and flogged her through all the market places of Caesarea. Firmilianus forbade the burial of these martyrs, provoking (it was alleged) the pillars of public buildings in the city to weep miraculously.[46]

The next few months witnessed the most severe bout of persecution. On 14 December 309 Firmilianus condemned some Egyptians arrested at Ascalon on their way to comfort the confessors in Cilicia: most lost the use of their left foot and right eye; three were beheaded. On 10 January 310 two Christians from the Christian village of Anaia, near Eleutheropolis, were burned alive, the ascetic Peter and Asclepius, a Marcionite bishop.[47] A month later, on 16 February, came the martyrdom of Pamphilus and six companions. Pamphilus and two disciples had been in prison for more than two years, subject to frequent torture and exhortations to sacrifice: the arrival of five Egyptians, who had succored the confessors in Cilicia, provided the occasion for their final trial. The Egyptians were tried first, then Pamphilus and his disciples from prison: when they were executed, four more members of Pamphilus' household, who had not been imprisoned, provoked and obtained martyrdom by gestures of sympathy for those already condemned. Shortly afterward (on 5 and 7 March 310) two Christians from Batanaea were executed at Caesarea, after they attempted to visit the confessors of the city. They were the very last martyrs to be executed at Caesarea before Galerius' edict of toleration became known.[48]

Eusebius does not explain the sudden cessation of executions; significantly, it coincides with a change of governor.[49] In the military zone, however, persecution continued. At Phaeno, on 19 September 310, the *dux* of Palestine executed four Egyptians to terrify their fellow confessors, who numbered about one hundred and fifty and had dared to build a church at Zoar for Christian worship. Again, on 4 May 311, Silvanus of Gaza, condemned to the copper mines sometime before, was finally beheaded, together with another thirty-nine confessors.[50] When Silvanus died, Galerius had already issued his edict of toleration, and within a few weeks persecution ceased in Palestine.

Eusebius' *Martyrs of Palestine* is not quite what its conventional title seems to imply. Its author did not set out to give a complete list of Christians in Palestine who were executed for their faith between 303 and 311. Eusebius himself entitled the work "About those who suffered martyrdom in Palestine," and his intention was to preserve the memory of martyrs whom he knew, rather than to give a comprehensive account of how persecution affected the Roman province in which he lived. The preface of the long recension states the author's purpose clearly:

> It is meet, then, that the conflicts which were illustrious in various districts should be committed to writing by those who dwelt with

the combatants in their districts. But for me, I pray that I may be able to speak of those with whom I was personally conversant, and that they may associate me with them—those in whom the whole people of Palestine glories, because even in the midst of our land the Savior of all men arose like a thirst-quenching spring. The contests, then, of those illustrious champions I shall relate for the general instruction and profit.[51]

In accordance with his stated plan, Eusebius concentrated on individual martyrs, even though incidental references in the text sometimes reveal that the martyr whose death Eusebius describes was accompanied by a large number of other martyrs whom he does not name.[52] The personal bias of the *Martyrs* explains the disproportionately long accounts of Apphianus and of Pamphilus and his disciples, whom Eusebius knew intimately as a member of the same household. It also explains the inclusion of some Christians who suffered martyrdom outside Palestine. Romanus died at Antioch, but he was a deacon and exorcist of the church at Caesarea.[53] Aedesius assaulted a prefect of Egypt who was trying Christians in Alexandria, and was tortured and executed there, but he was the brother of Apphianus and, like him, had studied under Pamphilus' direction.[54] It is more than doubtful, therefore, whether the *Martyrs of Palestine* can safely be made the basis for any general estimate of how many martyrs perished during the persecution between 303 and 311.[55] The selection of material is personal: the *Martyrs* is less a history of the persecution in Palestine than a memorial to the friends of Eusebius who died for their faith.[56]

The long recension of the *Martyrs of Palestine* has not survived exactly as Eusebius wrote it in 311, for a number of passages allude to the deaths of Maximinus and his supporters in 313 or speak of the emperor in terms which would be treasonable while he lived.[57] Eusebius presumably retouched the original text in 313/4 when he was engaged in producing the short recension. This second version of the *Martyrs of Palestine* was not originally intended to stand as a separate work. In the summer of 313, when the persecution finally ended, Eusebius decided to continue his *Ecclesiastical History* with an account of the martyrs of his own day. He did so by rewriting the *Martyrs* in a shorter version, designed to stand in the *History* in the place which Book Eight now occupies— hence the present state of the short recension of the *Martyrs of Palestine,* without proper beginning or end, which can, however, be identified as the present preface to Book Eight of the *History* and the passage conventionally printed as an appendix to that book.

The new version of the *Martyrs of Palestine* differed in intent and sometimes in scope from the first. It began by evoking briefly the historical context of the persecution: in the late third century Christianity was prosperous, socially acceptable, confident of worldly success.[58] Moreover, Eusebius described explicitly the three persecuting edicts of 303.[59] For the most part, however, he merely rewrote and adapted his earlier work. From the martyrdom of Procopius (7 June 303) to that of Silvanus (4 May 311), the two versions run closely parallel, but with some significant alterations. The death of Maximinus allowed Eusebius to describe that emperor's role in persecution more frankly; the short recension names Maximinus or notes his presence in Caesarea on several occasions where the long does not,[60] and it alone reports Urbanus' boast that Maximinus held him in high esteem because he persecuted Christians zealously.[61]

There are also deliberate changes of emphasis. Eusebius subtly moves his readers' attention from the governors of Palestine, who oppressed only a single province, to the emperor who ruled the whole of Oriens. And he abbreviates sections of primarily local interest, sometimes drastically, as when he removes a long passage on the life and imprisonment of Pamphilus and his disciples.[62] Nor is the rewritten *Martyrs* exclusively Palestinian. Between the brothers Apphianus and Aedesius, a brief insertion notes the martyrdom of Ulpianus at Tyre (which reflects Eusebius' visit to the city), and John, a blind Egyptian, receives as much prominence as Silvanus of Gaza in the final chapter.[63] At the end, as at the beginning, Eusebius set the persecution in Palestine in a more general context. He surveyed the course of the persecution (it lasted only two years in the West), quoted the imperial edict which ended it, and described briefly how each of the emperors ruling in 303 subsequently died.[64]

The eighth book of the *Ecclesiastical History* represents Eusebius' attempt to transform the rewritten *Martyrs of Palestine* into a general account of the persecution. The process of adaptation has produced vagueness, confusion, even outright error. The narrative of the *Martyrs* (in both recensions) noted the abdication of Diocletian as approximately contemporaneous with a martyrdom on 24 March 305, in the second year of the persecution.[65] But the general historical summary following the short recension carelessly stated that Diocletian and Maximian abdicated less than two whole years after persecution began.[66] That is a clear error, since the persecution began in Palestine shortly before Easter 303, while Diocletian and Maximian abdicated on 1 May 305. Nevertheless, Book Eight of the *History* takes over the error and makes it more explicit: the Augusti "had not yet completed a second year of such a disturbance" when they retired into private life.[67] Eusebius' reworking of his material explains how the mistake has arisen.

Still more disturbing in Book Eight of the *History* is a pervasive tendency to disregard strict chronological sequence and to conflate the periods before and after 311. The rewritten *Martyrs* glances forward to the renewal of persecution after May 311 in a striking passage which records how bishops were compelled to tend the imperial camels and to serve as stableboys for the imperial horses.[68] But the eighth book of the *History* alludes to events after 311 so frequently that any sense of chronological development is destroyed, and it omits important and relevant facts, such as the edict of February 304, which ordained universal sacrifice, and Maximinus' later attempts (in 306 and 309) to render it effectual.

Book Eight of the *Ecclesiastical History* reproduces the preface of its predecessor, probably almost unchanged, except that Eusebius has added an introductory sentence to explain that this book is devoted to the persecution.[69] The influence of an approach more appropriate to the *Martyrs of Palestine* is evident when Eusebius circumscribes his subject matter: "We decided to make no mention of those who have been tempted by the persecution or have *made* utter *shipwreck* of their salvation (1 Timothy 1:19) and by their own decision were plunged in the depths of the sea; we shall add to the general history only those things which may be profitable, first to ourselves, and then to those who come after us."[70] That is a hagiographer or a panegyrist speaking, not a historian. By his own admission, Eusebius has produced not a history of the persecution between 303 and 311 but a "summary description of the sacred conflicts of the martyrs of the divine word." Apostasies and dissension within the Church he consigns to oblivion, for moral or didactic reasons. What remains is a selective account, an impression, a subjective reaction.

Reproduction of earlier material also distorts the arrangement of that material and produces an illogical order. Having begun to copy the short recension of the *Martyrs of Palestine,* Eusebius continues beyond its preface and describes the three persecuting edicts of 303 in phrases modified only slightly for their new context. But then, after he has described the effects of the third edict in the autumn of 303, he begins to speak of the martyrs in general terms—and suddenly goes back in time to 299 to introduce the purge of Christians from the army which preceded the first persecuting edict by almost four years. The narrative then switches to Nicomedia in late February and March 303 before returning to the second and third persecuting edicts, at which point Eusebius complements his earlier remarks.[71] Strangely, Eusebius here fails altogether to mention the fourth edict, although subsequent sections in Book Eight of the *History* assume that it was in operation.

After the third edict, the arrangement of the book becomes geographical, with separate chapters devoted to different provinces. Eusebius alludes to the martyrs of Palestine only to pass to the martyrdom of a group of Egyptians in Tyre—an event which may have occurred after 311. He next speaks of martyrs in Egypt and in the Thebaid, alluding to his own visit to Egypt. Again Eusebius appears to transgress the implied temporal limits of the book and to include events later than 311. He next names the martyrs Philoromus and Phileas, bishop of Thmuis (executed on 4 February 307), and quotes a letter of the latter to his congregation which describes persecution in Alexandria. Then Eusebius glances briefly at other regions. In Phrygia, soldiers burned a whole town with its inhabitants, magistrates included, and the imperial official Adauctus, who was then *rationalis* of the province, was executed. In Arabia Christians were killed with the axe, in Cappadocia by breaking their legs, in Mesopotamia by slow suffocation as they hung upside down over a fire, in Alexandria by the gradual dismemberment of their bodies. Eusebius devotes more space to persecution in Antioch, especially to four virgin martyrs, of whom two drowned themselves to escape the brothel and two were executed by drowning. And he notes the various refinements of torture in Pontus and, toward the end of the persecution, the mutilation of Christians, whose right eyes were put out and left ankles maimed.[72] The section ends with another survey, arranged geographically, of martyrs who were leaders of the Church, principally bishops. Again, strict chronology is disregarded, since Eusebius includes some men who died only after Maximinus resumed persecution in late 311.[73]

Eusebius continues Book Eight with an outline of the political history of the Roman Empire designed to introduce the edict of toleration, quoted in Greek, with which he concludes. Again he goes beyond 311, in order to propound the thesis that persecution brought disaster. Before 303 (Eusebius cheats a little on the chronology) there was peace, plenty, and prosperity; after 303 came dissension, civil war, and finally (in 312) famine and pestilence. Eusebius, like Lactantius, saw the last illness of Galerius as divine retribution on the main instigator of persecution.[74]

The eighth book of the *Ecclesiastical History* is unsatisfactory as a history of the persecution from 303 to 311. Its defects partly reflect its indebtedness to the *Martyrs of Palestine*. But Eusebius should not be blamed for failing to provide a full account of the persecution. He never attempted to give one: "It is not our task to commit to writing the conflicts of those who fought on behalf of piety towards the Deity throughout the whole world and to record in detail everything which befell them: that would be the duty of those who were eyewitnesses to the events."[75] Eusebius was aware of how little he could discover about the persecution outside Palestine, except for notorious barbarities or for the martyrdoms of prominent men. Regrettably, no well-informed observer in any other province emulated Eusebius, and hagiographical fiction soon began to swamp the facts. In consequence, it is impossible to make any precise estimate of how many victims the "Great Persecution" claimed.[76] Of set purpose, Book Eight of the *Ecclesiastical History* gives no more than an impressionistic sketch of the general course of persecution between 303 and 311.

The ninth book of the *Ecclesiastical History* is far more successful than the eighth. It has an immediacy which the latter lacks. An original composition which Eusebius wrote almost immediately after the events, it covers the last two years of the reign of Maximinus (311–313), concentrating on the emperor's religious policies and quoting Greek translations of the documents through which the emperor proclaimed and justified his actions to his subjects. In this book, Eusebius' provincial viewpoint ceases to be a disadvantage; since he can quote documents, he can describe with admirable clarity how Maximinus continued persecution despite the disapproval of his imperial colleagues. Moreover, his narrative neatly complements that of Lactantius, who knows more about Maximinus' court and his conduct in Asia Minor but is not well acquainted with events in the diocese of Oriens. As for chronology, a consistent framework emerges from the cross-references between the quoted documents.[77]

The edict of toleration issued in the name of the whole imperial college in late April 311 was published throughout the Danubian lands and Asia Minor. Maximinus, however, declined to publish the text of Galerius' pronouncement in his territory. Instead, he ordered his praetorian prefect to issue instructions to provincial governors to end persecution, but in a far less straightforward fashion. The edict of Galerius allowed Christians to assemble and build churches again and requested them to pray for the safety of the emperor and the state. Sabinus, the praetorian prefect of Maximinus, wrote to governors throughout Oriens bidding them to release Christians who were in custody, to cease to treat Christianity as a crime, and to instruct the local magistrates in each city to disregard the earlier imperial letter ordering Christians to perform pagan worship. All the Christians in prison or the mines were forthwith released. But, strictly construed, Maximinus' apparent grant of toleration merely annulled the requirement that Christians be compelled to sacrifice. Since it did not explicitly provide that Christians might again assemble or build churches, these rights were still implicitly denied, and not six months passed before Maximinus ruled that Christians were not allowed to assemble even in their cemeteries.[78]

Active persecution recommenced. The first victims were chosen for their prominence. On 26 November 311, Peter, bishop of Alexandria, was arrested by imperial agents sent especially for the purpose, tried summarily, and executed.[79] On 7 January 312 at Nicomedia, Maximinus himself presided over the trial of Lucian of Antioch, who was put to death in prison.[80] Provincial governors took their cue and acted; among the many martyrs who died in consequence Eusebius notes the aged Silvanus, who had been bishop of Emesa for forty years, and many Egyptian bishops.[81]

Various steps designed to strengthen pagan cults and discredit Christianity accompanied the repression. Maximinus tried to organize paganism as a cohesive religion. He had already, in late 309, decreed that disused temples and shrines be repaired;[82] now he established a pagan ecclesiastical hierarchy. The high-priests of the provincial councils received a general supervision of religious affairs, their new powers being marked by the constant attendance of a military escort as if they were government officials. Maximinus also appointed municipal priests from the leading citizens of each city to perform daily sacrifice to the gods and to aid in restoring ancient cults and priesthoods. Both priests and high-priests were granted the right to wear resplendent white cloaks—and were encouraged to compel Christians to join in their sacrifices.[83] Maximinus ordered that the *Acts of Pilate* (an apocryphal work of recent composition, but already in circulation) be posted publicly everywhere and that all teachers in schools make their pupils learn the *Acts* by heart. The *dux* of Phoenicia produced evidence of Christian debaucheries extracted under torture from prostitutes at Damascus, and this memorandum too Maximinus gleefully ordered to be set up everywhere.[84] At Antioch, the *curator* Theotecnus erected a statue of Zeus Philios, created a cult around it, and devised an oracle—which duly proclaimed that the Christians, as enemies of the god, should be expelled from the city and its territory.[85]

Persecution itself was represented as a response to the requests of Maximinus' subjects. Eusebius asserts that the emperor used agents to induce the citizens of Antioch to petition him for measures against the Christians.[86] Lactantius generalizes the charge.[87] Neither writer probably possessed accurate information about Maximinus' private dealings with his political supporters. The emperor did not need to suborn petitions, since he did not conceal his own prejudices, and his reaction to the embassy from Antioch created a precedent. City magistrates and governors alike urged the subjects of Maximinus to beseech the emperor to embark on a policy which he clearly desired.[88] Rescript answered petition, and persecution again obtained legal sanction. The text of the petition which the provincial council of Lycia and Pamphylia submitted survives on stone,[89] and Eusebius quotes the rescript posted at Tyre: the two dovetail perfectly, and almost identical texts must have been engraved in many eastern cities.[90]

The petitioners are brief and sharp. They habitually pray on behalf of the emperors to the gods, to whom the emperors are related. But the Christians avoid such worship; for the benefit of all, therefore, let the Christians be compelled to worship like everyone else. Maximinus is effusive and windy. He thanks the city of Tyre pompously and verbosely, and he expatiates on the evils which Christianity has inflicted on the world. What he calls "the baneful error and vain folly of unhallowed men" used to cause failure of crops, war, storms, and earthquakes. But now peace and plenty reign because of the emperor's devotion to the gods. Let his loyal subjects, therefore, expel persistent Christians, rid themselves of pollution and impiety, and worship the immortal gods with due reverence. Moreover, as a reward, the Tyrians may make any request which they wish; Maximinus will grant it as proof of his piety and generosity.

The rescript to Tyre betrays itself as a form letter. Maximinus represents the Tyrians as inspired by Zeus, "who presides over your far-famed city".[91] The patron god of Tyre was Hercules.[92] More unfortunate still was Maximinus' argument from current prosperity. If success was the criterion of truth, Christians were soon able to claim that the observable facts supported their God against his pagan rivals. Maximinus uttered his optimistic remarks in the summer of 312. During the following autumn and winter came war, drought, famine, and pestilence.

The inhabitants of the regions beyond the Tigris acquired by Rome in 298/9 refused to obey Maximinus' command to worship the gods and perhaps sheltered Christian refugees: Maximinus conducted an unsuccessful expedition to Mesopotamia in an attempt to enforce his religious policies in these quasi-independent and heavily Christian areas.[93] Within the empire, as a result of drought, the price of wheat rose in places to two thousand five hundred *denarii* for one measure.[94] Throughout the provinces of the East, thousands died of starvation or of its concomitant, an ulcerous disease which caused blindness.

Such circumstances produced religious toleration, at least informally and at the local level, for Christians tended the sick, buried the dead, and distributed bread to the living, without regard to creed.[95]

In describing these events, Eusebius has again departed from strict chronological order. Maximinus' campaign on the eastern frontier belongs to autumn 312,[96] but the famine resulted from the failure of the winter rains[97]—and cannot, therefore, have become serious before the following spring. By then, however, Maximinus had again stayed persecution and was at war with one of his imperial colleagues.

After Constantine defeated Maxentius and entered Rome, he wrote to Maximinus demanding that persecution cease.[98] In response, in December 312 the eastern emperor issued instructions to Sabinus, which the praetorian prefect transmitted to provincial governors and which they published. Maximinus' insincerity and plain mendacity shine through the resplendent phrases. Diocletian and Maximian had rightly (Maximinus avers) given orders that all who deserted the worship of the gods be recalled to it by threat of punishment. But Maximinus substituted exhortation for violence immediately on his accession; from 305 to 311 "no one in the eastern provinces was either banished or injured" and "no severe measures were employed." In 311, however, an embassy from Nicomedia pressed him to expel the Christians from their city. At first he refused. But the people of Nicomedia and many other cities persisted and compelled the reluctant emperor to accede to their loyal request on behalf of their ancestral gods. Now, therefore, Maximinus reaffirms his earlier policy towards the Christians: no harsh measures shall be taken against them by any official under his authority. Those who follow their own worship may be induced to worship the gods by words and exhortations, but violence and compulsion are disallowed.[99]

Maximinus' apologia lacked credibility (though it has found believers in a more recent age).[100] Christians who had suffered under his rule since 305 knew what value to set upon these false professions of humanity.[101] Moreover, the letter to Sabinus claimed to do no more than annul the rescripts to the cities issued in the preceding year. Hence it represented merely a return to the legal position of 311: neither persecution nor toleration. Again, as in 311, Maximinus refrained from authorizing Christians to assemble, to hold services, or to build churches. On this occasion, however, Christians interpreted his words strictly: they did not yet venture to assemble or to appear in public.[102] Safety came only when Maximinus was defeated in war.

In the spring of 313, Maximinus invaded Europe in an attempt to surprise Licinius before he could mount an offensive against him. The strike failed. On 30 April 313 Maximinus was defeated near Adrianople.[103] As he fled eastward, he finally conceded the toleration which he had so long withheld. Unwilling to the end to admit the truth, Maximinus pretended that subordinates had misunderstood his instructions. Now, however, he proclaimed that he intended to remove "all suspicion or doubt arising from fear": he granted all his subjects freedom to worship as they pleased, he explicitly granted Christians the right to build churches, and he even ordered the restitution of all property seized from the Christians, whether in the possession of the imperial treasury, a city, or private persons.[104]

Soon after uttering this pronouncement, Maximinus was defeated again and died, ignominiously and miserably. A purge of his supporters followed; Christians wrought vengeance on their former tormentors.[105] The "Great Persecution" ended in the East after a full decade of intermittent, but brutal, enforcement.

Persecution came both as a shock and as a novelty to Eusebius. But the deaths of the emperors who persecuted the Christians ultimately strengthened his prior belief that God intervenes in history to ensure that the Christian church shall prosper. Unpleasant as it was, therefore, persecution brought benefits. In 311 Eusebius stressed the continuing role of the martyrs, who walk with God and can assist their brethren on earth with their prayers; persecution created a link with the first apostles, who themselves suffered martyrdom.[106] In the rewritten *Martyrs of Palestine* and in Book Eight of the *Ecclesiastical History,* Eusebius took a broader view and interpreted persecution as God's rebuke to the Christians for dissensions within the Church.[107] This view he reiterated, in a fuller and subtler form, in a speech which forms the greater part of Book Ten of the *History;* he delivered the speech in Tyre about 315, when the rebuilt basilica was dedicated.[108]

Eusebius entitled the speech "Panegyric on the Building of the Churches, Addressed to Paulinus, Bishop of Tyre," and it has some recognizable elements of a formal panegyric on God. But Eusebius devotes much of the speech to exploring the implications of a threefold parallelism: the church built by Paulinus is an image of the worldwide Church founded by the Son of God, which the temple in Jerusalem prefigured, so that Paulinus is a new Solomon or new Zerubbabel, who appropriately built a new and larger structure on the site where the old had stood.[109] Eusebius describes the magnificent new building, and its symbolic meaning, in some detail.[110] The old church was destroyed when the Devil, resentful that Jesus had led mankind from gloomy darkness into light, attacked Christians through the threats of tyrannical emperors and the ordinances of impious governors.[111] Yet the Church was not wholly guiltless. Though at the Devil's prompting, the Church had chosen evil of her own free will. Hence God abandoned her to be an easy prey to her enemies, who despoiled her. The divine Word rescued and restored her when she had paid the just penalty for her sins. The prime agents were the emperors (Eusebius alludes to Constantine and Licinius, but does not name them) who cleansed the world of all who had oppressed the Christians.[112] These imperial champions, unlike their predecessors, have abandoned paganism and adopted Christianity; they acknowledge God, confess that Christ is king of the universe, and style him Savior. Eusebius adduces the statue and inscription in Rome which ascribed Constantine's victory over Maxentius to the *labarum,* but he implies that Licinius was no less of a Christian.[113]

In its interpretation of recent history, the speech equates the policies of Constantine with those of Licinius, the policies of Maxentius with those of Maximinus, just as Book Eight of the *Ecclesiastical History* does at greater length.[114] In both cases, the equation implies an ignorance of realities. Eusebius repeats a stereotype, a conventional opinion, a comforting simplification of the truth. Eusebius lived in Palestine, remote from Rome and from the court of Licinius. Even had he desired, he might not have been able to discover how Maxentius really treated the Christians of Italy and Africa, or what were Licinius' true religious beliefs. He repeats what Constantine and Licinius deemed politically advantageous. Yet that fact should not be allowed to damage his credit when he speaks of events in the East of which he had personal experience. The account given by Eusebius in the *Martyrs of Palestine* and in Book Nine of the *Ecclesiastical History* of the persecution which afflicted eastern Christians from 303 to 313 is irreplaceable.

X

EUSEBIUS AS APOLOGIST

Eusebius was not primarily an apologist for Christianity. He began as a biblical scholar, and he composed the first editions of both the *Chronicle* and *Ecclesiastical History* when the social and intellectual standing of Christians seemed secure and in no need of defense.[1] His historical views, therefore, which he maintained virtually unchanged until the end of his life, were not originally a product either of the age of Constantine or even of the early years of the fourth century; rather, they reflect the optimism which prevailed in Christian circles during the first fifteen years of Diocletian's reign. Writing then, Eusebius could assume or state briefly an interpretation of the course of human history as culminating in Christianity. It was only when the Christian church came under attack, both through legislation and from hostile polemics, that Eusebius felt obliged to set forth his views at length and to argue them fully. Eusebius was by instinct and training a scholar; he became an apologist only because circumstances demanded that he do so, and his style of argument in apology and polemic continually betrays the biblical exegete.

The earliest of Eusebius' apologetical works was *Against Hierocles*, which modern editors print under the inauthentic but more informative title "Against the Life of Apollonius of Tyana Written by Philostratus, Occasioned by the Comparison Drawn by Hierocles between Him and Christ."[2] Eusebius composed it shortly before 303, after the army had been purged of Christians but apparently before Diocletian issued persecuting edicts which affected Christian civilians.[3] Sossianus Hierocles (it is known from other evidence) was governor of a province, probably of Augusta Libanensis, *vicarius* of a diocese, *praeses* of Bithynia in 303, and prefect of Egypt seven years later.[4] Eusebius twice alludes to his adversary's official post in a way which implies that Hierocles was *vicarius Orientis* at the time of writing—and hence that before 303 he had already circulated his attack on Christianity in the East.[5] After persecution began, Hierocles also published his polemic in the imperial capital of Nicomedia, this time in two books. Lactantius was there and later described the contents of the work. His report reveals more about its style and nature than does Eusebius' deliberately selective presentation.[6]

Hierocles presented himself as an impartial "Lover of Truth," and addressed his work, not "against the Christians," but "to the Christians." He denied that he was attacking the Christians in a hostile fashion; his aim was to give them sound advice, and he warned them gravely not to be deceived by the Bible, which was wholly false and self-contradictory. Hierocles exhibited such knowledge of the Bible that Lactantius wondered whether he had once been a Christian himself. Yet Hierocles wrote sharply and ridiculed Jesus as a brigand with nine hundred followers, his disciples as low-class, uneducated liars, some of whom used to be fishermen. Hierocles did not deny that Jesus performed miracles. But he contended that Apollonius of Tyana had done the same or better. The refusal of most pagans to consider Apollonius a god proved them less credulous than Christians, who made a man into a god on the strength of a few miracles and prophecies. However, Hierocles was not a naive pagan of the traditional sort but a philosophical monotheist; in the epilogue to his work, he invoked a single supreme god who was the creator of the universe, the source of good, the begetter and sustainer of all life, whom the gods of the traditional cults, such as Jupiter, served as ministers or angels.

Eusebius made no serious attempt to report Hierocles' overall argument or to refute it directly. He addressed his answer to a friend, whom he depicts as admiring the comparison of Jesus and Apollonius.[7] Whether that is fact or literary artifice cannot be discerned; at all events, Eusebius airily dismisses the rest of Hierocles' arguments plagiarized from Celsus, and as refuted in advance by Origen's eight books *Against Celsus*—to which he refers anyone who wishes, with a genuine "love of truth," to understand his own position. Eusebius confines his attention to the one point where he concedes Hierocles' treatment any originality: Hierocles is the only denigrator of Christianity known to him who has compared and contrasted Apollonius and Jesus.[8] Eusebius then establishes the status of the text he intends to discuss. He quotes part of Hierocles' introduction of Apollonius: "They [that is, the Christians] babble incessantly, glorifying Jesus as having made the blind see and worked some similar wonders ... But let us consider how much better and more sensibly we inter-pret such things, and the view we hold of men gifted with remarkable powers ... In the time of our ancestors, during the reign of Nero, there flourished Apollonius of Tyana, who from early boyhood, when he became the priest of Asclepius, the lover of mankind, at Aegaeae in Cilicia, performed many re-markable feats, of which I shall omit the greater number and mention a few ..." Eusebius then quotes Hierocles' appeal to Philostratus:

> Why then have I recorded these facts? So that it may be possible to compare our accurate and solid judgment on each point with the frivolity of the Christians. For we hold that a man who has done such things is not a god, but a man favored of the gods, while they proclaim Jesus a god because of a few tricks ... And it is worth noting that, whereas Peter and Paul and a few like them, fellows known to be uneducated liars and cheats, have exaggerated the do-ings of Jesus, the deeds of Apollonius have been reported by Max-imus of Aegaeae, Damis, the philosopher who lived with him, and Philostratus of Athens, who were supremely well educated and re-spected the truth, and who, because they loved their fellow men, did not wish the achievements of a noble man, loved by the gods, to fall into oblivion.[9]

Eusebius lacked the critical acumen to question the credentials of Damis, whose testimony he accepts as that of a genuine associate of Apollonius from Assyria.[10] Nor could he raise the dangerous general question of what consti-tutes adequate attestation of a miracle—in the first or any other century.[11] He was content that the argument could proceed from evidence which Hierocles regarded as authoritative.

Before turning to a close examination of Philostratus' *Life of Apollonius* it-self, Eusebius permits himself some prefatory remarks. Even the most skepti-cal, Eusebius observes, must admit that Jesus is remarkable for many reasons: his coming was prophesied, he converted many who became disciples willing to die for his teaching, his power has overcome bitter persecution, his doctrine prevails everywhere, and his name casts out evil spirits. The Apollonius of Phi-lostratus deserves to be regarded as neither a philosopher nor an honest man, and his biographer, despite his education, is no respecter of truth. Apollonius himself may have been a sage; Eusebius used to regard him as such and will still do so—if he can disbelieve the *Life,* which depicts him as a mendicant sophist and magician, not as a philosopher. Divinely ordained bounds circum-scribe what mere men can achieve, and since men are incapable of participat-ing in the divine nature except by revelation sent from heaven, God aids man-kind by sending trusted messengers to illumine the world. Apollonius, therefore, cannot be a divine emissary, because he was known only to a few and conferred no benefits on posterity.[12]

With the fundamental question thus prejudged, Eusebius commences his dissection of the text. He proceeds book by book, episode by episode. He documents the claims made for Apollonius, and pillories them. Apollonius (according to the first book of the *Life*) possessed superhuman gifts from birth, and when he died he ascended bodily into heaven; therefore, he was a god. Why then did Apollonius need an education, when he knew everything already? Either the stories of his teachers or the claim that he had a divine nature must be false. Some of the details in Philostratus are too ridiculous to be true. Nevertheless, Eusebius again professes willingness to believe that Apollonius was a blameless philosopher and an admirable man. But Philostratus continually forgets that Apollonius is supposed to be superhuman—which discredits both himself and his hero.[13]

Eusebius scrutinizes each of the eight books of the *Life* in similar fashion[14] and almost never digresses to wider topics, though he makes frequent sallies against the "lover of truth," who recklessly believes manifest absurdities. He summarizes an episode, then criticizes it. Often he will accept Philostratus' account as true and ridicule it, either as laughable in itself or proving that Apollonius had human failings. Other stories he dismisses as obviously false or mythical; one story, he scoffs, even makes *The Wonders beyond Thyle* (of Antonius Diogenes) sound like sober history.[15] Eusebius argues that the Apollonius depicted in the *Life* was a fraud, a flatterer, and a liar, a wizard who performed often illusory miracles by conjuring evil spirits.[16]

In conclusion, Eusebius attacks Philostratus for philosophical inconsistency. Although the *Life* continually denies men's responsibility for their actions, attributing them to necessity, destiny, and the Fates, Philostratus nevertheless praises and blames the characters in his narrative, thus constantly assuming that they do have free will and responsibility. But, on Philostratus' own premises, since Apollonius was a mere puppet of fate or plaything of destiny, he does not deserve to be an object of admiration. More seriously, Eusebius defends a viewpoint fundamentally different from Philostratus': he reasserts, quoting Epictetus' *Encheiridion* and Plato, the traditonal view that men have the power to do or not to do certain actions. To deny that entails atheism and destroys morality. Eusebius concludes by restating the initial dilemma: either Apollonius was a philosopher and admirable, or he was as Philostratus depicts him—a disreputable magician.[17]

Eusebius's *Against Hierocles* is an ephemeral work, composed in haste to meet the sudden needs of controversy. When Eusebius wrote it, he may already have begun to compose a far more substantial and systematic work of apologia, the *General Elementary Introduction* to Christianity in ten books, of which the last five either survive almost complete or can be substantially reconstructed. The four books of *Prophetic Extracts Concerning Christ* explicitly describe themselves as Books Six to Nine of the *Introduction*,[18] while much (probably the greater part) of the last book has been preserved as fragments in a catena of patristic comments on Luke compiled by Nicetas of Heraclea in the eleventh century.[19]

The external form of the *General Elementary Introduction* invites comparison with two other, almost contemporaneous philosophical works. Anatolius, a philosopher in Alexandria before he became bishop of Laodicea in approximately 268, composed an *Introduction to Arithmetic* in ten books,[20] and Iamblichus, the former pupil of an Anatolius who is probably the same man, arranged a series of works to form a *Collection of Pythagorean Doctrines* in ten books, which began with a *Life of Pythagoras* and an *Exhortation to Philosophy* and devoted eight treatises to various branches of mathematics, to physics, ethics, music, and astronomy.[21] Eusebius certainly knew of Anatolius' *Introduction,* and he can hardly have remained entirely unaware of the activities and writings of Iamblichus, who taught philosophy in Syria, at Antioch and then at Apamea, for three decades or more until he died about 320.[22] Although Iamblichus held himself aloof from politics, some of his pupils hailed him as a champion of Hellenism—and one of them may have published an attack on Christianity in 303.[23]

The *General Elementary Introduction* reflects the time and the place of its composition. Eusebius was writing when the Christian church seemed more seriously menaced than ever before, since, in obedience to imperial legislation, the clergy had ceased to minister openly and congregations no longer assembled for worship.[24] Emperors and governors, and behind them the "unseen spiritual rulers of this world," were attempting to destroy the truth as revealed in the teaching of Jesus Christ.[25] On the rational level, Eusebius interpreted persecution as a temporary phenomenon. Ever-watchful and ever-pitying, God allowed his servants to be chastised for imperfect devotion to him but gave them continual comfort and would never desert them.[26] Also on the rational level, Eusebius argued that God would avenge the present persecution as he had those of the past, by destroying whoever attacked God and his servants.[27]

The severity of persecution, however, shook Eusebius deeply. For forty years the Christian church had enjoyed prosperity and security; now, if not technically abolished, it was officially disbanded. Some of the most primitive elements in Christianity suddenly became attractive to a man who prided himself on his rationality. Perhaps the course of history was nearing its end, perhaps the day of judgment was approaching, perhaps Christ would soon appear to vindicate his oppressed adherents.[28] The surviving books of the *General Elementary Introduction* have an insistent emphasis on Christ's second coming in glory which is far more urgent than in any of Eusebius' other works. During the persecution, Eusebius yearned for a "new age," when the children of God would be released from their enslavement in corruptible bodies, when creation would revert to its pristine state, freed from its present condition, redeemed, exalted, translated to a higher existence.[29]

Eusebius addressed his *Introduction* to Christianity to sympathetic pagans, whom he wished to convince of two main points—the superiority of the Judaeo-Christian tradition to paganism and the correctness of the Church's teachings within that tradition. The first five books were devoted to the first task, the last five to the second. Unfortunately, the first five books are lost, except for exiguous fragments of Book One; these are nevertheless significant, for one of them argues that human nature needs "the holy Word of God" to attain virtue.[30] The extant books assume that the reader grants the authority and inspiration of Scripture but needs assistance in comprehending it correctly; he is, or is assumed to be, a lover of true learning, one who wishes to form a right judgment, one who has made progress but not yet attained perfect understanding.[31] A reader who fitted this description was no disinterested pagan. In its historical context, the *General Elementary Introduction* had a precise and definite function: it replaced the formal, organized instruction of catechumens which was now forbidden by law.

Eusebius argues, both explicitly and implicitly, against three separate groups of adversaries or opposing points of view, which he describes, or rather disparages, in a way which indicates that he is not addressing them, but an independent audience capable of comparing his views with theirs. The adversaries named most frequently are "the circumcised": Eusebius consistently rejects Jewish interpretations of the Old Testament as too literal—always inadequate and often obviously stupid.[32] Eusebius also expressly repudiates the opinions of two types of Christian. The Marcionites construe God's utterances too mythically and wish to destroy the harmony of the Old and New Testaments, while the adherents of "godless heresies"—Ebionites and the followers of Artemon and Paul of Samosata—deny the divinity of Christ and assert that the Savior was a mere man who did not exist before the Incarnation.[33] Why does Eusebius concentrate on rebutting precisely these three positions? His concerns presumably reflect the situation in Caesarea. The phrase "the circumcised" may not be chosen merely for its offensiveness; it includes not only Jews but also Samaritans, of whom there were many in the city.[34] Marcionite communities (it is known) flourished in Palestine, while a schismatic church of Paulianists maintained some sort of corporate existence in Antioch and may have had sympathizers elsewhere.[35]

The four books of *Prophetic Extracts Concerning Christ,* which comprise Books Six to Nine of the *General Elementary Introduction,* commence with a preface (unfortunately now lacunose) in which Eusebius explains the relationship of these books to the first five, proffers his credentials as an exegete (the chronological tables of the *Chronicle* have qualified him), and states his basic theological assumptions. He also describes what he intends to do by interpreting a biblical text in the terminology of Stoic philosophy. Like the wise bee (Proverbs 6:8), he has extracted pollen from the meadows of God's word which will give health to both kings and others; but his *Prophetic Extracts* are far superior to mere honey:

For who of the faithful would not confess that the stores of salvation concerning the Word of God are incomparably superior to every bodily pleasure and benefit, being suited for the acquisition of truly beneficial and healthy correctness of belief? To respect this is necessary not only for those who have made moral progress and are called "kings" but also for those who are at a lower level and are just approaching the divine word for the first time. I think that my enterprise will be especially suitable for them, so that they may be able thereby to understand thoroughly the truth *of matters about which* they *have been informed* (Luke 1:4). Pure and simple faith possesses the firm force of conviction all the more when a man uses his reason and first lays foundations by demonstration and then receives elementary instruction in the certain apprehension and knowledge of what must be accepted on faith ... It seemed necessary to add as brief and concise an explanation as possible of each prophecy quoted, as befits an *Introduction* ... My exegesis will be brief and moderate, sometimes intended to prove that the holy predictions of God have been fulfilled in our Savior alone, at others stating the opinion I hold about what will be quoted.[36]

The four books of *Prophetic Extracts* proceed exactly as promised. Eusebius quotes biblical passages, first from the Pentateuch and the historical books of the Old Testament, discussing them in turn, occasionally at length but usually briefly (Book One), and then from the Psalms (Book Two). Eusebius treats the rest of the canonical Jewish Old Testament in the third book, and he devotes all of Book Four to Isaiah.[37] Throughout, Eusebius draws on the resources available to him in Caesarea. He refers interested readers who desire a full discussion of any biblical text to Origen's commentaries, which he commends as the work of that "wonderful" or "holy" man.[38] He takes his quotations from the Hexapla; thus he can, when he wishes, quote the original Hebrew of his proof text, at least in transliteration, can weigh the merits of translations other than the authoritative one quoted, and can note, where necessary, that part of the Greek Septuagint is obelized because there is no corresponding passage in the Hebrew.[39] Presumably, it was in Caesarea that Eusebius heard a Jew expounding some verses of Isaiah (7:10–17), not as a messianic prophecy but as foretelling Ezekiel's activities, and in Caesarea too that he heard Jewish polemics against the person and divine status of Jesus.[40] Such "slander and abuse" Eusebius confutes by combining the text "I will be fierce as a panther to Ephraim" (Hosea 5:14) with the statement (taken from Didymus of Alexandria) that the panther lulls its prey with its fragrance. Eusebius argues that Jesus is neither the son of a panther nor a man called Pantera (as Jews allege): Jesus himself is the panther, and the power of the divine Word is its fragrance.[41] How this conclusion can be proved is a question which Eusebius waives as too long to discuss in the present work.[42]

To the final book of the *General Elementary Introduction,* which followed the four books of *Prophetic Extracts,* Eusebius gave the significant title *Second Theophany,* that is, the second coming of Jesus at the last judgment. This last book surveyed the Gospels, and perhaps the rest of the New Testament, in a fashion similar to the preceding treatment of the Old: texts were quoted and then expounded. The *Prophetic Extracts* and the *Second Theophany* together advance an apologetical argument which is primarily historical. Eusebius contends that the Bible supplies the key to understanding human history, past, present, and future, because it reveals God's intentions for mankind.[43]

God, in the person of the divine Word, or Jesus, has revealed himself directly to man at only two periods, one remote and one recent. The patriarchs of Genesis saw God, and long afterward, God became man and lived on earth in the reigns of the emperors Augustus and Tiberius. During the intervening period, mankind was incapable of apprehending God directly; even Moses, who spoke with God, saw only the angels who surround God as a bodyguard. The patriarchs, being uncircumcised, were gentiles; the Jewish race came into existence only through the Mosaic dispensation. The Old Testament, therefore, and the Jewish way of life operate on a lower level of truth than Christianity. The laws of Moses conform to the historical situation in which they were given; they hint at the divine truth symbolically and figuratively, since the Jews of Moses' day, educated in Egyptian ways, could not receive a more mystical and spiritual teaching.[44]

Nevertheless, the Jewish Law, Jewish prophets, and the Jewish Old Testament predicted and prepared the way for the ultimate divine revelation when God became man: every historical event narrated in the Old Testament has a spiritual analog in the New, which it prefigures.[45] Interpreted aright, Moses and the prophets foretold every detail in the life of Jesus, and yet the Jews, who had God among them, blindly refused to recognize the promised Messiah.[46] Instead, they killed him. Hence God punished, and continues to punish, the Jews with political extinction, while ensuring that the Christian church, the repository of his truth, prospers everywhere.[47]

The contrast between the divergent fortunes of the Jewish nation and the Christian church is the constant refrain of both the *Prophetic Extracts* and the *Second Theophany:*

> This was uttered before the event; the Savior foretold what would
> be, and it soon came about, so that the fulfillment of the events was
> seen by men's eyes not long afterward. Since his time, throughout
> the whole inhabited world of man, among all races, the symbols of
> the kingdom of God have been visible through his churches, with
> myriads in them living according to the gospel of salvation and en-
> deavoring to worship God like the ancient prophets and Abraham
> himself, Isaac, and Jacob. For they too, though they preceded in
> time the laws of Moses, were conspicuous for living and conducting

themselves according to the gospel, since they despised the polytheistic error inherited from their fathers and received the knowledge of the supreme God. For this reason, it was said that the majority of the gentiles would come from east and west, and that they would become equal to Abraham and those other blessed men because of their equally good way of life. How the descendants and successors of those same men, called sons of the kingdom because of their forefathers (for potentially, like their forefathers, they had a share in the heavenly kingdom), have been deprived of their promised blessings is shown clearly by the sack of their city, the siege of their temple, their scattering among all the races of mankind, their enslavement to their enemies, and, in addition, their deprivation of worship according to Jewish custom, their ignorance of Christ, and their alienation from the teachings of the gospel. All these things should be manifest signs of the darkness which has enveloped them, into which they have stumbled because they opposed the light of salvation.[48]

The Jewish nation no longer exists, and Jews are forbidden to set foot in Jerusalem; both are God's punishment for their treatment of his son.[49] The Church, in contrast, rapidly filled the whole world by a divine and unspeakable power and proclaimed its message, not just to one or two nations or provinces, but everywhere to every nation.[50] For nearly three centuries the Church has been a civilizing force. Through its influence, the majority of mankind have been purged of base emotions and have changed their former animal wildness into humanity.[51] The Church continues to gain numerous converts even during persecution. For everyone can see, at this very moment, the firm, unyielding resolve of those who believe in Christ and resist the threats of emperors and governors, and everyone can see masses of ordinary people displaying a way of life embodying virtue and philosophy to a degree not easily found even among those who pride themselves on their scholarly or literary accomplishments.[52]

All significant historical events are, in Eusebius's view, prophesied in the Bible. The Old Testament foretold not only the Incarnation, Passion, and Resurrection but also the subsequent success of the Christian church, and even the persecution during which Eusebius wrote.[53] But to assume that Scripture has predicted only the past and the present would be illogical; it must also speak about events which still lie in the future. In particular, it speaks frequently and explicitly of the second coming of Christ, when the risen Lord will judge both the living and the dead.[54] Those who love God will be segregated from the godless and impious and will receive an eternal reward for their loyalty.[55] Eusebius envisages the second theophany in concrete, visual terms. The sea will dry up, and the watery element will vanish altogether. The Word of God will then appear with such bright glory that the stars, the moon, and even the sun will no longer be visible. There will thenceforth be perpetual day. The patriarchs and the prophets, the just and the worshipers of God will ascend into the ark of heaven, leaving the rest of mankind on earth to await God's vengeance; he will then, like an earthly monarch, order them to be executed.[56]

When will this happen? Eusebius warns that anyone who locates the last judgment in the distant future may be deceiving himself. The arrival of the day of the Lord will be "sudden and unexpected"—and even before then death may sneak up on a man like a robber. In readiness for that day, one must be ever alert and vigilant, always awaiting the Lord's coming, like a wise and faithful servant.[57] Eusebius lays especial stress on the text "Whoever is ashamed of me and my words, the Son of Man will be ashamed of him" (Luke 9:26; compare Matthew 10:32). He emphasizes that Jesus was speaking to men who would be tortured and perhaps executed for his sake, and that he promised his disciples eternal bliss in recompense for their suffering and martyrdom on earth.[58]

The emphasis on the second glorious theophany would not be lost on Eusebius' audience. Christians were no longer despised by their fellows as criminals who deserved torture and mockery, and their resistance won converts despite the repressive policies of emperors. Eusebius spoke bluntly and denounced the reigning emperor Maximinus for impiety in removing a bronze relief at Paneas believed to depict Jesus curing the woman with an issue of blood (Luke 8:43–48).[59] Christians everywhere believed that God would soon punish the persecutors, but the Eusebius of the *Second Theophany* sometimes writes as if that imminent vindication will coincide with the end of the world.

The technique of the *General Elementary Introduction,* at least in the five surviving books, is deliberately discursive, the overall argument emerging from a long succession of proof texts. The individual discussions, however, all proceed from a consistent method of interpreting the Bible and from a systematic interpretation of history. They also assume certain basic theological premises which are of great importance in understanding Eusebius' later standing in ecclesiastical politics. Eusebius was writing not only before the controversy began over Arius' teachings in Alexandria, but also before Eusebius realized that Origen's theology needed to be defended against charges of heresy.[60] All his later apologetical and theological works, including even the *Preparation for the Gospel,* were written at a time when Eusebius may have muted his views in order to avoid appearing heterodox. In the *Prophetic Extracts* and *Second Theophany,* however, he expresses himself freely and without inhibition. His philosophical formulations, predictably, derive from Origen.[61]

God the Father was "the first cause," the creator or demiurge of the universe, uncreated and the father of all things, the "first and uncreated God."[62] God the Son, the divine Word, or Logos, so Eusebius repeatedly states, is different from and inferior to God the Father.[63] Although the Son is Lord and God, and the only Lord and God apart from the Father, he occupies second place after the Father, he is a minister of his Father's will, and his power was given him by the Father.[64] He may be the "angel of mighty counsel" (Isaiah 9:6) who performs and announces the will of the Father to every created thing, but he is essentially different from the Father; he has a substance (*hypostasis*) of his own which differs from that of the Father, he is a separate being from the Father who sent him, and though he is called God, he is "the first of all created things after the uncreated beginning."[65] The Word assisted the Father in creation, since it was the Word that formed man, but the Word was merely the second cause.[66] Eusebius comes perilously close to an explicit statement that the second person of the divine Trinity is a second God, especially when he is discussing what was later to be the prime Arian proof text (Proverbs 8:22):

> The whole book of Proverbs seems to be spoken in the character of Wisdom, which in some passages commends the moral life, in others utters speeches appropriate to another, and sometimes propounds riddles, sometimes again teaches about herself and gives instruction concerning her divinely inspired calling. Of these we shall select the passage by which we learn that Wisdom is a divine creature with a wholly remarkable nature, being identical with the second cause of all after the first God, the *Word* which *was in the beginning with God* (John 1:1) and with the providence of God, which manages and governs everything and reaches even to affairs on earth, and which was created before every essence and substance, the *beginning of ways* of the whole act of creation.[67]

The substance of the divine Word is different from and inferior to the "first and uncreated" substance of the Father and God of all, and the divine Word is capable of suffering because it suffered together with the man whose form it took on earth.[68] Admirers of Eusebius's theology assert fervently that he was no Arian.[69] That was not the opinion of Eusebius's contemporaries, and the *General Elementary Introduction* repeatedly affirms two propositions which the Council of Nicaea condemned as heretical: that God the Son differs in substance from God the Father, and that the Son belongs to the created order. Writing in the earliest years of the fourth century, Eusebius could innocently regard both these opinions as orthodox.

Eusebius wrote both *Against Hierocles* and the *General Elementary Introduction* before he had any knowledge of the most notorious polemic against Christianity. The philosopher Porphyry wrote his vast *Against the Christians* in Sicily either shortly before or shortly after Diocletian issued the first of the persecuting edicts.[70] When Porphyry's work became known in the East, Methodius in Lycia and Eusebius in Palestine came out with refutations, which have perished.[71] Even though Eusebius filled no fewer than twenty-five books, three of them (Eighteen, Nineteen, and Twenty) devoted to the "abomination of desolation" (Daniel 6:20),[72] his *Against Porphyry* must have been an ephemeral and hasty work. When the decade of persecution ended in 313, Eusebius commenced work on a systematic and definitive refutation of Porphyry which comprised two separate and complementary works in fully thirty-five books: the extant *Preparation for the Gospel* in fifteen, and the *Proof of the Gospel* in twenty, of which the first ten books survive complete. The enormous work is the most majestic and disdainful of all polemics.

Eusebius' adversary was born in Tyre, probably in 234.[73] Porphyry originally bore the Semitic name of Malchus, and he may have been able to speak Syriac and to understand other Semitic languages.[74] In his youth he had close contacts with Christianity; he met Origen, perhaps studied with him, and may even have become a Christian for a period.[75] Still a young man, Porphyry left the Levant and studied in Athens for some time; here he attended a dinner party to celebrate Plato's birthday at which the host was Longinus, later a minister of Zenobia and executed by Aurelian as a traitor.[76] In 263 Porphyry went to Rome and became a pupil of Plotinus. Five years later he departed to Sicily, taking up residence at Lilybaeum, and he was in Sicily in the summer of 270 when Plotinus died.[77] After 270 Porphyry may have continued to reside in Sicily for most of the rest of his life.[78] For, although he returned to Rome, either briefly or for a period of years, the *Isagoge* (an introduction to Aristotle's *Categories*), probably *On Abstinence from Animal Foods,* and certainly *Against the Christians* were composed in Sicily.[79] Porphyry was still alive in or after 301, when he wrote the *Life of Plotinus* and published the definitive edition of Plotinus' writings.[80] He died, reportedly in Rome, not many years thereafter.[81]

Porphyry discussed the status of Christianity in at least two works. Many years before he wrote *Against the Christians,* even before he became a pupil of Plotinus, he had composed *On Philosophy from Oracles* in three books, which depicted Jesus in a far more favorable light.[82] This work is difficult to evaluate; because it is known mainly from Christian authors who quote it for polemical purposes, the surviving quotations may not give an accurate impression of the whole.[83] Porphyry collected oracles which he promised to reproduce either exactly or with small metrical or stylistic changes not affecting their sense, and he intended to demonstrate the essential harmony of Greek philosophical insight with divine revelation, even where the revelation had been vouchsafed to Egyptians, Phoenicians, Chaldaeans, Lydians, or Jews: "The present collection will register how the gods have declared that many of the dogmas of philosophy attain the truth, and I will briefly discuss the science of oracles, which will be of benefit both for contemplation and for the other purification of life. What profit the collection has, they will best know who, after laboring for the truth, have at some time prayed to receive a revelation from the gods and thus obtain relief from perplexity through the teaching of those who speak."[84] Porphyry saw no difficulty in integrating Jesus into this scheme. Apollo had declared that the God of the Jews was indeed a god: although Jesus had been executed, he was nevertheless a holy and pious man and a worthy teacher, whose immortal soul ascended into heaven to join the souls of other pious men. His followers, on the other hand, were unclean, polluted, and enmeshed in error, blasphemers against the gods who endowed men like Jesus with immortality; the Christians deserved pity for their stupidity in mistaking a good man for a god.[85]

Between writing *On Philosophy from Oracles* and *Against the Christians*, Porphyry abandoned this optimistic integration of Christianity into Greco-Roman culture. He began to fear that the Greeks and their gods were seriously endangered; he abandoned any desire for synthesis, claimed that Christianity and Greek culture were fundamentally incompatible, and transformed his favorable evaluation of Jesus into systematic denigration. His work *Against the Christians* comprised fifteen books, and Eusebius and Jerome state that Book Three attacked Origen, Book Four discussed the date of Moses, and Books Twelve and Thirteen that of Daniel;[86] perhaps, therefore, Porphyry began with three books of philosophical argument, and followed them with twelve which examined the Old and New Testaments in detail. It was Porphyry's emphasis on the Bible which made his attack so dangerous: he knew enough about the Bible and contemporary Christianity to be able to criticize Christian exegesis of the sacred text, compare it with other methods of interpretation, and ruthlessly expose errors of fact and reasoning. Although *Against the Christians* cannot be reconstructed, the surviving evidence reveals enough about its tenor to understand Eusebius' treatment of Porphyry as an adversary.[87]

Porphyry, like other Platonists of the period, objected to the elevation of faith above reason. He sneered that Christian teachers inculcated in their followers a blind and unreasoning acceptance of whatever they might say, and he claimed that their inability to provide rational proof of their position betrayed the essential falsity of their beliefs.[88] He rejected both the Christian conception of God and the Christian interpretation of history. If God were omnipotent (he argued), then God could lie—which is absurd.[89] He judged it equally absurd to claim a special historical significance for the Jews; the providence of the Demiurge provided oracles and prophecies everywhere, and those of the Jews were not significantly different from those of any other race.[90] Moreover, the claim that Jesus saves men's souls makes no provision for the innumerable blameless and virtuous men who lived before the Incarnation; Christianity, therefore, postulates in God an immoral lack of concern for men who, through no fault of their own, are ineligible for salvation simply because they were not Jews by race and lived too early to be able to become Christians.[91] More fundamentally still, Porphyry contended that the Incarnation was a logical impossibility; God, who was by definition impassible, could not become man and thus subject himself to suffering.[92]

Porphyry attacked the Old Testament on various levels, and he questioned the historical basis from which Christian interpretation proceeded. Whereas Eusebius, with appeal to Josephus and Justus, Clement, Africanus, and Tatian, made Moses a contemporary of Inachus, four hundred years before the Trojan War, Porphyry placed Moses before Semiramis and almost eight hundred and fifty before the Trojan War.[93] Porphyry claimed to possess an independent source for the Jews almost contemporary with Moses, namely, the history of Sanchuniathon, which Philo of Byblos translated from Phoenician into Greek in the second century.[94] Eusebius does not explain precisely how Porphyry exploited this evidence, but he presumably used it to impugn the alleged uniqueness of the Jews.

Porphyry also examined the credentials of individual books of the Bible. He demonstrated that Daniel was not written at the time of Cyrus, as it claims, but three and a half centuries later; significantly, Porphyry appears to draw heavily on Syrian or Syriac exegesis of Daniel and to misdate the transition from *post eventum* "prophecy" to real prophecy by one year.[95] Porphyry denied that Daniel in any sense prophesied the coming of Christ, and it seems probable that *Against the Christians* discussed all the passages claimed by Christians as messianic prophecies.[96] Porphyry attacked not only the factual assumptions of Christian exegesis but also its favorite method. Allegory (he argued) could prove anything. Porphyry applied allegory to the *Iliad* and showed that Homer's depiction of Achilles and Hector could be understood as an allegory of Christ and the Devil.[97] It was presumably by application of allegory to the Bible that Porphyry obtained a striking *reductio ad absurdum:* Solomon stated clearly that "God has no son."[98]

When he turned to the New Testament, Porphyry accused the four Gospels of frequent inconsistency and contradiction, and he ridiculed Jesus' parables.[99] He compared Jesus to Apollonius of Tyana and to Apuleius of Madaura, suggesting that they wrought greater miracles than Jesus, and he mocked the apostles as uneducated rustics, incapable of telling truth from falsehood.[100] Worse, both master and followers were "cheats and impostors" who set out to deceive mankind with a fraudulent web of lies and inventions.[101] Porphyry also derided the disciples, who provided the sole evidence for the exploits of Jesus, as ignorant illiterates who wrote nonsense and whose testimony was worthless.[102]

Nor did Porphyry omit contemporary Christians from his attack. He complained of the prominent role of women in Christianity, of Christian attacks on pagan religious practices,[103] and of the conduct of individual Christians. Origen had been a pupil of Ammonius, from whom he learned his skill in disputation; but whereas Ammonius, born a Christian, adopted a lawful way of life as soon as he touched wisdom and philosophy, Origen, though a Greek and educated in Greek culture, lapsed into "barbarian rashness": "He prostituted himself and his education. As far as external life went, he lived as a Christian and illegally, but in his opinions about things and the divine he was a Greek and corrupted Greek views with alien myths. For he always consorted with Plato, he frequented the works of Numenius, Cronius, Apollophanes, Longinus, Moderatus, Nicomachus, and distinguished Pythagoreans, and he used the books of Chaeremon the Stoic and Cornutus, from whom he learned the allegorical interpretation of Greek mysteries and applied it to the Jewish Scriptures."[104] Porphyry's two main charges are false—and all the more significant for that reason. Origen had probably been born a Christian; at the very least, he was a Christian by the age of seventeen, and both his parents were Christians. Furthermore, Origen drew on a Christian and, before that, a Jewish tradition of allegorical interpretation.[105] Porphyry implicitly denied both of these indisputable facts by his tendentious claim that Origen was an apostate from the Greek tradition to which he rightfully belonged.

The accusation of apostasy appears to have been Porphyry's principal charge against the Christians, and by it he justified the renewal of persecution. The worship of Jesus (he contended) rendered prayers to the traditional gods ineffectual; no wonder there was continual plague in Rome![106] Porphyry, like Diocletian in 302, branded all religious innovation as immoral. The Christians broke the law by impiously refusing to recognize the obvious manifestations of divine power, and it was right that the laws should prescribe death for their transgression.[107] Porphyry's intellectual arguments had very practical, and very unpleasant, corollaries, for he denied the social and intellectual respectability which Christians had enjoyed for a century. Like Celsus in the second century, Porphyry presented Christians as apostates, both from Greco-Roman religion and culture and from Jewish religion and culture, who forsook the established cults of city and country, patronized by kings, lawgivers, and philosophers, for atheism and impiety.[108] Christians had first made common cause with the impious Jews, the enemies of all mankind, and then abandoned even the Jews for something newfangled and irrational. Such men deserved brutal punishment—and between 303 and 313 many of them received brutal punishment.[109]

When persecution ceased in 313, Eusebius began to compose a systematic refutation of Porphyry, which should not so much controvert the arguments advanced against Christianity as address itself to Porphyry's basic assumptions and to the underlying issues.[110] Eusebius set out to provide a definitive statement of the relationship between Greek culture, Judaism, and Christianity. He dedicated the resulting twofold apologetical treatise, the *Preparation for the Gospel* and the *Proof of the Gospel,* to Theodotus, bishop of Laodicea in Syria.[111] His real audience was the same as that for which he composed the *General Elementary Introduction*—sympathetic pagans who might read attentively an explanation of why Christianity was superior to both pagan and Jewish religion.[112] The *Preparation for the Gospel* and the *Proof of the Gospel* also cover the same ground as the two parts of the *Introduction.* The first considers the relationship of Christianity to Greco-Roman civilization and culture; the second, its relationship to Judaism. But the argument has been reformulated to take account of Porphyry.

Eusebius writes with a deliberate, even ostentatious, parade of erudition and refers not infrequently, but for the most part anonymously, to the philosopher who is his main adversary. Porphyry is not, however, Eusebius' only intellectual opponent. When Eusebius states that anyone can collect prophetic passages from the Old Testament and "immediately silence those of the circumcision who say that the promises of God were given to them alone," his vivid language is not merely a rhetorical flourish; in Caesarea and many other cities of the East, there must have been Jews who advanced precisely this argument, not only to contradict Christians but also to win proselytes to Judaism.[113] Eusebius complains that Jews still curse Christ in their synagogues, that they mock, denigrate, and insult the Son of God.[114] In such passages a strongly felt resentment is obvious, and the scale and style of the *Proof of the Gospel* partly reflect the presence of Jewish teachers and scholars in the milieu in which Eusebius worked.[115] Porphyry's charge that Christians were apostates from Hellenism to Judaism who had reneged even on their substitute religion clearly rankled.

In any polemic, the opening statement is important, often decisive. The obvious procedure was to state the criticisms and objections, and then to refute them systematically by expounding the Scriptures, discussing the various points at issue, and propounding the Christian case. Despite the model of Origen's *Against Celsus,* Eusebius chose another style of argument. He stated the truth first, and then Porphyry's main objections.[116] But, of set purpose, he did not name Porphyry; instead, he presented a summary of his views as something that any Greek "who has no true understanding of either his religion or ours" might ask.[117] He then answered three philosophical objections, each in a chapter, still without alluding more specifically to Porphyry. Christians (he argued) have chosen their religion after sufficient examination, they have espoused useful beliefs out of conscious choice, and they have renounced superstitious error after sober reflection.[118] After this introduction, Eusebius commences the main argument of the *Preparation for the Gospel* with the documentation of the falsity of paganism from pagan writers themselves.[119] But only after three more chapters does Eusebius name Porphyry, whom he describes as "that famous contemporary of ours who seeks celebrity by his abuse of us"—in order to introduce a quotation from Porphyry's *On Abstinence from Animal Foods* which Eusebius can exploit in favor of his own argument.[120] Similarly, *Against the Christians* is quoted to establish the credentials of Philo of Byblos, whom Eusebius then uses as evidence for primitive Phoenician religion.[121]

The treatment of Porphyry in Book One of the *Preparation for the Gospel* illustrates Eusebius' technique throughout its fifteen books. If the aim of polemic is not to refute but to obliterate an adversary, Eusebius succeeds magnificently. The argument advances inexorably, with incessant refutation of Porphyry who, however, is rarely named. Eusebius quotes a wide range of authors (sometimes at immense length), including Porphyry himself, whose other works (principally *On Philosophy from Oracles,* for which Eusebius is the main source of fragments) are mercilessly exploited where they confute or contradict the arguments Porphyry used against the Christians. Throughout, Eusebius has one main polemical aim: to demonstrate, against Porphyry, an essential harmony or identity between Christianity and all that is best in Greco-Roman civilization. The quotations of Greek writers thus form an integral part of the overall argument, which Eusebius has ordered into a carefully designed structure.

The first three books of the *Preparation for the Gospel,* apart from the introduction, discuss the origin of pagan religion. Eusebius summarizes their argument as follows:

> Thinking it important to refute at the beginning of the *Preparation for the Gospel,* the polytheistic error of all the nations, in order to justify and excuse the separation which we have with good reason and judgment made from them, first of all, in the first three books, I thoroughly examined not only the myths concerning their gods, which the sons of their theologians and poets have ridiculed, but also their solemn and secret physical theories, which have been elevated high to heaven and to a cosmic scale by their noble philosophy, even though the theologians themselves declared that there was no need at all for solemnity on these matters. One must observe, therefore, that the very oldest of their theologians were proved to have no special historical knowledge, but to rely on mere myths. Hence appropriately, in all cities and villages, according to the narratives of the ancients, rites and mysteries of the gods conforming to the mythical narratives of the earlier authors have been handed down by tradition, so that even now people still accept the marriages of gods and their procreation of children, their lamentations and drunkenness, the wanderings of some, the infatuations of others, the rages of some, and others' disasters and adventures of every other type, in accordance with what is recorded by the most ancient writers in their rites, in their hymns, and in the odes composed for their gods. Nevertheless, at the same time, as a work of supererogation, I brought into the open the boastful dramatizations of these very writers in physical interpretations and the ingenious explanations of sophists and philosophers.[122]

The actual argument of the first three books is more specific and historical than this summary implies. Eusebius identified the earliest version of paganism as the astral religions of Phoenicia and Egypt, as described by Philo of Byblos and Diodorus Siculus.[123] All other types of paganism are later than this primitive religion, and Eusebius adduces abundant evidence to show that Greek religion, even in its earliest stage, was imported from Phoenicia and Egypt. Hence he can conclude that Greek religion is a secondary superstition, a mélange of Phoenician and Egyptian notions with no originality of its own, and that Greek theories about the gods represent merely a vain attempt to rationalize an obviously false worship of the material world from which the religions of Egypt and Phoenicia originated.[124]

Books Four to Six have a more diffuse thesis. In the preface to Book Four, Eusebius declares that, having refuted the mythical or historical theology of the poets and the physical or theoretical theology of the philosophers, he will now discuss official religion as established by law in every city and country.[125] In Book Fifteen, however, Eusebius identifies the subject matter of these three books as oracles and false views about fate.[126] The divergence between the two statements reflects an attempt by Eusebius, which is not quite successful, to equate oracles and official religion. In Books Four and Five, he argues that official religion is younger than the other types of paganism; its creation was rendered possible by the increasing power of evil demons, to whom the shrines belong. He adduces as proof the silence of the oracles, documented by Plutarch, which is a result of the advent of Christ, whose worship has rendered the gods of the official pantheon useless and ineffectual.[127] Combined, or rather interlaced, with these theses are two others. First, Eusebius constantly suggests that Christianity represents progress. Christianity is morally superior to paganism, and its influence is responsible for purifying other religions by putting an end to human sacrifice.[128] Second, he repeatedly argues that oracles are fraudulent, and to substantiate their fraudulence he appeals both to recent events and to Greek writers such as Diogenianus and Oenomaus of Gadara, whose *Detection of Impostors* he quotes at length.[129] Book Six, which argues against astral determinism, appears to be a digression, though Eusebius may again be obliquely answering Porphyry.[130]

In Books Seven to Nine, Eusebius examines the dogmatic theology and the history of the Old Testament. He claims, in brief, that the philosophy to be found in the Old Testament is superior to Greek philosophy in each of the traditional three branches of the subject (physics, metaphysics, and ethics), and he supports the claim not only from Christian and Jewish writers but also from gentile writers of the Hellenistic and Roman periods.[131] Book Seven also contains the clearest statement of what Eusebius thinks Christianity is. He turns on its head Porphyry's charge that Christians are renegades from both Hellenism and Judaism. Christianity (he holds) is identical with the religion of the Hebrew patriarchs, who saw the truth while the first pagans wallowed in error. Hence it is of greater antiquity than Judaism, which is a way of life founded by Moses, the last of the ancient Hebrews, as a temporary dispensation to allow knowledge of the Old Testament to circulate so that all mankind can embrace the religion of the Hebrew patriarchs revealed fully and to all in Christianity.[132]

Book Ten stands alone, occupying a pivotal position in the argument, for it provides the crucial proof that the Greeks derived their learning, as well as their philosophy, from the Hebrews. Eusebius quotes Clement of Alexandria and Porphyry to show that Greeks were plagiarists, he documents many varied examples of Greek borrowing from the Orient and he shows that Moses and the prophets lived earlier than the Greek philosophers.[133] The next three books compare the doctrines of Greek philosophers with those of the Old Testament. Eusebius concentrates on Plato and contends, with detailed illustration, that Plato derived the central features of his philosophy from the Hebrews but went astray in those areas, admittedly few, where he diverged from Hebrew philosophy.[134] Books Eleven to Thirteen thus argue for the essential harmony of Platonism and Christianity, while presenting the latter as superior. The last two books consider other Greek philosophical schools, including Aristotle and the Stoics; Eusebius quotes Plato, Numenius and many other philosophers, including Plotinus, to show the uselessness of all Greek philosophy other than Platonism.

Eusebius did not intend the *Preparation for the Gospel* to stand as a separate work. The introduction to Book Fifteen describes the *Proof of the Gospel,* which will immediately follow, as a "more complete argument";[135] whereas the *Preparation* concerns itself with the relation of Christianity to Greek religion and philosophy, the *Proof* considers its relation to Judaism. Eusebius himself characterizes Books One and Two of the *Proof* as an extended introduction.[136] The first book argues that the new covenant of Christ has superseded the Mosaic system, which was given to a single race and which the gentiles could not adopt even if they wished; the second book, that the Old Testament itself predicts that the coming of Christ will reveal knowledge of God to all mankind and will thus remove the Jews from their privileged position as the repositories of God's favor. Having established that Christianity is the fulfillment of the Old Testament, and hence that Christians have as much right to use it as the Jews, Eusebius proceeds to his main theme: the New Testament and subsequent history as the fulfillment of Old Testament prophecies.

Book Three establishes to Eusebius' satisfaction the fact that the Incarnation was foretold, while Books Four and Five deduce from the Old Testament a Christology which Eusebius describes as "more secret doctrines pertaining to the more mystical theology of our Savior."[137] Books Six to Ten can then proceed to the detailed exposition of proof texts: passages of the Old Testament, duly quoted, glossed, and expounded, prophesying God's presence on earth (Book Six), the place and mode of his human birth (Seven) and its date (Eight), every detail of Jesus' life on earth (Nine), and of his Passion, including the name and fate of his betrayer (Ten). Here, unfortunately, the text breaks off: the ten remaining books presumably interpreted the history of the Church from the Resurrection to Eusebius' own day as the fulfillment of Old Testament prophecies, for the *Proof of the Gospel,* like the *General Elementary Introduction,* included a substantial discussion of the end of the world and of the second coming of the Lord in glory and for judgment.[138]

Eusebius repeatedly draws his readers' attention to the progress of his argument, and he aids their comprehension by means of a scholarly device normal in his writings.[139] Each chapter is preceded by a brief heading which describes its contents and sometimes adds information not explicitly given in the text.[140] Moreover, each book is preceded by an index, or list of contents, composed of the collected chapter headings of that book.[141] By this device Eusebius made his apologetical work into a manual of reference for others to use in controversy with Jews or pagans. Nor was this result accidental; Eusebius cannot have been unaware of his good fortune in enjoying constant access to the library of Pamphilus or of the desirability of making the contents available to Christians elsewhere.

Eusebius composed the *Preparation* and the *Proof* (it may be imagined) in the library of Caesarea with the aid of pupils and friends. The *Preparation* especially reads as if Eusebius instructed someone to read the relevant passage and then commented on it aloud, with an amanuensis copying down both the passage read and Eusebius' comments.[142] The range of the *Preparation* clearly reflects the interests of Origen and of Pamphilus, who formed the library; Eusebius never quotes directly from Greek tragedy, comedy, or lyric poetry and shows no direct acquaintance with early Stoic or Epicurean philosophers, but he quotes copiously from historians and from Plato and recent Platonic philosophers.[143] Hence a strong modern interest in the *Preparation,* to the neglect of works which reveal more about its author. The quotations preserve much of great value which would otherwise have perished—fragments of Philo of Byblos, which reflect, at whatever remove, myths and legends of the second millennium B.C. now documented on tablets from Ras Shamra,[144] Hellenistic writings about the Jews,[145] parts of an otherwise lost work by Philo of Alexandria,[146] most of the surviving fragments of Numenius of Apamea and the Platonist Atticus,[147] important extracts from other philosophers and Christian writers,[148] and even a passage of Plotinus which is missing in all extant manuscripts of the *Enneads.*[149]

The quotations, besides being of inestimable value for their contents, indicate Eusebius' intellectual milieu. They attest his indebtedness to Middle Platonism; under the influence of Numenius, mediated through Origen, Eusebius constantly regards the venerable East as the source of Greek philosophy, exalts Plato above all other philosophers, and interprets Plato in terms of two Gods.[150] Eusebius' knowledge of Porphyry may be due to an especial effort to procure as many works as possible of his adversary, for he quotes the *Letter to Anebo,* which cannot have been written many years before 300.[151] Of Plotinus, however, he knows only two or three treatises, which probably circulated separately,[152] and there is no sign that he had read any of Iamblichus' works, although he must have known of Iamblichus' philosophical activity in nearby Syria.[153] The conceptual universe of Eusebius is not that of contemporary pagan philosophy, but still that of the Middle Platonists of the second and early third centuries, whom Origen had studied closely.

Eusebius' contribution to the argument of the *Preparation* is mainly architectonic. Nor, either in his own statements or in his treatment of quotations, does he show any interest in style for its own sake; he is completely impervious to the stylistic dictates of the Second Sophistic movement.[154] Nevertheless, there are sections where Eusebius speaks at length in his own person, and to good effect. Most important is an impassioned defense of free will which explains how Eusebius envisions God's intervention in human history.[155] Much of the philosophical material here may derive from Philo's *On Providence,* though Eusebius does not here invoke Philo's authority or utter his name.[156] The central argument is one Eusebius had employed when discussing Philostratus' account of Apollonius of Tyana: if we cannot choose between right and wrong, then there can be no moral responsibility, no true piety, for we are like lifeless puppets, wholly manipulated by an external power.[157] But how can we have free will when God's providence ordains the course of history? After describing the constraints which the body and human society impose on the free soul, Eusebius gives his answer: God allows us to choose, but his providence overrides our deliberate actions in a mysterious way, changing many natural consequences to suit the occasion.[158] Eusebius thinks of God as intervening in human affairs directly, but not continuously.

The *Proof of the Gospel* is composed according to a different prescription. The surviving books rework the *Prophetic Extracts* in a moderately systematic fashion, whereby the proof texts are arranged by topic rather than by the order of their occurrence in the Bible. And Eusebius develops at length the positive statement of what Christianity is which the *Preparation* sketched only briefly. The liveliest and most eloquent section of the *Proof*, however, is a long refutation of the allegation that Christ was a charlatan or wizard. Eusebius takes each charge and subjects it to a majestic *reductio ad absurdum*, drawing out at length the inconsistencies, implausibilities, and contradictions which the hypothesis appears to entail.[159] Eusebius here explicitly takes issue with Porphyry, but it may be presumed that many Jews in Caesarea shared Porphyry's opinion of Jesus.

The *Preparation for the Gospel* and the *Proof of the Gospel* are the apologia of a historian and a biblical scholar. Their central thesis is one which the *Ecclesiastical History* had stated succinctly and which the *Prophetic Extracts* began to refine and develop.[160] Here, it is fully articulated and amplified. What is Christianity? In Eusebius' view, it is the religion of the Hebrew patriarchs, and hence not only true but also primeval. And around this central idea Eusebius has constructed a detailed interpretation of the course of human history from the Fall to his own day.[161]

The earliest men were savage and uncivilized; they lived like beasts without morality or political organization. Most of them could think of nothing higher than their pressing physical and material needs. But some, through a natural instinct, realized that there must be a god and began to worship the heavenly bodies as divine, while others observed that some of their contemporaries possessed unusual powers or gifts and elevated them to divine status. Yet even at the dawn of recorded history some men (in fact, only a very few, and all among one race) were able, with unperverted reasoning, to see that God must transcend the created world. They were the Hebrew patriarchs of Genesis: Enoch, Noah, Seth and Japheth, Abraham, the priest Melchizedek, Isaac, Jacob, Joseph, Job, and Moses, the last of the ancient patriarchs. The unenlightened contemporaries of the patriarchs were the original pagans, and from their two original types of religion (worship of the heavenly bodies and divinization of men) derived all the varieties of pagan religion and superstition which filled the Greco-Roman world.[162]

The ancient patriarchs were the original Christians, living at a time when the prevailing level of civilization precluded a universal revelation of the truths which they alone perceived. Christianity is identical in content with the original and authentic religion of the patriarchs, except for some obvious differences, explicable on historical grounds. The patriarchs lived at the dawn of history and consequently needed to practice polygamy and beget large families in order to multiply the human race, particularly by rearing children who would transmit true religion to future generations, and the patriarchs could worship God without being distracted by domestic worries; now, Eusebius writes, the world is drawing to its close, and Christians must always be prepared for the advent of their Lord. Christians do not burn incense and sacrifice animals as the patriarchs did, because the ancient sacrifices symbolically prefigured the greater, divine sacrifice of Christ as the lamb of God (Isaiah 53:4–9), which immediately abolished sacrifice of the ancient type. But the patriarchs themselves did not merely prefigure Christianity; they actually were Christians. For, on the one hand, the patriarchs knew both God the Father, the unbegotten creator of the universe, and his Son, the divine Word, who protected the Hebrews while other angel-guardians watched over the other races of mankind. On the other hand, the patriarchs espoused the truth without needing the external props characteristic of the Jewish law.[163]

Judaism comes into Eusebius' scheme as a purely transitional stage, to prepare the way for the new covenant of Jesus which diffused the religion of the patriarchs to all mankind. The patriarchs were few, and the power of evil demons was increasing, so that successive generations gradually receded from the true knowledge of God and increased the varieties and the sway of polytheistic error. Even the descendants of the original Christians shared in the universal decline; as the Hebrews lived in Egypt, they were corrupted, adopted Egyptian customs, and were no longer able to follow the precepts of their ancestors. God, therefore, gave them the laws of Moses to serve as "a guardian and housekeeper of childish and imperfect souls." The Mosaic dispensation, unlike the religion of the patriarchs, was tied to the Jewish race and to the land of Israel. Life under Mosaic Law was a "lower and less perfect way of life," but necessary in the historical circumstances. Whatever their effects on the Jews, the Laws and Writings of Moses had a civilizing effect on the gentiles, so that when the Roman Empire created suitable political conditions, men of every nation, already familiar with the Greek translation of the Old Testament, could immediately embrace the full revelation of God's truth in the new covenant of Jesus, which was identical to God's ancient covenant with the Hebrew patriarchs.[164]

Eusebius divides mankind into three classes: the completely idolatrous and polytheistic, those who have reached the first stage of holiness, and those who have ascended on high through the teaching of the gospel.[165] And he argues that Christianity is superior to both the pagan and the Jewish religion of his time on three grounds: it is anterior in time, it is intellectually and morally preferable, and it is more effective and successful. It may be suspected that the third argument appealed most to Eusebius himself. The observable success of Christianity provides a theme with many variations which permeates all his writings: the Christian churches are numerous and flourishing, while Judaism has suffered political extinction as a direct result of its failure to accept Jesus for what he really was.[166] The Old Testament predicted it all; hence Eusebius can constantly argue that history validates the divine inspiration of Scripture. None of this was new in Eusebius' writings.[167] That fact is important. When Eusebius argued that the Church's success guarantees the truth of its teaching, he was voicing not a recent conviction adopted because he could see a Christian emperor on the throne but a fundamental assumption reflecting the secure conditions under which he grew to maturity in the late third century.[168]

The *Preparation for the Gospel* and the *Proof of the Gospel* also reflect basic theological ideas which Eusebius had long held. As in the *General Elementary Introduction,* he virtually ignores the Holy Spirit when speaking of God and thinks of God the Father and God the Son in terms of the First and Second Gods of Middle Platonism.[169] God the Father is the first God, without beginning and uncreated; the King; the one Father; the One or the Monad, the first, supreme, and only truly Good; the cause of all; the origin and source of all good; beyond the world; inaccessible to the sight or comprehension of men.[170] The Son is a second God, with a different substance and essence from the Father.[171] He is the Word, the second cause, the servant and subordinate of the Father, begotten before all ages by a process beyond man's understanding.[172] The oracles of the Hebrews explain what the Word is: "After the essence of the God of the universe, which has no beginning and is uncreated, which is unmingled and beyond all human apprehension, they introduce a second essence and divine power, the beginning of all created things, coming into existence first and created out of the first cause, calling it the Word and Wisdom and Power of God."[173] Eusebius thus repeats two opinions voiced in the *General Elementary Introduction* which some of his contemporaries were already denouncing as heretical: he asserts that the Son has a different substance from the Father, and he implies that the Son is part of creation and hence mutable.

The *Preparation for the Gospel* and the *Proof of the Gospel* were not Eusebius' final statement of the rational case for Christianity. They were (and are) too unwieldly and too erudite for easy reading. Moreover, some passages in the *Proof* reflected too clearly the time of its composition, when Christians were again being threatened and persecuted.[174] When Constantine conquered the East, Eusebius could revert to the unrestrained optimism of his youth—and he could now, in addition, hail the Christian Empire as the fulfillment of Old Testament prophecy. Shortly after 324, Eusebius distilled the essence of his apologetics into a work in five books addressed to a popular audience. The *Theophany*, which survives as a continuous text only in a Syriac translation,[175] is approximately contemporaneous with the last major revision of the *Ecclesiastical History* and the second edition of the *Chronicle,* which concluded with the *vicennalia* of Constantine (325/6).[176] The *Theophany* represents Eusebius' final opinions. When, in September 335, he delivered a speech at the dedication of the Church of the Holy Sepulcher in Jerusalem, he drew his material from the first three books of the *Theophany,* from which he merely transcribed the larger part of his speech, with virtually no alteration even in the wording.[177]

The *Theophany* adopts a tone more protreptic than apologetic, and it stresses theology rather than history. Nevertheless, Eusebius reiterates all the central themes which the *Preparation* and the *Proof* had developed more fully and with greater erudition.[178] Book One argues, by analogy, that the design of the created world presupposes a creator, and that there must be a mediator between God and man, namely, the Word of God. Eusebius then considers the nature of the world and of man. Both are twofold: visible and invisible, material and spiritual. Man was created in the image of God, and thus possesses an innate superiority to the rest of creation; by nature, therefore, he is capable of achieving perfection through his rational faculties. In fact, however, men were dragged down by their bodily desires and descended into the depths of evil. Book Two argues that they could be rescued only by a superhuman savior, the Incarnate Word. For, when men sank into the errors of irrationality and polytheism and worshiped natural phenomena, qualities, and products, their own faculties and desires, mere men and animals, even lifeless images as gods, the Greek philosophers who ought to have known the truth joined them in error. Hence, throughout the Mediterranean world a multiplicity of obnoxious cults and incessant warfare prevailed for centuries. Nevertheless, God intermittently revealed himself through prophecies and natural disasters and prepared the way for the liberation of mankind. When the time was ripe, and when the Roman Empire had created political unity, the Word of God appeared on earth and revealed to all mankind the God of truth.

Book Three describes at length the beneficial effects of the Incarnation: success for the Roman Empire, the decline of paganism, the destruction of those who persecuted the Church, the universal triumph of Christianity and the present prosperity of the Church. Eusebius then argues that the Incarnation did not affect the divinity of the incorporeal Word (who still pervaded and guided the universe during his lifetime on earth), and he justifies Jesus' death and resurrection. The Resurrection showed the disciples that they too would receive immortality and that Jesus could overcome death, for Jesus died as a sacrificial victim to atone for the impiety of mankind and, thus, to destroy the power of the demons. Books Four and Five prove the divinity of Jesus from his deeds and words as recorded in the New Testament. Eusebius sees many of Jesus' predictions as fulfilled in the Christian Empire, where the Roman army,

Roman officials, and even the imperial family have acknowledged the God of the Hebrew patriarchs, and Eusebius draws the inevitable contrast with the pitiable state of the Jews, whom God has rejected and cast down.[179]

If the interpretation of human history in the *Theophany* does little more than summarize Eusebius' earlier views, its theology shows an observable change. Eusebius emphasizes, even more than in earlier works, God's transcendence; he removes God from any direct contact with the universe after its initial creation, and thus conforms his ideas still more closely to Middle Platonic theories of the First and Second God.[180] In the *Theophany* and the speech of 335, the Word is interposed between God and the world as a necessary mediator:

> One must marvel at the hidden and invisible Word, the designer and organizer of the world, the only begotten son of God, whom the maker of the universe, the one beyond and above all existence, himself begetting from himself, established as the ruler and pilot of this world. For it was not possible for the perishable essence of bodies and the nature of recently created rational beings to approach the all-ruling God because of their excessive inferiority to the higher power; for God was unbegotten, above and beyond the universe, indescribable, incomprehensible, inaccessible, dwelling in unapproachable light, as the divine words say (1 Timothy 6:16), while it, having been brought forth from what did not exist, was very remote and far separated from unbegotten nature. For this reason, the wholly good and God of the universe sends forth the divine and omnipotent power of his only begotten Word as a kind of intermediary; this power associates as perfectly and closely as possible with the Father and enjoys his secrets from inside, but most graciously descends among and somehow makes itself like those who fall short of perfection. In no other way would it be proper or holy for him who is beyond and above the universe to be joined to perishable matter and a human body. Thus the divine Word, coming into this world indiscriminately and taking up the reins of the universe, drives it to and fro with an incorporeal and divine power, handling the reins with perfect skill, just as seems fitting to him.[181]

Eusebius originally formulated these sentences as the expression of his own opinions; in 335 he was emboldened to claim that they also represented the beliefs of Constantine.[182]

THREE

THE CHRISTIAN EMPIRE

XI

BEFORE CONSTANTINE

When Constantine conquered the East in 324, the Christian church which he rescued from persecution was not a small and insignificant sect, nor did his patronage alone immediately raise it to a position of dominance.[1] Christianity was powerful and respectable long before it acquired an imperial champion. By the end of the third century there were completely Christian villages in Palestine and Phrygia,[2] and in most eastern cities and provinces Christians constituted either a majority of the population or at least an influential minority.[3] Throughout the East, the Christian bishop had become a respected figure of the urban establishment whom provincial governors treated with respect or deference, and bishops acted as judges in legal disputes within the local Christian community.[4] When Constantine turned the impending war against Licinius into a Christian crusade, he happily united personal conviction with political advantage. A pagan emperor could no longer govern without the acquiescence and good will of his Christian subjects.[5]

Eusebius had completed the original edition of his *Ecclesiastical History* toward the close of the third century.[6] The books which he subsequently added do not constitute a proper history of the eastern Church between the reign of

Probus (where the first edition ended) and Constantine's conquest of the East; their aim is the more circumscribed one of narrating the persecutions which eastern Christians suffered under Diocletian and Galerius, under Maximinus and Licinius.[7] Eusebius neither intended nor attempted to describe fully the internal condition of the Christian church in the late third and early fourth century, so that he left the history of Greek Christendom during this important period largely unwritten, apart from the persecution and its direct effects. What Eusebius added to Book Seven in later editions of the *History* reflects a personal and provincial viewpoint.

Eusebius brought the lists of emperors and bishops in the *History* down to the persecution, though in an unsystematic fashion. Probus (he noted) was succeeded by Carus and his sons, then came Diocletian and his colleagues, under whom occurred the persecution and the destruction of the churches.[8] At Rome, the bishop Gaius was succeeded by Marcellinus, who still held the see when the persecution began.[9] At Antioch, Cyrillus was followed by Tyrannus, in whose time the churches stood siege.[10] In Jerusalem, Zabdas succeeded Hymenaeus for a brief period; then came Hermon, who still occupied the episcopal throne when Eusebius added the relevant notice.[11] At Alexandria, Maximus held the see for eighteen years after Dionysius, Theonas for nineteen after Maximus, and Peter for twelve years after Theonas. Peter guided his church through the difficult days of persecution until he died as a martyr in its ninth year.[12] Eusebius also notes that as bishop of Caesarea, Theotecnus was followed by Agapius, a wise pastor who gave to the poor with openhanded generosity.[13]

One substantive addition to the *History* has a very sharp tone. A new heresy arose in the late third century at the prompting of Satan. The mad Mani posed as Christ, claimed to be the Holy Spirit, and sent out twelve apostles from Persia to infect the Roman world with deadly poison. His system, a patchwork of false and godless doctrines from countless moribund heresies, enjoyed a distressing popularity—and proved that "knowledge falsely so-called" (1 Timothy 6:20) was still a danger.[14] A later writer supplies the precise information that Manichees settled in Eleutheropolis in the very year of Mani's death.[15]

For the most part, however, the additions to the *History* commemorate Eusebius' friends. Dorotheus was a priest in the church of Antioch who had learned Hebrew to understand the Old Testament better. He was also well educated in the Greek classics and a eunuch by birth—a combination which induced the emperor to appoint him superintendent of the purple-factory at Tyre. Eusebius heard Dorotheus expounding the Scriptures in church, either in Antioch or in Tyre.[16] From Eusebius' presentation it is not at all clear whether he is the same Dorotheus who was in the imperial household in Nicomedia in March 303, and whose outspoken defense of Christianity occasioned his arrest and execution with other eunuchs of the palace.[17]

The achievements of Pamphilus at Caesarea deserved brief notice, though Eusebius described them in full in a formal biography.[18] Pamphilus had been a pupil of Pierius, a priest in Alexandria who was a noted philosopher. It was probably through Pamphilus that Eusebius came to know Pierius and his fellow priest, Achillas, who taught in the catechetical school there.[19] Eusebius also records Meletius, metropolitan bishop of the churches in Pontus, as an accomplished orator and scholar; he spent seven years during the persecution hiding in remote areas of Palestine.[20] Eusebius' selection of notable Christians is personal, and he has allowed his own prejudices of later years to affect his choice and presentation. When describing the persecution, he deliberatedly excluded apostates from his purview, consigning them to oblivion.[21] Yet he makes an exception for a bishop of Laodicea whom he disliked. Stephanus, who succeeded Anatolius, was admired by many for his skill in philosophy and for his general culture, but the years of persecution revealed him to be a dishonest coward, not a true philosopher. God, however, intervened to protect the church of Laodicea and gave it Theodotus as its bishop, a doctor who could heal souls as readily as bodies.[22] Eusebius lauds Theodotus' mastery of divine learning; it was to Theodotus that he dedicated his *Preparation for the Gospel* and *Proof of the Gospel.* In 325 both were to be excommunicated by a Church council as heretics.[23]

Eusebius' total omission of Methodius, bishop of Olympus in Lycia and perhaps later of Patara,[24] may also reflect personal animosity. Several of Methodius' works survive, either in the original or in medieval Slavonic translations. He was an avid, if often uncomprehending, reader of Plato, and composed Platonic dialogues with a Lycian setting, in which he propounded Christian doctrines and explored theological problems.[25] Methodius also produced tracts interpreting individual passages of the Old Testament allegorically, biblical commentaries, a refutation of Porphyry's *Against the Christians,* and other treatises.[26] Methodius died as a martyr, probably on 20 June 312 and perhaps after being tried by the emperor Maximinus, who traveled along the south coast of Asia Minor in the summer of that year.[27] Some of Methodius' writings contain ideas and imagery very reminiscent of Origen.[28] But even if Methodius borrowed from Origen in his earlier writings, he later explicitly rejected some of Origen's most striking ideas. His treatise *On Free Will* repudiates Origen's idea of an infinite succession of worlds, and the dialogue *Aglaophon,* or *On the Resurrection,* attacks at length and sometimes quite bitterly Origen's eschatology and his theories of the pre-existence of souls and of the spiritual body: Origen is here, by implication, derided for tendentious and violent interpretation of the Bible.[29] Eusebius knew of Methodius' hostility toward Origen,[30] and it is entirely understandable that one so devoted to the memory of Origen should remain silent about Methodius' writings and martyrdom.

Personal bias alone, however, will not account for all the omissions which can be uncovered. Eusebius never intended to chronicle all the Christian writers and scholars of his generation. If he quotes Phileas, the bishop of Thmuis in Egypt, it is to document the course of persecution in that province, not to illustrate the bishop's attainments as a writer or theologian.[31] Moreover, besides the conscious omissions, allowance must be made for possible ignorance. Eusebius may simply not have known what his contemporaries in Asia Minor and Greece were doing.[32] Although Christians everywhere needed copies of the Scriptures and aid in understanding them, most textual and exegetical work on the Bible was intended for local use in the church for which it was produced and became known to a wider audience only slowly.

In Egypt, one Hesychius produced texts of the Greek Old and New Testaments which later bore his name.[33] He may be identical with the bishop Hesychius, noted by Eusebius, who died in 307 as a martyr.[34] Lucian, a priest of the church at Antioch, also worked on the text of the Bible: toward the end of the fourth century Jerome claimed that Lucian's recension of the Septuagint prevailed throughout Asia Minor and Syria, just as Hesychius' did in Alexandria and Egypt. This "Lucianic recension" of the Old Testament, and even of the New, has received much discussion from modern scholars.[35] Yet, on a realistic assessment of the evidence, it seems doubtful whether Lucian did more than make minor additions to the pre-existing Antiochene text of the Bible.[36] In his own day, Lucian was probably less famous as a biblical scholar than as a teacher and theologian; his pupils incuded Eusebius, the bishop of Nicomedia, and probably Arius.[37] The career of Lucian, unfortunately, cannot be reconstructed. Much misunderstanding has resulted from a mistaken identification: the scholar Lucian is manifestly a different man from the Lucian who was bishop of the schismatic church in Antioch formed by supporters of the deposed Paul of Samosata.[38] Moreover, the fact that Lucian was once a priest at Antioch encourages the assumption that Antioch always remained the focus of his activities.[39] That inference ought to be doubted. Lucian was martyred at Nicomedia on 7 January 312, and a fragment of a letter preserved by the merest chance shows that he was in Nicomedia nine years earlier.[40] He may have taught in the imperial capital for many years. Helena, the mother of Constantine, displayed an especial veneration for Lucian after his martyrdom:[41] at Nicomedia, in the reign of Diocletian, Constantine and his mother may have been among those who heard Lucian teach and expound the Scriptures.

The nature of Christian devotion inevitably changed when the constant threat of persecution diminished and then disappeared. Asceticism replaced martyrdom as the highest ideal to which Christians could normally aspire. At the beginning of the third century, Clement of Alexandria was the first Christian writer to place the ascetic on the same level as the martyr.[42] During the two generations between 260 and 324 asceticism became a widespread way of expressing Christian piety, and religious communities were organized in which groups of Christians could withdraw from the world to concentrate on divine matters unhindered by worldly diversions. Many celibate, ascetic households must have existed in the late third century. In Caesarea, Pamphilus probably presided over a celibate confraternity devoted to sacred learning. Pamphilus and his pupils lived simply, copied and corrected the Scriptures, and carried on the intellectual traditions of Origen.[43]

Similar households probably existed in much of the East and Asia Minor. Methodius wrote his *Symposium* in the cultural backwater of Lycia. The work takes the form of a dialogue, modeled on Plato's *Symposium,* in which eleven women deliver discourses in praise of chastity, but its function is to provide a manual of Christian doctrine for a community of female ascetics. Methodius regards chastity, like the Platonic *eros,* as a means for achieving the ascent of the soul, enabling it to perceive the true, heavenly realities. For him, therefore, virginity becomes coterminous with Christian virtue. The eleven expositions include themes as diverse as the allegorical interpretation of Scripture, the nature of the hereafter, the divinity of Christ, astrology, and free will. Although the dialogue purports, on one level, to be set in apostolic times, with Thecla as one of the interlocutors, the epilogue bears a signature which marks its contemporary relevance: a "lady from Telmessus" was with Methodius when he questioned Arete, the daughter of Philosophy, about what happened at the banquet.[44] It is an attractive inference that this mysterious lady from Telmessus supported a community of virgins on her country estate, which Methodius presents as a new Eden.[45] The *Symposium* both celebrates this sorority and provides for the instruction of its members.

The household of Pamphilus and the retreat presupposed in Methodius represent a form of community which depended on the wealth and continuing patronage of its founder. A striking passage in the *Ecclesiastical History* implies that before 300 Eusebius also knew of organized monastic communities in Palestine. He quotes long extracts from Philo's description of the Therapeutae of the first century, who organized themselves in celibate communities of men and women, living in separate establishments of their own and devoting themselves exclusively to the worship of God and philosophy.[46] Eusebius claims the Therapeutae as Christian (not Jewish) ascetics because the way of life described by Philo so perfectly matches the life of contemporary Christian ascetics.[47] Such reasoning demonstrates securely, if indirectly, that some form of monastic life existed in Palestine when Eusebius wrote the passage, before the end of the third century.

The Christian monasticism of the later Roman Empire appears to derive ultimately from first-century Judaism, whose traditions of asceticism, preserved in Mesopotamia, may have been reintroduced to Syria, Palestine, and Egypt by Manichean missionaries.[48] It was in Egypt, however, that these traditions assumed the form which was to inspire and shape the great monastic orders of later centuries. By 324, the monk was an established figure in Egyptian village society.[49] The principal avatars of medieval monasticism were two Copts, Pachomius and Antony.

The biographer of Antony puts his hero, who died in 356, allegedly at the age of one hundred and five, into a pre-existing tradition of asceticism. When his parents died, the young Antony gave away his patrimony and entrusted his only sister to a community of virgins. When he began the ascetic life, he copied an old hermit from a neighboring village who had spent many years in a solitary existence. Antony, too, took up his abode just outside the village. He cut all ties with his family. He labored with his hands to earn enough to buy his daily bread, and he gave any surplus to the needy. He lived alone, practicing self-discipline and praying incessantly.[50] At the age of almost thirty-five, Antony withdrew to the edge of the desert, where he lived in an abandoned fort in total isolation. After nearly twenty years—about 305, on the chronology of the *Life of Antony*—the door was broken down and Antony emerged like an initiate from a shrine, full of God. He healed the sick, cast out demons, comforted the sorrowing, reconciled enemies, and urged all to put the love of Christ before anything in this world. He thus persuaded many to choose the solitary life.

Soon there were monasteries in the mountains, and "the desert was made a city" by monks who left their homes and relatives to enroll themselves in the community of heaven.[51] When Maximinus resumed persecution, Antony and his monks made a political demonstration in Alexandria, appearing in court when the prefect was trying Christians. When persecution ended, Antony returned to his monastery, where crowds of visitors, among them a Roman army commander, thronged his door seeking cures for their ills. Antony decided to escape, fell in with a Saracen caravan, and came to the remote mountain near the Red Sea where he spent the rest of his life.[52]

Antony was a hermit, an anchorite. He was probably not the first Christian ascetic to migrate to the desert. Jerome had heard of one Paul of Thebes who preceded Antony, and Jerome's composition of an utterly fictitious *Life of Paul* does not suffice to prove that Paul never existed.[53] But Antony was the first famous monk to enjoy political power and influence by virtue of his status. He wrote to Constantine to intercede on ecclesiastical matters, and the emperor replied with letters justifying his policy.[54]

Pachomius, a Copt from the Thebaid, was conscripted into the army of Maximinus at the age of twenty.[55] Previously a pagan, he was converted by Christians who brought food and drink to the recruits incarcerated in the camp at Luxor. After Maximinus' defeat in 313, Pachomius was discharged from the army, returned to the Thebaid, and soon sought baptism. Shortly thereafter, he decided to embark on a monastic life. At first, Pachomius was an anchorite like Antony. By 320, however, he was organizing the monks who flocked to join him into a community which shared tasks and worship within a walled enclosure.[56] The original *coenobium* was at Tabennesis, but very soon Pachomius founded other communities, and a finely regulated rhythm of life commenced whose principles later crystallized in the first known monastic rule.[57]

If Coptic monks from Egypt set the tone of piety in the Christian empire, thinkers from the Greek milieu of Alexandria determined the direction of theological debate. A Platonic philosopher writing in Alexandria about 300 prefaced a critique of Manichean doctrines with some observations on the state of Christianity which presumably reflect conditions in that city. He characterized Christianity as a simple philosophy, chiefly devoted to ethical instruction, which tells ordinary people how to behave and thus inculcates genuine virtue, piety, and desire for the good. He complained, however, that Christianity lacked a proper theoretical basis, either for theology or in ethics. Since they had no agreed basis for deciding theological issues, the leaders of sects sought novelty for its own sake, thereby converting a simple philosophy into something hopelessly complicated and ineffectual.[58] Eusebius confirms the philosopher's strictures. In retrospect, Eusebius presented the advent of persecution as being, at least in part, a chastisement sent from God because the Church had fallen into sinful ways. Christians envied, abused, and insulted one another, bishop attacked bishop, and communities were divided into bitter factions.[59] In Alexandria and elsewhere, the central theological issues which divided Christians arose from the teaching of Origen.

When Heraclas became bishop of Alexandria shortly after 230, he was succeeded as head of the catechetical school there by Dionysius, a former pupil of Origen.[60] Some fifteen or sixteen years later, Dionysius succeeded Heraclas as bishop.[61] He occupied the see during the decade when Decius and Valerian persecuted the Christians, and he obtained a rescript from Gallienus ordering the return of confiscated Christian property.[62] Dionysius was a vigorous administrator who participated in the disciplinary disputes which the Decian persecution occasioned.[63] Enough survives of three philosophical and theological works to show that he also stood in the intellectual tradition of his master. His treatise On Nature set out to refute Epicurean materialism; he argued, in a pleasant and engaging manner, that the world is too marvelous to be the product of mere chance but attests the design of a creator.[64] A work On Promises, in two books, attacked the chiliastic views of Nepos, bishop of Arsinoe, whose Refutation of the Allegorists maintained that the Scriptural promises would be fulfilled literally. Dionysius' first book laid down what he considered to be the correct interpretation, and the second discussed the book of Revelation at length.[65]

Four books entitled Refutation and Defense explained Dionysius' beliefs about the Trinity to Dionysius, the bishop of Rome who had doubted his orthodoxy.[66] In letters denouncing the ideas of Sabellius, which were circulating in Libya, Dionysius had expressed himself in terms which suggested that he had fallen into the opposite heresy, namely, of postulating three Gods where Sabellius had confused the three persons.[67] He wrote his Refutation and Defense to dispel this suspicion.[68] The work, unfortunately, is known mainly from a pamphlet written about 350 to prove Dionysius orthodox in fourth-century terms, which perhaps adds anachronistic coloring to the third-century controversy. Direct quotations from Dionysius' Refutation and Defense, however, which must be accepted as authentic, establish his profound indebtedness to Origen: Dionysius refused to use the word homoousios, since he believed that the three persons of the Trinity had three substances, and though he denied that the Son was created, he justified his use of the word "maker" in describing the relationship of the Father to the Word.[69] It was not implausible, therefore, that the Arians of the fourth century should claim Dionysius as one who shared their fundamental views.[70]

When Dionysius died about 265, the traditions of Origen were continued by Theognostus and Pierius, who may have been successive heads of the catechetical school.[71] Theognostus wrote a large work in seven books, entitled *Hypotyposeis* (or "outlines"), which was a systematic exposition of Christian theology.[72] He devoted one book to each person of the Trinity, a fourth to angels and demons, two books to the Incarnation, and the final book to the creation of the world. The work (unfortunately known only from a brief summary and a few small fragments) was clearly intended to be a comprehensive exposition like Origen's *On First Principles,* and Photius expressly notes that Theognostus repeated dubious ideas which Origen had propounded. Theognostus denied the eternity of matter, limited the authority of the Son to rational beings only, and used expressions which later theologians construed as asserting that the Son was a creature. Despite his theology, however, Theognostus earned an accolade for style: in Photius' opinion, he wrote vigorously and always with relevance in an Attic Greek which never sacrificed dignity in attaining clarity and accuracy.[73]

Pierius was a still more controversial character. As a priest in Alexandria during the reigns of Carus and Diocletian, he led a life of poverty, learning, and philosophy, taught with great success, and published so many sermons on different subjects that he was called "Origen the younger."[74] When persecution came, Pierius was arrested and imprisoned, but it seems that he obtained release by some act of conformity (with which in February 307 the governor was able to taunt Phileas, bishop of Thmuis).[75] After that, Pierius presumably lived on in disgrace. He composed a eulogy of his former pupil Pamphilus, who died as a martyr on 7 February 310, but after the persecution Pierius removed himself from Alexandria to Rome, where he died.[76]

Pierius labored at biblical exegesis, and his theology, like that of Theognostus, had strong similarities to Origen's. Pierius asserted the pre-existence of souls, spoke of the Father and the Son as having two essences (*ousiai*), and was accused of making the Holy Spirit inferior to the Father and the Son. From the verdict of Photius, who read a volume of twelve of Pierius' discourses, which he found clear, brilliant, and spontaneous, it is clear that Pierius copied Origen in the freedom and boldness of his theological speculations. Photius soberly remarked that much of Pierius was "foreign to the present institutions of the Church," though he conceded that it may have been permissible when written.[77] Even while Pierius still lived, however, there were those in Alexandria who rejected the ideas of Origen which Pierius most liked to repeat.

A decisive reaction against Origen began when Peter became bishop of Alexandria.[78] Peter attacked Origen's ideas in the Easter letters which he sent each year to the churches throughout Egypt.[79] In these letters he criticized allegorical interpretation of Scripture[80] and wrote on the nature of God and the Incarnation, maintaining that, though the Savior was both God by nature and man by nature, he suffered no derogation from his divinity by becoming man.[81] It may be surmised that Peter repudiated any idea that the Logos was a second God, inferior to the Father. Peter also wrote two treatises which took specific issue with Origen. A treatise *On the Soul* rejected Origen's doctrine of the pre-existence of souls as an alien importation from Greek philosophy: the first man was not created by the union of flesh with a fallen soul from a higher world, but received a vital energy from the will and operation of God.[82] Similarly, *On the Resurrection* asserted the full identity of the resurrection body with the earthly body, a doctrine which Origen had denied.[83]

The attitude of Peter of Alexandria is highly relevant to the *Defense of Origen and His Opinions,* which Pamphilus and Eusebius undertook while Pamphilus was in prison.[84] The work was addressed to confessors condemned to work in the mines of Palestine. The circumstances which provoked its composition are nowhere clearly stated, but can be recovered by conjecture. The enemies of Pamphilus in Caesarea, among them probably the bishop, doubted his orthodoxy.[85] When his imprisonment as a confessor lent kudos to his views, his enemies appealed to the Egyptian confessors at Phaeno to intervene in their local quarrel. The Egyptians replied with an indictment of Origen, which they had perhaps learned from the bishop of Alexandria. They listed (it appears) ten heretical theses which Origen affirmed:

(1) One should not pray to the Son;
(2) The Son is not good in the strict sense of the word;
(3) The Son does not know the Father as the Father knows himself;
(4) Rational natures are inserted in the bodies of irrational animals;
(5) There is metempsychosis;
(6) The soul of the Savior was the soul of Adam;
(7) There is no eternal punishment;
(8) There is no resurrection of the flesh;
(9) Magic is not an evil;
(10) Astronomy is the effective cause of actions.[86]

Presumably, Pamphilus was invited to deny his master or admit the charge of heresy.

Pamphilus, with the assistance of Eusebius, who could consult Pamphilus' library and bring him books in prison, replied with the massive *Defense of Origen and His Opinions.* Significantly, the preface included a long answer to the allegation that some honest, religious, and blameless men (clearly Pamphilus himself) put Origen and his writings on the same level as the holy apostles and prophets.[87] Pamphilus divided the accusers of Origen into three classes. First, the ignorant: some unable to speak Greek at all, others completely uneducated, some too lazy to read Origen, others incapable of perceiving Origen's intended meaning, and many who merely repeat what others have told them. Pamphilus clearly alludes to the Egyptian confessors in general. Second are those who ignore everything in Origen of which they approve but commit to memory any phrase they can use in controversy. Pamphilus presumably alludes to the confessor who drew up the list of charges against Origen. Third, and most bitter, are those who once studied Origen carefully as disciples but have now disowned Origen after becoming teachers themselves. They pronounce curses and anathemas, and even publish pamphlets against Origen.[88] The generalized description surely has a very precise reference—to Peter of Alexandria.[89]

Pamphilus undertook the defense of Origen both against the charges made in 308/9 and against all Origen's detractors. Pamphilus arranged his apologia in five books. The first proved that Origen accepted the essential doctrines of Christianity; it quoted from his works, principally from *On First Principles*, and from his opinions on the rule of faith, on the Trinity, and on the Incarnation. Book Two documented Origen's career and teaching activity; Pamphilus showed that the condemnation of Demetrius and Pontianus did not represent the judgment of the whole Church, and he presented Origen, tendentiously, as a martyr of the Decian persecution. The next book (it appears) quoted the *Address to Origen* which Gregory had recited in Caesarea, perhaps with other testimony to Origen's standing among his contemporaries. The last two books considered the doctrinal charges against Origen, most of which Pamphilus answered in one of four ways: sometimes he quoted copiously to prove Origen's orthodoxy on the relevant point, sometimes he exculpated Origen by attributing the denounced passages to malicious interpolation, sometimes he argued that Origen regarded the offending thesis as merely a hypothesis for inquiry, and sometimes he showed that others, too, held the same views, especially Clement and Dionysius of Alexandria. On some issues, however, such as the pre-existence of souls, Pamphilus boldly defended Origen's controversial views as correct.[90]

After Pamphilus' death, Eusebius added a sixth book to the original five.[91] Its introduction mentioned Patermouthios, one of the Egyptian confessors to whom Pamphilus had addressed his work. The warm praise of Patermouthios in the *Martyrs of Palestine* suggests that, whatever his earlier views, he had been convinced by Pamphilus' defense.[92] Why then did Eusebius write? Since the sixth book upbraided Methodius for attacking Origen after earlier praising him,[93] it may be an answer to criticism of Origen by Methodius of which Eusebius had only recently become aware. It contained letters written by Origen—certainly one to Fabianus, bishop of Rome, and probably one addressed to his friends in Alexandria, in which he complained that his writings had been interpolated and his ideas falsified.[94]

The *Defense of Origen* is an important historical document. It shows that theological bickering did not cease during the "Great Persecution." Pagans and heretics (Pamphilus observed) might derive comfort from seeing Christian teachers, against whom they could not prevail, caught in virtual civil war within the Church.[95] When Pamphilus penned these words, there already existed a schismatic church among the Egyptian confessors to whom he was writing. Eusebius alluded to the schism in the *Martyrs of Palestine,*[96] but refused to allow the narration of such distasteful facts to mar his selective picture of a brave Church heroically withstanding persecution.

When the first persecuting edict arrived in the spring of 303, Peter of Alexandria went into hiding and perhaps fled Egypt.[97] He returned before Easter 306 and issued a circular letter to Egyptian bishops which laid down the approriate treatment of Christians who had compromised themselves during the persecution.[98] The provisions of this "Canonical Epistle" strongly resemble the decisions of a council held an Ancyra eight years later, after Licinius had officially ended persecution.[99] In the East, no blame attached to those who had surrendered the Scriptures in obedience to the imperial edicts; Peter and the council at Ancyra were concerned exclusively with those who sacrificed or participated in pagan festivals. Nor was it shameful to have fled persecution or bribed officials to avoid apostasy: Peter justified flight by examples from Scripture and commended those who offered bribes as serving God rather than mammon, as relinquishing their earthly goods to save their souls.

Many Christians, however, showed fortitude and determination. Between 303 and 311 many martyrs died in Egypt: local tradition states the plausible (though not verifiable) figure of six hundred and sixty for Alexandria alone.[100] Numerous confessors suffered imprisonment, torture, forced labor, especially in the Thebaid, or deportation to the mines in other provinces.[101] There were many who had provoked martyrdom by ostentatiously offering themselves for punishment.[102] Such hardy spirits, and those who admired them, might be less than sympathetic to a bishop who recommended light penance for their confrères who had weakened during torture—or even from fear of mere imprisonment.[103] When Maximinus began to enforce the persecuting edicts more efficiently in 306 by using the newly compiled census registers,[104] Peter again withdrew. Melitius, who had replaced an apostate as the bishop of Lycopolis, stepped in to perform the duties which the bishop of Alexandria abandoned.[105]

The full story of Melitius' activities will probably never be known. But two contemporary documents attest his intervention in Alexandria. Four bishops wrote to Melitius from prison: Hesychius, Pachomius, Theodorus, and Phileas of Thmuis, who was later executed by the prefect Clodius Culcianus, probably on 4 February 307.[106] The bishops salute Melitius as a "dear fellow minister in the Lord," but rebuke him for performing ordinations in the dioceses of other bishops without consulting them and without the metropolitan's permission. The result has been schism, since Melitius' ordinations displease many. Melitius (the bishops imply) was already in Alexandria. There he not only ordained priests but attempted to exercise authority over the local clergy in place of the absent bishop. Peter wrote to his congregation in Alexandria, instructing them not to communicate with Melitius until he could examine and approve Melitius' conduct.[107] He then returned to the city, convened a synod, and excommunicated Melitius.[108] Melitius, perhaps even before the synod, was imprisoned and was later deported to the mines of Palestine, where he continued to ordain priests, and even bishops, of what was now a schismatic "church of the martyrs."[109] Melitius and the other confessors returned to Egypt in 311, when toleration was decreed. But Peter refused to communicate with Melitius or to recognize the validity of baptism performed by the priests whom Melitius had ordained.[110] Melitius countered by organizing a separate ecclesiastical network throughout Egypt; within some twenty years there were Melitian monasteries, and a separate Melitian church continued to exist for centuries.[111]

Peter died as a martyr on 26 November 311. While few yet suspected a renewal of persecution, agents sent secretly by Maximinus arrested Peter and secured his rapid condemnation and execution.[112] The see of Alexandria probably remained vacant for some time, then Achillas died within a few months of his election as bishop.[113] Although persecution ceased in the summer of 313, the new bishop, Alexander, soon confronted a still more dangerous challenge to his authority than the Melitian schism.

By custom, the priests of Alexandria were licensed to preach, each in a separate church.[114] The Libyan Arius was a popular preacher at the church of Baucalis.[115] About Arius' education and his career before his sudden notoriety, nothing is known for certain. Arius may have studied outside Egypt, since he saluted Eusebius of Nicomedia as a "fellow Lucianist"—which appears to imply that Eusebius and Arius had studied together with Lucian, either in Antioch or in Nicomedia.[116] It was alleged much later that Arius and Isidorus (perhaps the brother of Pierius) had aided Melitius in 306 against Peter.[117] That charge need be no more than gossip or deliberate invention.[118] One of Arius' early associates, however, may link him indirectly to Eusebius of Caesarea: Achillas, or Achilles, also a priest of Alexandria, whom Alexander denounces in one document as joint leader with Arius of the dissident party.[119] The *Ecclesiastical History* praises an Achillas, who was a priest in Alexandria with Pierius and was head of the catechetical school.[120] This Achillas should be either the bishop who succeeded Peter or the priest who supported Arius. Since Eusebius wrote the relevant passage after Peter of Alexandria had died, his failure to record that his Achillas became bishop in Peter's stead inevitably implies that his Achillas is not the bishop. But if Eusebius' Achillas is identical with Arius' associate, he provides a link between Arius and Pierius, the teacher of Pamphilus.

The teachings of Arius are unfortunately known mainly from the hostile reports of his adversaries. Selective quotation, however, does not prove deliberate distortion in the passages quoted verbatim.[121] The central points of Arius' theology, as stated in later refutations and in the anathemas declared by

Church councils, are confirmed by the evidence of documents from the early stages of the controversy. Alexander, the bishop of Alexandria, summed up the objectionable features of Arius' teaching as follows:

> God was not always Father, but there was when God was not Father. The Word of God did not always exist, but came into existence out of nothing. For God, who existed, made him who did not exist out of what did not exist. Hence, too, there was a time when he was not. For the Son is a creature and an object. He is neither like the Father in substance, nor the true and natural Word of the Father, nor his true Wisdom, but one of the created objects, and he is improperly called Word and Wisdom, since he himself came into being by the proper Word of God and the Wisdom in God, in which God made both everything and him. Hence he is both mutable and changeable by nature, as are all rational creatures. The Word is alien to, different from, and separated from the substance of God, and the Father is invisible to the Son. For the Word neither knows the Father perfectly and exactly nor can see him perfectly. And the Son does not know the nature of his own substance. For he was made for our sake, so that God might make us by means of him, as by a tool. And he would not have existed had not God decided to make us.

Alexander also reports that the Arians said that the Word of God was "of mutable nature and created."[122] This report of Arius' teachings may be tendentious and designed to horrify rather than to inform. But its essential accuracy is confirmed by the formal creed which Arius and his followers subsequently drew up. This creed cleverly emphasized how much Arius agreed with orthodox doctrine, and it described itself as inherited from previous generations and learned from Alexander himself. Arius here dropped the assertion that the Son was mutable, but he reaffirmed other propositions to which Alexander had taken objection, though adding glosses designed to make his opinions more palatable. The Son, he wrote, was "a perfect creature of God, but not like other created objects." He received life and existence from the Father "before all ages": only the Father is without beginning; the Son is "begotten by the Father outside time," and hence neither eternal nor coeternal with the Father. Moreover, the three persons of the Trinity are three substances (*hypostaseis*).[123] Arius' creed lays emphasis on the nature of Christ—and it must be deduced that this was the question which perplexed and concerned him.[124]

Arius' ideas have often been traced to sources outside the Christian tradition.[125] That is neither a necessary nor an attractive hypothesis.[126] His concerns, as evinced in the creed which he formulated, are not with philosophical propriety, but with the avoidance of heresy. He wished to tread a careful path between several contrasting errors. For Arius, the Son was not a mere emanation from the Father, as Valentinus held. Nor was the Son part of the Father, of one substance with the Father; that was an error of Mani—whom Arius, significantly, regards as a Christian heretic. Nor could Arius accept either Sabellius' identification of Father and Son, or Hieracas' simile of one torch lit from another. Nor, finally, could Arius accept what he claimed to have heard Alexander assert publicly and frequently: that the Son existed before he became the Son. Nevertheless, Arius claimed to have learned from Alexander himself that the Father was prior to the Son, even though he disagreed with Alexander on how to express the precise relationship.[127]

All of Arius' central theses can be paralleled in Christian writings of the third century—in the writings of Origen and his followers. Dionysius and Theognostus had both styled the Son a creature.[128] Moreover, although Origen expressly denied that "there is when he was not," Dionysius once used the very formulation of this idea which Arius made famous.[129] Origen and Dionysius both rejected the idea that Father and Son were "of one substance": Dionysius advanced the Arians' later complaint that the word *homoousios* was not Scriptural, and Origen had said clearly that the Son had a different essence and substance from the Father.[130] And if Origen did not assert that the Father was invisible to the Son, he nevertheless held that the Son could not fully comprehend the Father.[131] These parallels are too striking and too many to have arisen by coincidence—and are not to be discounted because of Dionysius' later disclaimers. Arius drew on the Origenist tradition to combat Manichean and Sabellian ideas in Alexandria; if he fell into the opposing heresy of tritheism, his subsequent career demonstrates that many Christian bishops and thinkers outside Egypt judged his views at least permissible, and perhaps even deserving of admiration.

Trouble began early in Alexander's episcopate. Several clerics (among whom, it was later alleged, Melitius took a leading role) objected to Arius' teaching and complained to the bishop.[132] He summoned Arius to a meeting of all the clergy of Alexandria, confronted him with the complaints, and urged him to modify his views. Arius refused.[133] An open breach now unavoidable, Alexander convened a council of about one hundred bishops from Egypt and Libya.[134] This council drew up a creed which repudiated Arius' novel views. When Arius and others refused to accept this document, the council excommunicated them and banished them from Alexandria.[135] Arius sought allies outside Egypt. He wrote to Eusebius, the bishop of Nicomedia, who had recently left Berytus for that see, perhaps to be close to the court of Licinius, to whose praetorian prefect he was related.[136]

Arius claimed that he had been unjustly banished from Alexandria because of his refusal to assert publicly that the Son is coeternal with the Father; he further claimed to have the support of almost all eastern bishops: Eusebius of Caesarea, Theodotus of Laodicea, Paulinus of Tyre, Athanasius of Anazarbus, Gregorius of Berytus, and Aetius of Lydda all assert the prior existence of God the Father, a doctrine denied only by Philogonius of Antioch, Hellanicus of Tripolis in Phoenicia, and Macarius of Jerusalem, all three heretics who had never received a proper theological training.[137] Eusebius of Nicomedia replied favorably to Arius and wrote to many bishops soliciting their support for the exiled priest.[138] Eusebius of Caesarea, too, may have joined the fray at the outset: he believed that the Father existed before the Son, and at some stage he wrote to Euphrantion of Balaneae explaining his views.[139]

Alexander countered with a circular letter of his own, which he first presented to the clergy of Alexandria and the Mareotis for their endorsement. The step was necessary because two priests and four deacons had joined Arius since his condemnation.[140] Alexander's clergy duly subscribed his letter; in all, thirty-six priests and forty-four deacons. Alexander addressed himself to his fellow bishops of the catholic Church everywhere and asked them to show solidarity by refusing communion to the "lawless enemies of Christ" from his diocese whom he had been compelled to excommunicate. He wrote because Eusebius was taking up their cause, and Alexander requested that the recipients of the letter pay no heed to the bishop of Nicomedia. Alexander named the apostates (six priests, six deacons, and the Libyan bishops Secundus and Theonas), and he quoted their heretical opinions and explained why they must be erroneous.[141]

Eusebius of Nicomedia convened a council in Bithynia to reverse the verdict of the Egyptian synod. In preparation, Arius drew up a creed, in the form of a declaration addressed to Alexander, which emphasized how close the views of the two men were.[142] The council pronounced Arius orthodox, admitted him to communion, and instructed Alexander to do likewise.[143] Eusebius of Nicomedia then organized a lobby on behalf of Arius and wrote to Paulinus of Tyre, who wrote to Alexander on Arius' behalf.[144] Eusebius of Caesarea and Athanasius of Anazarbus wrote to Alexander, and so too did other bishops from Syria and Palestine.[145]

After his excommunication, and perhaps while he was in Nicomedia, Arius composed a work entitled the *Banquet,* laying his views before a wider public.[146] He wrote partly in verse, not in a stately or dignified meter, but in sotadeans set to music, which the educated despised as dissolute, effeminate, and vulgar.[147] He probably now returned to Alexandria. There he found that Colluthus, a priest foremost in denouncing him, had organized a schismatic group. Arius organized conventicles of his own. He sought and found support among the Alexandrian populace; a later report alleges that he attracted seven hundred virgins to his cause. His adherents were disorderly, daily threatening the orthodox with violence in the streets of the city.[148]

Alexander again appealed to bishops outside Egypt, dispatching to all bishops everywhere a circular letter with a far more impressive array of signatures than before: almost two hundred bishops appended their names to this denunciation of Arius, the majority doubtless Egyptian, but with a sprinkling of names from most of the Greek provinces of the Roman Empire, among them Philogonius of Antioch.[149] Alexander also wrote a long and detailed account and refutation of Arius to a bishop whose diocese had so far escaped the controversy.[150] The writer who quotes this letter identifies the addressee as Alexander of Byzantium.[151] Eusebius of Caesarea perhaps reacted to the circular letter by convening a council of bishops in Palestine to intervene again in Arius' behalf.[152]

No firm dates are attested for the early stages of the Arian controversy.[153] It was perhaps, therefore, at this point that Licinius' ban on Church councils supervened.[154] If the Christians obeyed (as Eusebius of Caesarea implies), then the progress of controversy was suddenly arrested while the tensions were most acute. When Constantine conquered the East in 324, controversy among Christians at once resumed with all the exuberance of factions desiring dominance in an already triumphant Church.[155]

Alexander of Alexandria was aided during his struggle with Arius by his secretary, Athanasius, who was a deacon in Alexandria and had subscribed his name to Alexander's first circular letter.[156] Alexander's later letters may have been not only penned but also composed by Athanasius; one letter evokes a novel image recurring in Athanasius' *Easter Letters*—that of the Arians dividing the robe of Christ which his executioners had left intact (John 19:23–24).[157] A story later circulated that Alexander discovered Athanasius as a boy playing on the beach and took him into his household.[158] Despite the fairy-tale motifs in the story, its essence can be accepted: Athanasius was Alexander's protégé from an early age, perhaps from the start of Alexander's episcopate. When Athanasius was elected bishop in 328, some protested that he was below the canonical age (which was presumably thirty).[159] Since the charge was soon dropped, it may be deduced that Athanasius was born in 298 or very shortly before. He made his literary début at the age of twenty with a twofold work of Christian apologetics.

Against the Pagans and *On the Incarnation of the Word* were composed about 318, for Athanasius alludes to the apotheosis of deceased emperors by the Roman Senate as still occurring—which seems explicable only if he had recently heard of the consecration of Maximian about 317.[160] Throughout the two interconnected treatises, Athanasius draws confidently on the language and ideas of Greek philosophy, expressing his position easily in the prevailing terminology of Middle Platonism.[161] Athanasius feels no continuing tension between Greek philosophy and Christian theology. On the contrary, he assumes and asserts the victory of the latter. The wisdom of the Greeks (he proclaims) is disappearing, and the demons have altogether lost their power.[162]

Why did Athanasius write these apologies? Since he proposes to show that belief in Christ is not unreasonable, it might be supposed that Porphyry's attempt to prove the opposite (in *Against the Christians*) provoked the work.[163] But Athanasius addresses a friend who has already embraced the Christian faith.[164] The audience envisaged should thus be primarily Christian.[165] More significant is Athanasius' puzzling assertion that the works of his teachers are not available.[166] With their cool and intellectual tone, the two treatises read like a private theological exercise or a demonstration that the author has read and understood his teachers.[167] Therein lay their practical value in Alexander's eyes. The bishop of Alexandria hoped that his protégé would establish his credentials as a theological expert. For half a century after Alexander died, Athanasius was to be a resolute, stalwart, and effective champion of orthodoxy against both Melitians and Arians.

XII

THE COUNCIL OF NICAEA

Constantine fought the war of 324 as a liberator: he came to rescue the eastern provinces from oppressive government, eastern Christians from both misgovernment and persecution.[1] Soon after his arrival in Nicomedia, he began to fulfill the promises which his progaganda implied. The new ruler of the East annulled the imperial constitutions of the defeated Licinius, replacing them with ancient practice and his own rulings.[2] He also repealed the legal enactments of Licinius' subordinates, subject to the normal proviso that just decisions and privileges secured by petition should stand.[3] The population of the East (it seems) enjoyed an immediate alleviation of its tax burdens: when Constantine undid Licinius' innovations, he automatically reduced the age of exemption from liturgies, and presumably from personal taxation, from seventy years to sixty.[4]

In the autumn of 324, Constantine addressed two important letters to the inhabitants of each eastern province. One went to its churches, the other to those outside the Church.[5] Eusebius preserves the copy of the document which the emperor wrote "to the provincials of Palestine"; though in form a letter, it concludes with a formula ordering publication throughout the East which, in an earlier period at least, was characteristic of edicts.[6] It is a deliberate, public statement of imperial policy.

Constantine begins the letter by observing that the power of God has always manifested itself in the success and prosperity of those who scrupulously keep the tenets of the Christian religion. Those who attack and persecute Christianity, however, receive retribution for their crimes; God dashes their hopes and dooms them to defeat in war and even to death. Recently, when impious tyranny oppressed the world, what alleviation did God devise? He chose Constantine as his servant, who from Britain and the setting of the sun advanced to the East to rescue it from affliction. Those who showed endurance and resolution under the persecutors will now have a more splendid and blessed existence under the servant of God.

The detailed provisions following this general statement remedy the effects of Licinius' policy toward the Christians. Constantine recalls to their homeland Christians who had been exiled, discharges those, presumably priests, who had been enrolled in city councils as a punishment, and restores those deprived of their property to their homes, to their families, and to their former wealth. Christians deported to deserted islands shall return from penury and degradation to freedom and security, those condemned to forced labor shall return to a normal, leisurely existence, and any who have forfeited liberty and privileges shall at once resume their lost status in society. Those who were expelled from the army because of their faith may choose either their former rank or an honorable discharge. Christians of high birth who were degraded and then condemned to toil in imperial woolen mills or linen factories or to be slaves of the treasury, shall recover their freedom, honors, and status, and all those of whatever station who have been enslaved shall again be free.

Christians had lost property under Licinius as well as status and liberty; Constantine makes equally detailed provisions for its restitution. He awards to their nearest relatives the confiscated property of Christians who died in the persecution, whether as martyrs or confessors, in exile or simply of natural causes, after losing their property. If no relative can claim the inheritance, it shall revert to the local church. To avoid ambiguity, Constantine explains to pagans that they must surrender with all speed any land, houses, gardens, or anything else in their possession which has been confiscated from a Christian, declaring how much income it has brought them. He threatens punishment for all who attempt to defend their possession of such property; they must hand it over, no matter how it was acquired.

A series of significant paragraphs concludes the letter. Constantine informs his subjects that even his own *fiscus* will make full restitution, that the churches, as corporate bodies, are fully entitled to repossess everything confiscated from them, and that the churches own all places where martyrs are buried. The emperor then promises, as a favor, to pardon anyone who has purchased the confiscated property of Christians or obtained it from the *fiscus* by petition, and he reminds his pagan addressees that it is the God of the Christians who has delivered everyone from misery and oppression.

Constantine's letter differs fundamentally from the letters of Licinius, some eleven years before, which ended persecution in the East and guaranteed toleration. In 313, pagans who surrendered property previously confiscated from Christians were promised compensation from imperial funds.[7] In 324, in contrast, not only is there no hint of compensation, but Constantine speaks as if a pagan's mere possession of former Christian property constitutes a crime. The letter does not disguise the religious sympathies of Constantine, who takes every opportunity to stress the truth of Christianity. An emperor with these convictions could not be expected to tolerate pagan practices which all Christians found morally offensive. Constantine soon followed his initial letters to his new subjects with actions establishing Christianity as the official religion of the Roman Empire.

Christians received preference in official appointments, and pagan magistrates, whether provincial governors, *vicarii* of dioceses, or praetorian prefects, were forbidden to sacrifice before commencing official business.[8] Moreover, Constantine instructed provincial governors and bishops to cooperate in providing churches in which the numerous converts he expected as a result of his victory might worship. He wrote to each bishop (or at least to each metropolitan), urging him to restore churches damaged in the persecution, to enlarge existing buildings, and to construct new ones where needed. Constantine subsidized the cost from imperial funds, directing governors to supply money to the bishops on demand.[9]

The political circumstances of 324 enabled Constantine to take a still more momentous step. Throughout the cities of the East, many prominent supporters of Licinius were killed, either with or without the formality of a trial, when the persecuted took revenge, as they had after the fall of Maximinus.[10] Paganism was now a discredited cause. Constantine forbade the erection of cult statues, the consultation of pagan oracles, divination of any sort, and sacrifice to the gods under any circumstances.[11] A change so sudden, so fundamental, so total shocked pagans. There were probably complaints and protests to the emperor, perhaps even formal petitions. Constantine then issued a justification of his policy, which still survives. This remarkable document is not (as commonly supposed) an edict of toleration in which the conqueror of Licinius guarantees that pagans may continue to perform traditional cults and rituals.[12] To be sure, it permits pagans to retain ownership of their temples and forbids the use of violence to compel them to become Christians. But Constantine uses harsh language throughout, continually denounces paganism (temples are "groves of falsehood"), and pointedly refrains from mentioning sacrifices. Against the background of the earlier law, Constantine's silence ineluctably implies that sacrifice remains totally prohibited.

The external form of the pronouncement is an imperial letter "to the provincials of Oriens," yet Constantine writes much of it as if addressing a prayer to

God. He states his aim at the outset; true philosophy leads to the knowledge of God, but the masses prefer perversity and folly; Constantine, therefore, will attempt, as best he can, to outline the nature of his own hopes. Of earlier emperors, Constantius alone was humane and pious. His colleagues, at a time of peace, plunged the empire into civil war by persecuting the truth. Apollo gave an oracle proclaiming that "the righteous on earth" prevented him from speaking the truth, and Constantine himself, then a mere boy, heard how Diocletian asked his bodyguard who were "the righteous on earth." When a pagan priest identified them as the Christians, Diocletian issued his bloody edicts; Christians were tortured indiscriminately and executed, and some were even forced to take refuge beyond the imperial frontiers.

The persecuting emperors, however, are now all dead and are being punished everlastingly in hell, because they succumbed to the delusive power of Apollo's oracles. Constantine owes all his successes (he avows) to God, whose holy house, defiled and destroyed by "those disgusting and most impious men," the emperor hastens to renew by his own efforts. He desires, therefore, that God's people live in undisturbed peace. Pagans too can enjoy the same blessings—as an incentive to become Christian. Constantine invokes God as the giver of all good gifts, and he closes by observing that, as a Christian emperor, he tolerates paganism only because to attempt complete suppression would cause rebellion and public disorder.

In this document Constantine defines a policy which he was to maintain until his death. Christianity is the emperor's religion, and Christians can expect him to give them preferential treatment.[13] Pagans may retain their temples, shrines, and sacred groves, but sacrifice, divination, and the dedication of new cult images are all illegal—precisely the activities which constituted the essence of the traditional religions of the Roman Empire. Also prohibited were certain sorts of attack on Christianity; Porphyry had overstepped the permissible bounds, and Constantine ordered all copies of *Against the Christians* to be burned, prescribing the death penalty for any who furtively retained the work.[14]

In many matters, Constantine showed a caution which has often seemed to imply a policy of religious toleration. He would not risk rebellion or civil disobedience, and in Italy and the West, where he had been emperor long before 324, he made no serious attempt to enforce the prohibition of sacrifice which Eusebius attests for the East.[15] More generally, he could not disappoint the expectations of subsidy or support which loyal subjects, whatever their creed, entertained of their ruler, for to do so would flout the etiquette of centuries. Constantine subsidized the travels of a priest of the Eleusinian mysteries who visited the tombs of the kings in Egyptian Thebes, welcomed a pagan philosopher at court, and honored a priest of Apollo at Delphi for conspicuous devotion to the imperial house.[16]

Yet none of this entailed toleration for the forbidden cult practices. Constantine allowed pagans to retain their beliefs, even to build new sacred edifices. But he allowed them to worship their traditional gods only in the Christian sense of that word, not according to the traditional forms hallowed by antiquity. The emperor made the distinction underlying his policy explicit when he answered a petition from the Umbrian town of Hispellum requesting permission to build a temple of the Gens Flavia. Constantine granted the request but specified that the shrine dedicated to the imperial family must never be "polluted by the deceits of any contagious superstition."[17] From 324 onward Constantine consistently evinced official disapproval of the sacrifices and other cultic acts which constituted the essence of Greco-Roman paganism: Christianity was now the established religion of the Roman Empire and its ruler, and paganism should now conform to Christian patterns of religious observance.

Constantine marked his victory over Licinius by founding a new city to be his capital. His action, though obviously also symbolic in other ways, had a religious dimension. The new capital was to be a Christian city in which Christian emperors could hold court in an ambience untainted by the buildings, rites, and practices of other religions.[18] On 8 November 324 Constantine invested his son Constantius with the imperial purple and formally marked out the perimeter of the new city.[19] The emperor named it "New Rome," but most of his subjects preferred to call it Constantinople after its founder.[20]

Shortly after the ceremonies of 8 November, Constantine left the environs of Nicomedia and traveled across Asia Minor. His journey was not unexpected and was probably desirable for both political and military reasons. The poet Publilius Optatianus Porfyrius, languishing in exile, spoke of Indians, Arabians, Ethiopians, Medes, and Persians doing homage to the conqueror of the East.[21] He hinted that Constantine would soon go to the ends of the earth, that the emperor intended to make the Medes pay tribute,[22] and in Egypt men prepared for an impending imperial visit.[23] Constantine proceeded (it seems) as far as Antioch.[24] He then returned to Nicomedia, where his presence is attested on 25 February 325.[25] He himself explains the change of plan: he did not wish to see and hear the theological bickering which divided the East.[26] The Arian controversy forced itself on his attention just at the period when he most wished to concentrate on converting pagans to Christianity. By 324 not only were bishops denouncing one another, but congregations were divided into two parties, and in the theater pagans taunted Christians about their dissensions.[27]

Constantine felt a moral duty to intervene in the dispute. He wrote a letter to Alexander and Arius urging them to settle their differences peaceably and entrusted it to Ossius of Corduba, who had probably remained constantly at court since 312.[28] In fact, no real possibility of compromise existed. If Constantine hoped to mediate the quarrel, it was because he set a lower value on theological definitions, which he considered pedantic, than on making the Roman Empire Christian.[29]

The letter which Ossius took to Alexandria repeatedly rebukes Alexander and Arius for quarreling over questions which are of no importance. The bishop ought not to have interrogated his priests about their exegesis of a single passage of Scripture, and Arius ought to have maintained silence; both question and answers were produced by the contentious spirit of idle leisure. Their dispute is far less serious than the Donatist schism which divides Africa.[30] For the central doctrines of the divine law are not in dispute, nor has anyone introduced a novel way of worshiping God. Since the debate is a philosophical one, Constantine urges Alexander and Arius to behave like philosophers; their agreement on the main issues far outweighs minor differences, especially because they disagree on a question where the feebleness of the human intellect hinders the clear exposition or apprehension of the truth.[31]

Constantine has sometimes been accused of failing to appreciate what was at stake in the controversy, or of an inability to detect manifest heresy.[32] The charge is unjust and anachronistic. Constantine believed that all people should be Christian, but that Christians might legitimately hold divergent opinions on theological questions and that sensible Christians could disagree about doctrine in a spirit of brotherly love. The letter does not necessarily indicate that in his private thoughts Constantine dismissed the issues as totally trivial; writing to the chief disputants, he naturally minimized their differences. Yet it was already too late to write in this fashion. In the third century an Origen could speculate freely about metaphysics: long before Constantine dispatched his letter, such speculations were being pounced upon as heresies with no place within the Christian church.[33]

Ossius' mission failed. Of his activities in Alexandria, it is known only that he presided over a synod which demoted the schismatic Colluthus from bishop to priest and declared Colluthus' ordinations invalid.[34] But this synod presumably made some decisions about Arius, Melitius, and their followers, for this synod (it seems) announced a great council to be held at Ancyra, where Marcellus, a fanatical opponent of Arius, had been bishop since at least 314.[35] Moreover, as Ossius was returning to court, he discovered that the church of Antioch was in total disorder.[36] The bishop, Philogonius, had died on 20 December 324,[37] and rioting ensued over the election of his successor.

Eustathius was chosen, either shortly before Ossius arrived or partly through his intervention. A council of more than fifty bishops from Palestine, Arabia, Phoenice, Syria Coele, Cilicia, and Cappadocia met in Antioch to settle the affairs of the Antiochene church. Ossius communicated their decisions to Alexander, bishop of New Rome. The bishops acted decisively to support Alexander, bishop of Alexandria, and they adopted an intricately phrased creed which defined orthodox belief. All the bishops present except three declared that this formulary represented the true apostolic teaching necessary for salvation. The recusants were Theodotus of Laodicea, Narcissus of Neronias, and Eusebius of Caesarea. Ossius interrogated them one by one; the council pronounced their views heretical and excommunicated all three. The excommunication, however, was not unconditional: at the "great and holy council at Ancyra," the three would have the opportunity to repent, recognize the truth, and be restored to communion.[38] Ossius returned to court, and preparations were made for the approaching council.

The council never met at Ancyra. Constantine transferred it to Nicaea and perhaps enlarged its scope so that it became the first "ecumenical council" of the Christian church.[39] He wrote to the bishops, many of whom had probably already departed for Ancyra, instructing them to come to Nicaea with all haste. Constantine gave three reasons for changing the venue: bishops from Italy and the West could reach Nicaea more easily, its climate was more agreeable than that of Ancyra, and he himself desired to watch and participate in the deliberations.[40] His real motives, however, may have been very different. The date of the letter is unfortunately not known, but there is a suspicious coincidence between Constantine's expression of a desire to attend the council and a political crisis which his action has almost succeeded in obliterating from the historical record.

In September 324 Licinius was sent to Thessalonica, with a promise of safety.[41] Some time later he was strangled, in circumstances which remain unclear.[42] The official version represented his death as merited punishment: Licinius was plotting insurrection, and Constantine's timely action prevented a resumption of civil war.[43] The story might be true, so far as it goes, though it resembles too much the fabricated account of how Maximian in 310 plotted secretly to assassinate the emperor who had just pardoned him for open insurrection.[44] Some of Constantine's subjects thought that the emperor had murdered Licinius in contravention of the oath he swore in September 324 to spare the life of his defeated brother-in-law.[45] But one of the ordinary consuls of 325 suffered *damnatio memoriae* in May and was replaced by Julius Julianus, who had served Licinius as praetorian prefect until the end.[46] The consul, whose name was erased from the *fasti,* appears to have belonged to the pagan nobility of Rome.[47] There may, therefore, have been a real danger of rebellion in the spring of 325, and Licinius was the obvious focus of resentment against Constantine. Since Licinius posed a threat as long as he lived, Constantine had him killed—probably together with his son, the former Caesar, a boy of nine.[48]

Constantine's presence at Nicaea helped to divert attention from such unpleasant facts. Few Christians grieved at the death of Licinius, however obtained. They basked in the light of a new glory. Bishops converged on Nicaea, nearly three hundred in all; the emperor allowed them free use of the *cursus publicus,* and he paid their living expenses during the council.[49] They came from all the eastern provinces and from most of the Danubian region. There were also a few from beyond the empire, and some from the western provinces. The bishop of Rome did not come, pleading old age as an excuse, but he sent two priests who represented him and occupied a place of honor.[50] In age, attainments, and character, it was a motley gathering.[51] Prestige did not depend mainly on a bishop's see nor on his subtlety in debate. Confessors, especially those whose missing eyes and maimed ankles manifested proof of their steadfastness during the persecution, enjoyed enormous authority.[52] Important contributions also came from some who were not technically members of the council. The bishop of Alexandria received advice throughout the proceedings from his deacon Athanasius,[53] and Constantine, though not even a baptized Christian, participated in the debates.[54]

The rival parties did not arrive at Nicaea unprepared. A hostile but credible report alleges that Alexander of Alexandria and Ossius of Corduba agreed in advance that the word *homoousios* should be the touchstone of orthodoxy.[55] The term was known to be totally unacceptable to Eusebius of Nicomedia.[56] On the other side, the bishops who had been provisionally excommunicated at Antioch set out to rehabilitate themselves. Eusebius of Caesarea drew up a formal creed to prove his orthodoxy, which he tendered to the council.[57] In it he affirmed that "the Father is truly Father, the Son truly Son, and the Holy Spirit truly Holy Spirit," and he swore that the creed represented what he had been taught and had always believed as catechumen, neophyte, priest, and bishop.[58] The vast majority of bishops, however, had no personal stake in the Arian controversy and came predisposed to accept almost any formula which would secure harmony within the Church.

The council commenced about the beginning of June.[59] The opening ceremony was held in the judgment hall of the imperial palace. The bishops took their places on benches arranged in rows along the length of the hall. In silence, Constantine's attendants entered—not the usual soldiers of the bodyguard, but friends of the emperor who were Christians—all unarmed. At a sign, all stood. Constantine entered, clad in the imperial purple, with a diadem and insignia of gold and diamonds. He advanced as far as the first seats in each row. A small stool of wood encrusted with gold was produced. After requesting permission from the bishops, Constantine sat down; the rest followed suit.[60] The bishop immediately to his left, Eusebius of Nicomedia, rose and delivered a panegyrical address of welcome.[61] After Eusebius resumed his seat, Constantine replied briefly and formally in Latin.

He expressed gratitude to God for allowing him to see the bishops assembled together in concord, and he deprecated violent dissension within the Church as more lamentable than even civil war. Could the Devil sully the Church even after all the persecutors had been destroyed? His own victories in war could be fully complete only when the consecrated servants of God united in peace and harmony. They should, therefore, state their disagreements openly in order to achieve a peaceful resolution of their differences, for only thus could they please God and show adequate gratitude to their liberator.[62] An interpreter translated the speech into Greek.[63] When Constantine finished (it appears), he received petitions from the bishops, many of whom had already approached him privately with accusations against one another. He sat with the petitions (which were later burned) in his lap and reproved the bishops for letting private animosities interfere with God's business.[64] The debates then began.

Ossius of Corduba presided.[65] Constantine sat apart from the bishops, but close enough to participate in the discussions.[66] Unfortunately, it appears that the proceedings of the Council of Nicaea were not recorded or published at the time.[67] As a result, the complex course of the debates cannot be reconstructed, and the few episodes which can be documented cannot be combined to produce any sort of coherent account.[68] The role of Constantine, however, is clear. Eusebius of Caesarea later praised the emperor for his patience: speaking in Greek, Constantine settled differences, urged all to concord, and praised those who spoke well.[69] Eustathius of Antioch, in contrast, complained that unnamed persons put forward the name of peace and thereby reduced to silence those who normally spoke best.[70] Eusebius and Eustathius appear to be describing the same facts in different ways: Constantine intervened with the voice of reason, to advise moderation.[71]

The council considered the Arian controversy first. Eusebius of Caesarea and two other bishops had arrived in Nicaea under a provisional ban of excommunication. Eusebius presented the previously prepared document as proof of his orthodoxy. His enemies could find no obvious blunder in this creed and its glosses. Constantine spoke first; he commended Eusebius' beliefs as orthodox, almost identical, in fact, with his own, and surely acceptable to all—if Eusebius would only add that the Son was of one substance with the Father.[72] Eusebius accepted the condition, unpalatable though he found it.[73] He thereby created a dilemma for his enemies. They were compelled either to receive Eusebius, whom they still considered heretical, back into communion or to brand Constantine as a heretic for sharing the unorthodox beliefs of the bishop of Caesarea. Eusebius, Theodotus, and Narcissus were admitted to membership of the council.

The orthodoxy of other bishops who sympathized with Arius may also have been discussed. At all events, a letter of Eusebius of Nicomedia was read in which he repudiated the term *homoousios*, a word now sanctioned by the emperor.[74] Moreover, Eustathius of Antioch reports the reading of something written by Eusebius (either of Nicomedia or, perhaps, of Caesarea) which shocked the assembly by its obvious heterodoxy. It was symbolically torn up.[75]

The debate on the theological issue dragged on for some days. Finally, a creed was produced. It may have been formulated in committee: Basil of Caesarea, fifty years later, remarks casually that the Cappadocian priest Hermogenes wrote the Nicene Creed.[76] The creed contained the word *homoousios* and the very specific statement that the Son was "begotten of the Father, that is, from the essence (*ousia*) of the Father." Anathemas were pronounced on Arius' main propositions. The creed excommunicated any who said that "there was when he was not," or "before being born he was not," or "he came into existence out of nothing," or who said that the Son was of another essence or substance from the Father, or was created, changeable, or mutable.[77]

When the creed was presented to the full council, Constantine made it clear that he expected all to accept it, even Arius himself.[78] The minority, therefore, requested a detailed explanation of what each new phrase signified, in what precise sense each word was employed. Eustathius and many others clearly wished to explain the creed in a way which those who thought like Eusebius of Caesarea could not accept. But Constantine contributed an exegesis which virtually every bishop present, even Eusebius, could accept as consistent with his own views.[79] On 19 June 325 Ossius promulgated the creed and subscribed his name.[80] Notaries supplied by the emperor carried round the document.[81] Only the two Libyan bishops associated with Arius from the outset (Secundus of Ptolemais and Theonas of Marmarica) refused to sign; they departed into immediate exile, together with Arius and some priests who also refused to repudiate his views.[82]

The Council of Nicaea had much other business and remained in session for another month. It was perhaps Constantine himself who had asked the council to determine the proper date of Easter. He took a prominent part in the discussion,[83] and afterward wrote a circular letter communicating the decision to the churches of each province in Syria and Palestine. In this letter Constantine evinces his concern that not all Christians celebrate the festival on the same day, and that some adopt the Jewish computation, which is tainted by its origin and can produce two Easters in a single astronomical year. The council shared the emperor's view that to allow different Easters in different places was absurd and sinful, and it legislated for uniformity, ordering all churches everywhere to adopt the calculation which prevailed throughout the West, Asia Minor, and Egypt.[84] Since no specific Easter cycle was prescribed, the council probably asked the bishops of Rome and Alexandria to cooperate in fixing the date of Easter each year.[85] Complete uniformity, however, was not attained: in Syria, the Protopaschites or Audiani continued to adhere to the forbidden practice of celebrating Easter on the Sunday following the Jewish Passover,[86] and, at least in some years after 325, the churches of Rome and Alexandria celebrated Easter on different days.[87]

Another problem too obvious to ignore was the status of schismatic groups. The council considered how to treat not only Melitius and those whom he had ordained, but also the followers of Novatian and of Paul of Samosata. Melitius himself was allowed to remain bishop of Lycopolis but was specifically denied any right to appoint or ordain priests in the surrounding countryside or in another city. Although the council accepted priests already ordained by Melitius as validly consecrated, it declared that in each town or village they were inferior in rank to all those ordained under Alexander of Alexandria, and it forbade them to appoint or propose the appointment of their candidates to the clergy, or even to do anything at all without the consent of the bishop of the Catholic church loyal to Alexander. Nevertheless, Melitian priests who forswore schism and acknowledged the authority of Alexander should have full clerical privileges and might replace a deceased priest of the universal church, provided that the congregation so wished and that the bishop of Alexandria agreed.[88]

The Novatianists were rigorists from an earlier persecution. The council investigated their orthodoxy, and Constantine interrogated Acesius, a bishop of the sect.[89] The council acknowledged Novatianist ordinations as valid and laid down that all bishops or priests of the sect who were willing to signify in writing their acceptance of normally accepted disciplinary standards, specifically the readmission of adulterers and apostates after penance, should be counted as bishops or priests of the Catholic church in any city or village where there was no Catholic clergy. Where there was a Catholic bishop, he should retain his episcopal powers, though he might confer the honorary title of bishop on the former Novatianist. Alternatively, he might make a former Novatianist a suf-fragan bishop or priest, so that there would not be two bishops in the city.[90] The followers of Paul of Samosata were heretics rather than schismatics. The council treated them more harshly, pronouncing their ordinations totally in-valid and ordering Paulianists who joined the Catholic church to be rebap-tized.[91]

The council also issued regulations on many other matters. When Licinius forbade Church councils and otherwise harried the Church, he thereby pre-vented the solution of some problems and created others. Collections of canon law register twenty canons of the Council of Nicaea, of which two deal with the Novatianists and Paulianists. Many of the other eighteen concern questions of liturgical practice[92] or problems of discipline and penitence, and much of their content is predictable. The council declared that voluntary self-castration, pre-viously undisclosed crimes, apostasy, and lending money at interest disqualify a man from belonging to the clergy.[93] The council prohibited the immediate ordination of the newly baptized as priests or bishops and forbade clergy to keep any women in their house except a mother, sister, aunt, or other female relative who would not arouse suspicion.[94] And it considered the appro-priate penance for the most eager of the apostates during the persecution under Licinius.[95] The bishops also endeavored to strengthen the ecclesiastical hierar-chy by enhancing the effective power of metropolitan bishops and of Church councils.

Bishops, priests, and deacons were all forbidden to move from one church to another.[96] Ideally, a bishop would be ordained by all the bishops of a prov-ince, but as few as three were allowed to consecrate, provided that the absent bishops accepted the choice in writing, with the metropolitan bishop possessing the right of veto.[97] Those whom the bishops of one province excommunicated were not to be received into communion elsewhere, and all the bishops of a province should meet twice a year (before Ascension and about the time of the autumn equinox) to consider offenses against ecclesiastical discipline.[98]

The council acted to preserve the traditional rights of metropolitan bishops which the division of the empire into smaller provinces had implicitly dimin-ished. The churches of Alexandria, Antioch, and other cities (it declared) were to retain their ancient privileges: thus the bishop of Alexandria would continue to have jurisdiction outside the Roman province of Egypt; his authority would extend, as it always had, throughout Egypt, Libya, and the Pentapolis, in the same way as the authority of the bishop of Rome extended over peninsular

Italy.[99] Eusebius of Caesarea, however, found his pre-eminence as metropolitan of Palestine potentially endangered. The bishop of Jerusalem traditionally enjoyed great prestige as the occupant of an apostolic see; the council, although acknowledging the status of Caesarea as the metropolitan see in Palestine, also decreed that Jerusalem should receive due honor.[100]

The decisions of the Council of Nicaea were communicated not only through synodal letters (as was the normal custom) but also by Constantine. Athanasius quotes a letter of the bishops at Nicaea written especially to the church of Alexandria and the Christians of Egypt, Libya, and the Pentapolis, and a letter of Constantine to the church of Alexandria, and Eusebius reproduces a circular letter of Constantine to the churches of each province.[101] The first letter reports all the major decisions of the council; the second, only the adoption of the creed; the third, only the regulations concerning the date of Easter. In adding his letters to those of the bishops, Constantine deliberately emphasized his role as a Christian emperor bringing unity and concord to a divided Church.

Before the bishops departed from Nicaea, Constantine conferred on them a signal honor. On 25 July 325 the celebration of the emperor's *vicennalia* began in nearby Nicomedia.[102] To mark the anniversary, Constantine invited all the bishops to a banquet; they came to the palace, swept past the soldiers standing guard with drawn swords, and feasted with the emperor—like the apostles surrounding Christ in paradise.[103] After the feast, Constantine gave each of his guests an appropriate present, and he summoned them to his presence yet again for a farewell discourse in which he commended charity, cooperation, and concord.[104]

The *vicennalia* were a time for general rejoicing, whatever a person's creed. Constantine gave generously to all, as custom required, and granted an amnesty, which released the poet Publilius Optatianus Porfyrius from his exile.[105] Moreover, Constantine proposed to complete the vicennial celebrations with a visit to Rome, which he had not seen for a decade. He remained at Nicomedia until September, then spent the autumn and winter in or near Constantinople, presumably supervising its construction.[106] In March 326 he traveled swiftly westward, reached Aquileia by 1 April, and prepared to enter Rome in triumph.[107] While he was in northern Italy, however, intrigue and scandal struck.

Constantine believed that sexual misdemeanors merited the harshest treatment, and his legislation removing legal disabilities from celibates sometimes seems to regard even marriage as sinful.[108] In 322, when a grandchild was born, he pardoned all criminals except murderers, practitioners of magic, and adulterers.[109] In 326, Constantine publicly committed himself to a cruel and unnatural policy. As late as 3 February 326, he issued a rescript which reflects traditional Roman attitudes: although the female owner of a tavern and her lovers can be guilty of adultery, a barmaid must be presumed so vile, shameful, and unchaste that she and her lovers do not infringe the laws of Augustus by their promiscuity.[110] But four surviving fragments indicate that shortly thereafter

Constantine issued a general edict of wide scope which comprehensively revised the existing law.[111]

The edict was dated 1 April and copies were prepared for officials throughout the empire. Constantine totally forbade married men to have concubines.[112] He restricted the right to bring a charge of adultery to husbands, fathers, brothers, uncles, and cousins.[113] He laid down that when a female ward grows up and wishes to marry, her guardian must furnish proof that she is a virgin inviolate; if the guardian has seduced her, he shall be deported and all his property confiscated.[114] Constantine decreed that rapists should be punished by being burned alive, and he disallowed any appeal against the sentence. Moreover, under the new law, a man who carried off a girl against her parents' wishes could no longer marry her, even if she was willing; on the contrary, her acquiescence rendered her too liable to be burned alive. Nurses who encouraged girls to elope were to have boiling lead poured down their throats, while anyone of either sex who aided the lover would also be burned alive. Constantine treated seduction like a ritual impurity which can in no way be cleansed. If parents of virgins who had been seduced concealed the crime, they became liable to deportation, and any slave who reported their attempts at concealment received a reward. Even a virgin who was violently raped deserved punishment, since she could have stayed safely at home. Professing clemency, the emperor ordained that she should lose the right to inherit property from her parents—and hence, presumably, any chance of a dowry and a respectable husband.[115]

This law is morbid and unwholesome. It disregards the natural appetites of men and women in favor of an abstract ideal of purity, deduced from Christian tenets of asceticism. More dangerous, it rendered criminal the normal behavior of many Roman aristocrats.[116] Hence it laid the indiscreet open to denunciation by their political and personal enemies. Important persons were soon accused, among them Constantine's own son and a young Roman aristocrat. Constantine tried the cases himself.[117] The Caesar Crispus was a married man, and his wife had given birth to at least one child.[118] Constantine sentenced him to death and he was executed at Pola.[119] The precise details of his crime have been obscured by legend and invention. Writers hostile to Constantine alleged that the empress Fausta fell in love with her stepson: when he repulsed her advances, like a second Phaedra she accused him of attempted rape.[120] That version of events ignores the fact that by 326 Crispus normally resided in Trier, far from his stepmother, who lived at his father's court. Moreover, apparently at the same time, Constantine tried and exiled the young Ceionius Rufius Albinus for adultery and magic.[121] The truth behind the accusations against Crispus and Albinus seems forever lost. It is clear, nevertheless, that Fausta or her agents must have played a large role in securing Crispus' condemnation: by the death of Crispus, Fausta's own sons lost a rival, and Constantine can only have executed his son on evidence which appeared irrefragable.[122]

The sequel ineluctably implies that Crispus was falsely accused. Helena, the mother of Constantine, had lived in Rome for many years. When Constantine entered Rome on 15 July 326 to celebrate the twentieth anniversary of his accession ten days later,[123] she approached him in mourning for her grandson. Helena either told Constantine facts he did not know about the condemnation of Crispus or at least planted in his mind the suspicion that the whole truth had not been disclosed. The emperor then (it must be assumed) confronted Fausta and accused her of deceiving him, but it is not clear that he formally tried her. Fausta went into the *caldarium* of the baths in the imperial palace. The room was heated far beyond the normal temperature; she suffocated in the steam and was carried out a corpse. Her death appears to have been suicide under compulsion.[124] The young aristocrat Albinus was abruptly recalled from exile and launched on a brilliant career (which took him to an ordinary consulate in 335 at the remarkably young age of thirty-two).[125]

Political embarrassment again induced Constantine to advertise the Christianity of the imperial court ostentatiously. While the emperor returned slowly to Nicomedia (which he reached during the summer of 327),[126] Helena went on a pilgrimage to the Holy Land. The dowager empress, a woman of almost eighty, left Rome in the autumn of 326 and played her role as imperial benefactress well. Her generosity was designed to make people forget recent events, and Constantine allowed her to act and spend freely.[127] In Palestine Helena endowed two churches: one in Bethlehem commemorated the nativity of Jesus, the other his ascension into heaven from the Mount of Olives.[128] From Jerusalem she traveled north to Syria, presumably intending to join the imperial court at Constantinople or Nicomedia. As she went, she gave generously to cities, to the soldiers, and to all individuals who approached her, especially to the poor. She released criminals from prison, from the mines, from exile. She dedicated gifts in churches everywhere, even in the smallest cities.[129]

Helena died with the memory of her good works still fresh—and legend was to enhance them greatly.[130] She reached the imperial court and died in the presence of her son, probably at Nicomedia.[131] Constantine constructed a magnificent sarcophagus of porphyry; a large military guard escorted it slowly and majestically to Rome, where it was laid in a mausoleum on the Via Labicana.[132]

Constantine renamed Drepanum in Bithynia, where his mother was born, Helenopolis; on 7 January 328, he refounded the city and transferred there the relics of Lucian of Antioch, whom his mother had venerated.[133] He probably also accompanied her embalmed body to Italy, for he had pressing business in the West. The removal of Crispus had created a dangerous void, which might tempt the ambitions of a usurper. Constantine wished to install the Caesar Constantinus, now almost twelve years of age, with a court and advisers in Trier to ensure the security of the western provinces.[134]

In the spring of 328 Constantine left Nicomedia. He spent some time on and near the Danube, perhaps at this time building the stone bridge from Oescus to Sucidava which announced his intention of carrying war beyond the river.[135]

By late September Constantine was at Trier, and during the autumn he conducted a German campaign, for which an imperial victory was proclaimed.[136] On 1 January 329, Augustus and Caesar entered on the consulate of the year at Trier amid the customary splendor.[137] Constantine soon departed, leaving Constantinus with the full apparatus of a court, including trusted advisers who would prevent the Caesar from showing any independence of policy.[138] By the spring of 329 Constantine was at Sirmium, and during the next year he remained in the vicinity of Naissus, Serdica, and Heraclea. When he entered New Rome again, he came to celebrate the formal dedication of his new capital.

The day chosen for the dedication (11 May 330) was significant.[139] It was the festival of Saint Mocius, a martyr of Byzantium under Diocletian or Licinius—and perhaps known to Constantine in his youth.[140] Local tradition reports that Constantine constructed a church in honor of Mocius from a temple of Jupiter.[141] Whether or not that story is true, Constantine certainly dedicated a martyrium to Mocius one mile outside his new city.[142] The date of the dedication emphasized the close connection between the foundation of Constantinople and the defeat of the last of the persecutors: Constantine consecrated the New Rome to "the God of the martyrs."[143]

Later legend offers a plethora of detail for the ceremonies of 11 May 330, in which pagan and Christian elements are inextricably entwined.[144] The early and reliable evidence more realistically stresses the Christian character of the foundation. If the statue of Constantine which stood atop a porphyry column in the center of the forum was (as is alleged) a reworked statue of Apollo from Phrygia, it had been remodeled for its new location.[145] From the start, Constantine endowed his new city with splendid churches, commissioning Eusebius of Caesarea to send fifty copies of the Bible for use in divine worship, and he refused to allow any trace of pagan rites.[146] The fountains and the public buildings reflected Christian, not traditional, art. Instead of the usual figures and scenes from Greek mythology, there were statues of the Good Shepherd, of Daniel in the lions' den, and other biblical characters, often in gilded bronze—and a cross of precious stones hanging in midair dominated the principal hall of the imperial palace.[147]

By the mere fact of its existence, Constantinople immediately became the capital of the Eastern Empire and one of the main cultural centers of the Greek world. Even pagan intellectuals felt the lure of the new city, despite its aggressively Christian ethos. In 340 Libanius decided to leave Athens for Constantinople, because he wished to bury himself in a small town no longer, and he felt that the new and rich capital needed teachers and orators.[148] In Constantinople, Libanius encountered Bemarchius, a sophist from Cappadocia, whom the city had hired as an official teacher for a large salary. Bemarchius may have been a pagan (Libanius claims that he sacrificed to the gods), but he wrote a laudatory history of Constantine in ten books and recited panegyrics on churches built by Constantine's son.[149]

Constantine gave the inhabitants of his new city privileges appropriate to its status as the eastern capital. He created a Senate of Constantinople whose members attained full equality of rank with senators of Rome within a generation.[150] On 18 May 332, he commenced the distribution of free grain; the harvests of Egypt, formerly transported to Italy, were diverted eastward, and the provinces in Asia, Syria, and Phoenicia also sent grain in payment of their tribute.[151] Constantine built a hippodrome adjacent to the palace. Here the amusements offered lacked any taint of overt paganism, and the spectators at the horse races had ample opportunity to applaud their imperial benefactor as a Christian emperor.[152]

XIII

ECCLESIASTICAL POLITICS

The Christianity which now constituted the established religion of the Roman Empire was of an exclusive type. From 312, Constantine confined his largess and fiscal privileges to Christians belonging to the Catholic church.[1] Further, when the Donatists finally refused to acknowledge a Catholic bishop of Carthage vindicated by councils of bishops and by the emperor himself, Constantine treated their schism as a crime and confiscated their property.[2] The victory of 324 permitted Constantine to make the principle underlying this decision explicit and universal. He legislated an end to all heretical sects. A letter explicitly addressed "to heretics" was publicly displayed. In it Constantine insulted Novatianists, Valentinians, Marcionites, Paulianists, Montanists, and all other heretics and declared their conduct intolerable. He ordained that they no longer meet, even in private houses, that their houses of prayer be surrendered to the Catholic church, and that any other real property they owned be confiscated.[3] The law was clearly not enforced, since Valentinian, Marcionite, and Montanist conventicles long continued to exist.[4] And a rescript of 326 exempted the Novatianists, whose beliefs Constantine had verified as orthodox at Nicaea; the rescript allowed them to retain houses and burial places which they had bought or acquired after their separation from the Catholic church.[5] Nevertheless, Constantine had stated that, in principle at least, heresy was now illegal. The relevance of this ruling to ecclesiastical politics escaped no one.

The Council of Nicaea failed to bring harmony to the eastern Church. On the contrary, it sharpened divisions and inaugurated a new phase of ecclesiastical politics. The actions, utterances, and beliefs of Constantine invested the Nicene Creed with a unique, inviolable status. A Christian emperor believed and affirmed that councils of bishops spoke with divine authority.[6] How then could any individual bishop challenge the definition of the faith adopted by the fathers at Nicaea? But a divinely inspired creed must be a guarantor as well as a touchstone of orthodoxy. Acceptance of the Nicene Creed and its anathemas now proved a man orthodox, at least in the eyes of the emperor. Yet Arius' opponents did not cease to believe that supporters of Arius who had subscribed to the Nicene Creed and its anathemas were heretical, and the creed itself (it emerged) was susceptible of diverse interpretations.

Constantine's respect for bishops as theological experts was naive and dangerous. It allowed Church councils to depose bishops in the confidence that the emperor would ensure that the deposition was carried into effect by exile, and the twelve years after Nicaea are a sad tale of how enduring enmities thwarted Constantine's desire for peace and concord within the Church. The reasons for the emperor's failure must not be misunderstood. Constantine did not fail because he attempted to impose a theological solution of his own by force,[7] but for the opposite reason. He acquiesced too often in the hasty verdicts of partisan councils—and he was totally unwilling to depose a bishop on his own authority.

The detailed course of events within the Church between 325 and 337 is very difficult to unravel. Ecclesiastical politics were complicated enough in reality, but legend and deliberate falsification have conspired to hide or distort many vital facts. The extant continuators of Eusebius' *Ecclesiastical History* belong to the fifth century and depend very heavily on Gelasius of Caesarea, whose lost work clearly projected the attitudes, inventions, and simplifications of the age of Theodosius back into that of Constantine.[8] Hence the similar narratives of Rufinus, Socrates, Sozomenus, Theodoretus, and Gelasius of Cyzicus can provide no basis for a genuine understanding, even though each of them preserves valuable facts and documents. The true course of events must be laboriously (and hesitantly) deduced from documents and reports of documents, from the partial and tendentious statements of interested parties, from contemporary hints and innuendos, from polemics and apologia which often disregard the canons of sincerity and truthfulness.[9]

Ecclesiastical politics after Nicaea are party politics. The Arian party, cowed and defeated in 325, suddenly recovered its power two years later and proceeded to dislodge its main opponents from their sees. When Constantine died in 337, though the heresiarch was dead, Arius' supporters enjoyed a supremacy in the eastern Church which appeared almost complete. The reversal can be explained by a significant change at court. Ossius of Corduba returned to Spain not long after Nicaea.[10] Eusebius of Nicomedia soon replaced him as Constantine's close and constant adviser on ecclesiastical matters—and Eusebius was the architect of his party's triumph.

While the Council of Nicaea was still in session, Eusebius of Caesarea wrote a letter which reveals deep embarrassment. He needed to explain his acceptance of the creed and its anathemas to his congregation, because many in Caesarea were likely to consider his action both unexpected and unwelcome. His letter asks its recipients to disregard any rumors which may have reached them. Eusebius promises an accurate account of what has happened. He presents the facts, however, in a highly selective and misleading fashion. He glosses over the debates at Nicaea in order to depict the creed adopted by the council as based on the creed which he had tendered as proof of his orthodoxy. Throughout the letter he shelters behind the authority of Constantine, whose presence and role at the council he continually recalls. Eusebius justifies at length his acceptance of the Nicene Creed, explaining in what precise sense he interprets each phrase, and he defends the anathemas appended to the creed as "harmless." It is predictably, however, in a fundamentally Arian sense that Eusebius interprets the phrases "of the substance of the Father" and "being of one substance with the Father." The opponents of Arius had inserted the word *homoousios* because they believed that the bishop of Caesarea and those who thought like him could never find it acceptable. Eusebius renders his *volte face* less surprising by giving the new phrases a broad and general sense. For him, "of the substance of the Father" means merely "of the Father": the Son is of the Father, but not part of him or of his substance. Similarly, "of one substance with the Father" should not be taken in any corporeal sense; it merely stresses the dissimilarity of the Son to the created order and asserts that he is "not of any other essence and substance, but of the Father." Eusebius, as a scholar, adds that the word *homoousios* has been used by respectable writers and bishops.[11]

Eusebius of Caesarea accepted the word *homoousios* by disregarding its implications. Others who sympathized with Arius salved their consciences in other ways. Eusebius of Nicomedia and Theognis of Nicaea subscribed to the creed but refused to subscribe to the anathemas appended to it.[12] The council did not depose or excommunicate them at once; it allowed them time for reflection and compliance.[13] When the council dispersed, however, Eusebius and Theognis imagined that they were safe. They communicated with some Alexandrian malcontents (presumably Melitians or supporters of Colluthus), whom Constantine had summoned to court for fanning the flames of schism.[14] When he discovered this challenge to the fragile unity of Nicaea, Constantine exiled the bishops of Nicomedia and Nicaea to distant parts of the empire. He did not convene another council to depose them but acted on the strength of the decisions made at Nicaea; he wrote to the church of Nicomedia to announce that Eusebius and Theognis had forfeited their sees and should be replaced by bishops who were holy, orthodox, and humane. The letter breathes an air of impatient annoyance and recites a long list of crimes previously forgiven or forgotten. Eusebius was a henchman of Licinius when he persecuted Christians, he spied on Constantine, he encouraged Arius from the outset of the controversy, he petitioned Constantine to save him after his condemnation. Constantine promises to curb any attempt to remember or praise the two miscreants.[15] Constantine also wrote to Theodotus of Laodicea to dissuade him from imitating the behavior of his former allies—a revealing letter, for it assumes that compliance with the Nicene decisions determines whether a believer shall hereafter gain rewards in heaven or punishment in hell.[16]

Eusebius and Theognis were exiled three months after Nicaea, in September or October 325.[17] A war of pamphlets had probably already begun. Bishops exchanged letters, confessing their anxiety about the new theological idea of consubstantiality or allowing its unclarity to encourage charges of blasphemy against those who interpreted it differently. Those who disliked the term *homoousios* accused its advocates of some form of monarchianism; its champions alleged that to reject the term implied polytheism or paganism. Nor were personal animosities absent. Eustathius of Antioch attacked Eusebius of Caesarea for adulterating the Nicene Creed, and Eusebius replied with a charge of Sabellianism.[18] When the theological issue was posed in such terms, compromise and toleration were impossible. Bishops who regarded themselves as orthodox had a sacred duty to depose those whom they derided as heretical. But it was difficult to proceed on charges of heresy against bishops who accepted the creed of Nicaea, whatever interpretation they might choose to put upon its formulations. The emperor would be more impressed by accusations of moral turpitude or infractions of canon law than by the squabblings of bishops over an issue he considered settled.

Eustathius of Antioch was vulnerable to such accusations, and a precious fragment of what appears to be a sermon on the Arian proof text *The Lord created me the beginning of his ways* (Proverbs 8:22) illuminates the circumstances of his downfall.[19] Eustathius contrasted the true and false exegesis of the text and argued that Eusebius (it is not certain which of the two) had used it to support heresy. Eusebius was exposed at Nicaea, but the Arian fanatics craftily suscribed to the creed to avoid disgrace and exile. They have thus (Eustathius complains) retained the ability to advocate the doctrines condemned by the council, and to attack their critics. Avoiding men of good sense and corrupting the secular rulers, they go to war with the champions of piety. Eustathius, however, draws comfort from Isaiah: even if the impious *become strong again, they will be defeated again* (8:9) by God's power.[20]

The clear implication of such utterances is that Eustathius has been accused before the emperor or the secular authorities, but expects that a council of bishops will soon vindicate him.[21] His confidence was misplaced. About two years after the Council of Nicaea, a council of bishops met at Antioch and conducted a purge in the Arian interest.[22] Eusebius of Caesarea presided, and Eustathius was deposed. His opponents believed him guilty of Sabellianism and included this among the counts against him.[23] Yet that was not the main charge. Eustathius was deposed for moral delinquencies; he dishonored the priesthood, he lived in a disorderly fashion, he kept a mistress, and he had spoken disrespectfully of the emperor's mother while she was in the East.[24] The charges may have been exaggerated or partly invented. But the council sustained them, and Constantine, who reviewed the case and examined Eustathius in person, raised no objection to the verdict of the council. The bishop of Antioch departed into exile in Illyricum.[25]

The same council deposed Asclepas of Gaza on unknown charges.[26] It probably also deposed several other bishops of Syria, Phoenicia, and Palestine who are known to have lost their sees under Constantine: Euphrantion of Balaneae, Cymatius of Paltos, Cymatius of Gabala, Carterius of Antarados, and Cyrus of Beroea.[27] One of the two Cymatii was a close associate of Eustathius and was apparently deposed for very similar moral reasons.[28]

The council replaced the deposed bishops with men whose theological beliefs the majority found more acceptable. But the church of Antioch was divided into two evenly balanced parties, and a serious attempt was subsequently made to reinstate Eustathius. Paulinus of Tyre, who succeeded Eustathius in 327, even though the Council of Nicaea forbade bishops to move from one see to another, died after six months.[29] Nor did the next bishop, Eulalius, last long.[30] When he died, dissension prevented an immediate election. Tension increased as the supporters of Eustathius canvassed for his recall. The struggle spread beyond the church of Antioch into the streets. At length, Constantine sent a trusted *comes* with letters to the opposing parties which reminded them of the crimes of Eustathius, affirmed that he must remain in exile, and urged the Christians of Antioch to compose their differences.[31]

Another council of bishops was then convened, perhaps at the emperor's behest. The church of Antioch and the council chose Eusebius as the new bishop.[32] The bishop of Caesarea demurred. Electors and reluctant candidate then appealed to Constantine, who received letters from the council and from Eusebius and, presumably at the same time, reports from the *comites* Acacius and Strategius.[33] In reply, the emperor wrote separately to the church of Antioch, to Eusebius, and to the council. He congratulated the Christians of Antioch on their unanimity in desiring Eusebius as their bishop, but tactfully suggested that they choose another.[34] Eusebius himself he complimented for respecting the rules which discouraged bishops from moving from one see to another.[35] Constantine invited the council to choose as bishop either Euphronius, a priest of Caesarea in Cappadocia, or George, a priest of Arethusa, or any other equally worthy person.[36] The council chose Euphronius. When he died, a year and some months later, Flaccillus became bishop—a man close enough to Eusebius to be honored with the dedication of Eusebius' last theological work.[37] By 330, therefore, the metropolitan see of Antioch was firmly in the Arian camp, and Flaccillus could ensure that any new bishop in Syria would sympathize with the Arian cause.[38]

The first council of Antioch had an immediate effect elsewhere. Arius, Eusebius of Nicomedia, and Theognis expressed a sudden desire to rejoin the Catholic church. Before the end of 327, their rehabilitation was effected through the mediation of Constantine. Arius indicated a willingness to accept the Nicene Creed and a desire to see the emperor. On 27 November 327, Constantine summoned Arius to court: he reminded the priest that only his intransigence prevented him from coming long ago, and he promised friendly assistance in securing his return to Alexandria.[39] When Arius arrived, Constantine demanded written proof of his orthodoxy. Arius and his fellow priest Euzoius submitted to Constantine a carefully worded statement of their beliefs. They avoided the word *homoousios,* but declared their belief in Jesus Christ, the only begotten Son of God, "begotten of God before all ages, divine Word, through whom everything was made." This creed (they affirmed) represented the teaching of the Catholic church and of Scripture. They accordingly begged Constantine to secure their reconciliation with the Church, their mother, putting an end to pointless speculations, so that they could join with the Church in prayer for the peaceful and pious rule of the emperor and all his family.[40] Constantine examined the letter and questioned Arius and Euzoius publicly.[41] Satisfied with their answers, he submitted their case to a council of bishops— which alone could revoke the condemnations pronounced at Nicaea.

Constantine (it appears) had already convened a large council of bishops to consider other business. The solution devised in 325 had not ended the Melitian schism; the emperor, therefore, summoned a second council on the same scale as the first to put an end to strife in Egypt.[42] At Nicomedia, in December 327, two hundred and fifty bishops assembled.[43] Constantine, who was residing in Nicomedia, attended their debates and participated as he had at Nicaea.[44] The council readmitted Arius and Euzoius, whereupon Eusebius and Theognis petitioned for reinstatement. In their letter to the council, they emphasized their acceptance of the Nicene Creed, including the term *homoousios;* they had not signed the anathemas because correspondence and conversation with Arius had convinced them that he did not hold the opinions attributed to him.[45] When the council restored Arius and acquitted him of heresy, it was inconsistent to refuse to pardon the exiled bishops. Eusebius and Theognis regained their sees, their successors being unceremoniously ejected.[46] As for the Melitians, another attempt was made to reintegrate them into the Catholic church of Egypt.[47]

Constantine endorsed the decisions of the council and announced them by letters.[48] But Alexander of Alexandria had not come to Nicomedia, and he was unwilling to comply with all the decisions of the council. Some progress may have been made toward receiving the Melitian clergy back into the ecclesiastical hierarchy,[49] but Alexander absolutely refused to readmit Arius to communion.[50] Constantine urged him to relent, vouching for Arius' orthodoxy himself, cajoling Alexander and demanding obedience to an emperor's wishes.[51] Alexander remained obdurate. But an imperial letter needed a reply, and Alexander dispatched Athanasius to court.[52] He carried the bishop's answer to Constantine, polite and respectful, but firm in its refusal to obey.

On 17 April 328, however, Alexander died,[53] while Athanasius was absent from Alexandria. Athanasius presumably returned with all speed as soon as he heard the news. Though still a deacon, Athanasius was the obvious candidate to become bishop of Alexandria, and Alexander had left instructions that no one else should succeed him.[54] But the election of so intransigent a character seemed likely to renew quarrels which had only recently been composed, and the bishops of Egypt and the Thebaid desired to avoid a renewal of schism. Some fifty-four bishops, therefore, supporters of both Alexander and Melitius, met to settle their differences and to consider who should be the new bishop.[55] Before they could all agree on a decision, six or seven acted. They went to the Church of Dionysius, barricaded the doors, and consecrated the returning Athanasius as bishop of Alexandria.[56] The date was 8 June 328, six weeks after Alexander had died.[57] A born politician, Athanasius at once wrote to Constantine, announcing that the Alexandrians had unanimously chosen him bishop and quoting a decree of the city to prove his assertion.[58] Constantine replied to the city and gave its choice his full approval.[59] The Melitian bishops, however, proceeded to elect a bishop of their own. The one writer who reveals this precious fact names him as Theonas and states that he died after three months.[60] The Melitians clearly replaced him, since the accidental find of a papyrus shows that a Melitian bishop of Alexandria existed in 334.[61] The later writings of Athanasius are deliberately silent about this schismatic bishop. But the complicated maneuvers to dislodge Athanasius from Alexandria between 328 and 335 become clearer when it is realized that a rival bishop claimed his see. The Melitians must have hoped that in accordance with the decisions recently reached at Nicomedia the deposition of Athanasius would automatically entail his replacement by the Melitian bishop of Alexandria.

Athanasius reacted by strengthening his position in Alexandria and Egypt. As metropolitan bishop of Alexandria, he could influence episcopal elections throughout Egypt and Libya; by 335, he controlled a phalanx of devoted bishops, who constituted a majority within Egypt and a reliable voting block in any wider dispute. In Alexandria itself, he maintained the popular support which he enjoyed from the outset and buttressed his position by organizing an ecclesiastical mafia. In later years, if he so desired, he could instigate a riot or prevent the orderly administration of the city. Athanasius possessed a power independent of the emperor which he built up and perpetuated by violence. That was both the strength and the weakness of his position. Like a modern gangster, he evoked widespread mistrust, proclaimed total innocence—and usually succeeded in evading conviction on specific charges. His opponents in Egypt could see how he operated, they believed with fervor that their cause was righteous, and they were determined to unseat the powerful bishop.

Athanasius confronted a delicate problem in his dealings with bishops outside Egypt. The Council of Nicomedia had readmitted Arius to communion, and both emperor and bishops were committed to securing his return to Alexandria. Eusebius of Nicomedia wrote to the new bishop of Alexandria requesting him to receive Arius and his followers. Athanasius refused, even though the messenger brought secret threats of retaliation against Athanasius if he did so. The grounds for refusal, though chosen for purely tactical reasons, were to have profound theological consequences: Athanasius declined to receive heretics "condemned by the ecumenical council," thus putting the Council of Nicaea on a higher level than any other council. Eusebius then approached Constantine, who wrote to Athanasius threatening exile if he persisted in refusing to receive Arius and his followers. The emperor desired all who wished to enter the Church to be allowed to do so: if he discovered that Athanasius prevented them, he would send someone to depose him and remove him from Alexandria. Athanasius replied by reasserting that Arius was a heretic and that there could be no place in the Catholic church for a heresy which attacked Christ.[62]

This interchange belongs to the beginning of Athanasius' episcopate. It preceded, and probably produced, an alliance between Arians and Melitians which involved Athanasius in a long battle on two fronts, within Egypt and without. A delegation of Melitian bishops went to court with a petition to Constantine, asking that they be permitted to hold meetings without violent disruption. The palace officials, not knowing what Melitians were, did not grant them access to the emperor. As the Melitians waited in the vicinity of Nicomedia and Constantinople, they became acquainted with the bishop Eusebius, whom they knew to have the ear of Constantine, put their case to him, and asked him for assistance. Eusebius promised to present their petition to the emperor, if they would admit Arius to communion with themselves. When they did so, Eusebius brought them before Constantine, explained their request, and obtained his permission for them to meet without hindrance.[63]

The writer who reports this episode implies that the Melitians came to the imperial court before Alexander of Alexandria died. That is impossible; even Athanasius concedes that the Melitians caused no trouble in the winter of 327/8, and Constantine left Nicomedia in the spring of 328, not returning to Asia Minor for fully two years.[64] Eusebius clearly befriended the Melitian bishops in the summer of 330 or later, after the emperor had dedicated his new capital of Constantinople and had taken up residence in the East again. The new alliance soon began to imperil Athanasius. At the instigation of Eusebius, the Melitians brought a criminal charge against the bishop of Alexandria.[65]

Men were found willing to swear that Athanasius had attempted to extort some sort of tax on linen tunics from the Egyptians, and that he had dunned them personally for payment.[66] They went to Constantine and made a formal accusation. Athanasius (it appears) prudently withdrew from Alexandria to the more remote Thebaid, from where he addressed his Easter letter of 331 to his congregation.[67] At court, two priests pleaded his case, doubtless sent there for this very purpose. Despite their advocacy, Constantine summoned Athanasius to his presence. He came, without any haste, in the course of the year 331, was heard by the emperor at Psamathia (a suburb of Nicomedia), and returned to Egypt, reaching Alexandria half way through Lent (about 13 March 332.)[68]

When Athanasius appeared before Constantine, he faced at least four charges. Eusebius of Nicomedia had persuaded Callinicus, Ision, Eudaemon, and Hieracammon to remain at court and reiterate their accusation of extortion. There was a complaint that Athanasius had been elected bishop below the canonical age (presumably thirty), and another that Macarius, one of the two priests who had earlier defended Athanasius, once broke a sacred chalice on Athanasius's orders. It was presumably Eusebius who made the most serious charge of all: Athanasius was alleged to have given a casket of gold to Philumenus for a treasonable purpose.[69]

Constantine patiently investigated the charges and heard both sides. He acquitted Athanasius. The bishop wrote his Easter letter of 332 from the imperial court; it announced his acquittal and was taken to Alexandria by a subordinate of Ablabius, the Christian praetorian prefect.[70] The emperor, too, wrote to the Catholic Christians of Alexandria. He urges them to love one another and put aside all hatreds, and he bitterly denounces the Melitians, though without naming them, for disturbing the peace of God's people. The wicked, however, have not prevailed against the bishop of Alexandria. They have wasted the emperor's time and deserve to be expelled from the Church. Athanasius, in contrast, so Constantine avers from personal conviction, is truly a man of God.[71]

With this impressive testimonial, Athanasius returned to Alexandria in triumph. His enemies were cowed and quiescent. Soon, probably during the course of 332, he visited the Pentapolis.[72] Since Arius was a Libyan, and the only two bishops who refused to subscribe to the creed at Nicaea were Secundus of Ptolemais and Theonas of Marmarica, both from the Pentapolis, the visit presumably had a political purpose.[73] Athanasius may have needed to intervene in Libyan episcopal elections against the Arian party.

By 332, nearly five years had passed since the emperor undertook to restore Arius to Alexandria. Yet Athanasius steadfastly refused to admit him, and he seemed no closer to his goal. Arius became impatient. From Libya he sent a petition to Constantine which complained about his continued exclusion and vented his frustration at the emperor's ineffectuality. He presented Constantine with an ultimatum: either he must be restored to communion, as the Council of Nicomedia had decreed, or he would form his large following into a separate church.[74] Accustomed to servility, not to threats or coercion, Constantine lost his temper.

Probably late in 332 or early in 333, the *agentes in rebus* Syncletius and

Gaudentius arrived in Alexandria with copies of two imperial letters. One was a brief circular letter to bishops and laity everywhere, the other a letter to Arius and the Arians, which the prefect Paterius read publicly in the governor's palace.[75] The circular letter declares that Arians should be called Porphyrians, since Arius has shown himself as much an enemy of Christianity as Porphyry; Arius' writings must be burned, and anyone who secretes a copy shall be liable to summary execution.[76] The other letter is long, rambling, and abusive, the work of a man who feels angry and affronted.

"An evil interpreter is a replica of the Devil." Constantine begins with a stark enunciation of principle and passes rapidly to a denunciation of Arius as the mouthpiece of Satan, spewing forth a message of perdition. Other equally offensive metaphors are employed: Arius, fierce like a serpent lurking in its lair, wrote to the emperor with a pen dipped in venom. Why such ire? Arius (it emerges) included in his letter a statement of his beliefs which offended Constantine profoundly. For Arius affirmed that the Son had "a different substance (*hypostasis*)" from the Father. Constantine reaffirms his strong conviction that the Father and Son had "one essence (*ousia*)" and scolds Arius for sundering the persons of the Divine Trinity. Arius has reasserted a belief anathematized at Nicaea; he is again, therefore, an excommunicate, no matter how many adherents he can claim.

Constantine ridicules Arius' theology at length. Nor does he spare his person, spattering his letter with a long series of insulting sobriquets which it was undignified for an emperor to apply to a subject. He depicts Arius as a dishonest fool, an impious ninny, an empty-headed chatterbox. But God exacts vengeance on the criminal who inflicts wounds and scars on his Church. Look at Arius! His wasting and emaciated flesh, his careworn countenance, his thinning hair, the pallor of his visage, his half-dead appearance—all these attest his vapidity and madness. Constantine, "the man of God," has seen through Arius, who has cast himself into utter darkness.

For Arius' followers, the emperor prescribes a harsh penalty. Every single layman who refuses to rejoin the Catholic church peaceably shall have ten *capita* added to his census assessment, and any clerics who remain in communion with Arius shall become liable to serve as decurions and to perform public liturgies. Arius himself is summoned to court, and the irate letter concludes on an unexpected note: the emperor will interview the heretic and either heal his madness or give thanks to God that he already has a healthy soul.[77] Arius presumably went to Constantine as the emperor commanded, but the result of the interview is not known for certain; Arius is next discovered in 335, traveling to Jerusalem there to be readmitted into communion by the bishops who were trying Athanasius at Tyre.[78]

Not long after this letter, the Melitians renewed their attack on Athanasius. They brought two charges against him: the first was that Athanasius had ordered Marcarius to break the chalice of Ischyras, a priest in the Mareotis whom Colluthus had ordained; the second, that he had arranged the murder of Arsenius, bishop of Hypsele in Upper Egypt.[79] The first charge was not new, and Athanasius knew how to refute it: he produced (or obtained) a written statement from Ischyras, witnessed by thirteen priests, forswearing the accusation. Ischyras swore before God that the Melitians had intimidated him into making a false accusation; no chalice had been broken, no holy altar overturned.[80] The charge of murder looked stronger, for the Melitians could exhibit an arm which they alleged to be the only recoverable remant of Arsenius, retained by Athanasius for magical purposes.[81]

The Melitians made their charges to Constantine in writing. Constantine dismissed the lesser charge, which he had heard before, but wrote to the *censor* Dalmatius, then residing in Antioch, and instructed him to investigate the accusation of murder. Dalmatius wrote to Athanasius and ordered him to prepare to defend himself.[82] When he received Dalmatius' letter, Athanasius withdrew from Alexandria to make himself inaccessible.[83] At the same time, he wrote to all the bishops of Egypt and sent a deacon in search of Arsenius, whom he had not seen for five or six years.[84] Constantine ordered a council of bishops to meet at Caesarea in Palestine.[85] Eusebius of Nicomedia naturally came with his allies, and the *censor* Dalmatius was to be there, occupying a position analogous to that of the emperor at Nicaea.[86] Constantine wrote to Egypt ordering bishops, priests, and others to present themselves at Caesarea. Among those summoned was the priest Aurelius Pageus, the prior of a Melitian monastery at Hipponon in the Heracleopolite nome; he wrote on 18 March 334 to inform another monastery that he appointed his brother as his deputy until his return.[87]

Aurelius Pageus describes the agenda of the council as "a decision about purification of the holy Christian body." Athanasius, like everyone else, knew what lay behind the decorous phrase. He refused to attend the council, facing with equanimity the prospect that the bishops would find him contumacious.[88] For he now knew that he could prove Arsenius still alive. His agents discovered that Arsenius had been hiding in the Thebaid at the monastery of Ptermenkurkis in the Antaeopolite nome. The prior, Pinnes, dispatched him by boat before he could be apprehended, but Athanasius' agents took Pinnes and the monk Elias to Alexandria. There the *dux* of Egypt tortured them separately, and they disclosed the truth. Pinnes then wrote to Johannes Archaph, the Melitian bishop of Memphis, urging him to drop the charge of murder. The letter found its way into Athanasius' possession, perhaps very quickly.[89] Arsenius himself was found at Tyre. Although he stoutly denied his identity at first, Paul, the bishop of Tyre, recognized him and at length induced him to admit that he was Arsenius.[90]

The bishops at Caesarea wrote to the emperor denouncing the absent Athanasius for contumacy and violent behavior.[91] But Athanasius had already sent the trusted Macarius with a letter to Constantine containing the proof of his innocence: he informed Constantine that Arsenius had been found alive and reminded him that he had dismissed the other charge against him two years before. The emperor dissolved the council, thereby annulling whatever verdict it might already have reached, and ordered the bishops to return home.[92] To Athanasius he sent a letter which he requested him to read often in public; it proclaimed his full belief in Athanasius' innocence and denounced the perverse and wicked Melitians for malicious accusation, threatening punishment under the criminal law should they cause further trouble.[93]

Athanasius received letters of congratulation from sympathizers outside Egypt, including the influential Alexander of Thessalonica.[94] He also secured a letter from Arsenius and his clergy at Hypsele, in which Arsenius submitted to the authority of Athanasius, acknowledged Athanasius' rights as metropolitan bishop, and disowned the schismatics who had not yet made their peace with the Catholic church.[95] The Melitians countered with a petition to Constantine, in which Johannes of Memphis affirmed that he belonged to the Church, was reconciled with Athanasius, and desired to see the emperor. In reply, Constantine complimented Johannes for putting aside pettiness and invited him to use the *cursus publicus* to come to court.[96] Thus the complicated events of 333/4 seemed to produce a stalemate: Athanasius had refuted the charges against him, but without totally discrediting his opponents. They soon renewed the attack, this time with success.

Eusebius of Nicomedia persuaded the followers of Melitius, Colluthus, and Arius to cooperate in writing a joint letter to Constantine with several charges against Athanasius.[97] The emperor ordered a council to meet in Tyre to put an end to the long and tiresome dispute.[98] He sent the *comes* Flavius Dionysius, a former governor of Syria, to supervise the conduct of the council, and provided him with a detachment of soldiers for the purpose. Constantine also took steps to ensure that all interested parties attended. Macarius, the henchman of Athanasius, was discovered at court, arrested, and sent to Tyre in chains under military guard. Constantine wrote to Athanasius and ordered him to attend the council.[99] Athanasius hesitated, while friends wrote to him from court, urging him to obey the emperor, and an attempt to rescue Macarius failed. Athanasius embarked and disembarked, greatly reluctant to leave the safety of Egypt.[100]

An invaluable document describes the situation in Alexandria in May 335, while both parties were preparing for the council.[101] It is a letter from the Melitian Callistus to Paieou and Patabeit, priests at the Melitian monastery of Hathor in the eastern desert of the upper Cynopolite nome. On 20 May (Callistus relates) Isaac, the bishop of Letopolis, came to dine with Heraiscus, the Melitian bishop of Alexandria, in the camp. Supporters of Athanasius came with soldiers of the *dux* and of the camp, not entirely sober, in an attempt to seize Heraiscus and his guests, but other soldiers hid the Melitians in their living quarters. The supporters of Athanasius, however, found four other Melitian monks, whom they beat, bloodied, almost killed, and threw out of the camp. Then they went to the hospice where the Melitians were staying, found another five, kidnaped them, and held them in the camp until the *praepositus* ordered their release. Finally, they turned their violence on the only two men in Alexandria who had been willing to give lodging to Melitian monks from outside the city, and warned them not to do so again. The *praepositus* apologized to Heraiscus for the attack, but the Melitians were not allowed to see their bishop, who was confined to the camp. Athanasius sent bishops who would support him to Tyre, but detained his opponents: he shut one bishop in the meat market, a priest in the prison of the camp, and a deacon in the main prison of the city. All this happened in May 335: it was 11 July before Athanasius himself sailed from Alexandria to Phoenicia.[102]

When the bishops had assembled at Tyre, the council opened with the reading of an imperial letter. Constantine reminded the holy council that its task was to restore peace, unity, and concord to the Church. The assembled bishops should complete their business with dispatch, since the emperor had provided everything which they requested: he had invited the bishops whom they wished to attend (that is, the Melitians), and he had sent Dionysius to ensure the attendance of those who ought to come (that is, Athanasius) and to supervise the conduct of the council. Condign punishment awaited any who disobeyed the imperial command to attend. It merely remained, therefore, for the bishops to act without fear or favor, in accordance with ecclesiastical practice, in order to heal the divisions of the Church. They could thus lighten the emperor's cares and bring glory on themselves.[103]

The issues could not be resolved so easily. His enemies accused Athanasius of a variety of crimes. Callinicus, the Melitian bishop of Pelusium, and Ischyras reiterated the charge that Athanasius had ordered the breaking of a chalice and the destruction of a bishop's throne, to which they added several counts of assault. Athanasius (they maintained) had often imprisoned Ischyras and once persuaded the prefect Hyginus to imprison him by falsely accusing him of stoning pictures of the emperor. Athanasius had deposed Callinicus, a bishop of the Catholic church with whom Alexander had been in communion, because Callinicus refused to communicate with Athanasius unless he cleared himself of the suspicion of breaking the chalice, and he had entrusted the church of Pelusium to the unfrocked priest Marcus, arranging for Callinicus to be arrested by soldiers, tortured, and tried. Five Melitian bishops (Euplus, Pachomius, Isaac, Achilleus, and Hermaeon) complained of violence against their persons. The complainants also justified their own past conduct. Athanasius had obtained his election by trickery, and instead of attempting to persuade those who believed his election invalid, he had assaulted and imprisoned them.[104]

As for Arsenius, the Melitians read out before the council a record of popular acclamations in Alexandria which implicitly denounced Athanasius for the murder.[105] Their suspicions (they argued) were justifiable, even if mistaken: Plusianus, a bishop of Athanasius' party, and acting on his orders, burned Arsenius' house and kept Arsenius himself, beaten and bound, in a hut. When he escaped secretly and went into hiding, it was reasonable to conclude that he had been killed; since Arsenius was a prominent man and a confessor, the Melitians had then approached the authorities.[106]

Athanasius and his Egyptian supporters contested the charges. Macarius denied breaking a chalice, and Arsenius accused the Melitians of acting in bad faith. It was proposed, therefore, to send a commission of inquiry to the Mareotis to discover the true facts. Although Athanasius objected, the *comes* Dionysius agreed. But who should go to Egypt? The composition of the commission would surely determine its findings, and dispute accordingly ensued. Athanasius produced a list of bishops whom he claimed were known Arians, and, therefore, prejudiced: they should be disqualified from membership on the commission. The council chose Theognis of Nicaea, Maris of Chalcedon, Theodorus of Heraclea, Macedonius of Mopsuestia, Ursacius of Singidunum, and Valens of Mursa, and the commission departed for Egypt with Ischyras and an escort of soldiers.[107]

Athanasius prepared to contest the inevitable verdict. He protested to Dionysius that he was being "wronged and framed," since his enemies had chosen precisely the commissioners whose names he rejected.[108] His allies added their complaints. The Egyptian bishops at Tyre, forty-eight in number, composed two almost identical letters, which they sent to the other bishops at the council and to the *comes* Dionysius. They denounced Eusebius of Nicomedia and his associates as acting out of sheer enmity towards Athanasius, and they complained of unfairness in the conduct of the council: it was wrong to send a commission of inquiry to Egypt, especially one whose members were chosen against their wishes.[109] Failing to obtain satisfaction from Dionysius or the other bishops, they then submitted to the *comes* a formal appeal to the emperor, on the grounds that he, unlike Eusebius and his associates, would render a just decision.[110] And they wrote to bishops who were not, or not yet, in Tyre explaining their appeal.[111] When he received the news, Alexander of Thessalonica wrote to Dionysius, arguing, like the Egyptian bishops, that Dionysius should do something to prevent the unholy alliance of Colluthians, Arians, and Melitians from producing an unjust decision.[112] Dionysius lacked the authority to countermand the decision of a Church council. But he wrote a letter of warning to the bishops of the majority. He reminded them that before the commission was established he had advised them to choose its members by unanimous vote. They had disregarded his advice, and Athanasius and Alexander were now complaining. He invited the bishops of the majority, therefore, to consider whether their actions could be open to challenge as biased.[113]

Protests were made in Egypt too. The commission was aided and accompanied by the prefect Philagrius, allegedly an apostate, but it refused to allow the Alexandrian clergy to represent the interests of Athanasius and Macarius.[114] Accordingly, sixteen priests and five deacons of the Alexandrian church composed a protest in the form of a petition; they addressed one copy to the commission and a second to Palladius, a high-ranking *agens in rebus,* presumably for transmission to the prefect or even to the emperor. They declared that the absence of the two accused infringed biblical precept: since the commission rejected the Alexandrians' attempt to ensure fair play, its bias and plotting were obvious.[115] When the commission arrived in the Mareotis, fifteen priests and fifteen deacons submitted a declaration to the prefect, to Palladius, and to Flavius Antoninus, a *biarchus* of the praetorian prefects, in which they swore before God, the emperor, and his sons that Ischyras was not a priest of the Catholic church, that he had no church, that no chalice was broken—in brief, that all the charges were invented.[116] The declaration did not stop the prefect and the commissioners. They declined to listen to the clergy of the Mareotis and found more compliant witnesses who, perhaps with the aid or threat of torture, confirmed at least some of the allegations.[117] The priests and deacons of the Mareotis, therefore, wrote to the Council of Tyre, setting out their view of the facts and affirming that the commission obtained its evidence from the relatives of Ischyras, from Arians, and from other witnesses under duress.[118]

The commission probably arrived in Egypt during August, for the clergy of the Mareotis loyal to Athanasius swore their declaration on 8 September.[119] At Tyre the council, which may have been considering other business, adjourned. A letter arrived from Constantine, inviting the bishops at Tyre to go with all haste to Jerusalem. There they celebrated the dedication of the Church of the Holy Sepulcher. Constantine himself was absent, but he sent the *notarius* Marianus, who had once been a confessor, to supervise the lavish ceremonies in appropriate style. The bishops, constituted as a council, consecrated the church while Marianus supervised the administration of Constantine's generosity: he dedicated rich fittings and ornaments of gold, silver, and precious stones in the church, entertained the bishops at sumptuous banquets, and distributed gifts of food and clothing to large numbers of needy men and women. The celebrations lasted for a full week (13–20 September), and many bishops delivered speeches or sermons in praise of the new church and its founder, among them Eusebius of Caesarea, whose oration survives.[120]

The Council of Jerusalem did more than dedicate a church. Before the ceremonies began, it had performed an act both symbolic and politically important. Arius and Euzoius had petitioned Constantine to be readmitted to the Church. The emperor examined and approved the statement of belief which they submitted, and he interviewed the two priests. But, scrupulous as ever to leave theological issues to theologians, he submitted the final decision to a council of bishops. He sent Arius to Jerusalem, requesting the council to readmit him and his associates into communion provided that their present beliefs were orthodox and that they disputed no past decisions against them. The council circulated Constantine's letter and its appended creed. It then readmitted Arius. The decision was communicated to the emperor and was announced in a synodical letter addressed to the church of Alexandria and to bishops, priests, and deacons in Egypt and elsewhere. The council averred that they all found Arius' statement doctrinally sound, in accordance with the teachings of the apostles and the Church; hence Arius and his followers should be welcomed into the Church to restore unity and peace.[121]

The bishops then returned to Tyre and completed their business in the absence of Athanasius, who had secretly fled. The commission of inquiry returned from Egypt and presented a list of specific acts of wrongdoing. They did not present the full minutes of their examination of witnesses, in which Athanasius and his supporters later claimed to find inconsistencies. They produced, as was normal, a summary of their findings, in which they complained that Athanasius had removed potential witnesses, but that they had discovered enough to sustain at least the charge that Macarius broke the chalice of Ischyras on Athanasius' orders. The council accepted the report and acted accordingly. The bishops found Athanasius guilty, deposed him from his see, and forbade him to reside in Alexandria. They received Johannes Archaph and his followers into communion, conferring the appropriate clerical rank on each, and probably appointed as bishop of Alexandria the Arian Pistus, who owed his ordination as priest to Secundus of Ptolemais.[122] They wrote to Constantine and sent a circular letter to bishops everywhere, warning them not to communicate with Athanasius. The statement of Athanasius' deposition comprised four counts: first, his flight and inability to answer the charges betrayed his guilt; second, his refusal to present himself at Caesarea in 334 showed contempt both for Church councils and for the emperor; third, he came to Tyre with a gang of followers who disrupted the synod while he obstructed the inquiry and heaped abuse on other bishops; fourth, a commission had found the charge of breaking a chalice abundantly proved.[123]

Athanasius fled from Tyre in an open boat and under cover of darkness, evading the soldiers who doubtless patrolled the harbor.[124] His enemies could easily guess his destination. They must, therefore, have hurried through the final formalities of the council. They could not risk entrusting their letter to Constantine to an ordinary messenger. Six of their number took it to Constantinople in person—Eusebius of Nicomedia, Theognis, Patrophilus, Eusebius of Caesarea, Ursacius, and Valens.[125]

Athanasius arrived in the capital on 30 October 335.[126] Constantine was absent, having left the city on 21 or 22 October and visited Nicopolis.[127] On 6 November, however, he returned.[128] Athanasius accosted the emperor as he entered Constantinople on horseback. He was disheveled and dressed in mourning, unrecognizable at first. When Constantine discovered who he was, he took pity on him and recalled how he had tried and acquitted him once before. Athanasius asseverated that his enemies were again attempting to disgrace him on false charges and begged the emperor to grant him one small request: let him face his adversaries before the emperor. Constantine, greatly affected by the pitiable mien of Athanasius, granted his request. He summoned all the bishops who had reassembled at Tyre to come to court with all haste, so that the case of Athanasius could be decided fairly and impartially in his presence. He did not yet know (he wrote) what the council had decreed, but he suspected that disorder and personal animosities had obscured the truth. The bishops needed to convince him that they had decided without fear or favor.[129] By implication, therefore, Constantine annulled the decisions already made by the council.[130]

Eusebius of Nicomedia and the other five bishops arrived from Tyre only a few hours after Constantine dictated and dispatched the letter. They saw at once that there was no point in presenting the synodical letter to the emperor. Moreover, when they secured an audience with Constantine, five Egyptian bishops who had supported Athanasius at Tyre were also admitted to the imperial presence. Swift and decisive action was needed to forestall disaster to their cause. The Eusebians therefore accused Athanasius of treason, asserting that he had threatened to prevent the grain ships from sailing from Alexandria to Constantinople.[131] The emperor ordered Athanasius to answer the new charge. The interview was bitter and reproachful. Athanasius lost his temper and warned Constantine that God would judge between emperor and bishop.[132] Enraged, Constantine sent Athanasius to Trier: he did not condemn, or even try him, but removed him until the truth of the various charges could finally be determined.[133] Athanasius left Constantinople on 7 November 335, still technically bishop of Alexandria but effectively debarred from exercising the power which he had wielded with such vigor and enjoyment.[134]

The departure of Athanasius did not bring peace to the Egyptian church. The populace of Alexandria, not once but repeatedly, rioted and demanded the bishop's return. The monk Antony added his prestige to the cause of the exile. Though a Copt who spoke Coptic, he sent letters to Constantine (presumably translated into Greek by his disciples) in which he maintained that Athanasius was innocent of the Melitian charges. Constantine rebuked the Alexandrians for their folly and disorderly behavior, and he refused to change his mind or recall Athanasius, a troublemaker condemned by an ecclesiastical tribunal. He wrote in equally firm terms to Antony: even if some of the bishops at Tyre were motivated by hatred, Athanasius had caused dissension and strife within the Church, and a large number of distinguished bishops had condemned him unanimously. On the other hand, when the Melitian clergy, in accordance with the decision at Tyre, attempted to occupy the places to which they considered themselves entitled, Constantine checked them sharply. Declaring that he would allow none to cause strife or dissension among Christians, he exiled Johannes Archaph—and perhaps others.[135]

The decisions of the Councils of Jerusalem and Tyre were not completely unanimous. There was one prominent dissenter: Marcellus, bishop of Ancyra for more than twenty years.[136] Although a strong opponent of Arius and his ideas, Marcellus had prudently refrained from committing his own theological views to writing and concentrated instead on establishing orthodoxy within his own province of Galatia.[137] In 335, however, he attended the Councils of Jerusalem and Tyre—an error of judgment which rapidly led to his downfall and exile.

In Jerusalem, Marcellus refused to communicate with Arius on the grounds that he was still a heretic. The council accordingly declared that he should forfeit his see unless he assented to its decisions and communicated with Arius within a certain time. Marcellus remained obdurate. Moreover, when the bishops reassembled at Tyre, Marcellus objected to their condemnation of Athanasius. It is not certain whether he was formally deposed or not, but the Council of Tyre complained about his conduct to the emperor.[138] Marcellus thereupon dispatched to Constantine a hastily written tract of some ten thousand lines, which flattered the emperor in the highest terms and argued that the Arian leaders were all heretical.[139] In the surviving fragments (all known only from Eusebius of Caesarea), Marcellus accuses Arius' principal supporters of polytheism. He establishes, by quotation and from his memory of conversations with them, that Paulinus of Tyre (now dead), Narcissus of Neronias, and Eusebius all believed in a multiplicity of gods: they asserted that the Father and the Son were two essences (*ousiai*) or substances (*hypostaseis*), and they used phrases like "first and second God" and "younger Gods."[140]

Marcellus appears to have mounted a particularly ferocious attack on Asterius, a sophist from Cappadocia who had become a Christian before 303 but who had sacrificed during the persecution and was hence debarred from ordination as a priest.[141] Asterius was an excellent orator and preacher (some thirty homilies and parts of a commentary on the Psalms survive);[142] he toured the East on behalf of the Arian cause, and he had once published a pamphlet arguing that there could not be two uncreated beings.[143] Arius (it is reported) used Asterius' pamphlet,[144] and Marcellus repeatedly and at length attacked its assertion that Father and Son had different substances (*hypostaseis*).[145] Marcellus claimed to diagnose the cause of his adversaries' heretical beliefs. Eusebius held opinions like those of Valentinus and Hermes Trismegistus; Narcissus, opinions like those of Marcion and Plato.[146] Eusebius, Narcissus, Paulinus, and Asterius were all followers of Origen, who corrupted Christian theology with alien importations from Greek philosophy.[147]

In one respect at least, Eusebius' quotations must be deliberately misleading. The fragments of Marcellus' tract which he reproduces contain no mention of Arius—who was surely Marcellus' main target. In the course of his attack, however, the bishop of Ancyra revealed his own theological position; it was an old-fashioned dynamic modalism, which his enemies at once classified as a reassertion of the views of Sabellius and Paul of Samosata.[148] For Marcellus so stressed the identity of the Father, Son, and Spirit in an indivisible monad, that he held them to be not merely one essence or substance, but a single person (*prosopon*) which expands into three by activity alone.[149] Constantine declined to arbitrate a theological dispute. He summoned a council of bishops which met in Constantinople in the summer of 336, with the emperor again present.[150] Marcellus' tract was examined and deemed heretical. The council deposed

Marcellus, who was exiled, and elected Basil to be bishop of Ancyra.[151] It also witnessed a sudden and unexpected end to Arius' attempts to return to Alexandria.

Arius had gone from Jerusalem to Alexandria, where the church, loyal to Athanasius, refused to admit him. He left Egypt again, therefore, and came to the emperor in Constantinople.[152] Eusebius of Nicomedia and his allies decided to force the issue of Arius' orthodoxy at the council which met in the summer of 336: they would compel Alexander of Constantinople to receive him into communion. Constantine again examined Arius and questioned him about the sincerity with which he subscribed to the views he professed. When Arius swore an oath, the emperor again pronounced him orthodox. The Arian bishops then requested Alexander to communicate with Arius. When Alexander refused to be reconciled to "the inventor of heresy," they declared that they would escort him to Alexander's church to take part in a Sunday service. Distraught, Alexander flung himself on the floor of his sacristy, wept, and prayed. Macarius, the trusted henchman of Athanasius, joined him. Their prayers were answered. Before he could reach the church, Arius collapsed and died. His enemies inevitably detected the hand of God, and it was claimed that Constantine deduced that Arius must have lied to him about his true beliefs.[153] Instead of the triumphant reinstatement which Arius and his supporters confidently expected, sudden, irreparable, and everlasting infamy became his lot.

Official pronouncements by any autocrat deserve to be treated with a certain skepticism. But Constantine's letters to bishops, priests, and churches fall into so consistent a pattern of respect tempered with frustration that it is difficult to regard them as mere products of tact, diplomacy, or policy.[154] The emperor's personal attitudes and convictions constantly obtrude, and he speaks as one conversant with philosophy and theology who nevertheless believes the conversion of the Roman Empire to worship of the Christian God far more important than a precise (and potentially exclusive) definition of the intellectual content of Christianity. Nowhere are the underlying principles of his ecclesiastical policy more explicit than in the opening paragraphs of the letter which announced the deposition of Eusebius of Nicomedia in 325:[155]

> Constantine Augustus to the Catholic Church of Nicomedia—
> You all, beloved brothers, obviously know very well that the Lord God and Christ the Savior are Father and Son—Father without beginning and without end, parent of the world itself, and Son, that is, the will of the Father, which has not been comprehended by any human conception nor received through any extraneous essence for the completion of his works.[156] He who understands this and keeps it in his mind will have indefatigable endurance of every sort of affliction. But Christ, the Son of God, the creator of all and

supplier of immortality itself, was begotten—or rather, he who also is ever in the Father came forth for the ordering of what he had created—Christ was begotten by an indivisible coming forth, for will is both permanently fixed in its dwelling place and acts on and arranges the things which need different attention according to the nature of each one. What then is there between God the Father and God the Son? Obviously nothing. For this completed creation has received by perception the command of the will but has not divided or separated the will from the essence of the Father. The next point is: who is there who rejects the suffering of Christ my Lord from shame rather than from foolishness?[157] When the dwelling of the holy body seeks to perceive its own holiness, does the divine suffer or does what is separated from the body fall under its touch? Is not what is removed from the lowness of the body physically distinct? Do we not live, though the glory of the soul summons the body to death? What then has untroubled and sincere faith received which deserves dispute? Or do you not see that God has chosen a most venerable body, by which he intended to manifest the proofs of the faith and examples of his own virtue, to remove the destruction in which fatal error had already enveloped the human race, to give new instructions for worship, to cleanse the unworthy deeds of the mind by an example of purity, and then to remove the torment of death and proclaim the rewards of immortality?

You, however, whom the fellowship of love rightly makes me now call brothers, are acquainted with me, your fellow servant, and acquainted with the stronghold of your salvation, whose care I have sincerely undertaken and by which I not only defeated the arms of our enemies but also imprisoned them, still living, to display the true faith of clemency. At these successes I rejoiced most for the renewal of the world. For it was truly worthy of wonder to bring into concord so many nations who were recently said not to know God. Yet what were these nations with no part in the conflict likely to perceive? What, beloved brothers, do you think is my complaint against you? We are Christians, and we quarrel in a pitiful state of mind. Is this our faith, this the teaching of our law? What is the cause by which the disaster of the present evil has been aroused? What perversity! What hatred, which far exceeds the measure of righteous indignation! What dreadful brigandage has been revealed, which denies that the Son of God has come forth from the indivisible essence of the Father? Is God not everywhere, and do we not perceive his presence ever with us? Does not the harmony of the universe exist through his power, without the deprivation of separation?

Constantine failed to bring unity to the eastern Church, whose divisions were deep (and partly along geographical lines). He gave the decisions of councils of bishops the force of law and ordered provincial governors to observe them.[158] But bishops disagreed violently among themselves, and the Egyptian church steadfastly (and with something close to unanimity) repudiated the theology which prevailed in most of the other eastern provinces of the Roman Empire. Constantine might have been able to impose genuine unity if he had been willing to use force to compel acceptance of his own views. He did not try. Instead, he recommended, exhorted, cajoled, and threatened—ultimately, in vain. Perhaps he judged the Church too powerful to be coerced. Whatever the cause, the effect is clear: when Constantine died in 337, the eastern Church was even more bitterly divided than when he rescued it from persecution.

XIV

THE NEW MONARCHY

A revolution or a reformation achieves permanence when the vested interests of its beneficiaries safely outweigh the losses and resentment of the dispossessed. The establishment of Christianity as the official religion had a different meaning and a different effect in the two halves of the Roman Empire. The war of 324 had little impact in the West, where Constantine came to power in 306 as an advocate of religious toleration.[1] Constantine became ruler of the West before his conversion to Christianity; inevitably, therefore, in the West, he conformed to patterns of behavior inherited from his pagan predecessors. In 307, on his promotion from Caesar to Augustus, Constantine automatically assumed the title of *pontifex maximus,* which he never relinquished until he symbolically resigned the imperial power on his deathbed.[2] Nor did Constantine's immediate successors discard the title, although they too were Christians.[3] Moreover, public subsidies for the ancient cults of Rome continued under Constantine and long after his death. When his son Constantius visited Rome in 357, he removed the altar of the goddess Victory from the Senate-house, where it had stood since the days of Augustus.[4] Yet even Constantius continued public support for pagan ceremonies and, by virtue of his office as *pontifex maximus,* appointed new members to the Roman priestly colleges.[5]

Pagan temples in the western provinces retained their treasures and endowments, and their votaries probably still openly celebrated traditional rites and sacrifices. An imperial letter of 341 reiterated the prohibition of sacrifice which Eusebius attests for the East in 324/5.[6] Since the letter was addressed to Crepereius Madalianus, the *vicarius* of Italy, it must be suspected that, even if the law of 324/5 was promulgated throughout the Roman Empire, Constantine had made no serious attempt to enforce it in the West. Later still (probably in 343), Firmicus Maternus addressed a pamphlet *On the Error of Profane Religions* to the emperors Constantius and Constans.[7] The invocation of both brothers, recommended by etiquette, is misleading, for Maternus clearly intended his principal requests for the ears of Constans alone. With impassioned polemic, especially against the *taurobolium* and *criobolium* fashionable among the nobility, he entreats the emperors to stamp out pagan practices, which still persist, to seize the ornaments which adorn pagan temples, to melt down cult statues, to confiscate dedications in gold and silver, and to use the proceeds to mint money for the government to spend.[8]

Western Christians lacked the supreme self-confidence, the assured sense of superiority to traditional culture which the writings of a Eusebius or an Athanasius constantly exude. The Spaniard C. Vettius Aquilinus Juvencus was, to judge from his name, related to the Vettius Aquilinus who held the ordinary consulate in 286.[9] Juvencus renounced a political career to become a priest, and shortly after 324 he turned the Gospels into Latin hexameters.[10] The versification is smooth and accomplished; Juvencus echoes Virgil, frequently alludes to Ovid, Lucan, and Statius, and often writes with warm and elegant feeling. But the most significant feature of his poem is the bare fact of its composition; the Greek analog occurred only in the reign of Julian, when the grammarian Apollinaris turned the Octateuch into a Homeric poem in twenty-four books and much of the rest of the Old Testament into dramatic or lyric poetry while his son, Apollinaris of Laodicea, rewrote the Gospels and Epistles as Platonic dialogues.[11] Significantly too, Juvencus speaks of Constantine in tones no different from an anonymous Latin poem composed at Autun shortly before the war of 324. The Gallic poet praises Constantine as a Christian emperor, and prays for his victory.[12] Yet, even more than Juvencus, he seems to assume that Christianity must still prove itself against its rivals.[13]

In the East, Constantine had already taken the action which Firmicus Maternus later urged on Constans. The persecution which began in 303 was far more severe and lasted longer in Asia Minor, the Syrian region, and Egypt than elsewhere—and it ended with the overthrow of the emperor Maximinus and a thorough purge of his most prominent pagan supporters.[14] Similarly, in 324, the renewed persecution ended with the defeat of Licinius and a purge of his supporters. The victorious Constantine, therefore, could forbid pagan sacrifice knowing that his Christian subjects would enforce the law wherever possible.[15] Moreover, eastern pagans soon discovered that their new master would not allow them to retain all their shrines or any of their temple treasures.

Not long after 324, Constantine sent specially chosen *comites* to each eastern province. They visited every city and village, and they scoured the countryside. They sought out the temples and shrines of the traditional gods and examined their priests and priestesses. The imperial commissioners compelled them to produce for inspection all dedications, cult objects, and statues which lay inside the hallowed walls. They then confiscated whatever gold, silver, or precious stones they found. They removed everything of value: gold plate from gilded statues, roofs and doors of bronze, public statues of gods, goddesses, and heroes. Much was melted down into ingots for ease of transport, and when the *comites* departed from a place, they left its traditional gods only what they deemed worthless.[16] The proceeds of this systematic confiscation were enormous; four decades later a writer claimed that as a result gold coins, instead of bronze, came into use for the most trivial commercial transactions.[17]

The commissioners, if Eusebius may be believed, did not need to employ force as they despoiled the temples of wealth that had accumulated over many centuries. Constantine, however, was prepared to use armed force to suppress certain cults which he and many of his subjects regarded as particularly offensive. At Aphaca in Phoenicia, high and remote in the mountains of Lebanon, was a shrine of Aphrodite where homosexuality and all kinds of sexual license had long been practiced. Constantine acted swiftly and decisively. He sent a detachment of soldiers, who destroyed the temple utterly and compelled the lascivious devotees of Aphrodite to adopt more modest ways.[18] In like fashion, the Christian emperor prohibited ritual prostitution at Heliopolis in Phoenicia, and razed the temple of Asclepius at Aegaeae in Cilicia, famous for its cures by incubation and for its association with Apollonius of Tyana.[19] Nor were these three the only shrines which Constantine destroyed for moral or political reasons; he ordered soldiers to explore and profane all secret shrines and caves everywhere, revealing to all the nature of the superstition there practiced.[20]

Constantine's religious policy was coherent and comprehensive. He did not merely suppress paganism and establish Christianity as the official religion of the state; he set out to ensure that Christianity replaced the cults which it ousted. Constantinople was adorned by cult objects displayed in a context which deprived them of their original religious significance. Statues of Apollo and the Muses beautified public squares and the imperial palace, and the hippodrome was graced both by the tripod from Delphi, dedicated by the Greeks who defeated Xerxes, and by a statue of Theophanes, the client and historian of Pompey, whom the city of Mytilene had honored as a hero.[21] When Constantine ordered the inhabitants of Heliopolis to desist from ritual prostitution, he also urged them to adopt chastity and belief in God. More important, he began to build the first church in the city, and he provided, through the new bishop and his clergy, funds to support the poor—and to encourage them to become Christians.[22] Such a redirection of religious sentiment, combined with material inducements to conversion, can be documented elsewhere and should be presumed typical.[23] In Egypt, Constantine forbade castrated priests to perform the normal rites which were believed to ensure the annual flooding of the Nile, or even to appear in public at all.[24] He also ordered that the sacred cubits which measured the heights of the Nile's flood be dedicated each year not in the Serapeum to Serapis, as before, but in the church of Alexandria to God, the giver of every good gift.[25] Moreover, he gave the bishops of Egypt and Libya a supply of grain for the support of widows and the poor which they were to distribute under the supervision of the bishop of Alexandria.[26]

Imperial officials everywhere had standing instructions to disburse public funds, now abundant from the confiscation of temple treasures, to support Christian charitable activities and to construct churches.[27] Constantine had already encouraged bishops to build churches, and they rapidly transformed the appearance of many eastern cities. Constantine selected certain cities for especially grand foundations. He built a great church in Nicomedia to commemorate the martyrs of that city (many of whom he must have known), and a spectacular octagonal church at Antioch, gleaming with bronze and gold.[28] But the Holy Land benefited most from imperial generosity. The emperor's mother founded the Church of the Nativity at Bethlehem, and a church on the Mount of Olives to commemorate Christ's Ascension into heaven.[29] Another imperial pilgrim was Constantine's mother-in-law Eutropia. She informed Constantine of the pagan ceremonies at the Oak of Mamre, where God once appeared to Abraham (Genesis 18:1–33). The emperor wrote to the *comes* Acacius, instructing him to destroy the altar, burn the idols, and purify the place; Acacius was then, after consulting the bishops of Palestine, to whom Constantine also wrote, to build a basilica worthy of the catholic and apostolic Church.[30] A pilgrim who visited the site in 333 reports that the basilica was "of wonderful beauty."[31]

Constantine reserved to himself the credit for the most splendid of his constructions in Palestine, which covered both the site of the Crucifixion and what was believed to be Christ's tomb.[32] The pilgrim of 333 reports a basilica, again "of wonderful beauty," with reservoirs of water along the side and a baptistery behind.[33] A shrine of Aphrodite occupied the site until Constantine ordered its demolition. Excavations were made under the ruins until a tomb was discovered, which appears to have contained not a body, but some wood, which its finders identified as the cross on which Christ was crucified. Constantine, and Christians in general, hailed the discovery as manifest proof of Christ's death, burial, and resurrection. The emperor commissioned the construction of a lavishly appointed church and wrote to Macarius, the bishop of Jerusalem, asking him to supervise what should be a complex of buildings to outshine the architectural màrvels of any other city on earth.[34] Eusebius called the resulting edifice a "new Jerusalem" and described its interior as shimmering with gold and jewels.[35] The Church of the Holy Sepulcher was formally dedicated by a council of bishops in September 335 as part of the celebrations which marked Constantine's thirtieth year as a Roman emperor.[36]

Eusebius had long been accustomed to treat contemporary events as the fulfillment of Old Testament prophecy.[37] His overall interpretation of human history, formed when he was a subject of Diocletian, needed only slight modification when a Christian emperor ruled the east. The *Commentary on the Psalms* interprets the text "Dost thou work wonders for the dead?" (Psalm 87 [88]:11) as foretelling the wonders accomplished after 324 around the tomb of the Savior, and it claims the cessation of pagan sacrifices as the fulfillment of two separate predictions, one in the Psalms (17:9), the other by the apostle Paul (2 Corinthians 11:14).[38] The *Commentary on Isaiah* more consistently and more thoroughly endows Isaiah with foreknowledge of the Christian Roman Empire. Isaiah repeatedly prophesied the utter downfall of the persecutors.[39] He foretold that the worship of demons would cease in Areopolis and other cities of Arabia, that there would be churches in Petra, though it is inhabited by obstinate pagans, and that churches would be built in the countryside around Petra and among the Saraceni of the desert.[40] Isaiah further prophesied the appointment of Christians as provincial governors and generals—and it is in fulfillment of his prophecy that a Christian occupies the Roman imperial throne, showers gifts and dedications on God's Church, and grants it a supply of food to use for humanitarian purposes.[41]

Eusebius states his view of the living Constantine's place in history most fully in the speech which he delivered at the dedication of the Church of the Holy Sepulcher.[42] The greater part of the speech repeats, often almost unchanged, long sections from his *Theophany*, composed nearly a decade earlier.[43] But the concluding chapters of the speech attempt to relate the apologetic generalities repeated from the *Theophany* to the specific occasion which Eusebius is celebrating. The pagan emperors went to war against God and destroyed his churches. But God, with a single stroke, cast the persecutors down at the height of their felicity and filled the world with houses of prayer to celebrate Constantine's victory.

Eusebius presents the reign of Constantine as the culmination of human history. He evokes the Hebrew prophets, the ruin of the Jews, the humble fishermen who converted the world despite persecution, Galerius' confession of failure, the countless monks, dedicated virgins, and other ascetics of his own day, the unification of the Roman Empire under a single monarch, and the Christianity of the northern barbarians. In all things, God displays the hidden power of his mighty right hand. Constantine has legislated the gods and heroes of pagan antiquity out of existence and made the whole world worship the true God together, receiving divine instruction every Sunday. Constantine has seen the Savior often, both while awake and in dreams, and the emperor directs his policies by the revelations God vouchsafes him—God, his champion and guardian, who protects him in battle and from secret plots, who sustains him in perplexity, who guides his administration of state and armies, who inspires him to issue laws and spend money for the good of all. The Church of the Holy Sepulcher is Constantine's homage to God. He has built it to commemorate the Savior's victory over death, to proclaim to all nations in loud and unmistakable tones his belief in the heavenly and triumphant Word of God.[44]

Constantine regarded the city which bore his name as both his capital and his permanent residence, spending long periods there after its dedication.[45] Nevertheless, he did not entirely renounce the peripatetic existence of earlier years. He had rebuilt Trajan's bridge across the Danube, thereby revealing his design of reconquering lost territory beyond the river.[46] Three campaigns (in 332, 334, and 336) enabled him to proclaim that objective fulfilled.

Dissension among the barbarians offered opportunities which Constantine eagerly seized. The Sarmatians requested Roman aid against the Goths, who (it appears) had been in receipt of an annual subsidy from Rome for several years. Constantine took the field in the late winter of 332. After cold and starvation killed almost one hundred thousand of their number, the Goths submitted to Roman suzerainty and surrendered hostages, including the son of their king, Ariaricus.[47] Two years later, in 334, Constantine again waged a campaign across the Danube, this time against the Sarmatians, whom social conflicts had enfeebled. The ruling tribes (presumably in 331) had armed their subjects to aid in defense against the Goths. After the defeat of the Goths, these "slaves" turned their weapons against their "masters" and expelled them. The exiles appealed to Constantine, who welcomed them into the Roman Empire, enrolling some as tribal regiments in the Roman army and settling the rest as farmers in the Balkans and Italy. One writer puts the number of refugees in excess of three hundred thousand, including women and children.[48] Although details of the fighting are regrettably lost, it appears that Constantine both won a Sarmatian victory and extended Roman hegemony.[49] Nor was that the end of warfare. Traces of camps and fortifications indirectly attest aggressive Roman expansion,[50] and a chance allusion discloses that Constantine made extensive, if ephemeral, conquests north of the Danube.[51] In 336 Constantine took the title of Dacicus maximus: that implies at least a partial reconquest of the Dacia which Trajan had added to the Roman Empire two centuries before.[52]

For the political history of Constantine's last years any sort of ancient narrative is totally lacking. Nevertheless, the bare record of appointments and distinctions conferred on imperial relatives attests a battle for power and influence behind the bland façade of imperial unanimity. When Constantine executed Crispus in 326, he was a man of fifty-three or fifty-four whose eldest remaining son had not yet reached his tenth birthday. There was, therefore, an interval before the young Caesars could be entrusted with political power, and Constantine appears to have employed praetorian prefects to supervise the government of different regions of the empire—Bassus, the prefect of Crispus, in Gaul, Aemilianus and later L. Papius Pacatianus in Italy, Evagrius at Nicomedia, and Flavius Constantius at Antioch, whose name suggests kinship with the emperor.[53] But Constantine intended these quasi-regional prefectures as merely a temporary measure. As soon as it seemed practicable, he installed his sons in regional centers with praetorian prefects, armies, and civil and military administrations of their own. Constantinus began to reside at Trier in 328/9, and Constantius may have been established in a Danubian city not long after.[54] By the end of the reign, however, Constantine's sons were not the only heirs apparent. Other imperial relatives had broken their monopoly.

The emperor Constantius had divorced Constantine's mother to marry Maximian's daughter, Theodora, who bore him three sons and three daughters who survived infancy and childhood. Constantine found his half sisters a political asset, his half brothers at first an embarrassment. Constantia married Licinius in 313 and lived on at the court of Constantine after her husband was deposed and then executed; it was later alleged that her dying wishes induced her brother to recall Arius from exile.[55] Anastasia married into the Roman aristocracy; her husband was Bassianus, whom Constantine in 315/6 proposed to appoint Caesar, but abruptly discarded and disgraced.[56] Eutropia too married into the Roman aristocracy. Since she was the mother of Julius Nepotianus, who was proclaimed emperor briefly at Rome in 350, Eutropia presumably married Virius Nepotianus—only a name on the *fasti* as ordinary consul in 336, yet clearly a man of importance and influence in the western provinces.[57]

Of the three sons of Constantius and Theodora, Hannibalianus appears to have died young.[58] Flavius Dalmatius and Julius Constantius spent some years in provincial towns as virtual exiles. Dalmatius lived at Tolosa, and his sons learned rhetoric from a Gallic professor in nearby Narbo,[59] while Constantius resided in Corinth.[60] The brothers appear to have been recalled in 326, since Gallus, the son of Constantius, born in that year, first saw the light of day at the Massa Veternensis in Etruria—presumably while Constantine and his court were in Italy.[61] Dalmatius and Constantius became ordinary consuls and received the antique titles of *censor* and *patricius,* which Constantine revived in a new sense. For some years Dalmatius, consul in 333, resided at Antioch and performed broad administrative duties. He suppressed a rebellion in Cyprus and investigated a charge of murder against Athanasius. His title of *censor* (conferred in 333) marked him out as higher in rank than a praetorian prefect, but conveniently excluded him from the imperial college.[62] Constantius, consul in 335, received the title of *patricius,* which served the same function.[63] The first *patricius,* however, was Flavius Optatus, consul in 334;[64] that fact and the allegation that he married the daughter of a Paphlagonian innkeeper suggest that he may have been a relative of Constantine's mother.[65] The bestowal of the novel titles may be connected with Constantine's investiture of his youngest son as Caesar (25 December 333).[66] On 18 September 335, the emperor appointed the son of Flavius Dalmatius to be a fourth Caesar.[67]

When the young Dalmatius became a Caesar, Constantine made a territorial division of the empire which recalled the Diocletianic Tetrarchy. Africa was a special case, where since 333 a praetorian prefect administered all the African provinces.[68] But the rest of the empire was divided into four, even though Constantine himself retained overall control. In the West, Constantinus at Trier governed Britain, Gaul, and Spain. Constans probably resided at Milan, administering Italy and the Pannonian diocese, with Papius Pacatianus (consul in 331) as his praetorian prefect. On the lower Danube, probably at Naissus, was the new Caesar Dalmatius, assisted by Valerius Maximus, already a praetorian prefect for several years. Dalmatius' sphere of authority embraced the dioceses of Moesia and Thrace. The Caesar Constantius now took up residence in Antioch, with the able assistance of Flavius Ablabius (consul in 331), who had been praetorian prefect at Constantinople for several years.[69]

Constantine also arranged dynastic marriages for his sons. The identity of the woman Constantinus married has unfortunately escaped all record.[70] In July 336, however, Constantius married his cousin, the daughter of Julius Constantius, the half brother of the emperor.[71] And although Constans, whose birth probably fell in 323, was too young for wedlock in his father's lifetime, he was betrothed to Olympias, the daughter of Ablabius.[72] These matches clearly reflect Constantine's intention to leave his sons under the tutelage of advisers he had himself chosen.

Among Constantine's subjects, there is evidence of disquiet, discontent, and even open rebellion. The Christian empire brought significant changes in the status of Jews. Admittedly, Constantine allowed the Jews to set foot in Jerusalem again, but only on one day each year, in order to bewail their fate.[73] More generally, Constantine translated Christian prejudice against Jews into legal disabilities. He forbade Jews to own Christian slaves and to seek or accept converts to Judaism, and he prescribed that any Jew who attempted forcibly to prevent conversions from Judaism to Christianity should be burned alive.[74] Moreover, he granted the rank of *comes* to one Josephus of Tiberias, who had been an adviser of the Jewish patriarch. Josephus became a Christian, approached Constantine, and obtained permission and money to build churches in the predominantly Jewish towns of Galilee.[75] That marked a clear departure from the previous imperial policy of toleration toward the Jewish religion. Perhaps as a result, a group of zealots made a forlorn attempt, which was quickly suppressed, to seize Jerusalem and rebuild the temple.[76]

In Cyprus there was an open revolt, perhaps fanned by the resentment of pagans who interpreted an earthquake which destroyed the city of Salamis as divine condemnation of the Christian régime.[77] The keeper of the imperial camels, who bore the propitious name of Calocaerus, rebelled and seized the island. When he crossed to the mainland of Asia Minor, he was easily defeated by the *censor* Dalmatius, who burned him alive at Tarsus.[78]

There were troubles too at court, even apart from dynastic maneuvers. Constantine had outlawed a soldier in his bodyguard suspected of conspiring against him, and the soldier fled to the mountains of Bithynia—which implies that he had been accused of taking part in an attempt to assassinate the emperor.[79] And the philosopher Sopater provoked resentment from those who envied his easy familiarity with the emperor. Sopater, a pupil of Iamblichus, had frequented the court of Licinius; he came to the court of Constantine after his master's death.[80] Despite Sopater's paganism, the emperor held him in high esteem, conversed long with him, and used him as an adviser when conducting public business. However, one autumn the grain ships were delayed by the weather, and the hungry crowd in the hippodrome evinced its displeasure with the emperor. Sopater's enemies pounced. They accused the philosopher of fettering the winds. Constantine condemned Sopater to be beheaded (perhaps about the same time as Athanasius' enemies secured his removal by accusing him of threatening the grain supply).[81]

Eusebius visited Constantinople twice in the last years of Constantine's reign. He came in the autumn of 335, in haste from the Council of Tyre, to accuse Athanasius before the emperor.[82] After Athanasius departed for Gaul, Eusebius delivered a speech before Constantine in which he praised and described the recently dedicated Church of the Holy Sepulcher.[83] Eusebius came from Caesarea to Constantinople again in the summer of 336, as a member of the council of bishops which declared Marcellus of Ancyra heretical and deposed him from his see.[84] After the council, he remained to celebrate, on 25 July 336, the thirtieth anniversary of Constantine's accession. Outside the palace (presumably in the hippodrome), rank upon rank of foreign ambassadors offered precious gifts. Eusebius saw fair-skinned barbarians from the north, Nubians blacker than ebony or pitch, and richly appareled emissaries from India. The envoys of each nation or tribe in turn set before Constantine their gifts of homage: golden crowns, diadems with precious stones, fair-haired slaves, statues and paintings, exotic garments woven with golden flowers, horses and strange animals, shields and weapons of war. Constantine received the gifts graciously, gave rich presents in return, and bestowed high Roman rank on the leading ambassadors, some of whom he thus persuaded to remain at his court.[85] Inside the palace, speeches in praise of Constantine were recited before an audience which comprised not only courtiers, officials, and senators, but also the bishops who had attended the recently concluded council.[86] Eusebius' speech survives.

Eusebius prefaces his *Panegyric to Constantine* with a careful renunciation of the traditional panegyrical form. Let others, with the voice of Sirens, soothe the ears of the audience with conventional, mortal praises of the emperor's actions toward his fellow men. Eusebius promises a new song. He will travel a path which those with unwashed feet may not tread. He will praise Constantine's godlike virtues and God-loving deeds.[87] This preface sets the tone for what follows. Eusebius deliberately eschews exclusively Christian terminology, never uttering the name of Jesus or the word "Christ."[88] This feature of the speech must not be misconstrued. Eusebius was not suffering from diffidence, nor did he (or Constantine) fear to offend the pagans among those present; he does not propound a deliberately vague theology, nor adopt a tone of religious moderation.[89] On the contrary, Eusebius coolly appropriates the terminology of Greek philosophy to justify the Christian empire and the suppression of paganism.

The greater part of the *Panegyric* consists of variations and elaborations on a single theme: the similarity of Constantine to Christ.[90] The empire of Constantine is a replica of the kingdom of heaven, the manifestation on earth of that ideal monarchy which exists in the celestial realm. Constantine governs with his eyes ever gazing upward, patterning himself on the divine model of monarchical rule. He is the friend and ally of "the only-begotten Word of God, who rules with his Father from ages without beginning to endless ages without end." The length of Constantine's reign reflects the Word's eternity of rule. Like the Savior of the world, Constantine prepares men for the kingdom of God. Eusebius contrasts the *tricennalia* of 336 with similar celebrations of earlier emperors. Unlike his pagan predecessors, Constantine does not pollute his palace with the blood of sacrifice, with burnt offerings to the spirits of the underworld, or with any other sign of superstitious error. He repays God for the many blessings which God has showered on him by offering the sacrifice of a pure heart and mind.[91]

Eusebius did not invent the notion that monarchy reflects the supernatural order. Indeed, in origin the idea is not even Christian, but appears to derive from Hellenistic theories of kingship.[92] But Eusebius has given this idea an aggressively Christian content.[93] Just as the Word of God not only confers benefits on those who welcome his aid, but also wards off the unseen powers which fly above the earth and menace human souls, so Constantine both promotes piety and subjugates the visible opponents of truth by force of arms. The Constantine of Eusebius' speech is no benevolent tolerator of religious pluralism: he has "cleansed all the filth of godless error from his kingdom on earth."[94]

Eusebius was not content to leave his comparison of Constantine to Christ as a vacuous simile. He devoted a section of his speech to describing, praising, and justifying the suppression of paganism. The exposition proceeds from the observation that demons are spiritual barbarians who destroy human souls: Constantine has defeated these invisible foes as thoroughly as he conquered the barbarians who used to threaten the lives and property of his subjects. Eusebius presents the "Great Persecution" as the logical outcome of traditional religion, whose adherents murdered those dedicated to the king of the universe for the benefit of their demons, and he presents the rise of Constantine to supreme power as God's answer to the persecution. It was God who vanquished the unseen demons, Constantine who, as his prefect, stripped their corpses after defeat and freely distributed the spoils among the soldiers of the victor. The emperor decided to demonstrate to all the impotence of paganism. He sent a few trusted subordinates to confiscate and melt down idols everywhere in gold, silver, and bronze and sent a detachment of soldiers to suppress the shameful shrine of Aphrodite at Aphaca; they performed their tasks without resistance from any demon or god, any oracle or prophet.

In place of polytheism, Constantine has established monotheism. Pagan oracles are silent, pagan rites extinguished, the statues of the gods melted down to coin money for useful purposes. Constantine reigns under the saving and life-giving sign of the Cross, he sets one day in seven aside as a day of prayer, and his armies pray to God and fight with the *labarum* as their standard. The emperor has replaced the houses of prayer torn down in the persecution with grander edifices, he has embellished the great cities of the east with magnificent churches, and he everywhere fosters Christian worship and learning. The change is symbolized by the speaker and his audience: not godless men who babble idly, as of old, but initiated priests of God who celebrate the festival by praising the emperor's piety.[95]

Constantine carried through a religious reformation which could never be undone. But it is no easy matter to assess what changes he wrought in the administration of the empire and its secular institutions. The evidence is partial, fragmentary and unsatisfactory. Although Eusebius and Eunapius both describe his government, their accounts hardly coincide at a single point. Eusebius gives an extravagant panegyric. His Constantine was generous in every way. He gave freely to all, bestowing money, land, and status on any who asked and never refusing any request. From the emperor, some received consular rank, others membership in the Senate, many a provincial governorship; some became *comites* of the first, second, or third rank while countless others received the rank of *eminentissimus* or some other title. Eusebius' Constantine reduced taxation on agricultural land by one quarter, appointed officials to ensure fairness in the census, and always gave the loser in civil cases which he adjudicated a present equal in value to the claim lost.[96]

Eunapius' Constantine was antithetical. He divided the empire into four praetorian prefectures and appointed *magistri militum* who deprived the prefects of their military role, thus ruining the administration of the empire in both war and peacetime. He transferred the troops whom the wise Diocletian had stationed along the frontiers to cities of the interior which did not need protection, thus allowing barbarians to invade Roman territory freely and exposing the soldiers to a luxury and indiscipline which soon corrupted them. Dissolute and unwarlike, this Constantine spent public funds on private donations to unworthy and useless persons. Worse still, in order to fuel his misguided liberality, Constantine devised new and oppressive taxes. He imposed on all the inhabitants of cities the *chrysargyron* (a tax, more informatively known as the *auri lustralis collatio,* levied every four years, on businesses of every sort) which, Eunapius claimed, forced mothers to sell their sons into slavery, and fathers to prostitute their daughters. The emperor ordained that praetors give games to mark their tenure of that now pointless office, or at least provide a large sum of money instead, and he compelled all senators to pay a special tax on their property (the *follis senatorius* or *collatio glebalis*). By these means, Eunapius argued, Constantine ruined the majority of Roman cities.[97]

The contrasting pictures of Constantine are stereotypes which reproduce predictable features of the ideal ruler and the textbook tyrant. The former is always just, generous, and wise; the latter, always unjust, oppressive, and imprudent. Moreover, Eunapius' indictment of Constantine contains at least one clear anachronism: it was only under the sons of Constantine that the four regional praetorian prefectures of Eunapius' day came into existence.[98] What then were the innovations which Constantine introduced into the Roman state? The evidence of documents and contemporaries indicates a gradual reorganization of government by Diocletian and his successors; in administration, it seems, Constantine completed reforms already begun, or modified in detail arrangements which he found already in existence.[99]

Constantine had a palace official with the title *tribunus et magister officiorum* at least as early as 320,[100] and Martinianus was *magister officiorum* in 324 when Licinius raised him to the purple:[101] it may, therefore, have been Diocletian who created the post.[102] The *magister officiorum* controlled the three main secretarial departments of the palace (*memoria, epistulae* and *libelli*), each of which had a *magister* at its head. The *magister officiorum* controlled the *officium admissionum* and thus regulated audiences with the emperor. He also commanded most of the *scholae palatinae,* which included both imperial bodyguards in the palace and couriers (the *agentes in rebus*) for use on imperial business throughout the provinces.[103] Independent of the *magister officiorum* was the corps of notaries, who kept the minutes of the imperial consistory and could also be used as imperial messengers or agents.[104] The only innovation in the palace administration which the ancient evidence unequivocally attributes to Constantine is the appointment of the first *quaestor sacri palatii,* an official who aided the emperor in drafting imperial constitutions.[105]

In the last years of Constantine, the praetorian prefects (except the prefect in Africa) were still attached to emperors.[106] Hence, although they had lost their military functions, they had not yet acquired either a secure place in the civil administration or most of the duties which supervision of governors and taxation in each regional prefecture later entailed.[107] Dioceses and provinces remained largely as before, with minor changes of name, boundaries, and status.[108] But Constantine introduced a new flexibility by instituting three orders of *comites,* whom he could use either in regular administration or for a wide variety of special tasks.[109]

Under Constantine, the military hierarchy came to be entirely separate from the civil. Constantine appointed the first *magistri militum* to assume the purely military duties which the praetorian prefects relinquished (though the latter retained responsibility for recruitment and supply).[110] At a lower level, every province or group of provinces had, as under Diocletian, a *dux* in command of the local troops.[111] The army itself had changed significantly. Constantine disbanded the praetorian guard at Rome in 312, because he considered it an anachronism and a political menace.[112] But he greatly enlarged the central field army for use as a striking force.[113] This "select army" had existed as early as 270.[114] Constantine put his *comitatenses* under the command of the new *magister peditum* and *magister equitum* and gave them privileges superior to those of the *ripenses,* the soldiers of the frontier armies.[115] Constantine commenced his military reforms very early; in 312 it seems that he could already put fully one quarter of all the troops under his command into the field at once without unduly weakening the frontier defenses.[116]

Since the days of Augustus, Roman senators had gradually filled fewer of the important posts in the imperial administration. Diocletian excluded them almost totally from provincial governorships. Constantine chose his provincial governors from both senatorial and equestrian orders.[117] However, since the rank of *praeses* appeared too humble for most senators, Constantine revived the title of *consularis* for the governors of certain provinces which senators of Rome most desired to administer.[118] As a corollary of this implicit fusion of the two orders, senators held previously equestrian offices, becoming *praefecti annonae* and *praefecti vigilum* at Rome and *vicarii* of dioceses.[119]

The traditional, originally Republican, offices of quaestor, tribune, aedile, and praetor continued to exist at Rome, and at least quaestors and praetors were soon created at Constantinople.[120] But how men now normally entered the Senate is not wholly clear: sons of senators or *viri clarissimi* presumably did so automatically, as they had for centuries, while men of nonsenatorial families might be adlected by the emperor, who perhaps also augmented the Senate by other means.[121] There were now two types of consulate. Perhaps through a deliberate reform, the suffect consulate fell in esteem and was normally no longer deemed worthy of record in the statement of a man's career.[122] The ordinary consulate, by contrast, became one of the highest honors to which anyone outside the imperial family could aspire. It had lost its functions but enhanced its prestige. In Rome itself, the *praefectus urbi* had also gained in stature: he administered the old capital and presided in the Senate.[123] The new alignment of offices was soon reflected in the definition of nobility: a *nobilis* of the later Roman Empire was the descendant of a man who had been ordinary consul, praetorian prefect, or *praefectus urbi,* either at Rome or (later) at Constantinople.[124]

Changes in the assessing and raising of taxes are even harder to establish.[125] Although Eunapius denounced him for introducing the *collatio lustralis* and *follis senatorius,* Constantine may have done no more than extend taxes which Maxentius had first devised in Italy and Africa.[126] Nevertheless, the institution of the *collatio lustralis,* combined with the reduction in agricultural assessments attested by Eusebius, marks a significant shift in the balance of taxation from land to cities.[127] Galerius in 306 had sought to achieve the same end by including the landless inhabitants of cities in the census. The political consequences were disastrous.[128] Constantine learned from Galerius' mistake. He also (it may be conjectured) changed the five-year cycle on which censuses were conducted by postponing a census for one year.[129] Neither the cause nor the effect of that step is at all clear. But Constantine's religious policies enabled him to spend freely without taxing more heavily. The confiscation of temple treasures produced a sudden flow of capital into the imperial treasury. Constantine used it to build a solid foundation for the new, Christian monarchy.[130]

Benefactor of Christianity, enemy of the Church's enemies, Constantine regarded himself as the protector of Christians everywhere, entrusted with a divine mission to evangelize.[131] Such a conviction began, after 330, to influence his foreign policy. When he concluded a treaty with the Goths in 332, he insisted on the inclusion of religious stipulations. Two years later, he acted similarly with the Sarmatians.[132] In 335, therefore, Constantine felt entitled to claim that he had converted the northern barbarians; through fear of him, they now knew and worshiped God, who protected the emperor in all his undertakings.[133] In the spring of 337, Constantine, now aged sixty-four or sixty-five, was about to embark on a war whose motivation may have been partly religious.

The early history of Christianity in Parthian and Persian Mesopotamia lies shrouded in darkness, once the false illumination of a forgery is removed.[134] In the third century, however, the career of Mani presupposes a strong Christian element in southern Mesopotamia.[135] Born on 14 April 216, Mani lived for twenty years (220–240) among the Elchasaites;[136] later he preached his new religion to the Persian aristocracy and visited the court of King Shapur (240–272).[137] Mani's theological system, with its basic dualism of light and darkness, of the good soul and evil matter, though probably Gnostic in origin,[138] had an obvious appeal to Zoroastrians. The Zoroastrian clergy, however, saw that Mani's success threatened the status of Zoroastrianism as the official religion of the Persian Empire. Not long after Shapur died, the Zoroastrian clergy led by Kartir persuaded or compelled King Vahram to execute the dangerous visionary and, subsequently, to persecute Christians who were not Manichees.[139]

The persecution of Christians in the Persian Empire ceased not long after 290.[140] A generation later, religious changes on Persia's borders portended a change in the status of Christianity in Persia. Armenia became officially Christian in 314,[141] and shortly after Constantine conquered the East in 324, the kingdom of Iberia in the Caucasus embraced Christianity and a Roman alliance.[142] Constantine wrote to Shapur (who had been king of Persia from his birth in 309) asserting his patronage of Shapur's Christian subjects. The letter was polite and personal, not dictated (as was normal), but written in Constantine's own hand, its gentle phrasing designed to allow the two monarchs to reach an agreement without either appearing to lose face.

In this letter, Constantine is deliberately aphoristic, allusive, and indirect. He affirms an alliance with God, who has given the emperor success in order to secure peace for those who believe in him. Constantine reminds Shapur how God has punished every Roman emperor who persecuted the Christians, from Valerian to his own immediate predecessors and erstwhile colleagues. And he concludes with a commendation of the Christians in Persia: if Shapur, who is noted for his piety, helps them, God will favor him; therefore, let his good will match his generosity.[143] The date and precise political context of this letter are unfortunately both unclear. Shapur certainly persecuted the Christians of Persia vigorously and bitterly, but the inception of persecution falls after Constantine's death.[144]

War between Rome and Persia began in Constantine's lifetime. Shapur, who desired to recover what Narseh had lost nearly forty years before, took the initiative. There were border raids, and in 335 Constantine sent Constantius to reside in Antioch and guard the eastern frontier.[145] More serious still, probably in the next year, a Persian expedition under the royal prince, Narseh, invaded Armenia and installed a Persian nominee on the throne.[146] Constantine resolved to campaign against the Persians himself, and he proposed to wage the war as a Christian crusade. He solicited bishops (who agreed with alacrity) to accompany the army, he prepared a tent in the shape of a church to accompany him everywhere, and he intended, before invading Persia, to be baptized in the waters of the River Jordan.[147] Persian ambassadors arrived at Constantinople during the winter of 336/7, seeking to avoid war. The emperor repulsed their overtures.[148] Instead, he produced a candidate for the Persian throne. Hannibalianus, the son of Flavius Dalmatius, had perhaps already received the title of *nobilissimus* and the hand of Constantina, the emperor's elder daughter.[149] He was now proclaimed a king. Two writers of the fourth century make him ruler over the tribes of Pontus or Armenia and the surrounding lands.[150] It is more probable that the title "king of kings" conveyed a claim to replace Shapur.[151]

Constantine knew that his death could not be many years distant, and he had made provision for his memory. He constructed the Church of the Holy Apostles to serve as both a mausoleum and a shrine. The church was richly finished, with a roof of bronze and an abundance of gold and rare marble covering the interior and exterior walls. Around the church lay a large courtyard open to the air, with colonnades facing the church. Inside, in two equal rows, were twelve empty sarcophagi, one for each apostle. In secret, Constantine prepared a sumptuous sarcophagus to hold his own body and to stand in the center; he would thus be associated with the apostles by any who came to pray there.[152]

The end came far more suddenly than Constantine expected. Soon after Easter 337 (which fell on 3 April) the emperor became ill.[153] He went to take the waters at Aquae, as often before, then to Helenopolis in Bithynia where he prayed earnestly before the shrine of the martyr Lucian. Sensing the close approach of death, he prepared to meet his creator in a state of grace. He fell on his knees, confessed his sins, and sought admission to the Church as a catechumen.[154] From Helenopolis he proceeded to Nicomedia and there requested bishop Eusebius to baptize him. After the requisite preliminaries, Constantine received the eternal seal, laid aside the imperial purple, and donned plain robes of brilliant white. Now he was truly happy, now worthy of eternal life, now illumined with divine light. When his generals came to him, as he lay on his bed, and lamented their imminent loss, praying that he might live many years longer, he rebuked them. Constantine desired to go to God without delay. The festival of Christ's bodily ascension into heaven came; toward noon on the day of Pentecost (22 May 337) Constantine died.[155]

XV

EUSEBIUS AND CONSTANTINE

Constantius was in Antioch when his father's fatal illness began.[1] Probably informed secretly by the chamberlain Eusebius, the Caesar traveled westward in great haste. When he arrived in Nicomedia, the Augustus was already dead.[2] The Caesar and the eunuch, who seems at once to have become his chief minister,[3] turned to their own political advantage the profound feelings of grief which all felt at the loss of a loved and respected monarch. The body of Constantine was placed in a golden coffin draped with the imperial purple. Constantius escorted the soldiers who carried the coffin to Constantinople, where it lay in state in the main audience hall of the palace, adorned with the full imperial regalia. Generals, officials, senators, and people came and performed homage. Constantius himself conducted the funeral ceremonies. A military guard carried the body of Constantine to the Church of the Holy Apostles, where amid prayer and mourning he was laid to rest on a high platform.[4] His tomb at once became a place of pilgrimage.[5]

Constantine's dynastic arrangements did not long outlast his death. During 337 Flavius Dalmatius received a law issued at Naissus; it was presumably issued by his son, the Caesar Dalmatius, and it implies that Flavius Dalmatius held administrative office under his son.[6] On 2 August, Valerius Maximus was the praetorian prefect of Dalmatius.[7] Five weeks later, on 9 September, the three sons of Constantine were saluted as Augusti, and Roman armies everywhere, together with the Senate in Rome itself, acknowledged them as the sole emperors.[8] A military coup had eliminated the dynastic rivals of the new Augusti.[9] Dalmatius Caesar, his father, and his praetorian prefect perished—and with them, doubtless, any who showed loyalty to their cause.[10] Seven other members of the imperial family were also killed, the majority in Constantinople itself.[11] There was no formal trial; the murders were justified merely by the allegation that jealous relatives had poisoned Constantine, who realized their crime on his deathbed and left secret instructions for revenge.[12] The dead included Julius Constantius and his eldest son, the Caesar Dalmatius' brother Hannibalianus, and Flavius Optatus.[13]

Only two male members of the imperial house survived, both sons of Julius Constantius, preserved partly by their tender years, partly by the fact that their sister was Constantius' wife.[14] Who ordered the murders? Constantius clearly profited most from the elimination of rivals in Constantinople and on the Danube, and Julian later attributed the responsibility to him directly.[15] In the circumstances of 337, however, an imperial directive may not have been needed.[16] It is probably significant that the ordinary consuls of 338 were not two of the new Augusti, as custom prescribed, but two men who were probably generals[17]—and that they displaced an Italian senator, who had received a formal designation to office before May 337.[18]

Constantius left Constantinople to confer with his brothers. Constantinus was still in Trier on 17 June, and Constans apparently still in Italy on 31 August.[19] They met Constantius in Pannonia and agreed upon a new division of the empire.[20] Constantinus received some mark of pre-eminence in the imperial college,[21] but that was an empty honor. It was his younger brothers who gained territory. Constantinus now governed Britain, Gaul, and Spain, as before; Constans, Africa, Italy, and most of the Danubian lands; Constantius, Asia Minor and the dioceses of Thrace and Oriens.[22]

An inscription discloses a vitally important fact about the military situation in 337. By 340 both Constantius and Constans acquired the title *Sarmaticus,* which implies that they both claimed to have won a victory over the Sarmatians.[23] A joint campaign of Constantius and Constans in 337 might be inferred.[24] On a more plausible reconstruction, Constantius conducted an expedition across the Danube during the summer or early autumn of 337, and Constans took the field in the following year.[25] Both the motive and the ultimate result of these campaigns are clear: Constantine's conquests north of the Danube were lost.[26]

Constantius did not tarry long in Pannonia. He was soon in Constantinople again; there he convened a council of bishops which translated Eusebius from the see of Nicomedia to the imperial capital. He also ordered the murder of the former prefect Ablabius, whom he had already dismissed from office.[27] Constantius then returned to Antioch for the winter.[28] Soon he tackled the war against the Persians bequeathed by his father. The Roman position was worse than two years before, when Constantius first came to Antioch. In 336 the Persians had expelled Arsaces from the throne of Armenia; in 337 King Shapur invaded Roman Mesopotamia and besieged Nisibis for two months.[29] In 338, Constantius proceeded to Cappadocia and supervised the restoration of the Armenian king.[30] That completed successfully, Constantius settled into a routine which would vary little for a decade: he resided in Antioch, and sallied forth every summer into Mesopotamia to do battle with Rome's enemy.[31]

Constantinus returned to Trier.[32] Discontented with the settlement reached with his brothers, he soon decided to challenge Constans. Early in 340 he invaded his brother's territory, but was killed near Aquileia.[33] Constans then ruled the whole of the western empire until a usurper supplanted him a decade later.[34] Constantius reasserted his control over the whole empire, but only by appointing as Caesars the sons of Julius Constantius, who so narrowly escaped the fate of their massacred relatives. The elder, Gallus Caesar, ruled in the East for four years (351–354); he was then removed, accused of misgovernment and treason, and executed.[35] Gallus' brother, Julian, ruled in Gaul as Caesar for four years (6 November 355–January 360), then proclaimed himself Augustus, and finally marched against Constantius. His resentment against Christianity nourished by Constantius' selective piety, Julian had become a convert to the old religion. Yet he continued to profess Christianity until after his army had proclaimed him Augustus. Once Constantius was dead, Julian declared his true beliefs and began to attack Christianity with a vigor which dismayed even some of his loyal pagan supporters. The Church again had martyrs—and again had vengeance from on high: Julian died during an invasion of Persia which had failed.[36] No pagan ever again sat upon the throne of the Caesars.

Eusebius died before Constantinus attacked Constans, for the unfinished *Life of Constantine* assumes throughout that the three sons of Constantine rule the Roman Empire in harmony. The day of his decease is certified as 30 May;[37] the year must be 339 rather than 338 because of the volume of work which he composed after Constantine died. Between 22 May 337 and his own death, Eusebius not only labored on a life of the dead emperor, but completed two theological tracts for use in current controversy. The two books *Against Marcellus* and three entitled *Ecclesiastical Theology,* directed against the same target, have their genesis in a reversal of Constantine's ecclesiastical policy.

As soon as Constantine died, his sons pardoned all bishops exiled in their father's reign and restored them to their sees. It was Constantinus who issued the law, but he did so in the name of all the emperors and neither of his brothers openly demurred.[38] In Trier on 17 June 337, Constantinus also gave Athanasius a personal letter of recommendation to the church of Alexandria.[39] Athanasius hurried east, contacting other exiles and attempting to build up a party. At Viminacium, he encountered Constantius, sought an audience with him, and paid his respects.[40] In Constantinople, where he found that the bishop

Alexander had recently died, he helped to ordain Paul as Alexander's successor in a disputed election, and he intervened in the affairs of other churches along his route.[41] Athanasius reached Alexandria on 23 November.[42] He resumed his duties and began to reassert his control over the Egyptian church. His opponents complained, even accused him of murder, and it seems that during the course of 338 Constantius summoned him to Caesarea in Cappadocia to try him on the charge.[43] Though acquitted, Athanasius enjoyed little respite. A group of bishops met in Antioch in the winter of 338/9, denounced and deposed him, and ordained a successor.[44] Finally, on 18 March 339, Athanasius was driven out of his church by soldiers acting on imperial orders, and one week later he left Egypt for an exile which was to last more than seven years.[45]

Eusebius of Caesarea may have had no direct part in these events. The return of another exile, however, induced him to take up his pen in the Arian cause. Eustathius of Antioch had died in exile, at Trajanopolis in Thrace.[46] But Marcellus of Ancyra, removed from his see by the Council of Constantinople in 336,[47] was alive, and there were many who believed that the council had deposed him without valid justification. When Marcellus returned to Ancyra in 337, several bishops asked Eusebius, who had subscribed to the condemnation of Marcellus, to justify the actions of the council.[48] Eusebius complied with their request. The result was his tract *Against Marcellus,* whose preface, doubtless containing a fuller description of the circumstances of writing, is unfortunately lost.[49] Eusebius never intended an open-minded theological or philosophical discussion of Marcellus' views; he simply sets out to prove that Marcellus is a demonstrable heretic, with Jewish or Sabellian opinions, who brought his exile upon himself.[50] Although Eusebius appears at times to envisage as his audience those who do not yet know Marcellus' views,[51] he presumably sent the work to friends who might use it against Marcellus and his supporters. His technique is to quote Marcellus at length, interspersing brief comment to show how Marcellus damns himself with his own words.[52]

Eusebius devotes most of the first book to discrediting Marcellus personally. He derides his inaccuracy in quoting Scripture and his use of Greek proverbs in interpreting it.[53] But he spends far more space on a charge more relevant to the situation in 337: Marcellus has impertinently abused respected bishops and priests who, unlike himself, uphold the true teaching of the Church. Eusebius defends Asterius, Paulinus of Tyre, Eusebius of Nicomedia (now bishop of Constantinople), Narcissus of Neronias, himself, and Origen. Marcellus (it emerges) had quoted Origen's *On First Principles* and his *Commentary on Genesis* to establish his charge that the Arians derived their theology from pagan sources. Eusebius sets out to prove that Marcellus employed selective quotation and tendentious glosses in order to ascribe to his adversaries opinions which they never in fact held.[54]

The second book addresses itself to Marcellus' theology. Eusebius makes three separate charges of heresy, each documented by copious extracts. First, Marcellus denies that God the Son had an existence separate from the Father before his Incarnation. Second, his attempts to explain how the Word of God took flesh implicitly deny the reality of the Incarnation. Third, he asserts that the kingdom of Christ will have an end and that Christ will be reunited with the Father. Such manifest heresy (Eusebius argues) compelled an unwilling council in Constantinople to anathematize Marcellus and his doctrines.[55]

The *Ecclesiastical Theology* is a sequel to the *Against Marcellus,* and Eusebius describes it, in a prefatory letter addressed to Flacillus of Antioch, as a brief and positive statement of trinitarian theology. It may be presumed that Eusebius composed the work for a practical purpose. When Eusebius wrote, Marcellus was in Ancyra, in active possession of his see.[56] Marcellus is next discovered in exile again, at Rome, where he appears to have arrived in late 339 or early 340, after being deposed by a council of bishops.[57] The *Ecclesiastical Theology* prepares the way for a second deposition, for it argues at length that Marcellus' views fall outside the spectrum of theological views which the church can legitimately tolerate. Eusebius has nothing new to say; he merely reiterates that Marcellus' views are Sabellian and Jewish in turn, always contrary to Scripture and the teachings of the Church. The argument is tedious, repetitive, and wearisome.[58] Even the most casual reader, however, cannot fail to see that it is an Arian orthodoxy which Eusebius represents as the accepted teaching of the Church: the Son is not the same as the Father but different from him, since they are two substances (*hypostaseis*).[59] Eusebius more than once uses a striking simile drawn from Roman public life: the Son stands in the same relationship to the Father as the official laureled image publicly displayed everywhere stands to the exemplar which it depicts, the unique emperor who rules the whole Roman Empire.[60]

Eusebius may have begun his *Life of Constantine* while the emperor still lived, and he may even have taken up his pen in response to the emperor's express wishes.[61] But when Eusebius died in 339, he left the *Life* unfinished. Another hand, perhaps that of Acacius, who succeeded him as bishop of Caesarea, tidied the manuscript, added the chapter headings, and published the text as it stood.[62] Hence the four books of the *Life*, as extant, contain doublets and inconsistencies which show that the author was still engaged in revision when he died.[63] At least two distinct designs can be detected: a formal panegyric in the appropriate rhetorical style, and an account of Constantine's religious activities illustrated by documents quoted in their entirety.[64] Which of these two conceptions was the original? Presumably, the more conventional panegyric on the dead ruler. Eusebius then decided to transform the oration into something which more closely resembled a biography. The fact that the revision was never completed must not be ignored in any evaluation.

The historical value of the *Life of Constantine* has often been discussed—or rather, the portrait of Constantine which the *Life* explicitly depicts has often been analyzed.[65] Strangely, however, the picture of Eusebius himself which is implicit in the *Life* has usually been taken on trust. Eusebius suggests that he was close to the emperor; hence he becomes, in many modern accounts, a constant adviser of Constantine, a close confidant, his principal counselor on ecclesiastical matters.[66] Basic facts of geography and chronology contradict this conventional portrait. Eusebius of Caesarea did not, like his namesake of Nicomedia, reside near the imperial capital, come to court when he chose, or have ready access to the emperor's presence. He was no courtier, still less a trusted counselor from whom Constantine sought constant advice on ecclesiastical policy. Under Constantine, as under the pagan emperors who ruled the East before 324, Eusebius lived in Palestine, active as a scholar and a bishop. He probable met and conversed with the emperor on no more than four occasions.

When Eusebius saw Constantine in 301 or 302 traversing Palestine in the entourage of Diocletian, the scholar was merely one among thousands of spectators gazing on the young prince whom they expected to become their next emperor.[67] The two men first met in 325, when they both attended the Council of Nicaea; the bishop arrived under a provisional ban of excommunication, and the emperor helped him to rehabilitate himself and to prove his orthodoxy.[68] In 325, therefore, the two men spent the months of June and July in the same city. It was probably on this occasion that Constantine described to Eusebius the vision to which he owed his conversion.[69] But Eusebius need not have been either the unique or a solitary recipient of this narration. During and after the council, Constantine had abundant opportunity to explain how and why he respected bishops. Not only did he attend the formal sessions and intervene in the debate, but after the council he invited all the bishops to dine in the imperial palace, and he conversed with them freely.[70] The scholar and the emperor probably met again in December 327, for Eusebius presumably attended the Council of Nicomedia, which readmitted Arius.[71] After that, however, nearly eight years intervened before their next encounter. In November 335, Eusebius and five other bishops arrived from Tyre and accused Athanasius of treason.[72] After Athanasius departed for Gaul, Eusebius delivered a speech on the Church of the Holy Sepulcher, whose dedication he had helped to perform in September. Eusebius expatiated on the generosity of the emperor in building the church and endowing it richly with objects made of gold, silver, and precious stones, which Eusebius described in flowery rhetoric.[73] As a mark of respect, Constantine insisted on standing while Eusebius recited the speech—which is regrettably lost.[74]

In the summer of 336, Eusebius again came to Constantinople. He participated in the council which deposed Marcellus of Ancyra, with Constantine present. When the council finished its business, the bishops celebrated the thirtieth anniversary of the emperor's accession. As eleven years before at Nicaea, Constantine entertained the bishops and honored them publicly. And as part of the festivities, on 25 July 336, Eusebius delivered his *Panegyric to Constantine,* celebrating the Christian empire and the suppression of paganism.[75] Significantly, this speech was only the second which Eusebius delivered in the imperial palace.[76]

Nor were exchanges of letters between the two men any less formal or any more frequent. Eusebius received a letter from Constantine for the first time in 324; it was a proclamation addressed to the provincials of Palestine undoing the effects of Licinius' legislation against the Christians.[77] A second letter came not long after; the emperor wrote to all eastern bishops individually, urging them to enlarge their churches with funds which provincial governors would supply.[78] The third letter which Eusebius quotes as written to him by Constantine was in fact written to Macarius of Jerusalem and all the bishops of Palestine, instructing them to build a church over the Oak of Mamre.[79] The fourth letter is the first addressed to Eusebius alone; in it Constantine commended his refusal to become bishop of Antioch.[80] Eusebius also quotes two other letters which Constantine wrote to him personally. The one thanks Eusebius for the receipt of a treatise on Easter, the other requests him to prepare copies of the Bible for use in the churches of Constantinople.[81] Both have a tone of respect, but not of intimacy. Constantine doubtless regarded Eusebius highly as a scholar, writer, and theologian. There is no sign that he ever sought his advice on any political issue. Moreover, it is not unduly skeptical to suspect that Eusebius quotes all the important letters which he ever received from Constantine.[82]

The *Life of Constantine* clearly reflects the circumstances in which it was composed. That fact is most obvious in what Eusebius says, and does not say, about the events of summer 337. He presents Constantinus, Constantius, and Constans as a preordained trio of rulers. He carefully emphasizes that the sons of Constantine, appointed Caesars in their father's lifetime, have inherited by a law of nature the throne which Constantine had received from his father as his patrimony.[83] When Constantine died, the armies everywhere, with one accord and as if by divine inspiration, refused to acknowledge any emperor except his sons.[84] Likewise the Senate at Rome, when it declared that Constantine was now in heaven and requested that his coffin be brought to Italy, pronounced his sons and no others to be Augusti.[85] Eusebius cannot have been totally ignorant of the coup which thwarted Constantine's real intentions. There may be a hidden significance in his insistence that Constantine continued to reign even after his death.[86] Whether Eusebius realized it or not, that fiction, which finds an echo in a contemporary document,[87] conveniently absolved Constantius of responsibility for the murders which removed his rivals for power. Eusebius' account of 337 conceals the fact that Constantius arrived in Constantinople before his relatives were killed. More dishonest still, Eusebius states outright that before he died Constantine divided the empire among his three sons and established them with courts, advisers, and armies as his sole intended successors.[88]

Equally clearly, the *Life* betrays its unfinished state in many passages which are alien to their context and which spoil the structure of Eusebius' final design. Relics of the abandoned panegyric can be detected. Eusebius originally compared Constantine to all the other emperors of the early fourth century in turn. Hence he described the deaths of the persecutors Galerius and Maximinus, transcribing long passages from his *Ecclesiastical History,* composed a quarter of a century before.[89] From the same source he also copied out a detailed account of Maxentius' oppression of the Senate and a chapter on Licinius' fiscal policies.[90] Significantly, Eusebius utters the names of Maxentius and Licinius twice each—isolated lapses in a work which otherwise (except in quoted documents) totally avoids naming any individuals except Constantine and his immediate kin.[91]

To the panegyric which Eusebius decided to discard also belong passages where he celebrates Constantine's triumphs in war,[92] and allusions, misplaced in their present context, to the death and *damnatio memoriae* of Maximian and to the alleged plot of Bassianus, which God revealed to Constantine in a dream.[93] Similarly, three chapters now interrupt the account of the Arian controversy; here Eusebius contrasts Constantine's conduct, item by item, with that of Licinius, whom he presents, under a plural designation, as "those emperors who apostatized and compelled their subjects to worship gods who do not exist."[94] Another passage also apparently written for a conventional panegyric depicts Constantine as possessing all the traditional virtues of a Roman emperor: he gave presents and privileges to all who asked, he reduced taxation, he compensated those who lost cases before him, he defeated the barbarian Goths and Sarmatians, he received homage from the ends of the earth.[95]

The final version of the *Life of Constantine* would have discarded all this. On mature reflection, Eusebius decided to pass in silence over the deaths of the emperors who perpetrated the "Great Persecution"; such matters were inappropriate for the revised design, in which Eusebius would not defile the memory of the good by a contrast with the bad.[96] Eusebius proposed, moreover, to omit most of the conventional material of biography or panegyric. He would exclude warfare, treaties, and triumphs, he would exclude the emperor's acts and laws through which in time of peace he produced success for the state or prosperity for his subjects; instead, he would concentrate on Constantine's most notable achievement, his pursuit of piety.[97]

Eusebius arranged his material in part chronologically, in part thematically. The *Life* attempts to observe strict temporal order in narrating Constantine's rise to supreme power, from a precarious position at the court of Diocletian to the defeat of Licinius.[98] Much of the account is predictable. Eusebius exaggerates the protection which Constantine's father gave the Christians of Britain and Gaul, and Constantius' total dissimilarity from his imperial colleagues.[99] Eusebius repeats, from the *Ecclesiastical History,* his misdating of Constantius' elevation from Caesar to Augustus, which he puts "after the first year of the siege of the churches" when it should be "after the second."[100] He repeats the official story that Constantine reached his father on his deathbed, that his father appointed him his successor, and that he was proclaimed Augustus at once.[101] He likewise repeats the conventional story that Constantine invaded Italy to rescue its inhabitants from tyranny.[102] He duly gives Constantine the sole credit for ending persecution in the East.[103] He conflates the two wars against Licinius into a single war suspended briefly by an ineffectual truce, and he connects Licinius' execution as closely as possible with his defeat.[104] But Eusebius includes important information not known from other sources. He reproduces Constantine's own account of his conversion (which incidentally reveals that in 312 there were already bishops at the emperor's court), and he gives a detailed description of the *labarum* as he saw it long after 312.[105] He records, quite specifically, that Constantine not only began to give privileges and subsidies to the Christian church immediately after his conversion, but also that he attended a council of bishops before he had reigned for ten years.[106]

For the period after 324, Eusebius could quote documents. In a carefully constructed section of the *Life*, he shows how Constantine established Christianity as the official religion of the Roman Empire. First, Eusebius quotes the letter by which Constantine undid the effects of Licinius' persecution.[107] Then he registers three enactments, whose text he cannot quote. Constantine forbade praetorian prefects, *vicarii* of dioceses, and provincial governors to perform sacrifice before conducting official business.[108] The emperor also totally forbade the consecration of pagan cult statues, the consultation of pagan oracles and the performance of pagan sacrifice, and instructed governors to provide public funds for building churches.[109] Eusebius did not possess copies of these three laws; since they were addressed to imperial officials, that is natural enough, and his failure to quote their texts should not be allowed to call their existence into question.[110] Eusebius quoted what he did possess: a letter from Constantine encouraging him to make use of the third law to build a larger church.[111] He could also quote a letter (somewhat later in date), in which Constantine exhorted the inhabitants of Oriens to embrace true religion, while permitting them to retain their pagan shrines if they must.[112] The first four documents quoted or paraphrased all belong to the autumn of 324; Eusebius includes the fifth here because of its obvious thematic connection with what precedes.

Eusebius next turns to the Council of Nicaea. His account, in its present form, contains clear doublets, is interrupted by a rhetorical comparison of Constantine and Licinius, and is inartistically divided between two books.[113] Nevertheless, the design and interpretation of the account are clear. Eusebius carefully conceals the antecedents and the long history of the Arian controversy before 324. In the *Life*, envy and an evil demon suddenly disrupt a peaceful Church. The trouble began in Alexandria and rapidly spread, since in Egypt and the Thebaid there already existed a schism (that is, the Melitian schism) from a more ancient cause.[114] Constantine, deeply distressed, as if the controversy were a personal disaster, sent Ossius to Alexandria to attempt to reconcile the factions. Eusebius quotes the imperial letter which Ossius carried.[115] It shows Constantine's concern for the Church and the triviality of the dispute. There was also a more serious controversy over the date of Easter, which different Christians celebrated at different times.[116] Constantine, therefore, summoned an ecumenical council to meet at Nicaea; two hundred and fifty bishops came, with priests and deacons in attendance, from every race under heaven, to a gathering which Eusebius compares to the first Pentecost (Acts 2:5–11).[117]

The picture of the Council of Nicaea itself is deliberately selective. Eusebius focuses attention on the magnificent opening ceremony, on the letter in which Constantine communicated the council's decision on the date of Easter (quoted entire), and on Constantine's entertainment of the bishops after the council.[118] He allots the substantive debate on the creed only a few lines, and an epilogue alludes briefly to the Council of Nicomedia two and a half years later.[119] Eusebius' account is singularly uninformative. He intended it to be so. He did not desire to record his own excommunication and rehabilitation, the defeat of his party, or the exile of those whose views he shared.[120]

After Nicaea, the arrangement of material in the revised design becomes purely thematic until Eusebius comes to the end of the reign, where he passes, in chronological order, from the councils of Tyre and Jerusalem (335) to the *tricennalia* (336), and thence to a narrative of Constantine's death and burial.[121] The larger part of Books Three and Four falls into loosely connected sections and a miscellany. Eusebius expatiates at length on Constantine's building of churches in Palestine (with a brief mention of churches elsewhere), then he repeats with additions the section of the *Panegyric to Constantine* which described the suppression of paganism.[122] He turns next to the two Councils of Antioch (in 327 and 328) which deposed Eustathius and attempted to appoint Eusebius to the vacant see,[123] and the third book concludes with a letter in which Constantine deprived heretical sects of their property, apparently in 324.[124]

In Book Four, Constantine's letter to Shapur introduces a section where Eusebius records quite briefly many different actions by Constantine in favor of Christianity.[125] Among them are innovations introduced in the West before 324[126] and two important laws which attest Constantine's deepest convictions. One law, which survives in part, forbade Jews to buy Christian slaves, proclaiming that it was wrong for those who had killed the prophets and their Lord to own those redeemed by the Savior;[127] the other, which has not survived, gave the canons of Church councils legal force, forbidding governors to disregard synodical decisions, on the grounds that God's priests were superior to any civil magistrate.[128] Eusebius also records a witticism which Constantine made at dinner when he was entertaining bishops, presumably after the Council of Nicaea in 325: playing on the original meaning of *episcopos*, the emperor informed his guests that he too was ordained by God as a bishop or overseer—of those outside the church.[129]

The *Life of Constantine* omits much. Not all of the omissions are significant: it should occasion no surprise that Eusebius makes no allusion whatever to Crispus or to Fausta and even implicitly denies their existence; any imperial panegyrist would observe a similar silence, and dynastic politics fell outside the scope of the revised plan of the *Life*. The treatment of ecclesiastical politics is another matter. Constantine intervened often and to great effect in theological controversies.[130] Eusebius knew that, and elsewhere he records Constantine's part in the downfall of Marcellus of Ancyra.[131] The *Life* deliberately and consistently conceals the extent and the importance of controversy within the Christian church.

Eusebius approached the task of writing about Constantine with a historian's appreciation of its importance. Earlier emperors, even Nero and similar tyrants, had been glorified in voluminous histories by eager writers. How much more did Constantine deserve commemoration from a Christian author! Other historians described lives and actions which offered no moral improvement but tended to corrupt readers, and they wrote out of loyalty or hatred, or sometimes to display their own talents, adorning ugly narratives with gaudy rhetoric.[132] Eusebius promises moral improvement through the straightforward reporting of good deeds, for Constantine is a shining example of godly life for all.[133]

The *Life of Constantine* was not intended to be an entirely self-contained text. Eusebius proposed to append to it three speeches to illustrate Constantine's views and his own. First comes the *Speech to the Assembly of the Saints,* which Constantine delivered in Serdica or Thessalonica shortly before he conquered the East.[134] Eusebius also proposed to append the two speeches he recited in the imperial palace in November 335 and July 336, but his posthumous editor accidentally substituted the speech which Eusebius gave at Jerusalem in September 335 in place of the former.[135] The appended speeches establish two crucial theses: Eusebius is the authoritative interpreter of the Constantinian empire, and emperor and bishop agree on fundamental theological issues. The Constantine whom Eusebius quotes speaks of a first God and a second God who are "two substances with one perfection," and he asserts that the substance of the second God derives its existence from the first.[136] In 338 or 339, such views were unmistakably Arian. It is hard to believe that Eusebius did not intend his readers to infer that Constantine shared his own Arian views.

The Roman Senate in the fourth century had the custom of commending good emperors by comparison with two exemplary predecessors as "more successful than Augustus, better than Trajan."[137] Eusebius makes a still wider claim for his hero: Constantine surpassed all rulers in recorded history, whether Greek, Roman, or barbarian, and for the benefit of Greek readers Eusebius compares him to Cyrus and Alexander.[138] Eusebius' underlying conception, however, comes from the Jewish and Christian tradition. Constantine resembles Moses. Like Moses, the young Constantine grew up at a tyrant's hearth, and like Moses he fled.[139] His adversary and his army were drowned, like the Egyptian pharaoh in the Red Sea.[140] Again like Moses of old, Constantine prepared for battle with fasting and prayer.[141] Had Eusebius lived longer, he would doubtless have penetrated beneath these superficial resemblances to the deep similarity between the achievements of the two men: like "God's ancient prophet," Constantine was a law-giver who showed God's people how to live, prosper, and attain happiness, both in this world and hereafter.

EPILOGUE

Constantine has always been a controversial figure. In his own lifetime, and while his sons still occupied the imperial throne, pagans like Praxagoras of Athens and Libanius from Antioch, no less than Eusebius, presented his career as a paradigm of virtue rewarded by success. Constantine undertook all his wars from the highest of motives. When he learned that Maxentius was maltreating his subjects in Italy, he took pity on them and rescued them. When he discovered that Licinius was misgoverning the East in a harsh and inhuman manner, he made war on him and forced him to swear to treat his subjects with honesty and generosity. Only when Licinius totally disregarded these solemn promises did Constantine attack, defeat, and depose him. The Constantine of the panegyrists surpassed all earlier emperors in moral probity, in happiness, and in success.[1]

When the last of Constantine's sons died in 361, encomium was answered by invective. The emperor Julian, who had earlier echoed the conventional praises of Constantine,[2] gave the lead. He denounced his uncle bitterly as a reckless innovator who destroyed Rome's ancient way of life,[3] and he published a pamphlet entitled "Symposium, or the Saturnalia" (conventionally known as the *Caesars*) which directly contradicted the claim that Constantine was superior to his imperial predecessors. Julian compared Constantine with Alexander the Great, with Julius Caesar, with Augustus, Trajan, and Marcus Aurelius, always to Constantine's disadvantage. Julian's Constantine is a devotee of sensual pleasure whose idols are Luxury and Wantonness; he confesses his ambition to amass great wealth and to spend it liberally for the enjoyment of himself and his friends, and he goes gladly to a Jesus who promises instantaneous pardon to seducers, the unclean, and murderers.[4]

Eunapius of Sardis developed Julian's insinuations into a historical interpretation of the fourth century which blamed Constantine and his conversion to Christianity for the decline of the Roman Empire.[5] Writing after the crushing defeat at Adrianople in 378, Eunapius traced the process of disintegration to Constantine's failure to celebrate the Secular Games which fell due in 314, and he damned Constantine personally as immoral in both the personal and the political spheres. Born out of wedlock (and of a low-class mother), Constantine kept a mistress who bore his eldest son. This son he put to death, in defiance of the laws of nature, on suspicion of seducing his wife, and when his mother objected, he turned on his wife and ordered her to be suffocated while bathing. Eunapius, following Julian's hint, attributed Constantine's conversion to the two deaths: in vain the emperor sought purification for his wrongdoing, until a fraud from Spain, obtaining an entrée to the imperial palace through its womenfolk, persuaded him that Christianity would cleanse him from every stain.

In Eunapius' eyes, Constantine's political career strayed far from the path of virtue to which sycophants had confined it. Licinius gave no cause for offense; it was Constantine who broke treaties by attempting to seduce some of Licinius' officials from their allegiance, and when Licinius had been defeated, Constantine brutally murdered him, breaking a promise of safety. Constantine's reforms in army and state were a total disaster: he founded Constantinople out of pique so that he could live there in effete luxury; he divided the Roman Empire into four by his reforms of the praetorian prefecture; he invited barbarians to invade Roman territory, by removing troops from the frontiers; and he so lavished gifts of money on the useless and unworthy that he needed to invent new taxes, which ruined the worthy and respectable classes of the population.[6]

About the year 500, the pagan Zosimus repeated Eunapius' critique with embellishment. Otherwise, however, a far more favorable estimate of Constantine prevailed. The reason, regrettably, was not that historians corrected the appalling ignorance or disregard of facts which Eunapius and Zosimus often display, but that Constantine's position as the first Christian emperor was unassailable. In both East and West, Constantine embodied the standard against which medieval rulers were measured.[7]

When scholarship revived in the Renaissance, the divergence of the ancients soon found its echo in contradictory modern accounts of Constantine. The text of Zosimus was rediscovered by the German humanist Johann Löwenklau (Johannes Leunclavius), who published a Latin translation at Basel in 1576 and prefaced it with a "Defense of Zosimus against the Unjustified Charges of Evagrius, Nicephorus Callistus, and Others." He argued that Zosimus' picture of Constantine should be preferred to that of Eusebius and the ecclesiastical historians of the fifth century; Zosimus held a correct and judicious balance between the emperor's virtues and vices, whereas Eusebius was not a historian but a panegyrist, constrained to utter nothing except laudation—and therefore incapable of giving a true portrait of Constantine.[8]

Humanism was answered in the spirit of the Counter-Reformation. In a volume dedicated to the king of Spain and first published in the year of the Spanish Armada, Cardinal Baronius presented a Constantine who was the model of a Christian prince. The cardinal repeatedly denounced Zosimus for bias and falsehood (not always justifiably), and he characterized his work as a philippic against Constantine rather than a history. Baronius preferred Eusebius' picture of the pious ruler who fought Maxentius and Licinius only because they provoked him, and he based his account of Constantine primarily on Eusebius' *Life*. Although Baronius does indeed quote and discuss a wide range of other evidence, he always evaluates it against an *a priori* interpretation of Constantine. Moreover, so strong were Baronius' apologetical tendencies that he occasionally saw the hand of God in episodes which Eusebius had veiled in decent silence. The *Life of Constantine* betrays no hint of the deaths of Crispus and Fausta; simple omission of important facts being disallowed to a historian writing in the sixteenth century, Baronius reasoned that the deaths must represent God's punishment of Constantine for excessive toleration of paganism.[9]

The series of modern interpretations of Constantine which begins with Jacob Burckhardt in 1853 covers a spectrum of views only slightly wider than those already surveyed. On the religious plane, Constantine has been interpreted as an essentially unreligious politician motivated solely by ambition and cool intellect,[10] as a philosophical monotheist who derived his beliefs from a prevailing religious syncretism,[11] and as a man swept off his feet by a sudden conversion to Christianity, whose whole being became suffused with religious enthusiasm.[12] No less diverse are opinions about his capabilities as a statesman: he has been presented both as a weak-willed character dominated by a camarilla of anonymous advisers,[13] and as a dictatorial ruler of diabolical cleverness who held both Church and State firmly under his personal control.[14]

The present study of Constantine and Eusebius has sought to transcend the terms in which "the Constantinian question" has traditionally been posed.[15] Edward Gibbon attempted to "delineate a just portrait" of Constantine "by the impartial union of those defects which are confessed by his warmest admirers, and of those virtues which are acknowledged by his most implacable enemies," and he based his assessment on the contrasted narratives of Eusebius' *Life of Constantine* and Zosimus.[16] A broader and less subjective approach has here been essayed: to set in their context and exploit to the full the evidence of contemporary documents and literary works written during Constantine's lifetime, from very different (and therefore complementary) vantage points. Even so, a fully rounded portrait of Constantine has perhaps not been achieved. For much of his reign a reliable and detailed political narrative cannot be written, and a woeful lack of evidence for the secular administration of the Roman Empire under Constantine balances the plentiful documentation of his participation in ecclesiastical affairs.[17] A Roman emperor was constantly assailed by hosts of petitions, by a vast array of varied requests for legal rulings, for privileges, for charity.[18] Constantine was no exception, and the small proportion of his total correspondence which has been preserved attests the range of problems with which he had to concern himself: there survive, for example, fragments of more than forty letters to prefects of the city of Rome.[19] Constantine's administrative activities have here been largely neglected because of the intractability and fragmentary nature of the evidence. A full history of the period could not afford to be so selective.

The Constantine who has emerged in the preceding chapters was neither a saint nor a tyrant. He was more humane than some of his immediate predecessors, but still capable of ruthlessness and prone to irrational anger. As an administrator, he was more concerned to preserve and modify the imperial system which he inherited than to change it radically—except in one sphere. From the days of his youth Constantine had probably been sympathetic to Christianity, and in 312 he experienced a religious conversion which profoundly affected his conception of himself. After 312 Constantine considered that his main duty as emperor was to inculcate virtue in his subjects and to persuade them to worship God.[20] Constantine's character is not wholly enigmatic; with all his faults and despite an intense ambition for personal power, he nevertheless believed sincerely that God had given him a special mission to convert the Roman Empire to Christianity.[21]

CHRONOLOGICAL TABLE

Between 260 and 265	Birth of Eusebius
27 February 272 (or 273)	Birth of Constantine
20 November 284	Accession of Diocletian
1 March 293	Proclamation of Constantius and Galerius as Caesars
293?–305	Constantine in the East, in the army of Galerius, and at the court of Diocletian
Before 300	Eusebius composes the first editions of the *Chronicle* and *Ecclesiastical History* (in seven books)
299	Purge of Christians in the eastern armies
Shortly before 303	Eusebius writes *Against Hierocles*
24 February 303	First persecuting edict promulgated in Nicomedia
c. Easter 303	Persecution begins in Palestine
1 May 305	Diocletian and Maximian abdicate; Constantius and Galerius become Augusti; Severus and Maximinus proclaimed Caesars
25 July 306	Constantius dies at York; Constantine is proclaimed emperor and ends persecution in Gaul, Spain, and Britain
28 October 306	Maxentius seizes power in Rome

Winter 306/7	End of persecution in Italy and Africa
Late April 311	Galerius issues an edict of toleration ending persecution in Danubian provinces and in Greece
Summer/autumn 311	Eusebius writes the *Martyrs of Palestine* (long recension)
312	Constantine invades Italy and defeats Maxentius
313	Maximinus attacks Licinius (April) but is defeated and killed (c. July): Licinius finally ends persecution in Asia Minor and the East
Late 313?	Eusebius produces new edition of *Ecclesiastical History* incorporating revised version of the *Martyrs of Palestine* (short recension) and an account of Maximinus in 311–313 (Book Nine)
c. 313	Eusebius becomes bishop of Caesarea
c. 314–c. 318	Eusebius compiles the *Preparation for the Gospel*
c. 315	New edition of *Ecclesiastical History*, which includes the present Book Eight and 10.1–7
316/7	First war between Constantine and Licinius
c. 318–c. 323	Eusebius composes *Demonstration of the Gospel*
Between 321 and 324	Constantine delivers *Speech to the Assembly of the Saints*
c. 322	Sporadic persecution resumed in the territories of Licinius
324	Licinius defeated and deposed (September); Constantine becomes ruler of the whole Roman Empire and founds Constantinople
June–July 325	Council of Nicaea
325/6	Eusebius publishes final edition of *Ecclesiastical History* and second edition of the *Chronicle* (and probably writes the *Theophany*)
11 May 330	Formal dedication of Constantinople
c. 330	Eusebius at work on the *Commentary on Isaiah*
September 335	Eusebius delivers *Treatise on the Church of the Holy Sepulcher* in Jerusalem
25 July 336	Eusebius delivers *Panegyric to Constantine* in Constantinople
22 May 337	Death of Constantine; Eusebius at once begins his *Life of Constantine*
Summer 337	Dynastic rivals to Constantine's sons killed
9 September 337	Constantine's sons proclaimed Augusti
338	Eusebius writes *Against Marcellus* and *Ecclesiastical Theology*

30 May 339	Eusebius dies, leaving *Life of Constantine* unfinished
339	Acacius succeeds Eusebius as bishop of Caesarea and publishes *Life of Constantine*

EDITIONS AND TRANSLATIONS
OF EUSEBIUS

Detailed bibliographies of modern editions and studies of Eusebius' writings are available in J. Quasten, *Patrology* 3 (Utrecht and Antwerp, 1960), 309–345, and M. Geerard, *Clavis Patrum Graecorum* 2 (Turnhout, 1974), 262–275, nos. 3465–3505, and it would be superfluous to repeat such easily available information. Nevertheless, it may help readers if I provide a list of the editions which I have used and of modern translations of Eusebius. (The translations printed in Chapters VI–XI and XIII are my own except where attributed to a named translator, but my draft translations have often been improved by subsequent consultation of published versions.)

For Eusebius' biblical commentaries, letters and works which are either lost, fragmentary, or very brief, the Index of Passages of Eusebius Discussed should furnish sufficient guidance. For his main extant writings, I give: (1) the abbreviation which I have used in the notes to refer to the work in question; (2) its conventional Latin title; (3) the English version of the title which I have used in the text; (4) the edition or editions which I have consulted; and (5) brief details of modern English translations (usually the name of the translator, the place of publication, and the date).

C. Hier.: Contra Hieroclem, Against Hierocles
C. L. Kayser, *Flavii Philostrati Opera* 1 (Leipzig: Teubner, 1870), 369–413.
F. C. Conybeare, ed. and tr., *Philostratus, The Life of Apollonius of Tyana and the Treatise of Eusebius against Hierocles* 2 (Loeb Classical Library, 1912), 483–605.

C. Marc.: Contra Marcellum, Against Marcellus
E. Klostermann, *Eusebius' Werke* 4 (*Die griechischen christlichen Schriftsteller der ersten drei Jahrhunderte* 14, 1906), 1–54. Revised by G. C. Hansen (*GCS*, 1972), with additions but unchanged pagination.

Chron.: Chronicon, Chronicle
(a) The Armenian translation:
J. Karst, *Eusebius' Werke* 5: *Die Chronik aus dem Armenischen übersetzt mit textkritischem Kommentar* (*GCS* 20, 1911); references are given by page, or by page and line, in Karst's translation.
(b) Jerome's version of the *Canons:*
R. Helm, *Eusebius' Werke* 7: *Die Chronik des Hieronymus*[2] (*GCS* 47, 1956); references are given by page and line or by page and the superscript letter prefixed to the entry by Helm.
(c) Greek fragments:
Syncellus, ed. W. Dindorf, *Corpus Scriptorum Historiae Byzantinae* (Bonn, 1829).
J. A. Cramer, *Anecdota Graeca e Codd. Manuscriptis Bibliothecae Regiae Parisiensis* 2 (Oxford, 1839), 117–183.
A. Bauer, *Anonymi Chronographia Syntomos e Codice Matritensi No. 121 (nunc 4701)* (Leipzig: Teubner, 1909).
Eusebian fragments from Syncellus and the *Anec(dota) Par(isiensia)* are printed in A. Schoene, *Eusebi Chronicorum Libri Duo* 1 (Leipzig, 1875), 2 (1866), but I have given references to the separate editions.

DE: Demonstratio Evangelica, Proof of the Gospel
I. A. Heikel, *Eusebius' Werke* 6 (*GCS* 23, 1913).
W. J. Ferrar (London: Society for the Promotion of Christian Knowledge, 1920), 2 vols.

Eccl. Theol.: Ecclesiastica Theologia, Ecclesiastical Theology
E. Klostermann, *Eusebius' Werke* 4 (*GCS* 14, 1906), 59–182. Revised by G. C. Hansen (*GCS*, 1972), with additions but unchanged pagination.

Ecl. Proph.: Eclogae Propheticae, Prophetic Extracts
T. Gaisford, *Eusebii Caesariensis Eclogae Propheticae* (Oxford, 1842), reprinted in *PG* 22.1021–1262.

HE: Historia Ecclesiastica, Ecclesiastical History
E. Schwartz, *Eusebius' Werke* 2 (*GCS* 9.1, 1903; 9.2, 1908; 9.3, 1909).
Subsequent editions closely based on Schwartz's are:

K. Lake, Loeb Classical Library 1 (1926), 2 (1932), with English translation (vol. 2 translated by J. E. L. Oulton).

G. Bardy, *Sources Chrétiennes* 31 (1952); 41 (1955); 55 (1958); 73 (1960), with French translation.

In addition to the Loeb translation, there are the following English translations of Schwartz's text:

H. J. Lawlor and J. E. L. Oulton (London: Society for the Promotion of Christian Knowledge, 1927).

R. J. Deferrari, *Fathers of the Church* 19 (1953); 29 (1955).

J. A. Williamson (Harmsworth: Penguin, 1965).

Of these the version by Lawlor and Oulton is the most reliable.

Mart. Pal.: De Martyribus Palaestinae, Martyrs of Palestine
Short recension (S):
printed in their editions of *HE* by E. Schwartz, *GCS* 9.2 (1908), 907–950; G. Bardy, *Sources Chrétiennes* 55 (1958), 121–174.
Long recension (L):
(a) the Syriac text was edited by W. Cureton (London, 1861).
(b) Greek fragments were published by H. Delehaye, *Analecta Bollandiana* 16 (1897), 113–139, and are printed by Schwartz and Bardy in parallel with the corresponding sections of the short recension.

For the long recension I have used the German translation by B. Violet, *Texte und Untersuchungen* 14.4 (1896), and the composite English translation of both recensions which Lawlor and Oulton append to their version of the *Ecclesiastical History* (327–400).

Onom.: Onomasticon, On the Place-Names in Holy Scripture
E. Klostermann, *Eusebius' Werke* 3.1 (*GCS* 11.1, 1904).

PE: Praeparatio Evangelica, Preparation for the Gospel
K. Mras, *Eusebius' Werke* 8 (*GCS* 43.1, 1954; 43.2, 1956).
J. Sirinelli and others, *Sources Chrétiennes* (in progress). The following volumes have so far been published: *PE* 1, by J. Sirinelli and E. des Places (*SC* 206, 1974); *PE* 2–3, by E. des Places (*SC* 228, 1976); *PE* 4–5.17, by O. Zink and E. des Places (*SC* 262, 1979); *PE* 5.18–36 and 6, by E. des Places (*SC* 266, 1980): *PE* 7, by G. Schroeder and E. des Places (*SC* 216, 1975).
E. H. Gifford (Oxford, 1903); edition, translation, and commentary.

Theophany
H. Gressmann, *Eusebius' Werke* 3.2: *Die Theophanie: Die griechischen Bruchstücke und Übersetzung der syrischen Überlieferungen* (*GCS* 11.2, 1904).
The Syriac text was first edited by S. Lee (London, 1842), who also published an English translation (Cambridge, 1843).

Triac. 1–10: Oratio de Laudibus Constantini 1–10, Panegyric to Constantine
I. A. Heikel, *Eusebius' Werke* 1 (*GCS* 7, 1902), 195–223.

Triac. 11–18: Oratio de Laudibus Constantini 11–18, Treatise on the Church of the Holy Sepulcher

I. A. Heikel, *Eusebius' Werke* 1 (*GCS* 7, 1902), 223–259.

H. A. Drake, *In Praise of Constantine: A Historical Study and New Translation of Eusebius' Tricennial Orations* (Berkeley, 1976), 83–127.
    The *Panegyric* and the *Treatise* are separate works, but they are normally edited together as an appendix to the *Life of Constantine;* I have, therefore, retained the conventional consecutive numbering of the chapters.

VC: Vita Constantini, Life of Constantine
F. Winkelmann, *Eusebius' Werke* 1.1^2 (*GCS*, 1975).
    There has been no English translation of the *Life* since that by E. C. Richardson, *A Select Library of Nicene and Post-Nicene Fathers*, Second Series 1 (Oxford and New York, 1890), 481–540, which was a revision, in the light of the edition by F. Heinichen (Leipzig, 1869) of the anonymous translation first published by S. Bagster (London, 1845).

ABBREVIATIONS

For modern works of reference and for articles in scholarly periodicals, conventional abbreviations which should be easily recognizable are used, but as an additional aid the bibliography includes the full titles of all books and periodical publications which the notes cite in an abbreviated form. For the abbreviations used in citing Eusebius, see Editions and Translations of Eusebius. The following are the principal abbreviations used in adducing ancient evidence:

ACW	*Ancient Christian Writers* (Westminster, Md., 1946–)
AE	*L'Année Épigraphique*
BHL	*Bibliotheca Hagiographica Latina* (Brussels, 1898–1911)
CCL	*Corpus Christianorum,* Series Latina
CIL	*Corpus Inscriptionum Latinarum*
CJ	*Codex Justinianus*
CSEL	*Corpus Scriptorum Ecclesiasticorum Latinorum*
CTh	*Codex Theodosianus*

Chr. Min.	*Chronica Minora Saec. IV. V. VI. VII.*, ed. T. Mommsen (*Monumenta Germaniae Historica*, Auctores Antiquissimi 9, 1892; 11, 1894; 13, 1898)
EOMIA	C. H. Turner and others, *Ecclesiae Occidentalis Monumenta Iuris Antiquissima* (Oxford, 1899–1939)
FGrH	F. Jacoby, *Die Fragmente der Griechischen Historiker* (Berlin/Leiden, 1923–)
FIRA²	S. Riccobono and others, *Fontes Iuris Romani Antejustiniani²* (Florence, 1941–1943)
GCS	*Die griechischen christlichen Schriftsteller der ersten (drei) Jahrhunderte* (Leipzig and Berlin, 1898–)
HA	*Historia Augusta*
ILCV	H. Diehl, *Inscriptiones Latinae Christianae Veteres* (Berlin, 1925–1931)
ILS	H. Dessau, *Inscriptiones Latinae Selectae* (Berlin, 1892–1916)
Opitz, *Urkunden*	H.-G. Opitz, *Athanasius' Werke 3.1: Urkunden zur Geschichte des arianischen Streites* (Berlin, 1934)
PG	J. P. Migne, *Patrologia Graeca*
PL	J. P. Migne, *Patrologia Latina*
PO	*Patrologia Orientalis*
RIC	*The Roman Imperial Coinage* (London, 1920–)
SC	*Sources Chrétiennes*
Soden, *Urkunden*	H. von Soden and H. Lietzmann, *Urkunden zur Entstehungsgeschichte des Donatismus²* (*Kleine Texte* 122, 1950)

NOTES

I. DIOCLETIAN AND MAXIMIAN

1. For the day, *CIL* 1^2, pp. 255, 258, 259; for the approximate year, Eusebius, *VC* 1.8.1; 4.53. For full discussion of the age, career, and family of Constantine, see *New Empire*, ch. IV.

2. Firmicus Maternus, *Math.* 1.10.16; *Origo* 2.

3. Julian, *Misopogon* 348d; cf. R. Syme, *BHAC 1971* (1974), 237 ff.

4. *Origo* 1 f.; Jerome, *Chronicle* 231^h.

5. *Origo* 2; *Pan. Lat.* 6(7).5.2; *HA, Carus* 17.6.

6. *Pan. Lat.* 10(2).11.4; 8(5).1.6 ff.

7. *Pan. Lat.* 8(5).2.2 ff.; *Chr. Min.* 1.229.

8. *Origo* 2.

9. *Pan. Lat.* 10(2).11.4.

10. *Origo* 14 shows that she was a married woman by 315/6 (cf. Chapter V).

11. On Anastasius and Anastasia as Jewish and Christian names, G. Delling, *TLZ* 76 (1951), 521 ff.

12. *Epitome* 39.7; Lactantius, *Mort. Pers.* 19.5.

13. Lactantius, *Mort. Pers.* 9.11, 19.5, 52.3; Eutropius, *Brev.* 9.19.2.

14. Victor, *Caes.* 39.1; *HA, Carus* 13.1; Zonaras 12.31.

15. On the rebellion and reign of Carus, Victor, *Caes.* 38; Eutropius, *Brev.* 9.18 f.; Festus, *Brev.* 24; Jerome, *Chronicle* 224^g; *HA, Carus* 8.1; Zosimus 1.71.4ff. For Carus' titles, *PIR²* A 1475. By 284 Carinus and Numerianus are attested as *Germanici maximi, Brittannici maximi, Persici maximi* (*ILS* 608: near Ostia).

16. *CJ* 8.53.5 (26 January 284); *ILS* 608.

17. *CJ* 5.52.2 (Emesa, 16 March 284). Coins of Cyzicus advertise *Adventus Augg. nn.* (*RIC* 5.2.177, 201).

18. Victor, *Caes.* 38.7 ff; Eutropius, *Brev.* 9.18.2 ff.; *Epitome* 38.4 ff. For the date and place, *P. Beatty Panopolis* 2.163 etc.; Lactantius, *Mort. Pers.* 17.1; 19.2 (as amended in *New Empire*, ch. V: Galerius, n. 73); Zosimus 1.73.2 = John of Antioch, frag. 162.

19. *AE* 1964.223.

20. *Chr. Pasch.* 509 Bonn = *Chr. Min.* 1.229; Syncellus 729 Bonn.

21. Observe old clichés in the extant speeches of 289 and 291: Diocletian acted *ad restituendam rem publicam* (*Pan. Lat.* 10(2).3.1), and the result was *res publica dominatu saevissimo liberata* (*Pan. Lat.* 11(3).5.3).

22. On Julianus, *PIR²* A 1538. The evidence is contradictory—which induces *PLRE* 1.474, 480, to posit two men called Julianus, both Augusti in 284/5.

23. Victor, *Caes.* 39.11 f.; Eutropius, *Brev.* 9.19 f.; *Epitome* 38.7 f.; Zosimus 1.73.3 = John of Antioch, frag. 163.

24. *RIC* 5.2.241 no. 204; Zonaras 12.31.

25. *AE* 1964.223; cf. *New Empire*, ch. VII.

26. Viz., M. Junius Maximus, apparently of a long-established senatorial family (*PIR²* J 774–776).

27. And conceivably praetorian prefect before 288 (*New Empire*, ch. VIII).

28. Victor, *Caes.* 39.15. Observe also C. Ceionius Rufius Volusianus, appointed *corrector* in Italy by Carus but retained in the past for eight years in all (*CIL* 10.1655; *ILS* 1213). He was a relative, probably nephew, of Ceionius Varus, the *praefectus urbi* replaced by Bassus (T. D. Barnes, *JRS* 65 [1975], 45).

29. *Epitome* 40.10 (birthplace); *Pan. Lat.* 10(2).2.5 f. (career); Victor, *Caes.* 39.17 (*fidum amicitia*).

30. Eutropius, *Brev.* 9.20.3; *Passio Marcelli* 2; cf. *New Empire*, ch. I.

31. For Diocletian's movements in 285–287, *New Empire*, ch. V.

32. *Pan. Lat.* 8(5).21.1 (before 288).

33. *Pan. Lat.* 10(2).7.5, 9.1, 10.6 f.; 11(3).5.4, 8(5).3.3. Hence Diocletian is styled *Persicus maximus* on a dedication made in 290 (*ILS* 618).

34. M.-L. Chaumont, *Recherches sur l'histoire d'Arménie de l'avènement des Sassanides à la conversion du royaume* (Paris, 1969), 49 ff., 93 ff.

35. *Pan. Lat.* 10(2).4.2 ff.; Victor, *Caes.* 39.19; Eutropius, *Brev.* 9.20.3. Maximian was at Milan on 10 February 286 (*CJ* 8.53(54).6 + 3.29.4 = *Frag. Vat.* 282).

36. Victor, *Caes.* 39.20 f.; Eutropius, *Brev.* 9.21; cf. *New Empire*, chs. I, II, and V: Maximian.

37. *Pan. Lat.* 10(2).6.2 ff. Observe a *protector* killed by a Frank on barbarian soil near Deutz (*ILS* 2784: undated).

38. *Pan. Lat.* 10(2).12.1 ff.

39. *Pan. Lat.* 10(2).9.1, 11(3).5.4, 7.1.

40. *Pan. Lat.* 10(2).10.3 f., 11.4 ff., 11(3).7.2, 8(5).21.1.

41. *Pan. Lat.* 10(2).12.1 ff.

42. *Pan. Lat.* 8(5).12.2.

43. *RIC* 5.2.550 ff., esp. 550 no. 1 (*Carausius et fratres sui*).

44. *Pan. Lat.* 11(3).4.2. For a possible visit to Rome by Maximian in 289 or 290, see *New Empire*, ch. V: Maximian.

45. *Pan. Lat.* 8(5).2.1: *a ponte Rheni usque ad Danubii transitum Guntiensem deusta . . . Alamannia.* Guntia appears to be the modern Günzburg, near Augsburg (M. Ihm, *RE* 7 [1912], 1943).

46. *Pan. Lat.* 11(3).2.4, 8.1 ff.

47. *Frag. Vat.* 315 implies his presence at Durocortorum (Reims) on 18 February 291. Carausius held Rouen till 293 (*RIC* 5.2.516 ff.).

48. *New Empire*, ch. V: Maximian.

49. For Diocletian's activities between 287 and 293, *New Empire*, ch. V: Diocletian.

50. Chapter II.

51. *New Empire*, ch. XI.

52. Gregory of Nazianzus, *Orat.* 4.46 (*PG* 35.570).

53. T. Mommsen, *Römisches Staatsrecht* 2^3 (Leipzig, 1887), 1135 ff.; B. Parsi, *Désignation et investiture de l'empereur romain, Ier et IIe siècles après J.-C.* (Paris, 1963), 8 ff.

54. *Pan. Lat.* 10(2).3.1, 4.1, 9.1 ff.; Lactantius, *Mort. Pers.* 8.1 (the Augusti as brothers); *ILS* 646; *AE* 1961.240; *Pan. Lat.* 7(6).14.4 ff. (the Caesars as sons of the Augusti).

55. Both marriages are dated to 293 by the narrative sources (*Origo* 1; Victor, *Caes.* 39.24 f.; Eutropius, *Brev.* 9.22.1; *Epitome* 39.2). That is disproved for Constantius by *Pan. Lat.* 10(2).11.4, and may be equally false for Galerius.

56. *Pan. Lat.* 10(2).14.1 f.

57. Viz., Valeria Maximilla (*ILS* 666, 671)—who could well be a child of Valeria, the daughter of Diocletian (*New Empire*, ch. IV). Maxentius married Maximilla before 305 (Lactantius, *Mort. Pers.* 18.9), and by 312 they had produced at least two sons (*ILS* 667; *Pan. Lat.* 12(9).16.5).

58. Lactantius, *Mort. Pers.* 18.9, implies his recent presence at the court of either Diocletian or Galerius.

59. *Origo* 2; *Pan. Lat.* 7(6).6.2.

60. *New Empire*, ch. V.

61. Lactantius, *Mort. Pers.* 7.2.

62. Victor, *Caes.* 39.31: *parti Italiae invectum tributorum ingens malum.* Lactantius, *Mort. Pers.* 23.5, implies that the suburbicarian provinces remained exempt from direct taxation until 306.

63. *New Empire*, chs. XII, XIII.

64. *New Empire*, ch. XIII.

65. A. H. M. Jones, *The Later Roman Empire* (Oxford, 1964), 1.43 ff.

66. *New Empire*, ch. IX. Between 293 and 305 the only other province which can be shown to have had a governor of senatorial status is the combined Phrygia and Caria.

67. Lactantius, *Mort. Pers.* 7.4; cf. *PLRE* 1.1062 ff.

68. E. Stein, *Histoire du Bas-Empire* 1[2] (Paris and Bruges, 1959), 67 ff.

69. C. H. V. Sutherland, *RIC* 6 (1967), 3 ff., 93 ff. The reorganization of the mint appears to be intimately connected with the creation of the dioceses; cf. M. Hendy, *JRS* 62 (1972), 65 ff.

70. For its official status, *CTh* 1.1.5 (429): *ad similitudinem Gregoriani atque Hermogeniani codicis cunctas colligi constitutiones decernimus, quas Constantinus inclitus et post eum divi principes nosque tulimus.* Note also the omission of Gregorius and Hermogenianus from the private jurists whose authority is weighed in *CTh* 1.4.3 (426).

Nothing is known about the career of Gregorius, and Hermogenianus is only explicitly attested as the holder of an official post by the fictitious *Passio Sabini* (*BHL* 7451–7454), which makes him (apparently) praetorian prefect of Maximian in 304 (cf. *New Empire*, ch. VIII). However, Aurelius Arcadius Charisius wrote on the duties of praetorian prefects while *magister libellorum*, probably under Diocletian (*Dig.* 1.11.1), and Eunapius reports that Innocentius of Sardis, grandfather of the philosopher Chrysanthius (born c. 315), enjoyed a "law-giving power" conferred by the emperors, i.e., presumably, Diocletian and his colleagues. He too may have held a post in the imperial chancery; see F. Schulz, *Roman Legal Science* (Oxford, 1946), 114, n. 6. The codes of Gregorius and Hermogenianus were not "private collections" (as stated by L. Wenger, *Die Quellen des römischen Rechts* [Vienna, 1953], 534 ff.); indeed, A. M. Honoré, *JRS* 69 (1979), 58 ff., argues that Hermogenianus himself drafted the rescripts of 293–295 as *a libellis* to Diocletian.

71. On Roman jurisprudence between 235 and 284, F. Wieacker, *Rev. Hist. du Droit* 49 (1971), 201 ff.

72. For the date of the codes, G. Rotondi, *Scritti giuridici* 1 (Rome, 1922), 111 ff.; on their sources, P. Krüger, *Geschichte der Quellen und Litteratur des römischen Rechtes* (Leipzig, 1888), 282 ff.; J. Gaudemet, *La formation du droit séculier et du droit de l'église au IVe et Ve siècles* (Paris, 1957), 40 ff. In March 292, Diocletian ordained that the originals of rescripts subscribed in the emperor's hand be retained in the imperial archives (*CJ* 1.23.3); previously, the originals were displayed in a public place; cf. U. Wilcken, *Hermes* 55 (1920), 1 ff.; *Archiv für Papyrusforschung* 9 (1930), 15 ff.; W. Williams *JRS* 64 (1974), 86 ff.

73. Respectively, O. Lenel, *Palingenesia Iuris Civilis* 1 (Leipzig, 1889), 266 ff., with D. Liebs, *Hermogenians Iuris Epitomae* (Göttingen, 1964); *FIRA*[2] 3.321 ff., with the fragment of the full text published by G. G. Archi, M. David, E. Levy, R. Marichal, and H. L. W. Nelson, *Pauli Sententiarum Fragmentum Leidense* (*Studia Gaiana* 4, 1956), 5 ff. R. Marichal, ibid., 57, dates the fragment c. 300 on palaeographical grounds.

74. *New Empire*, ch. XIII.

75. Viz., 1 lb. gold = 36,000 denarii; cf. S. Bolin, *State and Currency in the Roman Empire to 300 A.D.* (Stockholm, 1958), 291 ff.

By 16 February 300, 1 lb. gold was worth 60,000 denarii (*P. Beatty Panopolis* 2.215 ff.), and the price edict states the maximum price of 1 lb. gold, whether ingots, coin, or fashioned into jewelry, as 72,000 denarii (R. Naumann, *Der Rundbau in Aezani* [*Istanbuler Mitteilungen*, Beiheft 10, 1973] 57; M. H. Crawford and J. M. Reynolds, *ZPE* 34 [1979], 176). Most modern analyses of Diocletian's monetary policies are based on the erroneous premise that the price edict attests the equation 1 lb. gold = 50,000 denarii (as in the edition of S. Lauffer, *Diokletians Preisedikt* [*Texte und Kommentare* 5, 1971], 191). On the importance of recent discoveries as they invalidate all earlier theories, J. Jahn, *JNG* 25 (1975), 91 ff.

76. *AE* 1973.526; cf. E. Ruschenbush, *ZPE* 26 (1977), 193 ff. He identifies *PSI* 965, *P. Oslo* 83, and *P. Rylands* 607 as also referring to the currency reform (206 ff.).

77. *CIL* 3, pp. 802 ff.; S. Lauffer, *Diokletians Preisedikt* 90 ff. *ILS* 642 unfortunately abbreviates the preamble.

78. S. Lauffer, *Diokletians Preisedikt* 14 ff.

79. Published by M. H. Crawford and J. Reynolds, *JRS* 65 (1975), 160, with Plate II. Revisions to their text are proposed by J. H. Oliver, *AJP* 97 (1976), 174 f.

80. J. and L. Robert, *Bulletin Épigraphique* 1964.69.

81. L. C. West, *CP* 34 (1939), 239 ff.

82. Lactantius, *Mort. Pers.* 7.6 f. (blaming Diocletian for creating the high prices). The price of gold continued to rise, soon reaching 100,000 denarii per pound (*P. Oxy.* 2106).

83. W. Seston, *Dioclétien et la Tétrarchie* 1 (Paris, 1946), 193 ff.; H. P. L'Orange, *Art Forms and Civic Life in the Late Roman Empire* (Princeton, 1965), 46 ff.

84. *Pan. Lat.* 10(2).2.1, 11(3)10.5.

85. *Pan. Lat.* 10(2).11.6.

86. *ILS* 634 (the Arch of Galerius at Thessalonica). Note the neat formulation in *Pan. Lat.* 9(4).8.1: *Caesar Herculius* (sc. Constantius) *et avi Herculis et Herculi patris instinctu*.

87. *P. Argent.* 480, 1 verso 5 ff.

88. *ILS* 631–633; Lactantius, *Mort. Pers.* 8.9; Julian, *Orat.* 7, 228d; cf. H. Castritius, *Studien zu Maximinus Daia* (*Frankfurter althistorische Studien* 2, 1969), 25 ff.

89. For these sentiments, *Pan. Lat.* 9(4).18.1 ff., 11(3).15.3 f., 8(5).10.1 ff., 18.3.

90. *Pan. Lat.* 8(5).18.5, 10.4, 10(2).3.3 f.

91. Lactantius, *Mort. Pers.* 7.1 ff. Galerius has the nickname Armentarius ("shepherd-boy") in Victor, *Caes.* 40.1 ff.; *Epitome* 39.2, 40.1, but according to Eutropius, he was *vir et probe moratus et egregius re militari* (*Brev.* 10.2.1).

92. *Pan. Lat.* 8(5), 9(4); Lactantius, *Mort. Pers.* 8.7; Eusebius, *VC* 1.13.3 ff.

93. Jerome, *De Viris Illustribus* 80. On his *nomen* (Caecilius rather than Caelius), Schanz-Hosius, *Gesch. d. röm. Litt.* 3[3] (Munich, 1922), 414. For a conspectus of modern chronologies of his works, see M. Perrin, *Lactance: "L'Ouvrage du Dieu Createur"* (*SC* 213 [1974]), facing p. 220. The fact that Lactantius was *accitus cum Fabio grammatico* implies that the summons was official.

94. A. Wlosok, *Laktanz und die philosophische Gnosis* (Heidelberg, 1960), 191 f.; *TU* 79 (1961), 234 ff.; H. Kraft and A. Wlosok, *Laktanz: "Vom Zorne Gottes"*[2] (*Texte zur Forschung* 4 [1971]), viii ff.

95. *De Opificio Dei* 1.1 ff.; *Div. Inst.* 5.4.1; cf. S. Brandt, *Sb. Wien*, Phil.-hist. Klasse 120 (1890), Abh. 5.25; J. Stevenson, *TU* 63 (1957), 661 ff.

96. E. Heck, *Die dualistischen Zusätze und die Kaiseranreden bei Lactantius* (Heidelberg, 1972), has demonstrated that the invocations of Constantine (*Div. Inst.* 1.1.13 ff., 7.26.11 ff.) belong to a revision of the text by Lactantius begun in 324 and probably never completed. He has also demonstrated that Lactantius composed and published the seven books as a unity before 311 (143 ff.; see also P. Monat, *Lactance: "Institutions divines," Libre V* 1 [*SC* 204 (1973)], 11 ff., 87 ff.). The date of completion can be defined éven more precisely. Lactantius not only alludes to Galerius as an active persecutor (5.11.5 f.) but writes as if none of the persecuting emperors has yet perished (5.23.1 ff.). That implies a date before the death of Maximian c. July 310; see A. Ebert, *Berichte Leipzig,* Phil.-hist. Classe 22 (1870), 125 ff.; K. Jagelitz, *Über den Verfasser der Schrift "De Mortibus Persecutorum"* (Prog. Berlin, 1910), 5 ff. Hence Lactantius may have completed the work as early as 308 or 309 (S. Brandt, *Sb. Wien,* Phil.-hist. Klasse 125 [1892], Abh. 6.16, 134; S. Prete, *Gymnasium* 63 [1956], 498 ff.).

The milieu in which Lactantius wrote the *Divine Institutes* is harder to establish than the date. Many scholars have argued that the author of *On the Deaths of the Persecutors* was in Nicomedia, not only from 303 to 305 (*Div. Inst.* 5.2.2, 11.15), but also in 311 and 313 (so E. Heck, *Die dualistischen Zusätze,* 144, 158 f.). But the eyewitness account of Donatus' release in 311 (*Mort. Pers.* 35.1 f.) may derive from Donatus' report, not from Lactantius' own observation. Lactantius clearly left Bithynia (*Div. Inst.* 5.2.2, 5.11.5), and a Latin work of this compass appears to presuppose a Latin-speaking audience—which hardly existed in the East, except at Nicomedia. Moreover, many passages imply composition in the West (e.g., *Div. Inst.* 2.12.15, 3.3.14, 3.14.10, 4.9.1, 4.27.3 ff.: on *mali reges,* i.e., Diocletian and Galerius; 5.9.10, 6.20.16: *neque militare iusto licebit*). Consequently, it is an easy inference that Lactantius left Bithynia in or shortly after 305, went to Gaul, and completed the *Institutes* there (as argued by S. Brandt, *Sb. Wien,* Phil.-hist. Klasse 125 [1892], Abh. 6.18 ff.; R. Pichon, *Lactance: Étude sur le mouvement philosophique et religieux sous le règne de Constantin* [Paris, 1901], 356 ff.; V. Loi, *Mélanges C. Mohrmann* [Utrecht and Antwerp, 1973], 61 ff.; R. M. Ogilvie, *The Library of Lactantius* [Oxford, 1978], 2). But why then did he not dedicate the first edition to Constantine, whom he regarded as the protector of Christianity from the day of his accession in 306 (*Mort. Pers.* 24.9; *Div. Inst.* 1.1.13)?

Both *a priori* considerations and certain indications in the text suggest that Lactantius completed the *Divine Institutes* in Africa under the régime of Domitius Alexander. On the one hand, it is a legitimate conjecture that Lactantius returned to his native Africa when Galerius became ruler of Asia Minor in 305. On the other, the *Divine Institutes* alludes to the reputation of Apuleius as a magician (5.3.7), and perhaps to the disputed episcopal election at Carthage which began the Donatist schism (4.30.5), while a reference to visiting *populorum atque urbium principes* (6.12.12) may also reflect conditions in Carthage. It is clear that Lactantius was not writing in Rome (see *Div. Inst.* 3.17.12, 3.20.3, 6.9.4, 7.25.7 f.). Moreover, the hostile way in which he alludes to Maxentius' exile of a bishop of Rome (6.6.13 f.; cf. R. Pichon, *Lactance* 20 f.) implies that he did not complete the work while a subject of Maxentius. The hypothesis that Lactantius completed the *Divine Institutes* in Africa in 308/9, even though it cannot formally be proved, best satisfies the available evidence.

97. Jerome, *Chronicle* 230^e Helm; *De Viris Illustribus* 80. The date is normally assumed to be after 313 (J. Steinhauser, *Trierer Zeitschrift* 20 [1951], 127 ff.), but that date relies on the assumption that Crispus was born c. 305—which is vulnerable if not demonstrably erroneous (*New Empire,* ch. IV).

98. Under the terms of the *litterae Licinii* posted in Nicomedia in June 313 (*Mort. Pers.* 48.2 ff.; cf. Chapter V).

99. Lactantius wrote *On the Anger of God* after June 313 (16.4), perhaps when Licinius and Constantine became estranged in 316 (24.12 [23.26]; cf. J. Stevenson, *TU* 63 [1957], 675). He addresses this work to a Donatus who is presumably identical with the addressee of *On the Deaths of the Persecutors,* and he justifies assumptions about divine anger made in that book which Donatus' friends found philosophically repugnant (1.1 f., 22.1 ff.). The *Epitome,* but not the *Divine Institutes* which it abbreviates, shows acquaintance with the Middle Platonic theory of a First and Second God (37.4). Lactantius wrote the *Epitome* no earlier than c. 320 (61 [66].1 ff.) and in the East, for he assumes that crucifixion is still a normal punishment for *humiliores* (*Epit.* 46 [51].3; cf. Chapter IV, n. 83).

100. *Mort. Pers.* 1.1, 35.1 f. On the date, T. D. Barnes, *JRS* 63 (1973), 29 ff. Donatus may, like Lactantius, be an African; on the name, cf. R. Syme, *Historia* 27 (1980), 588 ff.

101. M. Gelzer, *Kleine Schriften* 2 (Wiesbaden, 1963), 378 ff. On Lactantius' invective, I. Opelt, *JAC* 16 (1973), 98 ff. J. Rougé, *TU* 115 (1976), 135 ff., characterizes the work as "un véritable cinquième livre des Macchabées."

102. H. Grégoire, *Revue de l'Université de Bruxelles* 36 (1930/1), 252 ff.; *Byzantion* 14 (1939), 341 ff.; J. Moreau, *Lactance: "De la mort des persécuteurs"* (*SC* 39 [1954]), 34 ff.; E. Heck, *Die dualistischen Zusätze,* 159.

103. See the full commentary of J. Moreau, *Lactance,* 187 ff.

104. J.-R. Palanque, *Mélanges J. Carcopino* (Paris, 1966), 711 ff.

105. T. D. Barnes, *JRS* 63 (1973), 39 ff. In 7.9 ff., the repeated *hic* should mean "here, in Nicomedia"; see J. Moreau, *Lactance,* 256 ff.

106. *Mort. Pers.* 18.1 ff., 24.9.

II. GALERIUS AND THE CHRISTIANS

1. E. N. Luttwak, *The Grand Strategy of the Roman Empire* (Baltimore and London, 1976) 176 ff.

2. *Pan. Lat.* 11(3).16.4 ff. In 17.2 Galletier and Mynors both print *adscitis Sacis et Rufiis et Gelis:* the second name should be emended to *Cusiis;* see J. Marquart, *Abh. Göttingen,* Phil.-hist. Kl., N.F. 3.2 (1901), 36, n. 2; E. Herzfeld, *Paikuli* (*Forschungen zur islamischen Kunst* 3, 1924), 91 f.

3. *Pan. Lat.* 8(5).6.1 ff., 6(7).5.2.

4. *Pan. Lat.* 6(7).5.3, 8(5).12.2; *RIC* 5.2.558 ff.

5. *Pan. Lat.* 8(5).8.1ff., 6(7).5.3; cf. *New Empire,* tables 4, 5, 7.

6. *Pan. Lat.* 8(5).9.3, 21.1.

7. *Pan. Lat.* 8(5).14.4 ff.; cf. D. E. Eichholz, *JRS* 43 (1953), 41 ff. For the role of Asclepiodotus (predictably not named in the speech of 297), Victor, *Caes.* 39.42; Eutropius, *Brev.* 9.22; Jerome, *Chronicle* 227^a.

8. *Pan. Lat.* 6(7).5.4, 8(5).19.1 ff.; *RIC* 6.167, Treveri 34.

9. *Pan. Lat.* 8(5).13.3.

10. Victor, *Caes.* 39.23; Eutropius, *Brev.* 9.22.

11. *P. Argent.* 480, 1 verso 3.

12. *Pan. Lat.* 8(5).5.3; cf. *ILS* 645 (Tubusuctu).

13. *Frag. Vat.* 41; *RIC* 6.422–426, Carthago 1, 2, 10–28; *Pan. Lat.* 9(4).21.2, 7(6).8.7 (Rome).

14. For Maximian's movements between 293 and 305, *New Empire,* ch. V:Maximian.

15. Lactantius, *Mort. Pers.* 8.4; cf. L. Poinssot, *MSNAF* 76 (1919–23), 299 ff.

16. *Pan. Lat.* 6(7).6.2 ff.; cf. T. D. Barnes, *Phoenix* 30 (1976), 179, 191.

17. Diocletian's movements are attested by very numerous laws of 293 and 294 (*New Empire,* ch. V: Diocletian). For the hypothesis that Galerius was invested as Caesar at Sirmium, not at Nicomedia, ibid., ch. V: Galerius, n. 73 (on Lactantius, *Mort. Pers.* 19.2; *Chr. Pasch.* 521 Bonn = *Chr. Min.* 1.229).

18. *Chr. Min.* 1.230, cf. A. Alföldi, *Arch. Ert.* 2³ (1941), 49 ff.

19. *Pan. Lat.* 8(5).5.1f. aludes to *Sarmaticae expeditiones* and *proxima illa ruina Carporum* (cf. *New Empire,* tables 4, 5, 7). For a full discussion of Diocletian's activities on the middle and lower Danube, see P. Brennan, *Chiron* 10 (1980), 562 ff.

20. *New Empire,* ch. V: Galerius. Eusebius provides the central item of evidence: in 311 Galerius possessed the titles *Aegyptiacus maximus Thebaicus maximus* for victories won in or shortly after 293 (*HE* 8.17.3).

The only evidence that Diocletian came to the East between 293 and 296 is *Mos. et Rom. Legum Collatio* 6.4 = *CJ* 5.4.17, which can be attributed to Galerius (*New Empire,* ch. V: Galerius, n. 76).

21. Viz., Hormizd (272–3), Vahram I (273–276), Vahram II (276–293), Vahram III (293); see T. Nöldeke, *Geschichte der Perser und Araber zur Zeit der Sasaniden* (Leiden, 1879), 414 ff.; M. Sprengling, *AJSL* 57 (1940), 197 ff.; *Third Century Iran: Sapor and Kartir* (Chicago, 1953), 47 ff.

22. Narseh had been governing the eastern portions of Armenia: on his seizure of power in 293 and subsequent policies, A. Christensen, *L'Iran sous les Sassanides*² (Copenhagen, 1944), 220 ff.; W. B. Henning, *BSOAS* 14 (1952), 517 ff.

23. Hence the title *Persici maximi* for all four emperors; see *New Empire,* tables 4, 5, revising the chronology proposed by T. D. Barnes, *Phoenix* 30 (1976), 186 f.

24. Ammianus 23.5.11; Zonaras 12.31. The Armenian historian Faustus appears to preserve details of Narseh's campaign misdated by forty years (3.20 f.); cf. P. Peeters, *Bull. Acad. Roy. de Belgique,* Classe des Lettres⁵ 17 (1931), 18 ff.

25. *P. Argent.* 480, 1 verso; cf. T. D. Barnes, *Phoenix* 30 (1976), 183.

26. Eutropius, *Brev.* 9.24; Festus, *Brev.* 25; Ammianus 14.11.10.

27. *P. Cairo Isid.* 1; cf. *New Empire,* ch. XIV.

28. On the date, *New Empire,* ch. II.

29. For full discussion of the evidence relating to the revolt, see J. D. Thomas, *ZPE* 22 (1976), 253 ff.

30. *Pan. Lat.* 9(4).21.2; Eutropius, *Brev.* 9.23, with the additions in Paeanius' translation (*MGH,* Auct. Ant. 2 [1878], 165).

31. For Diocletian's movements, *New Empire,* ch. V: Diocletian. A contemporary rhetorical handbook refers to the alliance with the Blemmyes and Erembi (O. Spengel, *Rhetores Graeci* 3 [Leipzig, 1856], 387), which is described in detail by Procopius, *Bella* 1.19.27 ff. On the military and political situation in Upper Egypt, see J. Desanges, *CE* 44 (1969), 139 ff.; L. Castiglione, *ZÄS* 96 (1970), 90 ff.; A. K. Bowman, *BASP* 15 (1978), 25 ff.; on the local effects of the treaty, W. Y. Adams, *Nubia, Corridor to Africa* (London, 1977), 389, 419 ff.

32. *P. Beatty Panopolis* 1; *CJ* 8.53(54).24, as emended by T. Mommsen, *Ges. Schr.* 2 (Berlin, 1905), 289.

33. Victor, *Caes.* 39.34 ff.; Eutropius, *Brev.* 9.25; Festus, *Brev.* 25. Hence Lactantius' taunt that Diocletian *hunc per Armeniam misit ipse in Oriente subsistens et aucupans exitus rerum* (*Mort. Pers.* 9.6).

34. Implied by imperial victory titles (*New Empire,* tables 4–7).

35. Joshua the Stylite, *Chronicle,* trans. W. Wright (Cambridge, 1882), 6.

36. *HA, Carus* 9.3; Constantine, *Oratio* 16.4 (quoted and discussed in *New Empire,* ch. IV, n. 59); cf. H. P. Laubscher, *Der Reliefschmuck des Galeriusbogens in Thessaloniki* (*Archäologische Forschungen* 1, 1975), 16 f.

37. Ammianus 24.1.10.

38. Petrus Patricius, frag. 13. It is wrong to doubt the flaying; cf. B. H. Stolte, *Rivista storica di antichità* 1 (1971), 159 ff.

39. Petrus Patricius, frag. 14, as elucidated by P. Peeters, *Bull. Acad. Roy. de Belgique,* Classe des Lettres[5], 17 (1931), 25 ff.; M.-L. Chaumont, *Recherches sur l'histoire d'Arménie* (Paris, 1969), 121 ff. Petrus names the five *Transtigritanae regiones* as Intilene, Sophene, Arzanene, Cardyene, and Zabdicene; Ammianus, as Arzanene, Moxoene, Zabdicene, Rehimene, and Cordyene (25.7.9; cf. Zosimus 3.31).

40. Lactantius, *Div. Inst.* 4.27.4 f.; *Mort. Pers.* 10.1 ff.; Eusebius, *HE* 8.1.7, 4.2 ff.; Jerome, *Chronicle* 227[d].

41. Lactantius, *Mort. Pers.* 12.3, 15.1 f.; Eusebius, *HE* 8.1.3, 6.2 ff.

42. Lactantius, *Mort. Pers.* 9.7 ff.

43. Lactantius, *Mort. Pers.* 10.6 ff., 31.1; Eusebius, *HE* 8, app. 1, 3; Constantine, *Oratio* 22, with the chapter heading as emended by T. D. Barnes, *JTS,* n.s. 27 (1976), 420.

44. *Chr. Min.* 1.290; *Chr. Pasch.* 514; *Mos. et Rom. Legum Collatio* 15.3, cf. *New Empire,* ch. V: Diocletian. Eusebius saw Constantine with Diocletian on the journey to or from Egypt (*VC* 1.19).

45. For the palace complex, see M. Vickers, *JRS* 62 (1972) 25 ff., 63 (1973) 111 ff.; for the arch, H. P. Laubscher, *Der Reliefschmuck des Galeriusbogens,* 103 ff. The mint of Thessalonica opened c. 299, closed in 303, and reopened c. December 308 (C. H. V. Sutherland, *RIC* 6 [1976], 501 ff.)—which suggests that Galerius resided there from 299 to 303, and again after the Conference of Carnuntum in 308 (*New Empire,* ch. V: Galerius). *Origo* 8 implies that Serdica became his main residence in the intervening years.

46. Victor, *Caes.* 39.26 ff., 45 ff.

47. J. P. Callu, *Genio Populi Romani* (*295–316*): *Contribution à une histoire numismatique de la Tétrarchie* (Paris, 1960), 9 ff.

48. H. I. Marrou, *Histoire de l'éducation dans l'antiquité*[6] (Paris, 1965),

376 ff. For the subsequent use (and decline) of Latin in the East, A. H. M. Jones, *The Later Roman Empire* 2 (Oxford, 1964), 988 ff.

49. On the general tenor of Diocletian's legislation, see the varying estimates of E. Albertario, *Studi di diritto romano* 5 (Milan, 1937), 195 ff., 205 ff.; E. Schönbauer, *ZSS*, Rom. Abt. 62 (1942), 267 ff.; *JJP* 9–10 (1955–56), 15 ff.; R. Taubenschlag, *Opera minora* 1 (Warsaw, 1959), 3 ff. (originally published in 1923); M. Amelotti, *Per l'interpretazione della legislazione privatistica di Diocleziano* (Milan, 1960), 109 ff.

50. *Mos. et Rom. Legum Collatio* 6.4 (partly quoted in *CJ* 5.4.17). For the hypothesis that Galerius (not Diocletian) issued the edict, *New Empire,* ch. V: Galerius, n. 76. The edict specifically forbids a man to marry his daughter, granddaughter, great-granddaughter, mother, grandmother, great-grandmother, paternal aunt, maternal aunt, sister, sister's daughter, sister's granddaughter, stepdaughter, stepmother, mother-in-law, daughter-in-law and "all others forbidden by ancient law" (cf. Gaius, *Inst.* 1.56 ff.; *Tituli ex Corpore Ulpiani* 5–7 [*FIRA*² 2.268–271]; *Sententiae Pauli* 2.19; *Dig.* 23.2). The main innovation was to forbid the marriage of siblings, which had long been customary in Greece, Egypt, and elsewhere in the Eastern Empire; see E. Weiss, *ZSS*, Rom. Abt. 29 (1908), 240 ff. But *CTh* 3.12.1 (324) shows that marriage between uncles and nieces continued, at least in Phoenicia.

51. K. Stade, *Der Politiker Diokletian und die letzte grosse Christenverfolgung* (Wiesbaden, 1926), 77 ff.

52. E. Volterra, *La Persia e il mondo greco-romano* (Rome, 1966), 27 ff.

53. T. D. Barnes, *HSCP* 80 (1976), 246 ff.

54. *Mos. et Rom. Legum Collatio* 15.3.

55. Eusebius, *Mart. Pal.* 2.1 ff. It is impossible to assess the relevance of the earthquake which devastated Tyre and Sidon shortly before persecution began (Jerome, *Chronicle* 228ᵃ).

56. Lactantius, *Mort. Pers.* 10.7 ff.; Constantine, in Eusebius, *VC* 2.50 f., cf. *I. Didyma* 306 (with the comments of A. Rehm); Eusebius, *PE* 4.2.11.

57. Lactantius, *Div. Inst.* 5.11.13, reports hearing governors boast that they had not executed a single Christian. In North Africa, it seems that the governor of Byzacena (in contrast to the governors of Africa and Numidia) executed very few Christians: see S. Lancel, *Cahiers de Tunisie* 12 (1964), 142.

58. T. D. Barnes, *Tertullian: A Historical and Literary Study* (Oxford, 1971), 158 ff.

59. *Passio Pionii* 7.1 ff.; *Passio Mariani et Jacobi* 2.2 ff.; *Passio Montani et Lucii* 2. Bishop Fructuosus, however, martyred at Tarraco in 259, was beloved of pagans and Christians alike (*Acta Fructuosi* 3.1).

60. Chapter XI.

61. The *Vita Plotini,* designed as an introduction to the *Enneads,* refers to Porphyry's sixty-eighth year (23.12 ff.); since Porphyry was in his thirtieth year in the summer of 263 (4.1 ff.; cf. T. D. Barnes, *GRBS* 17 [1976], 67 ff.), he must be writing in 300 or 301.

On the date of *Against the Christians,* T. D. Barnes, *JTS,* n.s. 24 (1973), 433 ff.; J. M. Rist, *Basil of Caesarea: Christian, Humanist, Ascetic,* ed. P. J. Fedwick (Toronto, 1981), 142 ff.

62. Eusebius, *PE* 1.2.2 ff., 4.1.3.

63. T. D. Barnes, *JTS,* n.s. 24 (1973), 431 ff. Composition in or near Rome is suggested by a brief quotation in Eusebius, *PE* 5.1.9 f.

64. Lactantius, *Mort. Pers.* 16.4; Eusebius, *C. Hier.* 4, p. 373, 10–11 Kayser; 20, p. 386, 30–1 Kayser.

65. Lactantius, *Div. Inst.* 5.2.13, 3.22; cf. T. D. Barnes, *HSCP* 80 (1976), 240 ff. Eusebius appears to have written his rebuttal of Hierocles before spring 303 (Chapter X).

66. Lactantius, *Div. Inst.* 5.2.12; *Mort. Pers.* 16.4.

67. T. D. Barnes, *GRBS* 19 (1978), 105. Against identifying the philosopher with Porphyry, *JTS,* n.s. 24 (1973), 439 f.

68. Lactantius, *Div. Inst.* 5.2.3 ff. Observe also that the Egyptian poet Soterichus composed both a panegyric on Diocletian and a life of Apollonius of Tyana (*Suda* Σ 877). J. Bidez, *Rev. phil.* 27 (1903), 82, identified the lost panegyric as the poem of 297/8 partially preserved in *P. Argent.* 480. In disproof, R. Keydell, *Hermes* 71 (1936), 466 f.

69. Lactantius, *Mort. Pers.* 12.2 ff.; Eusebius, *HE* 8.5.1; *PO* 10.13; cf. B. de Gaiffier, *Anal. Boll.* 75 (1957), 22 ff.

70. Lactantius, *Mort. Pers.* 13.1; Eusebius, *Mart. Pal.* (S), praef. 1, 2.1; *HE* 8.2.4; 9.10.8; Opatatus, app. 1, pp. 186–188 and app. 2, pp. 198–202 Ziwsa. On the edicts and their enforcement, see the fundamental study of G. E. M. de Ste Croix, *HTR* 47 (1954), 75 ff.

71. Lactantius, *Mort. Pers.* 15.7.

72. *Acta Felicis* (edited by H. Delehaye, *Anal. Boll.* 39 [1921], 241 ff.). Magnilianus is attested as *curator rei publicae* by *CIL* 8.23964 f. (Henchir bou Cha, about 30 miles south of Carthage); the town, therefore, cannot be Tibiuca, as is normally supposed, cf. R. P. Duncan-Jones, *JTS,* n.s. 25 (1974), 106 ff.

73. Optatus, app. 1, pp. 186–188 Ziwsa. Two papyri from Oxyrhynchus attest the imposition of oaths on all litigants (*P. Oxy.* 2601) and the seizure of church property (2673).

74. Hence the remark of the scribe who accompanied the *curator* of Cirta to Silvanus: *mortuus fueras, si non illas invenisses* (Optatus, app. 1, p. 187).

75. Optatus 3.8.

76. Optatus, app. 2, pp. 198.31–199.1: *eius temporis* (i.e., 303) *officium incumbebat, ut ex iussione proconsulari omnes sacrificarent et si quas scripturas haberent, offerrent secundum sacram legem.*

77. *CIL* 8.6700. Florus had ceased to be governor of that part of Numidia before 20 November 303 (*ILS* 644).

78. G. E. M. de Ste Croix, *HTR* 47 (1954), 82 ff.

79. *Acta Eupli* (the authentic part of the text breaks off at p. 101.6 Knopf-Krüger-Ruhbach = p. 312.16 Musurillo).

80. Chapter IX.

81. Eusebius, *HE* 8.6.8; Libanius, *Orat.* 11.158 ff.; 19.45 f.; 20.18 ff. Libanius' grandfather and great-uncle appear to have been executed for complicity in the revolt (*Orat.* 1.3).

82. Eusebius, *Mart. Pal.* (S), praef. 2; *HE* 8.2.5; 6.8 f.

83. Eusebius, *Mart. Pal.* (S), praef. 2; (S) 1.3 f.; (L) 1.5b; *HE* 8.2.5, 6.10. Similarly, Christian litigants could evade the edict of 23 February by having an agent perform sacrifice on their behalf (*P. Oxy.* 2601).

84. Eusebius, *Mart. Pal.* 3.1 (both recensions).

85. *Martyrion ton hagion Agapes, Eirenes kai Chiones*; Eusebius, *Mart. Pal.* 3.1.

86. Constantine, *Oratio* 25.1 ff.

87. Lactantius, *Mort. Pers.* 14.1 ff.; Eusebius, *HE* 8.5 f. The names of several more *palatini* and eunuchs executed at Nicomedia in early 303 are preserved in the *Martyrologium Hieronymianum* (B. de Gaiffier, *Anal. Boll.* 75 [1957], 17 ff.).

88. Eusebius, *HE* 8.6.6; *PO* 10.15.

89. *Chr. Pasch.* 516 Bonn; Eusebius, *HE* 9.6.3.

90. Lactantius, *Mort. Pers.* 16.3 ff., 35.2. If the text of 35.2 is sound (*cum tibi carcer sex annis pro domicilio fuerit*), then either (as assumed here) Donatus was imprisoned in 303, released, and imprisoned again later, or he was first imprisoned in 305–6.

91. Lactantius, *Mort. Pers.* 14.6 f.

92. Lactantius, *Mort. Pers.* 17.1 ff.; *Chr. Min.* 1.148, cf. H. P. L'Orange, *Röm. Mitt.* 53 (1938), 1 ff.

93. Lactantius, *Mort. Pers.* 17.3 f.

94. Lactantius, *Mort. Pers.* 17.4 ff.; cf. *CJ* 3.28.26 (28 August 304).

95. Lactantius, *Mort. Pers.* 18.1 ff. The fact that the conversation between Diocletian and Galerius (18.7 ff.) is an imaginative reconstruction does not impair the validity of the political analysis which it contains.

96. Chapter I.

97. *Origo* 2 f.; Constantine, *Oratio* 16.4; cf. *New Empire*, ch. IV.

98. Eusebius, *VC* 1.19.

99. Constantine, *Oratio* 25.1 ff.; Lactantius, *Mort. Pers.* 18.10 ff.

100. *Pan. Lat.* 7(6).5.3, 6(7).3.3. Lactantius, *Mort. Pers.* 18.10, describes him in 305 as *tribunus ordinis primi*, which is argued to be a conflation of his rank in the army (*tribunus*) and his title at court (*comes primi ordinis*) by J. Moreau, *Lactance: "De la mort des persécuteurs"* (*SC* 39 [1954]), 313 f.

101. On Maxentius' status as "César présomptif," see D. de Decker, *Byzantion* 38 (1968), 486 ff.

102. Lactantius, *Mort. Pers.* 18.9 ff.

103. Chapter III.

104. D. de Decker, *Byzantion* 38 (1968), 493 ff., argues from his refusal to perform *adoratio* to Maximian or Galerius (Lactantius, *Mort. Pers.* 18.9) that Maxentius was an avowed Christian.

105. Lactantius, *Mort. Pers.* 19.1 ff. For the emendation in 19.1 assumed here, *New Empire*, ch. V: Galerius, n. 73.

106. Lactantius, *Mort. Pers.* 18.12, 26.10; Eutropius, *Brev.* 9.27.2.

107. Lactantius, *Mort. Pers.* 18.12; *Origo* 9. Conceivably, Severus was Galerius' praetorian prefect (*New Empire*, ch. VIII).

108. Lactantius, *Mort. Pers.* 18.13 f., 19.6; *Epitome* 40.1,18; Zosimus 2.8.1.

109. Eusebius, *Mart. Pal.* 6.1.

110. *RIC* 6.636, Antiochia 134; 287, Ticinum 54a, b; 317, Aquileia 47a, b.

111. *ILS* 645, 646; *AE* 1961.240.

112. *Origo* 5; Eutropius, *Brev.* 10.1.1 f.; cf. *New Empire*, ch. XI.

113. Julian, *Orat.* 2, 51D; Orosius, *Hist. adv. Pag.* 7.25.15 (where Zangemeister wrongly deletes *Hispaniaque*).

114. *Origo* 5, 9; Eutropius, *Brev.* 10.1.1 (Severus); Lactantius, *Mort. Pers.* 19.6., 36.1; Eusebius, *HE* 9.1.1 (Maximinus).

115. Lactantius, *Mort. Pers.* 20.1 f. Galerius appears to be about ten years younger than Constantius (*New Empire*, ch. IV).

116. Lactantius, *Mort. Pers.* 19.6, 26.8; Eutropius, *Brev.* 9.27.2, 10.2.3; *Epitome* 39.6. Observe *CIL* 3.12900 (Salonae): [*Gr*]*atiani pr*[*otectoris d*]*omestici*— possibly Gratianus, the father of Valentinian and Valens (Ammianus 30.7.2), in attendance on Diocletian in his retirement.

117. *ILS* 666 f.; Eutropius, *Brev.* 10.2.3; *Epitome* 40.2.

118. Lactantius, *Mort. Pers.* 24.5 ff.; Victor, *Caes.* 40.2 ff.; *Epitome* 41.2 f; Zosimus 2.8.2 ff. *Origo* 4 has the story about the horses, but correctly makes Constantine reach his father, not *iam deficientem* (as in Lactantius) but still in Gaul.

119. *Pan. Lat.* 6(7).7.1 ff.; *Origo* 4; cf. J. Curle, *Proceedings of the Society of Antiquaries of Scotland* 66 (1931–32), 370 f. Constantius and Galerius were *Brittanici maximi II* by 7 January 306 (*AE* 1961.240).

120. *CIL* 1², pp. 268, 269; *Chr. Min.* 1.231; Socrates, *HE* 1.2.1 (day); Eutropius, *Brev.* 10.1.3 and Jerome, *Chronicle* 228ᵍ (place); Eusebius, *VC* 1.21.2 (sons and daughters).

121. *Pan. Lat.* 7(6).5.3, 6(7).2.4 ff.; Lactantius, *Mort. Pers.* 24.8, 25.5; Eusebius, *VC* 1.21 f. For the role of Crocus (or Erocus), *Epitome* 41.3—presumably repeating Eunapius. On the etiquette of *recusatio imperii*, see J. Béranger, *Recherches sur l'aspect idéologique du principat* (*Schweizerische Beiträge zur Altertumswissenschaft* 6, 1953), 137 ff.

III. THE RISE OF CONSTANTINE

1. Lactantius, *Mort. Pers.* 24.9; *Div. Inst.* 1.1.13 (a passage added in 324; see E. Heck, *Die dualistischen Zusätze und die Kaiseranreden bei Lactantius* [Heidelberg, 1972], 127 ff).

2. Lactantius, *Mort. Pers.* 25.1 f.

3. Lactantius, *Mort. Pers.* 23.1 ff. For the hypothesis that the census of 306 belongs to a well-established five-year cycle of empire-wide censuses, *New Empire*, ch. XIV.

4. Lactantius, *Mort. Pers.* 25.3 ff. In Galerius' territory, Constantine's official *dies imperii* fell after 28 August 306; see R. S. Bagnall and K. A. Worp, *Regnal Formulas in Byzantine Egypt* (*BASP*, Supp. 2, 1979), 31 ff.

5. *Pan. Lat.* 7(6).4.2, 6(7).10.2 ff., 4(10).16.4 ff. Both the orator of 310 and Nazarius in 321 speak as if the campaign belongs to the very beginning of Constantine's reign, i.e., the autumn of 306, but a date early in 307 cannot be excluded: see T. D. Barnes, *ZPE* 20 (1976), 149 f.

6. Lactantius, *Mort. Pers.* 23.5.

7. Lactantius, *Mort. Pers.* 26.1 ff.; Zosimus 2.9. Zosimus names Maxentius' associates as two *taxiarkhoi*, Marcellianus and Marcellus, and Lucianus, who supervised the distribution of pork to the people of Rome; T. Mommsen (as quoted by L. Mendelssohn in his edition of Zosimus) convincingly suggested that they were the three tribunes of the three urban cohorts, adducing *ILS* 722,

which attests a *tribunus cohortium urbanarum X XI et XII et fori suari* (between 317 and 337). Less circumstantial accounts mention only the praetorians, not the urban cohorts (Victor, *Caes.* 40.5; Eutropius, *Brev.* 10.2.3).

8. *RIC* 6.367–370; 432, Carthago 52.

9. Lactantius, *Mort. Pers.* 26.4.

10. *RIC* 6.371, Roma 162, 163.

11. *Chr. Min.* 1.66.

12. Lactantius, *Mort. Pers.* 26.5 ff.; Zosimus 2.10.1 ff. Maxentius' control of northern Italy in spring/summer 307 is attested by an issue of coins with Maxentius and Maximian as Augusti, but Constantine still as Caesar (*RIC* 6.293, Ticinum 84–88).

13. *Chr. Min.* 1.66 f.

14. Lactantius, *Mort. Pers.* 26.11 f.; Zosimus 2.10.3. Both wrongly imply that Severus was killed at once: Egyptian documents continue to employ dating formulas which name Severus as emperor and consul until at least 29 September 307 (*P. Mil.* 55), while the earliest known papyri whose dating formulas assume that he is no longer emperor belong to 24 December (*P. Merton* 31; *P. Columbia* 138).

15. *ILS* 695 (Sitifis); *CIL* 2.481 (Emerita) give Constantine the victory titles *Sarmaticus maximus, Germanicus maximus, Gothicus maximus;* the order implies a Sarmatian victory by Galerius between 25 July 306 and Constantine's first German victory (T. D. Barnes, *ZPE* 20 [1976], 149).

16. For variant versions, see D. J. A. Westerhuis, *Origo Constantini Imperatoris sive Anonymi Valesiani Pars Prior* (diss., Groningen, 1906), 20. That Severus died on 15 September seems to be implied by *Chr. Min.* 1.148; see W. Seston, *Carnuntina* (Graz, 1956), 178.

17. Lactantius, *Mort. Pers.* 27.1 (a very corrupt passage).

18. At least, the orator of 307 claims that a mosaic depicting Constantine and Fausta between 293 and 296 presaged their marriage (*Pan. Lat.* 7(6).6.1 ff).

19. *Pan. Lat.* 6(7). 4.1; *Epitome* 41.4; Zosimus 2.20.2; Zonaras 13.2.37.

20. *Pan. Lat.* 7(6); cf. T. D. Barnes, *JRS* 63 (1973), 41, n. 143.

21. Lactantius, *Mort. Pers.* 27.2 ff.; *Origo* 6 f.

22. R. S. Bagnall and K. A. Worp, *Chronological Systems of Byzantine Egypt* (Amsterdam, 1978), 105 f. The date at which Galerius summoned Diocletian out of retirement (Lactantius, *Mort. Pers.* 29.2) is conjectural.

23. From c. September the ordinary consuls for 307 in the territory of Constantine were Maximian, for the ninth time, and Constantine (*Chr. Min.* 1.60, 67, 231); from January to c. September they had probably been Galerius, for the seventh time, and Constantine (*New Empire,* ch. V: Constantine, n. 102; ch. VI).

24. *RIC* 6.498–500 (Serdica); cf. C. H. V. Sutherland, ibid., 60; R. S. Bagnall and K. A. Worp, *Regnal Formulas,* 32 f.; *ILS* 658 (Aquincum: undated).

25. *Chr. Min.* 1.60, 67, 76, 231: all reflect the later *damnatio memoriae* of both Diocletian and Maximian.

26. *Chr. Min.* 1.67.

27. Lactantius, *Mort. Pers.* 28.1 ff.

28. *Chr. Min.* 1.67, 231. The replacement of Insteius Tertullus as *praefectus*

urbi by Statius Rufinus on 13 April 308 is probably also relevant (*New Empire*, ch. VII).

29. *Pan. Lat.* 6(7).14.6; Lactantius, *Mort. Pers.* 29.1.

30. Galerius was *Carpicus maximus V* on 7 January 306 (*AE* 1961.240), *Carpicus maximus VI* by April 311 (Eusebius, *HE* 8.17.3). A more precise date must be inferred from the victory titles of Constantine and Licinius: cf. T. D. Barnes, *Phoenix* 30 (1976), 192.

31. Lactanius, *Mort. Pers.* 29.1 f.; Jerome, *Chronicle* 229ᶜ; *Chr. Min.* 1.231; Zosimus 2.10.3 ff. (who commits various confusions). Licinius, like Constantine, had fought in Galerius' Persian campaign of 298 (Eutropius, *Brev.* 10.4.1).

32. *ILS* 659.

33. *Pan. Lat.* 6(7).14.6; Lactantius, *Mort. Pers.* 29.2.

34. *Origo* 8; cf. Chapter II, n. 45.

35. *Origo* 8.

36. *RIC* 6.131 (Londinium), 220 (Treveri); 263–264 (Lugdunum); cf. C. H. V. Sutherland, ibid., 158.

37. Lactantius, *Mort. Pers.* 32.1 ff.; *RIC* 6.513–515 (Thessalonica); 562–563 (Nicomedia).

38. Constantine is attested as *filius Augustorum* on the coinage of Antioch and Alexandria (*RIC* 6.631–632, 678–680) and on Egyptian papyri of 309 (*P. Cairo Isid.* 47, 90, 91), but there appears to be no attestation of Maximinus as *filius Augustorum* from the territory he ruled.

39. Lactantius, *Mort. Pers.* 32.5; cf. C. H. V. Sutherland, *RIC* 6 (1967), 15 f.

40. An inference from the fragmentary *ILS* 660; *CIL* 3.12134; cf. T. D. Barnes, *ZPE* 21 (1976), 277 f. (reproduced as *New Empire*, ch. III, nos. 5 and 6).

41. *Origo* 13.

42. For the basic narrative of Alexander's revolt, Victor, *Caes.* 40.17 ff.; Zosimus 2.12.2 ff. On the dates of his proclamation and suppression, *New Empire*, ch. II. It is not certain whether Alexander or Maxentius controlled Mauretania when a basilica was constructed at Altava in 309 (*I. Altava* 19).

43. *AE* 1942/3.81; *I. Rom. Tripolitania* 464.

44. *ILS* 8936 (near Sicca?); *AE* 1966.169 (Sardinia); *Chr. Min.* 1.148 (*fames magna fuit*).

45. Victor, *Caes.* 40.28; cf. *ILS* 5570 (Cillium: shortly after 312).

46. *Epitome* 40.6.

47. The panegyrist of 313 alludes to the purge: *omni Africa quam delere statuerat exhausta* (*Pan. Lat.* 12(9).16.1). And verses displayed in the forum at Lambaesis praised Constantine for removing *cruces et proelia saeva tyranni* (*CIL* 8.18261).

48. Hence, probably, some of the Moorish troops which the Arch of Constantine depicts as being in his army in 312; cf. H. P. L'Orange, *Symbolae Osloenses* 13 (1934), 105 ff.—though others had been in Maxentius' army since he filched them from Severus in 307 (Zosimus 2.10).

49. Zosimus 2.14.4; cf. *RIC* 6.379–381 (Rome), 400–406 (Ostia).

50. C. H. V. Sutherland, *RIC* 6.276, 308.

51. A. Jeločnik, *The Čentur Hoard: Folles of Maxentius and of the Tetrarchy* (*Situla* 12, 1973), 163 ff.; cf. V. Picozzi, *Numismatica e antichità classiche* 5 (1976), 267 ff. (who denies that Maxentius recovered Istria).

52. *ILS* 678 = *Inscr. Ital.* 10.2.7; cf. *Inscr. Ital.* 10.1.45 (Pola: undated). Observe also the *protector* who died in a civil war in Italy and was buried near Promona (*ILS* 2776).

53. *ILS* 660; cf. T. D. Barnes, *Phoenix* 30 (1976), 192.

54. Lactantius, *Mort. Pers.* 33.1 ff. The bust of Galerius published by P. Dontas, *BCH* 99 (1975), 521 ff., depicts him as old, bloated, and despondent.

55. The aid of Apollo and Asclepius was invoked; according to Lactantius, the cure prescribed by Apollo made the patient worse (*Mort. Pers.* 33.5).

56. Maxentius appears to have recovered Sardinia after the fall of Alexander (*Pan. Lat.* 12(9).16.1, 25.2).

57. *RIC* 6.129, Londinium 82; 6.134–135, Londinium 133–145; Eusebius, *VC* 1.25.

58. *Pan. Lat.* 7(6).4.2, 6(7).10.2 ff.; Lactantius, *Mort. Pers.* 29.3; *Pan. Lat.* 4(10).16.5 ff.

59. *Pan. Lat.* 6(7).14 ff.; Lactantius, *Mort. Pers.* 29.3 ff. The only explicit evidence for the year of Maximian's death appears to be *Chr. Min.* 1.231.

60. *Pan. Lat.* 6(7)—delivered on the *natalis* of Trier, perhaps 1 August 310.

61. *Pan. Lat.* 6(7).2.1 ff.; cf. R. Syme, *BHAC 1971* (1974), 240 ff.

62. Constantine is *nepos divi Claudi* on two inscriptions erected by Italian officials (*ILS* 699, 702); but the *Origo Constantini imperatoris* makes his father *divi Claudi optimi principis nepos ex fratre*, Eutropius *per filiam nepos Claudi* (*Brev.* 9.22.1). Inscriptions honoring a son of Constantine have both *abnepos* and *pronepos* (*ILS* 723, 725)..

63. *Pan. Lat.* 6(7).4.2 ff.

64. *Pan. Lat.* 6(7).3.1 ff.

65. *Pan. Lat.* 6(7).7.1 ff.

66. *Pan. Lat.* 6(7).10.1 ff.

67. *Pan. Lat.* 21.2 f.

68. *Pan. Lat.* 6(7).1.4 f.

69. *Pan. Lat.* 6(7). 15.5 f. Contrast Constantine's own later denunciation of Diocletian (*Oratio* 25.1 ff.; Eusebius, *VC* 2.51).

70. *Pan. Lat.* 6(7).21.3; cf. C. Jullian, *Histoire de la Gaule* 7 (Paris, 1926), 107, n. 2; E. Galletier, *Panégyriques Latins* 2 (Paris: Budé, 1952), 43 ff.

71. *Pan. Lat.* 6(7).21.4: *vidisti enim, credo, Constantine, Apollinem tuum comitante Victoria coronas tibi laureas offerentem, quae tricenum singulae ferunt omen annorum. hic est enim humanarum numerus aetatum quae tibi utique debentur ultra Pyliam senectutem.*
On the interpretation of this passage, see especially J. Bidez, *L'Antiquité Classique* 1 (1932), 5 f.; H. Lietzmann, *Sb. Berlin*, Phil.-hist. K1. 1937, 264 ff.; E. Galletier, *REA* 52 (1950), 292 ff. Lietzmann and Galletier assume that Apollo offered Constantine three crowns. But the lifetime of Nestor, the old man of Pylos, spanned three generations (*Iliad* 1.250 ff.), and 120 years was the conventional limit of human existence (Lactantius, *Div. Inst.* 2.12.23; *HA, Tacitus* 15.2; Servius, on *Aen.* 4.654); therefore, the phrase *ultra Pyliam senectutem* implies four generations of thirty years and four laurel crowns.

72. *Pan. Lat.* 6(7).21.5: *et—immo quid dico 'credo'?—vidisti teque in illius specie recognovisti, cui totius mundi regna deberi vatum carmina divina cecinerunt.* Virgil, *Ecl.* 4.10 (*tuus iam regnat Apollo*) clinches the allusion. Lactantius

and Constantine himself were soon to interpret the Fourth Eclogue as foretelling the birth of Christ (Chapter V).

73. *Pan. Lat.* 6(7).21.7.

74. H. Lietzmann, *Sb. Berlin,* Phil.-hist. K1. 1937, 266.

75. *Pan. Lat.* 6(7).21.7: *iam omnia te vocare ad se templa videantur praecipue-que Apollo noster,* etc.

76. *Pan. Lat.* 6(7).22.1 ff., esp. 3: *dabis et illic munera, constitutes privilegia, ipsam denique patriam meam ipsius loci veneratione restitues.*

77. Chapter I.

78. *RIC* 6.130–132 (Londinium); 212–213, 217–218 (Treveri); 260–265 (Lugdunum).

79. J. Maurice, *Numismatique Constantinienne* 2 (Paris, 1911), xx ff. Against modern theories that Constantine experienced a conversion to solar monotheism or felt personal devotion to Sol Invictus, see also K. Aland, *TU* 63 (1957), 580 ff.

80. Compare the speech of 307: *dive Constanti, quem curru paene conspicuo, dum vicinos ortus repetit occasu, Sol ipse invecturus caelo excepit* (*Pan. Lat.* 7(6).14.3).

81. N. H. Baynes, *Constantine the Great and the Christian Church* (London, 1931), 95 ff.; J. H. W. G. Liebeschuetz, *Continuity and Change in Roman Religion* (Oxford, 1979), 281 ff.

82. Viz., C. Ceionius Rufius Volusianus, cos. 311, 314, who had been a *corrector* in Italy from c. 282 to c. 290 and proconsul of Africa in 305–306 or 306–307 (*ILS* 1213).

83. In September 311, that is, only after he declared war on Constantine, Maxentius named Rufinus and Volusianus ordinary consuls: the former is either Aradius Rufinus, who became *praefectus urbi* on 9 February 312, or Statius Rufinus, *praefectus urbi* from 13 April 308 to 30 October 309 (*New Empire,* ch. VII).

84. Maxentius was consul in 308 (from 20 April), 309, 310, and 312 (*Chr. Min.* 1.67). In 308 and 309 his colleague was his son, Valerius Romulus, who died in the course of 309 (*RIC* 6.377 ff. [Roma]; 6.400, 404 ff. [Ostia]).

85. *Pan. Lat.* 12(9).3.5 ff. (delivered in 313); *ILS* 1217 (Atina: 315); Eusebius, *HE* 8.14.3 ff. (written c. 315); *VC* 1.26, 33 ff. (c. 338).

86. On Maxentius, see especially E. Groag, *RE* 14 (1930), 2417 ff.

87. *RIC* 6.430–431, Carthago 47, 48a, 51a—erroneously styling Maxentius *nobilissimus Caesar.*

88. Alexander was *vicarius* of Africa at the time of his proclamation (Victor, *Caes.* 40.17; Zosimus 2.12.2); therefore, although his official name was L. Domitius Alexander, he should be presumed identical with the Val(erius) Alexander attested as *vicarius* in 303 (*AE* 1942/3.81: Aqua Viva, in Numidia) and again under Maxentius (*I. Rom. Tripolitania* 464: Lepcis). As for Alexander's origin, Victor plausibly states that he was the son of Pannonian peasants (*Caes.* 40.17). Eunapius, however, made him a Phrygian (*Epitome* 40.20; Zosimus 2.12.3). T. Kotula, *Klio* 40 (1962), 159 ff., postulates a source common to both whom he identifies as Onasimos (*FGrH* 216).

89. Zosimus 2.12; cf. *ILS* 668 (from Numidia).

90. *Pan. Lat.* 12(9).4.4 (*plebis Romanae fame necatae*); *Chr. Min.* 1.148 (*fames magna fuit*).

91. Eusebius, *HE* 8.14.3; Victor, *Caes.* 40.24.

92. *Chr. Min.* 1.148.

93. Victor, *Caes.* 40.26 f.; *Chr. Min.* 1.148; cf. E. Groag, *RE* 14.2459 ff.

94. Victor, *Caes.* 40.26 f. Victor states that Maxentius completed construction of both the Templum Romae and the basilica, but before its completion the basilica was altered considerably to receive a colossal statute of Constantine; see A. Minoprio, *PBSR* 12 (1932), 1 ff.

95. Victor, *Caes.* 40.24: *quos* (sc. Senate and people) *in tantum afflictaverat, uti . . . primusque instituto pessimo munerum specie patres aratoresque pecuniam conferre prodigenti sibi cogeret.* For *aratoresque,* E. Groag, *Wiener Studien* 45 (1926/7), 109, proposed *sacerdotesque.*

96. *Chr. Min.* 1.148: *Romanis omnibus aurum indixit et dederunt.* E. Groag, *RE* 14 (1930), 2453 f., argued that this imposition set a precedent for Constantine's *collatio lustralis* (Chapter XIV).

97. *CIL* 6.37118; *Notizie degli Scavi* 1917.22; cf. E. Groag, *Wiener Studien* 45 (1926/7), 102 ff.

98. Optatus, 1.18; cf. Eusebius, *Mart. Pal.* (S) 12.13 f.; *HE* 8.14. Most modern discussion of Maxentius' religious policies is vitiated by a failure to make the elementary distinction between toleration and restitution.

99. Optatus, app. 1, p. 194.12 Ziwsa; cf. S. Lancel, *Cahiers de Tunisie* 14 (1967), 185; *Rev. Ét. Aug.* 25 (1979), 217 ff.

100. Augustine, *Contra Litteras Petiliani* 2.92.202 (*CSEL* 52.125); *De Unico Baptismo* 16.27 (*CSEL* 53.28). The *Liber Pontificalis,* p. 162 Duchesne, states that he performed sacrifice but repented within a few days and was martyred. The charge is vigorously denied by A. Amore, *Antonianum* 32 (1957), 411 ff.

101. For discussion of the problems, see especially E. Caspar, *ZKG* 46 (1927), 321 ff.; A. Amore, *Antonianum* 33 (1958), 57 ff. E. H. Röttges, *ZKT* 78 (1956), 385 ff., argues that the bishops Marcellinus and Marcellus are identical.

102. *Chr. Min.* 1.75: *fuit persecutio et cessavit episcopatum ann. VII m. VI d. XXV.* A hiatus of seven years is impossible; hence E. Caspar, *ZKG* 46 (1927), 326, n. 2, very plausibly emended to *ann. III.* If that is correct, then a hiatus of three years, six months, and twenty-five days will correspond exactly to the interval between Marcellinus' *traditio* c. May 303 and the consecration of Marcellus soon after 28 October 306.

103. Deduced from the length of his episcopate as given in the Liberian catalogue (*Chr. Min.* 1.75 = *Liber Pontificalis,* p. 6 Duchesne: 8 years, 3 months, 25 days, from 30 June 296 to the consular year 304). The *Liber Pontificalis,* p. 162 Duchesne, gives 25 April 304 as the day of the bishop's death—perhaps through confusion with the priest Marcellinus who was martyred in the Diocletianic persecution (Damasus, *Epigrammata* 29 Ihm).

104. In the West, *traditio* counted as apostasy and disqualified a man from the priesthood (Arles, Canon 13). T. Mommsen, *MGH, Gesta Pontificum Romanorum* 1 (1898), liii, accepted the evidence of the forged Acts of the Council of Sinuessa that Marcellinus was deposed on 23 August 303.

105. Hence the absence of Marcellinus from both the *depositio episcoporum* and the *depositio martyrum* in the Chronographer of 354 (*Chr. Min.* 1.70–72 =

Liber Pontificalis, pp. 10–12 Duchesne); cf. E. Caspar, *ZKG* 46 (1927), 329 ff.

106. Damasus, *Epigrammata* 48 = *ILCV* 962. For the day of Marcellus' death, *Chr. Min.* 1.70 (with *Marcellini* in error for *Marcelli*); *Martyrologium Hieronymianum,* under 16 January (*Acta Sanctorum,* Nov. 2.2 [1931], 42); *Liber Pontificalis,* p. 164 Duchesne. The Liberian Catalogue has the following entry (*Chr. Min.* 1.76): *MARCELLUS annum unum m. VI d. XX. fuit temporibus Maxenti, a cons. X et Maximiano* [i.e., 308] *usque post consulatum X et septimum* [i.e., 309]. On the analysis adopted here, *m. VI* (one ms. has *m. VII*) is an error for *m. I* or *m. II,* and the consular dates are a later and mistaken addition to the original list (they are Constantinian in form; see *New Empire,* ch. VI). It is possible, however, to delete *annum unum* and to argue that Marcellus was bishop from 27 May or 26 June 308 to 16 January 309, Eusebius bishop from 18 April to 17 August in either 309 or 310, as do L. Duchesne, *Liber Pontificalis* 1 (Paris, 1883), ccxlix, and E. Schwartz, *Gött. Gel. Nach,* Phil.—hist. Kl. 1904.530, n. 1.

107. *Chr. Min.* 1.76: *m. IIII d. XVI a. XIIII Kal. Maias usque in diem XVI Kal. Sept.* On the year (308 rather than 309 or 310), H. Lietzmann, *Petrus und Paulus in Rom*[2] (Berlin, 1927), 8 ff.

108. Damasus, *Epigrammata* 18 = *ILCV* 963.

109. *Chr. Min.* 1.76.

110. Augustine, *Brev. Coll.* 3.18.34; *Contra Partem Donati post Gesta* 13.17 (*CSEL* 53:84, 113–114).

111. Eusebius, *HE* 10.5.15–17.

112. Lactantius, *Mort. Pers.* 34 = Eusebius, *HE* 8.17.3–10. Lactantius describes it as an *edictum* (35.1), but in the heading, quoted by Eusebius, the emperors send "greeting to their provincials." On the difficulty of distinguishing between letters and edicts at an earlier period, W. Williams, *ZPE* 17 (1975), 40 ff.

113. Lactantius, *Mort. Pers.* 35.2.

114. Lactantius, *Mort. Pers.* 35.3; *Chr. Min.* 1.148; *Epitome* 40.16.

115. *New Empire,* ch. V: Maximinus.

116. *ILS* 660; Eusebius, *HE* 8.17.3 (Galerius *Persicus maximus III* in 310/1); *Inscr. Lat. de l'Algérie* 1.3956 (Constantine and Maximinus both styled *Persicus* in 312–313); *RIC* 6.636, Antiochia 104 (*Iovio propag(atori) orbis terrarum*).

117. *New Empire,* ch. XIV.

118. Lactantius, *Mort. Pers.* 36.1; *CTh* 13.10.2; cf. *New Empire,* ch. XIV.

119. *FIRA*[2] 1.93. On this document, see especially D. van Berchem, *L'armée de Dioclétien et la réforme constantinienne* (Paris, 1952) 73 ff.; R. Egger, *Römische Antike und frühes Christentum* 2 (Klagenfurt, 1963), 51 ff. Its precise historical context is too often ignored in studies of Roman taxation.

120. Lactantius, *Mort. Pers.* 36.2.

121. Eusebius, *HE* 9.9a.4, 6.3.

122. Lactantius, *Mort. Pers.* 36.3 ff.

123. Eusebius, *HE* 9.1.1 ff.; cf. Lactantius, *Mort. Pers.* 36.3.

124. Eusebius, *HE* 7.32.31, 9.6.2f.; cf. *New Empire,* ch. V: Maximinus.

125. Lactantius, *Mort. Pers.* 37.1 ff.

126. Lactantius, *Mort. Pers.* 43.4; Zosimus 2.14. Maxentius' coinage proclaims simultaneously the apotheosis of Galerius and Maximian: *RIC* 6.382

(Roma), 404 (Ostia)—and Eutropius dates the beginning of the war against Maxentius to Constantine's fifth year, i.e., before 25 July 311 (*Brev.* 10.4.3). Observe also a milestone from the road between Carthage and Theveste with the names of Maxentius and Constantine, the latter being erased (*Inscr. Lat. de l'Algérie* 1.3949).

127. *Pan. Lat.* 6(7).14.2 ff., 20.3 f.

128. Lactantius, *Mort. Pers.* 42.1.

129. Lactantius, *Mort. Pers.* 30.1 ff. Lactantius alone has the two successive plots; later writers tend to muddle the open rebellion, which certainly occurred, with the attempted assassination, which is a deliberate invention, cf. J. Moreau, *Lactance: "De la mort des persécuteurs"* (*SC* 39, 1954), 373 ff.

130. Lactantius, *Mort. Pers.* 43.2 f., 44.10.

131. Lactantius, *Mort. Pers.* 42.2 f. On the date, *JRS* 63 (1973), 32 ff.; for other versions of Diocletian's death, J. Moreau, *Lactance* (*SC* 39, 1954), 420.

132. *Sylloge*[3] 900 (visits Stratonicea); Eusebius, *HE* 9.3; Malalas 311 Bonn (at Antioch); Eusebius, *HE* 9.8.4 (cf. Chapter V).

133. *Pan. Lat.* 12(9).8.1 ff.; 4(10).25.1 ff. Zosimus 2.14.1 implausibly alleges that Maxentius intended to advance into Raetia, win over the troops there and thus seize Dalmatia and Illyricum.

134. *Pan. Lat.* 12(9).2.4.

135. *Pan. Lat.* 12(9).3.3, 5.1 f. The figure of 100,000, which the same speech gives for Maxentius' army, presumably represents all the troops at his disposal (3.3).

136. *Pan. Lat.* 12(9).5.4 ff.; 4(10).21.1 f.

137. *Pan. Lat.* 12(9).6.2 ff.; 4(10).22.1 ff. On the precise site and importance of the battle, M.A. Levi, *Bolletino storico-bibliografico subalpino* 36 (1934), 4 ff.

138. *Pan. Lat.* 12(9).7.1 ff. On the importance of northern Italian patriotism, M. A. Levi, *Bolletino storico-bibliografico subalpino* 36 (1934), 9 f.

139. *Pan. Lat.* 12(9).8.1 ff.; 4(10).25.1 ff. The orator of 313 chides Constantine for risking his own life in the thick of the fight (9.3 ff.).

140. The killing of senators is alleged by *Pan. Lat.* 12(9).4.4; Eusebius, *HE* 8.14.3.

141. Eusebius, *HE* 8.14.2 ff., 16 f.; *VC* 1.34. Rufinus gives the woman's name as Sophronia (*HE* 8.14.16), but that probably derives from a misunderstanding of Eusebius; cf. E. Groag, *RE* 14 (1930), 2467.

142. *Chr. Min.* 1.67.

143. A Chastagnol, *Les Fastes de la Préfecture de Rome au Bas-Empire* (Paris, 1962), 59.

144. On the Battle of the Milvian Bridge, cf. G. Costa, *Bilychnis* 2 (1913), 197 ff.; K. von Landmann, *Konstantin der Grosse und seine Zeit* (*Röm. Quart.*, Supp. 19, 1913), 143 ff.; E. Groag, *RE* 14 (1930), 2475 ff.

The reconstruction offered here proceeds from two basic premises, which require discussion. First, the engagement at Saxa Rubra, nine miles outside the city, alleged by Victor, *Caes.* 40.24, is unhistorical; see J. Moreau, *Scripta Minora* (Heidelberg, 1964), 72 ff. It owes its existence to confusion between the events of 312 and those of 193, for which Victor produces an earlier and unhistorical Battle of the Milvian Bridge (*Caes.* 19.4). Second, the Milvian Bridge was cut before Constantine reached Rome. The Arch of Constantine clearly shows the bridge as broken; cf. H. P. L'Orange and A. von Gerkan, *Der spätantike Bildschmuck des Konstantinbogens* (*Studien zur spätantiken Kunstgeschichte* 10, 1939), 65 ff. Its testimony must outweigh that of the Gallic orator of 313 who assumes that the bridge existed on the day of the battle (*Pan. Lat.* 12(9).17.1: *hostes ... angustiis Mulvii pontis exclusi*). Lactantius states twice that the bridge was cut (*Mort. Pers.* 44.9: *pons a tergo eius scinditur ... ad pontem, qui interruptus erat*), though he errs in thinking that it was severed on the day of the battle. The *Epitome* locates the *pons navigiis compositus* slightly upstream from the Milvian Bridge itself (40.7).

A fragment of a relief from Caesarea in Mauretania is often taken to depict the Battle of the Milvian Bridge, with troops crossing the bridge in flight (G. Doublet, *Musée d'Alger* [Paris, 1890], 42 ff.). But *Pons Mulvi expeditio imperatoris* [*Co*]n[*stantini*] (*ILS* 686) was reread as *expeditio imperatoris in German.* by S. Gsell, *Rev. Afr.* 38 (1894), 232 (whence *CIL* 8.20941, accepted by H. Dessau, *ILS* 3, p. clxxi). Nor is the authenticity of the relief entirely exempt from doubt; see H. P. L'Orange and A. von Gerkan, *Der spätantike Bildschmuck*, 71, n. 10.

145. *Pan. Lat.* 12(9).16.1 ff.; Lactantius, *Mort. Pers.* 44.3 f., 7 ff.; Eusebius, *HE* 9.9.1 ff.; *Pan. Lat.* 4 (10).28.1 ff.; Libanius, *Orat.* 59.20; Zosimus 2.15.2 ff.

146. Lactantius, *Mort. Pers.* 44.4 ff. Lactantius' description of the *caeleste signum dei* is problematical. In 44.5 most editors print *facit ut iussus est et transversa X littera, summo capite circumflexo, Christum in scutis notat.* H. Grégoire (see M. Sulzberger, *Byzantion* 2 [1925], 406 f.) proposed to insert *I* either before *transversa* or after *littera*, A. Alföldi to insert *virgula* after *littera* (*Pisciculi* [Münster, 1939], 5). Neither is convincing; see J. Vogt, *Gnomon* 27 (1955), 46 f. More radically, J. Rougé, *Lactance et son temps* (*Théologie Historique* 48, 1978), 22, proposes to delete the virtually incomprehensible description and read *fecit ut iussus est et Christum in scutis notat.*

147. Perhaps inspired by the dream of Judas in 2 Maccabees 15; cf. J. Rougé, *TU* 115 (1975), 140.

148. Probably in 325 (Chapter XV). Eusebius' account gives no hint of where the cross appeared: despite Lactantius, therefore, it may have been as early as during the crossing of the Alps. The celestial phenomenon which the army saw was probably a solar halo; see A. H. M. Jones, *Constantine and the Conversion of Europe* (London, 1949), 96. For some recent photographs of solar halos, *Sky and Telescope* 54 (1977/8), 185 ff.

149. Eusebius, *VC* 1.27 ff. Eusebius, marking the anachronism (32.1), inserts a description of the *labarum* as he had seen it after 324 (31). Both the original form of the *labarum* and its original significance are disputed; see R. Egger, *Römische Antike* 2 (1963), 325 ff.; M. Black, *Apostolic History and the Gospel: Biblical and Historical Essays Presented to F. F. Bruce* (Exeter, 1970), 319 ff.

150. The word is first attested in Eusebius, *VC* 1.31, heading: "Description of the cross-like sign, which the Romans now call *labarum.*" In favor of a Celtic etymology, see J. J. Hatt, *Latomus* 9 (1950), 427, citing A. Holder, *Alt-celtischer Sprachschatz* 2 (Leipzig, 1904), 114, s.v. *labarus;* R. Egger, *Römische Antike* 2 (1963), 334 ff.

Zosimus 2.15.1 emphasizes the Western origin of Constantine's army—barbarian captives, Germans, Celts, and levies from Britain. The Arch of Constantine gives prominence to the German contingent of Cornuti; see A. Alföldi, *DOP* 13 (1959), 174 ff.

151. *Pan. Lat.* 12(9).17.1 ff.; Lactantius, *Mort. Pers.* 44.9; Eusebius, *HE* 9.9.4 ff.; *Pan. Lat.* 4(10).28.1 ff.; *Origo* 12. The orator of 313 states specifically that the battle was quickly over: *ad primum igitur adspectum maiestatis tuae primumque impetum toties tui victoris exercitus hostes territi fugatique* (17.1). Similarly, Eusebius, comparing Maxentius to Pharaoh crossing the Red Sea, ignores any fighting and reports only Maxentius' attempted flight over the bridge of boats (*HE* 9.9.4).

152. On the cross and *labarum* as talismans, R. MacMullen, *GRBS* 9 (1968), 81 ff.

IV. THE CHRISTIAN EMPEROR OF THE WEST

1. *CIL* 1^2, p. 274.

2. *Pan. Lat.* 12(9).19.1 ff.; cf. J. Straub, *Regeneratio Imperii* (Darmstadt, 1972), 100 ff.

3. Zosimus 2.29.5—assuming a date in 326. F. Paschoud, *Cinq études sur Zosime* (Paris, 1975), 24 ff., argues that Constantine first refused to ascend the Capitol neither in 312, as the silence of the panegyric of 313 implies, nor in 326, as Zosimus alleges, but during his visit to Rome in 315.

4. Eusebius, *VC* 1.41.3; cf. *Pan. Lat.* 4(10).31.1: *educti e carcere consulares.* F. Winkelmann, in his edition (Berlin, 1976), 37, mistakenly restricts Eusebius' reference to Constantine's treatment of Christians. Prudentius, *C. Symm.* 1.470, alleges that Maxentius had imprisoned no less than one hundred senators.

5. *Pan. Lat.* 12(9).18.3; 4(10).32.6 ff.; *Origo* 12; Zosimus 2.17.1.

6. Victor, *Caes.* 40.25; Zosimus 2.17.2.

7. Note the hints in *Pan. Lat.* 12(9).3.6, 14.2. For Constantine's visit to Rome in 303, Chapter II.

8. *Pan. Lat.* 12(9).20, 3.6 ff.

9. *CTh* 15.14.3^S, 4^S.

10. Viz., Annius Anullinus (on whose identity, see *New Empire*, ch. VII).

11. On the career of Volusianus, T. D. Barnes, *JRS* 65 (1975), 46 f. His predecessor was Aradius Rufinus, prefect from 9 February to 27 October 312.

12. For salient details, A. H. M. Jones, *The Later Roman Empire* (Oxford, 1964), 24 f., 45, 104 ff., 525 ff.

13. For Constantine as "restorer of order," J. Gaudemet, *Studi in onore di S. Solazzi* (Naples, 1948), 652 ff.

14. Lactantius, *Mort. Pers.* 44.11: *senatus Constantino virtutis gratia primi nominis titulum decrevit, quem Maximinus sibi vindicabat.* Constantine thereupon began to style himself *maximus Augustus*; cf. J. Babelon, *Mélanges Boissier* (Paris, 1903), 49 ff.

15. Observe that the three pairs of nonimperial consuls in 314, 316, and 317 are all westerners, viz., Rufius Volusianus and Petronius Annianus, Antonius Caecinius Sabinus and Vettius Rufinus, and Ovinius Gallicanus and Caesonius Bassus.

16. *Pan. Lat.* 12(9).25.4: *senatus signum deae et paulo ante Italia scutum et coronam, cuncta aurea, dedicarunt.* On the reading (many editors emend the

transmitted *dee*, i.e., *deae*, to *dei*), and its significance, see M. R. Alföldi, *JNG* 15 (1961), 19 ff.

17. Victor, *Caes*. 40.26: *basilicam Flavii meritis patres sacravere*. For changes in the original plan (including an apse on the north wall in addition to that on the west wall), A. Minoprio, *PBSR* 12 (1932), 1 ff.

18. Eusbius, *HE* 9.9.10 f. The Christian nature of this statue was impugned by H. Grégoire, *L'antiquité Classique* 1 (1932), 135 ff., who accused Eusebius of falsifying the inscription. The statue in question is the colossus of Constantine, of which fragments are displayed in the Museo del Campidoglio: H. Kähler, *JDAI* 67 (1951), 1 ff.; T. Buddensieg, *Münchener Jahrbuch der bildenden Kunst* 13 (1962), 37 ff.

Eusebius describes the object which the statue held in its hand as "a memorial of the Savior's passion" and "the sign of salvation" (*HE* 9.9.10) and as "a lofty spear in the shape of a cross" (*VC* 1.40.2). For its identification as the *labarum*, see A. Alföldi, *Pisciculi* (Münster, 1939), 7 ff.; *The Conversion of Constantine and Pagan Rome* (Oxford, 1948), 42.

19. *Pan. Lat.* 12(9): on which, see now J. H. W. G. Liebeschuetz, *Continuity and Change in Roman Religion* (Oxford, 1979), 285 ff.

20. The invocation of *Sancte Thybri* hardly counts as an exception (18.1).

21. *Pan. Lat.* 12(9).2.5

22. *Pan. Lat.* 12(9).26.1 ff.: *te, summe rerum sator, . . . (quem enim te ipse dici velis, scire non possumus)*.

23. The allusion to *Aeneid* 6.726 ff. is obvious (A. Klotz, *Rh. Mus.* N.F. 66 [1911], 524), while parallels in the *Corpus Hermeticum* are canvassed by F. Altheim, *ZRGG* 9 (1957), 225 f. J. Béranger, *Mus. Helv.* 27 (1970), 438 ff., characterizes the orator as a philosophical monotheist.

24. *ILS* 694: *instinctu divinitatis, mentis magnitudine*. On the meaning of the first phrase, H. Schrörs, *Konstantins des Grossen Kreuzerscheinung: Eine kritische Untersuchung* (Bonn, 1913), 7 ff. A contemporary cliché, it recurs in Calcidius' dedicatory letter to Ossius (p. 6 Waszink: *non sine divino instinctu*), and in the speech of 313 (*Pan. Lat.* 12(9).11.4: *divino monitus instinctu*).

25. W. J. G. Lubbe, *Incerti Panegyricus Constantino Augusto dictus* (diss., Leiden, 1955), 55 ff.; J. Ziegler, *Zur religiösen Haltung der Gegenkaiser im 4. Jh. n. Chr.* (*Frankfurter althistorische Studien* 4, 1970), 10 ff.

26. A. Giuliano, *Arco di Costantino* (Rome, 1955), Plates 34, 40; cf. H. P. L'Orange, *Röm. Mitt.* 53 (1938), 1 ff.

27. *Origo* 12; cf. *Epitome* 40.12.

28. *Pan. Lat.* 12(9).3.4, 4.3.

29. *RIC* 7.180 (Trier); 252 (Arles); 310–312 (Rome); 394–395 (Aquileia); 429–430 (Siscia); 502–503 (Thessalonica). An allusion to the formal consecration by the Roman Senate can perhaps be detected in Athanasius, *Contra Gentes* 9.50–53 Thomson.

30. F. Millar, *The Emperor in the Roman World* (London, 1977), 491 ff.

31. *Origo* 2: *natus . . . in oppido Naisso et eductus, . . . litteris minus instructus*. It is not always remembered that the writer refers specifically to the period before Constantine went to the court of Diocletian.

32. F. Millar, *Emperor*, 205 f.

33. Chapter V.

34. *Pan. Lat.* 6(7).23.2; Jerome, *Chronicle* 230[c]; *De Viris Illustribus* 80; cf. Chapter I.

35. Eutropius, *Brev.* 10.7.2; *Epitome* 41.14.

36. The poet Porfyrius was *praefectus urbi* in 329 and 333: for the hypotheses that his proconsulate of Achaea (attested by *AE* 1931.6) falls before 306, and that Porfyrius was exiled in 315 with Rufius Volusianus, T. D. Barnes, *AJP* 96 (1975), 174 ff., 186.

37. The poem does not survive: the extant poems addressed to Constantine (*Carm.* 1–20) form a cycle of twenty poems, which Porfyrius sent to the emperor from exile in 324/5; see T. D. Barnes, *AJP* 96 (1975), 177 ff.

38. *Epistula Constantini,* in the edition of Porfyrius' poems by G. Polara (Turin, 1973), 4–6.

39. Publilius Optatianus Porfyrius, *Carm.* 1.1 ff.

40. *Epistula Porfyrii*—which G. Polara prints before the *Epistula Constantini* in his edition (Turin, 1973), 1–3. Porfyrius refers to the favorable reception of an earlier poem by Constantine's "victorious hands" (*Ep.* 2).

41. Note esp. *Ep.* 6: *tot divinae maiestatis insignia, quibus et invictus semper et primus es*—where the stress on *primus* best suits a date of 312/3.

42. That Constantine's army remained pagan after 312 is often deduced from the acclamation of his entourage recorded in *CTh* 7.20.2: *Augustine Constantine, dii te nobis servent.* But the subscription (*dat. kal. Mart. in civitate Velovocorum Constantino Aug. VI et Constantino Caes. conss.*) contains a contradiction, since Constantine was nowhere near Beauvais on 1 March 320; it may accordingly be proposed that the law was in fact issued on 1 March 307 (*New Empire,* ch. V, n. 102)—more than five years before the army became officially Christian.

43. Eusebius, *VC* 4.18.3 ff.

44. Lactantius, *Mort. Pers.* 46.6; cf. Eusebius, *VC* 4.20.1. Lactantius attributes the prayer to the dictation of an angel in a dream (46.3 ff.); for the hypothesis that the prayer represents an "imperial creed" which the two emperors agreed upon in Milan, A. Piganiol, *L'empereur Constantin* (Paris, 1932), 76.

45. *Eusebius, VC* 1.42.1.

46. *RIC* 7.364, Ticinum 36; cf. K. Kraft, *JNG* 5/6 (1954/5), 151 ff.

47. Until c. 320; see P. Bruun, *Arctos,* n.s. 2 (1958), 15 ff. Sol reappears on the first issue minted at Antioch after the war of 324 (*RIC* 7.685, Antioch 49; 720, Antioch 49A).

48. As argued by H. P. L'Orange, *Symbolae Osloenses* 14 (1935), 86 ff. M.R. Alföldi, *Mullus: Festschrift T. Klauser* (Münster, 1964), 10 ff., deduces from the coins of 324/5 that "der Kaiser hat, wie seit eh und jeh, trotz allem an dem heidnischen Sol-Kult festgehalten."

49. On the slow introduction of Christian coin-types, P. Bruun, *Arctos,* n.s. 3 (1962), 5 ff. For the originally pagan ideology of *Sol comes,* A. D. Nock, *Essays on Religion and the Ancient World* (Oxford, 1972), 672 ff. On the sun as a Christian symbol (and on Christ as Sol Invictus) see F. J. Dölger, *Sol Salutis*[2] (*Liturgiegeschichtliche Forschungen* 4–5, 1925), esp. 336 ff.

50. One of Augustus' favorite maxims, according to Suetonius, *Div. Aug.* 25.4.

51. Lactantius, *Mort. Pers.* 44.11; Eusebius, *HE* 9.9.12, 9a.12. On the neces-

sity of identifying the "most perfect law" of Eusebius with the letter to which Lactantius refers, see N. H. Baynes, *CQ* 18 (1924), 193 f.

52. Eusebius, *HE* 9.9.12, 9a.12—where the manuscripts reveal that Eusebius later denied Licinius any credit. For the analogous phenomenon of a letter of Licinius which also bears the name of Constantine, *FIRA*² 1.93.

53. The latter document (Eusebius, *HE* 9.9a.1 ff.) was written before the end of December 312 (cf. *HE* 9.10.8).

54. Eusebius, *HE* 10.2.15–17 = Soden, *Urkunde* 7 (a letter to Anullinus).

55. Eusebius, *HE* 10.6.1–5 = Soden, *Urkunde* 8.

56. Eusebius, *VC* 1.42.2.

57. Incorporated by the *Liber Pontificalis* in its account of Silvester, bishop of Rome from 314 to 336 (pp. 170–187 Duchesne). The list appears to belong to the fourth century (L. Duchesne, *Le Liber Pontificalis* 1 [Paris, 1883], cxlix ff.). It cannot, however, be wholly Constantinian since it refers to *tremisses* (p. 177.9)—which were not minted until 383 (F. Vittinghoff, *RE* 7A [1948], 105). The statements in the *Liber Pontificalis* that Constantine's donations included images are impugned by R. Grigg, *Viator* 8 (1977), 2, 9 ff.

58. For the archaeological evidence relating to Constantinian churches in Rome, see esp. C. Pietri, *Roma Christiana: Recherches sur l'Église de Rome, son organisation, sa politique, son idéologie de Miltiade à Sixte III (311–440) (Bibliothèque des Écoles Françaises d'Athènes et de Rome* 224, 1976), 4 ff.; R. Krautheimer, *Rome: Profile of a City, 312–1308* (Princeton, 1980), 3 ff.

59. *Liber Pontificalis,* pp. 172–175; cf. A. Piganiol, *L'empereur Constantin,* 113; C. Pietri, *Roma Christiana,* 6, n. 1. The *Liber Pontificalis* calls the church *Basilica Constantiniana* (p. 172), a document written c. 370 *Basilica Lateranensis* (*CSEL* 35.1), and Prudentius *aedes Laterani* (*C. Symm.* 1.585). Jerome identifies the origin of the name: *basilica quondam Laterani qui Caesariano truncatus est gladio* (*Epp.* 77.4; cf. Tacitus, *Ann.* 15.60.1).

60. *Liber Pontificalis,* pp. 179–181. A document apparently written shortly after 501 calls the church *basilica Heleniana quae dicitur Sessorium* (L. Duchesne, *Le Liber Pontificalis* 1 (1883), 196).

61. *Liber Pontificalis,* pp. 176–178; cf. C. Pietri, *Roma Christiana,* 33 ff. The endowment of St. Peter's includes property in Syria, Euphratensis, and Egypt, regions which Constantine acquired only in 324; hence Pietri deduces that construction of the church probably did not begin until c. 327 (53 ff.). But an allusion to pilgrims visiting the shrine of Peter in Eusebius' *Theophany* (4.7, p. 175* Gressmann) should indicate a significantly earlier date, if that work was written c. 325 (as argued in chapter X). Moreover, a gold cross over the reputed tomb of Peter was dedicated by Constantine and Helena—presumably in 326 (*Liber Pontificalis,* p. 176; cf. R. Egger, *Römische Antike und frühes Christentum* 2 [Klagenfurt, 1963], 304 ff.).

F. W. Deichmann and A. Tschira, *JDAI* 72 (1957), 44 ff., argue on archaeological grounds that the basilica on the Via Labicana dedicated to the priest Marcellinus and the exorcist Peter, both probably martyred in 303/4 (cf. Chapter III), was begun in the decade 310–320; for its endowment, *Liber Pontificalis,* p. 182.

62. Eusebius, *VC* 1.43.

63. For the contrary assumption, see W. Ullmann, *JEH* 27 (1976), 1 ff. He

asserts that "the basic law in regard to the Christian church was the edict of Galerius in 311" and that Licinius' letters of 313 mark "the acknowledgement of the church as a *corpus* in a juristic sense" (3, with appeal to A. Ehrhardt, *ZSS*, Rom. Abt. 70 [1953], 299 ff.; 71 [1954], 21 ff.; 72 [1955], 171 ff.).

64. Observe, e.g., Tertullian, *Scap.* 2.3; *Refutatio omnium haeresium* 9.12.9 (Christian cemeteries in Carthage and Rome c. 200); Eusebius, *HE* 7.13 (Gallienus); 7.30.19 (Aurelian). Significantly, one of the charges leveled against a delinquent bishop between 254 and 257 was that he buried his sons in a pagan cemetery among *alienigeni* (Cyprian, *Epp.* 67.6).

65. Chapters III, V, IX.

66. A. H. M. Jones, *The Later Roman Empire*, 895.

67. *CTh* 16.2.4 (321); *habeat unusquisque licentiam sanctissimo catholicae venerabilique concilio decedens bonorum quod optavit relinquere. Non sint cassa iudicia. Nihil est quod magis hominibus debetur, quam ut supremae voluntatis, post quam aliud iam velle non possunt, liber sit stilus et licens, quod iterum non redit, arbitrium.*

68. On Constantine's religious legislation between 312 and 324, see especially J. Gaudemet, *Revue de l'Histoire de l'Église de France* 33 (1947), 25 ff. (though he tends to assume that the earliest surviving law on a subject was the earliest to be issued); S. Calderone, *Costantino e il Cattolicesimo* 1 (Florence, 1962), 230 ff.

69. Eusebius, *HE* 10.7.1–2; Augustine, *Epp.* 88.2 = Soden, *Urkunden* 9, 10; *CTh* 16.2.2[S]: *ab omnibus omnino muneribus excusentur, ne sacrilego livore quorundam a divinis obsequiis avocentur.* Constantine soon needed to forbid decurions, their sons, and others of similar wealth from avoiding *munera publica* through ordination (*CTh* 16.2.3, 6; cf. K. L. Noethlichs, *JAC* 15 [1972], 137 ff.).

70. *Leges Saeculares* 117 (*FIRA*[2] 2.794).

71. Thus C. Dupont, *RHE* 62 (1967), 739 ff. W. Goffart, *Caput and Colonate: Towards a History of Late Roman Taxation* (*Phoenix*, Supplementary Volume 12, 1974), 24, 124, argues that clerical exemption from *munera publica, munera civilia, obsequia publica* and *functiones publicae*, attested in laws probably issued in 320 and 329 (*CTh* 16.2.3, 6[S]), must have included exemption from payment of taxes in money.

72. Opitz, *Urkunde* 34. 39. By a law of 325, serving and retired soldiers enjoyed exemptions which ranged from one *caput* to four *capita* (*CTh* 7.20.4).

73. Sozomenus, *HE* 1.9.6.

74. *CJ* 1.13.1; cf. F. Millar, *Emperor*, 591.

75. *CTh* 4.7.1 = *CJ* 1.13.2 (321). On these two laws, F. Fabbrini, *La manumissio in ecclesia* (Università di Roma, *Pubblicazioni dell' Istituto di Diritto Romano* 40, 1965), 48 ff.; H. Langenfeld, *Christianisierungspolitik und Sklavengesetzgebung der römischen Kaiser von Konstantin bis Theodosius II* (*Antiquitas* 1.26, 1977), 24 ff.

76. T. Mommsen, *Römisches Staatsrecht* 3 (Leipzig, 1887), 226, 243; A. H. M. Jones, *The Greek City from Alexander to Justinian* (Oxford, 1940), 228 (priests); R. MacMullen, *Soldier and Civilian in the Later Roman Empire* (Harvard, 1963), 107 ff.

It is difficult to derive *manumissio in ecclesia* from any of the normal forms of manumission in Roman law; cf. W. H. Buckland, *The Roman Law of Slavery*

(Cambridge, 1908), 447 ff. Hence L. Mitteis, *Reichsrecht und Volksrecht in den östlichen Provinzen des römischen Kaiserreichs* (Leipzig, 1891), 375, argued that the model was the practice of manumitting slaves in pagan temples, long customary in the Greek world. But *manumissio in ecclesia* has no analogue of the sale or dedication to the god or goddess, which is a standard feature of that process (H. Bömer, *Untersuchungen über die Religion der Sklaven in Griechenland und Rom* 2 [*Abh. Mainz*, Geistes- u. Sozialwiss. Kl. 1960, Nr. 1], 177 ff.). It may derive, therefore, from the equally Greek practice of manumitting slaves in a public assembly or during a festival; cf. E. Weiss, *RE* 14 (1930), 1373.

77. Note Charisius' remark: *ab huiusmodi muneribus* (i.e., those levied on property) *neque primipilaris neque veteranus aut miles aliusve, qui privilegio aliquo subnixus, nec pontifex excusatur* (*Dig.* 50.4.18.24).

78. For modern discussions of laws on this topic, W. Selb, *ZSS*, Rom. Abt. 84 (1967), 162 ff.

79. 1 Corinthians 6:1–6. Constantine did not create episcopal jurisdiction; see Eusebius, *HE* 7.30.7 (Paul of Samosata bribed by litigants).

80. *CTh* 1.27.1. The transmitted subscription (*data VIII kal. Julias Constantinopoli . . . A. et Crispo Caes. conss.*) implies that the extant law was issued by Licinius in 318 (*New Empire*, ch. V: Licinius); if so, it presumably repeated an earlier enactment by Constantine.

81. *Const. Sirm.* 1; cf. W. Selb, *ZSS*, Rom. Abt. 84 (1967), 185 ff. The present exegesis lays stress on Constantine's repeated emphasis on age: *Sanximus namque, sicut edicti nostri forma declarat, sententias episcoporum quolibet genere latas sine aliqua aetatis discretione inviolatas semper incorruptasque servari . . . Sive itaque inter minores sive inter maiores ab episcopis fuerit iudicatum, . . . ad exsecutionem volumus pertinere.*

82. C. F. A. Jungk, *De Originibus et Progressu episcopalis iudicii in caussis civilibus laicorum usque ad Iustinianum* (diss., Berlin, 1832), 49, 70, restricted the law to ecclesiastical disputes between Christians—a notion reported and rejected by G. Haenel, *De Constitutionibus quas Iacobus Sirmondus Parisiis a. mdcxxxi edidit* (diss., Leipzig, 1840), 21 f. Observe that Sozomenus writes as if appeal to bishops was available to all litigants in private lawsuits (*HE* 1.9.5).

The following clauses need careful interpretation: *Testimonium etiam ab uno licet episcopo perhibitum omnis iudex indubitanter accipiat nec alius audiatur testis, cum testimonium episcopi a qualibet parte fuerit repromissum. Illud est enim veritatis auctoritate firmatum, illud incorruptum, quod a sacrosancto homine conscientia mentis inlibatae protulerit.* J. Gaudemet, *Revue de l'Histoire de l'Église de France* 33 (1947), 36 ff., argued that Constantine cannot have intended to make bishops privileged witnesses in court and the transmitted text must contain later interpolations. But Constantine's words mean merely that the arbitration of a single bishop shall be binding on the magistrate from whose court one party has made an appeal.

83. Victor, *Caes.* 41.4; Sozomenus, *HE* 1.8.13; *CTh* 9.40.2[S] (316). T. Mommsen, *Römisches Strafrecht* (Berlin, 1899), 921, argued that the prohibition of crucifixion, undated in Victor and Sozomenus, belongs late in the reign, because the edict *de accusationibus* shows Constantine prescribing crucifixion as a punishment after 312 (*FIRA*[2] 1.94; *CTh* 9.5.1). The edict was in fact issued by Licinius (Chapter V, n. 65).

84. *CTh* 2.8.1.; *CJ* 3.12.2 (3); cf. Eusebius, *VC* 4.18.2. Despite different dates in the *Codex Theodosianus* and *Codex Justinianus,* the two fragments, both addressed to Helpidius, *vicarius* of the city of Rome, ought to belong to the same law; in his edition of the *Codex Theodosianus* (Berlin, 1923), P. Krüger prints *CJ* 3.12.2(3) as *CTh* 2.8.1a.

85. For the known provisions of the *Lex Julia de maritandis ordinibus* of 18 B.C. and the *Lex Papia Poppaea* of A.D. 9, H. Furneaux, in his edition of Tacitus, *Annales* 1² (Oxford, 1896), 483 ff.; G. Rotondi, *Leges Publicae Populi Romani* (Milan, 1912), 443 ff., 457 ff.

86. Tertullian, *Apol.* 4.8; Dio 77(76).16.4 (Septimius Severus).

87. Augustus recited the speech of Q. Metellus (censor in 131 B.C.) *de prole augenda* in the Senate (Suetonius, *Div. Aug.* 89.2); Paul believed that marriage was morally inferior to celibacy (1 Corinthians 7:25–40). For subsequent Christian denigration of marriage, A. Depke, *RAC* 4 (1959), 659 ff.

88. Eusebius, *VC* 4.26.2 ff.; Sozomenus, *HE* 1.9.1 ff.

89. *CTh* 8.161.1 (321).

90. *CTh* 3.16.1 (331). The law specifically denies women the right to divorce for drunkenness, gambling, or philandering. For Christian influence on Late Roman marriage law, H. J. Wolff, *ZSS,* Rom. Abt. 67 (1950), 261 ff.

91. J. Ziegler, *Zur religiösen Haltung,* 48 f.

92. *Pan. Lat.* 12(9).2.2.

93. *CTh* 9.16.1 (320^S).

94. *CTh* 9.16.3 (318^S), 2 (319).

95. *CTh* 16.10.1.

96. J. Gaudemet, *Revue de l'Histoire de l'Église de France* 33 (1947), 48 ff.

97. *CTh* 9.16.1: *superstitioni enim suae servire cupientes poterunt publicae ritum proprium exercere.*

98. *CTh* 9.18.1. For the tone, compare *CTh* 9.15.1 (318), which reiterates the traditional and barbaric method of execution for parricides.

99. G. Ville, *MEFR* 72 (1960), 273 ff. The Councils of Elvira (Canon 62) and Arles (Canons 4, 5) excommunicated actors and pantomimes; their failure to mention gladiators attests their disappearance or unimportance in the West by 300 (G. Ville, 313).

100. *CTh* 15.12.1; Eusebius, *VC* 4.25.1. The excerpt quoted in the *Codex* contains an anacolouthon: J. Gascou, *MEFR* 79 (1967), 649 ff., interprets the text not as abolishing gladiatorial combats but as merely forbidding the use of criminals as gladiators.

101. G. Ville, *MEFR* 72 (1960), 312 ff. Panolbius, the maternal uncle of Libanius, ostentatiously put on gladiatorial games as Syriarch in 328—which his nephew did not attend (Libanius, *Orat.* 1.5).

102. For the great change in public entertainments in the fourth century (though he does not attribute any role to Constantine), see A. Cameron, *Circus Factions: Blues and Greens at Rome and Byzantium* (Oxford, 1976), 214 ff. The fourth century also saw the disappearance of the gymnasium from Greek life; cf. H. I. Marrou, *L'histoire de l'éducation dans l'antiquité*⁶ (Paris, 1965), 201 ff. Christian pressure is commonly identified as the main cause, as by E. G. Turner, *Greek Papyri: An Introduction* (Oxford, 1968), 84.

103. For surveys of what is known about Christianity in the West before

Constantine, see above all A. Harnack, *Die Mission und Ausbreitung des Christentums in den ersten drei Jahrhunderten*[4] (Leipzig, 1924), 198 ff.; K. Baus, *From the Apostolic Community to Constantine* (*Handbook of Church History*, ed. H. Jedin and J. Dolan, 1 [Freiburg and London, 1965]), 379 ff. Adducing Cyprian, Harnack estimated that in about 250 Christians formed 3 to 5 percent of the population of African towns (948, n. 1). That estimate is probably far too low.

104. T. D. Barnes, *Tertullian: A Historical and Literary Study* (Oxford, 1971), 67 ff., 195 f.

105. M. M. Sage, *Cyprian* (*Patristic Monograph Series*, no. 1, 1975), 47 ff.

106. Eusebius, *HE* 6.43.11 (quoting a letter of bishop Cornelius to Fabius of Antioch); cf. A. Harnack, *Die Mission und Ausbreitung des Christentums*,[4] 806.

107. On early Christianity in Gaul, see E. Griffe, *La Gaule chrétienne à l'époque romaine* 1 (Paris, 1964); *Les Martyrs de Lyon (177)* (Paris, 1978), esp. 211 ff. (C. Pietri, on the origins of Christianity at Lyon). Gregory of Tours, *Liber in Gloria Confessorum* 90; *Hist.* 1.31, states that Leocadius of Bourges, the leading senator of Gaul, and his son Lusor became Christians shortly after 250. For Christians in the Senate before Constantine, see the survey by W. Eck, *Chiron* 1 (1971), 381 ff.

108. M. J. Routh, *Reliquiae Sacrae*[2] 4 (Oxford, 1846), 258 ff.; *PL* 84.301 ff. For two styles of modern exegesis, C. J. Hefele and H. Leclercq, *Histoire des conciles* 1 (Paris, 1907), 212 ff., and S. Laeuchli, *Power and Sexuality: The Emergence of Canon Law at the Synod of Elvira* (Philadelphia, 1972), who detects "a crisis of male identity" (104) and interprets the council as inaugurating "Christianity's Constantinian period" (114).

L. Duchesne, *Mélanges Renier* (Paris, 1877), 159 ff., showed that the absence of any allusion to recent persecution entails a date before 303. An attempt to deny the inference, and to establish the date as 306, was made by H. Koch, *ZNW* 17 (1916), 61 ff. The date of 309 adopted by H. Grégoire, *Les persécutions dans l'empire romain*[2] (Brussels, 1964), 78, and by S. Laeuchli, *Power and Sexuality*, 86 f., depends on the mistaken belief that Severus and then Maxentius ruled Spain from 305 to 309 (cf. *New Empire*, ch. XI).

109. No fewer than seventeen canons deal with adultery (7–10, 14, 19, 30, 31, 47, 63–65, 68–70, 72, 78). The offenders included bishops (19). The council allowed former prostitutes to be baptized, provided they had acquired husbands (44), but forbade male Christians to gamble (79) or to be charioteers or pantomimes (62), female Christians to have fancy hairdressers (67).

110. E.g., beating a slave to death (5), murder (6), prostituting a daughter (12), buggering boys (71).

111. E.g., failure to attend church on Sundays (21), fasting (23, 26), clerical celibacy (33), cemeteries (34, 35), paintings in church (36).

112. Canons 15–17.

113. Canons 55, 56.

114. Canons 2–4; cf. L. Duchesne, *Mélanges Renier*, 159 ff.

115. Canon 60: *si quis idola fregerit, et ibidem fuerit occisus, . . . placuit in numero eum non recipi martyrum.*

116. Athanasius, *Hist. Ar.* 44.1 (quoting a letter of Ossius).

117. Note the prominence of Datianus in Spanish hagiography; cf. B. de

Gaiffier, *Anal. Boll.* 72 (1954), 378 ff. Spain was under the rule of Maximian until 305, of Constantius in 305-306, and of Constantine from 306 (*New Empire,* ch. XI).

118. Optatus, app. 2, p. 198.31-199.1 Ziwsa (quoted in Chapter II, n. 76); *CIL* 8.6700 (*dies turificationis* at Milevis under Florus before 20 November 303); Optatus 3.8.

119. Optatus 1.13 ff. presents all the Donatist leaders as self-confessed *traditores,* while the Donatist who gave the *Passio Saturnini* its present form (*BHL* 7492, best edited by P. Franchi de' Cavalieri, *Note agiografiche* 8 [*Studi e Testi* 65, 1935], 49 ff.) states both that Fundanus, the bishop of Abitina, surrendered the Scriptures to be burned (3.5), and that the *traditor* Mensurius stationed his deacon Caecilianus outside the prison with whips to prevent the martyrs from receiving visitors (20.3 ff.).

The partial text of two official inquiries survives: (1) the *Acta Purgationis Felicis* (Optatus, app. 2, pp. 197-204 Ziwsa = Soden, *Urkunde* 19) record the investigation conducted in February 315 by Aelianus, the proconsul of Africa, which absolved Felix, bishop of Abthungi, of the Donatist charge that he had surrendered the Scriptures in 303; (2) the *Gesta apud Zenophilum* (Optatus, app. 1, pp. 185-197 Ziwsa = Soden, *Urkunde* 28) record the investigation conducted at Cirta in December 320 by Domitius Zenophilus, the *consularis* of Numidia, which produced evidence that the Donatist bishops had committed the very same offense they alleged against Felix. The *Gesta,* incomplete at the end, and the *Acta,* whose beginning is lost, form the extant part of a dossier which Optatus appended to his work in full (1.14). For a detailed analysis of its probable contents, L. Duchesne, *MEFR* 10 (1890), 625 ff. Both the oral testimony and the documents presented in court before Zenophilus have some extremely suspicious features; see T. D. Barnes, *JTS,* n.s. 26 (1975), 14 ff.; S. Lancel, *Actes de la Conférence de Carthage en 411* 1 (*SC* 194, 1972), 96 f.; *Rev. Ét. Aug.* 25 (1979), 217 ff.

120. The letters of Mensurius and Secundus are reported by Augustine, *Brev. Coll.* 3.13.25 = Soden, *Urkunde* 4.

121. *Acta Eupli* (*BHG*[3] 629); cf. H. Delehaye, *Les origines du culte des martyrs*[2] (*Subsidia Hagiographica* 20, 1933), 311.

122. Optatus, app. 1, p. 192.24 ff., p. 194.10 ff. = Soden, *Urkunde* 28.269 ff., 333 ff.; cf. S. Lancel, *Cahiers de Tunisie* 15 (1967), 183 ff.

123. Optatus 1.14; cf. Augustine, *Contra Partem Donati post Gesta* 14.18. On the date, see S. Lancel, *Rev. Ét. Aug.* 25 (1979), 217 ff.

124. Optatus 1.17; cf. T. D. Barnes, *JTS* n.s. 26 (1975), 18 ff. The emperor who summoned Mensurius might have been Severus, who ruled Italy and Africa from May 305 to October 306.

125. Optatus 1.18 f.

126. Augustine, *Brev. Coll.* 3.12.24. = Soden, *Urkunde* 13(C). The evidence that Donatus was a Numidian is very tenuous; see T. D. Barnes, *JTS,* n.s. 26 (1975), 16 f.

127. Augustine, *Epp.* 44.4.8; cf. *Sermo* 46.15 (*PL* 38.279). Significantly, Optatus omits this episode entirely.

128. Optatus 1.19 f., partly reproduced as Soden, *Urkunde* 6(B); Augustine, *Brev. Coll.* 3.14.26; *Contra Fulgentium* 26 = Soden, *Urkunde* 6(A), (C). Neither

party disputed the principle that *traditores* be excluded from the priesthood in perpetuity (Council of Arles, Canon 13).

129. As argued by T. D. Barnes, *JTS,* n.s. 26 (1975), 18 ff. The standard date of 311/2 for the beginning of the Donatist schism (recently restated by W. H. C. Frend and K. Clancy, *JTS,* n.s. 28 [1977], 104 ff.) depends on three erroneous premises: the argument misinterprets *tyrannus imperator* (1.17) as "usurper" (it here means "persecuting emperor"), it identifies the *tyrannus* with Maxentius (Optatus 1.17/18 distinguishes the two), and finally it confuses Maxentius' grant of toleration in 306/7 with his restoration of church property in 311 (Chapter III).

For the chronology of Constantine's dealings with the Donatists, *New Empire,* ch. XV. For full discussion of many details in the Donatist controversy, see the "notes complémentaires" by E. Lamirande and A. C. de Veer, *Oeuvres de Saint Augustin* 32 (Paris, 1965), 689 ff.; 31 (Paris, 1968), 741 ff.

130. Eusebius, *HE* 10.5.15–17 = Soden, *Urkunde* 7.

131. Eusebius, *HE* 10.6.1–5 = Soden, *Urkunde* 8.

132. Eusebius, *HE* 10.7.1/2 = Soden, *Urkunde* 9.

133. Optatus states that the Donatist petition of April 313 found Constantine *harum rerum adhuc ignarum* (1.22). Modern scholars have been strangely reluctant to doubt this tendentious allegation.

134. Augustine, *Epp.* 88.2 = Soden, *Urkunde* 10.

135. Optatus 1.22 = Soden, *Urkunde* 11. It is not altogether clear whether the *facinus* from which "Gaul is immune" is persecution or schism resulting from persecution; see T. D. Barnes, *JTS,* n.s. 26 (1975), 20 f.; F. Millar, *Emperor* (1977), 585. The petitioners clearly meant to request bishops as *iudices* (Augustine, *Epp.* 43.5.14; 53.2.5; 76.2).

136. Optatus 1.3; Eusebius, *HE* 10.5.18–20 = Soden, *Urkunde* 12. Optatus, app. 3, p. 204.18 ff., also describes the episode, but the crucial sentence is hopelessly corrupt; see H. Schrörs, *ZSS,* Kan. Abt. 11 (1921), 431 ff.; C. H. Turner, *JTS,* 27 (1926), 283 ff.; E. Caspar, *ZKG* 46 (1927), 335 ff.

137. E. Caspar, *Geschichte des Papsttums* 1 (Tübingen, 1930), 109 ff.; C. Pietri, *Roma Christiana* (1976), 160 ff.

138. *Optatus* 1.23 = Soden, *Urkunde* 13(A): *convenerunt in domum Faustae in Laterano;* cf. C. Pietri, *Roma Christiana,* 5 ff.; E. Nash, *Röm. Quart.* 71 (1976), 1 ff.

139. Soden, *Urkunde* 13, from Optatus 1.23; Augustine, *Contra Partem Donati post Gesta* 33.56; *Brev. Coll.* 3.12.24, 17.31; *Epp.* 43.5.16. On the proceedings of the council, cf. G. Roethe, *Zur Geschichte der römischen Synoden im 3. und 4. Jahrhundert (Forschungen zur Kirchen- und Geistesgeschichte* 11: *Geistige Grundlagen römischer Kirchenpolitik,* Heft 2, 1937), 51 ff., 118 ff.

140. Optatus, app. 3 (to the *vicarius*); Eusebius, *HE* 10.5.21–24 (to Chrestus, the bishop of Syracuse) = Soden, *Urkunden* 14, 15.

141. Eusebius, *VC* 1.44.

142. Optatus, app. 4 = Soden, *Urkunde* 16 (conciliar letter to Silvester, bishop of Rome); *Concilia Galliae A.314–A.506,* ed. C. Munier (*CCL* 148, 1963), 9 ff. (canons and subscriptions as preserved in collections of canon law).

The bishops excommunicated soldiers who refuse to fight, charioteers, theatrical performers (3–5), and girls who marry pagans (11); they also provided that

Christian provincial governors should carry *litterae ecclesiasticae communica-toriae,* be welcomed by local bishops, and excluded from communion if they offended against Christian moral standards (7).

143. Optatus, app. 5 = Soden, *Urkunde* 18.

144. Optatus, app. 2, p. 198.19 ff. = Soden, *Urkunde* 19.37 ff.

145. Optatus, app. 2, p. 197.16 ff.; Augustine, *Epp.* 88.4; *Contra Cresconium* 3.70.81 = Soden, *Urkunde* 19(B) 1 ff.; 20.3 ff.

146. Optatus, app. 2 = Soden, *Urkunde* 19(B). The date is wrongly given as 15 February 314 by Augustine, *Contra Partem Donati post Gesta* 33.56 = Soden, *Urkunde* 19(A).

147. Constantine's letter of early May 315 (Optatus, app. 6 = Soden, *Urkunde* 21) refers both to *amici* whom he had agreed to send to Africa to decide the case, and to the imminent arrival of the previously summoned Caecilianus.

148. Optatus, app. 8 = Soden, *Urkunde* 22.

149. Optatus, app. 6 = Soden, *Urkunde* 21. The correct relationship between the two documents was seen by L. Duchesne, *MEFR* 10 (1890), 619 f.

150. Augustine, *Epp.* 88.4; *Contra Cresconium* 3.70.81 = Soden, *Urkunde* 20.

151. Optatus 1.26.

152. Augustine, *Epp.* 43.7.20.

153. Optatus 1.26.

154. Optatus, app. 7 = Soden, *Urkunde* 23.

155. Augustine, *Contra Cresconium* 3.71.82; *Contra Partem Donati post Gesta* 33.56 = Soden, *Urkunde* 25.

156. Augustine, *Epp.* 88.3 = Soden, *Urkunde* 26. Augustine elsewhere calls it a *lex severissima* (*Epp.* 105.2.9).

157. *Sermo de Passione Donati* (*PL* 8.752 ff.).

158. For Leontius and Ursacius as persecutors of Donatists, *Sermo de Passione Donati* 2; Optatus 3.1, 4, 10; *Coll. Carth.* 3.258.

Ursacius' activities are dated shortly after 316 by Optatus 3.10; Augustine, *Contra Cresconium* 3.30.34. Augustine also reveals that Ursacius was killed in battle fighting barbarians (*Contra Litteras Petiliani* 2.92.202). Leontius is dated only by a passage in the *Sermo* which, suspiciously, also names a *tribunus* Marcellinus (see *New Empire,* ch. X). Leontius might be identical with the pagan Flavius Leontius, *dux per Africam,* who made a dedication to Jupiter *ob reportatam ex gentilibus barbaris gloriam* (*ILS* 2999).

159. Optatus, app. 1 = Soden, *Urkunde* 28. The *comes* Ursacius cooperated with Zenophilus in exiling Silvanus, presumably as soon as the inquiry brought in its verdict against him (Augustine, *Contra Cresconium* 3.30.34, quoting Cresconius).

160. Augustine, *Brev. Coll.* 3.21.29 = Soden, *Urkunde* 29, records a petition, probably written between 316 and 321, in which the Donatists derided Caecilianus as Constantine's worthless stooge and professed readiness to suffer whatever hardships he might inflict on them.

161. Augustine, *Contra Partem Donati post Gesta* 31.54, 33.56 = Soden, *Urkunde* 30.

162. Optatus, app. 9 = Soden, *Urkunde* 31.

163. Eusebius, *VC* 2.66.2 = Soden, *Urkunde* 32.

164. Optatus, app. 10 = Soden, *Urkunde* 36. Part of the instructions sent on

the same day to the *consularis* of Numidia survives in *CTh* 16.2.7 = Soden, *Urkunde* 35.

165. Augustine, *Epp.* 93.10.43 = Soden, *Urkunde* 38. Donatus wrote to Gregorius, praetorian prefect of Africa in 336–337, insulting him as *macula senatus et dedecus praefectorum* (Optatus 1.3 = Soden, *Urkunde* 37).

V. CONSTANTINE AND LICINIUS

1. Lactantius, *Mort. Pers.* 45.1; cf. 43.2. Constantine was still in Rome on 6 January 313 (*CTh* 15.14.3[S]), but must have departed very soon (*Pan. Lat.* 4(10).33.6: *bimestris fere cura*).
2. Lactantius, *Mort. Pers.* 45.1; Theomnestus, *Hippiatrica Berolinensia* 34.12.
3. Eusebius, *HE* 9.9a.10 f.
4. Antecedent legislation for Licinius' territories is implied by the reference in Lactantius, *Mort. Pers.* 48.1 ff. = Eusebius, *HE* 10.5.4 ff., to the meeting of the emperors at Milan. The unfortunate modern term "the edict of Milan" (defended by M. Anastos, *Revue des Études Byzantines* 25 (1967), 13 ff.) implies that the Christians of the western provinces still lacked what Constantine granted in 306 and Maxentius in 311 (Chapter III).
5. Eusebius, *HE* 9.8.2 ff.; cf. *New Empire*, Chapter V: Maximinus.
6. Lactantius, *Mort. Pers.* 45.2 ff. His distances differ by one or two miles from those attested by the majority of manuscripts of the *Itinerarium Burgidalense*, p. 569.8 ff. Wesseling, which give seventeen miles as the distance between Heraclea and the *mansio* Tunorullum, sixteen between the *mansiones* of Tunorullum and Drizupara.
7. Lactantius, *Mort. Pers.* 46.1 ff. The prayer (46.6) resembles the prayer which Constantine administered to his non-Christian soldiers (Eusebius, *VC* 4.20.1); on its probable origin, Chapter IV, n. 44.
8. Lactantius, *Mort. Pers.* 46.11 ff.
9. Lactantius, *Mort. Pers.* 49.1 ff.; Eusebius, *HE* 9.10.13 ff.; Eutropius, *Brev.* 10.4.4; Zosimus 2.17.2. His death was known in Karanis by 13 September (*P. Cairo Isid.* 103.20).
10. Lactantius, *Mort. Pers.* 48.1, 13.
11. Eusebius, *HE* 9.11.2 ff.; cf. Gregory of Nazianus, *Orat.* 4.96 (*PG* 35.629).
12. Lactantius, *Mort. Pers.* 50.2 ff.
13. Lactantius, *Mort. Pers.* 50.6.
14. Eusebius, *HE* 9.11.4; *Mart. Pal.* (S) 11.31. On the career of Hierocles, Chapter X. Peucetius may have been proconsul of Asia from 311 to 313 (*New Empire*, ch. IX).
15. Eusebius, *PE* 4.2.11; cf. Chapter II.
16. Eusebius, *HE* 9.2 f.; 9.11.5 f.; *PE* 4.2.6 ff.
17. Lactantius, *Mort. Pers.* 48.2 ff.; Eusebius, *HE* 10.5.2 ff. (described as translated from a Latin original).
18. Chapters IX, XI.
19. An inference from *ILS* 8942 (Semta: 315); 696 (near Sitifis, 318); cf. *New Empire*, Ch. V: Licinius, n. 145.
20. J. Lebon, *Le Muséon* 51 (1938), 89 ff.; P. Ananian, *Le Muséon* 74 (1961),

43 ff., 317 ff.; M. L. Chaumont, *Recherches sur l'histoire d'Arménie* (Paris, 1969), 147 ff.

21. *ILS* 8942; 696. [Julian], *Epp.* 186, 421A may allude to a panegyric which celebrated Licinius' crossing into Europe; see T. D. Barnes, *GRBS* 19 (1978), 103 f.

22. *ILS* 8938: *Tropeensium civitas auspicato a fundamentis feliciter opere constructa est.* For the hypothesis that the reliefs are a fourth century reworking of the originals, C. Cichorius, *Die römischen Denkmäler in der Dobrudscha: Ein Erklärungsversuch* (Berlin, 1904), 9 ff. It has not commended itself to most subsequent inquirers; see I.A. Richmond, *PBSR* 35 (1967), 37 ff.

23. [Julian], *Epp.* 185–187; cf. T. D. Barnes, *GRBS* 19 (1978), 102 f.

24. *Epitome* 41.4, and Zosimus 2.20.2, state that he was nineteen months old when proclaimed Caesar on 1 March 317—which implies birth in July or August 315. But both writers also describe Constantinus as being only a few days old: their source, therefore, may have reckoned from the beginning (not the end) of the war of 316–317. If so, Licinius Caesar was born c. February 315.

25. He was still at Milan on 10 March (*CTh* 10.8.1).

26. *New Empire*, ch. VI.

27. *Frag. Vat.* 291[S].

28. *Pan. Lat.* 12(9).21.5 ff.

29. *RIC* 7.97–98, London 1, 21; *ILS* 8942, 696; cf. T. D. Barnes, *ZPE* 20 (1976), 153 f.

30. Eusebius, *VC* 1.44; Optatus, app. 4, p. 208.16 Ziwsa; cf. *New Empire,* ch. V: Constantine.

31. *RIC* 7.124, 163–164, 166–167, 362–364; cf. Eusebius, *VC* 1.46. This appears to be the occasion when Constantine took the title *Germanicus maximus* for the third time (*ILS* 696; cf. T. D. Barnes, *ZPE* 20 [1976], 150 f.).

32. *CTh* 6.35.1, 1.2.1; *RIC* 7.164, Trier 12; Optatus, app. 8.

33. *CIL* 1², pp. 268, 272.

34. During Constantine's visit, the Senate dedicated the triumphal arch which they had decreed in 312; its inscriptions laud the emperor as a *liberator urbis* and *fundator quietis* who rescued the state from a tyrant in a just war (*ILS* 694).

35. He was in Milan on 19 October (*Frag. Vat.* 273) and at Trier by 11 January 316 (*CTh* 1.22.1).

36. Constantine is attested at Cabillunum on 21 March (*CTh* 9.40.2[S]), at Vienne on 6 May (*CTh* 2.6.1).

37. *CIL* 1², p. 271 (day); *Epitome* 41.4; Zosimus 2.20.2 (place).

38. *Origo* 15; Eusebius, *HE* 10.8.5; *VC* 1.50.2.

39. *Origo* 14 f. For a recent attempt to elucidate the episode, V. Neri, *Rivista storica di antichità* 5 (1975), 79 ff. He unfortunately dates the War of Cibalae to 314 (106).

40. Istria, though technically part of the Italian diocese, was ruled by Licinius (*Origo* 15).

41. Chapter III.

42. On the careers of Volusianus and Rufinus (consul in 316), see *New Empire,* ch. VI.

43. Firmicus Maternus, *Math.* 2.29.10 ff.; cf. T. D. Barnes, *JRS* 65 (1975), 40 ff.

44. Publilius Optatianus Porfyrius, *Carm.* 1–20; Jerome, *Chronicle* 232[e]; cf. T. D. Barnes, *AJP* 96 (1975), 184 ff. Volusianus and Porfyrius both occur in a list of seven names, perhaps the members of a Roman priesthood under Maxentius (*Notizie degli Scavi* 1917.22; cf. E. Groag, *Wiener Studien* 45 [1926/7], 102 ff.). Relationship, perhaps by marriage, is implied by the nomenclature of Publilius Caeionius Caecina Albinus, *consularis* of Numidia from 364 to 367 (*PLRE* 1.34 f.), who is conventionally identified as the son of C. Caeionius Rufius Volusianus, *praefectus urbi* in 364–365 (following O. Seeck, *MGH, Auct. Ant.* 6.1 [1883], clxxviif.).

45. Constantine is attested at Arles on 13 August (*CTh* 11.30.5, 6).

46. *Frag. Vat.* 290 (year not stated); *Chr. Min.* 1.231 (giving 8 October 314, in error). Complementary details of the campaign are preserved in *Origo* 15 ff.; Zosimus 2.18.1 ff.; Petrus Patricius, frag. 15. Coins show that Valens was proclaimed Augustus, not Caesar (*RIC* 7.644, Cyzicus 7; 706, Alexandria 19).

47. As Eutropius states: *bellum apud Cibalas instruentem repentinus oppressit* (*Brev.* 10.5). The *Epitome* alleges a nocturnal assault on Licinius' camp (41.5).

48. On the site of the battle, H. Grégoire, *Byzantion* 13 (1938), 586 (emending *in campo mardiense* in *Origo* 17 to *in campum Ardiensem*). Constantine had been in Serdica in early December (*CTh* 9.13.1; 1.13.1, as emended in *New Empire,* ch. V: Constantine, n. 116).

49. Eutropius, *Brev.* 10.4.1; *Origo* 7.

50. *Chr. Min.* 1.232; cf. *Pan. Lat.* 4(10).2.1 ff., 38.2.

51. [Julian], *Epp.* 184; Socrates, *HE* 1.6.33; Sozomenus, *HE* 4.16.6. *P. Oxy.* 889 appears to imply that Licinius fought the Sarmatians c. 318 (reprinted and discussed in *New Empire,* ch. XIV).

52. T. D. Barnes, *GRBS* 19 (1978), 99 ff.

53. [Julian], *Epp.* 181, 449A.

54. Ibid., 184, 416D–417A.

55. Libanius, *Orat.* 52.31 (Apamea); Malalas 312 Bonn (Antioch).

56. [Julian], *Epp.* 185–187.

57. Ibid., 184, 417D–418A.

58. Ibid., 181, 449B; 184, 419A.

59. Eusebius, *VC* 2.66.

60. Eusebius, *HE* 10.8.11 ff.; Praxagoras, *FGrH* 219; *Origo* 22.

61. Eusebius, *HE* 9.9.1, 9.12, 10.3, 11.8. Manuscript variants show that in 325 Eusebius revised these passages in order to attribute all the credit to Constantine—and Licinius' name was removed from the heading to Galerius' edict of 311 (*HE* 8.17.5).

62. Eusebius, *HE* 9.9.1; *VC* 1.49.2. On Latin accounts of Licinius, see R. Andreotti, *Hommages à L. Herrmann* (*Collection Latomus* 44, 1960), 105 ff.

63. R. Andreotti, *Studi in Onore di E. Betti* 3 (Milan, 1962), 41 ff. On imperial legislation beteen 305 and 324, see also A. Amelotti, *SDHI* 27 (1961), 252 ff.

64. *FIRA*² 1.94.

65. *CTh* 9.5.1 = *CJ* 9.8.3 (January 314) quotes part of a *sacrum edictum* also attested epigraphically (*FIRA*² 1.94). For its identification as a law ad-

dressed by Licinius to his praetorian prefect, T. D. Barnes, *ZPE* 21 (1976), 275 f.

66. *CTh* 12.1.5, 8.4.3.

67. *CTh* 10.20.1, 12.1.5.

68. *CTh* 10.7.1. An inscription from Lyttos in Crete contains an imperial letter designed to curb extortion by procurators and *Caesariani* (*I. Cret.* 1.189); it too may emanate from Licinius.

69. *CTh* 12.1.4 (19 January 317, addressed to Octavianus, *comes Hispaniarum*).

70. Eusebius, *HE* 10.8.13; *VC* 1.55.2. Similar allegations are made about Maximian (Lactantius, *Mort. Pers.* 8.5), Maximinus (*Mort. Pers.* 38.1 ff.; Eusebius, *HE* 8.14.12 ff.) and Maxentius (*Pan. Lat.* 12(9).3.6, 4.4; Eusebius, *HE* 8.14.2).

71. Eusebius, *HE* 10.8.12; *VC* 1.55.1.

72. For the five-year cycle of empire-wide censuses, *New Empire,* ch. XIV.

73. Eusebius, *VC* 4.3 (undated); *ILS* 1240–1242 (a *peraequator census provinciae Gallaeciae* shortly after 320). Note also three laws of 321 protecting provincials from excessive demands to provide transport (*CTh* 4.13.1–3).

74. Eusebius, *HE* 10.8.12; *VC* 1.55.1 f.

75. *P. Oxy.* 889, as interpreted in *New Empire,* ch. XIV.

76. *CTh* 8.4.1 (326). It is hard to assess the effect of Licinius' action in reducing the value of the *follis* from 25 to 12½ denarii c. 321 (P. Bruun, *RIC* 7 [1966], 12). Evidence from both Egypt and Palestine attests rampant inflation throughout the fourth century; see D. Sperber, *Archiv orientální* 34 (1966), 54 ff. The price of 1 lb. gold rose from 72,000 denarii in 301 (Chapter I, n. 75) to over 300,000 by 324 (*P. Oxy.* 1430).

77. Opitz, *Urkunde* 27.9 ff.

78. Opitz, *Urkunde* 4b.4; cf. Socrates, *HE* 1.6.33. If Licinius had already moved his capital from the Balkans to Nicomedia, then the date can be no earlier than the spring of 317.

79. The emperor Julian was related to Eusebius of Nicomedia (Ammianus 22.9.4); the kinship passed through his mother, Basilina, the daughter of Julius Julianus; see J. Bidez, *Mélanges P. Thomas* (Bruges, 1930), 54 ff.

80. Philostorgius, *HE* 1.9 (in 325); Rufinus, *HE* 10.12; Socrates, *HE* 1.25; Sozomenus, *HE* 2.27.2 (after Nicaea). It is not certain that Jerome had accurate information about the period before 324 when he asserted that *Arrius, ut orbem caperet, sororem principis ante decepit* (*Epp.* 133.4).

81. Lactantius, *Div. Inst.* 1.1.13 ff.; cf. E. Heck, *Die dualistischen Zusätze und die Kaiseranreden bei Lactantius* (Heidelberg, 1972), 127 ff.

82. Eusebius, *HE* 10.8.10. In *VC* 1.52 Eusebius writes as if a separate (and later) law exiled Christian courtiers and deprived Christian *palatini* of their rank and property.

83. Sozomenus, *HE* 4.16.6 ff.

84. Philostorgius, *HE* 5.2; *Suda* A 4450.

85. Eusebius, *HE* 10.8.10; *VC* 1.54.1; cf. N. H. Baynes, *Constantine the Great and the Christian Church* (London, 1931), 80 ff.

86. *ILS* 8940, with the revealing phrase *iussu sacro dd. nn. Licini Aug. et Licini Caes.*

87. *CTh.* 16.2.5[S]. The manuscripts have *dat. viii Kal. Jun. Sirmi Severo et*

Rufino conss., but the law's reference to *lustrorum sacrificia* implies a date close to the fifteenth anniversary of Licinius' *dies imperii* (11 November 323).

88. Eusebius, *VC* 1.51.1 f.

89. Ibid., 1.53.1.

90. Ibid., 1.53.2.

91. Ibid., 2.20.2, 30.1

92. On the persecution of Licinius, see H. Görres, *Kritische Untersuchungen über die licinianische Christenverfolgung: Ein Beitrag zur Kritik der Märtyreracten* (Jena, 1875), and E. Honigmann, *Patristic Studies* (*Studi e Testi* 173, 1953), 6 ff. Both writers inexplicably overlook Eusebius' *Proof of the Gospel.*

93. Chapter X.

94. Eusebius, *DE* 3.5.78 ff., 5.3.11, 6.20.17 ff.; cf. 2.3.155, 3.7.36 ff., 7.1.132, 8.1.61.

95. *Pan. Lat.* 4(10).38.3.

96. E. Honigmann, *Patristic Studies,* 20 ff.

97. Eusebius, *HE* 10.8.15 ff.; *VC* 2.1.1 ff.

98. Eusebius, *HE* 10.8.18 f.; *VC* 2.2.3.

99. For Constantine's attested movements between 317 and 324, *New Empire,* ch. V: Constantine.

100. Petrus Patricius, *Excerpta Vaticana* 190 = Anon. post Dionem, frag. 15.1.

101. *Origo* 18; Eutropius, *Brev.* 10.5.

102. Julian, *Orat.* 1, 8 CD.

103. *Orientis Graeci Inscriptiones Selectae* 720 f., with J. Baillet, *CRAI* 1922, 282 ff.; cf. P. Graindor, *Byzantion* 3 (1926), 209 ff.; F. Millar, *JRS* 59 (1969), 17.

104. *FGrH* 219.

105. C. Jan, *Musici Scriptores Graeci* (Leipzig, 1895), 285. Observe also that Constantine reaffirmed the traditional immunity from taxation of doctors, *grammatici,* and other teachers (*CTh* 13.3.1).

106. G. Évrard, *MEFR* 74 (1962), 607 ff. Bassus probably served as prefect from 318 to early 332 (*New Empire,* ch. VIII). Either as consul in 331 or later, Bassus dedicated a basilica in Rome (*CIL* 6.1737). He is claimed as a pagan by R. von Haehling, *Die Religionszugehörigkeit der hohen Amtsträger des römischen Reiches seit Constantins I. Alleinherrschaft bis zum Ende der Theodosianischen Dynastie* (*Antiquitas* 3.23, 1978), 289.

107. *Pan. Lat.* 4(10).17.2; cf. 37.3; Publilius Optatianus Porfyrius, *Carm.* 10.24 ff.; *RIC* 7.185, Trier 237–241.

108. *RIC* 7.196, Trier 362–366; 475, Sirmium 49–52 proclaim *Alamannia devicta* in 323.

109. *CTh* 9.38.1; Publilius Optatianus Porfyrius, *Carm.* 10, *versus intexti*; cf. T. D. Barnes, *AJP* 96 (1975), 181.

110. Crispus' wife is known only from *CTh* 9.38.1: *propter Crispi atque Helenae partum omnibus indulgemus praeter veneficos homicidas adulteros.*

111. *RIC* 7.470, Sirmium 19, 20A; *Pan. Lat.* 4(10).36.4 ff.; cf. *New Empire,* ch. V: Crispus.

112. *New Empire,* ch. VI.

113. On their careers, *New Empire,* ch. VI.

114. *Pan. Lat.* 4(10): it is the fifteenth year of Constantine's reign (2.2).

115. Eusebius, *VC* 4.32, promises to append to the *Life,* as a specimen of Constantine's Latin orations officially translated into Greek, the speech which the emperor delivered "to the assembly of the saints," and a speech with this title duly follows the *Life* in the manuscripts. Modern scholars (e.g., F. Winkelmann, in his edition of the *Life* [1976], 132) have often denied that the extant speech is the speech promised by Eusebius; for a survey of the controversy, see N. H. Baynes, *Constantine the Great and the Christian Church* (London, 1931), 50 ff.; D. de Decker, *Lactance et son temps* (*Théologie Historique* 48, 1978), 75 ff. Practically all the arguments advanced against authenticity have unfortunately been either *a priori* or based on a misunderstanding of historical allusions in the text; see T. D. Barnes, *JTS,* n.s. 27 (1976), 414 ff.

In 1976 I argued that Constantine delivered the speech in Serdica on 12 April 317. Subsequent inquiry into the residences and movements of emperors has convinced me that, although my central argument is sound (viz., that Constantine is speaking in a city where Galerius had resided before 311), it allows Thessalonica an equal claim with Serdica to be regarded as the place of delivery. Moreover, the hostile tone of Constantine's reference to Licinius (25.4) should exclude a date before the open rupture of 321. Consequently, although I incline to believe that Constantine probably delivered the speech at Serdica on 31 March 321, delivery in Thessalonica on 5 April 323 or 27 March 324 cannot be excluded (as proposed by A. Piganiol, *RHPR* 12 [1932], 370 ff.).

116. *Pan. Lat.* 4(10).17.2, 37.1 ff. Nazarius held the official chair of rhetoric at Rome (Ausonius, *Prof.* 14.7 ff.), and may have had a hand in forming *Pan. Lat.* 4–12 (mss. order) into a collection; see Schanz-Hosius, *Gesch. d. röm. Litt.* 3³ (Munich, 1922), 138, 150.

117. *Pan. Lat.* 4(10).3–35, including a digression on Constantine's campaigns in Gaul before 312 (16.3–19.1); 38.

118. J. H. W. G. Liebeschuetz, *Continuity and Change in Roman Religion* (Oxford, 1979), 289 f. Observe that Jerome enters the floruit of both Nazarius and his daughter (*Chronicle* 231ᶜ, 233ᵉ).

119. J. M. Pfättisch, *Die Rede Konstantins des Grossen an die Versammlung der Heiligen auf ihre Echtheit untersucht* (*Strassburger theologische Studien* 9.4, 1908), 66 ff.; *Theologische Quartalschrift* 92 (1910), 399 ff., argued that the verbal echoes of Plato proved thorough rewriting by a Greek. N. H. Baynes accepted his conclusion and therefore refrained from using the *Speech* as evidence for Constantine's religious beliefs (*Constantine the Great,* 56).

120. V. Schultze, *ZKG* 14 (1894), 541 ff.; W. Hartmann, *Konstantin der Grosse als Christ and Philosoph in seinen Briefen und Erlassen* (Prog., Fürstenwalde, 1902), 17 ff., 29 ff. Similarly, A. Kurfess, *ZNW* 19 (1919/20), 77: "Selbständiges Studium Platos traue ich dem Kaiser nicht zu." Kurfess, therefore, attempted to derive Constantine's knowledge of the *Timaeus* from Cicero's partial translation (72 ff.).

121. Chapters I, II.

122. Chapter I.

123. A. Kurfess, *Theologische Quartalschrift* 130 (1950), 148 ff.; D. de Decker, *Lactance et son temps,* 80 f. The *Speech* is, however, argued to be completely independent of Lactantius by A. Bolhuis, *Vig. Chr.* 10 (1956), 25 ff.

124. A. Kurfess, *ZRGG* 4 (1952), 42 ff.

125. J. H. Waszink, *Plato Latinus* 4: *Timaeus a Calcidio translatus commentarioque instructus* (Leiden, 1962), xiii ff., argued strenuously for a date c. 400 and another dedicatee. This conclusion has been widely accepted: see, e.g., E. Mensching, *Vig. Chr.* 19 (1965), 55 f.; *PLRE* 1.172/3; J. H. Waszink, *JAC* 15 (1972), 236 ff.; P. Courcelle, *Romanitas et Christianitas* (Amsterdam and London, 1973), 45 ff.; A. Cameron, *Christianisme et formes littéraires de l'Antiquité tardive en Occident* (*Entretiens sur l'Antiquité Classique* 23, 1977), 21 f. For proof of a date early in the fourth century, J. Dillon, *The Middle Platonists* (London, 1977), 401 ff.; J. M. Rist, *Basil of Caesarea: Christian, Humanist, Ascetic,* ed. P. J. Fedwick (Toronto, 1981), 151 ff.

126. Calcidius compliments Ossius on his fluency in Greek (p. 5.8 ff. Waszink).

127. P. Wendland, *Berl. phil. Woch.* 22 (1902), 229 ff., argued that a literary adviser wrote the *Speech* under the emperor's close supervision.

128. For the crucial distinction between assistance during composition and later interpolation, too often ignored in modern discussions of Constantinian documents, see S. Calderone, *Costantino e il Cattolicesimo* 1 (Florence, 1962), 265, n. 2.

129. H. Dörries, *Das Selbstzeugnis Kaiser Konstantins* (*Abh. Göttingen,* Phil.-hist. Klasse[3] 34, 1954), 129 ff. The chapter headings, and probably the division into chapters, are the work of Eusebius or his literary executor; see E. Schwartz, *RE* 6 (1909), 1427 f.

130. Constantine, *Oratio* 1.1 ff.

131. *Oratio* 2.1 f.; cf. Valesius, as reported in *PG* 20.1237: on this interpretation, Constantine invokes Protogenes of Serdica (the captain who possesses holy virginity), his church, and the assembled priests and laymen ("you who truly worship God").

132. On the structure of the *Speech,* J. M. Pfättisch, *Konstantin der Grosse und seine Zeit,* ed. F. J. Dölger (*Röm. Quart.,* Supp. 19, 1913), 100 ff.; A. Kurfess, *Pastor Bonus* 41 (1930), 116 f.

133. J. M. Rist, *Basil of Caesarea,* 155 ff.

134. Numenius, frags. 12–22 des Places. His exegesis of Plato proceeds from an obscure passage in the Second Letter attributed to Plato (312d–313a), whose author is very plausibly identified as the Neopythagorean Thrasyllus by J. M. Rist, *Phronesis* 10 (1965), 79 ff.

135. Constantine, *Oratio* 9.3.

136. Numenius, frags. 1–21 des Places (mainly from Eusebius' *Preparation for the Gospel*). Constantine begins his argument with a sentence full of philosophical allusions: "The good for which everything yearns, God who exists forever above reality, does not have a coming into being, and therefore does not have a beginning" (3.1).

137. Constantine, *Oratio* 3–10.

138. *Oratio* 11–21.

139. *Oratio* 16.4.

140. Lactantius, *Div. Inst.* 7.16–25; cf. A. Kurfess, *Theologische Quartalschrift* 117 (1936), 11 ff. (the Sibylline Oracles); 130 (1950), 138 ff. (Virgil's Fourth Eclogue).

141. *Oratio* 18, quoting *Orac. Sib.* 8.217 ff.

142. Lactantius quotes lines 8, 20–21, 23, and 25–26 of the acrostic, always in Greek (*Div. Inst.* 7.19.9, 16.11, 20.3). Augustine, *Civ. Dei* 18.23, quotes a Latin translation into hexameters; its initial letters almost reproduce the acrostic, but this Latin version omits the last seven verses quoted by Constantine. A. Kurfess, *Sokrates,* N.F. 6 (1918), 99 ff., argued that Constantine cited only the acrostic, the actual verses being added by the Greek translator, who perhaps also composed the verses unknown to Augustine.

143. *Oratio* 19–21. The Greek translation of Virgil is very corrupt; for improvements in I. A. Heikel's text, see A. Kurfess, *Mnemosyne,* n.s. 40 (1912), 283 f.; *Phil. Woch.* 50 (1930), 366 ff.; 54 (1934), 1247; 56 (1936), 364 ff. The same scholar has established that the commentary often presupposes Virgil's Latin and cannot be based on the Greek translation: A. Kurfess, *Mnemosyne,* n.s. 40 (1912), 277 ff.; *Sokrates* N.F. 7 (1919), 337 f.; *Jahresberichte des philologischen Vereins zu Berlin* 64 (1920), 90 ff.; *ZNW* 35 (1936), 97 ff.; *Glotta* 25 (1936), 274 ff.; *Mnemosyne*³ 5 (1937), 283 ff. His conclusions are contradicted (but not disproved) by A. Bolhuis, *Vergilius' Vierde Ecloga in de "Oratio Constantini ad Sanctorum Coetum"* (diss., Amsterdam, 1950), 27 ff. On other Christian interpretations of the Fourth Eclogue, P. Courcelle, *REA* 59 (1957), 294 ff. C. Monteleone, *L'egloga quarta da Virgilio a Costantino: Critica del testo e ideologia* (Manduria, 1975), 75 ff., argues that the transmitted text of Virgil contains Christian interpolations.

144. *Oratio* 22–25. For the allusions to Galerius (22.1 ff.) and to Licinius (25.4), T. D. Barnes, *JTS,* n.s. 27 (1976), 421 ff. S. Mazzarino, *Antico, tardoantico ed èra costantiniana* 1 (Bari, 1974), 99 ff., detects allusions to Licinius in both passages and holds that Constantine delivered the *Speech* in Constantinople at Easter 325. That is impossible for many reasons, and the index and heading name the persecutor described in Chapter 22 as Galerius (p. 151 Heikel, as emended in *JTS,* n.s. 27 [1976], 420).

145. *Oratio* 24; cf. Lactantius, *Mort. Pers.* 4–6.

146. *Oratio* 25.1 ff. Constantine notes his own presence in Nicomedia in 303, when part of the palace burned down (25.2; cf. Chapter II).

147. Most explicitly in the peroration (*Oratio* 26).

148. *Oratio* 11.1. At p. 166.8, the transmitted *ei pou* misrepresents the train of thought. Presumably, therefore, the original had *siquidem* in a causal sense ("I wish that this revelation had been vouchsafed to me long ago, since happy is he who from childhood has been steadfast and has rejoiced in the knowledge of things divine and the beauty of virtue"). Constantine surely alludes to and combines Genesis 48.15 and Psalm 70(71):5.

149. *Oratio* 25.4 f.

150. Zosimus 2.22.1; P. Bruun, *Studies in Constantinian Chronology* (*Numismatic Notes and Monographs* 146, 1961), 74 ff.

151. *Origo* 21, calling the invaders Goths.

152. *CTh* 7.1.1, 12.1 (28 April 323). *CTh* 4.8.6 = *CJ* 8.46.10 attests his presence at Thessalonica on either 15 February or 18 May 323.

153. *Origo* 21; Zosimus 2.21.

154. Publilius Optatianus Porfyrius, *Carm.* 6.14 ff.

155. *AE* 1934.158; cf. *New Empire,* table 7; *RIC* 7.135, Lyons 202–222; 201–202, Trier 429, 435–438; 262, Arles 257–258; 475, Sirmium 48.

156. *Origo* 21; Petrus Patricius, *Excerpta Vaticana* 187 = Anon. post Dionem, frag. 14.1 Müller.

157. *CTh* 16.2.5[S] attests his presence there on 25 December 323. Observe also coins celebrating the consular procession of the Caesar Crispus on 1 January 324 (*RIC* 7.473, Sirmium 43; 476, Sirmium 57).

158. The campaign of 324 is principally reconstructed from *Origo* 23–28; Zosimus 2.22–28; cf. E. Pears, *EHR* 24 (1909), 3 ff.

159. For 3 July as the day of the battle, *CTh* 7.20.1; *Chr. Min.* 1.232; *CIL* 1², p. 268.

160. There may also have been fighting elsewhere: a coin hoard implies that Constantine stationed troops on Delos, which technically belonged to the province of Achaea, despite its proximity to the Asiatic coast; cf. P. Bruun, *Studies in Constantinian Chronology*, 78 ff.

161. For coins of Martinianus as Augustus, *RIC* 7.608, Nicomedia 45–47; 645, Cyzicus 16. The absence of coinage in his name at Antioch and Alexandria confirms the brevity of his rule.

162. For the date, *Chr. Min.* 1.232; *CIL* 1², p. 272.

163. *Origo* 28; *Epitome* 41.7; Philostorgius, p. 180. 12 ff. Bidez.

164. *RIC* 7.609, Nicomedia 52.

165. Eusebius, *VC* 2.19.2. For the numerous inscriptions which confirm Eusebius' statement, A. Chastagnol, *Latomus* 25 (1966), 543 ff.; E. Guadagno, *Rendiconti Lincei*[8] 25 (1970), 111 ff.; G. Camodeca, *Atti dell'Accademia di Scienze morali e politiche, Napoli* 82 (1971), 30 ff.

VI. ORIGEN AND CAESAREA

1. On Caesarea, L. I. Levine, *Revue Biblique* 80 (1973), 75 ff.; *IEJ* 24 (1974), 62 ff.; *Caesarea under Roman Rule* (*Studies in Judaism in Late Antiquity* 7, 1975); *Roman Caesarea: An Archaeological-Topographical Study* (*Qedem* 2, 1975); J. Ringel, *Césarée de Palestine: Étude historique et archéologique* (Paris, 1975); B. Lifshitz, *ANRW* II.8 (1977), 490 ff.; E. Schürer, *The History of the Jewish People in the Age of Jesus Christ* (*175 B.C.–A.D. 135*), revised by G. Vermes, F. Millar, and M. Black, 2 (Edinburgh, 1979), 115 ff.

2. Josephus, *BJ* 1.408 ff.; *AJ* 15.331 ff.; cf. L. I. Levine, *Roman Caesarea* (Jerusalem, 1975), 5 ff.

3. *Expositio Totius Mundi et Gentium* 32.

4. E. Shürer, *History of the Jewish People,* revised by G. Vermes and F. Millar, 1 (Edinburgh, 1973), 361.

5. Aristo of Pella, quoted by Eusebius, *HE* 4.6.3; Justin, *Apol.* 1.47.5; *Dial.* 40.2, 92.2; Tertullian, *Apol.* 21.5; Jerome, *Chronicle* 201ᵉ; cf. E. Schürer, *History,* rev. G. Vermes and F. Millar, 1.521 ff., 553.

6. Pliny, *NH* 5.69; *Dig.* 50.15.8.7 (Paulus); 50.15.1.6 (Ulpian); cf. L. I. Levine, *Caesarea* (1975), 34 ff.

7. Timisitheus, the praetorian prefect of Gordian III, had been *proc. prov. Syriae Palaestinae ibi exactor reliquor(um) annon(ae) sacrae expeditionis* (*ILS* 1330: Lugdunum), i.e., in 232/3, during Severus Alexander's expedition against Persia; cf. H.-G. Pflaum, *Les carrières procuratoriennes équestres sous le Haut-Empire romain* 2 (Paris, 1960), 814 f. Observe also the recent discovery of

a Mithraeum (L. M. Hopfe and G. Lease, *Biblical Archaeologist* 38 [1975], 2 ff.).

8. Eusebius, *Mart. Pal.* 6.1 ff.; (S) 7.7; 8.3.

9. L. Kadman, *The Coins of Caesarea Maritima* (*Corpus Nummorum Palaestinensium* 2, 1957), 50 ff.

10. On the Jewish community, see L. I. Levine *Caesarea* (1975), 61 ff., and *Christianity, Judaism and Other Greco-Roman Cults* 4 (Leiden, 1975), 56 ff.; I. M. Levey, *Studies in the History of Caesarea Maritima* (Missoula, Mo., 1975), 54 ff.. On the Samaritans, L. I. Levine, *Caesarea* (1975), 107 ff.

11. Acts 8:40, 10:1–48.

12. Eusebius, *HE* 5.22, 25; cf. A. Harnack, *Die Mission und Ausbreitung des Christentums in den ersten drei Jahrhunderten*[4] (Leipzig, 1924), 647.

13. As emerges implicitly but clearly from Origen's biblical commentaries; see A. Harnack, *TU* 42.3 (1918); 42.4 (1919).

14. Eusebius, *HE* 6.1 f. Laetus (2.2) is attested as prefect from May 200 to the middle of 203 (G. Bastianini, *ZPE* 17 [1975], 304).

Eusebius described his account of Origen as based on letters and on the reminiscences of Origen's friends, with whom he had conversed (2.1); for an acute analysis, see P. Nautin, *Origène: Sa vie et son oeuvre* (*Christianisme Antique* 1, 1977), 19 ff. Nautin's reconstruction of Origen's life (409 ff.) is, however, vitiated in part by both constant hypercriticism and occasional lapses: he denies that the martyr Leonidas was Origen's father (32, 208) and that Origen himself bore the nickname Adamantius (47, n. 15)—but he bases his chronology of Origen's travels in Greece on Eusebius, *HE* 6.32 (87, 342).

15. Origen, *Homilies on Ezekiel* 4.8 (*GCS* 33.368).

16. Eusebius, *HE* 6.2.13 ff.

17. Eusebius, *HE* 6.19.6, 13 f.

18. Eusebius, *HE* 6.3.1 ff., 4.1 ff.; cf. Origen, *Homilies on Judges* 9.1 (*GCS* 30.518). Aquila is attested as prefect from late 206 to early 211 (G. Bastianini, *ZPE* 17 [1975], 305 f.). Claudius Julianus, who governed Egypt between Laetus and Aquila, was probably far more sympathetic to Christianity than either Laetus or Aquila: the anonymous *Epistle to Diognetus* appears to be addressed to an imperial procurator in Egypt during his prefecture; cf. *PIR*² C 852; H. I. Marrou, *À Diognète*² (*SC* 33bis, 1965), 241 ff.; T. D. Barnes, *Tertullian: A Historical and Literary Study* (Oxford, 1971), 104.

19. Eusebius, *HE* 6.3.8; cf. P. Nautin, *Origène*, 39. It is probably an anachronism when Eusebius speaks of "the catechetical school" at Alexandria in 203 (3.1).

20. Eusebius, *HE* 6.3.8 ff.

21. *HE* 6.8.1 ff.—probably based on the letter which Alexander of Jerusalem and Theoctistus of Caesarea wrote c. 231 to Pontianus, bishop of Rome; cf. P. Nautin, *Lettres et Écrivains chrétiens des IIe et IIIe siècles* (*Patristica* 2, 1961), 121 ff. H. Chadwick, *Early Christian Thought and the Classical Tradition: Studies in Justin, Clement and Origen* (Oxford, 1966), 67 f., doubts the story on the mistaken premise that Eusebius "depends on an unwritten tradition." More skeptical still, M. Hornschuh, *ZKG* 71 (1960), 1 ff., 193 ff., has argued that Eusebius' picture of Origen is almost wholly legendary or invented.

22. Eusebius, *HE* 6.19.15.

23. *HE* 6.19.16 ff. P. Nautin, *Origène*, 425 ff., dates Origen's first visit to Palestine to 230, arguing that Eusebius' "no small war" which flamed up in Alexandria (*HE* 6.19.16) is the hostility of the bishop and his clergy towards Origen (366). But Eusebius must surely allude to Caracalla's massacre of Alexandrians in 215; on which, see F. Millar, *A Study of Cassius Dio* (Oxford, 1964), 156 f.

24. Eusebius, *HE* 6.14.10; cf. *Chr. Min.* 1.74. Eusebius puts the death of Zephyrinus in the first year of Elagabalus, i.e., presumably, 218/9 (*HE* 6.21.1).

25. Origen's own account of the discovery is preserved in catenae on the Psalms: *PG* 80.30; G. Mercati, *Note di letteratura biblica e cristiana antica* (*Studi e Testi* 5, 1901), 29; P. Nautin, *Origène*, 310. Nautin argues that Origen visited Nicopolis in 245 (ibid., 411, 435). But Origen's numeration of the Greek versions of the Psalms implies otherwise; the version which he discovered at Nicopolis he called the fifth, one found near Jericho in the reign of Caracalla the sixth. Hence, to save his hypothesis, Nautin must argue that the sixth version remained unknown to Origen for thirty years after its discovery (ibid., 344).

26. Eusebius, *HE* 6.18.1 ff., 23.1 ff.; cf. P. Nautin, *Origène*, 49 ff. Adducing the extant preface to the sixth tome on John (*GCS* 10.107 f.) and the lost ninth tome on Genesis, Eusebius assigns the following works to the period before Origen finally left Alexandria (*HE* 6.24): the first five tomes of his commentary on John and the first eight of his commentary on Genesis, a commentary on Psalms 1–25 (cf. P. Nautin, *Origène*, 262 ff.), a commentary on Lamentations (fragments in *GCS* 6.235–279), which referred to *On the Resurrection, On First Principles,* and ten books of *Stromateis* (cf. P. Nautin, *Origène*, 293 ff.). To this period also belong the *Dialogue with Candidus* (Jerome, *Contra Rufinum* 2.19) and probably *On Natures*; see P. Nautin, *Origène*, 170, 370.

27. A. C. McGiffert, *Select Library of Nicene and Post-Nicene Fathers*[2] 1 (Oxford and New York, 1890), 395 ff.; H. J. Lawlor and J. E. L. Oulton, *Eusebius: The "Ecclesiastical History"* 2 (London, 1928), 218 ff.

P. Nautin, *Origène*, 65 ff., 366 ff., 410, 427 ff., posits a very different reconstruction from that assumed here, viz., interview with Mamaea in winter 231–232, return to Alexandria, almost immediate departure in spring 232, ordination in Palestine, stay in Athens in spring 233, return to Caesarea in 234. But the imperial court left Rome during the course of 231 (*BMC, R. Emp.* 6.192, Sev. Alex. 781), traveled overland by way of Illyricum (Herodian 6.4.3), and may not have reached Syria before the spring of 232.

28. Eusebius, *HE* 6.23.4; cf. P. Nautin, *Origène*, 428.

29. Eusebius, *HE* 6.8.4, 23.4.

30. Origen completed the commentary on Ezekiel and composed the first five tomes of the commentary on the Song of Songs in Athens (Eusebius, *HE* 6.32.1). P. Nautin, *Origène*, 410, 435, assigns these works to a visit to Athens in 245/6.

31. Origen, *Ep. ad Caros Suos* (*PG* 17.625 f.) = Rufinus, *De Adulteratione Librorum Origenis* 7 (*CCL* 20.11 f.).

32. Eusebius, *HE* 6.21.3 f. The interview may be assigned to the winter of 232–233: Severus Alexander celebrated a triumph on his return to Rome in 233 (*BMC, R. Emp.* 6.207, Sev. Alex. 949; *ILS* 482).

33. Photius, *Bibliotheca* 118; Jerome, *Epp.* 33.4 f.—reporting Pamphilus and Eusebius' *Defense of Origen* (cf. *HE* 6.23.4).

34. An inference from Eusebius, *HE* 6.8.1 ff., 19.17 f., 27.1; Jerome *Epp.* 33.5.

35. Eusebius, *HE* 6.19.12–14, quotes a fragment from what appears to have been a long autobiographical letter to Alexander which provided him with most of his information about Origen's career; cf. P. Nautin, *Lettres et écrivains* (Paris, 1961), 126 ff., and *Origène* (Paris, 1977), 21 ff. For the "Letter to his Friends in Alexandria," see P. Nautin, *Origène,* 161 ff., combining and translating Jerome, *Contra Rufinum* 2.18 (*PL* 23.460 ff.) and Rufinus, *De Adulteratione Librorum Origenis* 7 ff. (*CCL* 20.11 ff.).

36. Eusebius, *HE* 6.26, giving the date as "shortly after" Origen's removal from Alexandria to Caesarea in the tenth year of Severus Alexander (231/2). But Eusebius has an inconsistent chronology for Heraclas: he places his death, after sixteen years as bishop, in the third year of Philip, i.e., 246/7 (*HE* 6.35). The figure is presumably inaccurate.

37. Photius, *Interrogationes Decem* 9 (*PG* 104.1229); cf. P. Nautin, *Origène,* 167 f., 386 f.

38. Origen, *Commentary on John* 6.2 (*GCS* 10.107 f.); Eusebius *HE* 6.28, 30.

39. P. Nautin argues that the *Address to Origen* was composed by a Theodorus (*Origène,* 183 ff.), who is not identical with the Gregory to whom a letter of Origen survives (ibid., 155 ff.), and he denies that either of these two men can be identical with Gregory the Thaumaturge (81 ff.). But the manuscripts expressly describe the work as "Address to Origen of Gregory the Thaumaturge, which he spoke in Caesarea of Palestine, when about to depart for his native land after many years of study with him," and the only evidence for Theodorus is Eusebius' statement that Origen's pupils included the bishops of Pontus, whom he knew personally, Athenodorus and his brother Theodorus, "who was the very same person as Gregory, the renowned bishop of our day" (*HE* 6.30).

40. On the career of Gregory, H. Crouzel, *Grégoire le Thaumaturge: Remerciement à Origène* (*SC* 148, 1969), 14 ff.

41. *Address to Origen* 31 ff.

42. *Address* 73 ff.

43. Gregory himself refers to "an eight-year period" in which he has listened only to "these holy men who have embraced lovely philosophy" (3), while Eusebius states that the two brothers stayed with Origen for five years (*HE* 6.30). Gregory's words appear to exclude the hypothesis that his eight years include three studying law (as argued by H. Crouzel, *SC* 148 (1969), 20, with appeal to P. Koetschau and A. Harnack); Eusebius has simply misremembered the number (P. Nautin, *Origène,* 82). The precise dates of Gregory's arrival in and departure from Caesarea are unknown.

44. *Address* 93 ff.; cf. A. Knauber, *Münchener theologische Zeitschrift* 19 (1968), 182 ff.; H. Crouzel, *BLE* 71 (1970), 15 ff.

45. *Address* 184 ff. Origen's *Letter to Gregory* (*PG* 11.88–92; *Philocalia* 13) implies that Gregory embarked on a secular career on his return to Pontus; see H. Crouzel, *SC* 148 (1969), 86 ff., 186 ff. (text).

46. The evidence is, unfortunately, late and largely legendary, but genuine

traditions are reflected in the passage which Rufinus inserted after his translation of Eusebius, *HE* 7.28.2 (*GCS* 9.2.953 ff.), and in Gregory of Nyssa, *Vita Gregorii* (*PG* 46.893 ff.).

47. The *Canonical Letter* (M. J. Routh, *Reliquiae Sacrae*² 3 [Oxford, 1846], 251 ff.; *PG* 10.1019 ff.) refers to depredations of Goths and Boradi: the latter are the Borani, who are named by Zosimus in his narrative of the 250s (1.27.1, 31.1, 34.1).

48. Eusebius, *HE* 6.30, 7.14, 7.28.1.

49. Origen, *Ep. ad Africanum* (*PG* 11.48 ff.). Origen had discussed the story of Susanna with one Bassus in the presence of Africanus (*Ep. ad Origenem* 1, *PG* 11.41), perhaps somewhere in Asia Minor. Origen's visit to Firmilianus, bishop of Caesarea in Cappadocia, may belong to the same journey (Eusebius, *HE* 6.27).

50. Origen, *Commentary on John* 6.40 (*GCS* 10.149); Eusebius, *HE* 6.33 (Beryllus of Bostra), 37 (a second visit to Arabia). Eusebius probably alludes to Origen's interrogation of Heracleides preserved in *P. Cairo inv.* 88745 (edited by J. Scherer, *SC* 67 [1960], 52 ff).

51. Eusebius, *HE* 6.36.2; cf. H. Chadwick, *Origen: "Contra Celsum"* (Cambridge, 1953), xiv f.

52. Eusebius, *HE* 6.39.5.

53. Eusebius, *HE* 6.46.2, 7.1; Jerome, *De Viris Illustribus* 54; *Epp.* 84.7. Epiphanius, *Pan.* 64.3.3 (*GCS* 31.406); *De Mensuris et Ponderibus* 18 (*PG* 43.268), makes Origen reside in Tyre for twenty-eight years after leaving Alexandria.

54. Origen, *Princ.* 1, praef. 2 f.

55. For formal condemnations in the later fourth, fifth, and sixth centuries, F. X. Murphy, *Rufinus of Aquileia* (Washington, 1945), 59 ff.; F. Diekamp, *Die origenistischen Streitigkeiten im 6. Jahrhundert* (Münster, 1899).

56. J. Daniélou, *Message évangelique et culture hellénistique au IIe et IIIe siècles* (Tournai, 1961), 344 ff.; E. von Ivanka, *Plato Christianus: Übernahme und Umgestaltung des Platonismus durch die Väter* (Einsiedeln, 1964), 101 ff.; H. Chadwick, *Early Christian Thought and the Classical Tradition* (1966), 100 ff. Porphyry, who derided Origen for barbarizing the teachings of Numenius and other Greek philosophers (Eusebius, *HE* 6.19.8), reveals that contemporaries accused Plotinus of plagiarizing Numenius (*Vita Plotini* 17.1 ff.).

57. There are several good French studies of Origen's thought: J. Daniélou, *Origène* (Paris, 1948); H. de Lubac, *Histoire et Esprit: L'intelligence de l'Écriture d'après Origène* (Paris, 1950); H. Crouzel, *Théologie de l'image de Dieu chez Origène* (Paris, 1956); M. Harl, *Origène et la function révélatrice du verbe incarné* (Paris, 1958); H. Crouzel, *Origène et la "Connaissance mystique"* (Bruges and Paris, 1961); *Origène et la philosophie* (Paris, 1962); *Virginité et mariage selon Origène* (Bruges and Paris, 1963). For a brief but illuminating synthesis, H. Chadwick, *Early Christian Thought*, 74 ff., and *Cambridge History of Later Greek and Early Medieval Philosophy* (1967), 182 ff.

58. J. M. Rist, *Basil of Caesarea: Christian, Humanist, Ascetic,* ed. P. J. Fedwick (Toronto, 1981), 137 ff.

59. H. Crouzel, *BLE* 76 (1975), 161 ff., 241 ff. Origen identifies the dualistic and deterministic positions which he attacks as held by disciples of Marcion, Valentinus, and Basilides (*Princ.* 2.9.5; cf. 7.1).

60. *Princ.* 1, praef. 3 ff. The chapter divisions appear not to be Origen's; see M. Harl, *TU* 78 (1961), 57 ff.

61. *Princ.* 1.1.

62. *Princ.* 1.2; cf. *Contra Celsum* 8.12: the Father and Son "are two distinct existences, but one in mental unity, in agreement, and in identity of will" (trans. H. Chadwick). Elsewhere, too, Origen repudiates the notion that Father and Son have a single *ousia* or *hypostasis*: *Commentary on Matthew* 17.14 (*GCS* 40.624); *Commentary on John* 10.37(21) (*GCS* 10.212); *Orat.* 15.1 (*GCS* 3.334).

63. *Princ.* 1.3.

64. *Princ.* 1.4.3.

65. *Princ.* 1.5, 1.8, 1.7.

66. *Princ.* 2.1, 1.6, 3.1.

67. *Princ.* 2.2–3, 3.6.

68. *Princ.* 2.2.2.

69. *Princ.* 2.4–11, 3.2–6.

70. *Princ.* 2.6.3 ff.

71. *Princ.* 2.11.6 f.

72. *Princ.* 4.1. The argument from the success of Christianity is important for Origen—but not central to his thought: H. Chadwick, *TU* 64 (1957), 331 ff.

73. *Princ.* 4.2.

74. Pamphilus, *Defense of Origen*, praef. (*PG* 17.545); cf. P. Nautin, *Origène* (Paris, 1977), 253 ff. (list of known homilies); 389 ff. (occasions for their delivery). Eusebius, *HE* 6.36.1, states that Origen would not permit the shorthand writers to take down his homilies until he was more than sixty, i.e., until after 244.

75. Jerome describes briefly the three types of exegesis in the preface to his translation of Origen's *Homilies on Ezekiel* (*GCS* 33.318).

76. Eusebius, *HE* 6.23.1 f.; cf. E. Preuschen, *Archiv für Stenographie* 56 (1905), 6 ff., 49 ff.

77. But the difference of level between commentaries and homilies should not be exaggerated; cf. E. Klostermann, *TLZ* 72 (1947), 203 ff.; H. Crouzel, *BHE* 70 (1969), 241 ff.

78. Only exiguous fragments survive; see esp. G. Mercati, *Opere minori* (*Studi e Testi* 76, 1937), 325 ff., and *Psalterii Hexapli Reliquiae* (Vatican, 1958–1965); P. Nautin, *Origène,* 303 ff. However, the classic repertory of individual readings derived from the Hexapla (F. Field, *Origenis Hexapla quae Supersunt* [Oxford, 1867–1875]) can be supplemented greatly from subsequent publications; see S. Jellicoe, *The Septuagint and Modern Study* (Oxford, 1968), 129 ff.

79. Epiphanius, *Pan.* 64.2.2; Jerome, *Comm. Tit.* 3.9 (*PL* 26.595); Rufinus, *HE* 6.16.4. P. Nautin, *Origène,* 312 ff., discounts these witnesses and argues, partly from its absence in the surviving fragments, that Origen never included the Hebrew text in Hebrew characters, only in Greek transliteration.

80. S. Jellicoe, *Septuagint,* 76 ff., 94 ff.

81. J. A. Montgomery, *A Critical and Exegetical Commentary on the Book of Daniel* (Edinburgh, 1927), 46 ff.; S. Jellicoe, *Septuagint,* 83 ff.

82. Epiphanius, *De Mensuris et Ponderibus* 17 (*PG* 43.265). On the diacriti-

cal signs (borrowed from Alexandrian scholarship), H. B. Swete, *An Introduction to the Old Testament in Greek*[2] (Cambridge, 1902), 69 ff.; R. Devreesse, *Introduction à l'étude des manuscrits grecs* (Paris, 1954), 73 ff.

83. For Origen's description, *PG* 80.30; G. Mercati, *Note di letteratura biblica* (Vatican, 1901), 29; P. Nautin, *Origène*, 310. In the *History*, Eusebius counted the variants of the fifth version as the sixth, and Origen's sixth as the seventh (*HE* 6.16.2), but commenting on Psalm 61:4–5 he speaks of "another version" after "the fifth version" as if it might be different from the sixth (*PG* 23.592).

84. Eusebius, *HE* 6.16.4.

85. P. Nautin, *Origène*, 314 ff.

86. On the date of his visit to Nicopolis, see n. 25. H. M. Orlinsky, *Proceedings of the First World Congress of Jewish Studies* 1 (Jerusalem, 1952), 173 ff., argues that "Tetrapla" is merely another term for the Hexapla.

87. P. Nautin, *Origène*, 333 ff. On the Jewish origin of the second column, P. Kahle, *The Cairo Geniza*[2] (Oxford, 1959), 157 ff.

88. P. Nautin, *Origène*, 341.

89. Eusebius, *HE* 6.17 (reporting Origen). Palladius, *Historia Lausiaca* 64 (p. 160 Butler), quotes Origen as saying: "I found this book in the house of the virgin Juliana at Caesarea when I was hiding with her: she said she had received it from Symmachus the Jewish translator himself." That quotation may be authentic—but it does not support Palladius' assertion that Origen was in Cappadocian Caesarea fleeing persecution. If Origen obtained Symmachus' work in Caesarea, the date may be assumed to be 215/6 (n. 23).

90. Africanus, *Ep. ad Origenem* (*PG* 11.41 ff.).

91. Origen, *Ep. ad Africanum* 4 (*PG* 11.57).

92. S. Brock, *TU* 107 (1970), 215 ff.

93. *Commentary on Matthew* 15.14 (*GCS* 40.387).

94. N. R. M. de Lange, *Origen and the Jews: Studies in Jewish-Christian Relations in Third-Century Palestine* (Cambridge, 1976), 15 ff.

95. R. P. C. Hanson, *Vig. Chr.* 10 (1956), 103 ff.

96. P. Nautin, *Origène*, 351 ff.

97. Commenting on Psalm 3:8 and Ezekiel 7:27, he argues that the translators of the Septuagint either had a different Hebrew text from that otherwise attested or changed it deliberately (*PG* 12.1129, 13.796).

98. Jerome, *Epp.* 106.7, notes that Origen's critical signs can be found in editions of Greek and Latin poets.

99. *Homilies on Genesis* 2.3, 6.4–6 (*GCS* 29.30 ff., 61 ff.); *Homilies on Psalm 37* 1.1 (*PG* 12.1319); *Commentary on Matthew* 16.9–11 (*GCS* 40.501 ff.).

100. A. Zöllig, *Die Inspirationslehre des Origenes* (Freiburg, 1902), 101 ff.

101. R. P. C. Hanson, *Allegory and Event: A Study of the Sources and Significance of Origen's Interpretation of Scripture* (London, 1959), 11 ff.

102. H. A. Wolfson, *Philo* 1 (Cambridge, 1947), 115 ff. Origen complains that Celsus has not read Philo (*Contra Celsum* 4.51), and he commends Philo's *De Somniis* as "worthy of intelligent and wise study by those who wish to find the truth" (6.21).

103. Eusebius, *HE* 6.19.6 (translated in Chapter X).

104. R. P. C. Hanson, *Allegory and Event*, 162 ff.

105. *Princ.* 2.11.2, 4.2.4 ff.

106. *Princ.* 4.3.1 ff. (a long list of examples from the Pentateuch and New Testament).

107. R. P. C. Hanson, *Allegory and Event,* 242 ff.; cf. H. Crouzel, *BLE* 61 (1960), 81 ff.

108. Eusebius, *HE* 7.14.

109. Eusebius, *Mart. Pal.* (L) 11.1 ff.; Photius, *Bibliotheca* 118, 119. Eusebius, *HE* 7.32.30, dates Pierius' teaching at Alexandria to the time of bishop Theonas (282/3–300/1).

110. A. Ehrhardt, *Römische Quartalschrift* 5 (1891), 221 ff.; C. Wendel and W. Göher, *Handbuch der Bibliothekswissenschaft²* 3.1 (Wiesbaden, 1955), 131 ff. Isidore of Seville states that the library contained 30,000 rolls (*Etym.* 6.6.1).

111. K. Mras, *Anzeiger Wien,* Phil.-hist. Kl. 1956, 209 ff.

112. Jerome, *De Viris Illustribus* 3.

113. Jerome, *De Viris Illustribus* 75.

114. Jerome, *Epp.* 33; cf. P. Nautin, *Origène,* 227 ff. Pamphilus may not have recovered everything Origen wrote: the commentary on Isaiah, though comprising thirty tomes, broke off at Isaiah 30:6 (Eusebius, *HE* 6.32.1; *In Is.,* p. 195.20–21 Ziegler).

115. G. Mercati, *Nuove note di letteratura biblica e cristiana antica* (*Studi e Testi* 95, 1941), 1 ff.; R. Devreesse, *Introduction* (Paris, 1954), 122 ff. For an attempt to assess Pamphilus' influence on the textual history of the New Testament, W. Bousset, *TU* 11.4 (1894), 45 ff.

116. Codex Sinaiticus, fol. 19: a subscription to Esther quoting a subscription in a "very ancient copy" written in the hand of Pamphilus himself (reproduced by W. Bousset, *TU* 11.4 [1894], 45; G. Mercati [*Studi e Testi* 95, 1941], 18 f.).

117. Arethas, in a scholium on *PE* 1.3.6 (*GCS* 43.2.427, from Parisinus Graecus 451, fol. 188ʳ); cf. E. H. Gifford, *Eusebii Pamphili Evangelicae Praeparationis Libri XV* 3.1 (Oxford, 1903), ix ff. A sermon on the anniversary of his death by Eusebius of Emesa implies that Eusebius was of respectable birth (*PG* 24.1068).

118. See *HE* 7.14, 7.26.3.

119. *HE* 5, praef. 2, 5.20.5; cf. 6.32.3. There is no reason to suppose that the speech which Rufinus put into the mouth of Lucian in January 312 (*HE* 9.6) comes from Eusebius' *Collection of Ancient Martyrdoms,* as argued by A. Harnack, *Geschichte der altchristlichen Litteratur bis Eusebius* 2 (Leipzig, 1893), 529, 556.

120. Chapter XI.

121. *HE* 6.32.3, 8.13.6; *Mart. Pal.* (S) 11.3; Jerome, *De Viris Illustribus* 81; *Contra Rufinum* 1.9.

122. Eusebius is first attested as bishop between 313 and 316 (*HE* 10.4.1 ff.). His silence about his immediate predecessor suggests that the predecessor was hostile to Pamphilus (Chapter XI).

123. H. B. Swete, *Introduction²* (Cambridge, 1902), 76 ff.; S. Jellicoe, *Septuagint* (Oxford, 1968), 134 ff.

124. *PG* 30.81–104, reprinted from the Maurist edition by J. Garnier (Paris,

1721–1730). M. Richard, *Bulletin d'information de l'Institut de Recherche et d'Histoire des Textes* 5 (1956), 88 f., drew attention to Garnier's attribution to Eusebius (*PG* 29. ccii). Substantial portions can also be found in Montfaucon's edition of Eusebius' *Commentary on the Psalms* (*PG* 23.337–345).

References to the Psalms and to the comments of Origen and Eusebius on them normally state the number of the psalm and of the relevant verse or verses in both the Greek Psalter and then (in parentheses) in standard modern English and American translations wherever these differ.

125. *PG* 12.1319–1410. Rufinus states elsewhere that his version of these homilies is a straight translation without alterations (*PG* 14.1292 f. = *CCL* 20.276).

126. *PG* 30.89–90, 93, 96. In his homilies, Origen followed the standard Greek text, but in his serious commentaries, when surrounded by his own pupils, he inquired into the Hebrew original (Jerome, *Hebraicae Quaestiones in Libro Geneseos,* praef. [*CCL* 72.2]).

127. C. A. and E. G. Briggs, *International Critical Commentary: Psalms* 1 (Edinburgh, 1906), 336 ff.

128. Respectively, S. Mowinckel, *The Psalms in Israel's Worship,* translated by D. R. Ap-Thomas (Oxford, 1962), 2.9 ff.; W. R. Taylor and J. R. P. Slater, *The Interpreter's Bible* 4 (New York, 1955), 199 ff.

129. Hebrew: *mizmor l^edawid l^ehazkir,* rendered into Greek in the Septuagint as *eis anamnesin* (whence *per recordationem* in Rufinus' Latin translation). The standard modern view takes the infinitive to mean something like "to sing while bringing to the memorial offering" (of Leviticus 2:2); see W. L. Holladay, *A Concise Hebrew and Aramaic Lexicon of the Old Testament*[4] (Grand Rapids, 1978), 89, s.v. *zkr.* But that view appears to depend on the unproven assumption that all the Psalms have a liturgical function: the heading only occurs twice (also to Psalm 69 [70]), and the precise meaning of the infinitive hifil *hazkir* is unclear. It should also be noted that the Hebrew *mizmor l^edawid* does not in fact imply that King David was considered the author of the Psalm.

130. *PG* 12.1319 f. = *CCL* 20.251.

131. *PG* 12.1369 ff. Note his comment on verse 11: *sciens post exitum vitae quae poena immineat peccatori, haec dicit* (1380).

132. *PG* 30.88; cf. *PG* 12.1373 f. On Eusebius' habit of using for his own purposes passages from Origen on the same psalm, see R. Cadiou, *Commentaires inédits des Psaumes: Étude sur les textes d'Origène contenus dans le manuscrit Vindobonensis 8* (Paris, 1936), 36 ff.

133. *PG* 30.84–86.

134. *PG* 30.89 (Absalom); 101 (verse 19); 92 ("This verse teaches us not to conceal our own misdoings," etc.).

135. The fragments printed in *PG* 24.529 ff. as from a "Commentary on Luke" belong to the tenth book of the *General Elementary Introduction* (Chapter X). The *Commentary on the Psalms* as published by B. Montfaucon in 1713 and reprinted in *PG* 23 and 24.9–76 both contains much that is not by Eusebius and omits much that can confidently be attributed to him; see M. Rondeau, *Dictionnaire de Spiritualité* 4 (Paris, 1961), 855 ff.; M. Geerard, *Clavis Patrum Graecorum* 2 (Turnhout, 1974), 263 f. (no. 3467). For convenience, the present exposition largely confines itself to the indubitably Eusebian section of Mont-

faucon's edition (*PG* 23.441–1221). Montfaucon's edition of the *Commentary on Isaiah* (*PG* 24.89–526) exhibited the same defects; see R. Devreesse, *Revue Biblique* 42 (1933), 540 ff. Fortunately, however, A. Möhle discovered an almost complete text in the margin of a manuscript at Florence (*ZNW* 33 (1934), 87 ff.), and it has been edited by J. Ziegler (*GCS,* 1975).

136. Chapter XIV.

137. J. Ziegler, *Eusebius' Werke* 9: *Der Jesajakommentar* (*GCS,* 1975), 443 f., registers more than seven hundred references.

138. Approximately fifty times in the *Commentary on Isaiah* (J. Ziegler [*GCS* 1975], 444).

139. For example, the phrases *and may he pity us* in Psalm 66:3 and *in the gates of the daughter of Sion* in Psalm 72:28 (*PG* 23.673, 849).

140. On Origen's onomasticon, Chapter VII. Eusebius glosses *Basan* (Psalm 67:23) as "shame" (*PG* 23.708); on his knowledge of Hebrew, E. Nestle, *ZAW* 29 (1909), 57 ff.

141. *PG* 23.592.

142. *PG* 23.876 f.

143. *In Ps.* 88:3 (*PG* 23.1072).

144. *In Ps. 64:2–3 (PG* 23.625).

145. *In Ps.* 88:30–35 (*PG* 23.1105 ff.).

146. *In Ps.* 60:6 (*PG* 23.580).

147. *In Ps.* 80:14–15 (*PG* 23.981).

148. *PG* 23.469 ff.

149. *In Ps.* 68:2–3 (*PG* 23.721 ff.).

150. *In Is.* p. 16.11 ff.

151. R. P. C. Hanson, *Allegory and Event* (1959), 235 ff. He concludes that Origen's use of allegory is "unchartably subjective" (245).

152. *In Is.* p. 191.34 ff., p. 211.20 ff.; *In Ps.* 71:16 (*PG* 23.816).

153. *PG* 23.796.

154. *In Is.* p. 344.37 f., p. 213.6 f., p. 263.30 ff.

155. *PG* 23.752; *In Is.* 344.20 ff., 376.30 ff.

156. *PG* 23.725.

157. *PG* 23.896 ff.

158. *PG* 23.917, 961.

159. *PG* 23.961, 516.

160. *PG* 23.569.

161. On Eusebius' theology, see esp. H. G. Opitz, *ZNW* 34 (1935), 1 ff.; H. Berkhof, *Die Theologie des Eusebius von Caesarea* (Amsterdam, 1939): A. Weber, *APXH: Ein Beitrag zur Christologie des Eusebius von Cäsarea* (Rome, 1964); F. Ricken, *Theologie und Philosophie* 42 (1967), 341 ff.

162. E.g., *In Ps.* 57:7–9 (*PG* 23.524 f.), on providence and free will.

163. *In Ps.* 97:21–25 (*PG* 23.920); cf. Origen, *Princ.* 1.3.5 ff. Observe also a passage like *PE* 7.18.7 ff., where the Platonic language almost implies the doctrine of the pre-existence of souls.

164. *In Ps.* 56:5 (*PG* 23.509).

165. F. Ricken, *Theologie und Philosophie* 42 (1967), 341 ff. On his debt to Numenius, see further E. des Places, *TU* 116 (1975), 19 ff.

166. Numenius, frags. 11, 16, 19–21 des Places; Porphyry, *Vita Plotini* 3.30

ff.; cf. K. O. Weber, *Origenes der Neuplatoniker* (*Zetemata* 27, 1962), 74 ff. For opinions on the status of the demiurge, J. Dillon, *The Middle Platonists* (London, 1977), esp. 252 ff., 284 ff., 363 ff.

167. Respectively, *In Ps.* 64:3 (*PG* 23.628), 93:8–11 (*PG* 23.1200).

168. *Princ.* 4.1.

169. D. S. Wallace-Hadrill, *Eusebius of Caesarea* (London 1960), 72 ff., 168 ff.

170. Thus, in Psalm 65 (64), "the Holy Spirit sang and played with joy through the prophetic soul which received him" (*PG* 23.647).

171. For Origen's views on the Old Testament, R. P. C. Hanson, *Allegory and Event* (1959), 187 ff., 287 ff.

172. *In Is.* 1:1, p. 3.26 ff.

173. *In Ps.* 91:3, 80:4 (*PG* 23.1165 ff., 973); *In Is.* 66:23, p. 409.16 ff.; *In Ps.* 68:36–7 (*PG* 23.765 ff.).

174. *In Ps.* 93:8–11 (*PG* 23.1200); *In Is.* 34:3–4, p. 221.4 ff. *In Ps.* 90:3–9 (*PG* 23.1145 ff.). For Origen, the air between earth and heaven was the temporary abode of holy souls (*Princ.* 2.11.6).

175. *In Ps.* 94:8 (*PG* 23.1216). Origen believed that the goodness of God will ensure the salvation of all, even the Devil (*Princ.* 1.6.1, 3.6.1 ff.).

176. Thus the Psalms "habitually and in the present instance foretell the future as if it were already past"; *In Ps.* 73:12 (*PG* 23.861).

177. *In Is.* 22:2–3, p. 144.22 ff.; 3:4–11, p. 23.15 ff.; 2:5–9, p. 18.6 ff.; 6:11–13, p. 42.30 ff.; *In Ps.* 68:26–29, 70:12–16 (*PG* 23.753 ff.; 780 ff.).

178. *In Is.* p. 273.9 ff.; *PG* 23.568 f.

179. D. S. Wallace-Hadrill, *Eusebius of Caesarea* (1960), 62.

180. *In Is.* p. 335.1 ff.

181. *PG* 23.781.

182. *In Ps.* 86:7 (*PG* 23.1049).

183. *In Is.* p. 3.1 ff.

184. *In Is.* p. 108.19 (on 15:1–16:4); p. 128.26 f. (on 19:5–7).

185. *In Is.* 21:1–2, p. 138.27 ff.; *In Ps.* 76:20–21 (*PG* 23.90 f.).

186. *PG* 23.864.

187. Origen, *Commentary on Matthew*, frag. 140 (*GCS* 41.71 f.). Philo had argued that Moses' Ethiopian wife (Numbers 12:1) stands for fixed and unalterable resolve, because "the soul's power of vision is called 'Ethiopian woman,'" in the same way as the seeing part of the eye is black" (*Leg. All.* 2.67).

188. *In Ps.* 56:2 (*PG* 23.501 ff.).

189. E.g., *In Ps.* 51:2, 53:3–4 (*PG* 23.441 ff., 464 f.).

190. *In Ps.* 86:2–4 (*PG* 23.1040 ff.).

191. *PG* 23.821–836—an introduction to Psalms 72–82. For Eusebius' commentary on Psalm 49, which has the same heading, R. Devreesse, *Revue Biblique* 33 (1924), 78 ff.

192. For Eusebius' introduction to the "gradual" psalms, G. Mercati, *Opere minori* 2 (*Studi e Testi* 77, 1937), 61 ff.

193. The former is implied by histories and handbooks which assign Eusebius to the "entourage of Constantine" or to "the Golden Age of Greek patristic literature from the Council of Nicaea to the Council of Chalcedon," as do A.

Puech, *Histoire de la littérature grecque chrétienne* 3 (Paris, 1930), 167 ff., and J. Quasten, *Patrology* 3 (Utrecht; Antwerp; and Westminster, Md., 1960), 309 ff. The classic example of the latter fallacy is M. Faulhaber, *Die griechischen Apologeten der klassischen Väterzeit. I. Buch: Eusebius von Caesarea* (diss., Würzburg, 1895). Both are combined in H. Berkhof, *Die Theologie des Eusebius von Caesarea* (Amsterdam, 1939), esp. 60 ff.

VII. BIBLICAL SCHOLARSHIP AND THE *CHRONICLE*

1. The edition by E. Klostermann, *Eusebius' Werke* 3.1 (*GCS* 11.1, 1904), though the best available, needs to be used with care; see E. Nestle, *Berl. phil. Woch.* 24 (1904), 1156 ff.; *ZDPV* 28 (1905), 41 ff.; P. Thomsen, *Berl. phil. Woch.* 25 (1905), 621 ff. For fragments of an early Syriac translation, see I. E. Rahmani, E. Power, E. Tisserant, and R. Devreesse, *Revue de l'Orient Chrétien* 23 (1922–23), 225 ff.

2. M. Avi-Yonah, *RE*, Supp. 13 (1973), 427. The classic modern counterpart is P. Thomsen, *Loca Sancta: Verzeichnis der im 1. bis 6. Jahrhundert n. Chr. erwähnten Ortschaften Palästinas mit besonderer Berücksichtigung der Lokalisierung der biblischen Stätten* 1 (Halle, 1907). Eusebius' identifications and comments are naturally sometimes erroneous or confused; see F.-M. Abel, *Revue Biblique* 43 (1934), 347 ff.

3. I.e., in all probability a detailed study of Genesis 10; see E. Nestle, *Berl. phil. Woch.* 24 (1904), 1157 f. What appear to be fragments of this work quoted by Theodoretus of Cyrrhus and Procopius of Gaza can be found in F. Wutz, *Onomastica Sacra* 2 (*TU* 41.2, 1915), 1063 ff.

4. Eusebius describes the work as a *katagraphe;* see A. Schulten, *Die Mosaikkarte von Madaba* (*Abh. Göttingen,* Phil.-hist. Kl., N.F. 4.2, 1900), 41 ff. (list); M. Avi-Yonah, *The Madaba Mosaic Map* (Jerusalem, 1954), 31 (map). For use of Eusebius by the cartographers of the mosaic map at Madaba, W. Kubitschek, *Mitteilungen der kaiserlichen königlichen geographischen Gesellschaft in Wien* 43 (1900), 354 ff.

5. *Onom.* p. 2.14 ff. Klostermann; cf. his addenda (205).

6. *Onom.* pp. 164, 166 (with exact references supplied in accordance with modern convention; Eusebius himself did not supply even chapter numbers). For the identification of "Tina" as an error for *Kina* in Joshua 15:22, and "Tessam" as *Asem* in Joshua 15:29, T. D. Barnes, *JTS*, n.s. 26 (1975), 414.

7. Josephus, *AJ* 1.39: Eusebius has transposed into Greek the etymology which Josephus deduces from Aramaic and Hebrew.

8. The layout is presumably original; having begun, as usual, with formal headings for the entries for each book, Eusebius observed the paucity of names beginning with *T* and changed at this point to a more economical arrangement without formal headings.

9. *Onom.* p. 110.27.

10. E. Klostermann, *TU* 23.2b (1902), 9 ff.

11. Hence the frequent discussion of variant readings in the translations of the Old Testament by Aquila and Symmachus (registered by Klostermann, in the index to his edition, pp. 194, 201).

12. Listed in Klostermann, in his index, p. 187.

13. P. Thomsen, *ZDPV* 26 (1903), 140.

14. *Onom.* p. 10.15-24, p. 12.11-15.

15. P. Thomsen, *ZDPV* 26 (1903), 140; M. Noth, *ZDPV* 66 (1943), 34 ff.

16. W. Kubitschek, *JÖAI* 8 (1905), 119 ff. In response, Thomsen considerably modified his original opinion, *ZDPV* 29 (1906), 130.

17. Origen, *Commentary on John* 6.40 (*GCS* 10.149).

18. P. Thomsen, *ZDPV* 26 (1903), 162 f., lists most of the passages which refer to troops (to which add *Onom.* p. 24.9-11). Only once does Eusebius supply a name or title, when he notes the stationing of the Tenth Legion at Aila (p. 6.20).

19. W. Kubitschek, *JÖAI* 8 (1905), 125, noted that a disproportionate number of mileages are measured from Eleutheropolis.

20. E.g., the tombs of Miriam the sister of Moses at Kadesh Barnea (*Onom.* p. 112.10 f.) and of Habakkuk at Keilah (p. 114.17 f.).

21. For works on the geography of Palestine which Eusebius could have consulted, see H. Fischer, *ZDPV* 62 (1939), 169 ff.

22. C. W. Wolf, *Biblical Archaeologist* 27 (1964), 89, argues that Eusebius used an ealier list, originally Jewish, which pupils of Origen had expanded, and that the extant text also contains revisions by both Eusebius' pupils and Jerome. He appeals to E. Z. Melamed, *Tarbiz* 3 (1931/2), 314 ff., 393 ff.; 4 (1932/3), 78 ff., 249 ff. (in Hebrew).

23. P. Thomsen, *ZDPV* 29 (1906), 131.

24. The work is dedicated to Paulinus, "holy man of God" (*Onom.* p. 2.3-4), later bishop of Tyre and Antioch.

25. J. Tolkiehn, *RE* 12 (1925), 2432 ff.; C. Wendel, *RE* 18 (1939), 507 ff.

26. For lexicons preserved in papyri, M. Naoumides, *Classical Studies Presented to B. E. Perry* (Urbana, 1969), 181 ff. Absolute alphabetical order had been attempted before Eusebius (by Galen and Harpocration in the second century) but did not become normal for centuries later; see L. W. Daly, *Contributions to a History of Alphabetization in Antiquity and the Middle Ages* (*Collection Latomus* 90, 1967), 32 ff.; J. J. Keaney, *GRBS* 14 (1973), 415 ff.

27. Diogenianus' work is known from the *Suda* Δ 1140 (2.101 Adler). No other works of this type appear to be specifically attested, although they have been posited as sources for Stephanus of Byzantium; see E. Honigmann, *RE* 3A (1929), 2388 f.

28. On the variety and complicated history of Homeric lexicons, see A. Henrichs, *ZPE* 7 (1971), 99 ff.

29. *Onom.* p. 58.18-20; cf. E. Klostermann, *TU* 23.2b (1902), 13 ff.; P. Thomsen, *ZDPV* 26 (1903), 138 f.

30. Origen, *Commentary on John* 6.40 (*GCS* 10.149).

31. R. Cadiou, *REG* 45 (1932), 274 ff.

32. Edited by P. de Lagarde, *Onomastica Sacra*[2] (Göttingen, 1887), 26-111 (reprinted in *CCL* 72 [1969], 59-161). Jerome's preface, though disingenuous, seems to reveal Origen's purpose clearly enough: *in hoc laboravit, ut quod Philo quasi Iudaeus omiserat, hic ut Christianus impleret* (*CCL* 72.60). However, that Origen compiled an onomasticon at all is denied by F. Wutz, *Onomastica Sacra* 1 (*TU* 41.1, 1914), 50, 142 f., and R. P. C. Hanson, *Vig. Chr.* 10 (1956), 103, 120.

33. *P. Oxy.* 2745, with the comments of E. G. Turner, *Oxyrhynchus Papyri*

36 (London, 1970), 2 f. The editor of the papyrus (D. Rokeah) identifies the fragment as part of an anonymous onomasticon compiled c. 200 B.C. (see also D. Rokeah, *JTS,* n.s. 19 [1968], 70 ff.). But its gloss on Iemuel agrees with Jerome's *Liber Interpretationis Hebraicorum Nominum* (*CCL* 72.68: *Iamuhel dies eius deus*) against the normal glosses "right hand of God / the mighty" and "sea of them / God himself" (P. de Lagarde, *Onomastica Sacra*[2] 178.88, 168.52; F. Wutz, *Onomastica Sacra* [1914–15], 504 f.).

34. E. Preuschen, *Real-Encyclopädie für protestantische Theologie und Kirche*[3] 5 (Leipzig, 1898), 616. E. Nestle rightly protested against Klostermann's phrase "the geographical works of Eusebius" (*Berl. phil. Woch.* 24 (1904), 1157).

35. As in the lengthy studies of the city territories of Eleutheropolis, Diospolis, and Nicopolis by G. Beyer, *ZDPV* 54 (1931), 209 ff.; 56 (1933), 281 ff.

36. P. Thomsen, *ZDPV* 29 (1906), 131; E. Schwartz, *RE* 6 (1909), 1434; D. S. Wallace-Hadrill, *Eusebius of Caesarea* (London, 1960), 59.

37. These features were duly noted by P. Thomsen, *ZDPV* 26 (1903), 101.

38. *Onom.* p. 144.7–9, s.v. Rekem (Numbers 31:8); p. 142.7–8, s.v. Petra (Judges 1:36); p. 36.13–14, s.v. Arkem (2 Kings 17:30), quoting Josephus, *AJ* 4.161. In the entry for Kadesh-Barnea (p. 112.8–9, from Numbers 32:8), Jerome and Procopius of Gaza (*PG* 87.1021) show that Eusebius wrote "Petra, a city of Arabia."

39. *New Empire,* ch. XIII.

40. T. D. Barnes, *JTS,* n.s. 26 (1975), 412 ff. If Eusebius composed the work as argued here, then the entries describing Petra as belonging to Arabia were compiled before that attributing it to Palestine.

41. *Onom.* p. 3.1–3 Klostermann. Jerome's translation of c. 390 (it may be noted) was not the first: he himself alludes to an earlier translation (p. 3.14–18), whose use can be detected in the *Peregrinatio Egeriae;* see J. Ziegler, *Biblica* 12 (1931), 70 ff. (whose conclusion that the *Peregrinatio* used Jerome's version is unlikely on chronological grounds); J. Wilkinson, *Egeria's Travels* (London, 1971), 6.

42. *Chronicle* 6.17–7.3, 231[f] Helm.

43. Chapter VIII.

44. *Chronicle* 223[i, k] Helm.

45. On the eras, H. Seyrig, *Antiquités Syriennes* 4 (Paris, 1953), 72 ff. (Antioch), 92 ff. (Laodicea); M. Rostovtzeff, *Social and Economic History of the Hellenistic World* (Oxford, 1941), 846 f., 1534 f. (Tyre); A. R. Bellinger and C. B. Welles, *YCS* 5 (1935), 126, 131, 142 f. (Edessa); W. Benzinger, *RE* 2 (1896), 1609 (Ascalon).

46. Babylonian Talmud, *Sanhedrin* 97b; translated into English by H. Freedman (London, 1935), 2.658.

47. *Chronicle* 22[a], 46[b], 73[b], 109[n], 174[a], 223[h] Helm. Under the twelfth year of Severus (equated with year 251 of the Antiochene era) and again fifty and a hundred years later, Eusebius recorded jubilees celebrated according to the computation of *maiores nostri* (*Chronicle* 212[h]; 219[e]; 227[l] Helm).

48. *HE* 7.32.6 ff. Modern scholars are divided over whether Anatolius' nineteen-year Easter cycle (based on the Metonic cycle) began in 258 or 277; see V. Grumel, *Traité d'études byzantines* 1: *La Chronologie* (Paris, 1958), 31 ff.

49. R. Helm, *Abh. Berlin,* Phil.-hist. K1. 1923, Nr. 4. 42. Helm's suggestion

that the first edition of the *Chronicle* ended with A.D. 276/7 has been generally overlooked. It is discussed only to be rejected by R. M. Grant, *Eusebius as Church Historian* (Oxford, 1980), 7 ff.

50. The present treatment of the *Chronicle* owes much to A. A. Mosshammer, *The Chronicle of Eusebius and Greek Chronographic Tradition* (Lewisburg, Pa., and London, 1979), which the author most generously permitted me to consult in typescript.

51. For history of the text, see A. A. Mosshammer, ibid., 29 ff. E. Schwartz, *Abh. Göttingen,* Phil.-hist. Klasse 40.2 (1894), 33 f., and *RE* 6 (1909), 1378, asserted that Eusebius' original was hopelessly distorted before it reached Jerome's hands.

52. In the preface to the *Canons,* Eusebius described the first "book" as a collection of material for the *Canons* (*Chronicle* 8.7–20 Helm = Syncellus 122.16–123.8). The *Series regum* found between the two parts in the Armenian and some Latin manuscripts (144–155 Karst; A. Schoene, *Eusebi Chronicorum Libri duo* 1 [Berlin, 1875], app. 25–40) probably had no counterpart in the original and is accordingly ignored in this exposition.

53. J. Karst, *Eusebius' Werke* 5 (*GCS* 20, 1911). T. Mommsen, *Ges. Schr.* 7 (Berlin, 1909), 580 ff., argued that the manuscript from Etschmiadzin was the archetype of the other two—a claim which Karst overlooked in his edition, but then explicitly rejected, *TLZ* 36 (1911), 827 f.

54. J. Karst, *GCS* 20 (1911), xxxiv ff. A Syriac intermediary is denied by E. Preuschen, *Berl. phil. Woch.* 33 (1913), 964 ff.

55. J. N. D. Kelly, *Jerome: His Life, Writings and Controversies* (London, 1975), 72 ff.

56. J. K. Fotheringham, *Eusebi Pamphili Chronici Canones: Latine Vertit, Adauxit, ad Sua Tempora Produxit S. Eusebius Hieronymus* (London, 1923), xx ff.; R. Helm, *Eusebius' Werke* 7^2 (*GCS* 47, 1956), ix ff. Nevertheless, some genuine entries are omitted in the earliest manuscripts, surviving in the Latin tradition only in later ones; cf. A. A. Mosshammer, *CSCA* 8 (1976), 203 ff.

57. A. A. Mosshammer, *Chronicle* (1979), 75 ff., argues that Byzantine writers and the translators into Armenian and Syriac knew the *Chronicle* only through a revision produced in Alexandria c. 400.

58. J. A. Cramer, *Anecdota Graeca e Codd. Manuscriptis Bibliothecae Regiae Parisiensis* 2 (Oxford, 1839), 117 ff.; E. Hiller, *Rh. Mus.,* N.F. 25 (1870), 253 ff.—who identifies excerpts in Cyril of Alexandria, *Contra Julianum* 1 (*PG* 76.509 ff.); A. Bauer, *Anonymi Chronographia Syntomos e Codice Matritensi No. 121* (*nunc 4701*) (Leipzig, 1909); *Sb. Wien,* Phil.-hist. Klasse 162.3 (1909), 31 ff. See also L. Canet, *MEFR* 33 (1913), 119 ff. (a lengthy study of the versions of the entry 160^a Helm in *Chron. Pasch.* 1.358 Bonn, Georgius Monachus p. 301 de Boor, Syncellus 585, Georgius Cedrenus 1.323 Bonn). The edition of A. Schoene, *Eusebi Chronicorum Libri Duo* (Berlin, 1875 and 1866), conveniently prints Greek fragments in parallel with Jerome's Latin and a Latin translation of the Armenian version.

59. As in two fragments of Porphyry, *FGrH* 260 F2, 4 (with Jacoby's textual notes).

60. P. Keseling, *Oriens Christianus*[3] 1 (1926–27), 23 ff., 223 f.; 2 (1927), 33 ff.

61. There is an obvious and very large lacuna at the end of the *Chronog-*

raphy (143 Karst) and several in the *Canons* which, as extant, begin with the 344th year of Abraham (156, 177, 227 Karst).

62. *Chron.* 6.8–7 Helm.

63. R. Helm, *Abh. Berlin,* Phil.-hist. K1. 1923, Nr. 4; *Sb. Berlin,* Phil.-hist. K1. 1929, 371 ff.

64. E.g., *Chron.* 48ª, 50ª, where Dionysus is glossed *id est/qui Latine Liber pater.* On Jerome's method of working, see especially A. Schoene, *Die Weltchronik des Eusebius in ihrer Bearbeitung durch Hieronymus* (Berlin, 1900), 32 ff.

65. On Jerome's additions and his Latin sources, see R. Helm, *Rh. Mus., N.F.* 76 (1927), 138 ff., and *Hieronymus' Zusätze in Eusebius' Chronik und ihr Wert für die Literaturgeschichte* (*Philologus,* Supp. 21.2, 1929). In his edition, Helm conveniently marks with an asterisk the entries which betray the hand of Jerome.

66. *Chron.* 34.2–3, 62.3–5 Karst; 6–7, 231 Helm. A third edition is postulated, with neither proof nor probability, by D. S. Wallace-Hadrill, *JTS,* n.s. 6 (1955), 250 ff.

67. E.g., by A. Harnack, *Chronologie der altchristlichen Litteratur bis Eusebius* 2 (Leipzig, 1904), 112; E. Schwartz, *RE* 6 (1909), 1376; J. N. D. Kelly, *Jerome* (1975), 73.

68. Above, at nn. 44–49.

69. *PE* 10.9.1 ff.; cf. K. Mras, *GCS* 43.1 (1954), 585; 43.2 (1956), 466.

70. The preface to the *Canons* as translated by Jerome contains a passage (12.14 ff.) which expands the corresponding section in the *Preparation for the Gospel* (10.9.9 f.)—and it includes two quotations of Homer duly rendered by Jerome into Latin hexameters (13.1 ff., from *Iliad* 20.115, 223 f.). Moreover, the *Preparation* quotes, then criticizes, a passage from Porphyry's *Against the Christians* (10.9.11 ff.), and the *Chronicle* summarizes both the passage quoted there and Eusebius' comments on it (8.1 ff. Helm). Eusebius' habits of quotation in the *Preparation* indicate that if the preface to the *Canons* had existed in its present form at the time of writing, he would have contented himself with a single long quotation (cf. K. Mras, *GCS* 43.1 [1954], 1v ff.).

71. For further arguments against interpreting the *Chronicle* as an apology, J. Laurin, *Orientations maîtresses des apologistes chrétiens de 270 à 361* (Rome, 1954), 106 ff.

72. *Chron.* 1.1 Karst; *Anec. Par.* 2.119.17.

73. *Chron.* 1–4 Karst, esp. 2.35–36.

74. *Chron.* 4–34 Karst.

75. *Chron.* 34–62, esp. 37; 39–40, 44–45 Karst (on textual variants).

76. *Chron.* 62–80 Karst; cf. *Anec. Par.* 2.120–133.

77. *Chron.* 80–124 Karst. Much of this section, including the list of Olympic victors (90–103) also survives in Greek (*Anec. Par.* 2.134–153). The discussion of the kings of Macedonia also lacks a formal ascription: that it derives from Diodorus (*Bibl.* 7, frag. 15), is proved by Syncellus' quotation which attributes the list of Macedonian kings to him (498–499). It may be, therefore, that Diodorus' name has fallen out during textual transmission.

78. *FGrH* 260 F 2, 3, 31, 32; cf E. Will, *Histoire politique du monde hellénistique* 2 (Paris, 1967), 462.

79. *Chron.* 125–143; cf. 3.30–31, with Karst's additional note on p. 240.

80. Something is badly amiss either with the text or with Eusebius' arithmetic, for the interval between the two pairs of consuls is stated as 460 years in the quotation of Castor (*Chron.* 143.1–2 Karst). F. Jacoby obelizes the numeral, *FGrH* 250 F 5; cf. *Kommentar zu Nr. 106-261* (Leiden, 1961), 825 f.

81. *Chron.* 32.20–28 Karst. F. Jacoby prints the immediately preceding passage (30.27–32.15 Karst) as a fragment of Castor but excludes the Median kings (*FGrH* 250 F 1 d). On the provenance of the list, which combines four names from Ctesias (Diodorus, *Bibl.* 2.32.6 ff.) with four from Herodotus (1.102, 107, 130), see H. Montzka, *Klio* 2 (1902), 388 f.; A. A. Mosshammer, *Chronicle* (1979), 145 (arguing that Eusebius' immediate source is Porphyry's *Chronicle*).

82. *Chron.* 9–10, 41.19–23 Karst.

83. *Chron.* 88.31–89.1 Karst; 20 Helm.

84. The text freely translated here is what appears to be the opening of the preface to the first edition, viz., *Chron.* 7.11–18 Helm = Syncellus 122.3–10, immediately followed by *PE* 10.9.2–4.

85. *Chron.* 18.14–19.7 Helm.

86. On the layout of the original *Chronicle,* see especially R. Helm, *Abh. Berlin,* Phil.-hist. Kl. 1923, Nr. 4; *Sb. Berlin,* Phil.-hist. Kl. 1929, 371 ff.; *GCS* 47 (1956), xxvi ff.; A. A. Mosshammer, *Chronicle* (1979), 22 ff. (Plates 1–5), 65 ff. Exigencies of space sometimes led Eusebius to enter items in the wrong *spatium historicum*: e.g., the quotations of Castor in the left-hand page (45ᵃ, 64ᵃ Helm) instead of the right (as 27ᵍ), or the notice of Eumelus (87ᶜ). Jerome did the same far more frequently (e.g., 88ᵃ⁻ᵈ).

87. For hypothetical reconstruction of the original, see R. Helm, *GCS* 47 (1956), xxx f.; A. A. Mosshammer, *Chronicle,* 27 (Plate 5).

88. *Ecl. Proph.* 1, praef. (*PG* 22.1024).

89. In the very first scholarly study of the *Chronicle,* Scaliger asserted roundly: "nihil enim luculentum, vetustum, excellens in eo est, quod non ex Africano deprompserit," *Thesaurus Temporum* (Leiden, 1606), v.

90. For the fullest exposition of this view, H. Gelzer, *Sextus Julius Africanus und die byzantinische Chronographie* 2.1 (Leipzig, 1885), 23 ff.

91. A. A. Mosshammer, *Chronicle,* 128 ff.

92. *Chron.* 34.10–13 Karst; 113ᵃ Helm.

93. R. Helm, *Eranos* 22 (1924), 1 ff. (arguing that Josephus is used only through the medium of Africanus).

94. Clement is quoted by name three times (*Chron.* 57.24–33 Karst; 100ᵃ, 105ᵈ Helm) besides being invoked in the preface to the *Canons* (7.15 Helm).

95. *FGrH* 239–260.

96. *Chron.* 125.6–26 Karst: although the numbers of Olympiads may well be wrong in three of the four cases (A. A. Mosshammer, *Chronicle,* 140 ff.), I have translated Karst's German, correcting only the misprint of "138" for "228" (see *FGrH* 259 T 1).

97. *Chron.* 34.10–13 Karst.

98. E. Schwartz, *RE* 6 (1909), 1378.

99. The Median kings appear in the *Chronography* (32.20–28 Karst), left, and Jerome's *Chronicle* (83–102), right, as follows:

Arbaces	28 years	Arbaces	28 years
Maudaces	20	Sosarmus	30
Sosarmus	30	Madydus	40
Artycas	30	Cardyceas	13
Deioces	54	Deioces	54
Phraortes	24	Phraortes	24
Cyaxares	32	Cyaxares	32
Astyages	38	Astyages	38
	256 years		259 years

Jerome's list was identified as Africanus' by H. Montzka, *Klio* 2 (1902), 398. (The Armenian has only the last four names; 183–187 Karst.)

100. *Chron.* 103.24–28 Karst = *Anec. Par.* 2.153.19–20.

101. Syncellus 400.7–8 = Africanus, frag. 39 Routh; cf. H. Gelzer, *Sextus Julius Africanus,* 2.24.

102. *PE* 10.9.2 (translated above, at note 84).

103. A. A. Mosshammer, *Chronicle,* 138 ff.

104. Syncellus 371.20–372.7, 399.21–400.11 = Africanus, frags. 37, 39 Routh.

105. On the nature of Africanus' work, see A. A. Mosshammer, *Chronicle,* 146 ff., arguing principally from Photius, *Bibl.* 34; Eusebius, *PE* 10.10.1 ff.; *Excerpta Barbara Scaligeri,* fol. 31 (A. Schoene, *Eusebi Chronicorum Libri Duo* 1 [1875], 207–208); Syncellus 488.19–489.14.

106. *PIR²* C 500; *PLRE* 1.514–5.

107. A. A. Mosshammer, *Chronicle,* 141 ff.

108. *FGrH* 4, 6.

109. On their role, see especially F. Jacoby, *Apollodors Chronik: Eine Sammlung der Fragmente (Philologische Untersuchungen* 16, 1902); E. Knaack, *RE* 6 (1909), 381 ff.; A. A. Mosshammer, *Chronicle,* 113 ff., 158 ff., 173 ff.

110. The *Canons* are very sparing of explicit references to authorities; apart from noting the divergence on the date of Homer (66ᵃ Helm), the text named only four secular sources: Castor three times (27ᵍ, 45ᵃ, 64ᵃ), Porphyry (84ᶜ) and Apollodorus (84ᶠ) once each. A. A. Mosshammer, *Chronicle,* 157 ff., argues that Eusebius' main source was an Olympiad chronicler, conjecturally identified as Cassius Longinus, from whom he derived all his dates for the foundation of Greek colonies and for most events in Greek and Roman history.

111. The dates in this section, at least as transmitted, are often erroneous; see T. D. Barnes, *JRS* 63 (1973), 33.

112. R. Helm, *Abh. Berlin,* Phil.-hist. Kl. 1923, Nr. 4.5 ff.

113. *Ecl. Proph.* 1, praef. (*PG* 22.1024).

114. A. A. Mosshammer, *Chronicle,* 16.

115. K. Mras, *Wiener Studien* 46 (1927/8), 200 ff. (a general warning); A. A. Mosshammer, *Chronicle,* 171 ff. (on Greek history before 400 B.C.). The dates given in Jerome's additions (not directly relevant here) are equally insecure as evidence; see R. Helm, *Rh. Mus.,* N.F. 76 (1927), 138 ff., 254 ff.; *Philologus,* Supp. 21.2 (1929).

116. E.g., Herod's thirty-seven years as king of Judaea and Archelaus' nine

as one of his successors are equated with the eleventh to fifty-sixth years of Augustus, i.e., 33 B.C.–A.D. 14, instead of 41 B.C.–A.D. 6. Josephus, whom Eusebius quotes copiously, dates the census after the deposition of Archelaus to the thirty-seventh year after Actium (*AJ* 18.26).

117. Chapter X.

118. Chapter XIV.

119. Chapter VI.

120. Conveniently available in E. Nestle and K. Aland, *Novum Testamentum Graece*[25] (London, 1969), 32*–37*; cf. H. H. Oliver, *Novum Testamentum* 3 (1959), 138 ff. (with an English translation of the letter to Carpianus); H. K. McArthur, *CBQ* 27 (1965), 250 ff.

121. J. B. Lightfoot, *Dictionary of Christian Biography* 2 (London, 1880), 335. Despite his forceful protest, the misleading term has persisted, as in the study of Syriac versions by G. H. Gwilliam, *Studia Biblica et Ecclesiastica* 2 (Oxford, 1890), 241 ff.

122. In fact, no model can be identified.

123. On the textual history of the canons, and on their accompanying illustrations, see especially E. Nestle, *Neue kirchliche Zeitschrift* 19 (1908), 40 ff., 93 ff., 219 ff.; C. Nordenfalk, *Die spätantiken Kanontafeln: Kunstgeschichtliche Studien über die eusebianische Evangelien-Konkordanz in den vier ersten Jahrhunderten ihrer Geschichte* (Göteborg, 1938); J. Leroy, *Cahiers Archéologiques* 9 (1957), 117 ff.; C. Nordenfalk, *Gazette des Beaux-Arts*[6] 62 (1963), 17 ff.

124. C. R. Gregory, *Textkritik des Neuen Testaments* 2 (Leipzig, 1902), 869 ff.; 3 (1909), 1160 Nr. 1582.

125. See his comments on Mark 16:9 in the *Quaestiones ad Marinum* 1.1 (*PG* 22.937–940).

126. On the manuscripts, A. Harnack, *Geschichte der altchristlichen Litteratur* (Leipzig, 1893), 579; A. Baumstark, *Oriens Christianus* 1 (1901), 378 ff. For the published texts, A. Mai, *Nova Patrum Bibliotheca* 4 (Rome, 1847), 219–303, whence *PG* 22.880–1016 (Greek); G. Beyer, *Oriens Christianus,* n.s. 12–14 (1925), 30 ff.; ser. III, 1 (1927), 80 ff.; 2 (1927), 57 ff. (Syriac). The date is established from cross-references in *Quaestiones ad Stephanum* 7.7 (*PG* 22.912); *DE* 7.3.18.

127. *HE* 2.18.1, 5.13.8. Philo's work survives only in an Armenian translation (rendered into English by R. Marcus, *Philo,* Supplement 1, 2 [Loeb Classical Library, 1953]). For a survey of the scholarly genre, G. Heinrici, *Abh. Leipzig,* Phil.-hist. K1. 27 (1909), 843 ff.

128. G. Bardy, *Revue Biblique* 41 (1932), 228 ff.

129. Acacius, who succeeded Eusebius as bishop and renovated the library at Caesarea, wrote six books of *Miscellaneous Questions* (Jerome, *De Viris Illustribus* 98; *Epp.* 34.1).

130. *PG* 22.937, 940, 948, 952. An English translation of the answer to the first question was made by J. Burgon, *The Last Twelve Verses of the Gospel According to S. Mark* (Oxford, 1871), 44–46; it has been reprinted by W. R. Farmer, *The Last Twelve Verses of Mark* (Society for New Testament Studies, Monograph Series 25, 1974), 4.

131. *Quaestiones ad Stephanum* 7.4 ff. (*PG* 22.908 ff.) with an explicit reference to the *Proof of the Gospel* (*DE* 1.3.1 ff.).

132. *Quaestiones ad Marinum* 2.1 (*PG* 22.940 f.); cf. *HE* 3.33.3.

133. *Questiones ad Marinum* 2.1–4, 1.1–2.

134. *Questiones ad Marinum* 2.7; cf. 3.1; *Quaestiones ad Stephanum* 16.1–3.

135. Hence the postulate of fighting between Constantine and Licinius in both 314 and 316/7 (R. Andreotti, *Diz. epig.* 4 (1962), 1002 ff.; *Latomus* 23 [1964], 543 ff.).

136. E.g., F. F. Bruce, *New Testament History* (London, 1969), 195 ff. (on where Jesus' disciples went after his crucifixion).

137. E. Schürer, *A History of the Jewish People*, revised by G. Vermes and F. Millar, 1 (Edinburgh, 1973), 399 ff. On modern attempts to show that P. Sulpicius Quirinius (Luke 2:1) conducted a census before A.D. 6, see also R. Syme, *Akten des VI. Internationalen Kongresses für Griechische und Lateinische Epigraphik* (*Vestigia* 17, 1973), 585 ff.

138. *VC* 4.36.

139. *VC* 4.37. For modern interpretations of the phrase *trissa kai tetrassa*, C. Wendel, *Zentralblatt für Bibliothekwesen* 56 (1929), 168 ff.; B. M. Metzger, *The Text of the New Testament: Its Transmission, Corruption and Restoration*[2] (Oxford, 1968), 7. The normal meaning of these words in Eusebius' day was "in three / four copies" (F. Preisigke, *Wörterbuch der griechischen Papyrusurkunden* 2 [Berlin, 1927], 618, 595).

140. On the ancient chapter divisions and chapter headings; see C. R. Gregory, *Textkritik des Neuen Testaments* 2 (1902), 858 ff.; H. von Soden, *Die Schriften des Neuen Testaments* 1.1[2] (Göttingen, 1911), 402 ff.

141. For the vast bibliography on the subject, B. M. Metzger, *Chapters in the History of New Testament Criticism* (*New Testament Tools and Studies* 4, 1963), 1 ff.

142. For a list of titles, H. von Soden, *Schriften des Neuen Testaments* 1.1[2], 405 ff.

143. T. D. Barnes, *JTS*, n.s. 27 (1976), 418 ff.

144. See W. H. P. Hatch, *The Principal Uncial Manuscripts of the New Testament* (Chicago, 1939), Plates XVII–XIX (Alexandrinus), XXVII–XXIX, XXXIV ff. (later mss.). In the Codex Sinaiticus (Plates XV, XVI) and Codex Bezae (XXII) the small numbered sections and Eusebius' canons have been added by a subsequent hand.

145. H. von Soden, *Schriften des Neuen Testaments* 1.1[2], 426 ff.

146. B. H. Streeter, *The Four Gospels: A Study of Origins* (London, 1924), 102 ff.; J. H. Ropes, *The Text of Acts* (*The Beginnings of Christianity*, ed. F. J. Foakes Jackson and K. Lake, 1.3 [London, 1926]), cclxxvi ff.; S. Jellicoe, *The Septuagint in Modern Study* (Oxford, 1968), 134 ff.; B. M. Metzger, *The Text of the New Testament*[2] (Oxford, 1968), 7 f.

147. H. Dörrie, *ZNW* 39 (1940), 92 ff.; M. Spanneut, *TU* 79 (1961), 171 ff.; J. W. Wevers, *Text History of the Greek Genesis* (*Abh. Göttingen*, Phil.-hist. Kl.[3] 81, 1974), 158 ff.; A. Pietersma, *Vetus Testamentum* 28 (1978), 66 ff. (Psalms).

148. S. Jellicoe, *Septuagint*, 124 ff.

149. For divergent interpretations of the evidence, D. S. Wallace-Hadrill, *HTR* 49 (1956), 105 ff.; *Eusebius of Caesarea* (London, 1960), 61 ff.; M. J.

Suggs, *JBL* 75 (1956), 137 ff.; *Novum Testamentum* 1 (1956), 233 f.; *HTR* 50 (1957), 307 ff.

150. *In Ps.* 77:1 (*PG* 23.901). In Matthew 13:35, the name of Isaiah, which Eusebius states to be lacking "in the accurate copies," is found in the Sinaiticus as a later correction, the Koridethi ms. and Families 1 and 13, i.e., the prime witnesses of the "Caesarean text" (B. H. Streeter, *Four Gospels,* 77 ff.; B. M. Metzger, *Chapters* [Leiden, 1963], 42 ff.).

VIII. THE HISTORY OF THE CHURCH

The text of the present chapter was composed in 1978 and the annotation added in 1979, before the publication of R. M. Grant, *Eusebius as Church Historian* (Oxford, 1980). Grant detects "six important points in regard to which Eusebius changed his mind between the first edition [of the *Ecclesiastical History*] and the second," and he specifies these as the death of James, the nature of the book of Revelation, the reliability of Papias, the date of Hegesippus, the date of the martyrdoms at Lugdunum (*HE* 5.1 ff.), and the circumstances of the death of Origen (15). Although such conclusions would greatly, if only indirectly, strengthen my contention that the first edition of the *Ecclesiastical History* belongs to the 290s, I do not believe that Grant has established them satisfactorily.

1. For a systematic exposition, J. Sirinelli, *Les vues historiques d'Eusèbe de Césarée durant la période prénicéenne* (Dakar, 1961), with the comments of M. Harl, *REG* 75 (1962), 522 ff.

2. *HE* 1.1.8. The preface to the *Chronicle* attributed the founding of pagan religion to Cecrops the contemporary of Moses (12.5 ff. Helm).

3. *HE* 1.2.2 ff. On the equation of Christianity with "true" Judaism, M. Simon, *Verus Israel: Étude sur les relations entre Chrétiens et Juifs dans l'empire romain (135-425)*[2] (Paris, 1964), 105 ff. In this scheme, Melchizedek inevitably plays a crucial role as the first Christian priest; cf. J. Sirinelli, *TU* 81 (1962), 233 ff.; F. L. Horton, *The Melchizedek Tradition* (Cambridge, 1976), 87 ff.

4. E. Schwartz, *Ges. Schr.* 1 (Berlin, 1938), 110 ff.

5. A. Momigliano, *The Conflict between Paganism and Christianity in the Fourth Century* (Oxford, 1963), 90.

6. *HE* 1.4.1. ff.

7. *HE* 5, praef. 3 f.

8. *HE* 1.1.4 ff.

9. T. D. Barnes, *GRBS* 21 (1980), 191 ff. For the structure of the whole work, E. Schwartz, *GCS* 9.3 (1909), 11 ff.; for a more detailed analysis of Book Six, D. S. Wallace-Hadrill, *Eusebius of Caesarea* (London, 1960), 160 ff.

10. On the hypothesis of completion c. 295, the following passages of Books One to Seven must be or must contain subsequent additions: 1.1.2, 2.27, 9.3/4, 11.9, 4.7.14, 6.19.2–15, 23.3/4, 32.3, 33.4, 36.4–7, 7.18.3, 30 index and chapter heading, 30.22, 32.1 ff. Two other passages in Book One (2.14–16 and 13) also appear to be later additions (see n. 15).

Most modern analyses of the purpose and theology of the *History* proceed from the erroneous premise that Eusebius wrote the whole of it after 303: e.g., G. Bardy, *RHE* 50 (1935), 5 ff.; W. Völker, *Vig. Chr.* 4 (1955), 157 ff. Even

H. Eger, *ZNW* 38 (1939), 97 ff., who argued that the *History* displays a very different attitude toward the Roman Empire from works written after 313, implicitly assumed a date after 303. According to G. F. Chesnut, *The First Christian Histories* (*Théologie Historique* 46, 1977), 94 ff., the perspective of the work runs "from Eden to the Milvian Bridge."

11. *HE* 1.1.1–2, omitting the reference to the persecution of 303–313.

12. *HE* 3.3.3. For a parallel but contrasting analysis of how Eusebius treats his seven "themes," see R. M. Grant, *Eusebius as Church Historian*, 45 ff.

13. *HE* 2, praef. 1.

14. *HE* 1.5.3. ff., 6.2., 9 f., 10.4 f., 11.5 ff. (Josephus); 6.2, 7.1 ff. (Africanus). Eusebius' quotation of Josephus on Jesus (11.8, from *AJ* 18.63 f.) contains the statement that Jesus was the Messiah—which Josephus cannot have made. It seems clear that Josephus' description of Jesus was rewritten by a Christian who found it unflattering; see P. Winter, in E. Schürer, *History of the Jewish People in the Age of Jesus Christ*, revised by G. Vermes and F. Millar, 1 (Edinburgh, 1973), 428 ff. Origen expressly states that Josephus denied that Jesus was the Messiah (*Commentary on Matthew* 10.17 [*GCS* 40.22]; *Contra Celsum* 1.47).

15. *HE* 1.13, drawing on an earlier version of the Syriac *Doctrine of Addai*, the extant form of which seems to date from c. 400; see I. Ortiz de Urbina, *Patrologia Syriaca*[2] (Rome, 1965), 44. Eusebius describes how Thaddaeus went to Edessa after the Ascension (13.11 ff.): the preface to Book Two states "let us now consider the events after his ascension" (2, praef. 2).

16. E. Schwartz, *GCS* 9.3 (1909), 3 ff.

17. *HE* 4.5.3, 5.12.2, from *Chronicle* 198[k], 208[l] Helm—where Eusebius remarks that he cannot compute the exact dates "because up to the present day the years of their episcopates are not preserved." The names appear to come from a single list which must be at least partly artificial; see C. H. Turner, *JTS* 1 (1900) 529 ff.

18. Thus Babylas succeeded Zebennus in the reign of Gordian (6.29.4) and died in prison under Decius (6.39.4). If the day of his death was 24 January (*PO* 10.12), then the year must be 251.

19. Eusebius' chronology of the bishops of Rome and Alexandria is conveniently tabulated by E. Schwartz, *GCS* 9.3 (1909), 6 f., 9. For attempts to establish the correct dates, A. Harnack, *Chronologie der altchristlichen Litteratur bis Eusebius* 1 (Leipzig, 1904), 70 ff.; C. H. Turner, *JTS* 17 (1916), 338 ff.; 18 (1917), 103 ff.; E. Caspar, *Die älteste römische Bischofsliste* (*Schriften der Königsberger Gelehrten Gesellschaft*, Geisteswissenschaftliche Klasse 2.4, 1926); H. J. Lawlor and J. E. L. Oulton, *Eusebius: The "Ecclesisastical History" and the "Martyrs of Palestine"* 2 (London, 1928), 40 ff. The dates of all bishops of Rome before 235 are somewhat uncertain; see L. Koep, *RAC* 2 (1954), 410 ff. For them, the present work adopts the conventional modifications of the consular dates in *Chr. Min.* 1.74, which cannot be greatly in error for the late second and early third centuries.

20. *HE* 2.17.2 ff., with copious quotation of Philo, *De Vita Contemplativa*.

21. *HE* 2.4.2 f., 17.1, 18.1 ff.; cf. H. J. Lawlor, *Eusebiana* (Oxford, 1912), 138 ff. A manuscript of Philo's *De Opificio Mundi* notes that Euzoius, who became bishop of Caesarea in 366, "renewed" the text of the work (L. Cohn and

P. Wendland, *Philonis Alexandri Opera quae Supersunt* 1 [Berlin, 1896], iii; cf. xxxv ff.). Jerome records the efforts of Euzoius and his predecessor Acacius to preserve Pamphilus' library (*Epp.* 34.1; *De Viris Illustribus* 113).

22. *HE* 3.9.1 ff.; cf. 1.5.3 ff., 6.2, 6.9 f., 8.4 ff., 9.4, 10.4 f., 11.5 ff.; 2.4.1 ff., 6.3 ff., 10.2 ff., 11.2 ff., 19.1, 20.1 ff., 21, 23.20 ff., 26; 3.5.4 ff.

23. *HE* 4.8.1 f., 11.7, 22.1 ff.; cf. 2.23.3 ff., 32.2 ff., 3.11, 16, 19 f. (Hegesippus); 4.8.3. ff., 16.1 ff.; cf. 2.13.2 ff.; 3.26.3 (Justin); 4.21; 5.4.1 f., 5.8 ff.; cf. 2.13.5 ff.: 3.18.2 f., 23.2 ff., 26.2, 28.6, 36.12, 39.1, 39.13; 4.7.4, 7.9, 10f., 14.1 ff. (Irenaeus).

24. E.g., Aristo of Pella, who is adduced as the source for Hadrian's permanent banishment of Jews from Jerusalem (4.6.3). Clement of Alexandria quoted Aristo's *Dialogue between Jason and Papiscus* in the sixth book of his *Hypotyposeis* (Maximus the Confessor, *PG* 4.421 = *GCS* 17.199), a work which was in the library of Caesarea (*HE* 6.13.1 ff.).

25. A. Harnack, *TU* 8.4 (1892), 1 ff.

26 *HE* 2.2.4. Tertullian in fact addressed magistrates on the hill of the Byrsa in Carthage (*Apol.* 1.1).

27. *HE* 2.2.4 ff.

28. *HE* 2.25.4, 3.20.7, 33.3. Eusebius also quotes Hegesippus on Domitian (3.20.1 ff.).

29. *HE* 5.5.5 ff. Apollinarius is also adduced (4).

30. *HE* 1.4.1 ff.

31. *HE* 3.18.4; cf. Dio 67.14.1 f. In the *Chronicle*, Eusebius adduces Bruttius (192ᵉ Helm: the name is given as Brettius in the Armenian and Syncellus 650 Bonn). He is presumably Bruttius Praesens, the correspondent of Pliny (*Epp.* 7.3), who may have had reason to commemorate friends who died under Domitian (on his career, see R. Syme, *Roman Papers* [Oxford, 1979], 490 ff.) Bruttius Praesens would not have classified Domitilla as a Christian.

32. *HE* 5.21.1.

33. *HE* 2.3.1: "Thus, by a heavenly power and operation, the word of salvation immediately began to illumine the whole world like a ray of sunlight."

34. Book Two, with 3.18.1, 20.9, 23 (John), 30 f., 37.1 (Philip).

35. *HE* 3.36–39.

36. *HE* 5.23–25; cf. P. Nautin, *Lettres et écrivains chrétiens des IIᵉ et IIIᵉ siècles* (Paris, 1961), 65 ff.; *HE* 6.1–5, 8, 15–19, 23–29; cf. Chapter VI.

37. Irenaeus, *Adv. Haer.* 3.1 ff.

38. *HE* 1.1.1.

39. On the nature of Hegesippus' work, which Epiphanius also appears to have used c. 375, H. J. Lawlor, *Eusebiana* (1912), 1 ff.; N. Hyldahl, *Studia Theologica* 14 (1960), 70 ff.; B. Gustafsson, *TU* 78 (1961), 227 ff.

40. *HE* 4.22.4 f.

41. *HE* 2.1.10 ff., 14 f. Eusebius quotes Justin, *Apol.* 1.26 (13.3 f.) and adduces Irenaeus, *Adv. Haer.* 1.23.1 ff. (13.5).

42. *HE* 3.26, again adducing Irenaeus and quoting Justin, *Apol.* 1.26.

43. *HE* 3.27–29.

44. *HE* 4.7.

45. *HE* 4.10 f. Eusebius registers Cerdon and Valentinus as flourishing when

Hyginus was bishop of Rome (10); Marcion, under Anicetus, who became bishop fifteen years after Hyginus died (11.6 ff.).

46. *HE* 4.29, quoting Irenaeus, *Adv*. *Haer*. 1.28.1.

47. *HE* 5.14–20.

48. *HE* 5.16.2 ff., naming Gratus as the proconsul in whose year Montanus began to prophesy (7); cf. T. D. Barnes, *JTS*, n.s. 21 (1970), 403 ff. On the enigmatic inscription of Abercius Marcellus, H. Strathmann and T. Klauser, *RAC* 1 (1950), 12 ff.

49. *HE* 5.18.1 ff. (Apollonius); 16; 19. In 17.5 Eusebius registers Miltiades, whom the anonymous anti-Montanist mentioned (17.1).

50. *HE* 5.15, 20.

51. *HE* 5.28; cf. 7.30.16; *Ecl. Proph.* 3.19, 4.22.

52. *HE* 5.28.3 ff.; cf. Theodoretus, *Haer. Fab. Comp.* 2.5 (*PG* 83.392). On the date (and in favor of attribution to Hippolytus), R. H. Connolly, *JTS* 49 (1948), 73 ff.

53. *HE* 5.28.9, 14. On Galen's attitude towards Christians (moral respect tempered by intellectual contempt), see R. Walzer, *Galen on Jews and Christians* (Oxford, 1949), 10 ff. For commentary on the extract quoted in *HE* 5.28.13 ff., H. Schöne, *Pisciculi* (Münster, 1939), 252 ff.

54. *HE* 7.30.17 (synodical letter of 268); cf. R. H. Connolly, *JTS* 49 (1948), 76 ff.

55. *HE* 6.33.

56. *HE* 6.37. A papyrus seems to preserve part of the record of this synod; see J. Scherer, *Entretien d'Origène avec Héraclide* (*SC* 67, 1960), 19 ff.

57. *HE* 6.38. On the Elchasaites, see now A. Henrichs, *HSCP* 83 (1979), 361 ff.

58. M. M. Sage, *Cyprian* (Philadelphia, 1975), 249 ff.

59. *HE* 6.43; cf. 7.3 f.

60. *HE* 7.6, 26.1.

61. *HE* 6.22; cf. *Refutatio Omnium Haeresium* 9.12.15 ff. Photius, *Bibl.* 121, enables the work by Hippolytus to which Eusebius refers to be reconstructed from [Tertullian], *Adv. Omn. Haer.* (*CCL* 2.1401–1410), Epiphanius, Filastrius, and the *Contra Noetum*; cf. R. A. Lipsius, *Zur Quellenkritik des Epiphanios* (Vienna, 1865), 33 ff.; C. Martin, *RHE* 37 (1941), 5 ff.; P. Nautin, *Hippolyte: Contre les hérésies (fragment): Étude et édition critique* (Paris, 1949), 22 ff.

P. Nautin has contested the traditional attribution of the *Refutatio* to Hippolytus in a series of studies: P. Nautin, *Hippolyte et Josipe: Contribution à l'histoire de la littérature chrétienne du 3e siècle* (Paris, 1947); *Rech. Sci. Rel.* 35 (1947), 100 ff., 347 ff.; *RHE* 47 (1952), 5 ff.; *Le dossier d'Hippolyte et de Meliton dans les florilèges dogmatiques et chez les historiens modernes* (Paris, 1953); *Rech. Sci. Rel.* 42 (1954), 226 ff.; *Mél. Sci. Rel.* 11 (1954), 215 ff.; *Lettres et écrivains* (1961), 177 ff. His arguments have been subjected to damaging criticisms, principally by G. Bardy, *Mél. Sci. Rel.* 5 (1948), 63 ff.; M. Richard, *Mél. Sci. Rel.* 5 (1948), 294 ff.; B. Capelle, *Recherches de théologie ancienne et médiévale* 17 (1950), 145 ff.; 19 (1952), 193 ff.; B. Botte, ibid., 18 (1951), 5 ff. Nevertheless, his main thesis is probably correct; see A. Amore, *Antonianum* 36 (1961), 3 ff.; V. Loi and others, *Ricerche su Ippolito* (Rome, 1977), esp. 155 (M. Simonetti).

62. *Refutatio Omnium Haeresium* 9.12.

63. Chapter XI.

64. *HE* 1.1.2.

65. *HE* 1.8.3 ff.

66. *HE* 2.4–6. God also punished Pilate, who committed suicide under Caligula (2.7).

67. *HE* 2.19–23, 26; 3.5–8.

68. *HE* 2.10, quoting Josephus, *AJ* 19.343 ff.; *HE* 2.23.20, quoting a passage not found in the transmitted text of Josephus, but known to Origen (*Commentary on Matthew* 10.17 [*GCS* 40.22]; *Contra Celsum* 1.47), which contradicts Josephus' interpretation of the episode (*AJ* 20.199 ff.). Eusebius' immediate source may be Origen himself; cf. H. Chadwick, *Origen: Contra Celsum* (Cambridge, 1953), 43.

69. *HE* 3.5.3. Eusebius omits the return from Pella after A.D. 70 attested by Epiphanius, *De Mensuris et Ponderibus* 15 (*PG* 43.261). Both are drawing on Hegesippus; see H. J. Lawlor, *Eusebiana* (Oxford, 1912), 25 ff., 101 f.

70. *HE* 3.5–7.

71. *HE* 7.1. Chapter 6 quotes successively Josephus, *BJ* 5.424–438 , 512–519, 566; 6.199–213.

72. *HE* 4.2.

73. *HE* 4.6. On the Jewish war of 115–117, see E. M. Smallwood, *The Jews under Roman Rule* (Leiden, 1976), 412 ff.; on that of 132–135, G. W. Bowersock, *Approaches to Ancient Judaism* 2 (*Brown Judaic Studies* 9, 1980), 131 ff. Eusebius is wrong in assuming that Jerusalem was refounded as the *colonia Aelia Capitolina* only after the revolt: the refoundation probably occurred in A.D. 130; see G. W. Bowersock, ibid., 135 ff.

74. E.g., *Ecl. Proph.* 3.36; *DE* 2.3.71 ff. (quoting Joshua 6:3–12), *DE* 6.13.2 ff.; *Theophany* 4.20 = frag. 12 (pp. 197*, 31* Gressmann). Some Jews in fact visited Jerusalem during the third century; cf. M. Avi-Yonah, *The Jews of Palestine* (New York, 1976), 79 ff.

75. Chapter IX.

76. He speaks of crowded churches in every city and village in the reign of Tiberius (*HE* 2.3.2).

77. *HE* 3.5.2.

78. *HE* 2.25.

79. *HE* 3.17–20. Eusebius misreports the identity of Flavia Domitilla (18.4), making her the niece of Flavius Clemens instead of his wife (*PIR*² F 418). Hegesippus states that Domitian interviewed the grandsons of Jude in person (20.1); the story is suspect (see T. D. Barnes, *Tertullian: A Historical and Literary Study* [Oxford, 1971], 150)—but perhaps not wholly fictitious. The information about John may also come from Hegesippus; see H. J. Lawlor, *Eusebiana*, 95.

80. *HE* 3.32, quoting Hegesippus. The governor was Atticus (32.3, 6), who governed the province from c. 99 to c. 103 (E. Schürer, *History*, rev. G. Vermes and F. Millar, 1.516).

81. *HE* 3.33, based on and quoting Tertullian, *Apol.* 2.5.

82. *HE* 4.3, 8.6 ff. (from Justin, *Apol.* 1.68). On the rescript to Minicius Fundanus, proconsul of Asia in 122–123, R. Freudenberger, *Das Verhalten der*

römischen Behörden gegen die Christen im 2. Jahrhundert (Münchener Beiträge zur Papyrusforschung 52, 1967), 216 ff.

83. *HE* 4.13. The letter as quoted by Eusebius bears the names of Marcus Aurelius and Lucius Verus as Augusti, though the text preserved in the manuscript of Justin (printed in *GCS* 9.1.328) attributes the letter to Antonius Pius in his twenty-fourth *tribunicia potestas,* i.e., between 10 December 160 and 7 March 161. Whether the letter is authentic or not, it refers to earthquakes which certainly occurred in 160/1; cf. G. W. Bowersock, *HSCP* 72 (1967), 289 ff.

84. *HE* 4.15–17. Eusebius partly paraphrases (15.4–14), partly quotes (15.3, 15–45) the extant *Martyrdom of Polycarp;* for the correct dates of these martyrs, see below, at nn. 136–142.

85. *HE* 4.26.4 ff. Eusebius quotes extracts from the apology which Melito addressed to Marcus Aurelius, probably in 175/6, when the emperor visited Asia (M. Sordi, *Studi romani* 9 [1961], 368 ff.).

86. *HE* 5.1–2; cf. above, at n. 7.

87. *HE* 5.5.1. In the same chapter Eusebius quotes Apollinarius and Tertullian, *Apol.* 5.5 for the miraculous rain and victory produced by the prayers of the "Thundering Legion."

88. R. M. Grant, *TU* 115 (1975), 416, suggests that Eusebius has "sacrificed historical fact" in order to curry favor with Constantine.

89. H. J. Lawlor and J. E. L. Oulton, *Eusebius* 2 (London, 1928), 129, 161.

90. A. R. Birley, *Marcus Aurelius* (London, 1966), 152 ff.

91. *HE* 5.21.

92. *HE* 6.1–5.

93. *HE* 6.21.3 f.; cf. Chapter VI. It is now known that Hippolytus addressed a work, presumably a letter, to Mamaea (M. Richard, *Symbolae Osloenses* 38 [1963], 79 f., no. 3).

94. *HE* 6.28. For the true extent of "the persecution of Maximinus" (unknown to Lactantius), G. W. Clarke, *Historia* 15 (1966), 445 ff.

95. *HE* 6.34, 39.1. The story that Philip confessed his sins, performed penance, and attended a paschal vigil (34) probably comes from one of the two letters which Origen wrote to Philip and his wife, Otacilia Severa (36.3); see H. Crouzel, *Gregorianum* 56 (1975), 545 ff.; P. Nautin, *Origène* (1977), 172 f. But there is no reason to believe that Philip reigned as a Christian (as claimed by Jerome, *Chronicle* 217ᶜ); Origen referred to Philip's passing interest in Christianity while a private citizen.

96. *HE* 6.40–42. Chapter 39 notes the martyrdoms of bishops Fabianus at Rome, Alexander of Jerusalem (at Caesarea), and Babylas at Antioch, and the imprisonment and torture of Origen. On Decius' legislation and its enforcement, especially in Italy and Africa, see G. W. Clarke, *Antichthon* 3 (1969), 63 ff.; *Historia* 22 (1973), 650 ff.; *BICS* 20 (1973), 118 ff.

97. *HE* 7.1, quoting Dionysius. Cyprian's correspondence confirms the exile of the bishop of Rome with some clergy, as well as the expectation at Carthage in 252 that persecution would recommence (*Epp.* 58–62).

98. *HE* 7.10–12.

99. *HE* 7.13, 15–16.

100. G. W. Anderson, *Cambridge History of the Bible* 1 (1970), 135 ff.

101. See the introductions to each book in R. H. Charles, *Apocrypha and Pseudepigrapha of the Old Testament in English* (Oxford, 1913). The Dead Sea Scrolls contain many fragments of the original Hebrew, for the most part otherwise lost; see A. Dupont-Summer, *Essene Writings from Qumran,* trans. G. Vermes (Oxford, 1961), 295 ff. The writings of Philo and Josephus were similarly preserved only by Christians, not by Jews.

102. *HE* 3.9.5 ff., 4.26.14, 6.25.1 f. On Origen's indebtedness to Hebrew scholars, N. R. M. de Lange, *Origen and the Jews* (Cambridge, 1976), 15 ff.

103. *HE* 3.25; cf. M. Müller, *Theologische Studien und Kritiken* 105 (1933), 425 ff.; D. S. Wallace-Hadrill, *Eusebius* (London, 1960) 63 ff.; R. M. Grant, *Cambridge History of the Bible* 1 (1970), 284 ff.

104. H. J. Lawlor and J. E. L. Oulton, *Eusebius* 2 (London, 1928), 101.

105. *HE* 3.3.1, 4.

106. *HE* 2.23.24 f.; cf. R. M. Grant, *Cambridge History of the Bible* 1 (1970), 306.

107. E.g., the Acts, Gospel, Preaching, and Apocalypse of Peter (*HE* 3.3.2), the Acts of Paul, and Shepherd of Hermas (3.3.5 f.).

108. *HE* 3.39.17, 4.22.8 (Gospel of the Hebrews), 6.14.1 (Clement). Clement also used Barnabas in his *Stromateis* (*HE* 6.13.6). The Gospel of the Hebrews was the only gospel admitted by the Ebionites (3.27.4, from Irenaeus, *Adv. Haer.* 1.22.2, 3.11.10). Irenaeus calls it "the Gospel according to Matthew," as do Epiphanius (*Pan.* 29.9.4, 30.3.7, 51.5.3) and Jerome (*De Viris Illustribus* 3), who attest its use by the Nazoreans in the late fourth century. Eusebius knew the work at first hand (*PG* 24.685, from the *Second Theophany; Theophany* 4.12, p. 183* Gressmann).

109. *HE* 2.15.2, 3.36.2, 39, cf. H. J. Lawlor, *Hermathena* 43 (1922) 167 ff. The fragments of Papias are collected in F. X. Funk and K. Bihlmeyer, *Die apostolischen Väter* 1 (Tübingen, 1924), 133 f., and are translated and discussed by J. A. Kleist, *ACW* 6 (1948), 105 ff. E. Gutzwenger, *ZKT* 69 (1947), 385 ff., argues that Papias wrote in the 90s—before Revelation was written. He infers from Eusebius' silence that Papias never mentioned Revelation—not a secure inference, and its premise is probably disproved by *HE* 3.39.13 f.

110. *HE* 3.39.1, 6.13.4 ff., 25.3 ff.

111. *HE* 3.24.5 ff. Eusebius may be correct; see J. M. Rist, *On the Independence of Matthew and Mark* (Society for New Testament Studies, *Monograph Series* 32, 1978), 100.

112. *HE* 3.24.6, 39.16 (Papias), 5.8.2 (Irenaeus), 10.3 (Pantaenus), 6.25.4 (Origen). (By *Hebrew,* Eusebius and other writers should mean Aramaic.) According to Jerome, a manuscript at Caesarea contained what was believed to be the original Aramaic Matthew (*De Viris Illustribus* 3; *Dialogus contra Pelagianos* 3.2 [*PL* 23.597]). His testimony must be discounted, for he confuses the hypothetical original Matthew with the well-attested Aramaic Gospel According to the Hebrews—which was in the library at Caesarea (A. Harnack, *Chronologie der altchristlichen Litteratur bis Eusebius* 1 [Leipzig, 1896], 625 ff.). On patristic evidence for gospels in Aramaic, see now A. F. J. Klijn, *Text and Interpretation. Studies in the New Testament Presented to M. Black* (Cambridge, 1979), 169 ff.

113. *HE* 2.15, 3.39.15 (Papias); cf. T. Y. Mullins, *Vig. Chr.* 14 (1960), 216 ff.; 5.8.3 (Irenaeus, *Adv. Haer.* 3.1.1), 6.14.6 f. (Clement), 25.5 (Origen). Eusebius

was naturally ignorant of what purports to be part of a letter of Clement attesting an otherwise unknown secret gospel of Mark, published by M. Smith, *Clement of Alexandria and a Secret Gospel of Mark* (Harvard, 1973), 448 ff. The fact that the letter is known only from photographs is highly suspicious; see Q. Quesnell, *CBQ* 37 (1975), 48 ff.; 38 (1976), 200 ff. M. Smith seems to concede that no one besides himself has seen the original (*CBQ* 38 [1976], 196 ff.). The letter is thus exempt from the scientific examination of writing material and ink which has damned so many modern forgeries.

114. *HE* 2.22.6, 3.4.6. Papias appears to have said nothing about Luke (*HE* 3.39), but Irenaeus noted his closeness to Paul (*Adv. Haer.* 3.11, quoted at *HE* 5.8.3) and Origen that he wrote for non-Jewish converts (*HE* 6.25.6, from the lost beginning of Origen's *Commentary on Matthew*).

115. *HE* 3.24, 6.14.7 (from Clement). The anti-Marcionite prologue states that John dictated his Gospel to his disciple Papias at the very end of his life (D. de Bruyne, *Rev. Bén.* 40 [1928], 198, 206 ff.).

116. *HE* 3.3.5.

117. *HE* 6.20.3 (Gaius), 25.11 (Origen). The latter argued that, since the thought is Pauline (12), Hebrews was written by a disciple of Paul trying to reproduce his teaching (13), perhaps Clement of Rome, or Luke (14).

118. *HE* 3.38. Eusebius later quotes Clement's explanation of why Hebrews does not (like the other thirteen Pauline epistles) call itself a letter of Paul: Paul suppressed his name because of the recipients' prejudice against him (6.14.3).

119. *HE* 3.3.1, 24.17. Papias quoted both (39.17).

120. *HE* 3.24.18, 25.2, 4.

121. *HE* 3.18.2 f., 5.8.5 ff. (Irenaeus, *Adv. Haer.* 5.30.3), 4.18.8 (Justin), 6.25.9 (Origen). Eusebius also notes that Theophilus of Antioch and the anti-Montanist Apollonius draw proof texts from Revelation (*HE* 4.24, 5.18.14).

122. *HE* 3.39.3 ff.; 7.25. Dionysius was attacking Nepos, who argued from Revelation that there will be an earthly millennium (7.24.1 f.).

123. Eusebius traces millenarianism to Papias' misunderstanding of the teaching of the Apostles (3.39.12 f.)—and he knew that persecution produced eschatological fervor (6.7, on Judas, who argued that the seventy weeks of Daniel 9:24 ended in the tenth year of Septimius Severus).

124. See the collective volume *Les Martyrs de Lyon* (*177*) (Paris, 1978).

125. *HE* 4.23, 6.11; cf. P. Nautin, *Lettres et écrivains* (Paris, 1961), 13 ff., 105 ff.

126. The quotations from *HE* 6.40–7.25 and elsewhere are collected in C. E. Feltoe, *The Letters and Other Remains of Dionysius of Alexandria* (Cambridge, 1904), and are translated into German with an introduction and notes by W. A. Bienert, *Dionysius von Alexandrien: Das erhaltene Werk* (*Bibliothek der griechischen Literatur* 2, 1972); cf. W. A. Bienert, *Dionysius von Alexandrien: Zur Frage des Origenismus im dritten Jahrhundert* (*Patristische Texte und Studien* 21, 1978).

127. *HE* 1.1.3 f.

128. H. J. Lawlor and J. E. L. Oulton, *Eusebius* 2 (1928), 19 ff. On the principles which Eusebius observes in using his sources, see also B. Gustafsson, *TU* 79 (1961), 429 ff.

129. H. J. Lawlor and J. E. L. Oulton, *Eusebius* 2 (1928), 28 ff.

130. As in works like H. Grégoire, *Les persécutions dans l'empire romain*[2] (Brussels, 1964); M. Sordi, *Il Cristianesimo e Roma* (Rome, 1965); W. H. C. Frend, *Martyrdom and Persecution in the Early Church* (Oxford, 1965).

131. *HE* 5.27.

132. T. D. Barnes, *JTS*, n.s. 30 (1979), 47 ff.

133. *PIR*[2] B 54.

134. *HE* 4.30.

135. For discussion of *HE* 4.30, *PE* 6.10.1 ff., and their relevance to the "Book of the Laws of Countries" extant in Syriac, see H. J. W. Drijvers, *Bardaisan of Edessa* (Assen, 1966), 60 ff.

136. *HE* 4.17, quoting Justin, *Apol.* 2.2.

137. Viz., Q. Lollius Urbicus (*PIR*[2] L 327).

138. *HE* 4.15.

139. *HE* 4.15.1.

140. *Mart. Pol.* 21.

141. T. D. Barnes, *JTS*, n.s. 18 (1967), 433 ff.; 19 (1968), 511 ff.

142. *Passio Pionii* 2.1, 9.4, 23; cf. T. D. Barnes, *JTS*, n.s. 19 (1968), 529 ff.

143. R. Freudenberger, *Theologische Zeitschrift* 23 (1967), 97 ff.

144. Tertullian, *Scap.* 4.5 ff.; Eusebius, *HE* 6.19.15; cf. T. D. Barnes, *Tertullian* (Oxford, 1971), 69 f.

145. P. Brown, *The World of Late Antiquity* (London, 1971), 60 ff. Significantly, church councils begin to be validly attested shortly after 180; cf. J. A. Fischer, *Annuarium Historiae Conciliorum*, 6 (1974), 241 ff.; 9 (1977), 241 ff.

146. T. D. Barnes, *JTS*, n.s. 26 (1975), 111 ff.

147. T. D. Barnes, *Tertullian*, 5 ff.

148. Irenaeus and this dossier provide almost all the material for *HE* 5.1–8.

149. T. D. Barnes, *Tertullian*, esp. 60 ff.; 211 ff.

150. H. Dessau, *Hermes* 15 (1880), 471 ff.

151. M. M. Sage, *Cyprian* (Cambridge, Mass., 1975), 95 ff.

152. Cyprian, *Epp.* 39.3; cf. T. D. Barnes, *Tertullian*, 156 ff.

153. *HE* 7.12.

154. *HE* 7.15.

155. *HE* 7.16.

156. *HE* 7.18 f. Maximinus destroyed the relief shortly after 305 (*PG* 24.541, from the *General Elementary Introduction*).

157. *HE* 7.27.1.

158. *HE* 7.29.2. For the synodical acts to which Eusebius refers (29.2), H. de Riedmatten, *Les Actes du Procès de Paul de Samosate: Étude sur la Christologie du III*e *au IV*e *siècle* (*Paradosis* 6, 1952), 15 ff.; 135 ff.

159. *HE* 7.30.2 ff.

160. P. Galtier, *Rech. Sci. Rel.* 12 (1922), 30ff. For attempts to reconstruct Paul's theology, G. Bardy, *Paul de Samosate: Étude Historique* (Louvain and Paris, 1923), 305 ff.; F. Loofs, *Paulus von Samosata: Eine Untersuchung zur altkirchlichen Literatur- und Dogmengeschichte* (*TU* 44.5, 1924), 202 ff.

161. Hilary of Poitiers, *De Synodis* 81 f. (*PL* 10.534); Athanasius, *De Synodis* 25, 45; Basil, *Epp.* 52.1. The reliability of this information is doubted by F. Loofs, *Paulus von Samosata* (*TU* 44.5, 1924), 155 f.; H. de Riedmatten, *Les*

Actes du Procès de Paul de Samosate (*Paradosis* 6, 1952), 107; G. C. Stead, *Divine Substance* (Oxford, 1977), 216 f.

162. *HE* 7.30.6 ff.; cf. F. Millar, *JRS* 61 (1971), 14 ff.

163. H. Chadwick, *JTS*, n.s. 23 (1972), 132 ff.

164. F. Millar, *The Emperor in the Roman World* (London, 1977), 551 ff.

165. *HE* 7.30.20 f.

166. The chapter on Manichaeism (*HE* 7.31) probably did not appear in the first edition.

167. Dorotheus (*HE* 7.32.2 f.) was probably not mentioned in the first edition; on him, see Chapter XI.

168. A. Harnack, *Chronologie* 2 (Leipzig, 1904), 75 ff.

169. Anatolius, the teacher of Porphyry (Eunapius, *Vit. Phil.* 5.1.2., p. 457), must be the Anatolius to whom Porphyry dedicated Book One of his *Homeric Questions* and Iamblichus his *On Justice* (Stobaeus, *Ecl.* 3.9.35 f.). In favor of identification with the Christian Anatolius, J. Dillon, *Iamblichi Chalcidensis in Platonis Dialogos Commentariorum Fragmenta* (*Philosophia Antiqua* 23, 1973), 9. R. M. Grant, *Romanitas et Christianitas* (Amsterdam and London, 1973), 184 ff., argues that it was Anatolius who brought the early works of Porphyry to Caesarea.

170. *HE* 7.32.5 ff.

171. Chapter VII, at nn. 44–49.

172. *HE* 7.32.22, 24.

173. *HE* 7.27.1, 32.1; cf. H. J. Lawlor and J. E. L. Oulton, *Eusebius* 2 (1928), 255, 261.

174. *HE* 7.29.1, 30.2; cf. C. H. Turner, *JTS*, 17 (1916), 348 f.

175. J. Molthagen, *Der römische Staat und die Christen im zweiten und dritten Jahrhundert* (*Hypomnemata* 28, 1970), 98 ff.

176. *HE* 8.1.1 ff. An inscription of Eumeneia (*ILS* 8881) attests a Christian soldier in the *officium* of Castrius Constans, governor of Phrygia and Caria shortly after 293; see L. Robert, *Noms indigènes dans l'Asie-mineure greco-romaine* 1 (Paris, 1963), 361 ff.

177. Lactantius, *Mort. Pers.* 12.3, 14.1 ff.

IX. PERSECUTION

1. Chapter VIII.

2. *Mart. Pal.* 4.8; Photius, *Bibl.* 118.

3. The *Commentary on Isaiah* may allude to such a visit (p. 110.6 ff.). It was perhaps at Phaeno that Eusebius heard the blind Egyptian John, who was martyred in May 311: *Mart. Pal.* (S) 13.8.

4. *HE* 8.7.2; 9.4. The section 9.1–5 reads like an insertion into its context.

5. *HE* 9.7.3.

6. Athanasius, *Apol. sec.* 8.3; Epiphanius, *Pan.* 68.8.3 ff.

7. Chapter I.

8. *Mart. Pal.* 6.1 ff., (S) 7.7, 8.3.

9. Published by W. Cureton (London, 1861). The edition of the short recension by E. Schwartz, *GCS* 9.2 (1908), 907–950, prints the Greek fragments of the long recension published by H. Delehaye, *Anal. Boll.* 16 (1897), 113 ff. An

English translation of both recensions together is printed by H. J. Lawlor and J. E. L. Oulton, *Eusebius* 1 (London, 1927), 327–400.

10. *Mart. Pal.* (L) 13.11: the chapter headings (327–328 Lawlor and Oulton) provided explicit dates for most episodes by "years of the persecution in our days." Eusebius' system was elucidated by G. W. Richardson, *CQ* 19 (1925), 96 ff.

11. Chapter III.

12. Below, at n. 79.

13. Chapter V.

14. T. D. Barnes, *GRBS* 21 (1980), 191 ff. That is, the second edition of the *History* comprised *HE* 1.1–8.2.3 + *Mart. Pal.* (S) + Galerius' edict (= *HE* 8.17.3–10) + *HE* 8 app. + *HE* 9, perhaps arranged in eight books rather than nine; cf. R. Laqueur, *Hermes* 46 (1911), 189 ff.

15. Respectively, *HE* 10.4 and 10.5–7.

16. *HE* 8.13.7 describes it as "another work."

17. *HE* 9.17.5, 9.1, 9.12, 9a.12, 10.3, 11.8.

18. *HE* 10.8–9. Rufinus, the Syriac translation, and two of the seven primary Greek manuscripts omit 10.5–7.

19. *HE* 10.9.4, 6. Crispus' name is omitted in the Syriac translation, published by W. Wright and N. McLean (Cambridge, 1898). The manuscript evidence for a multiplicity of editions is conveniently set out by E. Schwartz, *GCS* 9.3 (1909), xlvii ff.

20. *Mart. Pal.* (S), praef. 1.

21. *Mart. Pal.* (L) 1.1 ff. The diurnal dates present a problem: either the *Martyrs* is four times mistaken about the day of the week on which a martyr died (1.2, 4.15, 6.1, 7.1), or the Julian equivalents of the local Caesarean calendar stated in the text are systematically erroneous. The latter hypothesis is adopted by J. P. Rey-Coquais, *Anal. Boll.* 96 (1978), 55 ff., who reconstructs the calendar of Caesarea on the assumption that Eusebius states the day of the week correctly in all four places. Unfortunately, this reconstruction requires the improbable hypothesis of systematic interpolation by a scribe using an Antiochene calendar (ibid., 57). Moreover, only the short recension states the days of the week; the days of the week, therefore, are a secondary element in these four dates, added carelessly by Eusebius as he revised; see H. J. Lawlor and J. E. L. Oulton, *Eusebius* 2 (London, 1928), 327.

22. *Mart. Pal.* (S), praef. 2.

23. *Ecl. Proph.* 1.8.

24. *Mart. Pal.* (L) 1.5bc, (S) 1.3f. Observe, however, that in Caesarea the Christians appear to have retained possession of churches (*Mart. Pal.* [L] 11.28: February 310).

25. Chapter VI.

26. *Mart. Pal.* (L) 1.5.

27. *Mart. Pal.* 3.1 (both recensions). A chapter heading attests the dates as 21 May "in the second year of the persecution in our time," i.e., 21 May 304; B. Violet, *TU* 14.4 (1896), 15. H. J. Lawlor and J. E. L. Oulton, *Eusebius* 2, 327, wrongly emend the date to 21 March—which is not "in the second year."

28. *Mart. Pal.* 3.2 ff. (both recensions).

29. *Mart. Pal.* (L) 3.2. The short recension omits this valuable detail.

30. Lactantius, *Mort. Pers.* 19.1.
31. G. E. M. de Ste Croix, *HTR* 47 (1954), 97, 113.
32. Lactantius, *Mort. Pers.* 23.1 ff.
33. *CTh* 13.10.2^S; cf. *New Empire,* ch. XIV.
34. *Mart. Pal.* 4.1 ff. (both recensions).
35. Ibid., 6.1 ff.
36. Ibid., 7.1 f.
37. Ibid., 7.3 ff.
38. *Mart. Pal.* (L) 8.1, (S) 11.31. Firmilianus presumably perished in the purge of 313 (Chapter V).
39. *Mart. Pal.* 8.1 (both recensions). S. Lieberman, *Annuaire de l'Institut de Philologie et d'Histoire Orientales et Slaves* 7 (Brussels, 1939–1944), 410 ff., argued that the episode occurred at Lydda (Diospolis). But Eusebius states specifically that the whole population of the city where the incident took place was Jewish. Lydda had a Christian bishop in 325, while Diocaesarea long remained wholly Jewish (Epiphanius, *Pan.* 30.10.10 (*GCS* 25.347); Theodoretus, *HE* 4.22.35: a letter of Peter of Alexandria, the successor of Athanasius).
40. *Mart. Pal.* 8.2 ff. (both recensions).
41. Ibid., 9.1.
42. G. M. Richardson, *CQ* 19 (1925), 100.
43. *Mart. Pal.* 11.5 (both recensions).
44. Chapter III.
45. *Mart. Pal.* 9.2 f. (both recensions).
46. Ibid., 9.4 ff. On the weeping pillars, see S. Lieberman, *Annuaire de l'Institut de Philologie et d'Histoire Orientales et Slaves* 7 (1939–44), 397 ff., and *JQR* 36 (1945–46), 246 ff. It cannot be deduced, however, that Rabbi Abbahu of Caesarea died precisely in 309; see I. Sonne, *JQR* 36 (1945–46), 148 ff.; 37 (1946–47), 308 ff.
47. *Mart. Pal.* 10.1 ff. (both recensions).
48. Ibid., 11.1 ff.
49. One Valentinianus, whom Eusebius nowhere names, is attested as *praes(es) provinc(iae) Syr(iae) Pal(aestinae)* before the decease of Galerius (*AE* 1964.198: Scythopolis).
50. *Mart. Pal.* 13.1 ff. (both recensions).
51. *Mart. Pal.* (L), praef. 8 (translated by J. E. L. Oulton in H. J. Lawlor and J. E. L. Oulton, *Eusebius,* 1.331).
52. *Mart. Pal.* (L) 1.1, 3.3, 7.1, 8.4.
53. *Mart. Pal.* 2.1 ff. (both recensions).
54. Ibid., 5.2 f.
55. As by E. Gibbon, *The Decline and Fall of the Roman Empire,* chap. XVI (ed. J. B. Bury [London, 1896], 2.137 f.). The argument is reiterated by G. E. M. de Ste Croix, who argues that the *Martyrs* "gives a complete list of all the Palestinian martyrdoms of the Great persecution" (*HTR* 47 [1954], 100 ff.).
56. For a list of martyrs named by Eusebius in the *Martyrs* and the *History,* E. Keller, *Eusèbe, historien des persécutions* (Geneva and Paris, 1912), 89 ff.
57. *Mart. Pal.* (L) 3.5 ff., 4.1, 6.1 ff., 7.7.
58. *HE* 8.1.1 ff.
59. *Mart. Pal.* (S), praef. 1 f.

60. Ibid., 8.3, 8.13, 13.10.

61. Ibid., 7.7. Similarly 11.31, on the deaths of Maximinus and Firmilianus.

62. *Mart. Pal.* (L) 11.1a–n.

63. *Mart. Pal.* (S) 5.1, 13.6 ff. H. J. Lawlor and J. E. L. Oulton, *Eusebius* 1 (1927), 352, 398, explain the divergences by marking lacunae in the long recension.

64. *Mart. Pal.* (S) 13.11 ff; *HE* 8 app. The concluding sentence of *Mart. Pal.* (S) 13.14 runs: "the recantation also must be placed on record."

65. *Mart. Pal.* 3.5.

66. *HE* 8, app. 2.

67. *HE* 8.13.10 f.; cf. G. W. Richardson, *CQ* 19 (1925), 100. H. J. Lawlor, *Eusebiana* (Oxford, 1912), 179 ff., made this synchronism the basis of an aberrant chronology of the persecution.

68. *Mart. Pal.* (S) 12.

69. *HE* 8, praef.

70. *HE* 8.2.3.

71. *HE* 8.2.4/5 (edicts), 3 (effects of third edict), 4 (299), 5–6.7 (Nicomedia), 6.8–10 (second and third edicts).

72. *HE* 8.7–12. Lactantius, *Div. Inst.* 5.11.10, also alludes to the Phrygian massacre. W. M. Ramsay, *Cities and Bishoprics of Phrygia* 2 (Oxford, 1897), 505 ff., identified the town as Eumeneia. But Eusebius' description of the place as a small town or village hardly fits populous Eumeneia. The governor who perpetrated the atrocity may be the *praeses* of the combined Phrygia and Caria whose name is erased on *IGRR* 4.814 (Hierapolis) and *AE* 1932.56 (Laodicea).

73. *HE* 8.13.1 ff. Anthimus (2) died on 24 April 303, Lucian (2) on 7 January 312, Silvanus of Emesa (3) in 312, Silvanus of Gaza (5) on 4 May 311, Pamphilus (6) on 16 February 310, Peter of Alexandria (7) on 26 November 311, Phileas (7) in 307.

74. *HE* 8.13.9–17.11, esp. 13.9 f. (change in 303); 16.2 ff. (Galerius). The blockade and preparations for naval warfare which Eusebius records in 15.1 ought to belong to either 311 or 313.

75. *HE* 8.13.7.

76. Hagiographical documents which draw on a dossier compiled c. 368 speak of more than 600 martyrs, e.g., *Passio Petri* 7 (published by P. Devos, *Anal. Boll.* 83 [1965], 167, 180; cf. W. Telfer, *Anal. Boll.* 67 [1949], 124). The figure appears to refer to the number of martyrs who died in Alexandria before Peter (i.e., before 26 November 311)—and could be approximately correct.

77. *New Empire,* ch. V: Maximinus.

78. *HE* 9.1 f. Some (but not all) manuscripts quote Maximinus' letter to Sabinus (1.3–6).

79. *HE* 9.6.2; cf. 7.32. 31; 8.13.7. On the exact day (not 24 or 25 November), F. H. Kettler, *RE* 19 (1938), 1283.

80. *HE* 9.6.3; cf. 8.13.2; *PO* 10.12; *Acta Sanctorum,* Nov. 2.2 (1931), 29.

81. *HE* 9.6.1 ff.

82. *Mart. Pal.* 9.2 (both recensions).

83. *HE* 8.14.9, 9.4.2; Lactantius, *Mart. Pers.* 36.4 ff.; cf. R. M. Grant, *Christianity, Judaism and other Greco-Roman Cults* 4 (Leiden, 1975), 157 ff.

An inscription from Laodicea Combusta attests Diogenes, the governor of

Pisidia, torturing a Christian of high social standing under Maximinus (*Monumenta Asiae Minoris Antiqua* 1.170, cf. W. M. Calder, *Gnomon* 10 [1934], 503 f.). Valerius Diogenes was appointed by Galerius, since he honored Galerius' wife, Valeria, as Augusta (*ILS* 8932: Apamea). Since Maximinus disgraced and exiled Valeria in 311 (Lactantius, *Mart. Pers.* 39.1 ff.), there is a chance that *epi Maximinou* in the inscription from Laodicea may be an error for *epi Maximianou,* i.e., "under Galerius."

84. *HE* 9.5, 7.1.

85. *HE* 9.3.

86. *HE* 9.2.

87. Lactantius, *Mort. Pers.* 36.3.

88. *HE* 9.4.3.

89. *CIL* 3.12132 = *Tituli Asiae Minoris* 2.3.785 (Arycanda). There is no good reason to believe that Constantine's name was omitted from the imperial college (as argued by R. M. Grant, *Christianity,* 153).

90. *HE* 9.7.3–14. Eusebius states that the petitions of cities against the Christians and the answering rescripts were published through every province (9.7.1, 15).

91. *HE* 9.7.7.

92. O. Eissfeldt, *RE* 7A (1948), 2282 f.; M. Chéhab, *Mélanges de l'Université Saint Joseph* 38 (1962), 16 f.

93. *HE* 9.8.2, 4. Constantine later referred to Christians who found refuge among the barbarians (*VC* 2.53); relevance to Maximinus was detected by N. H. Baynes, *Constantine the Great and the Christian Church* (Oxford, 1931), 91, n. 74.

Eusebius calls Maximinus' opponents in the war of 312 Armenians "who had long been friends and allies of the Romans." However, since Eusebius also states that they were Christians, whereas the previously pagan kingdom of Armenia officially adopted Christianity only in 314 (Chapter V), it seems clear that he refers to the *regiones Transtigritanae* of the treaty of 299 (Chapter II, n. 39); see L. Duchesne, *Mélanges Nicole* (Geneva, 1905), 107 ff.

94. That appears to be approximately three times the normal price c. 312; see D. Sperber, *Archiv orientální* 34 (1966), 59.

95. *HE* 9.8.1 ff.

96. *New Empire,* ch. V: Maximinus.

97. *HE* 9.9.1.

98. *HE* 9.9.12; cf. Chapter IV, at nn. 51–53.

99. *HE* 9.9a.1–10.

100. H. Castritius, *Studien zu Maximinus Daia (Frankfurter althistorische Studien* 2, 1969), 63 ff.; T.Christensen, *C. Galerius Valerius Maximinus: Studier over Politik og Religion i Romerriget 304–13* (Copenhagen, 1974), 66 ff., 229 ff.

101. *HE* 9.9a.10.

102. *HE* 9.9a.11.

103. *HE* 9.10.1 ff.

104. *HE* 9.10.7–11.

105. *HE* 9.10.13 ff. For a fuller account of these events, Chapter V.

106. *Mart. Pal.* (L), praef. 1 ff.

107. *HE* 8.1.7 ff.

108. *HE* 10.4: Constantine and Licinius still live in perfect amity (16, 60).
109. *HE* 10.4.3 ff., 36.
110. *HE* 10.4.25 ff., 37 ff. The physical description, however, lacks clarity; see R. Krautheimer, *DOP* 21 (1967), 132. On some of the terms which Eusebius uses, G. Downey, *Mélanges de l'Université Saint Joseph* 38 (1962), 191 ff.
111. *HE* 10.4.14.
112. *HE* 10.4.57 ff.; cf. 33 ff.
113. *HE* 10.4.16; cf. 9.9.10 f.
114. *HE* 8.14.

X. EUSEBIUS AS APOLOGIST

1. Chapters VI–VIII.
2. Edited by C. Kayser, *Philostrati Opera* 1 (Leipzig, 1870), 369–413. Kayser's text was reprinted, accompanied by an English translation, by F. C. Conybeare, *Philostratus: "The Life of Apollonius of Tyana"* 2 (Loeb Classical Library, 1912), 482–605.
3. T. D. Barnes, *HSCP* 80 (1976), 240 ff.
4. *CIL* 3.133 = 6661; *AE* 1932.79 (Palmyra); Lactantius, *Mort. Pers.* 16.4; *P. Oxy.* 3120; *P. Cairo Isid.* 69: *P. Berol. Inv.* 21654, published by H. Maehler, *Collectanea Papyrologica. Texts Published in Honor of H. C. Youtie* 2 (Bonn, 20, 1976), 527 ff.
5. *C. Hier.* 4, p. 373.10–11 Kayser; 20, p. 386.30–31.
6. Lactantius, *Div. Inst.* 5.2.12 ff.
7. *C. Hier.* 1, p. 369.1; 5, p. 373.19.
8. *C. Hier.* 1.
9. *C. Hier.* 2. Eusebius naturally accepts Hierocles' statement that Apollonius was a man; for evidence that he was regarded as a god or hero, see C. P. Jones, *JHS* 100 (1980), 190 ff.
10. *C. Hier.* 3. The existence of Damis was disproved by E. Meyer, *Hermes* 52 (1917), 371 ff. A lengthy attempt at rehabilitation was undertaken by F. Grosso, *Acme* 7 (1954), 333 ff. In fact, he may well be the invention of Philostratus himself; see E. L. Bowie, *ANRW* II 16.2 (1978), 1652 ff.
11. Christians have often been readier to believe in miracles in the remote and inaccessible past than in the verifiable present—as Gibbon very pertinently observed (*Decline and Fall*, ch. XVI).
12. *C. Hier.* 4–6. Many later Christians adopted a far more charitable view of Apollonius' magical powers; see W. Speyer, *JAC* 17 (1974), 53 ff.
13. *C. Hier.* 7–12.
14. *C. Hier.* 13–44.
15. *C. Hier.* 17, p. 384.20 ff.
16. *C. Hier.* 39, 43.
17. *C. Hier.* 45–48. Eusebius quotes the opening sentence of Epictetus' *Encheiridion* (p. 411.31–32) and paraphrases what follows, then quotes Plato, *Republic* 617e (p. 412.13).
18. The *Prophetic Extracts* were edited by T. Gaisford (Oxford, 1842), whence *PG* 22.1021–1262. For improvements to the text of various passages, H. Nolte, *Theologische Quartalschrift* 43 (1861), 95 ff.; W. Selwyn, *Journal of*

Philology 4 (1872), 275 ff.; on the lacuna in *Ecl. Proph.* 2, G. Mercati, *Mémorial L. Petit* (Bucarest, 1948), 1 ff.

19. *PG* 24.529–605, 653, 657–690; cf. D. S. Wallace-Hadrill, *HTR* 67 (1974), 55 ff.

20. *HE* 7.32.20.

21. H. Oppermann, *Gnomon* 5 (1929), 545, 557 f.; J. Dillon, *Iamblichi Chalcidensis in Platonis Dialogos Commentariorum Fragmenta* (Leiden, 1973), 3 ff.

22. [Julian], *Epp.* 184; Libanius, *Orat.* 52.31 (Apamea); Malalas 312 (Antioch): cf. T. D. Barnes, *GRBS* 19 (1978), 105. Eusebius probably visited Antioch before 303 (*HE* 7.32.4).

23. [Julian], *Epp.* 184; cf. Chapter II, at n. 67; Chapter V, at nn. 52–58.

24. *Ecl. Proph.* 1.8.

25. Ibid., 2.2; 4.24, 27.

26. Ibid., 1.20.

27. Ibid., 1.13, discussing Numbers 24:7–9.

28. Ibid., 1.8; 4.3, 8, 31.

29. *PG* 24.596 ff.

30. *PG* 22.1272 (from chapter 4).

31. *Ecl. Proph.* 2.13; 4.4, 7, 20, 26; *PG* 24.580 f.

32. E.g., *Ecl. Proph.* 2.9, 13; 3, praef., 24, 46; 4.4, 5, 7, 13. The sin of the Jewish people against the Savior is "indelible" (3.35).

33. Ibid., 3.19, 4.22; cf. 1.2, 3, 21 (the same charges without the names).

34. Jewish sources disclose that although in 304 Diocletian exempted Jews from the order to sacrifice, Samaritans were required to sacrifice—and did so; cf. S. Lieberman, *Annuaire de l'Institut de Philologie et d'Histoire Orientales et Slaves* 7 (Brussels, 1939–44), 402 ff.

35. *HE* 7.12; *Mart. Pal.* 10.3; cf. A. Harnack, *Marcion: Das Evangelium vom Fremden Gott*[2] (*TU* 45, 1924), 341* ff.; Opitz, *Urkunde* 14.36; cf. F. Loofs, *Paulus von Samosata* (TU 44.5, 1924), 180 ff.

36. *Ecl. Proph.* 1.2.

37. He confines himself to the twenty-two books accepted as inspired by "the circumcised" (Ibid., 3.6).

38. Ibid., 4.4, 5; cf. 2.1, 7; 4.7. Also "the most painstaking interpreter of the holy Scriptures" (3.6).

39. Ibid., 2.5; 1.13; 2.13; 3.11, 35; 4.20.

40. Ibid., 4.4, 27.

41. Ibid., 3.10, quoting "the first book of Didymus' *Physica.*" For Jewish polemic on the parentage of Jesus, see H. L. Strack, *Jesus, die Häretiker und die Christen nach den ältesten jüdischen Angaben* (Leipzig, 1910), 10* ff.; W. Horbury, *JTS*, n.s. 23 (1972), 457. M. Smith, *Jesus the Magician* (San Francisco, 1978), 47, has recently asserted that "it is possible, though not likely" that the tombstone of Ti. Julius Abdes Pantera, a soldier from Sidon (*ILS* 2751: near Bingen) is "our only genuine relic of the Holy Family."

42. Cf. *Ecl. Proph.* 3.23.

43. Like Origen, Eusebius constantly distinguishes between the literal meaning of a text and its true, inner, more spiritual meaning, which can be discovered through allegorical interpretation (e.g., *Ecl. Proph.* 1.6, 13; 4.24).

44. Ibid., 1.3–12; *PG* 24.540 f., 569 ff.

45. *Ecl. Proph.* 1.15.

46. E.g., Ibid., 3.26 (Jeremiah 17:1 named Judas as the betrayer of Jesus); 2.2 (Jewish "earthbound assumptions" about the nature of Christ's kingdom).

47. Ibid., 1.15.

48. *PG* 24.569.

49. *Ecl. Proph.* 1.8; 3.36.

50. Ibid., 1.18; 2.10; 4.24, 28, 30.

51. Ibid., 4.8; cf. 16.

52. Ibid., 4.27, 3.37.

53. Ibid., 1.8, 19.

54. Ibid., 2.15, 27, 28; 3.31, 42; 4. 14.

55. Ibid., 4.3, 31.

56. *PG* 24.584 ff.

57. *PG* 24.561 ff.

58. *PG* 24.548 ff.

59. *PG* 24.541 ff.

60. Chapter XI.

61. Chapter VI. The *Prophetic Extracts* are unfortunately ignored in some modern expositions of Eusebius' theology.

62. *Ecl. Proph.* 1.7, 2.5, 1.5, 1.11.

63. The Father is a "greater Lord," the Word "in second place after the Father" (Ibid., 1.12).

64. Ibid., 1.2–10, 3.30, 3.8.

65. Ibid., 3.30; 1.5, 25; 2.17; 4.23.

66. Ibid., 3.8, 2.18, 3.1.

67. Ibid., 3.1.

68. Ibid., 4.25.

69. H. Berkhof, *Die Theologie des Eusebius* (Amsterdam, 1939), 65 ff. The imperfect antithesis "nicht Arianer, sondern Origenist" was developed by M. Weis, *Die Stellung des Eusebius von Caesarea im arianischen Streit* (diss., Freiburg-im-Breisgau, 1919), 62 ff.

70. On the date of the work, T. D. Barnes, *JTS*, n.s. 24 (1973), 433 ff.; J. M. Rist, *Basil of Caesarea: Christian, Humanist, Ascetic,* ed. P. J. Fedwick (Toronto, 1981), 142 ff. Porphyry composed it as an old man (Libanius, *Orat.* 18.178).

71. Jerome, *De Viris Illustribus* 81, 83, and *Epp.* 70.3; Philostorgius, *HE* 8.14; Socrates, *HE* 3.23.35.

72. Jerome, *Commentary on Daniel,* praef. (*CCL* 75A.771); *Commentary on Matthew* 24:16 (*CCL* 77.226 f.).

73. Porphyry, *Vita Plotini* 4.1 ff.; cf. T. D. Barnes, *GRBS* 17 (1976), 68 f.

74. Porphyry, *Vita Plotini* 17.7 ff.: Porphyry was "called Malchus in his native language." On the role of Syriac in Roman Syria and Phoenicia, see F. Millar, *JRS* 61 (1971), 1 ff.

75. Eusebius, *HE* 6.19.5; Socrates, *HE* 3.23.37.

76. Quoted by Eusebius, *PE* 10.3.1 ff. For Longinus' political career, Libanius, *Epp.* 1078; *HA, Aurel.* 30.3; Zosimus 1.56.2 f. He was a Syrian by birth, the nephew of the Severan rhetor, Fronto of Emesa (*Suda* Φ 735).

77. Porphyry, *Vita Plotini* 4.1 ff., 5.1 f., 2.23 ff.

78. T. D. Barnes, *JTS*, n.s. 24 (1973), 432 f., 442.

79. J. Bidez, *Vie de Porphyre le philosophe néo-platonicien* (Ghent, 1913), 51 ff.

80. Porphyry, *Vita Plotini* 23.12 ff.

81. Eunapius, *Vit. Phil.* 4.2.6, p. 457.

82. J. Bidez, *Vie de Porphyre*, 15 ff.

83. For the fragments, G. Wolff, *Porphyrii de Philosophia ex Oraculis Haurienda Librorum Reliquiae* (Berlin, 1856), 109 ff. Other known oracles (including some attested epigraphically) can also be identified as having been included in Porphyry's collection; see L. Robert, *CRAI* 1968, 568 ff.; 1971, 597 ff.

84. *PE* 4.7.2; cf. 9.10.3 = 14.10.6.

85. *DE* 3.7.1 f.; Augustine, *De Consensu Evangelistarum* 1.15.23 (*CSEL* 43.22); *De Civitate Dei* 19.23.

86. *HE* 6.19.9; *PE* 10.9.12; *Chronicle* 8.1 ff. Helm; Jerome, *Commentary on Daniel*, praef. (*CCL* 75A. 771); *Commentary on Matthew* 24:16 (*CCL* 77.226).

87. The standard collection of ninety-seven fragments, by A. Harnack, *Abh. Berlin*, Phil.-hist. Kl. 1916, Nr. 1, contains more than fifty culled from Macarius Magnes which it is not legitimate to regard as direct quotations; see T. D. Barnes, *JTS*, n.s. 24 (1973), 428 ff.

88. *PE* 1.2.4; *DE* 1.1.12; cf. R. T. Wallis, *Neoplatonism* (London, 1972), 100 ff.

89. Didymus of Alexandria, *Commentary on Job* 10:13, edited by U. and D. Hagedorn and L. Koenen, *Papyrologische Texte und Abhandlungen* 3 (Bonn, 1968), 150; cf. D. Hagedorn and R. Merkelbach, *Vig. Chr.* 20 (1966), 86 ff.

90. *DE* 5, praef. 3 ff. *Against the Christians* probably presented Moses in a less favorable light than *On Philosophy from Oracles;* see J. G. Gager, *Moses in Greco-Roman Paganism* (Princeton, 1972), 69 ff.

91. Augustine, *Epp.* 102.8.

92. Frag. 84 Harnack, from a manuscript which preserves extracts from Methodius' *Against Porphyry* (printed by N. Bonwetsch in the apparatus criticus to *GCS* 27.503 line 2, 505 line 10).

93. Jerome, *Chronicle* 8.5 ff. Helm.

94. *PE* 1.9.21 = 10.9.12.

95. Frag. 43 Harnack; *FGrH* 260 F 35–58 (from scattered passages of Jerome's commentary on Daniel); cf. P. M. Casey, *JTS*, n.s. 27 (1976), 15 ff.

96. The anonymous allusions in *DE* 6.18.11 ff., 10.1.3 ff. imply that Porphyry rebutted the interpretation of passages in Zechariah and the Psalms as prophecies of the Incarnation.

97. Didymus of Alexandria, *Commentary on Ecclesiastes* 9:10, published by G. Binder, *ZPE* 3 (1968), 92.

98. Augustine, *Epp.* 102.28 = frag. 85.

99. Didymus of Alexandria, *Commentary on Psalm* 43:2, edited by M. Gronewald, *Papyrologische Texte und Abhandlungen* 12 (Bonn, 1970), 104.

100. Jerome, *Tractatus de Psalmo lxxxi* 225 ff. (*CCL* 78.89) = frag. 4; *De Principio Marci* 30 ff. (*CCL* 78.452) = frag. 9. Observe that Hierocles omitted Apuleius, of whom, as an easterner, he knew nothing (Lactantius, *Div. Inst.* 5.3.9). Porphyry had visited Africa (*De Abstinentia* 3.4).

101. *DE* 3.2.78–6.13 (stating and refuting the charge).

102. Jerome, *Epp.* 57.9 = frag. 2; Jerome, *Commentary on Matthew* 9:9, 21:21, 27:45 (*CCL* 77.55, 191, 273) = frags. 6, 3, 14. Porphyry complained that the evangelists knew their Old Testament so badly that they often attributed quotations or allusions to the wrong book (Jerome, *Tractatus de Psalmo lxxvii* 73 ff.; *De Principio Marci* 30 ff. (*CCL* 78.66, 452) = frags. 10, 9).

103. Jerome, *Commentary on Isaiah* 3:12 (*CCL* 73.52) = frag. 97; Augustine, *Epp.* 102.16 = frag. 79.

104. *HE* 6.19.5–8 = frag. 39 (part).

105. Chapter VI. Modern scholars tend to overestimate Porphyry's quality as a historian (e.g., W. den Boer, *CP* 69 [1974], 198 ff.).

106. *PE* 5.1.10 = frag. 80.

107. *PE* 4.1.3; cf. Chapter II. J. Bidez, *Vie de Porphyre,* 67 ff., assuming a date c. 270, too charitably interprets the work as an apolitical exercise of an unworldly philosopher profoundly preoccupied with God and his own soul.

108. *PE* 1.2.1 ff. U. von Wilamowitz-Moellendorf, *ZNW* 1 (1900), 101 ff., identified the passage as a quotation, and A. Harnack prints it as frag. 1. It is, rather, a summation of Porphyry's central thesis.

109. Chapter IX.

110. The composition of the *Preparation* and the *Proof* occupied most of the years from 313 to 324, with the *Preparation* presumably completed by about 318 and the *Proof* begun immediately thereafter. *PE* 4.2.11 ff. alludes to the purge of 313; *DE* 2.3.155, 3.5.78 f., 7.1.132, 8.1.61 to the renewal of persecution.

111. *PE* 1.1.1; *DE* 1, praef. 1.

112. *PE* 1.1.12; *DE* 2.3.178, 3.2.78; cf. J. Sirinelli, *Eusèbe de Césarée: La Préparation Évangelique* 1 (*SC* 206, 1974), 36 ff.

113. *DE* 2.3.43. Jews of course continued to proselytize despite legal prohibitions; see M. Avi-Yonah, *The Jews of Palestine* (New York, 1976), 81 ff.

114. *DE* 9.3.8, 10.8.55.

115. L. I. Levine, *Caesarea under Roman Rule* (Leiden, 1975), 80 ff.

116. *PE* 1.1–2.

117. *PE* 1.2.5.

118. *PE* 1.3.6–6.7. The conventional modern division into chapters and sections sometimes disregards Eusebius' careful articulation of the text by means of chapter headings; see K. Mras, *GCS* 43.1 (1954), viii f.

119. *PE* 1.6.8–9 introduces the Greek cosmogonies documented in 1.7.1 ff.

120. *PE* 1.9.6 ff.

121. *PE* 1.9.20 ff.

122. *PE* 15.1.1 ff.

123. *PE* 1.9.1–2.1.51.

124. For the sharpest formulations of the thesis, *PE* 1.9.19, 2.1.52. Documentation occupies almost the whole of Books Two and Three.

125. *PE* 4.1.1 f. On this "tripartite theology," see esp. J. Pépin, *Mythe et Allégorie: Les origines grecques et les contestations judéo-chrétiennes*[2] (Paris, 1976), 276 ff. He rightly emphasizes that, despite its familiar association with Varro, the threefold division must derive from earlier Greek sources. H. Lewy, *Chaldaean Oracles and Theurgy* (Cairo, 1956), 509 ff., identifies Porhyry's *Philosophy from Oracles* as the source of the "Hellenic theology" summarized in *PE* 4.5.1–2.

126. *PE* 15.1.3.

127. *PE* 5.16.3 ff., quoting Plutarch, *De Defectu Oraculorum* 411 d–f, 418e–420a. Eusebius gleefully observes that Plutarch dated the death of Pan to the reign of Tiberius—and precisely to the time of Jesus' ministry on earth (5.17.13).

128. *PE* 4.16.1 ff., with quotation of Porphyry, *De Abstinentia* 2.54–56, 27, 43; Philo of Byblos (a passage already quoted in 1.10.44); Clement of Alexandria, *Prot.* 3.42.1–43.1; Dionysius of Halicarnassus, *Ant. Rom.* 1.23.1–24.4, 38.2–3; Diodorus Siculus, *Bibl.* 20.14.4–6.

129. *PE* 4.2.1 ff., 3.1 ff. (Diogenianus, frag. 4); 5.18.1 ff. (Oenomaus).

130. Note the statement that Origen's excellence as an exegete is known "even to outsiders" (*PE* 6.10.50), and the conclusion that pagan gods who issue oracles are "cheats, impostors, and deceivers" (11.82)—precisely the words Porphyry used of Jesus and the apostles.

131. *PE* 7.9–22.

132. *PE* 7.2.8.

133. Book Ten quotes the following passages from earlier writers: Clement of Alexandria, *Strom.* 6.4.3–5.2, 16.1, 25.1–2, 27.5–29.2 (*PE* 10.2); Porphyry, *Recitatio Philologica*, frags. 1–4 (not known from elsewhere) (*PE* 10.3); [Plato], *Epinomis* 986e–987a, 987de (*PE* 10.4.21 f.); Democritus, from Clement, *Strom.* 1.69.5 (*PE* 10.4.23); Clement, *Strom.* 1.75.2–3, 74.2–6 (not in perfect order), 75.4–77.2 (*PE* 10.6); Josephus, *Contra Apionem* 1.6–26 (*PE* 10.7); Diodorus Siculus, *Bibl.* 1.96.1–6, 97.4–98.5 (*PE* 10.8); Porphyry, *Against the Christians*, frag. 41 (*PE* 10.9.12: already quoted in 1.9.21); Africanus, frag. 22 Routh (*PE* 10.10); Tatian, *Oratio ad Graecos* 31; 36–42 (*PE* 10.11); Clement, *Strom.* 1.101.2–107.6 (*PE* 10.12); Josephus, *Contra Apionem* 1.73–75, 82–90, 103–104 (*PE* 10.13). Chapters 9 and 14 also utilize the first edition of the *Chronicle* (cf. Chapter VII).

134. *PE* 11.28.17–19.

135. *PE* 15.1.8.

136. *DE* 3, praef. 1.

137. *DE* 4.1.1. J. E. Bruns, *Vig. Chr.* 31 (1977), 117 ff., argues that Book Three (which is clearly drawn from the lost *Against Porphyry*) makes extensive quotations from Ammonius, *On the Agreement between Jesus and Moses* (*HE* 6.19.10).

138. *DE* 15, frags. 1, 3, 5, 6; cf. 6.2.3, 9.17.8.

139. T. D. Barnes, *JTS*, n.s. 27 (1976), 418 ff.

140. Thus only the chapter heading identifies *PE* 4.3.1–13 as a quotation of Diogenianus (frag. 4: not known from elsewhere).

141. For cases where they differ, K. Mras, *GCS* 43.1 (1954), viii f.

142. Ibid., lviii.

143. K. Mras, *Anzeiger Wien*, Phil.-hist. Kl. 1956, 212 ff.; cf. Mras' register of passages quoted (*GCS* 43.2 [1956], 439–466). On the textual value of Eusebius' quotations from Plato's *Laws*, E. des Places, *Mélanges J. Saunier* (Lyon, 1944), 27 ff.; *Aegyptus* 32 (1952), 233 ff.

144. *FGrH* 790; cf. O. Eissfeldt, *Sb. Berlin*, Klasse für Sprachen, Lit. und Kunst 1952, Nr. 1 and *Kleine Schriften* 3 (Tübingen, 1966), 398 ff., 501 ff.; M. L. West, *Hesiod: Theogony* (Oxford, 1967), 24 ff.; L. Troiani, *L'opera storio-*

grafica di Filone da Byblos (Pisa, 1974); J. Barr, *Bulletin of the John Rylands Library* 57 (1974/5), 17 ff.

145. See the classic study of J. Freudenthal, *Hellenistische Studien* (Prog., Breslau, 1874–1875). He noted that Eusebius quotes far more accurately than Clement of Alexandria (1.7 ff.)—who sometimes improves the Greek of quotations which Eusebius reproduces unchanged; see K. Mras, *Rh. Mus.*, N.F. 92 (1944), 218 ff.

146. Viz., the *Hypothetica* (8.6 f.) and *Defense of the Jews* (8.11)—which appear to be different titles of the work called *On the Jews* in *HE* 2.18.6; cf. J. Bernays, *Gesammelte Abhandlungen* 1 (Berlin, 1885), 262 ff.

147. See the editions by E. des Places (Budé, 1973) and J. Baudry (Budé, 1931).

148. E.g., the quotations of the *Unmasking of Impostors* by the Cynic Oenomaus of Gadara (*PE* 5.18 ff., 6.6 f.), most of Africanus frag. 22 Routh (10.10), a fragment of Origen's *Commentary on Genesis* (7.20), and the fragments of Porphyry, *Adversus Boethum de Anima* (11.28, 14.10.3, 15.11, 15.16).

149. Viz., *Ennead* 4.7.8^5.1–50. Moreover, the majority of the manuscripts of Plotinus also omit *Enn.* 4.7.8.28–8^4.28, and it seems clear that the three manuscripts which contain all or most of this section derive it from a lost manuscript of Eusebius, *PE* 15.22.49 ff. For discussion of the implications of these facts, see P. Henry, *Recherches sur la Préparation Évangelique d'Eusèbe et l'édition perdue des oeuvres de Plotin publiée par Eustochius* (Paris, 1935), and *Études plotiniennes* 1: *Les États du texte de Plotin* (Brussels, 1938), 77 ff.; H. R. Schwyzer, *Gnomon* 32 (1960), 32 ff.

Porphyry divided his edition, often artificially, into six books, each comprising nine treatises (hence the title). Eusebius does not quote *Ennead* 4.7, which bears the title "On the Immortality of the Soul," from Porphyry's collected edition (published in or after 301), since he states that *Ennead* 4.7.1.1–8^4.28 is taken from "Plotinus' First Treatise on the Soul" (*PE* 15.22), 4.7.8^5.1–50 from "Plotinus' Second Treatise on the Soul" (*PE* 15.10); cf. P. Henry, *Recherches* (1935), 111 ff., and *États du texte* (1938), 18.

150. H. D. Saffrey, *Forma Futuri: Studi in onore del Cardinale M. Pellegrino* (Turin, 1975), 145 ff.

151. *PE* 3.4, 5.7.4 ff., 5.10, 14.10.1 f.; cf. H. D. Saffrey, *Philomathes: Studies and Essays in the Humanities in memory of P. Merlan* (The Hague, 1971), 227 ff.; B. D. Larsen, *Iamblique de Chalcis, exégète et philosophe* (Aarhus, 1972), 37.

152. Viz., Plotinus, *Enn.* 4.7 (cited as two separate treatises in *PE* 15.10, 22) and *Enn.* 5.1 (*PE* 11.17); cf. J. M. Rist, *Basil of Caesarea* (Toronto, 1981), 159ff. The edition of Plotinus by Eustochius, attested only by a scholium on *Ennead* 4.4.29.55 (O.C.T. 2.55) was not necessarily a complete edition.

153. Chapter V, and above, at nn. 21–23.

154. K. Mras, *Rh. Mus.*, N.F. 92 (1944), 226 ff.; *GCS* 43.1 (1954), ix. The most detailed study of Eusebius' language and style remains the brief Munich dissertation of E. Fritze, *Beiträge zur sprachlich-stilistischen Würdigung des Eusebios* (Borna-Leipzig, 1910).

155. *PE* 6.6. For an analysis of this chapter, A. Amand, *Fatalisme et liberté dans l'antiquité grecque* (Louvain, 1945), 368 ff.

156. P. Wendland, *Philos Schrift über die Vorsehung: Ein Beitrag zur Ges-*

chichte der nacharistotelischen Philosophie (Berlin, 1892), 40, argued direct use of Philo: the *De Providentia*, now fully extant only in an Armenian translation (M. Hadas-Lebel, *Les Oeuvres de Philon d'Alexandrie* 35 [Paris, 1973]), was certainly in the library of Caesarea (*HE* 2.18.6) and the *Proof of the Gospel* quotes it later at length (*DE* 7.21; 8.14). For Origen's views, which must also have influenced Eusebius, see esp. *Princ.* 3.1.

157. *PE* 6.6.46 ff., 20; cf. *C. Hier.* 45. The image of man as the plaything of God, controlled by his emotions as a marionette by its strings, goes back to Plato, *Laws* 644e, 803c. But Eusebius' words (20: *diken apsukhon . . . neurospastoumenous*) reproduce Clement, *Strom.* 2.11.1.

158. *PE* 6.6.45; cf. G. L. Chesnut, *The First Christian Histories* (*Théologie Historique* 46, 1977), 61 ff.

159. *DE* 3.2.78–5.109. For a recent restatement of Porphyry's thesis in the light of modern scholarship, M. Smith, *Jesus the Magician* (San Francisco, 1978), esp. 140 ff.

160. Chapter VIII, and above, at nn. 43–47.

161. J. Sirinelli, *Les vues historiques d'Eusèbe de Césarée durant la période prénicéenne* (Dakar, 1961), 139 ff.; cf. M. Harl, *REG* 75 (1962), 522 ff.

162. *PE* 2.5. f., 7.2 f.

163. *PE* 14.3.1 ff.; *DE* 1.2.1 ff., 1.6.1 ff., 1.9.1 ff. Eusebius had written a treatise on the polygamy and large progeny of the patriarchs (*PE* 7.8.29; *DE* 1.9.20); it is lost, except for a brief quotation in Basil, *De Spiritu Sancto* 29.72 (*PG* 32.204).

164. *PE* 7.8 ff., 8.1 ff.

165. *DE* 1.6.32 ff.

166. *DE* 7.1.79 ff., 8.3.10 ff.

167. Chapters VI, VIII.

168. Chapter VI.

169. F. Ricken, *Theologie und Philosophie* 42 (1967), 341 ff., 53 (1978), 323 ff.

170. *DE* 5.4.11, 4.3.8 f., 4.1.2 ff., 4.5.15 ff., 5.1.24, 4.7.4.

171. *DE* 5.1.28; *PE* 7.12.2, 7.15.1 ff.

172. *PE* 7.12.11 ff.; *DE* 4.10.16, 4.3.1 ff., 5.1.4 ff. Eusebius quotes with approbation a lost work of Philo which speaks of "the second God, who is the Word of [the Father of the universe]" (*PE* 7.13.1).

173. *PE* 7.12.2. The proof texts naturally include Proverbs 8:22, discussed at length in *DE* 5.1.4 ff.

174. Chapter V.

175. Published by S. Lee (London, 1842), and translated by him into English (Cambridge, 1843). For the Greek fragments and a German translation of the Syriac, H. Gressmann, *Eusebius' Werke* 3.2 (*GCS* 11.2, 1904).

176. The *Theophany* refers to the *Proof of the Gospel* (4.37; 5.1); a date very shortly after 324 is indicated by Eusebius' remark that sacred prostitution still survives at Heliopolis in Phoenicia (*Theophany* 2.14, p. 85*.10 ff. Gressmann).

177. H. Gressmann, *Studien zu Eusebs Theophanie* (*TU* 23.3, 1903), 38 ff.; *GCS* 11.2 (1904), xiv ff. The reverse order and a date after 337 are argued by D. S. Wallace-Hadrill, *Eusebius of Caesarea* (London, 1960), 52 ff.

178. For the overall argument of the *Theophany,* cf. H. Gressmann, *TU* 23.3 (1903), 1 ff.

179. *Theophany* 5.1 ff., however, again answer the charge that Jesus was a mere magician or impostor.

180. *Theophany* 1.21 ff. = *Triac.* 12.1 ff.; cf. F. Ricken, *Theologie und Philosophie* 42 (1967), 346 ff.

181. *Theophany* 1.4 f. = *Triac.* 11.11 ff.; cf. F. Ricken, *Theologie und Philosophie* 53 (1978), 326 ff.

182. *Triac.* 11.1 ff., 18.3. The crucial opening sentence (11.1: "Come, Constantine, greatest conqueror, let us put before you revelations about solemn mysteries in this royal treatise about the universal sovereign of all, not initiating you, who have been made wise by God, ... to whom, even before our speeches, God has revealed and disclosed the secrets of the holy rites ... by frequent divine visions") is mistranslated by H. A. Drake, *In Praise of Constantine* (Berkeley, 1976), 103.

XI. BEFORE CONSTANTINE

1. As assumed by A. H. M. Jones, *The Later Roman Empire* 1 (Oxford, 1964), 91, 96. He asserts that in 312 "Christians were still a tiny minority, especially in the West, and they were on the whole people of no importance" (81).

2. Chapters VII, at n. 37; IX, at n. 72.

3. A. Harnack, *Die Mission und Ausbreitung des Christentums in den ersten drei Jahrhunderten*[4] (Leipzig, 1924), 946 ff.; L. Hertling, *ZKT* 58 (1934), 243 ff.; K. Baus, *From the Apostolic Community to Constantine* (*Handbook of Church History,* ed. H. Jedin and J. Dolan, 1 [Freiburg and London, 1965]), 367 ff. For Egypt, see now E. A. Judge and S. R. Pickering, *JAC* 20 (1977), 47 ff. In Palestine, Jews and Samaritans outnumbered Christians until the fifth century; see M. Avi-Yonah, *The Jews of Palestine* (New York, 1976), 138 f., 220.

4. For the striking case of Paul of Samosata, Chapter VIII. The small town of Oxyrhynchus had two churches by 295 (*P. Oxy.* 43, verso). In a rescript to a Jew, dated 293, Diocletian totally denied the validity of decisions of private law courts (*CJ* 3.13.3).

5. Chapters III, V.

6. Chapter VIII.

7. Chapter IX.

8. *HE* 7.30.22. The addition is betrayed by the phrase "a little earlier than this" (30.23), which introduces a notice of bishops of Rome, interrupted by the addition of a paragraph on Manichaeism (31). Dionysius (30.23) was bishop of Rome from 260 to 268, Felix (30.23; 32.1) from 269 to 273 or 274, Eutychianus from 274 or 275 to 282 or 283; cf. C. H. Turner, *JTS* 17 (1916), 349 f.

9. *HE* 7.32.1. Gaius was bishop from 282 or 283 to 295 or 296 (C. H. Turner, *JTS* 17 [1916], 350 f.); on Marcellinus and his successors, Chapter III.

10. *HE* 7.32.4.

11. *HE* 7.32.29.

12. *HE* 7.32.30 f. It should not be necessary to reiterate that the Latin letter of Theonas *Ad Lucianum Cubiculariorum Praepositum* is a seventeenth century forgery (A. Harnack, *TU* 24.3 [1903], 93 ff.).

13. *HE* 7.32.24.

14. *HE* 7.31. In Jerome's *Chronicle* the notice of Manichaeism follows the synchronism with which the first edition probably ended (223[k, l]; cf. Chapter VII, at nn. 44–49).

15. Epiphanius, *Pan.* 66.1.1 f.

16. *HE* 7.32.2 ff. The unnamed emperor is presumably Diocletian; see A. H. M. Jones, *The Later Roman Empire* 1 (1964), 66, 834 ff. (on state factories).

17. *HE* 8.1.4; 6.1 ff. For eunuchs in the imperial palace executed in early 303, B. de Gaiffier, *Anal. Boll.* 75 (1957), 21 ff.

18. *HE* 7.32.25.

19. *HE* 7.32.26 f., 30.

20. *HE* 7.32.26 ff.

21. *HE* 8.2.3; cf. Chapter IX.

22. *HE* 7.32.23 f.

23. Chapter XII.

24. Jerome, *De Viris Illustribus* 83; cf. T. D. Barnes, *JTS*, n.s. 30 (1979), 54.

25. G. N. Bonwetsch, *Die Theologie des Methodius von Olympus* (*Abh. Göttingen,* Phil.-hist. Kl. N.F. 7.1, 1903); J. Farges, *Les idées morales et religieuses de Méthode d'Olympe* (Paris, 1929); M. Margheritis, *Studi dedicati alla memoria di P. Ubaldi* (Milan, 1937), 401 ff.; H. J. Musurillo, *St. Methodius, The Symposium: A Treatise on Chastity* (*ACW* 27, 1958), 5 ff.

26. G. N. Bonwetsch, *GCS* 27 (1917), 425 ff.

27. Jerome, *De Viris Illustribus* 83; *Acta Sanctorum,* Propylaeum ad Nov. (1902), 757 f. (day); cf. T. D. Barnes, *JTS,* n.s. 30 (1979), 54. Maximinus visited Stratonicea in Caria in 312 (*Sylloge*[3] 900).

28. H. J. Musurillo, *St. Methodius* (*ACW* 27, 1958), 180, doubts direct indebtedness.

29. A. Vaillant, *PO* 22 (1930), 649 ff.; H. Chadwick, *HTR* 41 (1948), 82 ff. Vaillant, however, misdates and misinterprets the dialogue commonly known as Adamantius' *On Right Faith in God*—which is here assumed identical with Maximus' lost work *On Matter* (as argued in *JTS*, n.s. 30 [1979], 47 ff.).

30. Jerome, *Contra Rufinum* 1.11 (*PL* 23.423).

31. *HE* 8.10.

32. Still less about Victorinus of Poetovio, who wrote biblical commentaries in Latin and died as a martyr in 303 or shortly thereafter (Jerome, *De Viris Illustribus* 74).

33. Jerome, in the preface to his translation of *Chronicles: Alexandria et Aegyptus in Septuaginta suis Hesychium laudat auctorem, Constantinopolis usque Antiochiam Luciani martyris exemplaria probat, mediae inter has provinciae Palaestinos codices legunt, quos ab Origene elaboratos Eusebius et Pamphilus vulgaverunt, totusque orbis hac inter se trifaria varietate compugnat* (*PL* 28.1392 f., edited critically in *Biblia Sacra iuxta Latinam Vulgatam Versionem* 7 [Rome, 1948], 4). The preface to the translation of the Gospels also alludes in passing to *eos codices, quos a Luciano et Hesychio nuncupatos paucorum hominum asserit perversa contentio* (*PL* 29.559, edited critically in *Novum Testamentum Latine,* ed. J. Wordsworth and H. J. White, 1 [Oxford, 1911], 2).

34. *HE* 8.13.7; cf. Chapter IX. For an attempt to identify readings peculiar to "the recension of Hesychius," W. Bousset, *TU* 11.4 (1894), 74 ff.

35. E.g., P. E. Kahle, *The Cairo Geniza*[2] (Oxford, 1959), 228 ff.; B. M. Metzger, *Chapters in the History of New Testament Textual Criticism* (*New Testament Texts and Studies* 4, 1963), 1 ff.

36. M. Spanneut, *TU* 79 (1961), 171 ff.

37. Philostorgius, *HE* 2.13; Opitz, *Urkunde* 1.5.

38. Opitz, *Urkunde* 14.36.

39. *HE* 8.13.2; cf. G. Bardy, *Recherches sur Saint Lucien d'Antioche et son école* (Paris, 1936), 33 ff.; P. E. Kahle, *The Cairo Geniza*[2] (1959), 221; T. E. Pollard, *Johannine Christology and the Early Church* (Cambridge, 1970), 121. For what it is worth, Epiphanius alleges that Eusebius of Nicomedia lived with Lucian in Nicomedia (*Pan.* 69.5.2).

40. *HE* 9.6.3; *Chr. Pasch.* 519 f.; *PO* 10.12; *Acta Sanctorum*, Nov. 2.2 (1931), 29. He wrote to Antioch from prison, announcing the martyrdom of Anthimus of Nicomedia in April 303 (*Chr. Pasch.* 519).

41. Philostorgius, *HE* 2.13.

42. E. E. Malone, *The Monk and the Martyr* (*Studies in Christian Antiquity* 12, 1950), 5 ff.

43. Chapter VI.

44. *GCS* 27.137.

45. *GCS* 27.4 ff.; cf. H. J. Musurillo, *ACW* 27 (1958), 10 ff., 240.

46. *HE* 2.17.3 ff. (from Philo, *De Vita Contemplativa*); cf. Chapter VIII.

47. *HE* 2.17.2: "he describes as accurately as possible the way of life of our ascetics."

48. A Vööbus, *History of Asceticism in the Syrian Orient* 2: *Early Monasticism in Mesopotamia and Syria* (*CSCO*, Subsidia 17, 1960), 66 ff.; L. Koenen, "Manichäische Mission und Klöster in Ägypten" (forthcoming). Mani's father was an *oikodespotes*, i.e., the prior of some sort of abbey among the Elchasaites in Mesopotamia (*Codex Manichaicus Coloniensis* 89.9 ff.; cf. A. Henrichs and L. Koenen, *ZPE* 32 [1978], 166 ff.).
In the East the cenobitic lifestyle normally preceded the eremetical; see A. Veilleux, *Monastic Studies* 6 (1968), 5 ff. The contrary is often assumed, as by P. Brown, *The Making of Late Antiquity* (Cambridge, Mass., 1978), 81 ff., and by P. Rousseau, *Ascetics, Authority and the Church in the Age of Jerome and Cassian* (Oxford, 1978), 33 ff.

49. *P. Coll. Youtie* 77 = *P. Columbia* 171; cf. E. A. Judge, *JAC* 20 (1977), 72 ff.

50. Athanasius, *Vita Antonii* 2 ff.

51. Ibid., 11 ff. The long discourse put into Antony's mouth (16–43) is wholly Athanasius' own; see H. Dörries, *Nachrichten Göttingen*, Phil.-hist. Kl. 1949, 378 ff.

52. Athanasius, *Vita Antonii* 46 f. The soldier who visited Antony (47), is named as Martinianus: he might conceivably be the Martinianus whom Licinius appointed Augustus in 324 (Chapter V).

53. Jerome, *Vita Pauli*, praef. (*PL* 23.17). Some of Jerome's contemporaries denied the existence of Paul (*Vita Hilarionis*, praef. [*PL* 23.30]). H. Delehaye, *Anal. Boll.* 44 (1926), 64 ff., detected an allusion to him in a document of 383/4 independent of Jerome (*Collectio Avellana* 2.93 f.). But that document attests a Paul of Oxyrhynchus, not a Paul from distant Thebes; see F. Cavallera, *Revue*

d'Ascétique et de Mystique 7 (1926), 302 ff. On the other hand, Jerome appears not to have invented Paul himself; see J. N. D. Kelly, *Jerome: His Life, Writings and Controversies* (London, 1975), 61. Pilgrims visited Paul's retreat, or at least a place described as such, not long after Jerome wrote (Sulpicius Severus, *Dial.* 1.17.1).

54. Athanasius, *Vita Antonii* 81; Sozomenus, *HE* 2.31.2 f. Antony must have dictated the letters in Coptic, with a disciple translating into Greek (cf. *Vita Antonii* 1, 72 ff.).

55. D. J. Chitty, *TU* 64 (1957), 379 ff.

56. *Epistula Ammonis* 12 ff.; *Sancti Pachomii Vita Prima* 4 ff. (ed. F. Halkin, *Subsidia Hapiographica* 19 [Brussels, 1932], 3 ff.). On the primacy of these two documents, D. J. Chitty, *JEH* 5 (1954), 38 ff.

57. D. J. Chitty, *The Desert a City* (London, 1966), 20 ff. For the earliest discoverable form of the rule, A. Boon and L. T. Lefort, *Pachomiana Latina* (Louvain, 1932), 11 ff., 155 ff.

58. Alexander of Lycopolis, *Contra Manichaeos* 1; cf. P. W. van der Horst and J. Mansfeld, *An Alexandrian Platonist against Dualism* (Leiden, 1974), 4 ff. Observe also the Christian denunciation of the Manichees partly preserved in a late third-century papyrus (*P. Rylands* 469).

59. *HE* 8.1.7.

60. *HE* 6.29.4.

61. *HE* 6.35.

62. *HE* 6.40–7.26. Observe that Gallienus was clearly answering a petition from Dionysius and other bishops (7.13).

63. P. Nautin, *Lettres et écrivains chrétiens des IIe et IIIe siècles* (*Patristica* 2, 1961), 143 ff.

64. C. L. Feltoe, *The Letters and Other Remains of Dionysius of Alexandria* (Cambridge, 1904), 127 ff. The treatise is known primarily from quotations in Eusebius, *PE* 14.23–27.

65. *HE* 7.24. Eusebius characterizes Nepos' exegesis as "too Jewish" (24.1), and quotes Dionysius at length (25), because he shares Eusebius' distrust of Revelation (Chapter VIII, nn. 120–123).

66. C. L. Feltoe, *Letters and Other Remains of Dionysius*, 165 ff.

67. Dionysius of Rome, quoted by Athanasius, *De Decr. Nic. Syn.* 26.2 ff.; cf. *Ep. de Sent. Dionysii* 16.1, 3.

68. It was addressed to Dionysius of Rome (*HE* 7.26.1).

69. Athanasius, *Ep. de Sent. Dion.* 18.1 ff.; cf. 4.1 ff.; Basil, *Epp.* 9, and *De Spiritu Sancto* 29.72 (*PG* 32.201). On Dionysius' theology, see W. A. Bienert, *Dionysius von Alexandrien: Zur Frage des Origenismus im dritten Jahrhundert* (*Patristische Texte und Studien* 21, 1978)—who paradoxically concludes that he was not a follower or admirer of Origen, but rejected and attacked some of Origen's principal opinions (222).

70. Athanasius wrote his *Epistula de Sententia Dionysii* to controvert the claim; others accepted the Arian interpretation of Dionysius and either argued that his writings had been interpolated (Rufinus, *De Adulteratione Librorum Origenis* 5 [*CCL* 20.10]) or denounced Dionysius as a heretic and *fons Arii* (Gennadius, *Liber Ecclesiasticorum Dogmatum* 4 [*PL* 41.1214 = 58.892, best edited by C. H. Turner, *JTS* 7 (1906), 90]).

71. Philippus of Side, fragment printed in Theodorus Lector, ed. G. C. Mansen (*GCS*, 1971), 160. Philippus makes Pierius precede Theognostus— which cannot be correct. Observe also that Eusebius mentions Pierius without noting that he taught at the school (*HE* 7.32.30).

72. For the testimonia and fragments, A. Harnack, *TU* 24.3 (1903), 74 ff.

73. Photius, *Bibliotheca* 106; cf. L. B. Radford, *Three Teachers of Alexandria: Theognostus, Pierius and Peter. A Study in the Early History of Origenism and Anti-Origenism* (Cambridge, 1908), 2 ff.

74. *HE* 7.32.30; Jerome, *De Viris Illustribus* 76.

75. *Acta Phileae* (Greek), col. 2.5 ff.

76. Philippus of Side, frag. 7 (ed. C. de Boor, *TU* 5.2 [1888], 170 f.); Jerome, *De Viris Illustribus* 76. The statement in Philippus, frag. 7, and Photius, *Bibliotheca* 118, 119, that Pierius and his brother Isidore were martyrs, in whose honor a large church stood in Alexandria, must be mistaken.

77. Photius, *Bibliotheca* 119; cf. L. B. Radford, *Three Teachers of Alexandria*, 49 ff.

78. L. B. Radford, ibid., 58 ff.

79. Two such fragments from the letter of 309 are printed by M. Richard, *Le Muséon* 86 (1973), 267 f.

80. Procopius of Gaza, *Commentary on Genesis* 3:21 (*PG* 87.221). The Greek fragments of Peter adduced here are conveniently collected in M. J. Routh, *Reliquiae Sacrae* 4^2 (Oxford, 1846), 46 ff.

81. See the passages quoted at the Council of Ephesus in 431 (*ACO* 1.1.2.39) and by Leontius, *Contra Nestorianos et Eutychianos* 1 (*PG* 86.1312).

82. Justinian, *Ep. ad Menam* (*ACO* 3.197).

83. For Syriac fragments and a Latin translation, J. B. Pitra, *Analecta Sacra* 4 (Paris, 1883), 189 ff., 426 ff.

84. The lost *Defense* is reconstructed from three principal sources: Rufinus' translation of the preface and Book One (*PG* 17.541–616), Photius' summary of the *Defense* in six books (*Bibliotheca* 118), and Photius' summary of what he states to be an anonymous work, *On Behalf of Origen and His Opinions*, in five books (*Bibliotheca* 117)—which must be Pamphilus' work; see P. Nautin, *Origène: Sa vie et son oeuvre* (*Christianisme Antique* 1, 1977), 108 ff.

85. Observe Eusebius' total silence about the bishop of Caesarea who succeeded Agapius (*HE* 7.32.24), apparently before 303; cf. H. J. Lawlor and J. E. L. Oulton, *Eusebius* 2 (London, 1928), 263. He was presumably the immediate predecessor of Eusebius himself.

86. Photius, *Bibliotheca* 117; cf. P. Nautin, *Origène*, 114 ff., 134 ff.

87. *PG* 17.543 ff.

88. *PG* 17.546 f.

89. P. Nautin, *Origène*, 144.

90. Photius, *Bibliotheca* 117; cf. Eusebius, *HE* 6.23.4 (Book Two); Socrates, *HE* 4.27.6 (the *Address* quoted). R. M. Grant, *Forma Futuri: Studi in onore del Cardinale M. Pellegrino* (Turin, 1975), 635 ff., argues that Book Six of the *Ecclesiastical History* is later than the *Defense of Origen*. Despite the cross-references (*HE* 6.23.3 f., 33.4, 36.4), it is earlier (Chapter VIII).

91. Photius, *Bibliotheca* 118.

92. *Mart. Pal.* (S) 13.3.

93. Jerome, *Contra Rufinum* 1.11 (*PL* 23.423).

94. *HE* 6.36.4; cf. P. Nautin, *Origène,* 161 ff., 172.

95. *PG* 17.547 f.

96. *Mart. Pal.* (S) 12.

97. The principal evidence for the origins of the Melitian schism derives from a dossier or documentary history compiled by associates of Athanasius c. 368, apparently to commemorate the fortieth anniversary of his consecration as bishop; see E. Schwartz, *Ges. Schr.* 3 (Berlin, 1959), 30 ff.; W. Telfer. *Anal. Boll.* 67 (1949), 117 ff. There survive (1) two letters of 306/7, best edited by F. H. Kettler, *ZNW* 35 (1936), 159–163; H. G. Opitz, *EOMIA* 1.634–6; (2) statements in Latin passions of Peter drawing on the dossier: L. Surius, *De Probatis Sanctorum Historiis* 6 (Cologne, 1575), 577 ff. (*BHL* 6696); A. Mai, *Spicilegium Romanum* 3 (Rome, 1842), 673 ff.; *Bibliotheca Casinensis* 3 (Cassino, 1877), Florilegium Casinense 187 ff. (*BHL* 6692/3). The medieval Neapolitan hagiographer Guarimpotus states that he has excerpted certain details about Peter *ex libello . . . qui vitam et gesta sanctissimi refert Athanasii* (Florilegium Casinense 3.189). For quotation and discussion of the relevant parts of these passions, W. Telfer, *Anal. Boll.* 67 (1949) 126 ff.; P. Devos, *Anal. Boll.* 76 (1958), 170 ff.; 83 (1965), 157 ff.

The various passions of Peter allege that he went to Palestine, Phoenicia, and Mesopotamia; see W. Telfer, *Anal. Boll.* 67 (1949), 126, and P. Devos, *Anal. Boll.* 83 (1965), 167 (*BHG*³ 1502a; *BHL* 6696). That is not impossible; Meletius came from Pontus to hide in Palestine for seven years (Eusebius, *HE* 7.32.27), and some Christians fled beyond the imperial frontiers (Constantine, quoted by Eusebius, *VC* 2.53). If Peter went to Mesopotamia, his destination was the Christian satrapies beyond the Tigris (Chapter IX, n. 93).

98. M. J. Routh, *Reliquiae Sacrae*² 4 (1846), 23 ff.; E. Schwartz, *Ges. Schr.* 3 (1959), 90 ff.

99. Council of Ancyra, Canons 1–9.

100. W. Telfer, *Anal. Boll.* 67 (1949), 126; P. Devos, *Anal. Boll.* 83 (1965), 167.

101. Eusebius, *HE* 8.6.10; 9.1 ff.; *Mart. Pal.* 8.1, 13 (both recensions).

102. Peter, Canon 11.

103. Peter, Canons 2–7.

104. Chapter IX.

105. Apollonius of Lycopolis sacrificed publicly, according to a Coptic passion of Colluthus, published and translated by E. A. E. Reymond and J. W. B. Barns, *Four Martyrdoms from the Pierpoint Morgan Coptic Codices* (Oxford, 1973), 147. His apostasy is also attested in a Coptic fragment of a letter ascribed to Peter (published, translated, and discussed by J. Barns and H. Chadwick, *JTS,* n.s. 24 [1973], 443 ff.). In the passion the governor asserts that Apollonius "is not at all ashamed, and everyone honors him"—which may be relevant to Melitius. Epiphanius describes Melitius as an archbishop in the Thebaid, subordinate only to the bishop of Alexandria (*Pan.* 68.1.5 f.—where K. Holl marks a lacuna, 69.3.3). E. Schwartz, *Ges. Schr.* 3 (1959), 113, deduced that Peter had "delegated his metropolitan functions" to Melitius—which is not plausible; see K. Müller, *Abh. Berlin,* Phil.-Hist. Kl. 1922, Nr. 3.18 ff.

106. For the day, *Acta Sanctorum,* Nov. 2.2 (1931), 77; for the year, Athana-

sius, *Ep. ad Episcopos Aegypti et Libyae* 22 (implying that the Melitian schism began nineteen years before the Council of Nicaea).

107. *EOMIA* 1.634–6. M. Richard, *Symbolae Osloenses* 38 (1963), 80, publishes a fragment of a letter of Peter to his clergy, in which Peter denounces Melitius for dividing the Church.

108. Athanasius, *Apol. Sec.* 59.1.

109. Epiphanius, *Pan.* 68.1.4 ff.; cf. K. Müller, *Abh. Berlin,* Phil.-hist. Kl. 1922, Nr. 3.12 ff.

110. Sozomenus, *HE* 1.15.2.

111. *P. Lond.* 1913, 1914, published and discussed by H. I. Bell, *Jews and Christians in Egypt* (London, 1925), 38 ff.

112. Eusebius, *HE* 9.6.2; W. Telfer, *Anal. Boll.* 67 (1959), 127 f.

113. Gelasius of Cyzicus, *HE* 2.1.13 ff., states that a year elapsed between Peter's death and the election of Achillas, and that the latter died after five months (cf. Theodoretus, *HE* 1.2.8).

114. Epiphanius, *Pan.* 69.2; Socrates, *HE* 6.22.43 ff.; cf. H.-I. Marrou, *CRAI* 1973, 535 ff.

115. Epiphanius, *Pan.* 68.4.2, 69.1.2. Arius' church appears to be the Church of Saint Mark, close to the agora, the market, and the docks; see H. Leclercq, *DACL* 1 (1924), 1099 f. (map), 1112.

116. Opitz, *Urkunde* 1.5; cf. above, at n. 37.

117. *EOMIA* 1.635 f.; Sozomenus, *HE* 1.15.2. Sozomenus adds that Arius abandoned Melitius and was ordained deacon by Peter, quarreled with Peter and was again excommunicated, then obtained readmission from Achillas, who ordained him priest. Even if false, that story suggests that Arius was born c. 282.

118. Athanasius alleges that Melitius was deposed for many illegalities— and for sacrificing to pagan gods (*Apol. Sec.* 59.1).

119. Opitz, *Urkunden* 14.3, 36.56. Similarly, a tract against Arius and Sabellius, published among the works of Gregory of Nyssa (*PG* 45.1281 ff.) but perhaps written by Didymus of Alexandria; see K. Holl, *Gesammelte Aufsätze* 2 (Tübingen, 1928), 298 ff.

120. *HE* 7.32.20. Jerome, *Dialogus contra Luciferanos* (*PL* 23.183) states that the Arian Achilles was a lector: the contemporary documents make him a priest like Arius himself (Opitz, *Urkunden* 4b.6, 6.5).

121. As appears to be argued by G. C. Stead, *JTS*, n.s. 29 (1978), 20 ff.

122. Opitz, *Urkunde* 4b.7–10.

123. *Urkunde* 6.

124. R. C. Gregg and D. E. Groh, *Anglican Theological Review* 59 (1977), 260 ff., argue that Arius was primarily interested in soteriology. Some of his sympathizers showed a far greater interest than Arius himself—for example, Athanasius of Anazarbus; for whose views see *PL* 13.621, frag. 16 (edited critically by D. de Bruyne, *ZNW* 27 [1928], 107), and the sermon published by R. P. Casey, *JTS* 36 (1935), 4 ff. (on the attribution, M. Tetz, *ZKG* 64 [1952/3], 209 ff.). Athanasius appealed to Dionysius of Alexandria for the proposition *ante esse patrem quam filius generaretur* (D. de Bruyne, *ZNW* 27 [1928], 107).

125. H. W. Gwatkin, *Studies of Arianism*[2] (Cambridge, 1900), 1 ff. (pagan sources); R. Lorenz, *Arius judaizans?* (Göttingen, 1980). For invocation of a

Christian but alien "Antiochene tradition," T. E. Pollard, *JTS*, n.s. 9 (1958), 103 ff.; *Johannine Christology and the Early Church* (Cambridge, 1970), 141 ff. The notion that Arius was "utterly illogical and unspiritual" is strongly disputed by M. F. Wiles, *JTS*, n.s. 13 (1962), 339 ff.

126. G. C. Stead, *JTS*, n.s. 15 (1964), 16 ff.; F. Ricken, *Theologie und Philosophie* 44 (1969), 321 ff.; E. P. Meijering, *God Being History* (Amsterdam, 1975), 81 ff.; J. M. Rist, *Basil of Caesarea: Christian, Humanist, Ascetic,* ed. P. J. Fedwick (Toronto, 1981), 170 ff.

127. Opitz, *Urkunde* 6.3.

128. Athanasius, *Ep. de Sent. Dion.* 4.2; Photius, *Bibliotheca* 106.

129. Origen, *Princ.* 1.2.9 f., 4.4.1; Athanasius, *Ep. de Sent. Dion.* 14.4.

130. Origen, *Orat* 15.1; *Contra Celsum* 8.12; Athanasius, *Ep. de Sent. Dion.* 4.2, 18.2; Basil, *De Spiritu Sancto* 29.72 (*PG* 32.201).

131. Origen, *Princ.* 4.4.8.

132. Epiphanius, *Pan.* 69.3.3 ff.

133. Sozomenus, *HE* 1.15.4 ff.

134. Opitz, *Urkunde* 4b.11.

135. Ibid., 1.2.

136. Ibid., 4b.4; cf. Chapter X.

137. Opitz, *Urkunden* 1. The letter was taken by one Ammonius, described by Arius as "my father," who had business in Nicomedia (1.2). He seems to be otherwise unknown.

138. Ibid., 2, 4b.4. The documents imply that Arius approached Eusebius directly. The statements in Epiphanius (*Pan.* 69.4.1 ff.) and Sozomenus (*HE* 1.15.7 ff.) that he first toured Palestine and Syria soliciting testimonials to his orthodoxy probably derive from confusion with his later activities; see W. Telfer, *JTS* 37 (1936), 62 f.

139. Opitz, *Urkunde* 3.

140. Ibid., 4a.

141. Ibid., 4b.

142. Ibid., 6.

143. Ibid., 5 = Sozomenus, *HE* 1.15.10.

144. Opitz, *Urkunden* 8, 9.

145. Ibid., 7, 11.

146. Athanasius, *De Synodis* 15.2: "after his expulsion and at the instigation of the Eusebians"; cf. C. Kannengiesser, *Kyriakon: Festschrift J. Quasten* 1 (Münster, 1970), 346 ff., who assumes, however, that Arius must have written before he left Alexandria.

147. For the fragments, G. Bardy, *Recherches sur Saint Lucien d'Antioche* (Paris, 1936), 252 ff. The verses quoted by Athanasius are analyzed as hexameters by P. Maas, *BZ* 18 (1909), 511 ff., as true sotadeans (a meter based on the ionic a maiore) by W. J. W. Koster, *Mnemosyne*[4] 16 (1963), 135 ff., and as partly accentual anapaests by G. C. Stead, *JTS*, n.s. 29 (1978), 40 ff.

148. Opitz, *Urkunde* 14.3 ff.; cf. Epiphanius, *Pan.* 69.3.2.

149. Opitz, *Urkunde* 15.

150. Ibid., 14.

151. Theodoretus, *HE* 1.3.3 f. H.-G. Opitz rejects the identification on the ground that Alexander of Byzantium was not yet bishop, and he prints *Ur-*

kunde 14 as a letter to Alexander of Thessalonica (which was in Constantine's territory). His premise is false: Alexander was bishop of Byzantium and then of Constantinople from 314 or 315 to 337 (Socrates, *HE* 2.6.1; cf. T. D. Barnes, *AJAH* 3 [1978], 66).

152. Opitz, *Urkunde* 10 = Sozomenus, *HE* 1.15.11.

153. On the chronological problems, see H.-G. Opitz, *ZNW* 33 (1934), 142 ff.; W. Telfer, *JTS* 47 (1946), 129 ff.; N. H. Baynes, *JTS* 49 (1948), 165 ff.; W. Telfer, *JTS* 50 (1949), 187 ff. Telfer adopts a different order for the documents from that assumed here, viz., Opitz, *Urkunden* 2, 3, 11–13, 6, 4a, 1, 4b, 7, 5, 8–10, 14.

For much fuller accounts of the early stages of the Arian heresy than the brief outline offered here, E. Boularand, *L' hérésie d'Arius et la "foi" de Nicée* (Paris, 1972); M. Simonetti, *La crisi ariana nel IV secolo* (Rome, 1975), 25 ff.

154. Eusebius, *VC* 1.51.1. Perhaps as early as 320 (Chapter V)—and perhaps at the instigation of Eusebius, in order to forestall a second expulsion of Arius from Alexandria.

155. *VC* 2.61.

156. Opitz, *Urkunde* 4b.21 (p. 11.1).

157. Ibid., 14.5; cf. M. Aubineau, *Kyriakon: Festschrift J. Quasten* 1 (Münster, 1970), 107 ff. No earlier Greek patristic writers appear to use Christ's robe as the symbol of a united Church.

158. Rufinus, *HE* 10.15; Socrates, *HE* 1.15; Sozomenus, *HE* 2.17.6 ff.; Gelasius of Cyzicus, *HE* 3.15.10 ff.; *Vita Athanasii* 2 (*PG* 25. clxxxvi); Photius, *Bibliotheca* 258.

159. *Epistula Ammonis* 13; cf. Council of Neocaesarea, Canon 11.

160. Athanasius, *Contra Gentes* 9; cf. *New Empire,* ch. IV.

161. E. P. Meijering, *Orthodoxy and Platonism in Athanasius: Synthesis or Antithesis?*[2] (Leiden, 1974), 5 ff., 114 ff.; J. M. Rist, *Basil of Caesarea,* 173 ff.

162. Athanasius, *De Incarnatione* 55.

163. As with Eusebius' *Preparation for the Gospel* and *Proof of the Gospel,* composed at the same period (Chapter X).

164. Athanasius, *Contra Gentes* 1, 46, 47; *De Incarnatione* 1; 56.

165. E. P. Meijering, *Orthodoxy*[2], 106 ff.

166. Athanasius, *Contra Gentes* 1, characterized as a "literary affectation" by R. W. Thomson, in his edition (Oxford, 1971), 3.

167. F. L. Cross, *The Study of Athanasius* (Oxford, 1945) 14; E. P. Meijering, *Orthodoxy*[2] 108.

XII. THE COUNCIL OF NICAEA

1. Praxagoras, *FGrH* 219; Eusebius, *VC* 2.1 ff.

2. *CTh* 15.14.1[S] (16 December 324).

3. *CTh* 15.14.2 (12 February 325).

4. *P. Oxy.* 889, as interpreted in *New Empire,* ch. XIV.

5. Eusebius, *VC* 2.23.2. 20–21 summarize the document quoted in 24–42; 22 appears to be a doublet of 43.

6. *VC* 2.24–42. On the concluding formula ("Let it be published in our east-

ern parts"), see F. Millar, *The Emperor in the Roman World* (London, 1977), 222, 319 f.

7. Chapter V.

8. *VC* 2.44. For Christians in the Roman Senate under Constantine, D. M. Novak, *Ancient Society* 10 (1979), 271 ff.

9. *VC* 2.45 f. Eusebius quotes the letter he received (46).

10. *VC* 2.18.

11. *VC* 2.45.1. Pagan reaction may be inferred from Iamblichus' belief that man cannot obtain release from plague, starvation, or want, or gain any benefit from the gods without sacrifice (*De Mysteriis* 5.6). Two generations later Libanius advanced the totally misleading claim that Constantine "made not a single change in the traditional forms of worship" (*Orat.* 30.6).

12. For the standard interpretation, H. Dörries, *Das Selbstzeugnis Kaiser Konstantins* (*Abh. Göttingen,* Phil.-hist. Kl.[3] 34, 1954), 51 ff. It depends on dating the document to October 324 (following O. Seeck, *Regesten der Kaiser und Päpste für die Jahre 311 bis 476 n. Chr.* [Stuttgart, 1919], 174) and forgetting or disbelieving the ban on sacrifice (*VC* 2.45.1). Eusebius indicates a clear temporal order: first the letter quoted in 24–42, then the measures described in 44–46, and later still (47.1) the letter quoted in 48–60. Moreover, Constantine's reference to the deaths of the persecuting emperors and their eternal punishment in hell appears to presuppose the execution of Licinius c. April 325 (2.54).

13. For a practical example, *Monumenta Asiae Minoris Antiqua* 7.305: in response to a petition, Constantine conferred the title and status of city on the village of Orcistus in Phrygia, declaring himself swayed by the fact that all its inhabitants were Christian.

14. Opitz, *Urkunde* 33 (datable to 332/3); *CTh* 15.5.66 = *ACO* 1.1.3.68 no. 111 (436). The law was presumably issued in 324/5.

15. Eusebius, *Triac.* 7.1 ff. In the West, sacrifices continued: Firmicus Maternus urged Constans to suppress them in 343 (*De Err. Prof. Rel.* 16.4, 28.1 ff.), scarcely two years after Constans had either reiterated his father's prohibition or extended it to Italy (*CTh* 16.10.2; cf. *ILS* 1228). Even in the East, later evidence suggests that enforcement of the prohibition depended largely on local initiative; see G. Fowden, *JTS,* n.s. 29 (1978), 53 ff.

16. Chapter V, at n. 103; Eunapius, *Vit. Phil.* 6.2.2 ff., pp. 462 f.; unpublished inscription from Delphi.

17. *ILS* 705 (between 25 December 333 and 18 September 335); cf. J. Gascou, *MEFR* 79 (1967), 651 ff. The petitioners also sought permission to put on stage performances and gladiatorial displays in Hispellum, as was customary in Vulsinii: Constantine appears to have allowed both forms of spectacle—which might indicate that he did not enforce his general prohibition on gladiatorial games in Italy and the West (cf. Chapter IV).

18. A Alföldi, *The Conversion of Constantine and Pagan Rome* (Oxford, 1948), 110 ff. Within a century it was believed that Constantine at first intended to rebuild Troy (Sozomenus, *HE* 2.3.2; Zosimus 2.30.1)—a story once told of Julius Caesar (Suetonius, *Divus Julius* 79.5). Later still, a story grew up that Constantine attempted to build his capital at Chalcedon, until eagles carried

the stones to Byzantium (Cedrenus 1.495 f. Bonn; Zonaras 13.5). Its debt to legends about the foundation of Byzantium and Rome is clear.

19. Themistius, *Orat.* 4, 58b; cf. *Chr. Min.* 1.232; *CIL* 1^2, p. 276.

20. *CTh* 13.5.7 (334): *urbis, quam aeterno nomine iubente deo donavimus*; *Origo* 30; Eutropius, *Brev.* 10.8.1 The title "New Rome" appears to be attested as early as 324/5 by Publilius Optatianus Porfyrius, *Carm.* 4.6; Opitz, *Urkunde* 18, where the standard retroversion of the Syriac into Greek unjustifiably emends the name to "Thessalonica"; see E. Schwartz, *Ges. Schr.* 3 (1959), 132, 136.

21. Porfyrius, *Carm.* 5.1 ff., 14.9 ff. Lines 25–27 of the latter poem imply that Constantine received Persian ambassadors at court.

22. Ibid., 18.4: *et Medi praestas in censum sceptra redire.*

23. *P. Oxy.* 1261 (13 January 325), 1626 (26 May 325).

24. *RIC* 7.685, Antioch 48; Malalas 318 f. Bonn; cf. T. D. Barnes, *AJAH* 3 (1978), 54 ff.

25. *CTh* 1.15.1.

26. *VC* 2.72.2 = Opitz, *Urkunde* 17.

27. *VC* 2.61.

28. *VC* 2.63; Socrates, *HE* 1.7.1; Sozomenus, *HE* 1.16.5.

29. Constantine, *Oratio* 11.1 ff.

30. Constantine alludes to an otherwise unattested mission of eastern bishops whom he sent to Africa in autumn 324 (*VC* 2.66). His attitude to theological controversy in Alexandria recalls the remarks of Alexander of Lycopolis (Chapter XI).

31. *VC* 2.64–72.

32. A. H. M. Jones, *Constantine and the Conversion of Europe* (London, 1949), 144: "he could not understand the metaphysical subtleties on which the dispute centred."

33. Chapter XI.

34. Athanasius, *Apol. sec.* 74.3 f., 76.3.

35. The synodical letter of the Council of Antioch presupposes that "the great and holy council at Ancyra" has already been convened (Opitz, *Urkunde* 18.14). Marcellus is first attested as bishop of Ancyra in 314 (*EOMIA* 2.30, 50, 51). There is no clear ancient evidence for the often repeated modern assertion that Constantine summoned the Council of Ancyra for the spring of 325 (e.g., O. Seeck, *Geschichte des Untergangs der antiken Welt* 3^2 [Stuttgart, 1921], 405 ff.). Indeed, his letter changing the venue to Nicaea implies that he had not summoned the bishops to Ancyra (*Urkunde* 20).

36. Opitz, *Urkunde* 18.3. For Ossius as the writer of the synodical letter of the Council of Antioch, H. Chadwick, *JTS,* n.s. 9 (1958), 292 ff.; on its general historical context, J. R. Nyman, *TU* 79 (1961), 483 ff.

37. John Chrysostom, *De Beato Philogonio* (*PG* 47.747–756); cf. Theodoretus, *HE* 1.7.10. Constantine may then have been in Antioch; see T. D. Barnes, *AJAH* 3 (1978), 56.

38. Opitz, *Urkunden* 18, 19. On the creed (which avoids the term *homoousios*), see E. Seeberg, *Die Synode von Antiochien im Jahre 324/25: Ein Beitrag zur Geschichte des Konzils von Nicäa* (*Neue Studien zur Geschichte der Theolo-*

gie und der Kirche 16, 1913), 120 ff. Theophanes, a.5816 (p. 21 de Boor), states that Eustathius was appointed bishop by the Council of Nicaea.

Disciplinary canons of the Council of Antioch are preserved in a Syriac translation published by F. Schulthess, *Abh. Göttingen*, Phil.-hist. Kl., N.F. 10 (1908), 164 ff. They are also incorporated in Basil, *Epp.* 217 as Canons 65-80, 82, and 83; see E. Schwartz, *Ges. Schr.* 4 (Berlin, 1960), 180 ff.

39. *VC* 3.6.1; cf. H. Chadwick, *JTS*, n.s. 23 (1972), 132 ff.

40. Opitz, *Urkunde* 20.

41. Chapter V.

42. *Epitome* 41.7; Zosimus 2.28.

43. *VC* 2.18; Socrates, *HE* 1.4.4. Another source speaks of a riot and the soldiers' demands for Licinius' head (*Origo* 29).

44. Chapter III. Orosius, *Hist. Adv. Pag.* 7.28.20, draws the parallel—and commends Constantine for forestalling any action by Licinius.

45. Eutropius, *Brev.* 10.6.1: *contra religionem sacramenti;* Jerome, *Chronicle* 231[b]: *contra ius sacramenti.*

46. *P. Oxy.* 3125 (between 27 March and 25 April) and *CTh* 2.25.1 (25 or 29 April) state the consuls of 325 as Proculus and Paulinus in place of the abundantly attested Paulinus and Julianus; cf. *New Empire*, ch. VI.

47. Viz., a Valerius Proculus (*P. Oxy.* 889; cf. T. D. Barnes, *ZPE* 21 [1976], 280 f.).

48. Eutropius, *Brev.* 10.6.3, and Jerome, *Chronicle* 231[d], implausibly associate the son's death with that of Crispus in 326, not with that of his father in 325.

49. *VC* 3.6.1, 9.

50. *VC* 3.7.1 ff. For the subscriptions to the creed as preserved in a variety of languages, H. Gelzer, H. Hilgenfeld, and O. Cuntz, *Patrum Nicaenorum Nomina* (Leipzig, 1898). Eustathius of Antioch estimated the number of bishops at Nicaea at about two hundred and seventy (frag. 32 = Theodoretus, *HE* 1.8.1) and Eusebius gives it as more than two hundred and fifty (*VC* 3.8). The subscriptions securely attest a still smaller number, but are clearly incomplete (H. Gelzer, H. Hilgenfeld, and O. Cuntz, lx ff.).

51. *VC* 3.9.

52. E.g., the Egyptian Paphnutius, and Maximus who succeeded Macarius as bishop of Jerusalem (Rufinus, *HE* 10.4, 12; Socrates *HE* 1.11.1 ff.; Sozomenus, *HE* 1.10, 23; Theodoretus, *HE* 1.7.6; 2.26.6; Gelasius of Cyzicus, *HE* 2.9).

53. *Coll. Antiariana Parisina* B.II.11.6 (*CSEL* 65.154); Socrates, *HE* 1.8.13; Sozomenus, *HE* 1.17.7. In his voluminous writings, Athanasius says surprisingly little about the debates at the council (only *De Decretis Nicaenae Synodi* 19 f., and *Ep. ad Episcopos Africae* 5 f.).

54. Opitz, *Urkunde* 22.7, 14 ff.; *VC* 3.13; Socrates, *HE* 1.10.1. ff.; Sozomenus, *HE* 1.22. Gelasius of Caesarea also alleged that pagan philosophers were present to tender expert advice (frag. 13 Winkelmann, whence Rufinus, *HE* 10.3; Sozomenus, *HE* 1.18). These "philosophers" are the Arians; see F. Winkelmann, *Byzantinische Forschungen* 1 (1966), 347.

55. Philostorgius, *HE* 1.7, 7a. On the obscure history of the term *homoousios* before 325, see esp. H. Kraft, *ZKG* 66 (1954/5), 1 ff.; G. C. Stead, *Divine Substance* (Oxford, 1977), 190 ff. It is possible that Alexander and Ossius did not

intend the council actually to adopt a creed which included the term, but were forced to insert it during the council—perhaps at Constantine's instigation.

56. Opitz, *Urkunde* 21 = Ambrose, *De Fide* 3.15.125.

57. For proof that the creed was specially prepared for use at Nicaea (not the baptismal creed of Caesarea), see H. von Campenhausen, *ZNW* 67 (1976), 126 ff. The same scholar had earlier protested against the prevailing modern tendency to construe most earlier creeds as baptismal formulae (*ZNW* 63 [1972], 210 ff.).

58. Opitz, *Urkunde* 22.

59. Not on 20 May; see E. Schwartz, *Ges. Schr.* 3 (Berlin, 1959), 79 ff.

60. *VC* 3.10.

61. *VC* 3.11: the chapter heading supplies the name. Eusebius describes the speaker as "the leading man of the right-hand row"—presumably with reference to his own position facing the emperor.

62. *VC* 3.12.

63. *VC* 3.13.1.

64. Rufinus, *HE* 10.2; Socrates *HE* 1.8.18 ff.; Sozomenus, *HE* 1.17.3 ff.; Theodoretus, *HE* 1.11.4 ff.; Gelasius, *HE* 2.8.1 ff.

65. T. D. Barnes, *AJAH* 3 (1978), 56 ff.

66. Opitz, *Urkunden* 23.2, 25.2, 26.1, 27.13, 32.2.

67. A Wikenhauser, *Konstantin der Grosse und seine Zeit* (*Röm. Quart.*, Supp. 19, 1913), 122 ff., postulated the existence of *acta* on *a priori* grounds.

68. J. N. D. Kelly, *Early Christian Creeds*[3] (London, 1972), 211 ff.

69. *VC* 3.13.2.

70. Frag. 32 = Theodoretus, *HE* 1.8.1 ff.; cf. T. D. Barnes, *AJAH* 3 (1978), 57 ff. Theodoretus, *HE* 1.7.10, implies that Eustathius led the anti-Arian party.

71. In Constantine's own words: "wishing nothing else than to produce concord among all" (Opitz, *Urkunde* 27.13).

72. Ibid., 22.7.

73. Hence his embarrassed letter to the church of Caesarea (ibid., 22—excellently analyzed by J. N. D. Kelly, *Early Christian Creeds*[3] (1972), 220 ff.).

74. Opitz, *Urkunde* 21. The document read may have been the extant letter to Paulinus of Tyre (*Urkunde* 8), as argued by G. C. Stead, *JTS*, n.s. 24 (1973), 92 ff.

75. Frag. 32; cf. T. D. Barnes, *AJAH* 3 (1978), 59 ff.

76. Basil, *Epp.* 81, 244.9, 263.3.

77. Opitz, *Urkunde* 24, prints the text of the creed with a simplified apparatus criticus; for a full critical edition, G. L. Dossetti, *Il Simbolo di Nicea e di Constantinopoli* (Rome, 1967), 216 ff.

78. Philostorgius, *HE* 1.9a.

79. Opitz, *Urkunde* 22.9 ff. The ecclesiastical historians state that seventeen bishops initially refused to accept the term *homoousios* (Rufinus, *HE* 10.5; Sozomenus, *HE* 1.20.1).

80. Athanasius, *Hist. Ar.* 42.3. For the date, E. Schwartz, *Ges. Schr.* 3 (Berlin, 1959), 79 ff.

81. Philostorgius, *HE* 1.9a. He names Philumenus, the *magister officiorum*, as supervisor of the signing.

82. Opitz, *Urkunden* 23.4 f., 25.5 f.; Philostorgius, *HE* 1.9 f.

83. Eusebius, *On the Feast of Easter* 8 (*PG* 24.701). Eusebius states that three-quarters of the bishops were in agreement at the start of the debate, and he identifies the minority who finally yielded as "those of the East who defended their ancient custom." Sozomenus, *HE* 1.16.4 f., states that Constantine had sent Ossius to try to resolve the difference before the council. But there is nothing on the subject in the synodical letter of the Council of Antioch (Opitz, *Urkunde* 18).

84. *VC* 3.17–20 = Opitz, *Urkunde* 26.

85. F. Daunoy, *Echos d'Orient* 24 (1925), 443. On the different computations of Easter in the fourth century, see M. Richard, *Le Muséon* 87 (1974), 307 ff.

86. Epiphanius, *Pan.* 70.10.1 ff. For proof that the council discussed Protopaschites, not Quartodecimans, F. Daunoy, *Échos d'Orient* 24 (1925), 428 ff.

87. E.g., in 343: *Chr. Min.* 1.63 (3 April); Festal Index 15 (1 Pharmouthi = 27 March).

88. Opitz, *Urkunde* 23.6 ff.; cf. A. Martin, *Politique et Théologie chez Athanase d'Alexandrie* (*Théologie Historique* 27, 1974), 33 ff. The Latin version in the Codex Veronensis LX (58) (also printed by Opitz) assumes a reference to bishops, not to priests (6).

89. Socrates, *HE* 1.10.1 ff.; Sozomenus, *HE* 1.22. Sozomenus later notes that, as Novatianist bishop of Constantinople, Acesius retained the favor of Constantine until he died (*HE* 2.32.5).

90. Canon 8.

91. Canon 19.

92. The council forbade deacons to administer the eucharist (18)—and ordered that worshipers stand, not kneel, to pray (20).

93. Canons 1, 9, 10, 17. Offenders already ordained were to be expelled from the clergy.

94. Canons 2, 3.

95. Canons 11, 12. The apostates in question are those who lapsed without compulsion or threats (Canon 11), and those who first left the army but later resumed their commissions (12); presumably, existing rules covered other types of apostates, except catechumens (Canon 14). The duration of the prescribed penance is very long—ten and thirteen years, respectively.

96. Canons 15, 16.

97. Canon 4.

98. Canon 5.

99. Canon 6. On the text and significance of this clause, H. Chadwick, *HTR* 53 (1960), 180 ff. For the relationship of civil and ecclesiastical provinces, K. Lübeck, *Reichseinteilung und kirchliche Hierarchie des Orients bis zum Ausgange des vierten Jahrhunderts: Ein Beitrag zur Rechts- und Verfassungsgeschichte der Kirche* (*Kirchengeschichtliche Studien* 5.4, 1901), 32 ff.

100. Canon 7.

101. Viz., Opitz, *Urkunden* 23, 25, 26.

102. Jerome, *Chronicle* 231[e].

103. *VC* 3.15.

104. *VC* 3.16, 21. It was probably on one of these occasions that Constantine described his conversion in 312 (Chapter XV).

105. Jerome, *Chronicle* 232[e] (misdated); cf. T. D. Barnes, *AJP* 96 (1975), 174 ff.

106. *New Empire,* ch. V: Constantine.

107. *CTh* 9.24.1, 9.8.1 (1 and 4 April). On 8 March he had still been in Constantinople (*CTh* 2.10.4).

108. *CTh* 8.16.1.

109. *CTh* 9.38.1.

110. *CTh* 9.7.1.

111. O. Seeck, *ZWT* 33 (1890), 71 ff.; *Regesten* (1919), 63—assuming, however, that the execution of Crispus preceded the law.

112. *CJ* 5.26 (published at Caesarea on 14 June).

113. *CTh* 9.7.2 (published at Nicomedia on 25 April).

114. *CTh* 9.8.1 (4 April).

115. *CTh* 9.24.1 (1 April).

116. J. F. Matthews, *Western Aristocracies and Imperial Court,* A.D. *364-425* (Oxford, 1975), 56 ff.

117. Victor, *Caes.* 41.11; Firmicus Maternus, *Math.* 2.29.18.

118. Known only from *CTh* 9.38.1 (322). Pubilius Optatianus Porfyrius, *Carm.* 10, with *versus intexti,* implies that Crispus' wife was again pregnant in 324; see T. D. Barnes, *AJP* 96 (1975), 181.

119. Ammianus 14.11.20.

120. Philostorgius, *HE* 2.4a; Zosimus 2.29.2. The *Epitome* also stresses the role of Fausta as accuser (41.11).

121. Firmicus Maternus, *Math.* 2.29.14 ff.; cf. T. D. Barnes, *JRS* 65 (1975), 40 ff.

122. P. Guthrie, *Phoenix* 20 (1966), 325 ff.

123. *CIL* 1[2], p. 268; Jerome, *Chronicle* 231[e]; *Chr. Min.* 1.232. Observe two dedications to Helena by the local Senate and people of Naples which style Constantine *victor* (*CIL* 10.1483 f.); Helena presumably visited the city for the dedication of the basilica, aqueduct, and forum which Constantine bestowed on Naples (*Liber Pontificalis,* p. 186 Duchesne).

124. *Epitome* 41.12; Philostorgius, *HE* 2.4, 4a: Zosimus 2.29.2.

125. Firmicus Maternus, *Math.* 2.29.10; cf. T. D. Barnes, *JRS* 65 (1975), 47 f.

126. *New Empire,* ch. V: Constantine.

127. *VC* 3.44. In Jerusalem she endowed a convent of nuns (*Suda* E 3213) and instituted a distribution of free bread to the poor (*CCL* 175.143).

128. *VC* 3.43. Eusebius specifically and repeatedly states that Helena founded only two churches.

129. *VC* 3.43.5 ff.

130. Gelasius of Caesarea told a picturesque story of how Helena sought and found the True Cross (frag. 20 Winkelmann, whence Socrates, *HE* 1.17; Sozomenus, *HE* 2.1). The story was known to Ambrose by 395 (*De Obitu Theodosii* 43 ff. [*CSEL* 73.393 f.]), but there is no hint of it in the *Itinerarium Egeriae,* which describes ceremonies involving the Cross a decade earlier (36 ff.); the story was presumably invented by Gelasius, or his uncle, Cyril of Jerusalem.

131. *VC* 3.46.

132. *VC* 3.47.1; cf. F. W. Deichmann and A. Tschira, *JDAI* 72 (1957), 44 ff.

The mausoleum was attached to the Church of the Martyrs Marcellinus and Peter and was probably begun not long after 312.

133. *Chr. Pasch.* 527 Bonn. Constantine also gave Helenopolis immunity from taxation.

134. On Constantine's movements in 328–330, *New Empire,* ch. V: Constantine.

135. *Chr. Pasch.* 527 Bonn = *Chr. Min.* 1.233.

136. *CTh* 1.4.2^S; *AE* 1934.158.

137. *RIC* 7.213, Trier 517; cf. 516, which shows that Constantine allowed his son a share of the glory.

138. *New Empire,* chs. V, VIII; cf. Libanius, *Orat.* 59.43 ff. (on Constantius and Constans as Caesars).

139. H. Delehaye, *Les origines du culte des martyrs* (*Subsidia Hagiographica* 20, 1933), 235.

140. For the day, *Acta Sanctorum,* Propylaeum ad Nov. (1902), 673. The *Passio Mocii,* published by H. Delehaye, *Anal. Boll.* 31 (1912), 163 ff., appears to be historically worthless.

141. T. Preger, *Scriptores Originum Constantinopolitanarum* (Leipzig: Teubner, 1901–1907), 19, 214 f.

142. Theophanes, a.5816 (p. 23 de Boor); cf. *VC* 3.48.1. For the site of the church, *Passio Mocii* 10.

143. *VC* 3.48.2.

144. For discussion, T. Preger, *Hermes* 36 (1901), 457 ff.; D. Lathoud, *Echos d'Orient* 27 (1924), 289 ff.; 24 (1925), 180 ff.; R. Frolow, *RHR* 127 (1944) 61 ff.; G. Dagron, *Naissance d'une capitale: Constantinople et ses institutions de 330 à 451* (*Bibliothèque Byzantine,* Études 7, 1974), 29 ff.

John Lydus, *De Mensibus* 4.2, has the ludicrous story that a major role in dedicating the city was taken by Sopater, the pupil of Iamblichus, and by Praetextatus the hierophant—i.e., Vettius Agorius Praetextatus, who was born c. 325/330.

145. *Chr. Pasch.* 528 Bonn. Malalas 320 Bonn and Zonaras 13.3.25 f. state that the statue came from Ilium. On its nature and significance, see J. Karayannopoulos, *Historia* 5 (1956), 341 ff.

146. *VC* 3.48, 4.36 f.

147. *VC* 3.49.

148. Eunapius, *Vit. Phil.* 16.1.6, p. 495.

149. Libanius, *Orat.* 1.31, 39 ff.; *Suda* B 259.

150. *Origo* 30; Sozomenus, *HE* 2.3.6; cf. G. Dagron, *Naissance d'une capitale,* 120 ff.

151. *Chr. Pasch.* 531 Bonn = *Chr. Min.* 1.234; Eunapius, *Vit. Phil.* 6.2.8, p. 462. Constantine gave *navicularii* legal privileges for transporting the corn (*CTh* 13.5.7).

152. Zosimus 2.31; cf. R. Janin, *Constantinople byzantine*^{2} (Paris, 1964), 183 ff.

XIII. ECCLESIASTICAL POLITICS

1. Eusebius, *HE* 10.5.16, 6.4, 7.2 (312/3); *CTh* 16.5.1 (326): *haereticos atque schismaticos non solum ab his privilegiis alienos esse volumus, sed etiam diversis muneribus constringi et subici.*
2. Chapter IV.
3. Eusebius, *VC* 3.64 f.
4. A. H. M. Jones, *Later Roman Empire* (Oxford, 1964), 953 ff.
5. *CTh* 16.5.2.
6. Rufinus, *HE* 10.5 = Gelasius, *HE* 2.27.10. Constantine had made a very similar assertion in 314 (Chapter IV, at n. 143).
7. As argued by E. Schwartz, *Kaiser Constantin und die christliche Kirche*[2] (Leipzig, 1936), 126 ff.
8. F. Winkelmann, *Byzantinische Forschungen* 1 (1966), 346 ff.; see also his *Untersuchungen zur Kirchengeschichte des Gelasios von Kaisareia* (*Sb. Berlin, Klasse für Sprachen, Literatur und Kunst* 1965, Nr. 3), and *Byzantinoslavica* 27 (1966), 104 ff.
9. See especially the series of papers "Zur Geschichte des Athanasius" by E. Schwartz (1904–1911), largely republished in his *Ges. Schr.* 3 (Berlin, 1959); for subsequent work, T. D. Barnes, *AJAH* 3 (1978), 53 ff. Philostorgius is important, for he writes from an Arian viewpoint; see W. G. Rusch, *Politique et théologie chez Athanase d'Alexandrie* (*Théologie Historique* 27, 1974), 161 ff.
10. V. C. de Clercq, *Ossius of Cordova: A Contribution to the History of the Constantinian Period* (Washington, 1954), 282 ff. Ossius presumably left the court when it was in Italy in 326—possibly in disgust at the execution of Crispus (Chapter XII).
11. Opitz, *Urkunde* 22. A scholiast on Socrates, *HE* 1.8.51 (who quotes the letter), states that the word *homoousios* was used by Theognostus of Alexandria.
12. Opitz, *Urkunde* 31.2.
13. Ibid., 27.16; cf. K. Müller, *ZKG* 24 (1925), 291.
14. Opitz, *Urkunde* 27.15. In his note on the passage, H.-G. Opitz argues that the Alexandrians must be Arius, Secundus, and Theonas. But they were already in exile (Philostorgius, *HE* 1.9c, 10).
15. Opitz, *Urkunde* 27.
16. Ibid., 28.
17. Philostorgius, *HE* 1.10.
18. Socrates, *HE* 1.23.6 ff.
19. On his career and theology, see R. V. Sellers, *Eustathius of Antioch and His Place in the Early History of Christian Doctrine* (Cambridge, 1928), 24 ff.
20. Frag. 32 Spanneut = Theodoretus, *HE* 1.8.1 ff. On the interpretation of this exceedingly difficult passage, see T. D. Barnes, *AJAH* 3 (1978), 58 f. When Eustathius contends that the Arians "ought to be kneeling among the penitents," he may allude primarily to Asterius, who had lapsed during the persecution (below, at n. 141).
21. T. D. Barnes, *AJAH* 3 (1978), 59. Since Eusebius of Nicomedia was still in exile, Eusebius of Caesarea is more likely to be Eustathius' target.
22. For the date, T. D. Barnes, *AJAH* 3 (1978), 60.
23. Cyrus of Beroea formally accused him of Sabellianism, according to

George of Laodicea in his panegyric of Eusebius of Emesa (Socrates, *HE* 1.24.2).

24. *CSEL* 65.66; Athanasius, *Hist. Ar.* 4.1; Philostorgius, *HE* 2.7; Sozomenus, *HE* 2.19.1; Theodoretus, *HE* 1.21.5 ff.

25. *VC* 3.59.4; Athanasius, *Hist. Ar.* 4.1; Theodoretus, *HE* 1.21.9 f.

26. *CSEL* 65.118 = Athanasius, *Apol. Sec.* 45.2. Asclepas was deposed seventeen years before the Council of Serdica (*CSEL* 65.56), which met in the winter of 343–344; see T. D. Barnes, *AJAH* 3 (1978), 67 ff.

27. Athanasius, *Apol. de Fuga* 3.3; *Hist. Ar.* 5.2; cf. E. Honigmann, *Patristic Studies* (*Studi e testi* 175, 1953), 36 ff.

28. *CSEL* 65.66: *Eustasio et Quimatio . . . de quorum vita infami ac turpi dicendum nihil est.*

29. Eusebius, *C. Marc.* 1.4.2; Philostorgius, *HE* 3.15.

30. Philostorgius, *HE* 3.15; Theodoretus, *HE* 1.22.1.

31. *VC* 3.59.1 ff.

32. *VC* 3.60.3.

33. *VC* 3.60.3, 61.1, 62.1.

34. *VC* 3.60.

35. *VC* 3.61.

36. *VC* 3.62.

37. Theodoretus, *HE* 1.22.1. Flacillus is the dedicatee of Eusebius' *Ecclesiastical Theology* (Chapter XV).

38. The canons and subscriptions transmitted as belonging to the "Dedication Council" in 341 (*EOMIA* 2.215 ff.) belong in fact to the council which deposed Eustathius and Asclepas; see E. Schwartz, *Ges. Schr.* 3 (1959), 216 ff.; H. Chadwick, *JTS* 49 (1948), 34 f. The bishops at Antioch in 327 forbade appeals to the emperor either by clergy dismissed by their bishop or by bishops deposed by a Church council (Canon 12), and laid down that new bishops must be ordained by a council at which the metropolitan is present (Canon 19).

39. Opitz, *Urkunde* 29.

40. Ibid., 30.

41. Ibid., 32.3.

42. *VC* 3.23. It was presumably in the months after Nicaea that Melitius drew up a list of his clergy for Alexander (Athanasius, *Apol. Sec.* 71.6).

43. Philostorgius, *HE* 2.7; cf. T. D. Barnes, *AJAH* 3 (1978), 60 f.; R. Lorenz, *ZKG* 90 (1979), 22 ff.

44. *VC* 3.23; cf. *CTh* 12.5.1^S, 14.24.1.

45. Opitz, *Urkunde* 31.

46. Socrates, *HE* 1.14.1 ff.; Sozomenus, *HE* 2.16.1 ff. Amphion had replaced Eusebius; Chrestus, Theognis.

47. Athanasius, *Apol. Sec.* 59.3.

48. *VC* 3.23.

49. Implied by Athanasius, *Apol. Sec.* 59.3; Sozomenus, *HE* 2.17.4.

50. Arius returned to Alexandria, according to Socrates, *HE* 1.27.1; Gelasius, *HE* 3.13.19.

51. Opitz, *Urkunde* 32.

52. Epiphanius, *Pan.* 68.7.2.

53. Festal Index, praef.

54. Sozomenus, *HE* 2.17.2 f. (quoting Apollinaris of Laodicea); Epiphanius, *Pan.* 68.7.3.

55. Sozomenus, *HE* 2.17.4, 25.6.

56. Athanasius, *Apol. Sec.* 6.4; Philostorgius, *HE* 3.11; Sozomenus, *HE* 2.17.4.

57. Festal Index, praef.; *Chr. Min.* 1.292; *Historia acephala* 17.

58. Philostorgius, *HE* 2.11.

59. Ibid., 2.11a.

60. Epiphanius, *Pan.* 68.7.3. He errs in making Theonas bishop between Alexander and Athanasius (4).

61. *P. Lond.* 1914.6 f.; cf. K. Holl, *Gesammelte Aufsätze zur Kirchengeschichte* 2 (Tübingen, 1928), 288 f. One of Athanasius' earliest letters to Constantine complained of "illegal ordinations" by the Melitians (Sozomenus, *HE* 2.22.3).

62. Athanasius, *Apol. Sec.* 59.4 ff.

63. Epiphanius, *Pan.* 68.6.1 ff.

64. Athanasius, *Apol. Sec.* 59.3; *New Empire,* ch. V: Constantine.

65. Athanasius, *Apol. Sec.* 60.1.

66. Ibid., 60.2.

67. *Festal Letter* 3; cf. Index 2. Constantine was in Nicomedia, according to Socrates, *HE* 1.27.8. This letter is redated to 342 by E. Schwartz, *Ges. Schr.* 4 (Berlin, 1960), 7 f.; V. Peri, *Aevum* 35 (1961), 45 ff. In favor of the transmitted date, L. T. Lefort, *Bull. Acad. Roy. de Belgique,* Classe des Lettres[5] 39 (1953), 646 ff.

68. Athanasius, *Apol. Sec.* 60.3 f.; Festal Index 3 (misplaced, since the content relates to *Festal Letter* 4).

69. For the charges, Athanasius, *Festal Letter* 4.5; *Apol. Sec.* 60.4; Festal Index 3 (cf. *Epistula Ammonis* 13); Socrates, *HE* 1.27.9; Sozomenus, *HE* 2.22.8. It can probably be deduced from Socrates, *HE* 1.13.4, with Photius, *Bibliotheca* 258, that Philumenus, who is attested as *magister officiorum* in 325 (Philostorgius, *HE* !.9a), was accused of plotting to assassinate Constantine.

70. *Festal Letter* 4.5.

71. Athanasius, *Apol. Sec.* 61 f.

72. Festal Index 4.

73. Secundus, and perhaps Theonas, appear to have returned to Libya not long after 325 (Philostorgius, *HE* 2.1, 1b).

74. Opitz, *Urkunde* 34, esp. 5, 20.

75. Athanasius, *De Decretis Nicaenae Synodi* 38.9, 40.43. Neither the beginning nor the end of Paterius' prefecture can be dated precisely: he is attested securely only in April 333 (*Festal Letter* 5, heading).

76. Opitz, *Urkunde* 33.

77. Ibid., 34. For some improvements in Opitz's text, see H. Chadwick, *JTS* 49 (1948), 169; F. Scheidweiler, *BZ* 47 (1954), 76 ff.

78. Sozomenus, *HE* 2.27.13. The story that Constantine recalled Arius from exile in obedience to his sister's dying wishes (Rufinus, *HE* 10.12; Socrates, *HE* 1.25; Sozomenus, *HE* 2.27.2 ff.; Theodoretus, *HE* 2.3.1 ff.; Gelasius, *HE* 3.12) may perhaps imply that in 333 Arius went into exile for a second time. But

the death of Constantia, presupposed by the renaming of Gaza in her honor (*VC* 4.38), cannot be dated at all precisely.

79. Athanasius, *Apol. Sec.* 65.1; Sozomenus, *HE* 2.23.1.

80. Athanasius, *Apol. Sec.* 64. Athanasius implies that. Ischyras made the declaration before the Melitians accused him for the second time (65.1).

81. Rufinus, *HE* 10.18; Socrates, *HE* 1.27.18; Sozomenus, *HE* 2.23.1.

82. Athanasius, *Apol. Sec.* 65.1 f.; Socrates, *HE* 1.27.20 f. Dalmatius' title of *censor* implies a date later than c. February 333 (T. D. Barnes, *AJAH* 3 [1978], 61 f.).

83. Festal Index 6: "In this year he went through the lower country."

84. Athanasius, *Apol. Sec.* 65.2.

85. Sozomenus, *HE* 2.25.1; Theodoretus, *HE* 2.28.1.

86. Athanasius, *Apol. Sec.* 65.4. For the identification of "the court of the *censor*" in Athanasius with the Council of Caesarea; see T. D. Barnes, *AJAH* 3 (1978), 62.

87. *P. Lond.* 1913.

88. Sozomenus, *HE* 2.25.1.

89. Athanasius, *Apol. Sec.* 67.

90. Ibid., 65.3.

91. Theodoretus, *HE* 1.28.3.

92. Athanasius, *Apol. Sec.* 65.4.

93. Ibid., 68.

94. Ibid., 66. Macarius had written Alexander from Constantinople (66.3).

95. Ibid., 69.

96. Ibid., 70.

97. For the cooperation of the three groups in 335, ibid., 77.5, 9; 78.5, 80.3.

98. Theodoretus, *HE* 1.28.4.

99. Athanasius, *Apol. Sec.* 71.2, 72.1.

100. *P. Lond.* 1914. 29 ff. Line 31 has a reference to Tyre which escaped the original editor; see K. Holl, *Gesammelte Aufsätze* 2 (1928), 286.

101. *P. Lond.* 1914.1 ff., 41 ff.

102. Festal Index 8.

103. *VC* 4.42.

104. Sozomenus, *HE* 2.25.3 ff.

105. Sozomenus, *HE* 2.25.7. The passage continues with a story that Athanasius was accused of fornication. The story clearly derives from Gelasius of Caesarea (cf. Rufinus, *HE* 10.18), for Sozomenus expressly remarks that there was no trace of it in the *acta* of the Council (*HE* 2.25.11).

106. Sozomenus, *HE* 2.25.12. Plusianus may be a former Melitian (Athanasius, *Apol. Sec.* 69.2).

107. Athanasius, *Apol. Sec.* 72.2 ff.

108. Ibid., 81.1.

109. Ibid., 77 f.

110. Ibid., 79.

111. Ibid., 79.4.

112. Ibid., 80. Alexander was already on his way to the council, since Eusebius notes his presence in Jerusalem in September (*VC* 4.43.3).

113. Athanasius, *Apol. Sec.* 81.

114. Ibid., 72.6. Philagrius had received a letter of instruction from Dionysius (72.4).

115. Ibid., 73.

116. Ibid., 76.

117. Ibid., 75.3 f.

118. Ibid., 74 f.

119. Ibid., 76.5.

120. *VC* 4.43.1 ff. For the date, A. Bludau, *Die Pilgerreise der Aetheria* (*Studien zur Geschichte und Kultur des Altertums* 15.1–2, 1927), 185 ff. Eusebius delivered two speeches on the new church, one in Jerusalem (*VC* 4.45.3), one before the emperor (46); although he intended to append the latter to his *Life of
Constantine* (*VC* 4.46), it is the former which survives and is printed by modern
editors as *Triac.* 11–18; see T. D. Barnes, *GRBS* 18 (1977), 342 ff.

121. Athanasius, *Apol. Sec.* 84; *De Synodis* 21.2 ff.; Sozomenus, *HE* 2.27.13 f.

122. Athanasius, *Apol. Sec.* 83.2 ff., 27.4, 28.4, 37.9, 44.4 f.; *Ep. ad Episcopos*
6.2; *Apol. Sec.* 24.1 ff. Athanasius places his own departure before the commission returned (82.1).

123. Sozomenus, *HE* 2.25.15 ff. Some of Athanasius' supporters were as vo-
ciferous as their leader: Paphnutius urged Macarius of Jerusalem, as a fellow
confessor, not to consort with criminals (Sozomenus, *HE* 2.25.20), and Potammon accused Eusebius of Caesarea of apostasy during the persecution (Athanasius, *Apol. Sec.* 8.3; Epiphanius, *Pan.* 68.8.3 ff.).

124. Festal Index 8; Epiphanius, *Pan.* 68.9.4; cf. P. Peeters, *Bull. Acad Roy.
de Belgique,* Classe des Lettres[5] 30 (1944), 148 ff.; *Anal. Boll.* 63 (1945), 131 ff.

125. Athanasius, *Apol. Sec.* 87.1.

126. Festal Index 8.

127. *CTh* 16.8.5; 16.9.1 = *Const. Sirm.* 4 (Constantinople, 21 October); *CJ*
1.40.4 (Nicopolis, 23 October).

128. Festal Letter 8.

129. Gelasius, *HE* 3.18.1 ff. When Athanasius quoted the letter (*Apol. Sec.*
86.2 ff.), he altered its wording at several points, removing Constantine's most
pointed allusions to his humbled condition; see N. H. Baynes, *JEA* 11 (1925),
63.

130. Hence Athanasius' exile should not be construed, in legal terms, as "the
execution of the judgment of Tyre," as it is by K. Girardet, *Kaisergericht und
Bischofsgericht: Studien zu den Anfängen des Donatistenstreites (313–315) und
zum Prozess des Athanasius von Alexandrien* (Bonn, 1975), 73.

131. Athanasius, *Apol. Sec.* 87.1 f. The charge of complicity with Philumenus may also have been revived (Photius, *Bibliotheca* 258).

132. Epiphanius, *Pan.* 68.9.5. Eyewitnesses reported that Constantine uttered threats while Athanasius wept and denied the charges, and that Eusebius
denounced Athanasius' wealth and political power (Athanasius, *Apol. Sec.* 9.3
f.).

133. Athanasius, *Apol. Sec.* 87.2 ff.

134. Festal Index 8. G. R. Sievers, *Zeitschrift für historische Theologie* 38
(1868), 98, emended the date to 5 February 336. In defense of the transmitted

date, P. Peeters, *Bull. Acad. Roy. de Belgique*, Classes des Lettres[5] 30 (1944), 166 ff. He rightly emphasizes Constantine's volatile temper (172).

135. Sozomenus, *HE* 2.31. For the importance of Constantine's desire to see the Church united, Socrates, *HE* 1.35.4.

136. He was already bishop of Ancyra in 314 (*EOMIA* 2.30, 50, 51).

137. Eusebius, *C. Marc.* 1.1.1 ff.

138. Sozomenus, *HE* 2.33.3. The eastern bishops at Serdica in 343/4 state that Protogenes of Serdica subscribed to condemnations of Marcellus on four occasions (*CSEL* 65.58): these must be the Councils of Jerusalem and Tyre in 335, the Council of Constantinople in 336, and the Council which deposed Marcellus again in 339.

139. *C. Marc.* 1.1.3, 1.4.1 ff., 2.4.29; *CSEL* 65.49 ff.

140. Frags. 40, 80–84 Klostermann.

141. Athanasius, *De Synodis* 18.2.

141. See the edition by M. Richard, *Symbolae Osloenses*, Supp. 16 (1956). Some sermons by Asterius the Sophist are published among those of Asterius of Amaseia and John Chrysostom; see J. Quasten, *Patrology* 3 (Utrecht; Antwerp; and Westminster, Md., 1960), 197.

143. For the fragments (culled from Marcellus and Athanasius), see G. Bardy, *Recherches sur Saint Lucien d'Antioche et son école* (Paris, 1936), 341 ff.

144. Athanasius, *De Decretis Nicaenae Synodi* 8.1.

145. Frags. 63 ff. Klostermann.

146. Frag. 85.

147. Frags. 37–40, 87–88.

148. Eusebius, *Eccl. Theol.* 1.1 ff., 1.20.6 ff.; *CSEL* 65.50, 52; Sozomenus, *HE* 2.33.4. Several of Marcellus' later works are preserved with incorrect attributions; see E. Klostermann, *Eusebius' Werke* 4: *Gegen Marcell*, revised by G. C. Hansen (*GCS*, 1972), 255 f.

149. Frags. 74, 78, 71. On Marcellus' theology, as revealed in Eusebius' quotations, see T. E. Pollard, *Johannine Christology and the Early Church* (Cambridge, 1970), 248 ff.

150. *CSEL* 65.50.

151. *C. Marc.* 2.4.30; Sozomenus, *HE* 2.33.1 f.

152. Socrates, *HE* 1.37.1; Sozomenus, *HE* 2.29.1.

153. Athanasius, *Ep. ad Episcopos Aeg. et Lib.* 18 f.; *Ep. ad Serapionem/De Morte Arii*. At the Council of Tyre, Alexander had been represented by the priest Paul, who succeeded him as bishop in 337 (*CSEL* 65.57; cf. T. D. Barnes, *AJAH* 3 [1978], 66).

154. H. Dörries, *Das Selbstzeugnis Kaiser Konstantins* (*Abh. Göttingen*, Phil.-hist. Kl.[3] 34, 1954), 241 ff.

155. Opitz, *Urkunde* 27.1 ff.

156. Compare Origen, *Princ.* 1.2.6, where the Son is likened to a will proceeding from the mind of the Father. Constantine used another phrase reminiscent of Origen when writing to the Alexandrian church in 332: "the only-begotten creator of our law, who presides over the life of all and hates discord" (Athanasius, *Apol. Sec.* 61.1).

157. H.-G. Opitz, *Athanasius' Werke* 2 (Leipzig and Berlin, 1935), 43 line 22

= 3.1 (1934), 58 line 16, prints I. A. Heikel's emendation *pathos* (for *opados* in the manuscripts).

158. *VC* 4.27.2.

XIV. THE NEW MONARCHY

1. Chapter III.

2. The earliest documentation of the title belongs to 311 (Eusebius, *HE* 8.17.4; *FIRA*[2] 1.93). On its possible relevance to Constantine's foundation of churches, L. Voelkl, *Die Kirchenstiftungen des Kaisers Konstantin im Lichte des römischen Sakralrechts* (Opladen, 1964), 9 ff.

3. Zosimus 4.36; cf. A. Cameron, *JRS* 58 (1968), 96 ff.

4. Symmachus, *Rel.* 3.3 ff.; Ambrose, *Epp.* 18.32 (*PL* 16.1022).

5. Symmachus, *Rel.* 3.7. On imperial appointment of Roman priests, see F. Millar, *The Emperor in the Roman World (31 B.C.-A.D. 337)* (London, 1977), 355 ff.

6. *CTh* 16.10.2; cf. *ILS* 1228 (Calama).

7. On the date of the work, see T. D. Barnes, *AJAH* 3 (1978), 75.

8. Firmicus Maternus, *De Err. Prof. Rel.* 16.2 ff., 20.7, 28.6 ff.

9. Various manuscripts attest Juvencus' full name (*CSEL* 24, v, n. 1). The consul of 286 is presumably a descendant of C. Vettius Aquilinus, attested as a senator under Commodus (*CIL* 6.2010).

10. Jerome, *Chronicle* 232[d] (under 328/9); *De Viris Illustribus* 84.

11. Socrates, *HE* 3.16.1 ff.; Sozomenus, *HE* 5.18.3 f.

12. *Laudes Domini* 143 ff. (*PL* 19.386 = 61.1094); cf. Juvencus, *Evangelia* 4.806 ff. The prayer to God *at tu . . . victorem laetumque pares mihi Constantinum* implies that Constantine did not yet have the title *victor*, which he assumed in September 324 (Eusebius, *VC* 2.19).

13. G. Bardy, *Mémoires de l'Académie de Dijon 1933* (1934), 36 ff.

14 Chapter IX.

15. Chapter XII.

16. Eusebius, *Triac.* 8.1 ff.; *VC* 3.54.4 ff. Eusebius describes the agents as "friends" of the emperor; Acacius and Strategius (*VC* 3.62.1) may be identified as the *comites* sent to Syria.

17. *De Rebus Bellicis* 2.1. The work appears to have been written in 368/9; see A. Cameron, *De Rebus Bellicis* 1 (*BAR*, International Series 63, 1979), 1 ff.

18. *Triac,* 8.4 ff.; *VC* 3.55.

19. *VC* 3.56 ff.; cf. *Theophany* 2.14, p. 85* Gressmann (Heliopolis); Philostratus, *Vita Apollonii* 1.7.

20. *VC* 3.57.4. The editor of the *Life of Constantine* entitled 3.54 "Destruction of Idols and Cult Statues Everywhere." Similarly, under the twenty-fifth year of Constantine, Jerome notes *edicto Constantini gentilium templa subversa* (*Chronicle* 233[b]).

21. *VC* 3.54.2; L. Robert, *CRAI* 1969, 42 ff. The forum contained statues of the Mother of the Gods from Mount Dindymus near Cyzicus and of Fortuna from Rome (Zosimus 2.31.2f).

22. *VC* 3.58.

23. *VC* 4.28.

24. *VC* 4.25.2.

25. Sozomenus, *HE* 5.3.3.

26. Athanasius, *Apol. Sec.* 18.2; cf. E. Schwartz, *Ges. Schr.* 3 (Berlin, 1959), 281, n. 1. The Melitians, as a tolerated Christian group, appear to have had a separate supply of grain under their control (*P. Lond.* 1914.48 ff.; cf. H. I. Bell, *Jews and Christians in Egypt* [London, 1924], 69 f.).

27. *In Is.* 49:23 (p. 316 Ziegler); *VC* 2.45.2, 46.3, 4.28; Theodoretus, *HE* 1.11.2; cf. L. Voelkl, *Riv. arch. crist.* 29 (1953), 49 ff., 187 ff.

28. *Triac.* 9.14; *VC* 3.50. On the church at Antioch (completed and dedicated in 341), G. Downey, *A History of Antioch in Syria* (Princeton, 1961), 342 ff.

29. *VC* 3.41 ff.

30. *VC* 3.51 ff.; Sozomenus, *HE* 2.4.

31. *Itinerarium Burdigalense* p. 599 Wesseling. Eusebius had noted pilgrimages to the Holy Land as a common phenomenon before 324 (*DE* 1.1.2 ff.). The earliest known pilgrim appears to be Melito of Sardis (*HE* 4.26.13 f.; cf. H. Windisch, *ZDPV* 48 [1925], 145 ff.). On early Christian pilgrims in Jerusalem, see J. Wilkinson, *PEQ* 108 (1976), 75 ff.

32. On the buildings, see esp. C. Coüasnon, *The Church of the Holy Sepulchre in Jerusalem* (London, 1974), 14 ff.

33. *Itinerarium Burdigalense* p. 594 Wesseling.

34. *VC* 3.25 ff.

35. *VC* 3.33 ff.

36. *VC* 4.43 ff.

37. Chapters VI and X.

38. *PG* 23.1061 ff., 681. The *Commentary on the Psalms* may originally have been composed before 324, since its comparatively few references to the Christian empire appear to be additions to a pre-existing text (e.g., the dedications of pure gold in churches, foretold by Psalm 71 [72]:15 [*PG* 23.813]).

39. *In Is.* pp. 203 f., 218, 235, 259 f., 294, 317, 333 f. Ziegler. Also the destruction of paganism (p. 20 f.) and the disappearance of oracles and idols (pp. 267, 298 f.).

40. *In Is.,* pp. 110, 273; cf. p. 89.

41. *In Is.,* pp. 91, 371, 375 ff., 316.

42. Viz., *Triac.* 11–18; cf. T. D. Barnes, *GRBS* 18 (1977), 341 ff.

43. Chapter X.

44. *Triac.* 17 f.

45. In 330/1, 332/3, 335 and 336/7; see *New Empire*, ch. V: Constantine.

46. *RIC* 7.331, Rome 298; Victor, *Caes.* 41.18; cf A. Alföldi, *ZfN* 36 (1926), 161 ff. *Chr. Pasch.* 527 = *Chr. Min.* 1.233 gives the date of 328. Observe also a milestone near Sucidava which appears to belong to the period 326–333 (D. Tudor, *Oltenia Romana*[3] [Bucarest, 1968], 506, no. 188).

47. *VC* 4.5; *Origo* 31; *Chr. Min.* 1.234; cf. *ILS* 820 (Constantinople). Constantine appears to have taken the title *Gothicus maximus* for the first time c. 328, for the second in 332 (*AE* 1934.158; cf. T. D. Barnes, *ZPE* 20 [1976], 151 f.).

48. *VC* 4.6; *Origo* 32; *Chr. Min.* 1.234.

49. He took the title *Sarmaticus maximus* for the second time (*AE* 1934.158).

50. D. Tudor, *Revista Istorică Romană* 11–12 (1941–2), 134 ff.; *Oltenia Romana*[3], 425 ff.

51. Julian, *Caes.* 329C: Constantine claims to have recovered the lost conquests of Trajan—and Silenus compares them to the gardens of Adonis.

52. *AE* 1934.158; cf. Festus, *Brev.* 26.

53. *New Empire*, ch. VIII.

54. *New Empire*, ch. V: Constantinus, Constantius.

55. Gelasius of Caesarea, frag. 22 Winkelmann, whence Socrates, *HE* 1.25; Sozomenus, *HE* 2.27.1 ff.

56. Chapter V.

57. Eutropius, *Brev.* 10.11; *Epitome* 42.3; Zosimus 2.43.2. Presumably a son of the Virius Nepotianus, consul in 301 (*New Empire,* ch. VI).

58. Philostorgius, *HE* 2.16a; *Chr. Pasch.* 520 = *Chr. Min.* 1.232; Zonaras 12.33.

59. Ausonius, *Professores* 17(16).9 ff. (with the misleading plural *Constantini fratres*); 18(17).10 f.; cf. D. R. Shackleton Bailey, *AJP* 97 (1976), 252; A. D. Booth, *Phoenix* 32 (1978), 244 ff.

60. Libanius, *Orat.* 14.29 ff. = Julian, *Epp.* 20 Bidez-Cumont. Constantius can hardly have gone to Corinth before 316/7 (cf. Chapter V).

61. Ammianus 14.11.27, cf. Chapter XII. Aemilius Magnus Arborius went from Tolosa to Constantinople, where he taught a Caesar and died (Ausonius, *Prof.* 17(16).13 ff.); his pupil was surely Dalmatius, who appointed Exsuperius, his teacher at Narbo, to a governorship in Spain (ibid., 18(17).12 f.).

62. Athanasius, *Apol. Sec.* 65.1 ff.; Theophanes, a.5825, p. 29 de Boor; cf. T. D. Barnes, *AJAH* 3 (1978), 61 f.

63. *P. Oxy.* 1206, 1265, 1470; Athanasius, *Apol. Sec.* 76.

64. Zosimus 2.40.2; cf. *P. Theadelphia* 24, 25; *P. Lond.* 1913.

65. Libanius, *Orat.* 42.26 f.

66. *Chr. Min.* 1.234.

67. *Chr. Min.* 1.235.

68. *New Empire,* ch. VIII.

69. For the territorial division, *Origo* 35; *Epitome* 41.20; cf. *New Empire*, chs. V, VIII, XI.

70. *VC* 4.49 attests the marriage and dates it before July 336.

71. *VC* 4.49; Julian, *Ep. ad Ath.* 272D.

72. Athanasius, *Hist. Ar.* 69; Ammianus 20.11.3; *Vita Olympiadis* 2 (ed. A.-M. Malingrey, *SC* 13[bis] [1968], 408).

73. *Itinerarium Burdigalense* p. 591.4 ff. Wesseling: *lapis pertusus, ad quem veniunt Iudaei singulis annis et unguent eum et lamentant se cum gemitu et vestimenta sua scindunt et sic recedunt.*

74. *CTh* 16.9.2, 16.8.6 (both dated 339 in the mss.), 16.8.1 (dated 315 in the mss.). O. Seeck, *Regesten der Kaiser und Päpste für die Jahre 311 bis 476 n. Chr.* (Stuttgart, 1919), 187, dated all three laws to 339; hence a contrast has been deduced between toleration of the Jews under Constantine and "new anti-Jewish legislation" after his death (M. Avi-Yonah, *The Jews of Palestine* [New York, 1976], 161 ff., 174 ff.). But all three fragments (perhaps all from the same law) are addressed to the praetorian prefect Evagrius and should probably be dated to 329 (*PLRE* 1.284f.): Eusebius explicitly ascribes the prohibition on

Jews' owning Christian slaves (*CTh* 16.9.2) to Constantine himself (*VC* 4.27.1).

75. Epiphanius, *Pan.* 30.4.1 ff.

76. John Chrysostom, *Adv. Jud.* 5.11 (*PG* 48.900), whence Cedrenus 1.499 Bonn; *Chronicon a.846*, a.654, translated by J. B. Chabot, *CSCO,* Scriptores Syri III.4 (1903), 148 f.; cf. M. Avi-Yonah, *The Jews of Palestine,* 173 f.

77. For the earthquake, Theophanes, a.5824, p. 29 de Boor; Malalas 313 Bonn. Malalas states that the emperor renamed Salamis Constantia and remitted four years' taxes (i.e., presumably, from 1 September 333 to 31 August 337).

78. Victor, *Caes.* 41.11 f.; Jerome, *Chronicle* 233^g; Theophanes, a.5825, p. 29 de Boor.

79. Socrates, *HE* 1.13.4 ff. The soldier was pardoned when the hermit Eutychianus went to Constantinople and petitioned the emperor in person. He was probably implicated in the alleged plot of Philumenus which occurred c. 331 (Chapter XIII, n. 69).

80. [Julian], *Epp.* 185, 184; Eunapius, *Vit. Phil.* 6.2.1, p. 462; cf. T. D. Barnes, *GRBS* 19 (1978), 102 ff.

81. Eunapius, *Vit. Phil.* 6.2.2 ff., pp. 462 f. Eunapius names the man who instigated Sopater's death as Ablabius (cf. Zosimus 2.40.3).

82. Chapter XIII.

83. *VC* 4.46; cf. T. D. Barnes, *GRBS* 18 (1977), 342 ff.

84. *C. Marc.* 2.4.28; cf. Chapter XIII.

85. *VC* 4.7. Eusebius does not state the occasion, but notes his own presence in Constantinople (*VC* 4.7.1). He records the Indian ambassadors again in the appropriate chronological place (*VC* 4.50).

86. *VC* 4.46.

87. *Triac.,* praef.

88. Which a later hand has interpolated in *Triac.* 1.3.

89. As argued by H. A. Drake, *In Praise of Constantine* (Berkeley, 1976), 78 f. He bases his interpretation of the whole speech on the erroneous premise that the audience was "composed of councilors, high officials, and public delegations" who were predominantly pagan (52).

90. Stated at the outset in the proposition: "This is a festival of the Supreme Sovereign" (*Triac.* 1.1). Observe the very strange claim that the proclamation of four Caesars fulfills a prophecy in Daniel (3.2 f.; cf. G. W. H. Lampe, *JTS* 49 [1948], 73).

91. *Triac.* 2–6.

92. N. H. Baynes, *Byzantine Studies and Other Essays* (London, 1955), 168 ff.; S. Calderone, *Le culte des souverains dans l'empire romain* (*Entretiens sur l'Antiquité Classique* 19, 1973), 220 ff. On the problem of dating the treatises on kingship attributed to Diotogenes, Ecphantus, and Sthenidas, whose ideas Eusebius echoes, see W. Burkert, H. Thesleff, and the ensuing discussion, in *Pseudepigrapha* 1 (*Entretiens sur l'Antiquité Classique* 18, 1972), 23 ff.

93. J. Straub, *Zum Herrscherideal in der christlichen Spätantike* (Berlin, 1939), 113 ff.; K. M. Setton, *Christian Attitude towards the Emperor in the Fourth Century* (New York, 1941), 47 ff.; R. Farina, *L'impero et l'imperatore cristiano in Eusebio di Cesarea: La prima teologica politica del Cristianesimo* (Zürich, 1966), 107 ff.; J.-M. Sansterre, *Byzantion* 42 (1972), 135 ff. For the sim-

ilarity of the formulations in the speech of 336 to those in Eusebius' earlier works, see F. E. Cranz, *HTR* 45 (1952), 51 ff.

94. *Triac.* 2.3, 5.

95. *Triac.* 7.1–10.7. Eusebius earlier described his hearers implicitly as "holy and pious men" (2.5).

96. *VC* 4.1 ff. Aurelius Victor adds specific details: Constantine removed the liability to provide oil and grain from the Tripolitanian cities and Nicaea (*Caes.* 41.19). And he confirms an alleviation of tax burdens—while obliquely criticizing liberality to the Church (41.20).

97. Zosimus 2.32 ff. The tendentiousness of the presentation is betrayed by the allegation that Constantine passed his last years in luxurious indolence in Constantinople without fighting any war (32.1).

98. *New Empire,* ch. VIII.

99. E. Stein, *Histoire du Bas-Empire* 1^2 (Paris and Bruges, 1959), 110 ff.

On the general tenor or specific aspects of Constantine's legislation outside the religious sphere, see esp. L. Mitteis, *Reichsrecht und Volksrecht in den östlichen Provinzen des römischen Kaiserreichs* (Leipzig, 1891), 204, 548 ff. (alleging a Hellenizing tendency); E. Vernay, *Études d'histoire juridique offerts à P. F. Girard* 2 (Paris, 1913), 263 ff.; M. Sargenti, *Il diritto privato nella legislazione di Costantino* (Milan, 1938), and *Accademia Romanistica Costantiniana: Atti del primo convegno internazionale* (Perugia, 1975), 229 ff.; C. Dupont, *Les constitutions de Constantin et le droit privé au début du IVᵉ siècle* (Lille, 1937); *Le droit criminel dans les constitutions de Constantin: Les infractions* (Lille, 1953); *Le droit criminel dans les constitutions de Constantin: Les peines* (Lille, 1955); *RIDA* 2 (1955), 327 ff. (sale); *RIDA* 9 (1962), 291 ff. (donations); *La réglementation économique dans les constitutions de Constantin* (Lille, 1963); *Iura* 15 (1964), 57 ff. (succession); *RHDFE 49 (1971), 586 ff. (edicts ad populum)*; J. Gaudemet, *Atti del Congresso Internazionale di diritto romano* 3 (Milan, 1951), 17 ff.; *Iura* 2 (1951), 44 ff. (decurions); E. Volterra, *Rendiconti Lincei*[8] 13 (1958), 61 ff.; *Mélanges H. Levy-Bruhl* (Paris, 1959), 325 ff.; D. V. Simon, *Konstantinisches Kaiserrecht: Studien anhand der Reskriptenpraxis und des Schenkungsrechts (Forschungen zur byzantinischen Rechtsgeschichte 2, 1977)*.

100. *CTh* 16.10.1 (320), 11.9.1 (323).

101. *Epitome* 41.6; Zosimus 2.25.2.

102. A. E. R. Boak, *The Master of the Offices in the Later Roman and Byzantine Empires (University of Michigan Studies, Humanistic Series 14.1, 1919)*, 25. Petrus Patricius knew of no *magister* before Martinianus; his successor was Palladius, who had served on the embassy to the Persian king in 298 (John Lydus, *De Mag.* 2.25). It may also be Diocletian who first appointed a eunuch as *praepositus sacri cubiculi;* see J. E. Dunlap, *The Office of the Grand Chamberlain in the Later Roman and Byzantine Empires (University of Michigan Studies, Humanistic Series 14, 1924)*, 180 ff.

103. A. H. M. Jones, *The Later Roman Empire* (Oxford, 1964), 368 f.; R. I. Frank, *Scholae Palatinae: The Palace Guards of the Later Roman Empire (Papers and Monographs of the American Academy in Rome 23, 1969)*, 47 ff.

104. A. H. M. Jones, *The Later Roman Empire,* 572 ff. The first attested imperial notary is Auxentius, under Licinius (*Suda* A 4450), the next Marianus,

who acted as master of ceremonies at the dedication of the Church of the Holy Sepulcher (*VC* 4.44).

105. Zosimus 5.32. Flavius Hermogenes, earlier a habitué of a pagan court and later proconsul of Achaea, may have been *quaestor sacri palatii* under Constantine; see F. Millar, *The Emperor in the Roman World* (London, 1977), 100 f. (on Himerius, *Orat.* 14.28 ff.).

E. Stein, *Histoire du Bas-Empire* 1^2, 114, and P. Bruun, *RIC* 7 (1966), 20, assign the first *comes sacrarum largitionum* to the last years of Constantine. But the first attestation of the title belongs to 345 (*CTh* 11.7.5), and the old title *rationalis summae rei* occurs as late as 349 (*CJ* 3.26.7; cf. *PLRE* 1.1064).

106. *New Empire*, ch. VIII.

107. A. H. M. Jones, *The Later Roman Empire*, 100 ff., 370 ff., 448 ff., 479 ff., 586 ff.

108. *New Empire*, ch. XIII.

109. A. H. M. Jones, *The Later Roman Empire*, 105; F. Millar, *The Emperor in the Roman World*, 117 f. For *comites* in charge of dioceses, A. Chastagnol, *REA* 70 (1968), 340 ff.

110. Zosimus 2.33. It could be conjectured that Polemius and Ursus, ordinary consuls in 338, were *magistri militum* (Chapter XV). The first *magistri* expressly attested as such belong to the reign of Constantius; see W. Ensslin, *Klio* 23 (1930), 306 ff.; 24 (1931), 102 ff.

111. The full and precise titles of few military commanders are attested: observe, however, a *dux per Africam* (*ILS* 2999: no date), a *dux limitis provinciae Scythiae* under Diocletian (*ILS* 4103), a *dux Aegypti et Thebaidos utrarumque Libyarum* both in 309 (P. Lacau, *Annales du Service des Antiquités de l'Égypte* 34 [1934], 22 f.) and again in 324 (*ILS* 701).

112. Victor, *Caes.* 40.25; Zosimus 2.17.2; cf. M. Durry, *Les cohortes prétoriennes* (Paris, 1938), 393 ff.

113. Zosimus 2.34.2.

114. *FGrH* 100 F 6.2—a passage overlooked by most writers about the army of Diocletian and Constantine.

115. *CTh* 7.20.4 (325).

116. *Pan. Lat.* 12(9).3.3, 5.1 f.; cf. Zosimus 2.15.1.

117. *New Empire*, ch. IX.

118. Viz., Campania, Sicilia, Byzacena, and Numidia (*New Empire* ch. IX).

119. For *viri clarissimi* (instead of *viri perfectissimi*) in those three offices under Constantine, see respectively *CTh* 14.28.1 (328); *ILS* 700 (between 324 and 337); *CIL* 2.4107 (probably between 324 and 337). Similarly, a *vir clarissimus* is found as prefect of Egypt in 334–336, viz., Flavius Philagrius (*P. Oxy.* 1470).

120. A. H. M. Jones, *The Later Roman Empire*, 537 ff.

121. A. Chastagnol, *Recherches sur les structures sociales dans l'Antiquité classique* (Paris, 1970), 187 ff.; *Atti del' Accademia Romanistica Costantiniana. 2° Convegno Internazionale* (Perugia, 1976), 53 ff.; F. Millar, *The Emperor in the Roman World*, 295 ff. Nazarius in 321 commended Constantine for enlarging the Senate (*Pan. Lat.* 4(10).35.2).

122. A. Chastagnol, *Revue Historique* 219 (1958), 221 ff.

123. A. Chastagnol, *La préfecture urbaine à Rome sous le Bas-Empire* (Paris, 1960), 21 ff.

124. T. D. Barnes, *Phoenix* 28 (1974), 444 ff.

125. For discussion, A. Déléage, *La capitation du Bas-Empire* (Macon, 1945); F. Lot, *Nouvelles recherches sur l'impôt foncier et la capitation personnelle sous le Bas-Empire* (*Bibliothèque de l'École des Hautes Études* 305, 1955); A. H. M. Jones, *JRS* 47 (1957), 88 ff.; F. Grelle, *"Stipendium vel tributum": L'imposizione fondiaria nelle dottrine giuridiche del II e III secolo* (Naples, 1963); A. Cerati, *Caractère annonaire et assiette de l'impôt foncier au Bas-Empire* (Aix-en-Provence, 1968); W. Goffart, *Caput and Colonate: Towards a History of Late Roman Taxation* (*Phoenix*, Supplementary Volume 12, 1974); R. MacMullen, *Roman Government's Response to Crisis A.D. 235–337* (Yale, 1976), 129 ff. Also, on changes in financial administration, J. Karayannopulos, *Das Finanzwesen des frühbyzantinischen Staates* (Munich, 1958), 53 ff.

126. Victor, *Caes.* 40.42: *uti . . . primusque instituto pessimo munerum specie patres aratoresque conferre prodigenti sibi cogeret.*

127. Zosimus 2.38.2; Eusebius, *VC* 4.3; cf. A. Chastagnol, *BHAC 1963* (1964), 46 ff.

128. Chapter III.

129. For documentation of censuses every five years from 301 to 321, *New Empire,* ch. XIV; for the quinquennial census attested from 362 onward, O. Seeck, *Deutsche Zeitschrift für Geschichtswissenschaft* 12 (1894), 279 ff.

130. Hence the jibe of Eunapius repeated in a later writer: in his last ten years Constantine was *pupillus ob profusiones immodicas nominatus* (*Epitome* 41.16).

131. Constantine, *Oratio* 11.1.

132. *VC* 4.5 f.

133. Gelasius, *HE* 3.10.10 = Athanasius, *Apol. Sec.* 86.10 f.

134. Viz., the *Chronicle of Arbela,* published by A. Mingana in 1907; cf. J.-M. Fiey, *L'Orient Syrien* 12 (1967), 265 ff. It is unfortunately employed as thoroughly trustworthy by A. Harnack, *Die Mission und Ausbreitung des Christentums in den ersten drei Jahrhunderten*[4] (Leipzig, 1924), 683 ff.; M. L. Chaumont, *RHR* 165 (1964), 165 ff. For an investigation of early Christianity in Persia which quite properly disregards the *Chronicle of Arbela,* see J.-M. Fiey, *Jalons pour une histoire de l'Église en Iraq* (*CSCO* 310 = Subsidia 36, 1970), 32 ff.

135. A. Henrichs, *HSCP* 77 (1973), 43 ff.

136. *Codex Manichaicus Coloniensis* 11.1 ff., 18.1 ff.; cf. A. Henrichs and L. Koenen, *ZPE* 5 (1970), 116 ff.

137. W. Sundermann, *Acta Orientalia* 24 (1971), 79 ff.; P. Brown, *Religion and Society in the Age of Saint Augustine* (London, 1972), 97 ff. Shapur tolerated Christians (John of Ephesus, *HE* 2.20; Elisaeus Vardapet 3.15 ff.; cf. F. Decret, *Recherches Augustiniennes* 14 [1979], 102 ff.).

138. A. Böhlig, *Mysterion und Wahrheit* (Leiden, 1968), 202 ff.; L. Koenen, *Illinois Classical Studies* 3 (1978), 161 ff. Both Eusebius, *HE* 7.31, and Alexander, *Contra Manichaeos* 1 (Chapter XI, at n. 58), classify Mani as a Christian heretic.

139. W. B. Henning, *BSOAS* 10 (1940–42), 941 ff. (Mani's death); S. Brock, *Anal. Boll.* 96 (1978), 167 ff. (the persecution).

140. J. Neusner, *A History of the Jews in Babylonia* 3 (Leiden, 1968), 8 ff.

141. Chapter V.

142. Gelasius of Caesarea, frag. 21, whence Socrates, *HE* 1.20; Sozomenus, *HE* 2.7; Theodoretus, *HE* 1.24; cf. P. Peeters, *Anal. Boll.* 50 (1932), 30 ff.; F. Winkelmann, *Byzantinische Forschungen* 1 (1966), 382.

143. *VC* 4.9 ff. The addressee of this letter is argued to be Tiridates, king of Armenia, by D. de Decker, *Persica* 8 (1979), 99 ff. To reach this conclusion he must dismiss the chapter headings of the editor of the *Life* (p. 11.9 ff. Winkelmann) as the work of a hypothetical "rédacteur anonyme de la recension byzantine" (106).

144. The letter could be as early as 324/5 (cf. Chapter XII). Sozomenus, *HE* 2.9 ff., makes it a riposte to violent persecution in Persia. He bases his account on Syriac passions, perhaps composed c. 400; see P. Devos, *La Persia e il mondo greco-romano* (Rome, 1966), 221 ff. But these, like the contemporary evidence of Aphraates, date Shapur's first repressive measures to his thirty-first year (339/40), the first martyrdoms to his thirty-second (340/1); see T. Noeldeke, *Geschichte der Perser und Araber zur Zeit der Sasaniden* (Leiden, 1879), 410 f.; J. Labourt, *Le christianisme dans l'empire perse sous la dynastie sassanide (224–632)* (Paris, 1904), 45 ff.; P. Peeters, *Revue des Études Arméniennes* 1 (1920–1), 26 ff.; *Anal. Boll.* 56 (1938), 118 ff.

145. Festus, *Brev.* 26; Eutropius, *Brev.* 10.8.2; Philostorgius, *HE* 3.1a. Ammianus 25.4.23 and Cedrenus 1.516 Bonn claim that Constantine was induced to go to war by the lies of the philosopher Metrodorus, who had visited India—presumably another *canard* from Julian or Eunapius.

146. Faustus 3.21; cf. W. Ensslin, *Klio* 29 (1936), 102 ff. Libanius, *Orat.* 59.60 ff., makes it clear that Constantius did not engage in any fighting before his father died.

147. *VC* 4.56, 62.2.

148. *VC* 4.57, chapter heading (there is a lacuna in the text); Festus, *Brev.* 26. The Persians proposed to retain the Transtigritane regions which they had already seized (Libanius, *Orat.* 59.71 f.).

149. Zosimus 2.39.2 (title); *Origo* 35; Ammianus 14.1.2; Philostorgius, *HE* 3.22 (marriage).

150. *Origo* 35; *Epitome* 41.20.

151. O. Seeck, *Geschichte des Untergangs der antiken Welt* 4 (Berlin, 1911), 25. Significantly, coins of Constantinople with *Regi Hannibaliano* on the obverse depict the River Euphrates on the reverse (*RIC* 7.584, 589 f.).

152. *VC* 4.58 ff.; cf. R. Krautheimer, *Mullus: Festschrift T. Klauser* (Münster, 1964), 224 ff.

153. *VC* 4.60.5.

154. *VC* 4.61. On the baptism of Constantine, cf. F. J. Dölger, *Konstantin der Grosse und seine Zeit* (*Röm. Quart.,* Supp. 19, 1913), 377 f.; H. Kraft, *TU* 63 (1957), 642 ff. Deathbed baptism appears to have been not unusual among upper-class Christians; see A. H. M. Jones, *Later Roman Empire,* 980 f.

155. *VC* 4.62 ff. For the date, Festal Index 10; *Chr. Min.* 1.235; Socrates, *HE* 1.39.2, 40.3.

XV. EUSEBIUS AND CONSTANTINE

1. Zonaras 13.4.

2. Julian, *Orat.* 1, 16D.

3. Socrates, *HE* 2.2.6; Sozomenus, *HE* 3.1.4.

4. Eusebius, *VC* 4.65 ff. For full discussion, A. Kaniuth, *Die Beisetzung Konstantins des Grossen* (*Breslauer historische Forschungen* 18, 1941).

5. *VC* 4.71.2; cf. J. Vogt, *Hermes* 81 (1953), 111 ff.; R. Krautheimer, *Mullus: Festschrift T. Klauser* (Münster, 1964), 224 ff.

6. *CJ* 5.17.7.

7. *CTh* 13.4.2; cf. *New Empire,* ch. VIII.

8. *Chr. Min.* 1.235; *VC* 4.68 f.

9. On the date, A. Olivetti, *Riv. fil.* 43 (1915), 67 ff.

10. Victor, *Caes.* 41.22; Julian, *Ep. ad Ath.* 270D; *Inscr. lat. de la Tunisie* 814; cf. *New Empire,* ch. VIII. The Caesar Dalmatius died *factione militari* (Eutropius, *Brev.* 10.9.1; cf. *Epitome* 41.18; Socrates, *HE* 3.1.8).

The dead in Constantinople included Aemilius Magnus Arborius, the uncle of Ausonius and tutor of Dalmatius (Ausonius, *Prof.* 17 [16].13 ff.; cf. R. P. H. Green, *BICS* 25 [1978], 20 f.).

11. Julian, *Ep. ad Ath.* 270CD, gives the list: six cousins, his father, his uncle (Flavius Dalmatius), and his otherwise unknown oldest brother (by Julius Constantius' first wife, not by Julian's mother). Apart from Dalmatius and Hannibalianus, the six dead cousins of Constantius and Julian cannot be identified with any certainty, but they may well include Flavius Constantius, consul in 327, Flavius Optatus, consul in 334 and *patricius,* and Virius Nepotianus, consul in 336 and probably husband of Constantine's half-sister Eutropia. Observe also the erasure of the name of Flavius Felicianus, consul in 337, on an inscription of Puteoli (*ILS* 6112).

12. Philostorgius, *HE* 2.4—clearly from Eunapius, whose lost *History* depicted Constantine's death as a punishment for honoring Ablabius (*Vit. Phil.* 6.3.8, p. 464).

13. Julian, *Ep. ad Ath.* 270C; Zosimus 2.40.2.

14. For the marriage, Chapter XIV, at n. 71. Gallus was born in 326 (Ammianus 14.11.27). The evidence for Julian indicates either 330, 331, or 332: in favor of 331, see G. W. Bowersock, *Gibbon et Rome à la lumière de l'historiographie moderne* (*Publications de la Faculté des Lettres de l'Université de Lausanne* 22, 1977), 203 f.

Eusebius of Nicomedia may have had a hand in saving Gallus and Julian: they were related to him through their mother (Ammianus 22.9.4).

15. Julian, *Ep. ad Ath.* 270CD; 281B. Similarly, Zosimus 2.40.2, reflecting the views of Eunapius.

16. Eutropius has the plausible diagnosis *sinente potius quam iubente* (*Brev.* 10.9.1).

17. Viz., Flavius Ursus and Flavius Polemius. About the latter nothing is known before 338, but Ursus appears in legends of Saint Nicholas as a general sent by Constantine to quell a revolt of Taifali in Phrygia (G. Anrich, *Hagios Nikolaos: Der heilige Nikolaos in der griechischen Kirche* 1 [Leipzig and Berlin, 1913], 67, 77, 83, 162, 226, 252). Identity of the consul of 338 with the general Ursus addressed by the veterinary writer Apsyrtus is proposed in *PLRE* 1.989;

cf. 90, and by T. D. Barnes, *Phoenix* 28 (1974), 227. But Apsyrtus probably belongs to a much earlier date; see G. Björck, *Upssala Universitets Årsskrift* 1944.4, 7 ff.

18. Viz., Q. Flavius Maesius Egnatius Lollianus Mavortius, subsequently consul in 355 (Firmicus Maternus, *Math.* 1, praef. 8; cf. T. D. Barnes, *JRS* 65 [1975], 49).

19. Athanasius, *Apol. Sec.* 87.4; *Frag. Vat.* 35; cf. *New Empire,* ch. V: Constantinus, Constans.

20. Julian, *Orat.* 1, 19A.

21. Zosimus 2.39.2; cf. O. Seeck, *ZfN* 21 (1898), 44 f.; J. M. C. Toynbee, *Roman Medallions* (New York, 1944), 199. Constantinus issued a constitution to a proconsul of Africa—which technically belonged to Constans (*CTh* 12.1.27: 8 January 339).

22. *VC* 4.51.1; Philostorgius, *HE* 3.1a; Zonaras 13.5.1 ff.

23. *ILS* 724 (Troesmis).

24. T. D. Barnes, *ZPE* 20 (1976), 154.

25. T. D. Barnes, *Phoenix* 34 (1980), 162 ff. For a medallion commemorating the victory of Constans, J. M. C. Toynbee, *Roman Medallions,* Plate 48.8.

26. Julian, *Caes.* 329CD.

27. Socrates, *HE* 2.7; Eunapius, *Vit. Phil.* 6.3.9 ff., p. 464; Zosimus 2.40.3. Jerome states that many nobles were also killed (*Chronicle* 234[c]). Septimius Acindynus is attested as praetorian prefect in the East on 27 December 338 (*CTh* 2.6.4) and held office until late 340 (*PLRE* 1.11), but it is not completely certain that he was Ablabius' immediate successor.

28. Julian, *Orat.* 1, 20C; Socrates, *HE* 2.7; cf. T. D. Barnes, *Phoenix* 34 (1980), 164.

29. Jerome, *Chronicle* 234[d.f]; *Chr. Pasch.* 533 Bonn = *Chr. Min.* 1.236; cf. P. Peeters, *Anal. Boll.* 38 (1920), 285 ff.

30. Julian, *Orat.* 1, 20–21; cf. P. Peeters, *Bull. Acad. Roy. de Belgique,* Classe des Lettres[5] 17 (1931), 10 ff.

31. Libanius, *Orat.* 18.207.

32. *CTh* 12.1.27 (8 January 339). In spring 337 Constantinus was *Alaman* (*nicus*) (*AE* 1934.158), before his death *A[laman.ma]x. G[erm.max.]* (*CIL* 3.12483, improving *ILS* 724; cf. *ILS* 3.2, p. clxxii). It follows that he waged a German campaign in 338 or 339 (otherwise unattested).

33. Eutropius, *Brev.* 10.9.2. Constantinus claimed suzerainty over Italy and Africa (*Epitome* 41.21; Zosimus 2.41.1).

34. Viz., Fl. Magnus Magnentius, a man of barbarian origin (*PLRE* 1.532).

35. Ammianus 14.11.19 ff. For an attempt to redress Ammianus' hostile portrait of Gallus, E. A. Thompson, *The Historical Work of Ammianus Marcellinus* (Cambridge, 1947), 56 ff.

36. On his personality and reign, see G. W. Bowersock, *Julian the Apostate* (Harvard, 1978), 33 ff.

37. *PO* 10.15.

38. Athanasius, *Hist. Ar.* 8.1. The bishops were permitted to use the *cursus publicus* to return to their sees.

39. Athanasius, *Apol. Sec.* 87.4 ff.—in the name of Constantinus alone.

40. Athanasius, *Apol. ad Const.* 5.

41. Athanasius, *Hist. Ar.* 7.1 ff.; cf. *CSEL* 65.54 f. The fact that Paul subscribed to the deposition of Athanasius in 335 (*CSEL* 65.57) has encouraged the assumption that he became bishop in 335 or even earlier (W. Telfer, *HTR* 43 [1950], 49 ff.; F. Winkelmann, *BZ* 59 [1966], 61). But Paul surely attended the Council of Tyre as a priest representing Alexander, the bishop of New Rome—in precisely the same way as two priests represented the bishop of Rome at Nicaea in 325 and subscribed to the creed immediately after Ossius (H. Gelzer, H. Hilgenfeld, and O. Cuntz, *Patrum Nicaenorum Nomina* [Leipzig, 1898], lii).

42. Festal Index 10; cf. T. D. Barnes, *AJAH* 3 (1978), 65.

43. Athanasius, *Apol. Sec.* 3.5 ff.; *Apol. ad Const.* 5; cf. *CSEL* 65.54 f. Athanasius was absent from Alexandria when he wrote his Easter letter for 338 (*Festal Letter* 10.1 ff.).

44. Socrates, *HE* 2.8.6 f. No attempt was made to reinstate Pistus, appointed to succeed Athanasius by the Council of Tyre in 335 (Athanasius, *Ep. ad Episcopos* 6.2).

45. Athanasius, *Ep. ad Episcopos* 2.1 ff.; Festal Index 11.

46. Jerome, *De Viris Illustribus* 85. Asclepas of Gaza, however, who was deposed with Eustathius (Chapter XIII), returned to his see, apparently being reinstated by a council of bishops over which Eusebius presided (Socrates, *HE* 2.23.40).

47. Chapter XIII.

48. *C. Marc.* 2.4.29 f. The eastern bishops in 343/4 complained that Marcellus' return to Ancyra was attended by arson and violence (*CSEL* 65.55).

49. The list of contents for Book One, the first chapter heading, and perhaps the beginning of the text are also lost.

50. *C. Marc.* 1.1.13 ff., 2.4.29.

51. *C. Marc.* 1.1.36.

52. *C. Marc.* 1.1.37.

53. *C. Marc.* 1.2 f.

54. *C. Marc.* 1.4.

55. *C. Marc.* 2.4.9.

56. *Eccl. Theol.* 2.22.4.

57. Epiphanius, *Pan.* 72.2 f. = Marcellus, frag. 129 Klostermann; cf. W. Schneemelcher, *Bonner Festgabe J. Straub* (Bonn, 1977), 324 ff. Protogenes of Serdica again subscribed to Marcellus' deposition (*CSEL* 65.58; cf. Chapter XIII, n. 138).

58. For a full and sympathetic presentation of the ideas in the *Ecclesiastical Theology,* T. E. Pollard, *Johannine Christology and the Early Church* (Cambridge, 1970), 268 ff.

59. *Eccl. Theol.* 1.20.17, 40; 2.7.1 ff.

60. Ibid., 2.17.6, 2.23.3. The analogy appears implicitly to deny the divinity of the Son; see T. E. Pollard, *Johannine Christology,* 279, n. 5.

61. As argued by P. Meyer, *Festschrift dem Gymnasium Adolfinum zu Moers* (Bonn, 1882), 23 ff.

62. G. Pasquali, *Hermes* 46 (1910), 386.

63. Ibid., 369 ff.; F. Winkelmann, *Eusebius' Werke* 1.1 (*GCS,* 1975), liii ff.

64. G. Pasquali, *Hermes* 46 (1910), 369 ff.

65. R. Storch, *Church History* 40 (1971), 145 ff. For a survey of the vast modern bibliography on the *Life,* F. Winkelmann, *Klio* 40 (1962) 187 ff.

66. E.g., K. Setton, *Christian Attitude towards the Emperor in the Fourth Century* (New York, 1941), 40 ff.; J. Quasten, *Patrology* 3 (Utrecht; Antwerp; and Westminster, Md., 1960), 310; P. Brown, *The World of Late Antiquity* (London, 1971), 82, 86.

A. Momigliano, *The Conflict between Paganism and Christianity in the Fourth Century* (Oxford, 1963), 85, can recognize "the shrewd and worldly adviser of the Emperor Constantine" even in the *Chronicle*—which was written before 300 (Chapter VII). Moreover, and by paradox, Eusebius' exaggeration of his own importance is taken at its face value by those who impugn the *Life* most vigorously. Thus J. Burckhardt argued that, since Eusebius knew Constantine's true nature (as defined by himself), he must have misrepresented Constantine's character deliberately (*Age of Constantine the Great,* trans. by M. Hadas [London, 1949], 283). Similarly, H. Grégoire envisaged Eusebius as a "good courtier" who could not have made the errors of fact which Grégoire claimed (often mistakenly) to detect in the *Life* (*Bull. Acad. Roy. de Belgique,* Classe des Lettres⁵ 39 [1953], 462 ff.). Indeed, all modern denials of Eusebius' authorship of the *Life* have depended on fallacious assumptions.

67. *VC* 1.19.

68. Chapter XII.

69. *VC* 1.28 ff.

70. *VC* 3.13, 15, 21.

71. Chapter XIII.

72. Athanasius, *Apol. Sec* . 87.1.

73. *VC* 4.46. Parts of the speech are presumably reproduced or summarized in *VC* 3.33 ff.

74. *VC* 4.33.

75. Chapter XIV.

76. *VC* 4.46.

77. *VC* 2.43.

78. *VC* 2.45.2.

79. *VC* 3.51.2.

80. *VC* 3.61.

81. *VC* 4.35, 36.

82. The letter of Eusebius to Constantia, compiled from quotations produced by iconoclasts in the eighth century (*PG* 20.1545 ff.), may not be genuine; see C. Murray, *JTS,* n.s. 28 (1977), 326 ff.

83. *VC* 1.1.3, 9.2.

84. *VC* 4.68.2.

85. *VC* 4.69. The consecration of Constantine as *divus* might appear to imply that the Roman state was not officially Christian; see P. Bruun, *Arctos,* n.s. 1 (1954), 19 ff. But the consecration was totally denuded of pagan symbolism, and Constans, who ruled Italy, declined to strike any consecration coins at his mints (L. Koep, *JAC* 1 [1958], 94 ff.).

86. *VC* 4.67.3.

87. *P. Oxy.* 3266, dated 13 August 337, refers forward to the impending thirty-second year of Constantine.

88. *VC* 4.51 f.

89. *VC* 1.58 f.

90. *VC* 1.35 ff., 54 ff.

91. *VC* 1.37.2, 38.2, 55.1, 59.2: cf. G. Pasquali, *Gött. Gel. Anz.* 171 (1909), 285 f.

92. *VC* 1.25, 46.

93. *VC* 1.47.1 f. After noting the *decennalia* of 315–316 (48), the *Life* again alludes to Bassianus, very obliquely (50.1).

94. *VC* 3.1 ff.

95. *VC* 4.1 ff.

96. *VC* 1.23.

97. *VC* 1.11.

98. *VC* 1.19 ff.

99. *VC* 1.13 ff. On the panegyrical nature of 1.14, H. Kloft, *Historia* 19 (1970), 509 ff.

100. *VC* 1.18.1; cf. Chapter IX, at nn. 65–67.

101. *VC* 1.21.

102. *VC* 1.26.

103. *VC* 1.28 ff., 41.

104. *VC* 1.48 ff., 2.15.

105. *VC* 1.28 ff.

106. *VC* 1.39 ff.; cf. Chapter IV.

107. *VC* 2.24–42.

108. *VC* 2.44.

109. *VC* 2.45.

110. As by H. Drake, *In Praise of Constantine* (Berkeley, 1976), 65, 150. On the documents which Eusebius quotes or reports, see C. Dupont, *Viator* 2 (1971), 1 ff.

111. *VC* 2.46.

112. *VC* 2.48–60; cf. Chapter XII.

113. On *VC* 2.61–3.24, see H. J. Sieben, *Die Konzilsidee der alten Kirche* (Paderborn, 1979), 438 ff. *VC* 3.1–3 are a relic of the earlier panegyric.

114. *VC* 2.61 f., 73, 3.4.

115. *VC* 2.64–72.

116. *VC* 3.5.

117. *VC* 3.6 ff.

118. *VC* 3.10 ff.

119. *VC* 3.13, 23.

120. Chapter XII.

121. *VC* 4.40 ff. 4.40.1 marks the *tricennalia,* observing that Constantine concluded each decade of rule by appointing one of his three sons to be Caesar.

122. *VC* 3.25–58.

123. *VC* 3.59–62.

124. *VC* 3.64 f. Clearly earlier than *CTh* 16.5.2 (326). Eusebius praises the enactment as securing the unity of the Church (*VC* 3.66). Those who acknowledged the Church as their mother and returned from exile (66.3) should be the

priests Arius and Euzoius, and the bishops Eusebius of Nicomedia and Theognis of Nicaea (Chapter XIII, at n. 40).

125. *VC* 4.8 ff.

126. Chapter IV.

127. *VC* 4.27.1 *CTh* 16.9.2, though transmitted with the date of 339, clearly comes from the law (Chapter XIV, n. 74).

128. *VC* 4.27.2.

129. *VC* 4.24. On modern interpretations of this deliberately obscure phrase, F. Vittinghoff, *Rh. Mus.*, N.F. 96 (1953), 365 ff.; J. Straub, *TU* 63 (1957), 678 ff.; S. Calderone, *Costantino e il Cattolicesimo* 1 (Florence, 1962), ix ff.; R. Farina, *L'impero e l' imperatore cristiano in Eusebio di Cesarea* (Zürich, 1966), 312 ff.; D. de Decker and G. Dupuis-Masay, *Byzantion* 50 (1980), 118 ff.

130. Chapters XII, XIII.

131. *C. Marc.* 2.4.31.

132. *VC* 1.10.

133. *VC* 1.3.4.

134. *VC* 4.32; cf. Chapter V. Eusebius quotes an official translation which Constantine had circulated (4.32).

135. *VC* 4.46; cf. T. D. Barnes, *GRBS* 18 (1977), 341 ff.

136. Constantine, *Oratio* 9.4.

137. Eutropius, *Brev.* 8.5.3.

138. *VC* 4.75, 1.7 f.

139. *VC* 1.12, 20.

140. *VC* 1.38.

141. *VC* 2.11 f., with quotation from Exodus 9:12 and allusion to Exodus 33:7.

EPILOGUE

1. Photius, *Bibliotheca* 62 = *FGrH* 219; Libanius, *Orat.* 59.19 ff. Libanius is argued to be copying Eusebius by R. Foerster, *Libanii Opera* 4 (Leipzig, 1908), 201, n. 3; P. Petit, *Historia* 1 (1950), 562 ff., copying Praxagoras by J. Moreau, *Scripta Minora* (Heidelberg, 1964), 124 ff. The truth is rather that all three writers independently reflect the same "official" version of Constantine's rise to supreme power.

2. *Orat.* 1, 7D–8C (written in 355). Julian's second oration on Constantius, composed in 358, obliquely but perceptibly criticizes Constantine; see J. Vogt, *Historia* 4 (1955), 339 ff.

3. Ammianus 21.10.8. Julian's charge that Constantine raised barbarians to the ordinary consulate is false (*New Empire*, ch. VI); therefore, presumably, Julian used *barbarian* as a synonym for Christian, as Porphyry had before him (Eusebius, *HE* 6.19.7).

4. Julian, *Symposium,* esp. 318A, 335B, 336AB.

5. Eunapius' views can be assumed to be identical with, and can therefore be deduced from, those of Zosimus, who copied him for the period 270–404 (Photius, *Bibliotheca* 98); see Z. Petre, *Studii Clasice* 7 (1965), 264 ff.

In *CP* 71 (1976), 267, and *The Sources of the Historia Augusta* (Brussels, 1978), 114 ff., I argued that Eunapius published the first edition of his *History*

c. 380. The traditional view that it went down to 395 is reiterated by F. Paschoud, *BHAC 1977/1978* (1980), 149 ff. His arguments do not suffice to reinstate the traditional date, but they may show that the first edition of Eunapius' *History* continued beyond the Battle of Adrianople in 378 down to c. 383.

6. Zosimus 2.7.2, 8.2, 20.2, 29.2–3, 18.1, 28.2, 30.1, 32–34, 38. Zosimus (and hence Eunapius) echo Julian's allegations of *truphe* and *asotia* (2.32.1, 38.2), and Zosimus commits so many gross factual errors as to suggest that Eunapius indulged in deliberate invention and falsification of history.

7. E. Ewig, *Historisches Jahrbuch* 75 (1956), 1 ff.; W. Kaegi, *Schweizerische Zeitschrift für Geschichte* 8 (1958), 289 ff.

8. The *Apologia pro Zosimo adversus Evagrii, Nicephori Callisti et aliorum acerbas criminationes* was published with Löwenklau's translation of Zosimus in a volume which also contained Procopius, Agathias, and Jordanes (for fuller details, see the *British Museum Catalogue of Printed Books* 263 [London 1966], 860). The *Apologia* was reprinted in the introductory matter to the edition of Zosimus which C. Keller (Cellarius) published at Zeitz in Saxony in 1679 (which reprints Sylburg's Greek text and Löwenklau's revised Latin translation of 1590). It was rendered into English for the introduction to the first English translation of Zosimus (London, 1684).

9. C. Baronius, *Annales Ecclesiastici* 3 (Antwerp, 1623), esp. 5, 108, 227 (on Zosimus); 74, 163 (the civil wars), 235 (Crispus and Fausta).

10. J. Burckhardt, *Die Zeit Constantins des Grossen* (Basel, 1853; second, revised and expanded edition, Leipzig, 1880).

11. A. Piganiol, *L'empereur Constantin* (Paris, 1932).

12. A. Alföldi, *The Conversion of Constantine and Pagan Rome* (Oxford, 1948), 16 ff.

13. A. H. M. Jones, *Constantine and the Conversion of Europe* (London 1949), 248.

14. E. Schwartz, *Kaiser Constantin und die christliche Kirche*[2] (Leipzig, 1936), 126 ff.; *Charakterköpfe aus der Antike*[2] (Leipzig, 1943), 223 ff.

15. On the vast bibliography (more than 1500 items in the first half of the twentieth century, according to K. Aland, *TU* 63 [1957], 549), see especially N. H. Baynes, *Constantine the Great and the Christian Church* (London, 1931), 30 ff. (the preface to the second edition [by H. Chadwick, 1972] discusses subsequent scholarship); J. Miller, *Bursians Jahresbericht* 236 (1935), 59 ff.; E. Gerland, *Konstantin der Grosse in Geschichte und Sage* (*Texte und Forschungen zur byzantinisch-neugriechischen Philologie* 23, 1937); W. Ensslin, *Klio* (1940), 353 ff.; J. Miller, *Bursians Jahresbericht* 279 (1942), 261 ff.; W. Ensslin, *Byzantion* 18 (1948), 264 ff.; A. Piganiol, *Historia* 1 (1950), 82 ff.; H. Karpp, *Theologische Rundschau*, N.F. 19 (1951), 1 ff.; K. F. Stroheker, *Saeculum* 3 (1952), 654 ff.; J.-R. Palanque, *Études médiévales offerts à M. le Doyen A. Fliche* (Montpellier, 1952), 133 ff.; J. Vogt and W. Seston, *Relazioni del X. Congresso Internazionale di Scienze Storiche* 6 (Florence, 1955), 733 ff.; F. Winkelmann, *Klio* 40 (1962), 187 ff.; J. Vogt, *Mullus: Festschrift T. Klauser* (Münster, 1964), 364 ff.; A. Alföldi, *The Conversion of Constantine and Pagan Rome*[2] (Oxford, 1969), viii ff.

16. E. Gibbon, *The Decline and Fall of the Roman Empire*, ch. XVIII. A note quotes C. Fleury, *Histoire Ecclésiastique* (edition not specified) 3.233: "On ne se

trompera point sur Constantin en croyant tout le mal qu'en dit Eusèbe, et tout le bien qu'en dit Zosime."

17. Chapters IV, XII, XIII.

18. F. Millar, *The Emperor in the Roman World* (London, 1977).

19. For a study of which, C. Dupont, *RHDFE* 47 (1969), 613 ff.

20. N. H. Baynes, *Constantine the Great,* 9 ff.; J. Straub, *Regeneratio Imperii* (Darmstadt, 1972), 70 ff.

21. Constantine, *Oratio* 11.1 This passage is omitted from three of the five primary manuscripts of Constantine's *Speech to the Assembly of the Saints* and occurs in no modern edition before that of Ivar Heikel in 1902 (p. 165.30 ff.). It was unknown to Jacob Burckhardt and is ignored by Eduard Schwartz. Unfortunately, even historians such as Norman Baynes who adopt an interpretation of Constantine very similar to the present one have abstained from exploiting the evidence of the speech (which is discussed in Chapter V).

BIBLIOGRAPHY

The following bibliography is designed solely as a guide to the present work. It lists only modern works cited in the notes, and among the works cited it lists only (1) reviews and articles published in periodicals, *Festschriften,* and collective volumes, (2) books and monographs which libraries frequently catalogue under the title of the series rather than under the name of the author, and (3) books and monographs especially pertinent to Constantine, Eusebius, and their contemporaries. General studies, articles in works of reference, and editions, translations, and commentaries are in principle excluded.

Abel, F. M. "La Question gabaonite et l'*Onomasticon.*" *Revue Biblique* 43 (1943), 347–373.

Aland, K. "Die religiöse Haltung Kaiser Konstantins." *Studia Patristica* 1. *Texte und Untersuchungen* 63 (Berlin, 1957), 549–600. Reprinted in his *Kirchengeschichtliche Entwürfe* (Gütersloh, 1960), 202–239.

Albertario, E. "Da Diocleziano a Giustiniano." *Conferenze per il XIV centenario delle Pandette,* 321–373. Milan, 1931. Reprinted in his *Studi di diritto romano* 5 (Milan, 1937), 205–253.

———— "Le classicisme de Dioclétien." *Studia et Documenta Historiae et Iuris* 3 (1937), 115–122. The Italian text is printed as "La Romanità di Diocleziano" in his *Studi* 5 (1937), 195–204.

Alföldi, A. "Die Donaubrücke Konstantins des Grossen und verwandte historische Darstellungen auf spätrömischen Münzen." *Zeitschrift für Numismatik* 36 (1926), 161–174.

────── " 'Hoc signo victor eris': Beiträge zur Geschichte der Bekehrung Konstantins des Grossen." *Pisciculi: Studien zur Religion und Kultur des Altertums F. J. Dölger dargeboten. Antike und Christentum,* Ergänzungsband 1 (Münster, 1939), 1–18.

────── "Epigraphica IV." *Archaeológiai Értesítö* 2³ (1941), 30–59.

────── *The Conversion of Constantine and Pagan Rome.* Oxford, 1948; 2nd ed., with note and supplementary bibliography, Oxford 1969.

────── "Cornuti: A Teutonic Contingent in the Service of Constantine the Great and Its Decisive Role in the Battle at the Milvian Bridge." *Dumbarton Oaks Papers* 13 (1959), 171–179.

Alföldi, M. R. "Signum Deae: Die kaiserzeitlichen Vorgänger des Reichsapfels." *Jahrbuch für Numismatik und Geldgeschichte* 15 (1961), 19–32.

────── "Die Sol-Comes-Münze vom Jahre 325: Neues zur Bekehrung Constantins." *Mullus: Festschrift T. Klauser. Jahrbuch für Antike und Christentum,* Ergänzungsband 1 (Münster, 1964), 10–16.

Altheim, F. "Konstantins Triumph von 312." *Zeitschrift für Religions- und Geistesgeschichte* 9 (1957), 221–231.

Amelotti, M. *Per l'interpretazione della legislazione privatistica di Diocleziano.* Milan, 1960.

────── "Da Diocleziano a Costantino. Note in tema di costituzioni imperiali." *Studia et Documenta Historiae et Iuris* 27 (1961), 241–323.

Amore, A. "Il preteso 'lapsus' di papa Marcellino." *Antonianum* 32 (1957), 411–426.

────── "È' esistito papa Marcello?" *Antonianum* 33 (1958), 57–75.

────── "La personalità dello scrittore Ippolito." *Antonianum* 36 (1961), 3–28.

Ananian, P. "La data e le circostanze della consecrazione di S. Gregorio Illuminatore." *Le Muséon* 74 (1961), 43–73, 317–360.

Anastos, M. V. "The Edict of Milan (313): A Defence of Its Traditional Authorship and Designation." *Revue des Études Byzantines* 25 (1967), 13–41.

Andreotti, R. "L'imperatore Licinio nella tradizione storiografica latina." *Hommages à L. Herrmann. Collection Latomus* 44 (Brussels, 1960), 105–117.

────── "L'imperatore Licinio ed alcuni problemi della legislazione costantiniana." *Studi in onore di E. Betti* 3 (Milan, 1962), 41–63.

────── "Recenti contributi alla cronologia costantiniana." *Latomus* 23 (1964), 537–555.

Archi, G. G.; David, M.; Levy, E.; Marichal, R.; and Nelson, H. L. W. *Pauli Sententiarum Fragmentum Leidense. Studia Gaiana* 4. Leiden, 1956.

Aubineau, M. "La tunique sans couture du Christ: Exégèse patristique de Jean 19:23–24." *Kyriakon: Festschrift J. Quasten* 1 (Münster, 1970), 100–127.

Babelon, E. "Un nouveau médaillon en or de Constantin le grand," *Mélanges Boissier* (Paris, 1903), 49–55.

Bagnall, R. S., and Worp, K. A. *Chronological Systems of Byzantine Egypt. Studia Amstelodamensia* 8. Zutphen, 1978.

—————— *Regnal Formulas in Byzantine Egypt. Bulletin of the American Society of Papyrologists,* Supplement 2. Missoula, 1979.

Baillet, J. "Constantin et le dadouque d'Éleusis." *Comptes Rendus de l'Académie des Inscriptions et Belles-Lettres* 1922, 282–296.

Bardy, G. "Les traditions juives dans l'oeuvre d'Origène." *Revue Biblique* 34 (1925), 217–252.

—————— "La *Thalie* d'Arius." *Revue Philologique*³ 1 (1927), 211–233. Reprinted in his *Recherches* (Paris, 1936), 246–274.

—————— "La littérature patristique des *'Quaestiones et Responsiones'* sur l'écriture sainte." *Revue Biblique* 41 (1932), 210–236, 515–537; 42 (1933), 14–30, 211–229, 328–352.

—————— "Les *Laudes Domini* (poème autunois du commencement du IVᵉ siècle)." *Mémoires de l'Académie de Dijon 1933* (1934), 36–51.

—————— "La théologie d'Eusèbe de Césarée d'après l' *'Histoire Ecclésiastique.'* " *Revue d'Histoire Ecclésiastique* 50 (1935), 5–20.

—————— *Recherches sur Saint Lucien d'Antioche et son école.* Paris, 1936.

—————— "L'énigme d'Hippolyte." *Mélanges de Science Religieuse* 5 (1948), 63–88.

Barnes, T. D. "A Note on Polycarp." *Journal of Theological Studies,* n.s. 18 (1967), 433–437.

—————— "Pre-Decian *Acta Martyrum.*" *Journal of Theological Studies,* n.s. 19 (1968), 509–531.

—————— "The Chronology of Montanism." *Journal of Theological Studies,* n.s. 21 (1970), 403–408.

—————— *Tertullian: A Historical and Literary Study.* Oxford, 1971.

—————— "Porphyry *Against the Christians:* Date and the Attribution of Fragments." *Journal of Theological Studies,* n.s. 24 (1973), 424–442.

—————— "Lactantius and Constantine." *Journal of Roman Studies* 63 (1973), 29–46.

—————— "Another Forty Missing Persons (A.D. 260–395)." *Phoenix* 28 (1974), 224–233.

—————— "Who Were the Nobility of the Roman Empire?" *Phoenix* 28 (1974), 444–449.

—————— "Two Senators under Constantine." *Journal of Roman Studies* 65 (1975), 40–49.

—————— "Publilius Optatianus Porfyrius." *American Journal of Philology* 96 (1975), 173–186.

—————— "The Beginnings of Donatism." *Journal of Theological Studies,* n.s. 26 (1975), 13–22.

—————— "The Embassy of Athenagoras." *Journal of Theological Studies,* n.s. 26 (1975), 111–114.

—————— "The Composition of Eusebius' *Onomasticon.*" *Journal of Theological Studies,* n.s. 26 (1975), 412–415.

—————— "The Chronology of Plotinus' Life." *Greek, Roman and Byzantine Studies* 17 (1976), 65–70.

—————— "The *Epitome de Caesaribus* and Its Sources." *Classical Philology* 71 (1976), 258–268.

———— "Sossianus Hierocles and the Antecedents of the Great Persecution." *Harvard Studies in Classical Philology* 80 (1976), 239–252.

———— "The Emperor Constantine's Good Friday Sermon." *Journal of Theological Studies,* n.s. 27 (1976), 414–423.

———— "The Victories of Constantine." *Zeitschrift für Papyrologie und Epigraphik* 20 (1976), 149–155.

———— "Imperial Campaigns, A.D. 285–311." *Phoenix* 30 (1976), 174–193.

———— "Three Imperial Edicts." *Zeitschrift für Papyrologie und Epigraphik* 21 (1976), 275–281.

———— "Two Speeches by Eusebius." *Greek, Roman and Byzantine Studies* 18 (1977), 341–345.

———— "A Correspondent of Iamblichus." *Greek, Roman and Byzantine Studies* 19 (1978), 99–106.

———— *The Sources of the Historia Augusta.* Collection Latomus 155. Brussels, 1978.

———— "Emperor and Bishops, A.D. 324–344: Some Problems." *American Journal of Ancient History* 3 (1978), 53–75.

———— "Methodius, Maximus and Valentinus." *Journal of Theological Studies,* n.s. 30 (1979), 47–55.

———— "Imperial Chronology, A.D. 337–350." *Phoenix* 34 (1980), 160–166.

———— "The Editions of Eusebius' *Ecclesiastical History.*" *Greek, Roman and Byzantine Studies* 21 (1980), 191–201.

———— *The New Empire of Diocletian and Constantine.* Cambridge, Mass., 1982.

Barns, J., and Chadwick, H. "A Letter Ascribed to Peter of Alexandria." *Journal of Theological Studies,* n.s. 24 (1973), 443–455.

Barr, J. "Philo of Byblos and His 'Phoenician History.'" *Bulletin of the John Rylands Library* 57 (1974–1975), 17–68.

Bastianini, G. "Lista dei prefetti d'Egitto dal 30ª al 299ᴾ." *Zeitschrift für Papyrologie und Epigraphik* 17 (1975), 263–328.

Batiffol, P. "Origines de règlement des conciles." *Études de Liturgie et d'Archéologie Chrétienne,* 84–153. Paris, 1919.

Bauer, A. *Beiträge zu Eusebios und den byzantinischen Chronographen. Sitzungsberichte der kaiserlichen Akademie der Wissenschaften in Wien,* Philosophisch-historische Klasse 162, Abhandlung 3. Vienna, 1909.

Baumstark, A. "Syrische Fragmente von Eusebios *peri diaphonias euangelion.*" *Oriens Christianus* 1 (1901), 378–382.

Baynes, N. H. "Two Notes on the Great Persecution." *Classical Quarterly* 18 (1924), 189–194.

———— "Athanasiana." *Journal of Egyptian Archaeology* 11 (1925), 58–69. Pages 61–65 are reprinted in his *Byzantine Studies and Other Essays* (London, 1955), 282–287.

———— *Constantine the Great and the Christian Church.* London, 1931. Reprinted from *Proceedings of the British Academy* 15 (1929), 341–442. (2nd ed. with preface by H. Chadwick, Oxford, 1972).

———— "Eusebius and the Christian Empire." *Mélanges Bidez. Annuaire de l'Institut de Philologie et d'Histoire Orientales et Slaves* 2 (Brussels, 1934), 13–18. Reprinted in *Byzantine Studies* (1955), 168–172.

——— "Sozomen *Ecclesiastica Historia,* I.15." *Journal of Theological Studies* 49 (1948), 165–168.

Bell, H. I. *Jews and Christians in Egypt.* London, 1924.

Bellinger, A. R., and Welles, C. B. "A Third-Century Contract of Sale from Edessa in Osrhoene." *Yale Classical Studies* 5 (1935), 93–154.

Béranger, J. *Recherches sur l'aspect idéologique du Principat. Schweizerische Beiträge zur Altertumswissenschaft* 6. Basel, 1953.

——— "L'expression de la divinité dans les *Panégyriques Latins.*" *Museum Helveticum* 27 (1970), 242–254. Reprinted in *Principatus: Études de notions et d'histoire politique dans l'Antiquité greco-romaine* (Geneva, 1973), 429–444.

Berchem, D. van. *L'armée de Dioclétien et la réforme constantinienne.* Institut Français d'Archéologie de Beyrouth, *Bibliothèque Archéologique et Historique* 56. Paris, 1952.

Berkhof, H. *Die Theologie des Eusebius von Caesarea.* Amsterdam, 1939.

Bernays, J. "Philons 'Hypothetika' und die Verwünschungen des Buzyges in Athen." *Monatsberichte der königlichen Akademie der Wissenschaften zu Berlin* 1876, 589–609. Reprinted in his *Gesammelte Abhandlungen* 1 (Berlin, 1885), 262–282.

Beyer, G. "Die evangelischen Fragen und Lösungen des Eusebius in jakobitischer Überlieferung und deren nestorianische Parallelen. Syrische Texte, herausgegeben, übersetzt und untersucht." *Oriens Christianus,* n.s. 12–14 (1925), 30–70; *Oriens Christianus*[3] 1 (1926–27), 80–97, 284–292; 2 (1927), 56–69.

——— "Das Stadtgebiet von Eleutheropolis im 4. Jahrhundert n. Chr. und seine Grenznachbarn." *Zeitschrift des deutschen Palästina-Vereins* 54 (1931), 209–271.

——— "Die Stadtgebiete von Diospolis und Nikopolis im 4. Jahrh. n. Chr. und ihre Grenznachbarn." *Zeitschrift des deutschen Palästina-Vereins* 56 (1933), 218–253.

Bidez, J. "Fragments nouveaux de Sotérichos?" *Revue de Philologie* 27 (1903), 81–85.

——— *Vie de Porphyre le philosophe néo-platonicien.* Ghent, 1913.

——— "Notes sur quelques passages des écrits de l'empereur Julien." *Mélanges P. Thomas,* 54–65. Bruges, 1930.

——— "À propos d'une biographie nouvelle de l'empereur Constantin." *L'Antiquité Classique* 1 (1932), 1–7.

Bienert, W. A. *Dionysius von Alexandrien: Zur Frage des Origenismus im dritten Jahrhundert. Patristische Texte und Studien* 21. Berlin and New York, 1978.

Binder, G. "Eine Polemik des Porphyrios gegen die allegorische Auslegung des Alten Testaments durch die Christen." *Zeitschrift für Papyrologie und Epigraphik* 3 (1968), 81–95.

Björck, G. *Apsyrtus, Julius Africanus et l'Hippiatrie grecque. Uppsala Universitets Årsskrift* 1944: 4. Uppsala, 1944.

Black, M. "The Chi-Rho Sign—Christogram and/or Staurogram?" *Apostolic History and the Gospel: Biblical and Historical Essays Presented to F. F. Bruce,* 319–327. Exeter, 1970.

Bludau, A. *Die Pilgerreise der Aetheria. Studien zur Geschichte und Kultur des Altertums* 15.1–2. Paderborn, 1927.

Boak, A. E. R. *The Master of the Offices in the Later Roman and Byzantine Empires. University of Michigan Studies,* Humanistic Series, 14.1. Ann Arbor, 1919. A revised edition with unaltered pagination appeared in the same series under the title *Two Studies in Later Roman and Byzantine Administration* (Ann Arbor, 1924), 1–160.

Böhlig, A. "Christliche Würzeln im Manichäismus." *Bulletin de la Société d'Archéologie Copte* 15 (1960), 41–61. Reprinted in his *Mysterion und Wahrheit: Gesammelte Beiträge zur spätantiken Religionsgeschichte* (Leiden, 1968), 202–221.

Bömer, F. *Untersuchungen über die Religion der Sklaven in Griechenland und Rom. Abhandlungen der Akademie der Wissenschaften und Literatur in Mainz.* Geistes- und Sozialwissenschaftliche Klasse 1957, Nr. 7; 1960, Nr. 1; 1961, Nr. 4. Mainz, 1957–1961.

Boer, W. den. "A Pagan Historian and His Enemies: Porphyry, 'Against the Christians.' " *Classical Philology* 69 (1974), 198–208.

Bolhuis, A. *Vergilius' Vierde Ecloga in de Oratio Constantini ad Sanctorum Coetum.* Diss., Amsterdam, 1950.

——— "Die Rede Konstantins des Grossen an die Versammlung der Heiligen und Lactantius *Divinae Institutiones." Vigiliae Christianae* 10 (1956), 25–32.

Bonwetsch, N. *Die Theologie des Methodius von Olympus. Abhandlungen der königlichen Gesellschaft der Wissenschaften zu Göttingen,* Philologisch-historische Klasse, N.F. 7.1. Göttingen, 1903.

Boor, C. de. "Neue Fragmente des Papias, Hegesippus und Pierius in bisher unbekannten Excerpten aus der Kirchengeschichte des Philippus Sidetes." *Texte und Untersuchungen* 5.2 (Leipzig, 1888), 165–184.

Booth, A. D. "Notes on Ausonius' *Professores." Phoenix* 32 (1978), 235–249.

Botte, B. "Note sur l'auteur du *De universo* attribué à Saint Hippolyte." *Recherches de Théologie Ancienne et Médiévale* 18 (1951), 5–18.

Boularand, E. *L'hérésie d'Arius et la "foi" de Nicée.* Paris, 1972.

Bousset, W. *Textkritische Studien zum Neuen Testament. Texte und Untersuchungen* 11.4. Leipzig, 1894.

Bowersock, G. W. "The Proconsulate of Albus." *Harvard Studies in Classical Philology* 72 (1967), 289–294.

——— "Gibbon and Julian." *Gibbon et Rome à la lumière de l'historiographie moderne.* Université de Lausanne, *Publications de la Faculté des Lettres* 22 (Geneva, 1977), 191–213.

——— "A Roman Perspective on the Bar Kochba War." *Approaches to Ancient Judaism* 2, ed. W. S. Green. *Brown Judaic Studies* 9 (Providence, 1980), 131–141.

Bowie, E. L. "Apollonius of Tyana: Tradition and Reality." *Aufstieg und Niedergang der römischen Welt,* ed. H. Temporini and W. Haase, II.16.2, 1652–1699. Berlin and New York, 1978.

Bowman, A. K. "The Military Occupation of Upper Egypt in the Reign of Diocletian." *Bulletin of the American Society of Papyrologists* 15 (1978), 25–38.

Brandt, S. *Über das Leben des Lactantius. Sitzungsberichte der kaiserlichen Akademie der Wissenschaften in Wien,* Philosophisch-historische Klasse 120, Abhandlung 5. Vienna, 1890.

────── *Über die Entstehungsverhältnisse der Prosaschriften des Lactantius und des Buches "De mortibus persecutorum." Sitzungsberichte der kaiserlichen Akademie der Wissenschaften in Wien,* Philosophisch-historische Klasse 125, Abhandlung 6. Vienna, 1891.

Brennan, P. "Combined Legionary Detachments as Artillery Units in Late-Roman Danubian Bridgehead Dispositions." *Chiron* 10 (1980), 553–567.

Brock, S. "Origen's Aims as a Textual Critic of the Old Testament." *Studia Patristica* 10. *Texte und Untersuchungen* 107 (Berlin, 1970), 215–218.

────── "A Martyr at the Sasanid Court under Vahran II: Candida." *Analecta Bollandiana* 96 (1978), 167–181.

Brown, P. R. L. "The Diffusion of Manichaeism in the Roman Empire." *Journal of Roman Studies* 59 (1969), 92–103. Reprinted in his *Religion and Society in the Age of Saint Augustine* (London, 1972), 94–118.

Bruns, J. E. "The 'Agreement of Moses and Jesus' in the 'Demonstratio Evangelica' of Eusebius." *Vigiliae Christianae* 31 (1977), 117–125.

Bruun, P. "The Consecration Coins of Constantine the Great." *Arctos,* n.s. 1 (1954), 19–31.

────── "The Disappearance of Sol from the Coins of Constantine." *Arctos,* n.s. 2 (1958), 15–37.

────── *Studies in Constantinian Chronology. Numismatic Notes and Monographs* 146. New York, 1961.

────── "The Ch. ..stian Signs on the Coins of Constantine." *Arctos,* n.s. 3 (1962), 5–35.

Bruyne, D. de. "Les plus anciens prologues latins des Évangiles." *Revue Bénédictine* 40 (1928), 193–214.

────── "Deux lettres inconnues de Theognius, l'évêque arien de Nicée." *Zeitschrift für die neutestamentliche Wissenschaft* 27 (1928), 106–110.

Buddensieg, T. "Die Konstantinsbasilika in einer Zeichnung Francescos di Giorgio und der Marmorkoloss Konstantins des Grossen." *Münchener Jahrbuch der bildenden Kunst* 13 (1962), 37–48.

Burckhardt, J. *Die Zeit Constantins des Grossen.* Basel, 1853; 2nd rev. ed. Leipzig, 1880 (frequently reprinted). Translated into English by M. Hadas as *The Age of Constantine the Great* (London, 1949).

Burkert, W. "Zur geistesgeschichtlichen Einordnung einiger Pseudopythagorica." *Pseudepigrapha* 1. *Entretiens sur l'Antiquité Classique* 18 (Vandoeuvres-Geneva, 1972), 23–55.

Cadiou, R. "Dictionnaires antiques dans l'oeuvre d'Origène." *Revue des Études Grecques* 45 (1932), 271–285.

Calder, W. M. Review of A. Wilhelm, "Griechische Grabinschriften aus Kleinasien." (*Sitzungsberichte der preussischen Akademie der Wissenschaften,* Philosophisch-historische Klasse 1927, Nr. 27). *Gnomon* 10 (1934), 502–504.

Calderone, S. *Costantino e il Cattolicesimo* 1. Florence, 1962.

────── "Theologia politica, successione dinastica e consecratio in età costantiniana." *Le culte des souverains dans l'empire romain. Entretiens sur l'Antiquité Classique* 19 (Vandoeuvres-Geneva, 1973), 215–261.

Callu, J.. P. *Genio Populi Romani (295–316): Contribution à une histoire numismatique de la Tétrarchie. Bibliothèque de l'École Pratique des Hautes Études,* Section des Sciences Historiques et Philologiques 314. Paris, 1960.

Cameron, A. "Gratian's Repudiation of the Pontifical Robe." *Journal of Roman Studies* 58 (1968), 96–102.

———— "Paganism and Literature in Fourth Century Rome." *Christianisme et formes littéraires de l'Antiquité tardive en Occident. Entretiens sur l'Antiquité Classique* 23 (Vandoeuvres-Geneva, 1977), 3–30.

———— "The Date of the Anonymus *De Rebus Bellicis." De Rebus Bellicis*: Part 1. *British Archeological Reports,* International Series 63 (Oxford, 1979), 1–10.

Camodeca, G. "Iscrizioni inedite di Pozzuoli." *Atti dell'Accademia di Scienze morali e politiche, Napoli* 82 (1971), 24–48.

Campenhausen, H. von "Das Bekenntnis im Urchristentum." *Zeitschrift für die neutestamentliche Wissenschaft* 63 (1972), 210–253.

———— "Das Bekenntnis Eusebs von Caesarea (Nicaea 325)." *Zeitschrift für die neutestamentliche Wissenschaft* 67 (1976), 123–139.

Canet, L. "Sur le texte grec des *Canons* d'Eusèbe." *Mélanges d'Archéologie et d'Histoire de l'École Française de Rome* 33 (1913), 119–168.

Capelle, B. "Hippolyte de Rome." *Recherches de Théologie Ancienne et Médiévale* 17 (1950), 145–174.

———— "À propos d'Hippolyte de Rome." *Recherches de Théologie Ancienne et Médiévale* 19 (1952), 193–202.

Casey, P. M. "Porphyry and the Origin of the Book of Daniel." *Journal of Theological Studies,* n.s. 27 (1976), 15–33.

Casey, R. P. "An Early Homily on the Devil Ascribed to Athanasius of Alexandria." *Journal of Theological Studies,* 36 (1935), 1–10.

Caspar, E. *Die älteste römische Bischofsliste. Schriften der Königsberger Gelehrten Gesellschaft,* Geisteswissenschaftliche Klasse 2.4 (Berlin, 1926), 209–472.

———— "Kleine Beiträge zur älteren Papstgeschichte." *Zeitschrift für Kirchengeschichte* 46 (1927), 321–355; 47 (1928), 162–202.

Castiglione, L. "Diocletianus und die Blemmyes." *Zeitschrift für Ägyptische Sprache* 96 (1970), 90–103.

Castritius, H. *Studien zu Maximinus Daia. Frankfurter althistorische Studien* 2. Kallmünz, 1969.

Cavallera, F. "Paul de Thèbes et Paul d'Oxyrhynque." *Revue d'Ascétique et de Mystique* 7 (1926), 302–305.

Chadwick, H. "The Fall of Eustathius of Antioch." *Journal of Theological Studies,* 49 (1948), 27–35.

———— "Athanasius, *De Decretis* XL. 3." *Journal of Theological Studies,* 49 (1948) 168–169.

———— "The Evidences of Christianity in the Apologetic of Origen." *Studia Patristica* 2. *Texte und Untersuchungen* 64 (Berlin, 1957), 331–339.

———— "Ossius of Cordova and the Presidency of the Council of Antioch, 325." *Journal of Theological Studies,* n.s. 9 (1958), 292–304.

——— "Faith and Order at the Council of Nicaea: A Note on the Background of the Sixth Canon." *Harvard Theological Review* 53 (1960), 171–195.

——— "The Origin of the Title 'Oecumenical Council.' " *Journal of Theological Studies,* n.s. 23 (1972), 132–135.

Chastagnol, A. "Observations sur le consulat suffect et la préture du Bas-Empire." *Revue Historique* 219 (1958), 221–253.

——— "Zosime II, 38 et l'Histoire Auguste." *Bonner Historia-Augusta-Colloquium 1964/65* (1966), 43–78.

——— "Un gouverneur constantinien de Tripolitaine: Laenatius Romulus, *Praeses* en 324–326." *Latomus* 25 (1966), 539–552.

——— "Les préfets du prétoire de Constantin." *Revue des Études Anciennes* 70 (1968), 321–352.

——— "Les modes de recrutement du sénat au IVᵉ siècle après J. C." *Recherches sur les structures sociales dans l'Antiquité classique,* 187–211. Paris, 1970.

——— "Constantin et le sénat." *Atti dell'Accademia Romanistica Costantiniana. 2° Convegno Internazionale,* 51–69. Perugia, 1976.

Chaumont, M. L. "L'inscription de Kartīr à la 'Ka'bah de Zoroastre.' " *Journal Asiatique* 248 (1960), 339–380.

Chéhab, M. "Tyr à l'époque romaine: Aspects de la cité à la lumière des textes et des fouilles." *Mélanges de l'Université Saint Joseph* 38 (1962), 13–40.

Chesnut, G. F. "Fate, Fortune, Free Will and Nature in Eusebius." *Church History* 42 (1973), 165–182. Reprinted in his *The First Christian Histories* (1977), 61–90.

——— *The First Christian Histories: Eusebius, Socrates, Sozomen, Theodoret and Evagrius. Théologie Historique* 46. Paris, 1977.

Chitty, D. J. "Pachomian Sources Reconsidered." *Journal of Ecclesiastical History* 5 (1954), 38–77.

——— "A Note on the Chronology of the Pachomian Foundations." *Studia Patristica 2. Texte und Untersuchungen* 64 (Berlin, 1957), 379–385.

Christensen, T. *C. Galerius Valerius Maximinus: Studier over Politik og Religion i Romerriget 305–13. Festskrift udgivet af Københavns Universitet i anledning af Hendes Majestaet Dronningens Fødselsdag 16. April 1974.* Copenhagen, 1974.

Clarke, G. W. "Some Victims of the Persecution of Maximinus Thrax." *Historia* 15 (1966), 445–453.

——— "Some Observations on the Persecution of Decius." *Antichthon* 3 (1969), 63–76.

——— "Double Trials in the Persecution of Decius." *Historia* 22 (1973), 650–663.

——— "Two Measures in the Persecution of Decius? Two Recent Views." *Bulletin of the Institute of Classical Studies* 20 (1973), 118–123.

Clercq, V. C. de. *Ossius of Cordova: A Contribution to the History of the Constantinian Period.* Catholic University of America, *Studies in Christian Antiquity* 13. Washington, D.C., 1954.

Connolly, R. H. "Eusebius, *H. E.* v. 28." *Journal of Theological Studies* 49 (1948), 73–79.

Costa, G. "La battaglia di Costantino a Ponte Milvio (28 Ottobre 312)." *Bilychnis* 2 (1913), 197–208.

Coüasnon, C. *The Church of the Holy Sepulchre in Jerusalem,* London, 1974.

Courcelle, P. "Les exégèses chrétiennes de la quatrième églogue." *Revue des Études Anciennes* 59 (1957), 294–319.

—— "Ambroise de Milan et Calcidius." *Romanitas et Christianitas. Studia I. H. Waszink Oblata,* 45–53. Amsterdam and London, 1973.

Cranz, F. E. "Kingdom and Polity in Eusebius of Caesarea." *Harvard Theological Review* 45 (1952), 47–66.

Crawford, M. H. and Reynolds, J. M. "The Publication of the Prices Edict: A New Inscription from Aezani." *Journal of Roman Studies* 65 (1975), 160–163.

—— "The Aezani Copy of the Prices Edict." *Zeitschrift für Papyrologie und Epigraphik* 34 (1979), 163–210.

Crouzel, H. "Origène devant l'Incarnation et devant l'histoire." *Bulletin de Littérature Ecclésiastique* 61 (1960), 81–110.

—— "Origène et le sens litéral dans ses 'Homélies sur l'Hexateuque.'" *Bulletin de Littérature Ecclésiastique* 70 (1969), 241–263.

—— "L'école d'Origène à Césarée: Postscriptum à une édition de Grégoire le Thaumaturge." *Bulletin de Littérature Ecclésiastique* 71 (1970), 15–27.

—— "Qu'a voulu faire Origène en composant le *Traité des Principes?*" *Bulletin de Littérature Ecclésiastique* 76 (1975), 161–186, 241–260.

—— "Le christianisme de l'empereur Philippe l'Arabe." *Gregorianum* 56 (1975), 545–550.

Curle, J. "An Inventory of Objects of Roman and Provincial Roman Origin Found on Sites in Scotland Not Definitely Associated with Roman Construction." *Proceedings of the Society of Antiquaries of Scotland* 66 (1931–32), 277–400.

Daly, L. W. *Contributions to a History of Alphabetization in Antiquity and the Middle Ages. Collection Latomus* 90. Brussels, 1967.

Daunoy, F. "La question pascale au concile de Nicée." *Échos d'Orient* 24 (1925), 424–444.

Decker, D. de. "La politique religieuse de Maxence." *Byzantion* 38 (1968), 472–562.

—— "Le 'Discours à l'Assemblée des Saints' attribué à Constantin et l'oeuvre de Lactance." *Lactance et son temps. Théologie Historique 48, (Paris, 1978),* 75–87.

—— "Sur le destinataire de la lettre au roi des Perses (Eusèbe de Césarée, *Vit. Const.,* IV, 9–13) et la conversion de l'Arménie à la religion chrétienne." *Persica* 8 (1979), 99–116.

Decker, D. de, and Dupuis-Masay, G. "L' 'épiscopat' de l'empereur Constantin." *Byzantion* 50 (1980), 118–157.

Decret, F. "Les conséquences sur le christianisme en Perse de l'affrontement des empires romain et sassanide. De Shâpûr Ier à Yazdgard Ier." *Recherches Augustiniennes* 14 (1979), 91–152.

Deichmann, F. W. and Tschira, A. "Das Mausoleum der Kaiserin Helena und die Basilika der heiligen Marcellinus und Petrus an der Via Labicana vor Rom." *Jahrbuch des deutschen Archäologischen Instituts* 72 (1957), 44–110.

Delehaye, H. "Eusebii Caesariensis de Martyribus Palaestinae Longioris Libelli Fragmenta." *Analecta Bollandiana* 16 (1897), 113–139.

⸻ "Saints de Thrace et de Mésie." *Analecta Bollandiana* 31 (1912), 161–300.

⸻ "La passion de S. Félix de Thibiuca." *Analecta Bollandiana* 39 (1921), 241–276.

⸻ "La personnalité historique de Saint Paul de Thèbes." *Analecta Bollandiana* 44 (1926), 64–69.

Delling, G. "Speranda futura: Jüdische Grabinschriften Italiens über das Geschick nach dem Tode." *Theologische Literaturzeitung* 76 (1951), 521–526.

Desanges, J. "Le statut et les limites de la Nubie romaine." *Chronique d'Égypte* 44 (1969), 139–147.

Dessau, H. "Über einige Inschriften aus Cirta." *Hermes* 15 (1880), 471–474.

Devos, P. "L'oeuvre de Guarimpotus, hagiographe napolitain." *Analecta Bollandiana* 76 (1958), 151–187.

⸻ "Une passion grecque inédite de Saint Pierre d'Alexandrie et sa traduction par Anastase le Bibliothécaire." *Analecta Bollandiana* 83 (1965), 157–187.

⸻ "Les martyrs persans à travers leurs actes syriaques." *La Persia e il mondo greco-romano.* Accademia Nazionale dei Lincei, *Problemi attuali di Scienza e di Cultura* 76 (Rome, 1966), 213–225.

Devreesse, R. "La chaîne sur les Psaumes de Daniele Barbaro." *Revue Biblique* 33 (1924), 65–81, 498–521.

⸻ "L'édition du commentaire d'Eusèbe de Césarée sur Isaïe." *Revue Biblique* 42 (1933), 540–555.

Dölger, F. J. "Die Taufe Konstantins und ihre Probleme." *Konstantin der Grosse und seine Zeit,* ed. by F. J. Dölger. *Römische Quartalschrift,* Supplementband 19, 377–447. Freiburg, 1913.

Dörrie, H. "Zur Geschichte der Septuaginta im Jahrhundert Konstantins." *Zeitschrift für die neutestamentliche Wissenschaft* 39 (1940), 57–110.

Dörries, H. "Die *Vita Antonii* als Geschichtsquelle." *Nachrichten der Akademie der Wissenschaften in Göttingen,* Philologisch-historische Klasse 1949, 357–410. Reprinted in his *Wort und Stunde* 1 (Göttingen, 1966), 145–224.

⸻ *Das Selbstzeugnis Kaiser Konstantins. Abhandlungen der Akademie der Wissenschaften in Göttingen,* Philologisch-historische Klasse[3] 34. Göttingen, 1954.

Dontas, G. "Collection Paul Canellopoulos IX: Portrait de Galère." *Bulletin de Correspondance Hellénique* 99 (1975), 521–533.

Downey, G. "Constantine's Churches at Antioch, Tyre and Jerusalem (Notes on Architectural Terms)." *Mélanges de l'Université Saint Joseph* 38 (1962), 191–196.

Duchesne, L. "Le Concile d'Elvire et les flamines chrétiens." *Mélanges Renier. Bibliothèque de l'École des Hautes Études* 73 (Paris, 1887), 159–174.

⸻ "Le dossier du Donatisme." *Mélanges d'Archéologie et d'Histoire de l'École Française de Rome* 10 (1890), 589–650.

⸻ "L'Arménie chrétienne dans l'*Histoire Ecclésiastique* d'Eusèbe." *Mélanges Nicole,* 105–109. Geneva, 1905.

Duncan-Jones, R. P. "An African Saint and His Interrogator." *Journal of Theological Studies* n.s. 25 (1974), 106–110.

Dunlap, J. E. *The Office of the Grand Chamberlain in the Later Roman and Byzantine Empires.* University of Michigan Studies, Humanistic Series 14: *Two Studies in Later Roman and Byzantine Administration,* 161–324. Ann Arbor, 1924.

Dupont, C. *Les constitutions de Constantin et le droit privé au debut du IVe siècle: Les personnes.* Lille, 1937.

—— *Le droit criminel dans les constitutions de Constantin: Les infractions.* Lille, 1953.

—— *Le droit criminel dans les constitutions de Constantin: Les peines.* Lille, 1955.

—— "La vente dans les constitutions de Constantin." *Revue Internationale des droits de l'Antiquité*[3] 2 (1955), 237–262.

—— "Les donations dans les constitutions de Constantin." *Revue Internationale des Droits de l'Antiquité*[3] 9 (1962), 291–324.

—— *La réglementation économique dans les constitutions de Constantin.* Lille, 1963.

—— "Les successions dans les constitutions de Constantin." *Iura* 15 (1964), 57–116.

—— "Les privilèges des clercs sous Constantin." *Revue de l'Histoire Ecclésiastique* 62 (1967), 729–752.

—— "Les textes constantiniens et le prefet de la ville." *Revue Historique de Droit Français et Étranger* 47 (1969), 613–644.

—— "Décisions et textes constantiniens dans les oeuvres d'Eusèbe de Césarée." *Viator* 2 (1971), 1–32.

—— "Les constitutions *ad populum.*" *Revue Historique de Droit Français et Étranger* 49 (1971), 586–600.

Ebert, A. "Über den Verfasser des Buches 'De mortibus persecutorum.' " *Berichte über die Verhandlungen der königlichen sächsischen Gesellschaft der Wissenschaften zu Leipzig,* Philologisch-historische Classe 22 (1870), 115–138.

Eck, W. "Das Eindringen des Christentums in den Senatorenstand bis zu Konstantin d. Gr." *Chiron* 1 (1971), 381–406.

Eger, H. "Kaiser und Kirche in der geschichtlichen Theologie Eusebs von Caesarea." *Zeitschrift für die neutestamentliche Wissenschaft* 38 (1939), 97–115.

Egger, R. "Aus dem Leben der donauländischen Wehrbauern." *Anzeiger der österreichischen Akademie der Wissenschaften,* Philosophisch-historische Klasse 86 (1949), Nr. 1, 1–26. Reprinted in his *Römische Antike und frühes Christentum* 2 (Klagenfurt, 1963), 51–68.

—— "Das Goldkreuz am Grabe Petri." *Anzeiger der österreichischen Akademie der Wissenschaften,* Philosophisch-historische Klasse 1959, Nr. 12, 182–202. Reprinted in his *Römische Antike* 2 (1963), 304–320.

—— *Das Labarum, die Kaiserstandarte der Spätantike. Sitzungsberichte der österreichischen Akademie der Wissenschaften,* Philosophisch-historische Klasse 234, Abhandlung 1. Vienna, 1960. Reprinted in his *Römische Antike* 2 (1963), 325–344.

Ehrhardt, A. "Die griechische Patriarchal-Bibliothek von Jerusalem: Ein Beitrag zur griechischen Paläographie." *Römische Quartalschrift* 5 (1891), 217–265, 329–331, 383–384; 6 (1892), 339–365.

Ehrhardt, A. A. T. "Das Corpus Christi und die Korporationen im spätrömischen Recht." *Zeitschrift der Savigny-Stiftung,* Romanistische Abteilung 70 (1953), 299–347; 71 (1954), 25–40.

————— "Constantin d. Gr. Religionspolitik und Gesetzgebung." *Zeitschrift der Savigny-Stiftung,* Romanistische Abteilung 72 (1955), 127–190. Reprinted in *Konstantin der Grosse,* ed. H. Kraft, *Wege der Forschung* 131 (Darmstadt, 1974), 388–456.

Eichholz, D. E. "Constantius Chlorus' Invasion of Britain." *Journal of Roman Studies* 43 (1953), 41–46.

Eissfeldt, O. *Taautos und Sanchunjaton. Sitzungsberichte der deutschen Akademie der Wissenschaften zu Berlin,* Klasse für Sprachen, Literatur und Kunst 1952, Nr. 1. Berlin, 1952.

————— "Art und Aufbau der phönizischen Geschichte des Philo von Byblos." *Syria* 33 (1956), 88–96. Reprinted in his *Kleine Schriften* 3 (Tübingen, 1966), 398–406.

————— "Phönikische und griechische Kosmogonie." *Éléments Orientaux dans la Religion Grecque Ancienne.* Paris, 1960, 1–16. Reprinted in his *Kleine Schriften* 3 (1966), 501–512.

Ensslin, W. "Zum Heermeisteramt des spätrömishen Reiches." *Klio* 23 (1930), 306–325; 24 (1931), 102–147, 467–502.

————— "Zu dem vermuteten Feldzug des rex Hannibalianus." *Klio* 29 (1936), 102–110.

————— "Literatur zur späteren Kaiserzeit aus dem Jahre 1939." *Klio* 33 (1940), 349–368.

————— "Bericht über deutsche Veröffentlichungen zur byzantinischen Geschichte aus den Jahren 1939–1947." *Byzantion* 18 (1948), 261–302.

Évrard, G. "Une inscription inédite d'Aqua Viva et la carrière des Iunii Bassi." *Mélanges d'Archéologie et d'Histoire de l'École Française de Rome* 74 (1962), 607–647.

Ewig, E. "Das Bild Constantins des Grossen in den ersten Jahrhunderten des abendländischen Mittelalters." *Historisches Jahrbuch* 75 (1956), 1–46. Reprinted in *Das byzantinische Herrscherbild,* ed. H. Hunger, *Wege der Forschung* 341 (Darmstadt, 1975), 133–192.

Fabbrini, F. *La manumissio in ecclesia.* Università di Roma, *Pubblicazioni dell'Istituto di Diritto Romano* 40. Rome, 1965.

Farina, R. *L'impero e l'imperatore cristiano in Eusebio di Cesarea: La prima teologica politica del Cristianesimo.* Zürich, 1966.

Faulhaber, M. *Die griechischen Apologeten der klassischen Väterzeit. I. Buch: Eusebius von Caesarea.* Diss., Würzburg, 1895.

Fiey, J.-M. "Auteur et date de la 'Chronique d'Arbèles.'" *L'Orient Syrien* 12 (1967), 265–302.

————— *Jalons pour une histoire de l'Église en Iraq. Corpus Scriptorum Christianorum Orientalium* 310, Subsidia 36. Louvain, 1970.

Fischer, H. "Geschichte der Kartographie von Palästina." *Zeitschrift des deutschen Palästina-Vereins* 62 (1939), 169–189.

Fischer, J. A. "Die antimontanistischen Synoden des 2./3. Jahrhunderts." *Annuarium Historiae Conciliorum* 6 (1974), 241–273.

—— "Angebliche Synoden des 2. Jahrhunderts." *Annuarium Historiae Conciliorum* 9 (1977), 241–252.

Fowden, G. "Bishops and Temples in the Eastern Roman Empire, A.D. 320–445." *Journal of Theological Studies*, n.s. 29 (1978), 53–78.

Franchi de' Cavalieri, P. "La *Passio* dei Martiri Abitinensi." *Note agiografiche* 8. *Studi e Testi* 65 (Vatican, 1935), 3–71.

Frank, R. I. *Scholae Palatinae: The Palace Guards of the Later Roman Empire. Papers of the American Academy in Rome* 23. Rome, 1969.

Frend, W. H. C., and Clancy, K. "When did the Donatist Schism Begin?" *Journal of Theological Studies*, n.s. 28 (1977), 104–109.

Freudenberger, R. "Der Vorwurf ritueller Verbrechen gegen die Christen im 2. und 3. Jahrhundert." *Theologische Zeitschrift* 23 (1967), 97–107.

—— *Das Verhalten der römischen Behörden gegen die Christen im 2. Jahrhundert. Münchener Beiträge zur Papyrusforschung* 52. Munich, 1967.

Fritze, E. *Beiträge zur sprachlich-stilistischen Würdigung des Eusebios.* Diss., Munich; publ. Borna-Leipzig, 1910.

Frolow, A. "La dédicace de Constantinople dans la tradition byzantine." *Revue de l'Histoire des Religions* 127 (1944), 61–127.

Gaiffier, B. de. "*Sub Daciano praeside*: Étude de quelques passions espagnoles." *Analecta Bollandiana* 72 (1954), 378–396.

—— "Palatins et eunuques dans quelques documents hapiographiques." *Analecta Bollandiana* 75 (1957), 17–46.

Galletier, E. "La mort de Maximien d'après le panégyrique de 310 et la vision de Constantin au temple d'Apollon." *Revue des Études Anciennes* 52 (1950), 288–299.

Galtier, P. "L'*homoousios* de Paul de Samosate." *Recherches de Science Religieuse* 12 (1922), 30–45.

Gascou, J. "Le rescrit d'Hispellum." *Mélanges d'Archéologie et d'Histoire de l'École Française de Rome* 79 (1967), 600–659.

Gaudemet, J. "La legislation religieuse de Constantin." *Revue de l'Histoire de l'Église de France* 33 (1947), 25–61.

—— "Constantin, restaurateur de l'ordre." *Studi in onore di S. Solazzi*, 652–674. Naples, 1948.

—— "Constantin et le recrutement des corporations." *Atti del Congresso Internazionale di Diritto Romano e di Storia di Diritto* 3 (Milan, 1951), 17–25.

—— "Constantin et les curies municipales." *Iura* 2 (1951), 44–75.

Gelzer, H. *Sextus Julius Africanus und die byzantinische Chronographie.* Leipzig, 1880–1898.

Gelzer, M. "Der Urheber der Christenverfolgung von 303." *Wesen und Wandel der Kirche. Festschrift E. Vischer*, 35–43. Basel, 1935. Reprinted in his *Kleine Schriften* 2 (Wiesbaden, 1963), 378–386.

Gerland, E. *Konstantin der Grosse in Geschichte und Sage. Texte und Forschungen zur byzantinisch-neugriechischer Philologie* 23. Athens, 1937.

Girardet, K. M. *Kaisergericht und Bischofsgericht: Studien zu den Anfängen des*

Donatistenstreites (313–315) und zum Prozess Athanasius von Alexandrien (328–346). Antiquitas 1.21. Bonn, 1975.

Goffart, W. *Caput and Colonate: Towards a History of Late Roman Taxation. Phoenix,* Supplementary Volume 12. Toronto, 1974.

Görres, F. *Kritische Untersuchungen über die licinianische Christenverfolgung: Ein Beitrag zur Kritik der Märtyreracten.* Jena, 1875.

Graetz, H. "Hillel, der Patriarchensohn." *Monatschrift für Geschichte und Wissenschaft des Judentums* 30 (1881), 433–443.

Graindor, P. "Constantin le Grand et le dadouque Nicagoras." *Byzantion* 3 (1926), 209–214.

Grant, R. M. "Porphyry among the Early Christians." *Romanitas et Christianitas. Studia I. H. Waszink Oblata,* 181–187. Amsterdam and London, 1973.

——— "Eusebius and His Lives of Origen." *Forma Futuri: Studi in onore del Cardinale M. Pellegrino,* 635–649. Turin, 1975.

——— "The Case against Eusebius or, Did the Father of Church History Write History?" *Studia Patristica* 12. *Texte und Untersuchungen* 115 (Berlin, 1975), 413–421.

——— "The Religion of Maximin Daia." *Christianity, Judaism and Other Greco-Roman Cults: Studies for M. Smith* 4. *Studies in Judaism in Late Antiquity* 12 (Leiden, 1975), 143–166.

Green, R. P. H. "Prosopographical Notes on the Family and Friends of Ausonius." *Bulletin of the Institute of Classical Studies* 25 (1978), 19–27.

Gregg, R. C., and Groh, D. E. "The Centrality of Soteriology in Early Arianism." *Anglican Theological Review* 59 (1977), 260–278.

Grégoire, H. "La 'conversion' de Constantin." *Revue de l'Université de Bruxelles* 36 (1930–31), 231–272.

——— "La statue de Constantin et le signe de la croix." *L'Antiquité Classique* 1 (1932), 135–143.

——— "Deux champs de bataille: 'Campus Ergenus' et 'Campus Ardiensis.' " *Byzantion* 13 (1938), 585–586.

——— "La vision de Constantin 'liquidée.' " *Byzantion* 14 (1939), 341–351.

——— "L'authenticité et l'historicité de la *Vita Constantini* attribuée à Eusèbe de Césarée." *Bulletin de l'Académie Royale de Belgique,* Classe des Lettres[5] 39 (1953), 462–479.

Gressmann, H. *Studien zu Eusebs Theophanie. Texte und Untersuchungen* 23.3. Leipzig, 1903.

Grigg, R. "Constantine the Great and the Cult without Images." *Viator* 8 (1977), 1–32.

Groag, E. "Der Dichter Porfyrius in einer stadtrömischen Inschrift." *Wiener Studien* 45 (1926/7), 102–109.

Grosso, F. "La 'Vita di Apollonio di Tiana' come fonte storico." *Acme* 7 (1954), 333–533.

Gsell, S. "Chronique africaine: Archéologie et histoire ancienne. Année 1893." *Revue Africaine* 38 (1894), 109–233.

Guadagno, E., and Panciera, S. "Nuove testimonianze sul governo della Campania in età constantiniana." *Rendiconti della Accademia Nazionale dei Lincei,*[8] Classe di Scienze morali, storiche e filologiche 25 (1970), 111–129.

Gustafsson, B. "Hegesippus' Sources and His Reliability." *Studia Patristica* 3. *Texte und Untersuchungen* 78 (Berlin, 1961), 227–232.

———— "Eusebius' Principles in Handling His Sources, as Found in His 'Church History,' Books I–VII." *Studia Patristica* 4. *Texte und Untersuchungen* 79 (Berlin, 1961), 429–441.

Guthrie, P. "The Execution of Crispus." *Phoenix* 20 (1966), 325–331.

Gutzwenger, E. "Papias: Eine chronologische Studie." *Zeitschrift für katholische Theologie* 69 (1947), 385–416.

Gwatkin, H. M. *Studies of Arianism Chiefly Referring to the Character and Chronology of the Reaction which Followed the Council of Nicaea*[2]. Cambridge, 1900.

Gwilliam, G. H. "The Ammonian Sections, Eusebian Canons, and Harmonizing Tables in the Syriac Tetraevangelium." *Studia Biblica et Ecclesiastica* 2 (Oxford, 1890), 241–271.

Hagedorn, D., and Merkelbach, R. "Ein neues Fragment aus Porphyrios 'Gegen die Christen.' " *Vigiliae Christianae* 20 (1966), 86–90.

Hanson, R. P. C. "Interpretations of Hebrew Names in Origen." *Vigiliae Christianae* 10 (1956), 103–123.

———— *Allegory and Event: A Study of the Sources and Significance of Origen's Interpretation of Scripture*. London, 1959.

———— "A Note on Origen's Self-Mutilation." *Vigiliae Christianae* 20 (1966), 81–82.

Harl, M. "Recherches sur le *Peri arkhon* d'Origène en vue d'une nouvelle édition: La division en chapitres." *Studia Patristica* 3. *Texte und Untersuchungen* 78 (Berlin, 1961), 57–67.

———— "L'histoire de l'humanité racontée par un écrivain chrétien au début du IVᵉ siècle." *Revue des Études Grecques* 75 (1962), 522–531.

Harnack, A. "Die griechische Übersetzung des 'Apologeticus' Tertullians." *Texte und Untersuchungen* 8.4 (Leipzig, 1892), 1–36.

———— "Die Hypotyposen des Theognost." *Texte und Untersuchungen* 24.3 (Leipzig, 1903), 73–92.

———— "Der gefälschte Brief des Bischofs Theonas an den Oberkammerherrn Lucian." *Texte und Untersuchungen* 24.3 (Leipzig, 1903), 93–117.

———— *Porphyrius, "Gegen die Christen", 15 Bücher: Zeugnisse, Fragmente und Referate. Abhandlungen der königlichen preussischen Akademie der Wissenschaften,* Philosophisch-historische Klasse 1916, Nr. 1. Berlin, 1916.

———— *Der Kirchengeschichtliche Ertrag der exegetischen Arbeiten des Origenes. Texte und Untersuchungen* 42.3 (Leipzig, 1918), 1–96; 42.4. Leipzig, 1919.

———— *Marcion: Das Evangelium vom Fremden Gott.*[2] *Texte und Untersuchungen* 45. Leipzig, 1924.

Hartmann, W. *Konstantin der Grosse als Christ und Philosoph in seinen Briefen und Erlassen*. Programm, Fürstenwalde, 1902.

Hatt, J.-J. "Le vision de Constantin au sanctuaire de Grand et l'origine celtique du labarum." *Latomus* 9 (1950), 427–436.

Hebbelynck, A. "Les *kephalaia* et les *titloi* des Évangiles." *Le Muséon* 41 (1928), 81–120.

Heck, E. *Die dualistischen Zusätze und die Kaiseranreden bei Lactantius: Untersuchungen zur Textgeschichte der "Divinae Institutiones" und der Schrift*

"De opificio dei." *Abhandlungen der Heidelberger Akademie der Wissenschaften,* Philosophisch-historische Klasse 1972, Abhandlung 2. Heidelberg, 1972.

Heinrici, G. "Zur patristischen Aporienliteratur." *Abhandlungen der königlichen sächsischen Gesellschaft der Wissenschaften,* Philologisch-historische Klasse 27 (1909), 841–860.

Helm, R. *Eusebius' "Chronik" und ihre Tabellenform. Abhandlungen der preussischen Akademie der Wissenschaften,* Philosophisch-historische Klasse 1923, Nr. 4. Berlin, 1924.

―――― "De Eusebii in Chronicorum libro auctoribus." *Eranos* 22 (1924), 1–40.

―――― "Hieronymus und Eutrop." *Rheinisches Museum,* N.F. 76 (1927), 138–170, 254–306.

―――― *Hieronymus' Zusätze in Eusebius' "Chronik" und ihr Wert für die Literaturgeschichte. Philologus,* Supplementband 21.2. Leipzig, 1929.

―――― "Die neuesten Hypothesen zu Eusebius' (Hieronymus') 'Chronik.'" *Sitzungsberichte der preussischen Akademie der Wissenschaften,* Philosophisch-historische Klasse 1929, 371–408.

Hendy, M. "Mint and Fiscal Administration under Diocletian, His Colleagues and His Successors, A.D. 305–24." *Journal of Roman Studies* 62 (1972), 75–82.

Henning, W. B. "Mani's Last Journey." *Bulletin of the School of Oriental and African Studies* 10 (1940–42), 941–953.

―――― "A Farewell to the Khagan of the Aq-Aqatärän." *Bulletin of the School of Oriental and African Studies* 14 (1952), 501–522.

Henrichs, A. "Scholia Minora zu Homer." *Zeitschrift für Papyrologie und Epigraphik* 7 (1971), 97–149, 229–260; 8 (1971), 1–12; 12 (1973), 17–43.

―――― "Mani and the Babylonian Baptists: A Historical Confrontation." *Harvard Studies in Classical Philology* 77 (1973), 23–59.

―――― "The Cologne Mani Codex Reconsidered." *Harvard Studies in Classical Philology* 83 (1979), 339–367.

Henrichs, A., and Koenen, L. "Ein griechischer Mani-Codex (P. Colon. inv. nr. 4780)." *Zeitschrift für Papyrologie und Epigraphik* 5 (1970), 97–216.

―――― "Der Kölner Mani-Codex (P. Colon. inv. nr. 4780) *Peri tes gennes tou somatos autou." Zeitschrift für Papyrologie und Epigraphik* 19 (1975), 1–85; 32 (1978), 87–199.

Henry, P. *Recherches sur la "Préparation Évangelique" d'Eusèbe et l'édition perdue des oeuvres de Plotin publiée par Eustochius.* Paris, 1935.

Hertling, L. "Die Zahl der Christen zu Beginn des vierten Jahrhunderts." *Zeitschrift für katholische Theologie* 58 (1934), 243–253.

Herzfeld, E. *Paikuli, Monument and Inscription of the Early History of the Sasanian Empire. Forschungen zur islamischen Kunst* 3. Berlin, 1924.

Hiller, E. "Eusebius und Cyrillus." *Rheinisches Museum,* N.F. 25 (1870), 253–262.

Holl, K. "Über die Gregor von Nyssa zugeschriebene Schrift 'Adversus Arium et Sabellium.'" *Zeitschrift für Kirchengeschichte* 25 (1904), 380–398. Reprinted in his *Gesammelte Aufsätze zur Kirchengeschichte* 2 (Tübingen, 1928), 298–309.

―――― "Die Bedeutung der neuveröffentlichten melitianischen Urkunden für die Kirchengeschichte." *Sitzungsberichte der preussischen Akademie der Wissenschaften,* Philosophisch-historische Klasse 1925, 18–31. Reprinted in his *Gesammelte Aufsätze* 2 (1928), 283–297.

Honigman, E. *Patristic Studies. Studi e Testi* 173. Vatican, 1953.

Honoré, A. M. " 'Imperial' Rescripts, A.D. 193–305: Authorship and Authenticity." *Journal of Roman Studies* 69 (1979), 51–64.

Hopfe, L. M., and Lease, G. "The Caesarea Mithraeum: A Preliminary Announcement." *Biblical Archaeologist* 38 (1975), 2–10.

Horbury, W. "Tertullian on the Jews in the Light of *De Spectaculis* xxx.5–6." *Journal of Theological Studies,* n.s. 23 (1972), 455–459.

Hornschuh, M. "Das Leben des Origenes und die Entstehung der alexandrinischen Schule." *Zeitschrift für Kirchengeschichte* 71 (1960), 1–25, 193–214.

Horst, P. W. van der, and Mansfeld, J. *An Alexandrian Platonist against Dualism: Alexander of Lycopolis' Treatise "Critique of the Doctrines of Manichaeus" Translated, with an Introduction and Notes.* Leiden, 1974. Reprinted from *Theta Pi* 3 (1974), 1–97.

Hyldahl, N. "Hegesipps Hypomnemata." *Studia Theologia* 14 (1960), 70–113.

Jacoby, F. *Apollodors "Chronik": Eine Sammlung der Fragmente. Philologische Untersuchungen* 16. Berlin, 1902.

Jagelitz, K. *Über den Verfasser der Schrift "De Mortibus Persecutorum."* Programm, Berlin, 1910.

Jahn, J. "Zur Geld- und Wirtschaftspolitik Diokletians." *Jahrbuch für Numismatik und Geldgeschichte* 25 (1975), 91–105.

Jeločnik, *Centurska zakladna najdba: Folisov Maksencija in Tetrahije [The Centur Hoard: Folles of Maxentius and of the Tetrarchy].* Situla 12. Ljubljana, 1973.

Jones, A. H. M. *Constantine and the Conversion of Europe.* London, 1949.

———— *"Capitatio* and *Iugatio." Journal of Roman Studies* 47 (1957), 88–94. Reprinted in his *The Roman Economy: Studies in Ancient Economic and Administrative History* (Oxford, 1974), 280–292.

Jones, C. P. "An Epigram on Apollonius of Tyana." *Journal of Hellenic Studies* 100 (1980), 190–194.

Judge, E. A. "The Earliest Use of Monachos for 'Monk' (P. Coll. Youtie 77) and the Origins of Monasticism." *Jahrbuch für Antike und Christentum* 20 (1977), 72–89.

Judge, E. A., and Pickering, S. R. "Papyrus Documentation of Church and Community in Egypt to the Mid-Fourth Century." *Jahrbuch für Antike und Christentum* 20 (1977), 47–71.

Kaegi, W. "Vom Nachleben Konstantins." *Schweizerische Zeitschrift für Geschichte* 8 (1958), 289–326.

Kähler, H. "Konstantin 313." *Jahrbuch des deutschen Archäologischen Instituts* 67 (1952), 1–30.

Kaniuth, A. *Die Beisetzung Konstantins des Grossen: Untersuchungen zur religiösen Haltung des Kaisers. Breslauer historische Forschungen* 18. Breslau, 1941.

Kannengiesser, C. "Où et quand Arius composa-t-il la *Thalie?" Kyriakon: Festschrift J. Quasten* 1 (Münster, 1970), 346–351.

Karayannopoulos, I. "Konstantin der Grosse und der Kaiserkult." *Historia* 5

(1956), 341–357. Reprinted in *Das byzantinische Herrscherbild,* ed. H. Hunger, *Wege der Forschung* 341 (Darmstadt, 1975), 109–132, and in *Romischer Kaiserkult,* ed. A. Wlosok, *Wege der Forschung* 372 (Darmstadt, 1978), 485–508.

Karpp, H. "Konstantin der Grosse und die Kirche." *Theologische Rundschau,* N.F. 19 (1950), 1–21.

Karst, J. "Notiz zu meiner Ausgabe der 'Chronik' des Eusebius." *Theologische Literaturzeitung* 36 (1911), 827–828.

Keaney, J. J. "Alphabetization in Harpocration's *Lexicon." Greek, Roman and Byzantine Studies* 14 (1973), 415–423.

Keller, E. *Eusèbe, historien des persécutions.* Geneva and Paris, 1912.

Keseling, P. "Die 'Chronik' des Eusebius in der syrischen Überlieferung." *Oriens Christianus*³ 1 (1926/7), 23–48, 223–241; 2 (1927), 33–56.

Kettler, F. H. "Der melitianische Streit in Ägypten." *Zeitschrift für die neutestamentliche Wissenschaft* 35 (1936), 155–193.

Keydell, R. *"Patria Hermoupoleos." Hermes* 71 (1936), 465–467.

Klijn, A. F. J. "Patristic Evidence for Jewish Christian and Aramaic Gospel Tradition." *Text and Interpretation. Studies in the New Testament Presented to M. Black,* 169–177. Cambridge, England, 1979.

Kloft, H. "Zur *Vita Constantini* I 14." *Historia* 19 (1970), 509–514.

Klostermann, E. *Eusebius' Schrift peri ton topikon onomaton ton en tei theiai graphei. Texte und Untersuchungen* 23.2b. Leipzig, 1902.

———— "Formen der exegetischen Arbeiten des Origenes." *Theologische Literaturzeitung* 72 (1947), 203–208.

Klotz, A. "Studien zu den 'Panegyrici Latini.'" *Rheinisches Museum,* N.F. 66 (1911), 513–572.

Knauber, A. "Das Anliegen der Schule des Origenes zu Cäsarea." *Münchener Theologische Zeitschrift* 19 (1968), 182–203.

Koch, H. "Die Zeit des Konzils von Elvira." *Zeitschrift für die neutestamentliche Wissenschaft* 17 (1916), 61–67.

Koenen, L. "Augustine and Manichaeism in Light of the Cologne Mani Codex." *Illinois Classical Studies* 3 (1978), 154–195.

———— "Manichäische Mission and Klöster in Ägypten." To appear in *Das römisch-byzantinische Ägypten. Ägyptica* 2. Trier, forthcoming.

Koep, L. "Die Konsekrationsmünzen Kaiser Konstantins und ihre religionspolitische Bedeutung." *Jahrbuch für Antike und Christentum* 1 (1958), 94–104. Reprinted in *Römischer Kaiserkult,* ed. A. Wlosok, *Wege der Forschung* 372 (Darmstadt, 1978), 509–527.

Koster, W. J. W. "De Arii et Eunomii sotadeis." *Mnemosyne*⁴ 16 (1963), 135–141.

Kotula, T. "En marge de l'usurpation africaine de L. Domitius Alexander." *Klio* 40 (1962), 159–177.

Kraft, H. *"Homoousios." Zeitschrift für Kirchengeschichte* 66 (1954/5), 1–24.

———— "Zur Taufe Kaiser Konstantins." *Studia Patristia* 1. *Texte und Untersuchungen* 63 (Berlin, 1957), 642–648.

Kraft, K. "Das Silbermedaillon Constantins des Grossen mit dem Christusmonogramm auf dem Helm." *Jahrbuch für Numismatik und Geldges-*

chichte 5/6 (1954/5), 151–178. Reprinted in *Konstantin der Grosse,* ed. H. Kraft, *Wege der Forschung* 131 (Darmstadt, 1974), 297–344.

Krautheimer, R. "Zu Konstantins Apostelkirche." *Mullus: Festschrift T. Klauser. Jahrbuch für Antike und Christentum,* Ergänzungsband 1 (Münster, 1964), 224–229.

—— "The Constantinian Basilica." *Dumbarton Oaks Papers* 21 (1967), 115–140.

Kubitschek, W. "Die Mosaikkarte Palaestinas." *Mitteilungen der kaiserlichen königlichen geographischen Gesellschaft in Wien* 43 (1900), 335–380.

—— "Ein Strassennetz in Eusebius' Onomastikon?" *Jahreshefte des österreichischen Archäologischen Instituts* 8 (1905), 119–127.

Kurfess, A. "Observatiunculae ad P. Vergilii Maronis eclogae quartae interpretationem et versionem Graecam." *Mnemosyne,* n.s. 40 (1912), 277–284.

—— "Das Akrostichon *Iesous Khreistos Theou Huios Soter Stauros.*" *Sokrates: Zeitschrift für das Gymnasialwesen,* N.F. 6 (1918), 99–105.

—— Summary of "Die christliche Deutung der vierten Ekloge Vergils in Kaiser Konstantins Rede an die heilige Versammlung." *Sokrates: Zeitschrift für das Gymnasialwesen,* N.F. 7 (1919), 337–338.

—— "Platos 'Timaeus' in Kaiser Konstantins Rede an die heilige Versammlung." *Zeitschrift für die neutestamentliche Wissenschaft* 19 (1919/20), 72–81.

—— "Vergils vierte Ekloge in Kaiser Konstantins Rede an die heilige Versammlung." *Jahresberichte des philologischen Vereins zu Berlin* 64 (1920), 90–96. Appendix to *Sokrates: Zeitschrift für das Gymnasialwesen,* N.F. 8 (1920).

—— "Kaiser Konstantins Rede an die versammelte Heiligen." *Pastor Bonus* 41 (1930), 115–124.

—— "Zu Kaiser Konstantins Rede an die Versammlung der Heiligen." *Philologische Wochenschrift* 50 (1930), 366–368.

—— "Ad versionem Graecam eclogae IV Vergilii." *Philologische Wochenschrift* 54 (1934), 1247.

—— "Latein-Griechisch." *Glotta* 25 (1936), 274–276.

—— "Ad Vergilii eclogae IV versionem Graecam." *Philologische Wochenschrift* 56 (1936), 364–367.

—— "Kaiser Konstantin und die Sibylle." *Theologische Quartalschrift* 117 (1936), 11–26.

—— "Der griechische Übersetzer von Vergils vierter Ekloge in Kaiser Konstantins Rede an die Versammlung der Heiligen." *Zeitschrift für die neutestamentliche Wissenschaft* 35 (1936), 97–100.

—— "Die griechische Übersetzung der vierten Ekloge Vergils." *Mnemosyne*[3] 5 (1937), 283–288.

—— "Zu Kaiser Konstantins Rede an die Versammlung der Heiligen." *Theologische Quartalschrift* 130 (1950), 145–165.

—— "Kaiser Konstantin und die Erythräische Sibylle." *Zeitschrift für Religions- und Geistesgeschichte* 4 (1952), 42–57.

Lacau, P. "Inscriptions latines du temple de Louxor." *Annales du Service des Antiquités de l'Égypte* 34 (1934), 17–46.

Laeuchli, S. *Power and Sexuality: The Emergence of Canon Law at the Synod of Elvira*. Philadelphia, 1972.

Lampe, G. W. H. "Some Notes on the Significance of *basileia tou theou, basileia Khristou* in the Greek Fathers." *Journal of Theological Studies* 49 (1948), 58–73.

Lancel, S. "Originalité de la province ecclésiastique de Byzacène au IVme et Vme siècles." *Cahiers de Tunisie* 12 (1964), 139–153.

——— "Aux origines du Donatisme et du mouvement des Circoncellions." *Cahiers de Tunisie* 15 (1967), 183–188.

——— "Les débuts du Donatisme: La date du 'protocole de Cirta' et de l'élection épiscopale de Silvanus." *Revue des Études Augustiniennes* 25 (1979), 217–229.

Landmann, K. von. "Konstantin der Grosse als Feldherr." *Konstantin der Grosse und seine Zeit,* ed. by F. J. Dölger. *Römische Quartalschrift,* Supplementband 19 (Freiburg, 1913), 143–154.

Laqueur, R. "Ephoros." *Hermes* 46 (1911), 161–206, 321–354.

Lathoud, D. "La consécration et la dédicace de Constantinople." *Échos d'Orient* 23 (1924), 289–314; 24 (1925), 180–201.

Laubscher, H. P. *Der Reliefschmuck des Galeriusbogens in Thessaloniki. Archäologische Forschungen* 1. Berlin, 1975.

Laurin, J.-R. *Orientations maîtresses des apologistes chrétiens de 270 à 361. Analecta Gregoriana* 61. Rome, 1954.

Lawlor, H. J. *Eusebiana: Essays on the "Ecclesiastical History" of Eusebius, Bishop of Caesarea*. Oxford, 1912.

——— "Eusebius on Papias." *Hermathena* 43 (1922), 167–222.

Lebon, J. "Sur un concile de Césaree." *Le Muséon* 51 (1938), 89–132.

Lefort, L.-T. "Les lettres festales de Saint Athanase." *Bulletin de l'Académie Royale de Belgique,* Classe des Lettres^5 39 (1953), 643–656.

Leroy, J. "Nouveaux témoins des 'Canons' d'Eusèbe illustrés selon la tradition syriaque." *Cahiers Archéologiques* 9 (1957), 117–140.

Levey, I. M. "Caesarea and the Jews." *The Joint Expedition to Caesarea Maritima* 1: *Studies in the History of Caesarea Maritima. Bulletin of the American Schools of Oriental Research,* Supplemental Studies 19 (Missoula, 1975), 43–78.

Levi, M. A. "La campagna di Costantino nell'Italia settentrionale (A. 312)." *Bolletino storico-bibliografico subalpino* 36 (1934), 1–10.

Levine, L. I. "À propos de la fondation de la Tour de Straton." *Revue Biblique* 80 (1973), 75–81.

——— "The Hasmonean Conquest of Strato's Tower." *Israel Exploration Journal* 24 (1974), 62–69.

——— "R. Abbahu of Caesarea." *Christianity, Judaism and Other Greco-Roman Cults: Studies for M. Smith* 4. *Studies In Judaism in Late Antiquity* 12 (Leiden, 1975), 56–76.

Lieberman, S. "The Martyrs of Caesarea." *Annuaire de l'Institut de Philologie et d'Histoire Orientales et Slaves* 7 (1939–44), 395–446.

——— "The Martyrs of Caesarea." *Jewish Quarterly Review* 36 (1945–46), 239–253.

Liebs, D. *Hermogenians Iuris Epitomae: Zum Stand der römischen Jurisprudenz im Zeitalter Diokletians. Abhandlungen der Akademie der Wissenschaften in Göttingen,* Philologisch-historische Klasse[3] 57. Göttingen, 1964.

Lietzmann, H. "Symbolstudien XIII." *Zeitschrift für die neutestamentliche Wissenschaft* 24 (1925), 193–202.

—— "Der Glaube Konstantins des Grossen." *Sitzungsberichte der preussichen Akademie der Wissenschaften,* Philosophisch-historische Klasse 1937, 263–275. Reprinted in his *Kleine Schriften* 1. *Texte und Untersuchungen* 67 (Berlin, 1958), 186–201.

Lifshitz, B. "Césarée de Palestine, son histoire et ses institutions." *Aufstieg und Niedergang der römischen Welt,* ed. H. Temporini and W. Haase, II.8, 490–518. Berlin and New York, 1977.

Lightfoot, J. B. "Eusebius of Caesarea." *Dictionary of Christian Biography* 2 (London, 1880), 308–348.

Loi, V. "Il libro quarto delle *Divinae Institutiones* fu da Lattanzio composto in Gallia?" *Mélanges Christine Mohrmann: Nouveau recueil offert par ses anciens élèves,* 61–79. Utrecht and Antwerp, 1973.

Loofs, F. *Paulus von Samosata: Eine Untersuchung zur altkirchlichen Literatur- und Dogmengeschichte. Texte und Untersuchungen* 44.5. Leipzig, 1924.

L'Orange, H. P. "Maurische Auxilien im Fries des Konstantinbogens." *Symbolae Osloenses* 13 (1934), 105–113.

—— "Sol Invictus Imperator: Ein Beitrag zur Apotheose." *Symbolae Osloense* 14 (1935), 86–114.

—— "Ein tetrarchisches Ehrendenkmal auf dem Forum Romanum." *Römische Mitteilungen* 53 (1938), 1–34.

L'Orange, H. P., and Gerkan, A. von. *Der spätantike Bildschmuck des Konstantinbogens. Studien zur spätantiken Kunstgeschichte* 10. Berlin, 1939.

Lorenz, R. "Das Problem der Nachsynode von Nicäa (327)." *Zeitschrift für Kirchengeschichte* 90 (1979), 22–40.

—— *Arius judaizans? Untersuchungen zur dogmengeschichtlichen Einordnung des Arius. Forschungen zur Kirchen- und Dogmengeschichte* 31. Göttingen, 1980.

Lot, F. *Nouvelles recherches sur l'impôt foncier et la capitation personelle sous le Bas-Empire. Bibliothèque de l'École des Hautes Études* 305. Paris, 1955.

Maas, P. "Die Metrik der 'Thaleia' des Areios." *Byzantinische Zeitschrift* 18 (1909), 511–515. Reprinted in his *Kleine Schriften,* 143–148. Munich, 1973.

MacMullen, R. "Constantine and the Miraculous." *Greek, Roman and Byzantine Studies* 9 (1968), 81–96.

Maehler, H. "Zur Amtszeit des Präfekten Sossianus Hierocles." *Collectanea Papyrologica: Texts Published in Honor of H. C. Youtie* 2. *Papyrologische Texte und Abhandlungen* 20 (Bonn, 1976), 527–533.

Malone, E. E. *The Monk and the Martyr.* Catholic University of America, *Studies in Christian Antiquity* 12. Washington, D.C., 1950.

Margheritis, M. "L'influenza di Platone sul pensiero e sull'arte di S. Metodio d'Olimpo." *Studi dedicati alla memoria di P. Ubaldi. Pubblicazioni della Università Cattolica del Sacro Cuore,* Serie Quinta: Scienze Storiche 16 (Milan, 1937), 401–412.

Marquart, J. *Ērānšahr nach der Geographie des Ps. Moses Xorenac'i. Abhand-*

lungen der königlichen Gesellschaft der Wissenschaften zu Göttingen, Philologisch-historische Klasse, N.F. 3.2. Göttingen, 1901.

Marrou, H.-I. "L'arianisme comme phénomène alexandrin." *Comptes Rendus de l'Académie des Inscriptions et Belles-Lettres* 1973, 533–542.

Martin, A. "Athanase et les Mélitiens (325–335)." *Politique et Théologie chez Athanase d'Alexandrie. Théologie Historique* 27 (Paris, 1974), 33–61.

Martin, C. "Le *Contra Noetum* de Saint Hippolyte: Fragment d'homélie ou finale du *Syntagma.*" *Revue d'Histoire Ecclésiastique* 37 (1941), 5–23.

Maurice, J. *Numismatique Constantinienne.* Paris, 1908–1912.

Mazzarino, S. *Antico, tardoantico ed èra constantiniana* 1. *Storia e civiltà* 13. Bari, 1974.

McArthur, H. K. "Eusebian Sections and Canons." *Catholic Biblical Quarterly* 27 (1965), 250–256.

Meijering, E. P. *Orthodoxy and Platonism in Athanasius: Synthesis or Antithesis?*[2] Leiden, 1974.

――― *"En Pote Hote Ouk En Ho Huios:* A Discussion on Time and Eternity." *Vigiliae Christianae* 28 (1974), 161–168. Reprinted in his *God Being History: Studies in Patristic Philosophy* (Amsterdam, 1975), 81–88.

Melamed, E. Z. "The *Onomastikon* of Eusebius." [In Hebrew] *Tarbiz* 3 (1931/2), 314–327, 393–407; 4 (1932/3), 78–96, 248–284.

Mensching, E. "Zur Calcidius-Überlieferung." *Vigiliae Christianae* 19 (1965), 42–56.

Mercati, G. "D'un palimpsesto Ambrosiano contenente i Salmi esapli e di un'antica versione latina del commentario perduto di Teodoro di Mopsuestia al Salterio." *Atti della Reale Accademia delle Scienze di Torino* 31 (1896), 655–676. Reprinted in his *Opere minori* 1. *Studi e Testi* 76 (Vatican, 1937), 318–338.

――― "Alcune note di letteratura patristica." *Rendiconti del Reale Istituto Lombardo di Scienze e Lettere*[2] 31 (1898), 1033–1052, 1191–1229. Reprinted in his *Opere minori* 2. *Studi e Testi* 77 (Vatican, 1937), 55–107.

――― *Note di letteratura biblica e cristiana antica. Studi e Testi* 5. Vatican, 1901.

――― *Nuove note di letteratura biblica e cristiana antica. Studi e Testi* 95. Vatican, 1941.

――― "Il problema della Colonna II dell'Esaplo." *Biblica* 28 (1947), 1–30, 173–215.

――― "La grande lacuna delle 'Ecloghe Profetiche' di Eusebio di Cesarea." *Mémorial L. Petit,* 1–3. Bucarest, 1948.

Meyer, E. "Apollonios von Tyana und die Biographie des Philostratos." *Hermes* 52 (1917), 371–424. Reprinted in his *Kleine Schriften* 2 (Halle, 1924), 131–191.

Meyer, P. "De Vita Constantiniana Eusebiana." *Festschrift dem Gymnasium Adolfinum zu Moers gewidmet,* 23–28. Bonn, 1882.

Millar, F. "P. Herennius Dexippus: The Greek World and the Third-Century Invasions." *Journal of Roman Studies* 59 (1969), 12–29.

――― "Paul of Samosata, Zenobia and Aurelian: The Church, Local Culture and Political Allegiance in Third-Century Syria." *Journal of Roman Studies* 61 (1971), 1–17.

———— *The Emperor in the Roman World (31 B.C.–A.D. 337)*. London, 1977.

Miller, J. "Bericht über die Literatur zur Geschichte des römischen Reiches von Diocletian bis Theodosius I. (284–395 n. Chr.) aus den Jahren 1915–1932." *Bursians Jahresbericht* 246 (1935), 43–130.

———— "Geschichte des römischen Reiches in der Zeit von Diokletian bis Theodosius I. (284–395 n. Chr.): Bericht über das Schrifttum der Jahre 1933 bis 1937." *Bursians Jahresbericht* 279 (1942), 237–365.

Minoprio, A. "A Restoration of the Basilica of Constantine, Rome." *Papers of the British School at Rome* 12 (1932), 1–25.

Möhle, A. "Der Jesaiakommentar des Eusebios von Kaisareia fast vollständig wieder aufgefunden." *Zeitschrift für die neutestamentliche Wissenschaft* 33 (1934), 87–89.

Molthagen, J. *Der römische Staat und die Christen im zweiten und dritten Jahrhundert. Hypomnemata* 28. Göttingen, 1970. (2nd ed., 1975)

Momigliano, A. "Pagan and Christian Historiography in the Fourth Century A.D." *The Conflict between Paganism and Christianity in the Fourth Century*, 79–99. Oxford, 1963.

Mommsen, T. "Über die Zeitfolge der Verordnungen Diocletians und seiner Mitregenten." *Abhandlungen der königlichen preussischen Akademie der Wissenschaften* 1860, 349–447. Reprinted in his *Gesammelte Schriften* 2 (Berlin, 1905), 195–291.

———— "Die armenischen Handschriften der 'Chronik' des Eusebius," *Hermes* 30 (1895), 321–328. Reprinted in his *Gesammelte Schriften* 7 (Berlin, 1909), 580–596.

Monteleone, C. *L'egloga quarta da Virgilio a Costantino: Critica del testo e ideologia*. Manduria, 1975.

Montzka, H. "Die Quellen zu den assyrisch-babylonischen Nachrichten in Eusebios' 'Chronik.' " *Klio* 2 (1902), 351–405.

Moreau, J. "Pont Milvius ou Saxa Rubra?" *Nouvelle Clio* 4 (1952), 369–373. Reprinted in his *Scripta Minora* (Heidelberg, 1964), 72–75.

———— "Zum Problem der *Vita Constantini*," *Historia* 4 (1955), 234–245. Reprinted in *Scripta Minora* (1964), 124–134.

Mosshammer, A. "Lucca Bibl. Capit. 490 and the Manuscript Tradition of Hieronymus' (Eusebius') 'Chronicle.' " *California Studies in Classical Antiquity* 8 (1976), 203–240.

———— *The "Chronicle" of Eusebius and the Greek Chronographic Tradition*. Lewisburg, Pa., and London, 1979.

Mras, K. "Nachwort zu den beiden letzten Ausgaben der 'Chronik' des Hieronymus." *Wiener Studien* 46 (1927/8), 200–215.

———— "Ein Vorwort zur neuen Eusebiusausgabe (mit Ausblicken auf die spätere Gräcität)." *Rheinisches Museum*, N.F. 92 (1944), 217–236.

———— "Die Stellung der 'Praeparatio Evangelica' des Eusebius im antiken Schrifttum." *Anzeiger der österreichischen Akademie der Wissenschaften*, Philosophisch-historische Klasse 1956, Nr. 17, 209–217.

Müller, K. *Beiträge zur Geschichte der Verfassung der alten Kirche. Abhandlungen der preussischen Akademie der Wissenschaften*, Philosophisch-historische Klasse 1922, Nr. 3. Berlin, 1922.

———— "Kleine Beiträge zur alten Kirchengeschichte." *Zeitschrift für die neutestamentliche Wissenschaft* 23 (1924), 214–246; 24 (1925), 278–292.

Müller, M. "Die Überlieferung des Eusebius in seiner *Kirchengeschichte* über die Schriften des N.T. und deren Verfasser." *Theologische Studien und Kritiken* 105 (1933), 425–455.

Mullins, T. Y. "Papias on Mark's Gospel." *Vigiliae Christianae* 14 (1960), 216–224.

Murray, C. "Art and the Early Church." *Journal of Theological Studies,* n.s. 28 (1977), 303–345.

Naoumides, M. "The Fragments of Greek Lexicography in the Papyri." *Classical Studies Presented to B. E. Perry. Illinois Studies in Language and Literature* 58 (Urbana, 1969), 181–202.

Nash, E. "Convenerunt in domum Faustae in Laterano: S. Optati Milevitani I, 23." *Römische Quartalschrift* 71 (1976), 1–21.

Naumann, R. *Der Rundbau in Aezani mit dem Preisedikt des Diokletian und das Gebäude mit dem Edikt in Stratonikeia. Istanbuler Mitteilungen,* Beiheft 10. Tübingen, 1973.

Nautin, P. "Notes sur la catalogue des œuvres d'Hippolyte." *Recherches de Science Religieuse* 34 (1947), 99–107, 347–359.

———— "La controverse sur l'auteur de l'*Elenchos.*" *Revue d'Histoire Ecclésiastique* 47 (1952), 5–43.

———— "L'auteur du comput pascal de 222 et de la chronique anonyme de 235." *Recherches de Science Religieuse* 42 (1954), 226–257.

———— "Encore le problème d'Hippolyte." *Mélanges de Science religieuse* 11 (1954), 215–218.

———— *Origène: Sa vie et son œuvre. Christianisme antique* 1. Paris, 1977.

Neri, V. "Un miliario liciniano ad Aquileia: Ipotesi sui rapporti tra Costantino e Licinio prima del conflitto del 314." *Rivista storica di antichità* 5 (1975), 79–109.

Nestle, E. Review of *Eusebius' Werke* 3 (Leipzig, 1904). *Berliner philologische Wochenschrift* 24 (1904), 1156–1163.

———— "Zum *Onomastikon* des Eusebius." *Zeitschrift des deutschen Palästina-Vereins* 28 (1905), 41–43.

———— "Die Eusebianische Evangelien-Synopse." *Neue kirchliche Zeitschrift* 19 (1908), 40–51, 93–114, 219–232.

———— "Alttestamentliches aus Eusebius." *Zeitschrift für die alttestamentliche Wissenschaft* 29 (1909), 57–62.

Nock, A. D. "The Emperor's Divine *Comes.*" *Journal of Roman Studies* 37 (1947), 102–116. Reprinted in his *Essays on Religion and the Ancient World* (Oxford, 1972), 653–675.

Noethlichs, K. L. "Zur Einflussnahme des Staates auf die Entwicklung eines christlichen Klerikerstandes: Schicht- und berufsspezifische Bestimmungen für den Klerus in den spätantiken Rechtsquellen." *Jahrbuch für Antike und Christentum* 15 (1972), 136–153.

Nolte, T. "Zu den *Eclogis Propheticis* des Eusebius von Cäsarea." *Theologische Quartalschrift* 43 (1861), 95–109.

Nordenfalk, C. *Die spätantiken Kanontafeln: Kunstgeschichtliche Studien über die eusebianische Evangelien-Konkordanz in den vier ersten Jahrhunderten ihrer Geschichte.* Göteborg, 1938.

—— "The Apostolic Canon Tables." *Gazette des Beaux Arts*[6] 62 (1963) 17–34.

Noth, M. "Die topographischen Angaben im *Onomastikon* des Eusebius." *Zeitschrift des deutschen Palästina-Vereins* 66 (1943), 32–63.

Novak, D. M. "Constantine and the Senate: An Early Phrase in the Christian-ization of the Roman Aristocracy." *Ancient Society* 10 (1979), 271–310.

Nyman, J. R. "The Synod at Antioch (324–325) and the Council of Nicaea." *Studia Patristica* 4. *Texte und Untersuchungen* 79 (Berlin, 1961), 483–489.

Ogilvie, R. M. *The Library of Lactantius.* Oxford, 1978.

Oliver, H. H. "The Epistle of Eusebius to Carpianus: Textual Tradition and Translation." *Novum Testamentum* 3 (1959), 138–145.

Oliver, J. H. "The Governor's Edict at Aezani after the Edict of Prices." *American Journal of Philology* 97 (1976), 174–175.

Olivetti, A. "Sulle stragi di Costantinopoli succedute alla morte di Costantino il Grande." *Rivista di filologia* 43 (1915), 67–79.

Opelt, I. "Formen der Polemik im Pamphlet *De Mortibus Persecutorum.*" *Jahrbuch für Antike und Christentum* 16 (1973), 98–105.

Opitz, H.-G. "Die Zeitfolge des arianischen Streites von den Anfängen bis zum Jahre 328." *Zeitschrift für die neutestamentliche Wissenschaft* 33 (1934), 131–159.

—— "Euseb von Caesarea als Theologe: Ein Vortrag." *Zeitschrift für die neutestamentliche Wissenschaft* 34 (1935), 1–19.

Oppermann, H. Review of [*Iamblichi*] *Theologoumena arithmeticae* (ed. V. de Falco [Leipzig: Teubner, 1922]). *Gnomon* 5 (1929), 545–558.

Orlinsky, H. M. "Origen's Tetrapla—A Scholarly Fiction?" *Proceedings of the First World Congress of Jewish Studies* 1 (Jerusalem, 1952), 173–182.

Palanque, J.-R. "Constantin, empereur chrétien, d'après ses récents his-toriens." *Études médiévales offerts à M. le Doyen A. Fliche. Publications de la Faculté des Lettres de l'Université de Montpellier* 4 (Montpellier, 1952), 133–142.

—— "Sur la date du *De mortibus persecutorum.*" *Mélanges d'archéologie, d'épigraphie et d'histoire offerts à J. Carcopino,* 711–716. Paris, 1966.

Paschoud, F. "Zosime 2,29 et la version paienne de la conversion de Constan-tin." *Historia* 20 (1971), 334–353. Reprinted in his *Cinq études sur Zosime* (Paris, 1975), 24–62.

—— "Quand parut la première édition de l'*Histoire* d'Eunape?" *Bonner Historia-Augusta-Colloquium 1977/1978* (1980), 149–162.

Pasquali, G. Review of I. A. Heikel, *Eusebius' Werke* 1 (Leipzig, 1902). *Göttingsche Gelehrte Anzeigen* 171 (1909), 259–286.

—— "Die Composition der *Vita Constantini* des Eusebius." *Hermes* 46 (1910), 369–386.

Pears, E. "The Campaign against Paganism, A.D. 324." *English Historical Review* 24 (1909), 1–17.

Peeters, P. "La légende de Saint Jacques de Nisibis." *Analecta Bollandiana* 38 (1920), 285–373.

—— "Le début de la persécution de Sapor, d'après Fauste de Byzance."

Revue des Études Arméniennes 1 (1920–1), 15–33. Reprinted in his *Recherches d'histoire et de philologie orientales. Subsidia Hagiographica* 27, 1.59–77. Brussels, 1951.

——— "L'intervention politique de Constance II dans la Grande Arménie, en 338." *Bulletin de l'Académie Royale de Belgique,* Classe des Lettres[5] 17 (1931), 10–47. Reprinted in his *Recherches* (Brussels, 1951), 1.222–250.

——— "Les débuts du Christianisme en Géorgie d'après les sources hagiographiques." *Analecta Bollandiana* 50 (1932), 5–58.

——— "La date du martyre de S. Syméon, archévêque de Séleucie-Ctésiphon." *Analecta Bollandiana* 56 (1938), 118–143.

——— "Comment S. Athanase s'enfuit de Tyr en 335." *Bulletin de l'Académie Royale de Belgique,* Classe des Lettres[5] 30 (1944), 131–177. Reprinted in his *Recherches* (Brussels, 1951), 2.53–90.

——— "L'épilogue du Synode de Tyr en 335." *Analecta Bollandiana* 63 (1945), 131–144.

Pépin, J. "La théologie tripartite de Varron." *Revue des Études Augustiniennes* 2 (1956), 265–294. Incorporated in his *Mythe et allégorie: Les origines grecques et les contestations judéo-chrétiennes*[2] (Paris, 1976), 276–307.

Peri, V. "La cronologia delle lettere festali di Sant'Atanasio e la quaresima." *Aevum* 35 (1961), 28–86.

Petit, P. "Libanius et la *Vita Constantini.*" *Historia* 1 (1950), 562–582.

Petre, Z. "La pensée historique de Zosime." *Studii Clasice* 7 (1965), 263–272.

Pfättisch, J. M. *Die Rede Konstantins des Grossen an die Versammlung der Heiligen auf ihre Echtheit untersucht. Strassburger theologische Studien* 9.4. Freiburg, 1908.

——— "Platos Einfluss auf die Rede Konstantins an die Versammlung der Heiligen." *Theologische Quartalschrift* 92 (1910), 399–417.

——— "Die Rede Konstantins an die Versammlung der Heiligen." *Konstantin der Grosse und seine Zeit,* ed. F. J. Dölger, *Römische Quartalschrift,* Supplementband 19 (Freiburg, 1913), 96–121.

Pichon, R. *Lactance: Étude sur le mouvement philosophique et religieux sous le règne de Constantin.* Paris, 1901.

Picozzi, V. "Una campagna di Licinio contro Massenzio nel 310 non attestata dalle fonti letterarie." *Numismatica e antichità classiche* 5 (1976), 267–275.

Pietersma, A. "Proto-Lucian and the Greek Psalter." *Vetus Testamentum* 28 (1978), 66–72.

Pietri, C. *Roma Christiana: Recherches sur l'Église de Rome, son organisation, sa politique, son idéologie de Miltiade à Sixte III (311–440). Bibliothèque des Écoles Françaises d'Athènes et de Rome* 224. Paris, 1976.

——— "Les Origines de la mission lyonnaise: Remarques critiques." *Les Martyrs de Lyon (177). Colloques Internationaux du Centre National de la Recherche Scientifique* 575 (Paris, 1978), 211–231.

Piganiol, A. *L'empereur Constantin.* Paris, 1932.

——— "Dates constantiniennes." *Revue d'Histoire et de Philosophie Religieuses* 13 (1932), 360–372. Reprinted in his *Scripta Varia* 3. *Collection Latomus* 133 (Brussels, 1973), 229–239.

——— "L'état actuel de la question constantinienne, 1939–49." *Historia* 1

(1950), 82–96. Reprinted in his *Scripta Varia* 3. *Collection Latomus* 133 (1973), 212–228.

Places, E. des. "La tradition indirecte des *Lois* de Platon (livres I–VI)." *Mélanges J. Saunier* (Lyon, 1944), 27–40.

———— "Les *Lois* de Platon et la *Préparation évangelique* d'Eusèbe de Césarée." *Aegyptus* 32 (1952), 223–231.

———— "Numénius et Eusèbe de Césarée." *Studia Patristica* 13. *Texte und Untersuchungen* 116 (Berlin, 1975), 19–28.

Poinssot, L. "La carrière de trois proconsuls d'Afrique contemporains de Dioclétien." *Mémoires de la Société Nationale des Antiquaires de France* 76 (1919–23), 264–341.

Pollard, T. E. "The Origins of Arianism." *Journal of Theological Studies,* n.s. 9 (1958), 103–11.

———— *Johannine Christology and the Early Church.* Society for New Testament Studies, *Monograph Series* 13. Cambridge, 1970.

Preger, T. "Konstantinos-Helios." *Hermes* 36 (1901), 457–469.

Prete, S. "Der geschichtliche Hintergrund zu den Werken des Laktanz." *Gymnasium* 63 (1956), 365–382, 486–509.

Preuschen, E. "Die Stenographie im Leben des Origenes." *Archiv für Stenographie* 56 (1905), 6–14, 49–55.

———— Review of J. Karst, *Eusebius' Werke* 5 (Leipzig, 1911). *Berliner philologische Wochenschrift* 33 (1913), 963–966.

Quesnell, Q. "The Mar Saba Clementine: A Question of Evidence." *Catholic Biblical Quarterly* 37 (1975), 48–67.

———— "A Reply to Morton Smith." *Catholic Biblical Quarterly* 38 (1976), 200–203.

Radford, L. B. *Three Teachers of Alexandria: Theognostus, Pierius and Peter. A Study in the Early History of Origenism and Anti-Origenism.* Cambridge, 1908.

Rahmani, I. E., with Tisserant, E., Power, E., and Devreesse, R. "L'*Onomasticon* d'Eusèbe dans une ancienne traduction syriaque." *Revue de l'Orient Syrien* 23 (1922–23), 225–270.

Rey-Coquais, J.-P. "Le calendrier employé par Eusèbe de Césarée dans les *Martyrs de Palestine.*" *Analecta Bollandiana* 96 (1978), 55–64.

Richard, M. "Bulletin de Patrologie." *Mélanges de Science Religieuse* 5 (1948), 273–308.

———— "Les premières chaînes sur le Psautier." *Bulletin d'Information de l'Institut de Recherche et d'Histoire des Textes* 5 (1956), 87–98. Reprinted as *Opera Minora* 3 (Turnhout, 1977), no. 70.

———— "Quelques nouveaux fragments des pères anténicéens et nicéens." *Symbolae Osloenses* 38 (1963), 76–83.

———— "Le florilège du Cod. Vatopedi 236 sur le corruptible et l'incorruptible." *Le Muséon* 86 (1973), 249–273. Reprinted as *Opera Minora* 1 (Turnhout, 1976), no. 4.

———— "Le comput pascal par octaétéris." *Le Muséon* 87 (1974), 307–339. Reprinted as *Opera Minora* 1 (1976), no. 21.

Richardson, G. W. "The Chronology of Eusebius: Addendum." *Classical Quarterly* 19 (1925), 96–100.

Richmond, I. A. "Adamklissi." *Papers of the British School at Rome* 35 (1967), 29–39.

Ricken, F. "Die Logoslehre des Eusebios von Caesarea und der Mittelplatonismus." *Theologie und Philosophie* 42 (1967), 341–358.

––––––– "Nikaia als Krisis des altchristlichen Platonismus." *Theologie und Philosophie* 44 (1969), 321–341.

––––––– "Zur Rezeption der platonischen Ontologie bei Eusebios von Kaisareia, Areios und Athanasios." *Theologie und Philosophie* 53 (1978), 321–352.

Riedmatten, H. de. *Les Actes du Procès de Paul de Samosate: Étude sur la Christologie du IIIe au IVe siècle. Paradosis* 6. Fribourg, 1952.

Rist, J. M. "Neopythagoreanism and 'Plato's' Second Letter." *Phronesis* 10 (1965), 78–81.

––––––– "Basil's 'Neoplatonism': Its Background and Nature." *Basil of Caesarea: Christian, Humanist, Ascetic,* ed. P. J. Fedwick (Toronto, 1981), 137–220.

Robert, J. and L. "Bulletin épigraphique." *Revue des Études Grecques* 77 (1964), 127–259.

Robert, L. "Trois oracles de la Théosophie et un prophète d'Apollon." *Comptes Rendus de l'Académie des Inscriptions et Belles-Lettres* 1968, 568–599.

––––––– "Théophane de Mytilène à Constantinople." *Comptes Rendus de l'Académie des Inscriptions et Belles-Lettres* 1969, 42–64.

––––––– "Un oracle gravé à Oinoanda." *Comptes Rendus de l'Académie des Inscriptions et Belles-Lettres* 1971, 597–619.

Roethe, G. *Zur Geschichte der römischen Synoden im 3. und 4. Jahrhundert. Forschungen zur Kirchen- und Geistesgeschichte* 11: *Geistige Grundlagen römischer Kirchenpolitik,* Heft 2. Stuttgart, 1937.

Röttges, E. H. "Marcellinus-Marcellus: Zur Papstgeschichte der diokletianischen Verfolgungszeit." *Zeitschrift für katholische Theologie* 78 (1956), 385–420.

Rokeah, D. "A New Onomasticon Fragment from Oxyrhynchus and Philo's Etymologies." *Journal of Theological Studies,* n.s. 19 (1968), 70–82.

Rotondi, G. "Studi sulle fonti del codice giustinianeo." *Bullettino dell'Istituto di Diritto Romano* 26 (1914), 175–246; 29 (1918), 104–180. Reprinted, with an appendix by V. Arangio-Ruiz, in his *Scritti giuridici* 1 (Pavia, 1922), 110–283.

Rougé, J. "Le *De Mortibus Persecutorum,* 5e livre des Macchabées." *Studia Patristica* 12. *Texte und Untersuchungen* 115 (Berlin, 1976), 135–143.

––––––– "À propos du manuscrit du *De Mortibus Persecutorum.*" *Lactance et son temps. Théologie Historique* 48 (Paris, 1978), 13–22.

Rusch, W. G. "À la recherche de l'Athanase historique." *Politique et Théologie chez Athanase d'Alexandrie. Théologie Historique* 27 (Paris, 1974), 161–177.

Ruschenbusch, E. "Diokletians Währungsreform vom 1.9.301." *Zeitschrift für Papyrologie und Epigraphik* 26 (1977), 193–210.

Saffrey, H. D. "Abamon, pseudonyme de Jamblique." *Philomathes: Studies and Essays in the Humanities in Memory of Philip Merlan,* 227–239. The Hague, 1971.

——— "Un lecteur antique des œuvres de Numénius: Eusèbe de Césarée." *Forma Futuri: Studi in onore del Cardinale M. Pellegrino*, 145–153. Turin, 1975.

Sage, M. M. *Cyprian. Patristic Monograph Series*, no. 1. Cambridge, Mass., 1975.

Ste Croix, G. E. M. de. "Aspects of the 'Great' Persecution." *Harvard Theological Review* 47 (1954), 75–109.

Sansterre, J.-M. "Eusèbe de Césarée et la naissance de la théorie 'césaropapiste.'" *Byzantion* 42 (1972), 131–195, 532–594.

Sargenti, M. *Il diritto privato nella legislazione di Costantino: Persone e famiglia.* Università di Roma, *Pubblicazioni dell'Istituto di Diritto Romano* 3. Milan, 1938.

——— "Il diritto privato nella legislazione di Costantino: Problemi e prospettive nella letteratura dell'ultimo trentennio." *Accademia Romanistica Costantiniana. Atti del Primo Convegno Internazionale*, 229–332. Perugia, 1975.

Scheidweiler, F. "Zur neuen Ausgabe des Athanasios." *Byzantinische Zeitschrift* 47 (1954), 73–94.

Schneemelcher, W. "Die Kirchweihsynode von Antiochien 341." *Bonner Festgabe J. Straub*, 319–346. Bonn, 1977.

Schönbauer, E. "Diokletian in einem verzweifelten Abwehrkampf? Studien zur Rechtsentwicklung in der römischen Kaiserzeit." *Zeitschrift der Savigny-Stiftung, Romanistische Abteilung* 62 (1942), 267–346.

——— "Untersuchungen über die Rechtsentwicklung in der Kaiserzeit." *Journal of Juristic Papyrology* 9–10 (1955–6), 15–96.

Schoene, A. *Die Weltchronik des Eusebius in ihrer Bearbeitung durch Hieronymus.* Berlin, 1900.

Schöne, H. "Ein Einbruch der antiken Logik und Textkritik in die altchristliche Theologie: Eusebios' *KG* 5, 28, 13–19 in neuer Übertragung erläutert." *Pisciculi: Studien zur Religion und Kultur des Altertums F. J. Dölger dargeboten. Antike und Christentum*, Ergänzungsband 1 (Münster, (1939), 252–265.

Schrörs, H. *Konstantins des Grossen Kreuzerscheinung: Eine kritische Untersuchung.* Bonn, 1913.

——— "Drei Aktenstücke in betreff des Konzils von Arles (314). Textverbesserungen und Erläuterungen." *Zeitschrift der Savigny-Stiftung, Kanonistische Abteilung* 11 (1921), 429–439.

Schulten, A. *Die Mosaikkarte von Madaba und ihr Verhältnis zu den ältesten Karten und Beschreibungen des heiligen Landes. Abhandlungen der königlichen Gesellschaft der Wissenschaften zu Göttingen*, Philologisch-historische Klasse, N.F. 4.2. Göttingen, 1900.

Schulthess, F. *Die syrischen Kanones der Synoden von Nicaea bis Chalcedon nebst einigen zugehörigen Dokumenten herausgegeben. Abhandlungen der königlichen Gesellschaft der Wissenschaften zu Göttingen*, Philologisch-historische Klasse, N.F. 10.2. Göttingen, 1908.

Schultze, V. "Quellenuntersuchungen zur *Vita Constantini* des Eusebius." *Zeitschrift für Kirchengeschichte* 14 (1894), 503–555.

Schwartz, E. *Die Königslisten des Eratosthenes und Kastor mit Excursen über die Interpolationen bei Africanus und Eusebios. Abhandlungen der königlichen Gesellschaft der Wissenschaften zu Göttingen,* Philologisch-historische Klasse 40.2. Göttingen, 1894.

—— "Zur Geschichte des Athanasius." *Nachrichten von der königlichen Gesellschaft der Wissenschaften zu Göttingen,* Philologisch-historische Klasse 1904, 333–401, 518–547; 1905, 164–187, 257–299, 305–374; 1911, 367–426, 469–522. Largely reprinted in his *Gesammelte Schriften* 3 (Berlin, 1959), except for 1904, 518–547, which is reprinted as "Der Aufstieg Konstantins zur Alleinherrschaft," in *Konstantin der Grosse,* ed. H. Kraft, *Wege der Forschung* 131 (Darmstadt, 1974), 109–144.

—— "Über Kirchengeschichte." *Nachrichten von der königlichen Gesellschaft der Wissenschaften zu Göttingen,* Geschäftliche Mitteilungen 1908, 106–122. Reprinted in his *Gesammelte Schriften* 1 (Berlin, 1938), 110–130.

—— "Eusebios von Caesarea." F. Pauly and G. Wissowa, *Realencyclopädie der classischen Altertumswissenschaft* 6 (Stuttgart, 1909), 1370–1439. Reprinted in his *Griechische Geschichtsschreiber*[2] (Leipzig, 1959), 495–598.

—— "Constantin." *Meister der Politik* 1[2] (Stuttgart and Berlin, 1923), 275–324. Reprinted in his *Charakterköpfe aus der Antike*[2] (Leipzig, 1943), 223–280.

—— "Zur Kirchengeschichte der vierten Jahrhunderts." *Zeitschrift für die neutestamentliche Wissenschaft* 34 (1935), 129–213. Reprinted in his *Gesammelte Schriften* 4 (Berlin, 1960), 1–110.

—— *Kaiser Constantin und die christliche Kirche*[2]. Leipzig, 1936.

—— "Die Kanonessammlungen der alten Reichskirche." *Zeitschrift der Savigny-Stiftung,* Kanonistische Abteilung 25 (1936), 1–114. Reprinted in his *Gesammelte Schriften* 4 (Berlin, 1960), 159–275.

Schwyzer, H. R. Review of *Plotins Schriften,* trans. by R. Harder (Hamburg, 1956–1958); Plotinus, trans. by S. MacKenna, 2nd ed., rev. B. S. Page (London, 1956), and K. Mras, *Eusebius' Werke* 8 (Berlin, 1954–1956). *Gnomon* 32 (1960), 31–48.

Seeberg. E. *Die Synode von Antiochien im Jahre 324/25: Ein Beitrag zur Geschichte des Konzils von Nicäa. Neue Studien zur Geschichte der Theologie und der Kirche* 16. Berlin, 1913.

Seeck, O. "Die Verwandtenmorde Constantins des Grossen." *Zeitschrift für wissenschaftliche Theologie* 33 (1890), 63–77.

—— "Zur Entstehung des Indictionencyclus." *Deutsche Zeitschrift für Geschichtswissenschaft* 12 (1894), 279–296.

—— "Zu den Festmünzen Konstantins und seiner Familie." *Zeitschrift für Numismatik* 21 (1898), 17–65.

—— *Regesten der Kaiser und Päpste für die Jahre 311 bis 476 n. Chr.: Vorarbeit zu einer Prosopographie der christlichen Kaiserzeit.* Stuttgart, 1919.

Selb, W. "Episcopalis audientia von der Zeit Konstantins bis zur Nov. XXXV Valentinians III." *Zeitschrift der Savigny-Stiftung,* Romanistische Abteilung 84 (1967), 162–217.

Sellers, R. V. *Eustathius of Antioch and His Place in the Early History of Christian Doctrine.* Cambridge, 1928.

Selwyn, W. "Emendations of Certain Passages of Eusebii '*Eclogae Propheticae.*'" *Journal of Philology* 4 (1872), 275–280.

Seston, W. *Dioclétien et la Tétrarchie* 1: *Guerres et réformes. Bibliothèque des Écoles Françaises d'Athènes et de Rome* 162. Paris, 1946.

———— "Die Constantinische Frage: B) Faits politiques, armées, finances." *Relazioni del X. Congresso Internazionale di Scienze Storiche* 6 (Florence, 1955), 781–799.

———— "La Conférence de Carnuntum et le 'Dies Imperii' de Licinius." *Carnuntina: Vorträge beim internationalen Kongress der Altertumsforscher Carnuntum 1955. Römische Forschungen in Niederösterreich* 3 (Graz, 1956), 175–186.

Setton, K. M. *Christian Attitude towards the Emperor in the Fourth Century, Especially as Shown in Addresses to the Emperor.* New York, 1941.

Shackleton Bailey, D. R. "Ausoniana." *American Journal of Philology* 97 (1976), 248–261.

Sieben, H. J. *Die Konzilsidee der alten Kirche.* Paderborn, 1979.

Sievers, G. R. "*Athanasii Vita Acephala:* Ein Beitrag zur Geschichte des Athanasius." *Zeitschrift für historische Theologie* 38 (1868), 89–162.

Simon, D. V. *Konstantinisches Kaiserrecht: Studien anhand der Reskriptenpraxis und des Schenkungsrechts. Forschungen zur byzantinischen Rechtsgeschichte* 2. Frankfurt, 1977.

Simonetti, M. *La crisi ariana nel IV secolo. Studia Ephemeridis "Augustinianum"* 11. Rome, 1975.

———— "A modo di conclusione: Una ipotesi di lavoro." *Ricerche su Ippolito,* ed. V. Loi, *Studia Ephemeridis "Augustinianum"* 13 (Rome, 1977), 151–156.

Sirinelli, J. *Les vues historiques d'Eusèbe de Césarée durant la période prénicéene.* Université de Dakar, Faculté des Lettres et Sciences Humaines, *Publications de la Section de Langues et Littératures* 10. Dakar, 1961.

———— "Quelques allusions à Melchisédech dans l'œuvre d'Eusèbe de Césarée." *Studia Patristica* 6. *Texte und Untersuchungen* 81 (Berlin, 1962), 233–247.

Smith, M. "On the Authenticity of the Mar Saba Letter of Clement." *Catholic Biblical Quarterly* 38 (1976), 196–199.

"Solar Halo Complexes." *Sky and Telescope* 54 (1977/8), 185–187.

Sonne, I. "The use of Rabbinic Literature as Historical Sources." *Jewish Quarterly Review* 36 (1945–46), 147–169.

———— "Word and Meaning—Text and Context." *Jewish Quarterly Review* 37 (1946–47), 307–328.

Sordi, M. "I nuovi decreti di Marco Aurelio contro i cristiani." *Studi Romani* 9 (1961), 365–378.

Spanneut, M. "La Bible d'Eustathe d'Antioche: Contribution à l'histoire de la 'Version lucianique.'" *Studia Patristica* 4. *Texte und Untersuchungen* 79 (Berlin, 1961), 171–190.

Sperber, D. "The Inflation in Fourth Century Palestine." *Archiv Orientální* 34 (1966), 54–66.

Speyer, W. "Zum Bild des Apollonios von Tyana bei Heiden und Christen." *Jahrbuch für Antike und Christentum* 17 (1974), 47–63.

Sprengling, M. "Kartīr, Founder of Sasanian Zoroastrianism." *American Journal of Semitic Languages and Literatures* 57 (1940), 197–228.

Stade, K. *Der Politiker Diokletian und die letzte grosse Christenverfolgung.* Wiesbaden, 1926.

Stead, G. C. "The Platonism of Arius." *Journal of Theological Studies,* n.s. 15 (1964), 16–31.

—— *Divine Substance.* Oxford, 1977.

—— "The *Thalia* of Arius and the Testimony of Athanasius." *Journal of Theological Studies,* n.s. 29 (1978), 20–52.

Steinhausen, J. "Hieronymus und Laktanz in Trier." *Trierer Zeitschrift* 20 (1951), 126–154.

Stevenson, J. "The Life and Literary Activity of Lactantius." *Studia Patristica* 1. *Texte und Untersuchungen* 63 (Berlin, 1957), 661–677.

Stolte, B. H. "The Roman Emperor Valerian and Sapor I, King of Persia." *Rivista storica di antichità* 1 (1971), 157–162.

Storch, R. "The 'Eusebian Constantine.' " *Church History* 40 (1971), 145–155.

Straub, J. "Konstantins christliches Sendungsbewusstsein." *Das Neue Bild der Antike* 2, ed. H. Berve (Leipzig, 1942), 374–394. Reprinted in his *Regeneratio Imperii: Aufsätze über Roms Kaisertum und Reich im Spiegel der heidnischen und christlichen Publizistik* (Darmstadt, 1972), 70–88.

—— "Konstantins Verzicht auf den Gang zum Kapitol." *Historia* 4 (1955), 297–313. Reprinted in his *Regeneratio Imperii* (1972), 100–118.

—— "Kaiser Konstantin als *episkopos ton ektos.*" *Studia Patristica* 1. *Texte und Untersuchungen* 63 (Berlin, 1957), 678–695. Reprinted in his *Regeneratio Imperii* (1972), 119–133.

Stroheker, K. F. "Das konstantinische Jahrhundert im Lichte der Neuerscheinungen 1940–1951." *Saeculum* 3 (1952), 654–680.

Suggs, M. J. "Eusebius' Text of John in the 'Writings against Marcellus.' " *Journal of Biblical Literature* 75 (1956), 137–142.

—— "The Eusebian Text of Matthew." *Novum Testamentum* 1 (1956), 233–245.

—— "Eusebius and the Gospel Text." *Harvard Theological Review* 50 (1957), 307–310.

Sulzberger, M. "Le symbole de la croix et les monogrammes de Jésus chez les premiers chrétiens." *Byzantion* 2 (1925), 337–448.

Sundermann, W. "Zur frühen missionarischen Wirksamkeit Manis." *Acta Orientalia* 24 (1971), 79–125.

Syme, R. "Pliny's Less Successful Friends." *Historia* 9 (1960), 362–379. Reprinted in his *Roman Papers* (Oxford, 1979), 477–495.

—— "The Titulus Tiburtinus." *Akten des VI. Internationalen Kongresses für griechische und lateinische Epigraphik. Vestigia* 17 (Munich, 1973), 585–601.

—— "The Ancestry of Constantine." *Bonner Historia-Augusta-Colloquium 1971* (1974), 237–253.

—— " 'Donatus' and the Like." *Historia* 27 (1978), 588–603.

Taubenschlag, R. "Das römische Privatrecht zur Zeit Diokletians." *Bulletin de*

438

l'Académie Polonaise des Sciences et des Lettres 1919–20 (Cracow, 1923), 141–281. Reprinted in his *Opera Minora* 1 (Warsaw, 1959), 3–177.

Telfer, W. " 'Arius Takes Refuge at Nicomedia.' " *Journal of Theological Studies,* 37 (1936), 60–63.

—— "When Did the Arian Controversy Begin?" *Journal of Theological Studies,* 47 (1946), 129–142.

—— "St. Peter of Alexandria and Arius." *Analecta Bollandiana* 67 (1949), 117–130.

—— "Sozomen I. 15, A Reply." *Journal of Theological Studies,* 50 (1949), 187–191.

—— "Paul of Constantinople." *Harvard Theological Review* 43 (1950), 31–92.

Tetz, M. "Eine arianische Homilie unter dem Namen des Athanasius von Alexandrien." *Zeitschrift für Kirchengeschichte* 64 (1952/3), 299–307.

Thesleff, H. "On the Problem of the Doric Pseudo-Pythagorica: An Alternative Theory of Date and Purpose." *Pseudepigrapha* 1. *Entretiens sur l'Antiquité Classique* 18 (Vandœuvres-Geneva, 1972), 57–87.

Thomas, J. D. "The Date of the Revolt of L. Domitius Domitianus." *Zeitschrift für Papyrologie und Epigraphik* 22 (1976), 253–279.

Thomsen, P. "Palästina nach dem *Onomasticon* des Eusebius." *Zeitschrift des deutschen Palästina-Vereins* 26 (1903), 97–141, 145–188. Also published separately as a Tübingen dissertation.

—— "Textkritisches zum *Onomasticon* des Eusebius." *Berliner philologische Wochenschrift* 25 (1905), 621–624.

—— "Untersuchungen zur älteren Palästinaliteratur." *Zeitschrift des deutschen Palästina-Vereins* 29 (1906), 101–132.

Tudor, D. "Constantin cel mare si recucerirea Daciei Traiane." *Revista Istorică Romană* 11–12 (1941–42), 134–148.

Turner, C. H. "The Early Episcopal Lists." *Journal of Theological Studies* 1 (1900), 181–200, 529–553; 18 (1917), 103–134.

—— "The *Liber Ecclesiasticorum Dogmatum* attributed to Gennadius." *Journal of Theological Studies,* 7 (1906), 78–99.

—— "The Papal Chronology of the Third Century." *Journal of Theological Studies* 17 (1916), 338–353.

—— "Adversaria critica: Notes on the Anti-Donatist Dossier and on Optatus, Books I, II." *Journal of Theological Studies,* 27 (1926), 283–296.

Ullmann, W. "The Constitutional Significance of Constantine the Great's Settlement." *Journal of Ecclesiastical History* 27 (1976), 1–16.

Veilleux, A. "The Abbatial Office in Cenobitic Life." *Monastic Studies* 6 (1968), 3–45.

Vernay, E. "Note sur le changement de style dans les constitutions impériales de Dioclétien à Constantin." *Études d'histoire juridique offerts à P. F. Girard* 2 (Paris, 1913), 263–274.

Vickers, M. "The Hippodrome at Thessaloniki." *Journal of Roman Studies,* 62 (1972), 25–32.

—— "Observations on the Octagon at Thessaloniki." *Journal of Roman Studies,* 63 (1973), 111–120.

Ville, G. "Les jeux de gladiateurs dans l'empire chrétien." *Mélanges d'Archéologie et d'Histoire de l'École Française de Rome* 72 (1960), 273–335.

Vittinghoff, F. "Eusebius als Verfasser der *Vita Constantini.*" *Rheinisches Museum,* N.F. 96 (1953), 330–373.

Völker, W. "Von welchen Tendenzen liess sich Eusebius bei Abfassung seiner 'Kirchengeschichte' leiten?" *Vigiliae Christianae* 4 (1955), 157–180.

Voelkl, L. "Die konstantinischen Kirchenbauten nach Eusebius." *Rivista di archeologia cristiana* (1953), 49–66, 187–206.

────── *Die Kirchenstiftungen des Kaisers Konstantin im Lichte des römischen Sakralrechts. Arbeitsgemeinschaft für Forschung des Landes Nordrhein-Westfalen,* Geisteswissenschaften 117. Opladen, 1964.

Vööbus, A. *History of Asceticism in the Syrian Orient: A Contribution to the History of Culture in the Near East* 2. *Early Monasticism in Mesopotamia and Syria. Corpus Scriptorum Christianorum Orientalium* 197, Subsidia 17. Louvain, 1960.

Vogt, J. "Der Erbauer der Apostelkirche in Konstantinopel." *Hermes* 81 (1953), 111–117. Reprinted in *Neue Beiträge zur klassischen Altertumswissenschaft: Festschrift B. Schweitzer,* 372–378. Stuttgart, 1954.

────── "Kaiser Julian über seinen Oheim Constantin den Grossen." *Historia* 4 (1955), 339–352.

────── Review of P. Franchi de' Cavalieri, *Constantiniana (Studi e Testi* 171, 1953). *Gnomon* 27 (1955), 44–48.

────── "Die Constantinische Frage: A) Die Bekehrung Constantins." *Relazioni del X. Congresso Internazionale di Scienze Storiche* 6 (Florence, 1955), 733–779. Reprinted in *Konstantin der Grosse,* ed. H. Kraft, *Wege der Forschung* 131 (Darmstadt, 1974), 345–387.

────── "Bemerkungen zum Gang der Constantinforschung." *Mullus: Festschrift T. Klauser. Jahrbuch für Antike und Christentum,* Ergänzungsband 1 (Münster, 1964), 374–379.

Volterra, E. "Intorno ad alcune costituzioni di Costantino." *Rendiconti della Accademia Nazionale dei Lincei,* Classe di scienze morali, storiche e filologiche[8] 13 (1958), 61–89.

────── "Quelques remarques sur le style des constitutions de Constantin." *Droits de l'antiquité et sociologie juridique. Mélanges H. Levy-Bruhl,* 325–334. Paris, 1959.

────── "La costituzione di Diocleziano e Massimiano contro i Manichei." *La Persia e il mondo greco-romano.* Accademia Nazionale dei Lincei, *Problemi Attuali di Scienza e di Cultura* 76 (Rome, 1966), 27–50.

Wallace-Hadrill, D. S. "The Eusebian *Chronicle:* The Extent and Date of Composition of Its Early Editions," *Journal of Theological Studies,* n.s. 6 (1955), 248–253.

────── "Eusebius and the Gospel Text of Caesarea." *Harvard Theological Review* 49 (1956), 105–114.

────── *Eusebius of Caesarea.* London, 1960.

────── "Eusebius of Caesarea's *Commentary on Luke:* Its Origin and Early History." *Harvard Theological Review* 67 (1974), 55–63.

Waszink, J. H. "Calcidius." *Jahrbuch für Antike und Christentum* 15 (1972), 236–244.

Weber, A. *APXH: Ein Beitrag zur Christologie des Eusebius von Cäsarea.* Rome, 1964.

Weis, M. *Die Stellung des Eusebius von Cäsarea im arianischen Streit: Kirchen- und dogmengeschichtliche Studie.* Diss., Freiburg-im-Breisgau, 1919.

Weiss, E. "Endogamie und Exogamie im römischen Kaiserreich." *Zeitschrift der Savigny-Stiftung,* Romanistische Abteilung 29 (1908), 340–369.

Wendel, C. "Der Bibel-Auftrag Kaiser Konstantins." *Zentralblatt für Bibliothekwesen* 56 (1939), 165–175.

Wendland, P. Review of I. A. Heikel, *Eusebius' Werke* 1 (Leipzig, 1902). *Berliner philologische Wochenschrift* 22 (1902), 226–236.

West, L. C. "Notes on Diocletian's *Edict.*" *Classical Philology* 34 (1939), 239–245.

Wevers, J. W. *Text History of the Greek Genesis. Abhandlungen der Akademie der Wissenschaften in Göttingen,* Philologisch-historische Klasse[3] 81. Göttingen, 1974.

Wieacker, F. "Le droit romain de la mort d'Alexandre Sévère à l'avènement de Dioclétien (235–284 apr. J.-C.)." *Revue Historique de Droit Français et Étranger* 49 (1971), 201–223.

Wikenhauser, A. "Zur Frage nach der Existenz von nizänischen Synodalprotokollen." *Konstantin der Grosse und seine Zeit,* ed. F. J. Dölger, *Römische Quartalschrift,* Supplementband 19 (Freiburg, 1913), 122–142.

Wilamowitz-Moellendorf, U. von. "Ein Bruchstück aus der Schrift des Porphyrius gegen die Christen." *Zeitschrift für die neutestamentliche Wissenschaft* 1 (1900), 101–105.

Wilcken, U. "Zu den Kaiserreskripten." *Hermes* 55 (1920), 1–42.

——— "Zur *propositio libellorum.*" *Archiv für Papyrusforschung* 9 (1930), 15–23.

Wiles, M. F. "In Defence of Arius." *Journal of Theological Studies,* n.s. 13 (1962), 339–347.

Wilkinson, J. "Christian Pilgrims in Jerusalem during the Byzantine Period." *Palestine Exploration Quarterly* 108 (1976), 75–101.

Williams, W. "Formal and Historical Aspects of Two New Documents of Marcus Aurelius." *Zeitschrift für Papyrologie und Epigraphik* 17 (1975), 35–78.

Windisch, H. "Die ältesten christlichen Palästinapilger." *Zeitschrift des deutschen Palästina-Vereins* 48 (1925), 145–158.

Winkelmann, F. "Zur Geschichte des Authentizitätsproblems der *Vita Constantini.*" *Klio* 40 (1962), 187–243.

——— *Untersuchungen zur Kirchengeschichte des Gelasios von Kaisareia. Sitzungsberichte der deutschen Akademie der Wissenschaften zu Berlin,* Klasse für Sprachen, Literatur und Kunst 1965, Nr. 3. Berlin, 1965.

——— "Die Quellen der *Historia Ecclesiastica* des Gelasius von Cyzicus (nach 475)." *Byzantinoslavica* 27 (1966), 104–130.

——— "Die Bischöfe Metrophanes und Alexander von Byzanz." *Byzantinische Zeitschrift* 59 (1966), 47–71.

——— "Charakter und Bedeutung der *Kirchengeschichte* des Gelasios von Kaisareia." *Polychordia: Festschrift F. Dölger* 1. *Byzantinische Forschungen* 1 (1966), 346–385.

Winter, P. "Josephus on Jesus." *Journal of Historical Studies* 1 (1968), 289–302. Reprinted in E. Schürer, *History of the Jewish People in the Age of Jesus Christ* 1 (revised by G. Vermes and F. Millar), 428–441. Edinburgh, 1973.

Wlosok, A. *Laktanz und die philosophische Gnosis: Untersuchungen zur Geschichte und Terminologie der gnostischen Erlösungsvorstellung. Abhandlungen der Heidelberger Akademie der Wissenschaften,* Philosophisch-historische Klasse 1960, Abhandlung 2. Heidelberg, 1960.

——— "Zur Bedeutung der nichtcyprianischen Bibelzitate bei Laktanz." *Studia Patristica* 4. *Texte und Untersuchungen* 79 (Berlin, 1961), 234–250.

Wolf, C. U. "Eusebius of Caesarea and the *Onomasticon.*" *Biblical Archaeologist* 27 (1964), 66–96.

Wolff, H. J. "Doctrinal trends in Postclassical Roman Marriage Law." *Zeitschrift der Savigny-Stiftung,* Romanistische Abteilung 67 (1950), 261–319.

Wutz, F. *Onomastica sacra: Untersuchungen zum "Liber Interpretationis Nominum Hebraicorum" des Hl. Hieronymus. Texte und Untersuchungen* 41. Leipzig, 1914–15.

Ziegler, J. "Die Peregrinatio Aetheriae und das *Onomastikon* des Eusebius. *Biblica* 12 (1931), 70–84.

INDEX OF PASSAGES OF
EUSEBIUS DISCUSSED

Against Hierocles, 164–167
Against Marcellus, 241, 263, 264–265
Against Porphyry, 174–175, 365n137

Canons (Gospel concordance), 121–122
Chronicle, 111–120
Collection of Ancient Martyrdoms, 94, 148,
  333n119
Commentary on Isaiah, 95–105, 121, 249,
  335n135, 355n3
Commentary on the Psalms, 95–105, 249,
  334n135

Defense of Origen, 94, 148, 199–201

Ecclesiastical History, 111
  Bks. 1–7: 126–147
  2.17: 195
  6.1–32: 82–86, 327n14, 327n21
  6.19.6: 177
  7.31–32: 192–194, 202
  Bks. 8–10: 149–150, 155, 156–163,
  191–192
    8.17: 39, 65

  9.8.2–4: 359n93
  9.9.9–11: 308n18
  9.9.12: 48–49
  9.9a.12: 48–49
  10.4: 162–163
  10.5.2–14: 64–65, 210
Ecclesiastical Theology, 263, 265

General Elementary Introduction, 151,
  167–174, 334n135

Letters
  To Carpianus, 121–122
  To Constantia, 401n82
  To the Church of Caesarea, 216, 226
  To Euphrantion, 205
Life of Constantine, 255, 263, 265–271, 274
  1.27–32: 43
  1.51–54: 70–71
  2.24–60: 208–211
  2.64–72: 212–213
  3.6–21: 214–219
  3.11: 380n61
  3.23: 229

Life of Constantine (cont.)
  3.54–58: 247
  3.60–62: 228
  3.64–65: 224
  4.9–13: 258–259
  4.19–20: 48
  4.36–37: 124–125, 222
  4.45–46: 253, 388n120
  See also Speech to the Assembly of the Saints
Life of Pamphilus, 94, 192

Martyrs of Palestine, 148–158, 162, 201

On the Place-Names in Holy Scripture, 106–111
On the Polygamy and Large Progeny of the Patriarchs, 367n163

Panegyric to Constantine, 247, 253–255, 270, 271

Preparation for the Gospel, 71–72, 93–94, 175, 178–186
Proof of the Gospel, 71–72, 175, 178–179, 182–186
Prophetic Extracts, 151, 167–174

Questions and Answers Addressed to Marinus, 122–124
Questions and Answers Addressed to Stephanus, 122–124

Second Theophany, 171–174, 334n135
Speech to the Assembly of the Saints (Constantine), 73–76, 271, 323–325, 405n21

Theophany, 187–188, 249, 310n61
Treatise on the Church of the Holy Sepulcher, 187, 188, 238, 249–250, 266, 271

GENERAL INDEX

Abantus, 76
Abellius, 30
Abercius Marcellus, 134
Abgar, king of Edessa, 129–130
Ablabius, praetorian prefect, 51, 232, 252, 262
Abraham, 115, 126, 171
Abthungi, 58
Abydenos, 114, 115, 118
Acacius, bishop of Caesarea, 265, 348n21
Acacius, *comes,* 228, 248
Acesius, Novatianist bishop, 217–218
Achaea, 10
Achaeus, governor of Palestine, 144
Achillas, associate of Arius, 202
Achillas, bishop of Alexandria, 202
Achillas, priest at Alexandria, 193, 202
Achilleus, Melitian bishop, 236
Achilleus, rebel, 17
Adam, 127
Adamantius, 141, 327n14, 369n29
Adauctus, 157
Adiabene, 18, 65
Adige, 42

Adraa, 108
Adrianople, 63, 67, 76, 161
Adultery, 52, 219–220, 314n109
Aedesius, martyr, 155
Aegaeae, 166, 247
Aelianus, proconsul of Africa, 58–59
Aelius Paulinus, 58
Aemilianus, praetorian prefect, 250
Aemilianus, rebel, 146
Aemilius Magnus Arborius, 392n61, 398n11
Aetius, bishop of Lydda, 204
Africa, 10, 12; Maximian in, 16; under Maxentius, 33, 37, 44; Christians in, 39, 54–61, 143; persecution in, 54–55; projected visit of Constantine to, 60; praetorian prefect of, 251–252
Africanus. *See* Julius Africanus
Agapius, bishop of Caesarea, 146, 192
Agapius, martyr, 151, 152
Agathonice, martyr, 137, 142
Agentes in rebus, 232, 238, 256
Alamanni, 6, 12, 66
Alexander, bishop of Alexandria, 202–207, 212–213, 215, 229–230

445

Alexander, bishop of Byzantium and Constantinople, 205–206, 213, 242, 264, 375n151
Alexander, bishop of Jerusalem, 84, 140
Alexander, bishop of Thessalonica, 235, 237
Alexander, of Lycopolis, 196–197
Alexander, usurper in Africa, 13, 33, 34, 37
Alexander the Great, 271
Alexander Polyhistor, 114, 115, 118
Alexandria, 93, 235–236, 263–264; rebellions in, 17, 146; visited by Diocletian, 17, 19, 20; persecution in, 82, 138, 157, 201; Origen active in, 82–84; bishops of, 84, 130, 132, 192, 218, 230; Christians and Manichees in, 196–197; schism in, 201–202
Alfius Caecilianus, 58
Allectus, 15–16
Allegory, 90, 93, 98–99, 193; criticized, 103, 177, 199
Alpheus, martyr, 151
Altava, 300n42
Amaseia, 72
Ambrosius, patron of Origen, 84–85, 91
Ammonius, associate of Arius, 375n137
Ammonius, biblical scholar, 121, 122
Ammonius, Christian writer, 365n137
Ammonius, philosopher, 83, 177
Amphion, bishop of Nicomedia, 227, 229
Anaia, 110, 154
Anastasia, 4, 251
Anatolius, bishop of Laodicea, 111, 146
Anatolius, teacher of Porphyry, 355n169
Angels, 87–89
Anicius Julianus, consul (322), 73
Annius Anullinus, C., 23, 54–55
Annius Anullinus, *praefectus urbi,* 45
Anthimus, bishop of Nicomedia, 24, 358n73
Antioch 84, 212; Galerius at, 9, 17; Diocletian at, 17, 19, 20–21; Maximinus at, 26, 39, 41, 64; Constantius at, 261, 262–263; churches in, 144–145, 248; bishops of, 130, 132, 144–145, 192, 218, 228–229; councils of bishops at, 144–145, 213, 227–228; persecution in, 157–158, 159–160
Antoninus, confessor, 94
Antoninus Pius, 137, 141
Antonius Diogenes, 167
Antony, hermit, 195–196, 240
Anullinus, praetorian prefect, 30
Anullinus, proconsul of Africa (303–305), 23, 54–55
Anullinus, proconsul of Africa (312–313), 49, 56–57
Apamea, 68

Aper, praetorian prefect, 5
Aphaca, 247, 255
Aphraates, 397n144
Aphrodite, shrines of, 247, 248, 255
Apollinaris, bishop of Laodicea, 246
Apollinaris, grammarian, 246
Apollinarius, bishop of Hierapolis, 131, 133, 134, 137
Apollo, 12, 36, 301n55; oracles of, 21, 64, 175, 211; priests of, 64, 211; statues of, 222, 247
Apollo Grannus, 36
Apollodorus, 120
Apollonius, anti-Montanist writer, 134
Apollonius, bishop of Lycopolis, 201
Apollonius, lexicographer, 109
Apollonius, martyr, 137
Apollonius, of Tyana, 164–167, 177, 247, 296n68
Apotheosis: of Constantius, 35, 47; of Maximian, 47, 206, 304n126; of Constantine, 267; of Galerius, 304n126
Apphianus, martyr, 152, 155
Apuleius, 177, 363n100
Aquae, 259
Aquila, prefect of Egypt, 83
Aquila, translator of Old Testament, 91, 92, 95, 102
Aquileia, 9, 33, 42, 219
Arabia, 83, 102, 110–111, 148, 157, 249
Aradius Rufinus, *praefectus urbi,* 45–46
Arbela, Chronicle of, 396n134
Areopolis, 108, 249
Arethas, 333n117
Ariaricus, 250
Aristides, apologist, 137
Aristo, of Pella, 348n24
Aristobulus, consul (285), 5–6
Aristotle, 134
Arius: beliefs and career before the Council of Nicaea, 194, 202–206, 212–213; exiles, rehabilitation, and death, 216–217, 229–233, 238–239, 241–242; denounced by Constantine, 233; ignored by Eusebius, 241, 402n124; supporters of, 204–205, 227–229, 232, 235, 237, 271
Arles, 34, 58
Armenia, 6, 17–18, 65, 72, 258
Army, 255, 256–257
Arsaces, 263
Arsacius, 71
Arsenius, bishop of Hypsele, 233–237
Artemon (Artemas), 134–135, 169
Asceticism, 83, 194–195
Asclepas, bishop of Gaza, 228
Asclepiodotus, praetorian prefect, 16
Asclepius, 247, 301n55
Asia, 10, 12, 137, 223

Asterius, sophist and Arian, 241, 264, 384n20
Astyrius, Christian senator, 144
Athanasius, bishop of Alexandria, 230–240, 253, 263–264, 266; early career, 206–207, 215; nature of his power, 230
Athanasius, bishop of Anazarbus, 204, 205, 374n124
Athenagoras, apologist, 142
Athenodorus, bishop of Pontus, 86
Athens, 71, 72, 76, 84, 222
Atticus, governor of Palestine, 136–137
Atticus, philosopher, 183
Audiani, 217
Augustus, 36, 52, 115, 271
Aurelian, 75, 145
Aurelius Pageus, 234
Autun, 36, 47, 246
Auxentius, 71

Babylon, 18, 75
Baetica, 54
Bagaudae, 6
Baptism, of Constantine, 260
Bar Kochba, 136
Barbarian, as synonym for Christian, 403n3
Bardesanes, 141
Baronius, Cardinal, 274
Basil, bishop of Amaseia, 72
Basil, bishop of Ancyra, 242
Basil, bishop of Caesarea, 216
Basilides, 134
Basilina, 321n79
Bassianus, 66–67, 251, 268
Bassus, consul (284), 5
Bassus, praetorian prefect, 72, 250
Batavia, 15
Baynes, Norman, 405n21
Bemarchius, 222–223
Beroea, 67
Beryllus, bishop of Bostra, 135
Berytus, 70, 85, 93
Bethabara, 109
Bethlehem, 221, 248
Bible: copies of, confiscated, 22–23, 55; authority of, 86; exegesis of, 90–91, 92–93, 94–104, 122–123; textual history of, 91–92, 94, 124–125, 194; canon of, 138–139; Eusebius and, 94–125; pagan knowledge of, 165, 176; Constantine's knowledge of, 325n148; onomastica, gazetteers, and concordances of, 98, 106–110, 121–122. See also Gospels; Old Testament
Bishops, 191, 210, 218–219, 314n109; at court, 43, 48, 70, 212, 231, 266; as judges, 51, 57, 145, 312nn78–82
Bithynia, 252

Blastus, schismatic, 134
Blemmyes, 18
Bononia (Boulogne), 6, 15, 16, 27
Bononia, on Danube, 76
Boradi (Borani), 330n47
Bostra, 83, 107, 108
Botrus, 55–56
Britain: rebellions in, 4, 7–8, 15; Christians in, 14; Constantius in, 16, 26–27; Constantine in, 27–29, 34, 65
Brixia, 59
Bruttius, cited by Eusebius, 132
Bruttius Praesens, 348n31
Burckhardt, Jacob, 274, 401n66, 405n21
Burgundians, 6
Byzacena, 295n57
Byzantium, 17, 63, 67, 76

Cabillunum, 34
Caecilianus, bishop of Carthage, 49, 56–59, 315n119
Caelestius, 55–56
Caesarea, in Cappadocia, 65
Caesarea, in Palestine, 39, 81–82, 143–144; bishops of, 82, 192, 219, 372n85; Origen in, 84–86; school of, 95, 121, 122; library at, 93–94, 109, 130, 170, 182–183, 347n21; martyrs in, 150–54
Caesarea Philippi, 144, 173
Caesariani, 69, 321n68
Caesonius Bassus, consul (284), 5
Calcidius, 74
Caligula, 135
Callinicum, 17
Callinicus, Melitian bishop of Pelusium, 232, 236
Callistus, bishop of Rome, 135
Callistus, follower of Melitius, 235–236
Calocaerus, 251, 252
Campania, 27
Campona, 76
Candidianus, 39, 64
Canons, enacted by church councils: Iliberris (before 303), 54; Arles (314), 58, 316n142; Ancyra (314), 201; Nicaea (325), 217–219; Antioch (327), 385n38; given legal force, 270
Capita, 40, 50, 233
Capitol, 44
Cappadocia, 65, 157, 263
Caracalla, 84, 138
Carausius, 6–8, 15
Carinus, 4–5
Carnuntum, conference at, 32, 153
Carpi, 12, 17, 32
Carpianus, 121, 122
Carpocrates, 134
Carpus, martyr, 137, 142

Carrhae, 17
Carterius, bishop of Antarados, 228
Carthage, 16, 33, 44, 49, 53, 54–61, 143
Carus, 4, 5, 192
Cassius Longinus, 118–119, 175
Castor, 114, 115, 118, 120
Catania, 55
Catholic church, recipient of official subsidies, 56, 60, 224
Catholic Epistles, authorship of, 139–140
Ceionius Rufius Albinus, 220–221
Ceionius Varus, 287n28
Celibacy, 52
Celsus, 21, 86, 165, 178, 332n102
Cemeteries, Christian, 49–50
Censor, 251
Census, 29, 39–40, 69–70, 151–152, 258
Cephalion, 114, 118
Cerdon, 134
Cerinthus, 134
Chaeremon, Stoic philosopher, 177
Chaibones, 6
Chalcedon, 76
Chaldaeans, 114, 115
Chamavi, 15
Chapter headings, Eusebius' use of, 124, 182, 324n129, 364n118
Charisius, jurist, 289n70
Chiliasm, 133–134
Chrestus, bishop of Nicaea, 227, 229
Christ. See God
Christian church: as owner of property, 49–50; defined by Eusebius, 126–128; contrasted with the Jews, 171–172, 188
Christian property: in the third century, 49–50; confiscated, 22–23, 50, 209; restored (306), 14, 28; (311/2), 38; (312/3), 56; (313), 62, 64–65, 70, 161–162; (324), 209–210
Christianity: as official religion, 50–53, 210–212, 224, 245–250; as defined by Eusebius, 126–128, 130, 181, 184–185
Christians: at the imperial court, 18–19, 24, 70–71, 138, 147, 249; in the Roman army, 19, 48, 71, 147, 209; in Roman society before 260, 21, 130–132, 134, 136, 142–143; in Roman society after 260, 21, 42, 49–54, 144–145, 155, 168, 178, 191; as holders of official posts, 147, 157, 187–188, 210, 249; political importance of, 37, 38–39, 70, 72, 191
Chrysargyron, 255, 257
Chrysopolis, 77
Churches: built and endowed by Constantine, 49–50, 210, 248–249, 259; founded by Helena, 221, 248
Cibalae, War of, 14, 67, 268–269
Cilicia, 153, 154

Circus, 53, 82, 223
Cirta, 23, 33, 38, 53, 60–61, 143
Claudius, emperor (41–54), 135
Claudius, emperor (268–270), 35, 47
Claudius Julianus, prefect of Egypt, 327n18
Clement, bishop of Rome, 132, 140
Clement, of Alexandria, 114, 115, 139, 142, 181, 368n157; forged letter of, 353n113
Clergy, privileges of, 50–51, 71, 209, 224, 233
Clodius Culcianus, 64, 201
Codex Gregorianus, 10
Codex Hermogenianus, 10
Codex Justinianus, 50
Codex Theodosianus, 50, 69
Collatio glebalis, 256, 257
Collatio lustralis, 255, 257
Colluthians, 233, 235, 237
Colluthus, priest at Alexandria, 213, 226
Comes sacrarum largitionum, 395n105
Comitatenses, 257
Comites, 46, 255; Constantine's use of, 228, 235, 247, 248, 256
Commodus, 132, 137
Consecration. See Apotheosis
Consilium, imperial, 21, 22
Constans, son of Constantine, 246, 252, 262–263, 267
Constantia, sister of Constantine, 41, 62, 70, 77, 251, 386n78
Constantina, daughter of Constantine, 259
Constantinople, 124, 212, 222–223, 231, 247, 250; council of, 241–242, 253, 264, 265, 266; Constantine buried in, 261; disputed episcopal election at (337), 262, 263, 264
Constantinus, son of Constantine, 66, 67, 221–222, 251, 252, 262–263, 267
Constantius, brother of Constantine, 251, 252, 262
Constantius, envoy of Constantine, 66
Constantius, father of Constantine: marriages and family, 3–4, 8–9, 251; as praetorian prefect, 3, 7–8; as emperor, 11, 12, 13, 15–16, 21, 23, 26–28; in Constantinian propaganda, 35–36, 47, 268
Constantius, praetorian prefect of Constantine, 250–251, 398n11
Constantius, son of Constantine, 67, 223, 251, 252, 261–263, 267; and Athanasius, 263–264; visits Rome (357), 245
Consulares, 257
Consulate, status of, 257
Consuls, as reflecting political events: (307–308), 30–32; (307–312), 37; (313), 65; (314–317), 307n15; (321–324), 60, 73; (325), 214; (338), 262

Conversion, of Constantine, 43, 75, 269, 275
Corinth, 251
Cornuti, 306n150
Cornutus, philosopher, 177
Correctores, 10
Councils of bishops: (before 260), 84, 86, 135, 354n145; Antioch (268/9), 144–145; Iliberris (shortly before 303), 53–54; Carthage (307/8), 56; Rome (313), 57; Ancyra (314), 201; Arles (314), 58; Caesarea, in Cappadocia (314), 65; Alexandria (c. 318), 204; in Bithynia (c. 319), 205; Alexandria (325), 213; Antioch (325), 213–214; Ancyra (325), 213–214; Nicaea (325), 214–219, 225, 231, 266, 269–270; Antioch (327), 227–228, 270; Nicomedia (327/8), 229, 231, 266, 270; Antioch (328), 228, 270; Caesarea (334), 234–235; Tyre (335), 235–241, 253, 270; Jerusalem (335), 238–239, 241, 248–249, 270; Constantinople (336), 241–242, 253, 264, 265, 266; Constantinople (337), 262, 271; Antioch (338/9), 264; Carthage (between c. 330 and c. 340), 61; attended by Constantine, 58, 65, 214–219, 229, 241–242, 270; Constantine's respect for, 58, 225, 270; forbidden by Licinius, 71, 206; status of, 237, 270
Court ceremonial, 48
Creation, 88
Creeds: use of, 216; Nicene, 216–217, 226
Crepereius Madalianus, 246
Crescens, philosopher, 137
Criobolium, 246
Crispus, 31, 66, 67–68, 72–73, 76; pupil of Lactantius, 13; in Eusebius, 150, 270, 274; death, 220, 250
Crocus, 27
Cross, 248, 382n130
Crucifixion, 51, 69, 292n99
Ctesiphon, 4, 18
Culcianus, prefect of Egypt, 64, 201
Cursus publicus, 59, 214, 235
Cusii, 292n2
Cymatius, bishop of Gabala, 228
Cymatius, bishop of Paltos, 228
Cyprian, bishop of Carthage, 53, 142, 143
Cyprus, 251, 252
Cyrillus, bishop of Antioch, 192
Cyrus, bishop of Beroea, 228, 384n23
Cyrus, king of Persia, 271

Dacia, 8, 250, 262
Dacia Ripensis, 3
Dalmatius, brother of Constantine, 234, 251, 252, 261–262

Dalmatius, Caesar (335–337), 251–252, 261–262, 392n61
Dalmatius, official under Licinius (311), 40
Damascus, 19, 107, 159
Damis, 166, 360n10
Daniel, 176, 177
Danube: defense of, 6, 8, 12, 25, 30, 32, 65; forts on, 17; bridge over, 221, 250
Danubian provinces, 12, 62
Dardania, 39
Darius, 116
Datianus, persecutor, 314n117
David, 95–97, 104
Decius, 75, 86, 138
Decurions, 69, 71, 209, 233
Delos, 326n160
Delphi, 211, 247
Demetrianus, bishop of Antioch, 144
Demetrius, bishop of Alexandria, 83–84
Demiurge, 74–75, 100
Devil, 87, 88–89, 134, 162, 215, 233
Didyma, 21
Didymus, of Alexandria, 170
Diocaesarea, 153
Dioceses, 9, 256
Diocles, 4
Diocletian, 4–26, 31–32, 41, 192; reforms, 9–11; Constantine's attitude toward, 36, 211
Diodorus Siculus, 114, 118, 180
Diogenes, governor of Pisidia, 358n83
Diogenianus, lexicographer, 109
Diogenianus, philosopher, 181
Dionysius, bishop of Alexandria, 135, 138, 140, 143, 146; theology of, 197–198, 204, 374n124
Dionysius, bishop of Corinth, 133, 140
Dionysius, bishop of Rome, 146
Dionysius, *comes,* 235–237
Dionysius, of Halicarnassus, 114
Dionysius, *praefectus urbi* (301/2), 16
Dionysius, writer on music, 72
Dionysus, 71
Diotogenes, 393n92
Divi, 35, 47, 206, 304n126, 401n85
Divination, 52–53, 210–211
Divorce, 52
Domitian, 131, 132, 136, 350n79
Domitianus, usurper, 17
Domitius Zenophilus, 60
Domninus, martyr, 152
Domnus, bishop of Antioch, 144
Donatism, 54–61, 213, 224
Donatus, confessor in Nicomedia, 13, 24
Donatus, episcopal candidate at Cirta, 55
Donatus, schismatic bishop of Carthage, 56–60

Dorotheus, martyr, 24, 192
Dorotheus, priest at Antioch, 192
Dositheus, 133
Drepanum, 3, 221
Duces, 10, 154, 159, 234, 256–257

Earthquakes, 252, 295n55, 351n83
Easter, date of, 146, 217
Ebionites, 91, 133–134, 169, 352n108
Ecphantus, 393n92
Edessa, 129
"Edict of Milan," 318n4
Egypt, 223, 244; rebellions in, 12, 17, 146;
    Galerius in, 17; Diocletian in, 17–18, 19,
    20; Eusebius in, 148–149; projected visit
    of Constantine to, 212; pagan religion in,
    180, 248
Elagabalus, 138
Elchasaites, 135, 258, 370n48
Eleutheropolis, 192
Eleutherus, bishop of Rome, 137
Emona, 66
Encratites, 134
Ennatha, martyr, 153
Ennathas, martyr, 154
Ephesus, 84, 132, 136
Epictetus, 84
Episcopalis audientia, 51, 145, 312nn78–82
Episcopos, 270
Equites, 46, 257
Eratosthenes, 119–120
Erembi, 294n31
Eschatology, of Eusebius, 101, 172–173
Euclid, 134
Eudaemon, accuser of Athanasius, 232
Euetius, martyr, 22
Eulalius, bishop of Antioch, 228
Eumelius, *vicarius* of Africa, 60
Eunapius, 255, 273, 398n12, 403n5
Eunomius, bishop, 59
Euphrantion, bishop of Balaneae, 205, 228
Euphrates, 12, 18
Euphronius, priest from Cappadocia, 228
Euplus, martyr, 55
Euplus, Melitian bishop, 236
Eusebius, bishop of Emesa, 333n117
Eusebius, bishop of Laodicea, 146
Eusebius, bishop of Berytus and Nicome-
    dia: related to Julian, 70, 398n14; at court
    of Licinius, 70, 77, 376n154; pupil of Lu-
    cian, 194, 202; ally of Arius, 204–205,
    231, 235, 237, 239, 242, 264; at Council
    of Nicaea, 215, 216; influence with Con-
    stantine, 226, 231, 260; deposed, 226–227;
    reinstated, 229, 402n124; bishop of Con-
    stantinople, 262, 264
Eusebius, bishop of Rome, 38
Eusebius, eunuch, 261

Eustathius, bishop of Antioch, 213, 216,
    227–228, 264, 270
Eutropia, sister of Constantine, 251, 398n11
Eutropia, wife of Maximian, 47, 248
Eutychianus, bishop of Rome, 146
Eutychianus, hermit, 393n79
Euzoius, associate of Arius, 229, 238,
    402n124
Euzoius, bishop of Caesarea, 347n21
Evagrius, praetorian prefect, 250
Exsuperius, 392n61

Fabianus, bishop of Rome, 200
Fabius, bishop of Antioch, 135
Fausta, 9, 31, 41, 66, 220–221; house in
    Rome, 57; ignored by Eusebius, 270, 274
Felix, African bishop and martyr, 23
Felix, bishop of Abthungi, 56, 58–59
Felix, deacon at Carthage, 55
Firmicus Maternus, 246, 377n15
Firmilianus, bishop of Caesarea (Cappado-
    cia), 144, 330n49
Firmilianus, governor of Palestine, 64,
    153–154
Fiscus, 65, 83, 209
Flaccillus, bishop of Antioch, 228–229, 265
Flaccinus, praetorian prefect, 24
Flamines, Christians as, 54
Flavia Domitilla, 132, 350n79
Flavianus, governor of Palestine, 150–151
Flavius Ablabius, 51, 232, 252, 262
Flavius Antoninus, *biarchus,* 238
Flavius Clemens, 132
Flavius Constantius, praetorian prefect,
    250–251, 398n11
Flavius Dalmatius, 234, 251, 252, 261–262
Flavius Dionysius, 235–237
Flavius Felicianus, 398n11
Flavius Hermogenes, 395n105
Flavius Leontius, *dux per Africam,* 317n158
Flavius Maesius Egnatius Lollianus, Q.,
    262
Flavius Optatus, 251, 262, 398n11
Flavius Polemius, consul (338), 262
Flavius Ursus, consul (338), 262
Florinus, 134
Florus, governor of Numidia, 23, 54
Follis senatorius, 256, 257
Franks, 6, 7, 29, 34, 35, 66, 72; under
    Probus, 12; as allies of Carausius and
    Allectus, 15–16
Free will, 167, 183–184
Frisii, 16
Fundanus, bishop of Abitina, 315n119

Gaetulians, 33
Gaius, bishop of Rome, 192
Galen, 134, 338n26

Galerius, 8–9, 12, 13, 17–34, 39; as instigator of persecution, 19, 21, 158; Constantine on, 75; apotheosis of, 304n126
Galilee, 252
Gallienus, 12, 138, 143
Gallus, emperor (251–253), 138
Gallus, nephew of Constantine, 251, 263
Gaudentius, *agens in rebus,* 232–233
Gaul, 6–8, 12, 15–16, 29, 34; Christians in, 14, 53, 137
Gelasius, bishop of Caesarea, 225, 382n130, 387n105
Gelasius, of Cyzicus, 225
Gennoboudes, 7
George, priest at Arethusa, 228
Germans, 4, 16, 35, 222
Germany, 7, 8, 65–66
Gibbon, Edward, 274, 357n55, 360n11
Gladiators, 51, 53
God, relationship of Father and Son defined: by Constantine, 74–75, 242–243, 271; by Origen, 87–89; by Eusebius, 99–100, 126, 173–174, 186, 188, 226, 265; by Sabellius, 135; by Arius, 203–204; by Marcellus, 241, 264–265
Good Friday speech of Constantine, 73–76
Gorgonius, 24
Gospels: concordance, 121–122; chapter headings, 124; textual history, 124–125; authorship, 139; Porphyry on, 177
Goths, 12, 22, 65, 250, 258, 330n47
Gratianus, *protector,* 298n116
Gratus, proconsul of Asia, 349n48
Greece, 12, 26
Greek, Constantine's knowledge of, 47, 74, 216–217
Greek religion, Eusebius' view of, 180–181
Grégoire, Henri, 308n18, 401n66
Gregorius, bishop of Berytus, 204
Gregorius, jurist, 10, 289n70
Gregorius, praetorian prefect, 318n165
Gregory, bishop in Armenia, 65
Gregory, bishop in Pontus, 85–86

Hadrian, 137
Hannibalianus, brother of Constantine, 251
Hannibalianus, nephew of Constantine, 259, 262
Harpocration, 338n26
Haruspices, 18, 52
Hebrew, Christian knowledge of, 92, 192, 335n142
Hebrews, as distinguished from Jews by Eusebius, 127, 181, 185
Hebrews, Epistle to, 140
Hegesippus, 131, 133, 136
Helena, mother of Constantine, 3, 49, 194, 220–221, 248

Helena, wife of Crispus, 72–73
Helenopolis, 221, 259
Heliopolis, 247, 367n176
Hellanicus, bishop of Tripolis, 204
Hellanicus, of Lesbos, 119
Hellenism, 68, 178, 181
Heraclas, bishop of Alexandria, 83, 84, 197, 329n36
Heraclea, 63, 222
Heracleides, heretic, 330n50
Heracleides, imperial procurator, 49
Heraclianus, *magister officiorum,* 256
Heraclius, rigorist at Rome, 38
Heraiscus, Melitian bishop of Alexandria, 230, 235–236
Hercules, 11, 160
Herculii, 12, 26, 36
Heresy, Constantine's treatment of, 212–213, 224–225, 270
Hermaeon, Melitian bishop, 236
Hermes Trismegistus, 241
Hermogenes, priest, 216
Hermogenianus, jurist, 10, 289n70
Hermon, bishop of Jerusalem, 192
Herod, king of Judaea, 81, 123, 135
Herod Agrippa, 135–136
Heruli, 6
Hesychius, biblical scholar, 194
Hesychius, bishop and martyr, 194, 201
Hexapla, 94, 95, 98, 102, 108, 120, 170; compilation of, 91–92; influence of, 125
Hieracammon, accuser of Athanasius, 232
Hieracas, 204
Hierapolis, 132
Hierocles, anti-Christian writer, 22, 24, 164–167, 363n100
Hippias, of Elis, 119
Hippolytus, 135, 349n61, 351n93
Hipponon, 234
Hispellum, 212
Holy Spirit, 87–90; as author of Scripture, 100–101, 104
Homer, 150–151, 341n70; lexicons to, 109
Homoousios, 145, 204, 215, 216–217, 226, 229
Honorary titles, 69, 255
Hyginus, prefect of Egypt, 236
Hymenaeus, bishop of Jerusalem, 192
Hypostasis, 203, 233, 241, 265, 331n62

Iamblichus, 22, 68, 168, 183, 377n11
Iberia, 18, 258
Ignatius, bishop of Antioch, 132
Iliberris, Council of, 53–54
Incarnation: Constantine on, 74, 75; importance for Eusebius, 102, 126–127, 172, 187; in the *Chronicle,* 114–116; date of, 123; ridiculed by Porphyry, 176

India, 139, 212
Inflation, 10–11, 160, 321n76
Ingentius, 59
Innocentius, 289n70
Insteius Tertullus, 299n28
Instinctus divinitatis, 308n24
Iovii, 12, 26
Irenaeus, bishop of Lugdunum, 131, 133, 134, 139, 140, 142
Isaac, Melitian bishop of Letopolis, 235, 236
Isaiah, Eusebius' exegesis of, 97–104, 249
Ischyras, priest in Mareotis, 233–234, 236–239
Isidorus, 202
Ision, accuser of Athanasius, 232
Istria, 33
Italy, 12, 33–34, 37–39, 41–42; assessed for taxation, 9, 29, 37–38

James, brother of Jesus, 132, 133
James, brother of John, 136
Jericho, 92
Jerome: as translator and adapter of Eusebius, 111, 112–113; on text of Bible, 194; *Life of Paul,* 196
Jerusalem: Jews excluded from, 82, 252, sack of, 104, 135–136; plan of, 106; bishops of, 130, 133, 144, 192, 219; Church of the Holy Sepulcher, 187, 238, 248–250; Church of the Ascension, 221; Council of, 238–239, 241, 248–249, 270
Jetheira, 110
Jesus, 127, 129, 165, 170, 175
Jews: in Spain, 54; rebellions of, 82, 134, 135–136, 252; in Caesarea, 82, 92, 169–170, 178–179, 184; role in history, Eusebius' view of, 104, 127, 171–172, 181–186, 188; legislation against, 252, 270
Johannes Archaph, Melitian bishop of Memphis, 234, 235, 239, 240
John, apostle, 132, 136; author of gospel, 139
John, blind martyr, 156, 355n3
Jordan, 144, 259
Josephus: as used in *On the Place-Names in Holy Scripture,* 107, 108, 110; as in the *Chronicle,* 114, 115, 118, 119; as used in the *Ecclesiastical History,* 129, 130, 131, 135–136, 138–139, 141; on Jesus, 347n14, 349n68
Josephus, of Tiberias, 252
Jubilees, 111
Judaea, 82, 106, 135–136
Judaism: Origen's view of, 90, 98; Eusebius' view of, 98, 101–102, 126–127, 171–172, 181–186
Judas, Christian writer, 353n123

Jude, brother of Jesus, 136
Julia Mamaea, 84, 138, 351n93
Juliana, 92
Julian, emperor (355–363), 263; on Constantine, 272–273
Julianus, proconsul of Africa (301/2), 20
Julianus, usurper (284/5), 5
Julius Africanus, 92, 114, 115, 117–119, 129
Julius Constantius, 251, 252, 262
Julius Julianus, 70, 214
Julius Nepotianus, 251
Junius Bassus, 72, 250
Junius Flavianus, 42
Junius Maximus, M., 5
Jupiter, 11, 35, 44, 63
Justin, apologist and martyr, 131, 132, 133, 137, 141
Justus, Jewish historian, 115
Juthungi, 12
Juvencus, Christian poet, 246

Kariatha, 110
Kartir, 258
King lists, 114, 116–117
Kingship, theories of, 254

Labarum, 43, 48, 255, 269; and statue of Constantine, 46, 162–163, 308n18; described by Lactantius, 306n146
Lactantius, 11, 12–13, 22–23, 165; career and writings, 13–14, 24, 70, 291–292nn96–99; acquaintance with Constantine, 14, 43, 74; tutor of Crispus, 47, 74; influence on Constantine, 74, 75; contrasted with Eusebius, 149, 158
Laetus, prefect of Egypt, 82
Lambaesis, 300n47
Last Judgment, 87, 89, 101, 172–173
Latin, as official language in East, 19, 215
Legacies: Church as recipient of, 50
Legions: II Parthica, 45; X Fretensis, 338n18
Leocadius, 314n107
Leonidas, father of Origen, 82
Leontius, *dux,* 60
Lexica, 109
Libanius, 222, 272, 313n101, 377n11; relatives executed (303), 296n81
Liber Pontificalis, 310nn57–61
Libya, 135, 197, 232
Licinius, 31–35, 39–41, 48, 62–72, 75–77; in Constantinian propaganda, 68; nature of government of, 68–72, 208; as persecutor, 70–72, 206, 209–210; in Eusebius, 150, 162–163; death of, 214
Licinius, Caesar (317–324), 65, 66, 214
Literature, Constantine as patron of, 47–48

Liturgies, 208; exemption of clergy from, 50, 71, 209
Löwenklau, Johann, 273–274
Lollius Urbicus, Q., 141
London, 15
Longinus. *See* Cassius Longinus
Lucan, 246
Lucania, 27
Lucian, of Antioch, 24, 40, 159, 194, 202, 358n73; relics and shrine of, 221, 259
"Lucianic recension," of the Bible, 124, 194
Lucianus, *tribunus fori suari*, 298n7
Lucilla, 56
Lucius, martyr, 141
Lucius Verus, 137
Lugdunum, 53, 137, 140
Luke, Gospel of, 123, 139, 140
Lusius Quietus, 136
Lusor, 314n107
Lycia, 193, 195
Lycia and Pamphylia, province of, 160
Lydda, 357n39

Macarius, associate of Athanasius, 232–235, 237, 239, 242
Macarius, bishop of Jerusalem, 204, 248, 267
Macedonius, bishop of Mopsuestia, 237
Macrianus, 138
Macrinus, 138
Magic, 165–167, 177, 199, 219, 220, 253
Magistri militum, 255, 256–257
Magistri officiorum, 52, 76, 256, 394n102
Magistri privatae, 10
Magnilianus, 296n72
Mainz, 6
Maiorinus, schismatic bishop of Carthage, 56–57
Malchion, priest at Antioch, 144
Mamaea, 84, 138, 351n93
Mamertinus, orator, 7, 9
Mamre, oak of, 110, 248, 267
Manetho, 114, 118
Mani, 20, 192, 204, 258
Manichees, 20, 192, 195, 196–197
Manumissio in ecclesia, 50–51, 52, 311n76
Marcellianus, tribune, 298n7
Marcellinus, bishop of Rome, 38, 192
Marcellinus, priest at Rome, 303n103, 310n61
Marcellus, bishop of Ancyra, 213, 240–242, 253, 264–265, 271
Marcellus, bishop of Rome, 38
Marcellus, tribune, 298n7
Marcion, 133, 134, 241
Marcionites, 143, 154, 169, 224
Marcus, associate of Valentinus, 134
Marcus, priest at Pelusium, 236

Marcus Aurelius, 131, 137, 141–142
Mareotis, 237–238
Margus, 5, 76
Marianus, *notarius*, 238
Marinus, bishop of Arles, 57
Marinus, martyr, 143–144
Marinus, recipient of work by Eusebius, 122
Maris, bishop of Chalcedon, 237
Mark, Gospel of, 123, 139; alleged secret gospel of, 353n113
Marriage laws, 19–20, 52, 69, 219–220
Mars, 12, 36
Martinianus, emperor (324), 76–77, 256
Martinianus, soldier, 370n52
Martyrs, number of, 155, 201, 358n76
Massilia, 34, 40–41
Maternus, bishop of Cologne, 57
Matthew, Gospel of, 123, 139; alleged Aramaic original, 94, 352n112
Mauretania, 16
Maxentius, 9, 25–26, 29–34, 37–39, 40–43, 44; in Constantinian propaganda, 37, 45, 47, 268; policy toward Christians, 38–39, 291n96
Maximian, 3, 6–8, 9, 11–13, 16, 25–27, 37; as persecutor, 23–24, 55; emperor for the second time, 30–32; rebellion and death, 34–36, 40–41, 67, 214, 268; apotheosis of, 47, 206, 304n126
Maximinus, emperor (235–238), 138
Maximinus, emperor (305–313), 26, 32–33, 39–41, 48–49, 62–64, 193; in Caesarea, 82, 152; and relief at Paneas, 144, 173; as depicted by Eusebius, 149–162
Maximus, accuser of Felix of Abthungi, 58
Maximus, author of treatise *On Matter*, 141, 369n29
Maximus, bishop of Alexandria, 192
Maximus, bishop of Jerusalem, 379n52
Media, 18, 65; kings of, 119, 342n99
Melchizedek, 184, 346n3
Meletius, bishop in Pontus, 193
Melitene, 23
Melitians, 202, 213, 217, 226, 229–240, 391n26; monasteries of, 234, 235
Melitius, bishop of Lycopolis, 201–202, 204, 213–217
Melito, bishop of Sardis, 133, 137, 139, 391n31
Memphis, 75
Meander, heretic, 133–134
Mensurius, bishop of Carthage, 54–55, 315n119
Mesopotamia, 17–18, 41, 62, 263; Christians in, 157, 160–161, 258
Messiah, 102, 171

Methodius, bishop in Lycia, 174, 193, 195, 200
Metrodorus, 397n145
Milan, 6, 8, 26, 42, 59–60, 62, 252; "edict" of, 318n4
Miletus, 21, 64
Milevis, 23
Miltiades, bishop of Rome, 38–39, 57
Milvian Bridge, 42–43, 305n144
Minervina, 31
Minicius Fundanus, 137
Minucius Felix, 53, 142, 143
Mithras, 32, 326n7
Mocius, martyr, 222
Moesia, 67
Monasticism, 130, 195–196, 202, 234, 235–236
Monotheism: solar, 36, 48; philosophical, 165
Mons Aureus, 5
Montanists, 134, 151, 224
Montanus, 134, 143
Moors, 16, 33
Moses: laws of, 90, 93, 101, 123, 127, 185; date of, 113–114, 115, 176–177, 181; prophesies the Incarnation, 127, 171; last of the Hebrew patriarchs, 171, 184; Constantine compared to, 271
Music, Constantine as patron of, 72

Naissus, 3, 222, 252, 261
Naples, 382n123
Narbo, 251
Narcissus, bishop of Neronias, 213, 216, 241, 264
Narseh, king of Persia (293–302), 17–19
Narseh, Persian prince, 259
Nazarius, 73
Nazoreans, 352n108
Nepos, millenarian, 353n122
Nero, 131, 136, 271
"New Rome," 212, 222, 378n20
Nicagoras, 72, 211
Nicolaitans, 134
Nicomedia, 4, 26, 27; residence of Diocletian, 6, 21, 24, 25, 147; Lactantius in, 13–14, 70; churches in, 19, 22, 147, 248; persecution in, 22, 24, 165, 192, 194; Maximinus in, 40, 41, 63, 161; residence of Licinius, 64, 68, 70, 71, 77; residence of Constantine, 74, 77, 194, 208, 212, 219, 221, 231; Council of, 229, 231, 266, 270; letter of Constantine to church of, 242–243; and Constantine's death, 259–261
Nicopolis, near Actium, 84, 91
Nicopolis, on the Black Sea, 239
Nile, 17, 248

Nisibis, 18, 263
Noah, 115
Nobatae, 18
Nobilis, 257
Noricum, 12
Notarii, 217, 238, 256
Novatian, 135, 142
Novatianists, 135, 217–218, 224
Novatus, 135
Nubians, 253
Numenius, 74–75, 100, 177, 182, 183, 330n56
Numerianus, 4–5
Numidia, 23, 54, 55, 60

Oenomaus, of Gadara, 181, 366n148
Oescus, 221
Old Testament: canonical books, 138–139; Eusebius' attitude toward, 96–104, 182, 186, 249
Olympias, daughter of Ablabius, 252
Olympic victors, 114, 119
Olympius, bishop, 59
Onasimos, 302n88
Oracles, 21, 64, 159–160, 175; consultation of, made illegal, 210–211, 255, 269
Orcistus, 377n13
Oriens, diocese of, 26, 39, 151
Origen, Christian writer: life and career, 82–86, 133, 135, 138, 142; knowledge of Greek philosophy, 86–87, 177, 183, 241; theology, 87–90, 204; and the Bible, 90–93, 94–96, 139, 170; Eusebius' debt to, 94–97, 99–101, 105, 110, 165, 183, 241; biblical onomasticon of, 98, 110; Porphyry and, 175, 176, 177–178; controversies over orthodoxy of, 193, 198–200, 241, 264; letter to Philip, 351n95
Origen, pagan philosopher, 100
Orontes, 64
Ossius, bishop of Corduba, 43, 51, 54, 56; patron of Calcidius, 74; in Alexandria and Antioch, 212–214; at Council of Nicaea, 215, 217; retirement, 225–226
Otacilia Severa, 351n95
Ousia, 216, 233, 241, 331n62
Ovid, 246
Oxyrhynchus, 296n73, 368n4

Pachomius, Egyptian bishop (306), 201
Pachomius, Melitian bishop (335), 236
Pachomius, monk, 196
Paganism, 46–47, 110, 144, 159–160; in the imperial army, 71, 309n42; Eusebius' view of, 180–186, 187; Constantine's policies toward, 210–212, 222–223, 246–248, 254–255, 269, 270

Palestine, 6, 8, 25, 106–111; Christian villages in, 111, 191; persecution in, 148–155
Palladius, *agens in rebus,* 238
Palmyra, 12
Pamphilus, 93–94, 183, 192–193, 194–195, 198; imprisonment and death, 153, 154, 155, 156, 358n73; *Defense of Origen,* 148, 199–201
Paneas. *See* Caesarea Philippi
Panegyrics, 11, 12, 223, 253–255, 265–268, 296n68; *Panegyrici Latini:* 10(2), 7, 9, 12; 11(3), 12, 15; 7(6), 31; 6(7), 34–36; 12(9), 41, 45, 46–47, 52, 307n3; 4(10), 73
Pannonia, 12, 41, 262
Panolbius, uncle of Libanius, 313n101
Pantaenus, 139
Pantera, alleged father of Jesus, 170
Paphnutius, bishop of Thebes, 379n52, 388n123
Papias, bishop of Hierapolis, 132, 139, 140
Papius Pacatianus, L., 250, 252
Papylus, martyr, 137, 142
Parentium, 33
Paterius, prefect of Egypt, 233
Patermouthios, 200
Patriarchs, 123, 126–127, 171, 181, 184–185
Patricii, 251
Patricius, *vicarius* of Africa, 49, 56
Patrophilus, bishop of Scythopolis, 239
Paul, apostle, 132, 140
Paul, bishop of Antioch, 134–135, 144–145, 169, 241
Paul, bishop of Cirta, 23
Paul, bishop of Constantinople, 264, 389n153, 400n41
Paul, bishop of Tyre, 234
Paul, heretic at Alexandria, 83
Paul, martyr of Caesarea, 153
Paul, of Samosata, 134–135, 144–145, 169, 241
Paul, of Thebes, 196
Paulianists, 169, 218, 224
Paulinus, bishop of Tyre and Antioch, 162, 204, 205, 228, 241, 264
Pella, 136
Pergamum, 137
Persecution: before 300, 21, 82–83, 136–138, 142–143, 145; instigated by Galerius, 19, 21, 24; decreed by Diocletian, 21, 22–23, 150–151; avoided by Constantius, 23, 28; under Maximian, 23, 38, 54; in the territory of Diocletian and Galerius, 23–24, 150–151; enforced by Maximinus, 49, 64–65, 151–154, 158–161; resumed by Licinius, 70–72, 209; Eusebius' reaction to, 148–163, 168; in Persia, 258, 397n144. *See also* Toleration

Persia, 6, 12, 72, 212; wars between Rome and, 4, 17–19, 25, 39, 82, 84, 259, 262–263; Christians in, 258–259
Peter, apostle, 132, 139
Peter, bishop of Alexandria, 40, 149, 159, 192, 198–202, 358n73
Peter, exorcist at Rome, 310n61, 383n132
Peter, martyr at Caesarea, 154
Peter, martyr at Nicomedia, 24
Petra, 102, 110–111, 249
Petronius Annianus, 46
Petronius Probinus, consul (322), 73
Peucetius, 64
Phaeno, mines at, 20, 152, 153, 154, 199, 202, 355n3
Philae, 18
Philagrius, prefect of Egypt, 237
Phileas, bishop of Thmuis, 157, 193, 198, 201, 358n73
Philip, apostle, 132
Philip, emperor (244–249), 138, 351n95
Philippopolis, 67
Philo, Jewish writer, 122, 130, 131, 135, 183–184, 195; Origen's debt to, 93, 94, 110, 332n102
Philo, of Byblos, 177, 179, 180, 183
Philogonius, bishop of Antioch, 204, 205, 213
Philoromus, martyr, 157
Philosophy, Constantine's acquaintance with, 47, 73–75, 242–243
Philostratus, 165–167
Philumenus, courtier, 59, 232, 393n79
Phlegon, 118–119
Phoenicia, 148, 180, 223
Photius, 198
Phrygia, 134, 157, 191
Phrygia and Caria, province of, 11, 288n66, 358n72
Picts, 27
Pierius, 93, 193, 198
Pilgrims, 221, 248
Pinnes, prior of Melitian monastery, 234
Pionius, martyr, 137, 142
Pistus, appointed bishop of Alexandria, 239, 400n44
Plato, 74, 94, 177, 193, 195, 241; in Eusebius' *Preparation for the Gospel,* 181–182, 183
Platonism, 74–75, 206; Origen's debt to, 86–87, 177; in Eusebius, 94, 100, 181–183, 186, 188
Pliny, 137
Plotinus, 21, 86, 175, 183, 330n56, 366n149
Plusianus, Egyptian bishop, 236
Polycarp, bishop of Smyrna, 132, 137, 142
Pompeianus, praetorian prefect, 42
Pomponius Januarianus, 5

Pontifex maximus, 245
Pontius Pilate, 131; *Acts of Pilate,* 159
Pontus, 72, 158
Porfyrius, poet, 47–48, 67, 212, 219
Porphyry, 181, 183, 184, 366nn148–149; life
    of, 175; *Against the Christians,* 21–22,
    174, 176–178, 193, 206, 211, 233, 341n70;
    Chronicle, 114, 118, 120, 340n59; *On Phi-
    losophy from Oracles,* 175–176, 179; on
    Origen, 177–178, 330n56, 403n3
Potammon, bishop of Heracleopolis, 149,
    388n123
Praefecti annonae, 257
Praefecti urbis, 42, 45–46, 257, 275
Praefecti vigilum, 257
Praepositus sacri cubiculi, 394n102
Praesides, 9–10, 257
Praetextatus, hierophant, 383n144
Praetorian guard, 29–30, 45, 257
Praetorian prefects, 3, 5, 22, 24, 159,
    250–252; as military commanders, 7–8,
    16, 33, 42; become civil administrators,
    255, 256
Praetors, 255–256, 257
Praxagoras, 72, 272
Price edict, 10–11
Priests. *See* Clergy
Prisca, wife of Diocletian, 19, 64, 147
Priscillianus, governor of Bithynia, 24
Probus, emperor (276–282), 4, 5, 12, 111,
    192
Probus, envoy of Galerius (307), 31
Proconnesus, 20
Proconsuls, 10
Procopius, martyr, 150–151
Prosopon, 241
Prostitution, 157–158, 314nn109–110
Protogenes, bishop of Serdica, 50–51,
    389n138, 400n57
Protopaschites, 217
Providence, 184
Provinces, 9–10, 256
Psalms, Eusebius' exegesis of, 95–104
Psamathia, 232
Ptermenkurkis, 234
Ptolemaeus, martyr, 141
Ptolemais, in Libya, 135
Publilius Optatianus Porfyrius, 47–48, 67,
    212, 219
Pythagoreanism, 177

Quadi, 12
Quadratus, apologist, 137
Quaestor sacri palatii, 256
Quindecimviri sacris faciundis, 43

Raetia, 7, 12
Rape, 220

Ras Shamra, 183
Rationales, 10, 124, 157, 395n105
Ravenna, 25, 30
Rebaptism, 57
Reticius, bishop of Autun, 57
Revelation, 134, 139, 140, 352n109
Rhine, 4, 6, 7, 12, 15, 16, 35–36, 65–66, 72
Rhodon, 122
Rhône, 34
Ripenses, 257
Roman Empire
    divisions of: (285), 6; (293), 8, 15, 19;
        (305), 26; (308), 32–33; (311), 39–40;
        (313), 63–64; (317), 67–68; (335),
        251–252; (337), 262
    Eusebius' view of, 185, 187
Roman law, 10, 19–20
Romanus, martyr, 20–21, 155
Rome, 27, 29–32, 245; Diocletian and Max-
    imian in, 16, 25, 45; under Maxentius, 33,
    37–39, 42–43; public buildings, 37–38, 46,
    47; persecution in, 38; bishops of, 38, 57,
    130, 132, 192, 218; Constantine in, 44–46,
    59, 66, 221; churches built by Constan-
    tine, 49; residence of Helena, 49,
    220–221; size of Christian community,
    53; early history of, 114–115
Romulianum, 39
Rufinus, consul (311), 302n83
Rufinus, ecclesiastical historian, 95, 96, 225
Rufius Volusianus (C. Ceionius Rufius Vo-
    lusianus), 33, 37, 45–46, 67, 287n28

Sabbath, 101
Sabellianism, 135, 197, 227, 228, 241,
    264–265
Sabellius, 135, 204
Sabinus, praetorian prefect, 40, 159, 161
Sacrifice, prohibition of, 210–211, 246,
    254–255, 269
Salamis, in Cyprus, 252
Salonae, 4
Samaritans, 82, 151, 169, 369n34
Sanchuniathon, 177
Saône, 34
Saraceni, 8, 102, 249
Sardinia, 33
Sarmatians, 12, 17, 22, 30, 33, 76, 250, 258,
    262
Saturninus, heretic, 134
Saxons, 6
Scheldt, 15
Schism, Constantine's attitude toward, 57,
    213, 224
Scholae palatinae, 256
Schwartz, Eduard, 274, 405n21
Scriptures. *See* Bible
Scythia Minor, 67

Second God, 74–75, 100, 173–174, 186, 188, 292n99
Second Sophistic movement, 183
Secundus, bishop of Ptolemais, 205, 217, 232, 239
Secundus, bishop of Tigisis, 54–55, 56
Segusio, 41
Senate, 5, 8, 257, 262, 271; attitude toward Maxentius, 37, 38, 42; relations with Constantine, 44–46; consecrates emperors, 206, 267; created at Constantinople, 223
Senecio, 66
Sententiae Pauli, 10
Septimius Acindynus, 399n27
Septimius Severus, 137–138
Septuagint, 91, 92, 95, 102, 114, 125
Serapion, bishop of Antioch, 134
Serapis, 248
Serdica, 26, 32, 40, 67, 72, 73, 222
Severianus, 64
Severus, consul (323), 73
Severus, emperor (193–211), 137–138
Severus, emperor (305–307), 26, 27, 29–30
Severus, rigorist, 134
Severus Alexander, 138
Shapur I, king of Persia (240–272), 17, 18, 258
Shapur II, king of Persia (309–379), 258–259, 263, 270
Sibylline books, 43
Sibylline Oracles, 74, 75
Sicily, 12, 174, 175
Sicorius Probus, 18
Silvanus, bishop of Cirta, 55
Silvanus, bishop of Emesa, 159, 358n73
Silvanus, bishop of Gaza, 152–153, 154, 156, 358n73
Silvester, bishop of Rome, 214
Simon, arch-heretic, 133–134
Sirmium: origin of Maximian, 6; imperial residence, 8, 9, 17, 32, 68, 72, 76, 222
Smyrna, 137
Socrates, ecclesiastical historian, 225
Sol, 12, 36, 48, 71
Sopater, 68, 252–253, 383n144
Sossianus Hierocles, 22, 24, 164–167, 363n100
Soterichus, poet, 296n68
Souls, 87, 88–90, 199, 200, 335n163
Sozomenus, 225
Spain, 12, 16, 27, 29; Christians in, 14, 53
Spalato, 27, 31
Statius, 246
Statius Quadratus, L., 142
Stenographers, 91, 144
Stephanus, bishop of Laodicea, 146, 193

Stephanus, recipient of work by Eusebius, 122
Sthenidas, 393n92
Stoicism, 87, 177
Strategius, *comes,* 228
Subatianus Aquila, 83
Sucidava, 221
Sulpicius Quirinius, P., 345n137
Sunday, 48, 51–52, 249
Susanna, story of, 92
Symeon, bishop of Jerusalem, 133, 136–137
Symmachus, translator of Old Testament, 91, 92, 95, 102
Syncletius, *agens in rebus,* 232–233
Synods. *See* Councils of bishops
Syracuse, 12
Syria, 8, 12, 17, 18, 23, 223

Tabennesis, 196
Tarsus, 63, 252
Tatian, 115, 122, 134
Tattooing, 51
Taurobolium, 246
Taxes, 37, 38, 39–40; innovations of Diocletian, 9, 17, 29; Christian clergy and, 50, 71; policies of Constantine, 69–70, 208, 255–256, 257–258; Athanasius and, 231–232
Telmessus, 195
Temples, Constantine's treatment of, 210–211, 246–247, 254–255, 257
Terminalia, 21
Tertullian, 53, 131, 137, 142–143
Tetrapla, 91–92, 94
Tetrarchy, ideology of, 8–13, 19–20, 33, 36, 66, 68, 251–252
Thallus, 118–119
Thebaid, 148, 201, 232
Thebes, in Egypt, 72, 211
Thebuthis, 133
Thecla, martyr, 151
Theoctistus, bishop of Caesarea, 84
Theodora, daughter of Maximian, 3, 7, 8–9, 251
Theodoretus, 225
Theodorus, bishop of Heraclea, 237
Theodorus, bishop of Tarsus, 71
Theodorus, Egyptian bishop, 201
Theodorus. *See* Gregory, bishop in Pontus
Theodosia, martyr, 152
Theodotion, translator of Old Testament, 91
Theodotus, bishop of Laodicea, 178, 193, 204, 213, 216, 227
Theodotus, Christian in Rome, 134
Theognis, bishop of Nicaea, 226–227, 229, 237, 239, 402–403n124
Theognostus, 198, 204

Theology, Constantine's interest in, 212–213, 242–243
Theonas, bishop of Alexandria, 192, 368n12
Theonas, bishop of Marmarica, 205, 217, 232
Theonas, Melitian bishop of Alexandria, 230
Theophanes, of Mytilene, 247
Theophilus, bishop of Antioch, 133
Theophrastus, 134
Theotecnus, bishop of Caesarea, 93, 144, 146, 192
Theotecnus, *curator* of Antioch, 64, 159–160
Therapeutae, 130, 195
Thessalonica, 24, 77; residence of Galerius, 19, 32; residence of Constantine, 72, 73, 76; executions at, 64, 214
Thrace, 6, 67
Thrasyllus, Neopythagorean, 324n134
Tiber, 43
Tiberius, 116, 131
Ticinum, 33
Tigris, 6, 18, 107
Timisitheus, 326n7
Timothy, martyr, 151
Tiridates, king of Armenia, 6, 17, 18, 65
Toleration, official: by Gallienus (260), 138, 143; by Constantine (306), 14, 28; by Maxentius (306/7), 38, 55–56; by Galerius (311), 39, 149, 159; by Licinius (313), 62, 149, 210; by Maximinus (313), 161–162; by Constantine (324), 209–210
Tolosa, 251
Traditio, 38, 54–59
Trajan, 65, 131, 136–137, 271
Transtigritanae regiones, 18, 160, 397n148
Tres Tabernae, 30
Tricennalia, of Constantine, 253–255, 266, 270
Trier, 7, 9, 16, 65; Lactantius in, 74, 292n97; residence of Constantinus, 221–222, 252, 262, 263
Tropaeum Traiani, 65
Turin, 41
Tyrannus, bishop of Antioch, 192
Tyre, 148, 149, 150, 160; Eusebius' sermon at, 162–163; Council of, 235–241, 253, 270

Ulpianus, martyr, 156
Urbanus, governor of Palestine, 151–153, 156

Ursacius, bishop of Singidunum, 237, 239
Ursacius, *comes,* 60

Vahram II, king of Persia (276–293), 6, 258
Valens, bishop of Mursa, 237, 239
Valens, emperor (316/7), 67
Valentina, martyr, 153
Valentinianus, governor of Palestine, 154
Valentinus, 134, 203, 241; followers of, 224
Valeria, daughter of Diocletian, 9, 19, 64, 147, 359n83
Valeria Maximilla, 9, 43
Valerian, 17, 18, 75, 138, 259
Valerius Diogenes, 358n83
Valerius Florus, 23, 54
Valerius Maximus, praetorian prefect, 252, 261, 262
Valerius Proculus, consul (325), 214
Valerius Romulus, 32, 302n84
Varro, 364n125
Verinus, *vicarius* of Africa, 60
Verona, 41, 42, 67
Vespasian, 82
Vettius Aquilinus, consul (286), 246
Vettius Aquilinus Juvencus, C., 246
Vettius Rufinus, consul (323), 73
Vicarii, 9–10, 257
Vicennalia, of Diocletian, 24–25, 47, 151; of Constantine, 111, 113, 219
Victor, bishop of Rome, 133, 134
Victory, 36, 46; altar of, 245
Vienne, 137
Viminacium, 5, 263
Virgil, 36, 75, 246
Virgines subintroductae, 145
Virius Nepotianus, 251, 398n11
Volusianus. *See* Rufius Volusianus

Word of God: in Eusebius, 100, 126–127, 174, 188; in Arius, 203

Xystus, bishop of Rome, 146

York, 27

Zabdas, bishop of Jerusalem, 192
Zacchaeus, martyr, 151
Zenophilus, *consularis* of Numidia, 60
Zephyrinus, bishop of Rome, 84, 134
Zeus, 64, 159–160
Ziatha, 18
Zoar, 154
Zoroastrians, 17, 258
Zosimus, 273–274